INTERPRETING COLONIAL AMERICA

Selected Readings

INTERPRETING COLONIAL AMERICA
Selected Readings
SECOND EDITION

Edited by
James Kirby Martin
Rutgers University

Harper & Row, Publishers
New York, Hagerstown, San Francisco, London

Sponsoring Editor: Marylou Mosher
Project Editor: Karla B. Philip
Designer: Michel Craig
Production Supervisor: Will C. Jomarron
Compositor: Maryland Composition Co., Inc.
Printer: } The Murray Printing Company
Binder:
Art Studio: J & R Technical Services Inc.

INTERPRETING COLONIAL AMERICA: Selected Readings, Second Edition

Library of Congress Cataloging in Publication Data

Martin, James Kirby, Date–   comp.
  Interpreting colonial America.

  Includes bibliographies.
  1. United States—History—Colonial period,
ca. 1600–1775—Addresses, essays, lectures.   I. Title.
El88.5.M26   1978   973.2   77-7111
ISBN 0-06-044209-3

For Edith H. Garrett,
and to the memory of
Frederick C. Garrett, and
Dora R. and William Martin,
my grandparents

CONTENTS

PREFACE

I have prepared this book of readings with the hope that the diversity of topics will assist students in understanding the colonial phase of American history. My hope, too, is that students will be stimulated by this collection to investigate more deeply the complex patterns and problems of national origins. With that in mind, four sections focus upon developments during the seventeenth century and four focus upon the eighteenth century. All eight sections together form a chronological chain of historical materials running from the first contact between Europeans and Indians in the New World to the emerging desire of English provincials on the mainland of North America to find more than token equality in the British empire during the years of the American Revolution.

Each of the sections has been designed to present a breadth of readings that will allow students to get beyond superficial matters and ask the crucial question *why*: Why were Europeans able to conquer the millions of Indians resident in the western hemisphere? Why did a pattern of genocide rather than that of acculturation evolve out of the confrontational course of Indian-white relations? Why were so many Europeans willing to leave behind Old World ties and begin life again in the New World? Why were black Africans permanently bonded as slaves when whites were not? Why did the provincial social and political structures permit more opportunity for advancement, when compared with the English and European models? Why did so many colonial Americans come to see themselves as called out to protect and defend human liberty, especially in the context of chattel slavery? Why did so many observers assert that a new kind of individual had been formed out of exposure to the American wilderness? Why was this kind of an individual, if a real person, a possible harbinger, in the late eighteenth century, of major historical change affecting the whole Western world? The readings provide perceptive, though differing, answers to such questions. The multiplicity of interpretive angles will allow us all to reflect upon the impact of colonial patterns of human existence as they affected the national years of United States history.

My basic function as an editor has been to assemble the readings from journals and books of more than momentary interest; naturally not all outstanding works could be included, yet I have tried to achieve a balance in choosing from among the most significant published materials. At the same time I have sought to avoid singling out any particular methodological approach. Thus the exciting writings of social and demographic historians stand beside the penetrating commentaries of scholars who drew upon traditional literary sources. If we are to comprehend the rich variety of possibilities in interpreting colonial America, then we must appreciate that no one methodological approach can be the complete basis of truth. We must regard all approaches as significant while deciding which can shed the most light in coming to terms with particular subjects.

As an editor I have benefited from many favors, and my debts are great. This volume's widespread acceptance in its first edition reflects directly upon the time and advice that a number of friends and colleagues have generously given. I wish to thank Merrill Jensen of the University of Wisconsin, Henry W. Bowden, Robert Gottfried, Philip J. Greven, Jr., Maurice D. Lee, Jr., Calvin Martin, Zenda Angelson, Shirley Meinkoth, Robert Rutter, Jill Schumann, Karen R. Stubaus, David Szatmary, and Michael Vaught of Rutgers University; James M. Banner, Jr., and John M. Murrin of Princeton University; Peter N. Stearns of Carnegie-Mellon University; Lawrence H. Leder of Lehigh University; Jackson Turner Main of the State University of New York at Stony Brook; Stephen Saunders Webb of Syracuse University; Kenneth J. Moynihan of Assumption College; Walter Boston of the State University College of New York at Brockport; James H. Levitt of the State University College of New York at Potsdam; friends Stanley J. Duane, Charles H. Woodford, John Greenman, and Mary Lou Mosher; and my wife, Karen W. Martin. Lastly, my gratitude is extended to the authors, journal editors, and publishers who kindly granted permission to reproduce the materials appearing in this volume.

James Kirby Martin

INTERPRETING COLONIAL AMERICA
Selected Readings

The Planting of English Settlements in North America— The Seventeenth Century

PART ONE

The Clash of Old and New World Peoples

SECTION 1

No one knows precisely, but as many as fifty million native American Indians, perhaps double that number, may have inhabited the western hemisphere on the pre-Columbian eve of Europe's westward expansion. The vast bulk of that population, representing hundreds of cultural and language groups, resided in central and southern America, where Spanish explorers, conquistadors, and their diseases, more so than their military weapons, devastated the landscape. By comparison, Indian population was much thinner along the eastern Atlantic seaboard region of North America. There Eastern Woodland cultures, largely hunting, fishing, and gathering peoples, lived harmoniously with nature, at least until they made contact with European fisherman, explorers, and settlers. Also ravaged by white diseases, these native Americans in turn suffered the same fate as those cultural groups in the Caribbean region. Rather than acculturation or balanced assimilation, the destruction of tribal values, customs, and life-styles came to characterize the nature of white-Indian relations as Europeans swept westward. By the end of the contact period in the seventeenth century, at least 90 percent of the native population had been eliminated, a staggering overall mortality rate by any measure.

Passing through an initial phase of curiosity, even fascination with Indian ways, white conquerers and settlers quickly adopted haughty attitudes about Indian habits and customs. The native American became the "savage," the "heathen," the "unclean animal" standing in the path of human progress. The European assumption was that "civilized" peoples had every legal and moral right to overrun, to enslave, and to exterminate men and women who structured their lives around "lower" attitudes and beliefs. Obviously, as we know today, European assumptions were grievously misplaced; native Indian cultures were *different* from those of Europeans, certainly not inferior. But that observation does not change the fact that sixteenth-century Europeans did not accept such neat distinctions. As contact between red and white peoples rapidly increased after 1492, so did the inflexibility of white attitudes. Lack of cultural appreciation fed the pattern of warfare, death, and destruction, but it only partially explains it.

In one sense, such massive human misery and waste came unexpectedly as an end product of forces that had been coalescing in Europe for several centuries—forces which exploded into the rush of westward expansion beginning in the late fifteenth century. New developments in science, in humanistic learning, and in the technologies of navigation and sailing allowed Europeans to move well beyond the coastlines of their confining boundaries for the first time. The rise of the cities, the emergence of a mercantile class, and the evolution of capitalist values coincidentally bred a broader quest for scarce trading goods. European merchants wanted to get their hands on rare spices, pharmaceuticals, metals, jewels, furs, ivory, and bullion, to name a few items capable of yielding handsome profits. At first merchants pursued trading routes to the East, but the expanding middle eastern Muslim world of the Mediterranean area became a threat to profitable expeditions. The Portuguese responded by coasting down Africa and developing a southeasterly route to the Orient—and the beginnings of a trade in black slaves in the process. But there were other mariners, such as Christopher Columbus, who believed that sailing west would prove to be the shortest, most economical trading route to the East. Queen Isabella of Spain had enough faith in the Genoese sailor's logic to sponsor him in what proved to be the first thrust in the creation of Spain's lucrative New World empire. Even though educated Europeans knew that the world was round before Columbus first sailed, they, like the "Admiral of the Ocean Sea," did not know that a massive native population living on two continents stood between them and the Orient.

Bumping into a "new world" came as a surprise to Columbus, who kept insisting that he had reached Japan. From the Spanish court's perspective, though, Columbus's error in calculating the earth's true circumference was not significant. What was significant was that great riches, especially in the form of gold and silver, began to flow in a torrential stream back to Spain, providing the capital base upon which sixteenth-century Spanish monarchs reigned as the most powerful in Europe.

Yet for the native Americans of central and southern America, Columbus's discovery of their world had grave consequences. Sophisticated cultural groups like the Aztecs of Mexico and the Incas of Peru soon faced extermination, though not because of superior Spanish manpower or military weaponry. Indeed, the secret, unknown, unintended weapon was disease. Having lived for centuries in isolation from virulent microbiological organisms that ravaged Europeans in such forms as smallpox, measles, diptheria, typhus, or plagues, native Americans lacked bodily immunities. Diseases rampaged everywhere once contact and exposure occurred, killing Indians by the millions. Tribes were so weakened and demoralized by the time that roving conquistadors appeared on the horizon that their will to resist sustained military incursions was gone. The few Indians who survived the pattern of rapid depopulation reluctantly accepted a fate of peonage and slavery.

Spain was the first European power to strike it rich in the New World on the funeral pyre of Indian nations. Given Spain's inordinate success in the sixteenth century, it seems strange that other Europeans were so slow in staking out their own claims. In fact, Englishmen took a full century after Columbus's voyages to plant an enduring, though admittedly feeble foothold at Jamestown, Virginia. Numerous factors seemed to hold back English and French adventurers, Spain's prime long-term New World competitors. One essential factor affecting the timing of westward advances was the rate of evolving central political stability in European states, characterized by the emergence of all-powerful dynastic heads of government. Ferdinand and Isabella were unifying Spain by breaking the power of localist forces long before a comparable pattern of national coalescence, identity, or allegiance surfaced in England and France. In time the challenge to Spanish

New World hegemony did come, greatly altering the nature of the European experience in America, an experience that began with the chilling, seemingly inexplicable decimation of millions of native peoples.

In the history of European westward expansion and the clash of Old and New World peoples, we must ask why events took the shape they did. For example, what was the total range of factors resulting in the destruction of the native population? What were the most important factors? Did any particular factor virtually presuppose a general pattern of cultural decimation, rather than some reasonable form of acculturation? Was there any way that native Americans might have defended or protected themselves more fully, especially given the unintended microbiological warfare? In turn, why was Spain, rather than England or France, the leader in the quest for New World riches? What factors seemed to hold Englishmen back? How much did the Spanish experience influence English attitudes and goals about what could be gotten from the New World? How much effect did the Spanish example have upon English or French relations with Indian natives? These and other important questions, raised in the introductory selections ahead, begin the process of learning more about the interpreting of colonial America.

1. Tudor Expansion: The Transition from Medieval to Modern History

A. L. Rowse

A. L. Rowse (b. 1903), a Fellow of All Souls College, Oxford University, has
devoted a lifetime of scholarly study to the subject of sixteenth-century England,
paying particular attention to those enterprising Elizabethan gentlemen who
formed a vanguard for English expansion into the New World. Rowse
hypothesizes below that the first steps in the English drive westward were taken
as the result of a conjunction of forces remolding the order of life in late
medieval Europe. Medieval society was parochial intellectually, and it was
divided politically. But a few men felt impelled to seek more knowledge about
the unknown in the world. At the same time dynastic monarchs such as the
Tudors were forcing their subjects to think in national rather than local terms.
The attack upon local allegiances made it possible for the Tudors to unify the
islands; for the first time since the early Middle Ages the dynamic westward
movement of peoples could begin.

Consolidation of political authority by dynastic heads of state, according to
Professor Rowse, was a condition necessary for English overseas expansion, as it
had been for the Spanish. This process formed part of a larger movement
restructuring the basis of life in early modern Europe. What are the implications
of this evolutionary portrait of change? Has Rowse understated the importance
of revolutions in altering the course of human events?

How much the greatest event it is that ever happened in the world! and how
much the best!" said Charles James Fox of the French Revolution. Charles Fox
was a man of notoriously bad judgment—and I am not sure that we historians are
not too generous in our estimate of the importance of revolutions. I am not speaking of their value or their merits, where bad is mixed with good, the destructive
with the constructive, losses with gains. I am speaking of the *importance* of revolutions as a factor in history and wondering whether we do not overrate it. I suppose that their chief contribution lies in the release they give to forces in society
that have been withheld or restrained—though not all is for the good when the
safety valve is blown off.

We historians attach much significance to the Puritan Revolution in England,
the Revolution of 1688, the French, the American, the Russian revolutions—many

Source: A. L. Rowse, "Tudor Expansion: The Transition from Medieval to Modern History,"
William and Mary Quarterly, 3rd ser., 14 (1957), pp. 309–316. Copyright 1957 by the Institute of
Early American History and Culture. Reprinted by permission of Curtis Brown, Ltd.

books, whole libraries, have been written about them. Yet I wonder whether there are not quieter, underlying movements, that attract less spectacular notice—the movements of peoples, the internal movements of population—which are more fundamental and achieve more durable results in the history of mankind. We in the twentieth century lie under the sinister shadow of the Russian Revolution: we are not likely to underestimate it. Yet it may well be that before long we shall come to think of the Russian colonization of Siberia, her expansion into the vast spaces of Northern Asia, as a matter of more solid and insurmountable importance for the world.

The fact is that people's attention is arrested by the drama of the revolutionary break in society: they are rather mesmerized by the cross section that is revealed and are apt not to grasp the long process in which revolution is a jolt, a disturbance, sometimes hurrying things up, sometimes obstructing or deflecting the current.

How many people have the historic imagination to realize that the making of the American nation must be the greatest single, homogeneous achievement of modern history?

Its appeal is epic rather than dramatic: a slower moving, in some ways a more subtle, appeal to the imagination. But one feels it no less strongly—and perhaps it is a deeper level of experience of life, of realization of the heroism and the pathos that it speaks to—as one moves across the prairies, down the Ohio and across the Mississippi, or out of the Cumberland Gap from Kentucky into southern Illinois and spreading fanwise across the Middle West, or along the trials from St. Louis to Oregon, to Santa Fé and across the passes into California. Again, to go back to an earlier phase, as one approaches the coast of America, one is touched to tears to think of all the effort and endurance, the sacrifice of men's lives that went into it, the hundreds and thousands of forgotten simple men along with the unforgotten— a Thomas Cavendish, most gifted young captain, second circumnavigator of the globe after Drake; a Stephen Parmenius, the Hungarian geographer, bedfellow of Hakluyt's in Oxford days, no less than a Humphrey Gilbert or a Henry Hudson, coming to his end in the ice floes of the bay now named after him. Or we remember how Gilbert beggared himself, spent his own fortune and his wife's, on his dream of the English colonization of North America; how Walter Raleigh spent similarly all that he won from the favor of the Queen upon the same great enterprise, and how, in circumstances of defeat, discouragement, disgrace, he wrote: "I shall yet live to see it an English nation."

We may regard the peopling of North America as an extension across the Atlantic of the process a thousand years before, in the time of the *Völkerwanderungen,* by which Britain was colonized by the original Anglo-Saxon stocks: a comparable process on a much smaller scale, occupying a much longer tract of time, by which forest was felled, the frontier extended, the nation took shape out of a creative mixing, a fusion of stocks. (It would be a fine subject for a book, to have a comparative study of these parallel processes, the naming of places and similar matters, separated by a thousand years.) I am to speak of the beginnings of that second process, of which the twentieth century has seen the consolidation, the fulfillment, rather than the end.

My story may be said to be concerned with the junction between the two processes, the transition from the medieval to the modern world. For, surely, this is where the transition comes between the Middle Ages and modern history, this is the factor that in the long run made the greatest difference: the discovery of the

new world. We are all aware of the long and fruitful discussion as to what constituted the Renaissance—nowhere better summed up than in Wallace K. Fer-
guson's admirable and discriminating book, *The Renaissance in Historical
Thought*—what were the factors out of which came the modern world and its
characteristic experience. Whatever we may think, however much we may
disagree, about the rediscovery of antiquity, the importance of the study of Greek,
the new standards of criticism and scholarship, the significance of humanism, of
Renaissance state and new monarchy, here is a *differentia* that is indisputable, the
significance of which grows with the expanding world, with which the Middle
Ages come to an end.

I often think how vividly it is brought home by that letter of a fourteenth-
century bishop of Exeter, John Grandison, to a friend at the papal court at
Avignon, describing the state of his remote diocese in the west: where in farthest
Cornwall the people speak a language that is not even English or understood by
the English, and beyond the Land's End is nothing but the great sundering flood.
It is the end of the known world.

A couple of centuries later, how all that has changed! The West Country now,
from being a remote backwater, is in the front line of all the maritime activity
launching out across the oceans: to the Canaries and the Guinea Coast, into the
South Atlantic to Brazil; from Guinea across to the Caribbean and out by the
Florida Channel; to Labrador and Hudson's Bay up into the gap between Green-
land and North America searching for a northwest passage to the Far East; to
Newfoundland and down the coast of New England into the unknown; to the
West Indies and up the coast to plant the Virginia colonies; at length direct to the
coast to plant the New England colonies; into the South Atlantic with Drake and
Cavendish, to penetrate the Pacific and establish contact with the Far East. All
these voyages took wing from Plymouth, in Bishop Grandison's diocese: in his
days a very inconsiderable place, confined to the small change of cross-channel
trade and tit-for-tat raiding, which has left its memento in the name of Bretonside
by Sutton Pool. These voyages made the name and fortune of Plymouth, under the
guidance of the remarkable Hawkins family and their brilliant poor relation,
Francis Drake. (He did not remain a poor relation for long.) The transition from
the medieval to the modern world stands well expressed in the change of name of
the fortified island off Plymouth Hoe: known to the medieval people as St.
Nicholas's island, to the moderns it is Drake's Island.

I realize that this is looking at the matter simply from an English perspective.
But a wider one makes my point all the stronger, when one considers that by this
time Portuguese and Spaniards had discovered half the world's coasts, were in
occupation of much of Central and South America, and had established a regular
route across the Pacific to the Far East. That brings home more powerfully than
ever the difference between the Middle Ages, in this sense circumscribed and
rather static, and the modern world, expansive and essentially dynamic.

The end of the Middle Ages in England was marked by contraction rather
than expansion: withdrawal from the long dream of conquest in France, and,
what is particularly significant, a marked shrinkage in the area of English control,
of English language and civilization, in Ireland. Gaeldom came once more lapping
like lake water up to the walls of the towns—Dublin, Waterford, Cork, Galway,
last outposts of earlier Anglo-Irish. In the early fifteenth century, with Owen
Glendower's rebellion, Wales achieved a temporary quasi independence; though it
was defeated and crushed, Wales remained resentfully aloof, unabsorbed. Nor was

any real progress made with the integration of Cornwall or the Scottish Borders, where they "knew no king but a Percy," into the fabric of the state. The fact was that the central institutions of the state were giving way under the strain of royal minorities, dynastic conflict, unsuccessful foreign war. The state's hold was contracting, government ineffectual, society itself inefficient and showing some signs of arrested development and decline.

The dynamic movement that initiates and motivates modern history reversed all that. The beginnings of this process form the subject of my book, *The Expansion of Elizabethan England,* and I have no wish to impose a summary of it here, apart from the unprofitability of such a procedure. But perhaps I may draw one or two conclusions from the detailed study made there.

By far the most important, the one that I had not realized before going into it, was the continuity of the process of expansion within the islands with that across the oceans, especially the phase of it which is crucial for modern history—Bismarck called it "the decisive fact in the modern world"—that across the Atlantic to the peopling of North America. These were two phases of the same movement, the second gathering momentum as it went forward, until it became the greatest single influence upon the home country in turn, a chief factor in transforming its society, making its fortune; today—it is not too much to say—constituting its fate. Without America the islands would have gone down to defeat and destruction twice in this century; without America I see no viable future for them.

The English state gathered its resources together under the Tudors and achieved an effective relation with society, particularly the leading middle elements in it—country gentry and town middle class—that enabled it to go forward with the work of expansion and internal integration.

We may see the process vividly brought home to us in the history of my native Cornwall. Small as it is, it was a little country on its own, with its own life, language, and culture. The Cornish were content with their Celtic ways—the remote people, who did not speak English, of Bishop Grandison's letter, wrapped up in their cult of the saints, their holy wells and wayside crosses, their feasts and pilgrimages, dreaming their dream of King Arthur and his return someday to the land. That self-regarding life was rudely shaken by the demand of Henry VII's government in 1497 for taxation for the defense of the Scottish Border. The Scottish Border was nothing to do with them, said the Cornish, and proceeded to raise a formidable rebellion which was only arrested outside of London, on Blackheath field. We see that the Cornish had an inadequate comprehension of the modern state, with its characteristic feature of central taxation for over-all state purposes. The Cornish were still living in the Middle Ages.

Nor were they any more reconciled half a century later when the central state imposed in 1549 a new religious uniformity upon the country with a prayer book in *English*. The English service was no better than a Christmas mumming, said the Cornish, and joined with the men of Devon in a rebellion that paralyzed government for several months in the summer of 1549, until it was crushed with some bloodshed. This time the repression was severe and the Cornish were taught a lesson they did not have to learn again. Indeed, the change of sentiment and of power within Cornwall was most marked, from the old inland families of Catholic sympathies to the newer coastal families, seafaring and Protestant, closely concerned in the ports and harbors engaged in the multifarious activities of oceanic expansion and sea warfare, their mouths open to the new world. It is surely very significant that all these families were to the fore in the voyages to America and the colonizing expeditions: one meets their names again and again in the records, Grenvilles, Killigrews, Tremaynes, Gilberts, Kendalls, Prideaux, Rouses.

Wales offers an example of integration with the state on a bigger scale, a much larger undertaking. Here the process was greatly helped and made much smoother by the Welsh capture of the throne in the person of Henry Tudor. Never the breath of a rebellion was raised against the dynasty that was Welsh—even when the representative of the central government, Bishop Rowland Lee, was repressing the age-long delights of Welsh society, thieving and cattle stealing, stringing up thieves in hundreds, stamping out blood feuds and affrays, reducing the Welsh to English ideas of law and order.

We do not find the Welsh so much to the fore as the West Country in the American voyages. All the same we come across their names on them—Morgans and Vaughans, Floyds and Trevors. And we remember that the Welsh Captain Middleton, who bore the news of the approaching Spanish fleet to Grenville in the Azores, finished his translation of the Psalms into Welsh *apud Scutum, insulam occidentalium Indorum*. The chief field for Welsh expansionist activity—after England, where they virtually bore rule with the Tudors and the Cecils—was Ireland, to which they sent captains and soldiers for the wars, undertakers and colonists, administrators, lawyers, a Lord Deputy, and even bishops.

Ireland was a far tougher proposition for the Tudor state with its exiguous resources. It seems that historians have not even yet realized how deep was the chasm between Tudor England, in essence a modern society, and the Celtic civilization of Ireland, in many parts not even a medieval society, but premedieval, nomadic and pastoral, with its tribal chieftains and their endemic warfare—a culture arrested in development and run down, closer to the England of the Anglo-Saxon heptarchy than it was to the England to Elizabeth. No doubt the subjugation of Ireland could have been effected by the Tudor state earlier—if that had been its intention; or with far less difficulty in the end, if it had been able to concentrate on the objective, instead of having to regard it as one sector of a continental and oceanic struggle with Spain.

However, in the end Ireland was subjugated and a basis laid for a fruitful intermixture of the two peoples which—in spite of disappointments and the subsequent frustrations of Irish history—has led to a distinguished contribution to the world in the shape of Anglo-Irish culture. Whatever anyone may say, the basis of modern Irish society, on the land, in its property system, in law and language, is not Celtic but English. The foundation was not laid until the accession of a Scottish king came to complete the lifework of an Anglo-Welsh queen: with the union of the two kingdoms, the settlement of Ulster could go forward along with the transformation of the Scottish Borders into the middle shires of a joint kingdom. It fell to a Scottish king to proclaim the union of Britain: "the Isle within itself hath almost none but imaginary bounds of separation, without but one common limit or rather guard of the Ocean sea, making the whole a little world within itself, the nations an uniformity of constitutions both of body and mind, especially in martial processes, a community of language (the principal means of civil society), an unity of religion (the deepest bond of hearty union and the surest knot of lasting peace)."

The unification of the islands gave the basis for the great lunge forward across the Atlantic, the exodus of stocks to North America, the open door for which the Elizabethans had fought. We are all aware of the part played by the West

Country, the Plymouth Company and its promoters—such men as Sir Ferdinando Gorges, John Trelawny, and John White of Dorchester—in the later beginnings of New England. But observe, what has been very little observed by historians, that it was the very people who were most deeply concerned with the plantation and colonization of Southern Ireland—Humphrey Gilbert, Walter Raleigh, Richard Grenville—who took the leading part in planting the first colonies in Virginia. It is as if Ireland were the blueprint for America.

The question of North America became one of national concern; that is to say, so many of the leading spirits of the age were interested, not a few of them engaged by it. The leading figures at Court were closely concerned—Leicester and Walsingham, Sir Christopher Hatton and Sir Philip Sidney, even Burghley in a watchful, conservative way; the Queen herself was less conservative, and she was interested in everything that affected America. She invested in at least two of Hawkins' voyages to the Caribbean, and one of Frobisher's towards the Northwest Passage. Unbeknown to her sage Lord Treasurer, she planned Drake's great voyage with him: in that she was the principal investor and the principal recipient of the booty. It was she who granted Humphrey Gilbert the patent to settle and colonize North America; on his death she passed it on to Walter Raleigh, to whom she permitted the land to be called Virginia after her. She would never make peace with Spain without security for the liberties of the Netherlands or the open door for English settlement in North America.

On the side of action, names are legion, so many of the most famous Elizabethans took part or were involved: Drake, Raleigh, the Gilberts, Grenville, Thomas Cavendish, Frobisher, the Hawkinses. On the side of science and intellect: John Dee, the leading mathematician and cosmographer of the early part of the reign; Thomas Hariot, first mathematician of the age; Richard Hakluyt, whose lifework it was to focus their minds upon America—the priority that the American school of thought and action came to have was due to a lifetime of concentrated, educated propaganda from his brain and pen. It has been given to few men to fertilize the history of their country so prodigiously. To him we owe the survival of nearly everything we know of the American voyages. His long life proved the one continuing figure that linked the two waves of Virginia enterprise, the successive attempts of the 1580's and those that gained a permanent foothold after the Queen's death. In literature, before Shakespeare died, the impact of America upon the English imagination is already rich and evident, in Spenser and Drayton, in Raleigh and Chapman and Donne, never more beautifully than in *The Tempest*.

Perhaps then we may leave the last word to a poet, Samuel Daniel—one of Sidney's circle and a West Countryman—who glimpsed something of the limitless possibilities to come out of the unimaginable future, in that process of which we have indicated the beginnings:

> And who in time knows whither we may vent
> The treasure of our tongue, to what strange shores
> This gain of our best glory shall be sent,
> To enrich unknowing nations with our stores?
> What worlds in the yet unformèd Occident
> May come refined with the accents that are ours?

But what a difference from the accent of the Middle Ages, what a world we are away now from the medieval world!

2. The European Impact on Indian Culture: An Ecological Interpretation

Calvin Martin

In our own modern world we constantly hear about the need for ecological balance, that is, protecting rather than despoiling and wasting vital natural resources. Rarely do we think of ecological balance as a theoretical concept which would assist in illuminating serious problems of the past. Yet Calvin Martin (b. 1948), an ethnohistorian concerned with the investigation of pre-Columbian North American Indian cultures who is also a member of the Rutgers University department of history, has employed that concept in the following selection as a means of attempting to understand the devastating impact that Europeans and their ways had upon native American Indian cultures. Taking a case study approach, Martin focuses in on the Micmac Indians of eastern Canada, Indians whose first contact with whites came when French fishermen, explorers, and Jesuit missionaries reached those northern shores.

Not surprisingly, the impact of Europeans upon the Micmac value structure, and by extension the value structures of other Eastern Woodland groups, was shattering. Yet what is most suggestive about Martin's analysis is the way in which contemporary themes from the field of cultural ecology help to clarify why such devastation occurred. In this context, how did European economic, social, and political values weaken and undermine the Micmac value structure? Was disease the decisive unhinging factor, predisposing other changes? Why did the Micmacs fail to unite with other native American groups in the region so as to more effectively resist white aggression upon the land? Did their traditional belief system somehow militate against successful intertribal responses?

As the drive for furs, known prosaically as the fur trade, expanded and became more intense in seventeenth-century Canada, complaints of beaver extermination became more frequent and alarming. By 1635, for example, the Huron had reduced their stock of beaver to the point where the Jesuit Father Paul Le Jeune could declare that they had none. In 1684 Baron Lahontan recorded a speech made before the French governor-general by an Iroquois spokesman, who explained that his people had made war on the Illinois and Miami because these Algonquians had trespassed on Iroquois territory and overkilled their beaver, "and contrary to the Custom of all the Savages, have carried off whole Stocks,

Source: From Calvin Martin, "The European Impact on the Culture of a Northeastern Algonquian Tribe: An Ecological Interpretation," *William and Mary Quarterly,* 3rd ser., 31 (1974), pp. 3–26. Footnotes omitted. Reprinted by permission of Calvin Martin and the *William and Mary Quarterly.*

both Male and Female." This exploitation of beaver and other furbearers seems to have been most intense in the vicinity of major trading posts and among the native tribes most affected by the trade (the Montagnais, Huron, League Iroquois, Micmac, and others), while those tribes which remained beyond European influence and the trade, such as the Bersimis of northeastern Quebec, enjoyed an abundance of beaver in their territories.

Even before the establishment of trading posts, the Micmac of the extreme eastern tip of Canada were engaged in lively trade with European fishermen. Thus areas that were important in the fishing industry, such as Prince Edward Island, the Gaspé Penninsula, and Cape Breton Island, were cleaned out of moose and other furbearers by the mid-seventeenth century. Reviewing this grim situation, Nicolas Denys observed that game was less abundant in his time than formerly; as for the beaver, "few in a house are saved; they [the Micmac] would take all. The disposition of the Indians is not to spare the little ones any more than the big ones. They killed all of each kind of animal that there was when they could capture it."

In short, the game which by all accounts had been so plentiful was now being systematically overkilled by the Indians themselves. A traditional explanation for this ecological catastrophe is neatly summarized by Peter Farb, who conceives of it in mechanistic terms: "If the Northern Athabaskan and Northern Algonkian Indians husbanded the land and its wildlife in primeval times, it was only because they lacked both the technology to kill very many animals and the market for so many furs. But once white traders entered the picture, supplying the Indians with efficient guns and an apparently limitless market for furs beyond the seas, the Indians went on an orgy of destruction." The Indian, in other words, was "economically seduced" to exploit the wildlife requisite to the fur trade.

Such a cavalier dismissal of northeastern Algonquian culture, especially its spiritual component, renders this explanation superficial and inadequate. One can argue that economic determinism was crucial to the course of Algonquian cultural development (including religious perception) over a long period of time. Yet from this perspective European contact was but a moment in the cultural history of the Indians, and it is difficult to imagine that ideals and a life-style that had taken centuries to evolve would have been so easily and quickly discarded merely for the sake of improved technological convenience. As we shall see, the entire Indian-land relationship was suffused with religious considerations which profoundly influenced the economic (subsistence) activities and beliefs of these people. The subsistence cycle was regulated by centuries of spiritual tradition which, if it had been in a healthy state, would have countered the revolutionizing impact of European influence. Tradition would doubtless have succumbed eventually, but why did the end come so soon? Why did the traditional safeguards of the northeastern Algonquian economic system offer such weak resistance to its replacement by the exploitive, European-induced regime?

When the problem is posed in these more comprehensive terms, the usual economic explanation seems misdirected, for which reason the present article will seek to offer an alternative interpretation. The methodology of cultural ecology will be brought to bear on the protohistoric and early contact phases of Micmac cultural history in order to examine the Indian-land relationship under aboriginal and postcontact conditions and to probe for an explanation to the problem of wildlife overkill.

Cultural ecology seeks to explain the interaction of environment and culture, taking the ecosystem and the local human population as the basic units of analysis. An ecosystem is a discrete community of plants and animals, together with the nonliving environment, occupying a certain space and time, having a flow-through of energy and raw materials in its operation, and composed of subsystems. For convenience of analysis, an ecosystem can be separated into its physical and biological components, although one should bear in mind that in nature the two are completely intermeshed in complex interactions. And from the standpoint of cultural ecology, there is a third component: the metaphysical or spiritual.

The ecosystem model of plant and animal ecologists is somewhat strained when applied to a human population, although, as Roy A. Rappaport has demonstrated in his *Pigs for the Ancestors,* the attempt can be very useful. The difficulties encountered include the assignment of definite territorial limits to the area under consideration (resulting in a fairly arbitrary delimitation of an ecosystem), the quantification of the system's energy budget and the carry capacity of the land, and the identification of subsystem interrelations. Assigning values to variables becomes, in many instances, quite impossible.

The transposition of the ecosystem approach from cultural anthropology to historical inquiry complicates these problems even further, for the relationships between a human population and its environment are seldom amenable to rigorous quantitative analysis using historical documents as sources. Yet this is certainly not always so. In the case of the fur trade, for example, one may in fact be able to measure some of its effects on the environment from merchants' records—showing numbers of pelts obtained from a region over a certain time period—and also from lists of goods given to the Indians at trading posts and by treaties. Even when available, such records are too incomplete to satisfy the rigorous demands of the ecologist, but to say that they are of limited value is not to say that they are useless.

Few historians have used the ecological model in their work. Recognizing the need for the environmental perspective in historiography, Wilbur R. Jacobs recently observed that "those who hope to write about such significant historical events [as the despoiling of the American west] . . . will need a sort of knowledge not oridinarily possessed by historians. To study the impact of the fur trade upon America and her native people, for instance, there must be more than a beginning acquaintance with ethnology, plant and animal ecology, paleoecology, and indeed much of the physical sciences."

In the case of the northeastern Algonquian, and the Micmac in particular, the fur trade was but one factor—albeit an important one—in the process of acculturation. Long before they felt the lure of European technology, these littoral Indians must have been infected with Old World diseases carried by European fishermen, with catastrophic effects. Later, the Christian missionaries exerted a disintegrative influence on the Indians' view of and relation to their environment. All three of these factors—disease, Christianity, and technology—which may be labeled "trigger" factors, must be assessed in terms of their impact on the Indians' ecosystem.

Among the first North American Indians to be encountered by Europeans were the Micmacs who occupied present-day Nova Scotia, northern New Brunswick and the Gaspé Peninsula, Prince Edward Island, and Cape Breton Island. According to the Sieur de Dièreville, they also lived along the lower St. John River with the Malecites, who outnumbered them. For our present purposes, the

Micmac territory will be considered an ecosystem, and the Micmac occupying it will be regarded as a local population. These designations are not entirely arbitrary, for the Micmac occupied and exploited the area in a systematic way; they had a certain psychological unity or similarity in their ideas about the cosmos; they spoke a language distinct from those of their neighbors; and they generally married within their own population. There were, as might be expected, many external factors impinging on the ecosystem which should also be evaluated, although space permits them only to be mentioned here. Some of these "supralocal" relations involved trade and hostilities with other tribes; the exchange of genetic material and personnel with neighboring tribes through intermarriage and adoption; the exchange of folklore and customs; and the movements of such migratory game as moose and woodland caribou. The Micmac ecosystem thus participated in a regional system, and the Micmac population was part of a regional population.

The hunting, gathering, and fishing Micmac who lived within this Acadian forest, especially along its rivers and by the sea, were omnivores (so to speak) in the trophic system of the community. At the first trophic level, the plants eaten were wild potato tubers, wild fruits and berries, acorns and nuts, and the like. Trees and shrubs provided a wealth of materials used in the fashioning of tools, utensils, and other equipment. At the time of contact, none of the Indians living north of the Saco River cultivated food crops. Although legend credits the Micmac with having grown maize and tobacco "for the space of several years," these cultigens, as well as beans, pumpkins, and wampum (which they greatly prized), were obtained from the New England Algonquians of the Saco River area (Abnakis) and perhaps from other tribes to the south.

Herbivores and carnivores occupy the second and third trophic levels respectively, with top carnivores in the fourth level. The Micmac hunter tapped all three levels in his seasonal hunting and fishing activities, and these sources of food were "to them like fixed rations assigned to every moon." In January, seals were hunted when they bred on islands off the coast; the fat was reduced to oil for food and body grease, and the women made clothing from the fur. The principal hunting season lasted from February till mid-March, since there were enough marine resources, especially fish and mollusks, available during the other three seasons to satisfy most of the Micmacs' dietary needs. For a month and a half, then, the Indians withdrew from the seashore to the banks of rivers and lakes and into the woods to hunt the caribou, moose, black bear, and small furbearers. At no other time of the year were they so dependent on the caprice of the weather: a feast was as likely as a famine. A heavy rain could ruin the beaver and caribou hunt, and a deep, crustless snow would doom the moose hunt.

Since beaver were easier to hunt on the ice than in the water, and since their fur was better during the winter, this was the chief season for taking them. Hunters would work in teams or groups, demolishing the lodge or cutting the dam with stone axes. Dogs were sometimes used to track the beaver which took refuge in air pockets along the edge of the pond, or the beaver might be harpooned at air holes. In the summer hunt, beaver were shot with the bow or trapped in deadfalls using poplar as bait, but the commonest way to take them was to cut the dam in the middle and drain the pond, killing the animals with bows and spears.

Next to fish, moose was the most important item in the Micmac diet, and it was their staple during the winter months when these large mammals were hunted with dogs on the hard-crusted snow. In the summer and spring, moose were tracked, stalked, and shot with the bow; in the fall, during the rutting season, the bull was enticed by a clever imitation of the sound of a female urinating. Another technique was to ensnare the animal with a noose.

Moose was the Micmacs' favorite meat. The entrails, which were considered a great delicacy, and the "most delicious fat" were carried by the triumphant hunter to the campsite, and the women were sent after the carcass. The mistress of the wigwam decided what was to be done with each portion of the body, every part of which was used. Grease was boiled out of the bones and either drunk pure (with "much gusto") or stored as loaves of moose-butter; the leg and thigh bones were crushed and the marrow eaten; the hides were used for robes, leggings, moccasins, and tent coverings; tools, ornaments, and game pieces were made from antlers, teeth, and toe bones, respectively. According to contemporary French observers, the Micmac usually consumed the moose meat immediately, without storing any, although the fact that some of the meat was preserved rather effectively by smoking it on racks, so that it would even last the year, demonstrates that Micmac existence was not as hand-to-mouth as is commonly believed of the northeastern Algonquian. Black bear were also taken during the season from February till mid-March, but such hunting was merely coincidental. If a hunter stumbled upon a hibernating bear, he could count himself lucky.

As the lean months of winter passed into the abundance of spring, the fish began to spawn, swimming up rivers and streams in such numbers that "everything swarms with them." In mid-March came the smelt, and at the end of April the herring. Soon there were sturgeon and salmon, and numerous waterfowl made nests out on the islands—which meant there were eggs to be gathered. Mute evidence from seashore middens and early written testimony reveal that these Indians also relied heavily on various mollusks, which they harvested in great quantity. Fish was a staple for the Micmac, who knew the spawning habits of each type of fish and where it was to be found. Weirs were erected across streams to trap the fish on their way downstream on a falling tide, while larger fish, such as sturgeon and salmon, might be speared or trapped.

The salmon run marked the beginning of summer, when the wild geese shed their plumage. Most wildfowl were hunted at their island rookeries; waterfowl were often hunted by canoe and struck down as they took to flight; others, such as the Canadian geese which grazed in the meadows, were shot with the bow.

In autumn, when the waterfowl migrated southward, the eels spawned up the many small rivers along the coast. From mid-September to October the Micmac left the ocean and followed the eels, "of which they lay in a supply; they are good and fat." Caribou and beaver were hunted during October and November, and with December came the "tom cod" (which were said to have spawned under the ice) and turtles bearing their young. In January the subsistence cycle began again with the seal hunt.

As he surveyed the seasonal cycle of these Indians, Father Pierre Biard was impressed by nature's bounty and Micmac resourcefulness: "These then, but in a still greater number, are the revenues and incomes of our Savages; such, their table and living, all prepared and assigned, everything to its proper place and quarter." Although we have omitted mention of many other types of forest, marine, and aquatic life which were also exploited by the Micmac, those listed above were certainly the most significant in the Micmacs' food quest and ecosystem.

Frank G. Speck, perhaps the foremost student of northeastern Algonquian culture, has emphasized that hunting to the Micmacs was not a "war upon the animals, not a slaughter for food or profit." Denys's observations confirm Speck's point: "Their greatest task was to feed well and to go a hunting. They did not lack animals, which they killed only in proportion as they had need of them." From this, and the above description of their effective hunting techniques, it would appear that the Micmac were not limited by their hunting technology in the taking of game. As Denys pointed out, "the hunting by the Indians in old times was easy for them. . . . When they were tired of eating one sort, they killed some of another. If they did not wish longer to eat meat, they caught some fish. They never made an accumulation of skins of Moose, Beaver, Otter, or others, but only so far as they needed them for personal use. They left the remainder [of the carcass] where the animals had been killed, not taking the trouble to bring them to their camps." Need, not technology, was the ruling factor, and need was determined by the great primal necessities of life and regulated by spiritual considerations. Hunting, as Speck remarks, was *"a holy occupation"*; it was conducted and controlled by spiritual rules.

The bond which united these physical and biological components of the Micmac ecosystem, and indeed gave them definition and comprehensibility, was the world view of the Indian. The foregoing discussion had dealt mainly with the empirical, objective, physical ("operational") environmental model of the observer; what it lacks is the "cognized" model of the Micmac.

Anthropologists regard the pre-Columbian North American Indian as a sensitive member of his environment, who merged sympathetically with its living and nonliving components. The Indian's world was filled with superhuman and magical powers which controlled man's destiny and nature's course of events. Murray Wax explains:

> To those who inhabit it, the magical world is a "society," not a "mechanism," that is, it is composed of "beings" rather than "objects." Whether human or nonhuman, these beings are associated with and related to one another socially and sociably, that is, in the same ways as human beings to one another. These patterns of association and relationship may be structured in terms of kinship, empathy, sympathy, reciprocity, sexuality, dependency, or any other of the ways that human beings interact with and affect or afflict one another. Plants, animals, rocks, and stars are thus seen not as "objects" governed by laws of nature, but as "fellows" with whom the individual or band may have a more or less advantageous relationship.

For the Micmac, together with all the other eastern subarctic Algonquians, the power of these mysterious forces was apprehended as "manitou"—translated "magic power"—much in the same way that we might use the slang word "vibrations" to register the emotional feelings emanating (so we say) from an object, person, or situation.

The world of the Micmac was thus filled with superhuman forces and beings (such as dwarfs, giants, and magicians), and animals that could talk to man and had spirits akin to his own, and the magic of mystical and medicinal herbs—a world where even inanimate objects possessed spirits. Micmac subsistence activities were inextricably bound up within this spiritual matrix, which, we are suggesting, acted as a kind of control mechanism on Micmac land-use, maintaining the environment within an optimum range of conditions.

In order to understand the role of the Micmac in the fur trading enterprise of the colonial period, it is useful to investigate the role of the Micmac hunter in the spiritual world of precontact times. Hunting was governed by spiritual rules and considerations which were manifest to the early French observers in the form of seemingly innumerable taboos. These taboos connoted a sense of cautious reverence for a conscious fellow-member of the same ecosystem who, in the view of the Indian, allowed itself to be taken for food and clothing. The Indian felt that "both he and his victim understood the roles which they played in the hunt; the animal was resigned to its fate."

That such a resignation on the part of the game was not to be interpreted as an unlimited license to kill should be evident from an examination of some of the more prominent taboos. Beaver, for example, were greatly admired by the Micmac for their industry and "abounding genius"; for them, the beaver had "sense" and formed a "separate nation." Hence there were various regulations associated with the disposal of their remains: trapped beaver were drawn in public and made into soup, extreme care being taken to prevent the soup from spilling into the fire; beaver bones were carefully preserved, never being given to the dogs—lest they lose their sense of smell for the animal—or thrown into the fire— lest misfortune come upon "all the nation"—or thrown into rivers—"because the Indians fear lest the spirit of the bones . . . would promptly carry the news to the other beavers, which would desert the country in order to escape the same misfortune." Likewise, menstruating women were forbidden to eat beaver, "for the Indians are convinced, they say, that the beaver, which has sense, would no longer allow itself to be taken by the Indians if it had been eaten by their unclean daughters." The fetus of the beaver, as well as that of the bear, moose, otter, and porcupine, was reserved for the old men, since it was believed that a youth who ate such food would experience intense foot pains while hunting.

Taboos similarly governed the disposal of the remains of the moose—what few there were. The bones of a moose fawn (and of the marten) were never given to the dogs nor were they burned, "for they [the Micmac] would not be able any longer to capture any of these animals in hunting if the spirits of the martens and of the fawns of the moose were to inform their own kind of the bad treatment they had received among the Indians." Fear of such reprisal also prohibited menstruating women from drinking out of the common kettles or bark dishes. Such regulations imply cautious respect for the animal hunted. The moose not only provided food and clothing, but was firmly tied up with the Micmac spirit-world—as were the other game animals.

Bear ceremonialism was also practiced by the Micmac. Esteem for the bear is in fact common among boreal hunting peoples of northern Eurasia and North America, and has the following characteristics: the beast is typically hunted in the early spring, while still in hibernation. It is addressed, when either dead or alive, with honorific names; a conciliatory speech is made to the animal, either before or after killing it, by which the hunter apologizes for his act and perhaps explains why it is necessary; and the carcass is respectfully treated, those parts not used (especially the skull) being ceremonially disposed of and the flesh consumed in accordance with taboos. Such rituals are intended to propitiate the spiritual controller of the bears so that he will continue to furnish game to the hunter. Among the Micmac the bear's heart was not eaten by young men lest they get out of breath while traveling and lose courage in danger. The bear carcass could be brought into the wigwam only through a special door made specifically for that purpose, either in the left or right side of the structure. This ritual was based on the Micmac belief that their women did not "deserve" to enter the wigwam through the same door as the animal. In fact, we are told that childless women actually left the wigwam at the approach of the body and did not return until it had been entirely consumed. By means of such rituals the hunter satisfied the soul-spirit of the slain animal. Of the present-day Mistassini (Montagnais) hunter, Speck writes that "should he fail to observe these formalities an unfavorable reaction would also ensue with his own soul-spirit, his 'great man' . . . as it is called. In such a case the 'great man' would fail to advise him when and where he would find his game. Incidentally the hunter resorts to drinking bear's grease to nourish his 'great man.'" Perhaps it was for a similar reason that the Micmac customarily forced newborn infants to swallow bear or seal oil before eating anything else.

If taboo was associated with fishing, we have little record of it; the only explicit evidence is a prohibition against the roasting of eels, which, if violated, would prevent the Indians from catching others. From this and from the fact that the Restigouche division of the Micmac wore the figure of a salmon as a totem around their neck, we may surmise that fish, too, shared in the sacred and symbolic world of the Indian.

Control over these supernatural forces and communication with them were the principal functions of the shaman, who served in Micmac society as an intermediary between the spirit realm and the physical. The lives and destinies of the natives were profoundly affected by the ability of the shaman to supplicate, cajole, and otherwise manipulate the magical beings and powers. The seventeenth-century French, who typically labeled the shamans (or *buowin*) frauds and jugglers in league with the devil, were repeatedly amazed at the respect accorded them by the natives. By working himself into a dreamlike state, the shaman would invoke the manitou of his animal helper and so predict future events. He also healed by means of conjuring. The Micmac availed themselves of a rather large pharmacopoeia of roots and herbs and other plant parts, but when these failed they would summon the healing arts of the most noted shaman in the district. The illness was often diagnosed by the *buowin* as a failure on the patient's part to perform a prescribed ritual; hence an offended supernatural power had visited the offender with sickness. At such times the shaman functioned as a psychotherapist, diagnosing the illness and symbolically (at least) removing its immediate cause from the patient's body.

It is important to understand that an ecosystem is holocoenotic in nature: there are no "walls" between the components of the system, for "the ecosystem reacts as a whole." Such was the case in the Micmac ecosystem of precontact times, where the spiritual served as a link connecting man with all the various subsystems of the environment. Largely through the mediation of the shaman, these spiritual obligations and restrictions acted as a kind of control device to maintain the ecosystem in a well-balanced condition. Under these circumstances the exploitation of game for subsistence appears to have been regulated by the hunter's respect for the continued welfare of his prey—both living and dead—as is evident from the numerous taboos associated with the proper disposal of animal remains. Violation of taboo desecrated the remains of the slain animal and offended its soul-spirit. The offended spirit would then retaliate in either of several ways, depending on the nature of the broken taboo: it could render the guilty hunter's (or the entire band's) means of hunting ineffective, or it could encourage its living fellows to remove themselves from the vicinity. In both cases the end result was the same— the hunt was rendered unsuccessful—and in both it was mediated by the same power—the spirit of the slain animal. Either of these catastrophes could usually be reversed through the magical arts of the shaman. In the Micmac cosmology, the overkill of wildlife would have been resented by the animal kingdom as an act comparable to genocide, and would have been resisted by means of the sanctions outlined above. The threat of retaliation thus had the effect of placing an upper limit on the number of animals slain, while the practical result was the conservation of wildlife.

The injection of European civilization into this balanced system initiated a series of chain reactions which, within a little over a century, resulted in the replacement of the aboriginal ecosystem by another. From at least the beginning of the sixteenth century, and perhaps well before that date, fishing fleets from England, France, and Portugal visited the Grand Banks off Newfoundland every spring for the cod, and hunted whale and walrus in the Gulf of St. Lawrence. Year after year, while other, more flamboyant men were advancing the geopolitical ambitions of their emerging dynastic states as they searched for precious minerals or a passage to the Orient, these unassuming fishermen visited Canada's east coast and made the first effective European contact with the Indians there. For the natives' furs they bartered knives, beads, brass kettles, assorted ship fittings, and the like, thus initiating the subversion and replacement of Micmac material culture by European technology. Far more important, the fishermen unwittingly infected the Indians with European diseases, against which the natives had no immunity. Commenting on what may be called the microbial phase of European conquest, John Witthoft has written:

> All of the microscopic parasites of humans, which had been collected together from all parts of the known world into Europe, were brought to these [American] shores, and new diseases stalked faster than man could walk into the interior of the continent. Typhoid, diphtheria, colds, influenza, measles, chicken pox, whooping cough, tuberculosis, yellow fever, scarlet fever, and other strep infections, gonorrhea, pox (syphilis), and smallpox were diseases that had never been in the New World before. They were new among populations which had no immunity to them. . . . Great epidemics and pandemics of these diseases are believed to have destroyed whole communities, depopulated whole regions, and vastly decreased the native population everywhere in the yet unexplored interior of the continent. The early pandemics are believed to have run their course prior to 1600 A.D.

Disease did more than decimate the native population; it effectively prepared the way for subsequent phases of European contact by breaking native morale and, perhaps even more significantly, by cracking their spiritual edifice. It is reasonable to suggest that European disease rendered the Indian's (particularly the shaman's) ability to control and otherwise influence the supernatural realm dysfunctional—because his magic and other traditional cures were now ineffective—thereby causing the Indian to apostatize (in effect), which in turn subverted the "retaliation" principle of taboo and opened the way to a corruption of the Indian-land relationship under the influence of the fur trade.

Much of this microbial phase was of course protohistoric, although it continued well into and no doubt beyond the seventeenth century—the time period covered by the earliest French sources. Recognizing the limitations of tradition as it conveys historical fact, it may nevertheless be instructive to examine a myth concerning the Cross-bearing Micmac of the Miramichi River which, as recorded by

Father Chrestien Le Clercq, seems to illustrate the demoralizing effect of disease. According to tradition, there was once a time when these Indians were gravely threatened by a severe sickness; as was their custom, they looked to the sun for help. In their extreme need a "beautiful" man, holding a cross, appeared before several of them in a dream. He instructed them to make similar crosses, for, as he told them, in this symbol lay their protection. For a time thereafter these Indians, who believed in dreams "even to the extent of superstition," were very religious and devoted in their veneration of this symbol. Later, however, they apostatized:

> Since the Gaspesian [Micmac] nation of the Cross-bearers has been almost wholly destroyed, as much by the war which they have waged with the Iroquois as by the maladies which have infected this land, and which, in three or four visitations, have caused the deaths of a very great number, these Indians have gradually relapsed from this first devotion of their ancestors. So true is it, that even the holiest and most religious practices, by a certain fatality attending human affairs, suffer always much alteration if they are not animated and conserved by the same spirit which gave them birth. In brief, when I went into their country to commence my mission, I found some persons who had preserved only the shadow of the customs of their ancestors.

Their rituals had failed to save these Indians when threatened by European diseases and intergroup hostilities; hence their old religious practices were abandoned, no doubt because of their ineffectiveness.

Several other observers also commented on the new diseases that afflicted the Micmac. In precontact times, declared Denys, "they were not subject to diseases, and knew nothing of fevers." By about 1700, however, Dièreville noted that the Micmac population was in sharp decline. The Indians themselves frequently complained to Father Biard and other Frenchmen that, since contact with the French, they had been dying off in great numbers. "For they assert that, before this association and intercourse [with the French], all their countries were very populous, and they tell how one by one the different coasts, according as they have begun to traffic with us, have been more reduced by disease." The Indians accused the French of trying to poison them or charged that the food supplied by the French was somehow adulterated. Whatever the reasons for the catastrophe, warned Biard, the Indians were very angry about it and "upon the point of breaking with us, and making war upon us."

To the Jesuit fathers, the solution to this sorry state of affairs lay in the civilizing power of the Gospel. To Biard, his mission was clear:

> For, if our Souriquois [Micmac] are few, they may become numerous; if they are savages, it is to domesticate and civilize them that we have come here; if they are rude, that is no reason that we should be idle; if they have until now profited little, it is no wonder, for it would be too much to expect fruit from this grafting, and to demand reason and maturity from a child.
>
> In conclusion, we hope in time to make them susceptible of receiving the doctrines of the faith and of the christian and catholic religion, and later, to penetrate further into the regions beyond.

The message was simple and straightforward: the black-robes would enlighten the Indians by ridiculing their animism and related taboos, discrediting their shamans, and urging them to accept the Christian gospel. But to their chagrin the

Indians proved stubborn in their ancient ways, no matter how unsuited to changing circumstances.

Since the advent of European diseases and the consequent disillusionment with native spiritual beliefs and customs, some Indians appear to have repudiated their traditional world view altogether, while others clung desperately to what had become a moribund body of ritual. We would suppose that the Christian message was more readily accepted by the former, while the latter group, which included the shamans and those too old to change, would have fought bitterly against the missionary teachings. But they resisted in vain for, with time, old people died and shamans whose magic was less potent than that of the missionaries were discredited. The missionary was successful only to the degree that his power exceeded that of the shaman. The nonliterate Indian, for example, was awed by the magic of handwriting as a means of communication. Even more significant was the fact that Christianity was the religion of the white man, who, with his superior technology and greater success at manipulating life to his advantage, was believed to have recourse to a great power (manitou) than did the Indian. Material goods, such as the trading articles offered the Indians by the French, were believed by the native to have a spirit within, in accord with their belief that all animate and inanimate objects housed such a spirit or power. Furthermore, there were degrees of power in such objects, which were determined and calibrated in the Indian mind by the degree of functionalism associated with a particular object. For example, the Micmac believed that there was a spirit of his canoe, of his snowshoes, of his bow, and so on. It was for this reason that a man's material goods were either buried with him or burned, so that their spirits would accompany his to the spirit world, where he would have need of them. Just as he had hunted game in this physical world, so his spirit would again hunt the game spirits with the spirits of his weapons in the land of the dead. Denys described an incident which emphasized the fact that even European trading goods had spirits, when he related how the brass kettle was known to have lost its spirit (or died) when it no longer rang when tapped. Thus Christianity, which to the Indians was the ritual harnessing all of this power, was a potent force among them. Nevertheless, the priests who worked among the Indians frequently complained of their relapsing into paganism, largely because the Micmac came to associate Christianity and civilization in general with their numerous misfortunes, together with the fact that they never clearly understood the Christian message anyway, but always saw it in terms of their own cosmology.

As all religious systems reflect their cultural milieux, so did seventeenth-century Christianity. Polygamy was condemned by the French missionaries as immoral, the consultation of shamans was discouraged, the custom of interring material goods was criticized, eat-all feasts were denounced as gluttonous and shortsighted, and the Indians were disabused of many of their so-called superstitions (taboos). The priests attacked the Micmac culture with a marvelous fervor and some success. Although they could not have appreciated it, they were aided in this endeavor by an obsolescent system of taboo and spiritual awareness; Christianity merely delivered the coup de grace.

The result of this Christian onslaught on a decaying Micmac cosmology was, of course, the despiritualization of the material world. Commenting on the process of despiritualization, Denys (who was a spectator to this transformation in the mid-seventeenth century) remarked that it was accomplished with "much difficulty"; for some of the Indians it was achieved by religious means, while others were influenced by the French customs, but nearly all were affected "by the need for the things which come from us, the use of which has become to them an indispensable necessity. They have abondoned all their own utensils, whether because of the trouble they had to make as well as to use them, or because of the facility of obtaining from us, in exchange for skins which cost them almost nothing, the things which seemed to them invaluable, not so much for their novelty as for the convenience they derived therefrom."

In the early years of the fur trade, before the establishment of permanent posts among the natives, trading was done with the coastwise fishermen from May to early fall. In return for skins of beaver, otter, marten, moose, and other furbearers, the Indians received a variety of fairly cheap commodities, principally tobacco, liquor, powder and shot (in later years), biscuit, peas, beans, flour, assorted clothing, wampum, kettles, and hunting tools. The success of this trade in economic terms must be attributed to pressure exerted on a relatively simple society by a complex civilization and, perhaps even more importantly, by the tremendous pull of this simple social organization on the resources of Europe. To the Micmac, who like other Indians measured the worth of a tool or object by the ease of its construction and use, the technology of Europe became indispensable. But as has already been shown, this was not simply an economic issue for the Indian; the Indian was more than just "economically seduced" by the European's trading goods. One must also consider the metaphysical implications of Indian acceptance of the European material culture.

European technology of the sixteenth and seventeenth centuries was largely incompatible with the spiritual beliefs of the eastern woodland Indians, despite the observation made above that the Micmacs readily invested trading goods with spiritual power akin to that possessed by their own implements. As Denys pointed out, the trade goods which the Micmac so eagerly accepted were accompanied by Christian religious teachings and French custom, both of which gave definition to these alien objects. In accepting the European material culture, the natives were impelled to accept the European abstract culture, especially religion, and so, in effect, their own spiritual beliefs were subverted as they abandoned their implements for those of the white man. Native religion lost not only its practical effectiveness, in part owing to the replacement of the traditional magical and animistic view of nature by the exploitive European view, but it was no longer necessary as a source of definition and theoretical support for the new Europe-derived material culture. Western technology made more "sense" if it was accompanied by Western religion.

Under these circumstances in the early contact period, the Micmac's role within his ecosystem changed radically. No longer was he the sensitive fellow-member of a symbolic world; under pressure from disease, European trade, and Christianity, he had apostatized—he had repudiated his role within the ecosystem. Former attitudes were replaced by a kind of mongrel outlook which combined some native traditions and beliefs with a European rationale and motivation. Our concern here is less to document this transformation than to assess its impact on the Indian-land relationship. In these terms, then, what effect did the trade have on the Micmac ecosystem?

The most obvious change was the unrestrained slaughter of certain game. Lured by European commodities, equipped with European technology, urged by European traders, deprived of a sense of responsibility and accountability for the land, and no longer inhibited by taboo, the Micmac began to overkill systematically those very wildlife which had now become so profitable and even indispensable to his new way of life. The pathos of this transformation of attitude and behavior is illustrated by an incident recorded by Le Clercq. The Indians, who still believed that the beaver had "sense" and formed a "separate nation," maintained that they "would cease to make war upon these animals if these would speak, howsoever little, in order that they might learn whether the Beavers are among their friends or their enemies." Unfortunately for the beaver, they never communicated their friendliness. The natural world of the Indian was becoming inarticulate.

It is interesting to note that Dièreville, who observed the Micmac culture at the beginning of the eighteenth century, was the only witness to record the native superstition which compelled them to tear out the eyes of all slain animals. Somehow, perhaps by some sort of symbolic transference, the spirits of surviving animals of the same species were thereby blinded to the irreverent treatment accorded the victim; otherwise, through the mediation of the outraged spirits, the living would no longer have allowed themselves to be taken by the Indians. The failure of the earlier writers to mention this particular superstition suggests that it was of fairly recent origin, a result of the overexploitation of game for the trade. To the Micmac mind, haunted by memories of a former time, the practice may have been intended to hide his guilt and insure his continued success.

Together with this depletion of wildlife went a reduction of dependency on the resources of the local ecosystem. The use of improved hunting equipment, such as fishing line and hooks, axes, knives, muskets, and iron-tipped arrows, spears, and harpoons, exerted heavier pressure on the resources of the area, while the availability of French foodstuffs shifted the position of the Micmac in the trophic system, somewhat reducing his dependency on local food sources as it placed him partly outside of the system. To be sure, a decreasing native population relieved this pressure to a degree, but, according to evidence cited above, not enough to prevent the abuse of the land.

Other less obvious results of the fur trade were the increased incidence of feuding and the modification of the Micmac settlement patterns to meet the demands of the trade. Liquor, in particular brandy, was a favorite item of the trade—one for which the Indians "would go a long way." Its effects were devastating. Both Jean Saint-Vallier (François Laval's successor as bishop of Quebec) and Biard blamed liquor as a cause for the increased death rate of the natives. Moreover, it was observed that drunkenness resulted in social disintegration as the Indians became debauched and violent among themselves, and at times, spilled over into the French community which they would rob, ravage, and burn. Drunkenness also provided a legitimate excuse to commit crimes, such as murdering their enemies, for which they would otherwise be held accountable.

European contact should thus be viewed as a trigger factor, that is, something which was not present in the Micmac ecosystem before and which initiated a concatenation of reactions leading to the replacement of the aboriginal ecosystem by another. European disease, Christianity, and the fur trade with its accompanying technology—the three often intermeshed—were responsible for the corruption of the Indian-land relationship, in which the native had merged sympathetically with his environment. By a lockstep process European disease rendered the Indian's control over the supernatural and spiritual realm inoperative, and the disillusioned Micmac apostatized, debilitating taboo and preparing the way for the destruction of wildlife which was soon to occur under the stimulation of the fur trade. For those who believed in it, Christianity furnished a new, dualistic world view, which placed man above nature, as well as spiritual support for the fur trade, and as a result the Micmac became dependent on the European market-place both spiritually and economically. Within his ecosystem the Indian changed from conservator to exploiter. All of this resulted in the intense exploitation of some game animals and the virtual extermination of others. Unfortunately for the Indian and the land, this grim tale was to be repeated many times along the moving Indian-white frontier. Life for the Micmac had indeed become more convenient, but convenience cost dearly in much material and abstract culture loss or modification.

The historiography of Indian-white relations is rendered more comprehensible when the Indian and the land are considered together: "So intimately is all of Indian life tied up with the land and its utilization that to think of Indians is to think of land. The two are inseparable." American Indian history can be seen, then, as a type of environmental history, and perhaps it is from this perspective that the early period of Indian-white relations can best be understood.

3. The Labor Problem at Jamestown, 1607-1618

Edmund S. Morgan

A fundamental problem in comprehending the evolution of society among transplanted Englishmen in North America is the impact of Old World patterns of life upon the organization of new European settlements in America. As Edmund S. Morgan (b.1916), Sterling Professor of History at Yale University, demonstrates here, there is no simple formula. In the case of the Virginia Company and the plantation at Jamestown, deeply ingrained English attitudes about work made it difficult for Company settlers to survive in the Chesapeake Bay environment. Assumptions about labor, about the abundance of America, and about the possibilities for enslaving Indian natives to use as a labor force help to explain why individuals faced starvation, disease, and death in Jamestown, yet preferred "bowling in the streets" to producing the staples of life. The author hypothesizes that settlers were slow to respond to the realities of a hostile environment because of such attitudes. The early adventurers remained attached to English models, despite the obvious and pressing need for survival.

Professor Morgan has made it possible to understand the irony of men not working even when they were confronting disease and starvation. He suggests, moreover, that attitudes about work carried by Englishmen to Jamestown were conditioning elements leading them to institutionalize chattel slavery for blacks later in the seventeenth century. Compare his reasoning about the origins of slavery with the writings of Carl N. Degler and Winthrop D. Jordan, farther along in this collection. From another point of view, if Morgan's assumptions about English habits of work are correct, then how do we account for the positive approach to labor and production evidenced by other early English settlement groups like the Puritans?

The story of Jamestown, the first permanent English settlement in America, has a familiar place in the history of the United States. We all know of the tribulations that kept the colony on the point of expiring: the shortage of supplies, the hostility of the Indians, the quarrels among the leaders, the reckless search for gold, the pathetic search for a passage to the Pacific, and the neglect of the crucial business of growing food to stay alive. Through the scene moves the figure of Captain John Smith, a little larger than life, trading for corn among the Indians and driving the feckless crew to work. His departure in October 1609 results in near

Source: Edmund S. Morgan, "The Labor Problem at Jamestown, 1607–1618," *American Historical Review*, 76 (1971), pp. 595–611. Reprinted by permission of Edmund S. Morgan.

disaster. The settlers fritter away their time and energy, squander their provisions, and starve. Sir Thomas Gates, arriving after the settlement's third winter, finds only sixty men out of six hundred still alive and those sixty scarcely able to walk.

In the summer of 1610 Gates and Lord La Warr get things moving again with a new supply of men and provisions, a new absolute form of government, and a new set of laws designed to keep everybody at work. But when Gates and La Warr leave for a time, the settlers fall to their old ways. Sir Thomas Dale, upon his arrival in May 1611, finds them at "their daily and usuall workes, bowling in the streets."[1]* But Dale brings order out of chaos. By enlarging and enforcing the colony's new law code (the famous *Lawes Divine, Morall and Martiall*) he starts the settlers working again and recues them from starvation by making them plant corn. By 1618 the colony is getting on its feet and ready to carry on without the stern regimen of a Smith or a Dale. There are still evil days ahead, as the Virginia Company sends over men more rapidly than the infant colony can absorb them. But the settlers, having found in tobacco a valuable crop for export, have at last gone to work with a will, and Virginia's future is assured.

The story probably fits the facts insofar as they can be known. But it does not quite explain them. The colony's long period of starvation and failure may well be attributed to the idleness of the first settlers, but idleness is more an accusation than an explanation. Why did men spend their time bowling in the streets when their lives depended on work? Were they lunatics, preferring to play games rather than clear and plow and plant the crops that could have kept them alive?

The mystery only deepens if we look more closely at the efforts of Smith, Gates, La Warr, and Dale to set things right. In 1612 John Smith described his work program of 1608: "the company [being] divided into tennes, fifteenes, or as the businesse required, 4 hours each day was spent in worke, the rest in pastimes and merry exercise." Twelve years later Smith rewrote this passage and changed the figure of four hours to six hours.[2] But even so, what are we to make of a six-hour day in a colony teetering on the verge of extinction?

The program of Gates and La Warr in the summer of 1610 was no more strenuous. William Strachey described it:

> it is to be understood that such as labor are not yet so taxed but that easily they perform the same and ever by ten of the clock have done their morning's work: at what time they have their allowances [of food] set out ready for them, and until it be three of the clock again they take their own pleasure,and afterward, with the sunset, their day's labor is finished.[3]

The Virginia Company offered much the same account of this period. According to a tract issued late in 1610, "the setled times of working (to effect all themselves, or the Adventurers neede desire) [requires] no more pains than from sixe of clocke in the morning untill ten, and from two of the clocke in the afternoone till foure."[4] The long lunch period described for 1610 was also a feature of the *Lawes Divine, Morall and Martiall* as enforced by Dale. The total working hours prescribed in the *Lawes* amounted to roughly five to eight hours a day in summer and three to six hours in winter.[5]

It is difficult, then, to escape the conclusion that there was a great deal of

* Notes, where used, appear at the ends of selections.

unemployment or underemployment at Jamestown, whether it was the idleness of the undisciplined in the absence of strong government or the idleness of the disciplined in the presence of strong government. How are we to account for this fact? By our standards the situation at Jamestown demanded hard and continuous work. Why was the response so feeble?

One answer, given by the leaders of the colony, is that the settlers included too many ne'er-do-wells and too many gentlemen who "never did know what a dayes work was."[6] Hard work had to wait until harder men were sent. Another answer may be that the Jamestown settlers were debilitated by hunger and disease. The victims of scurvy, malaria, typhoid, and diphtheria may have been left without the will or the energy to work. Still another answer, which has echoed through the pages of our history books, attributed the difficulty to the fact that the settlement was conducted on a communal basis: everybody worked for the Virginia Company and everybody was fed (while supplies lasted) by the company, regardless of how much he worked or failed to work. Once land was distributed to individuals and men were allowed to work for themselves, they gained the familiar incentives of private enterprise and bent their shoulders to the wheel.[7] These explanations are surely all valid—they are all supported by the testimony of contemporaries—and they go far toward explaining the lazy pioneers of Jamestown. But they do not reach to a dimension of the problem that contemporaries would have overlooked because they would have taken it for granted. They do not tell us what ideas and attitudes about work, carried from England, would have led the first English settlers to expect so little of themselves in a situation that demanded so much. The Jamestown settlers did not leave us the kind of private papers that would enable us to examine directly their ideas and attitudes, as we can those of the Puritans who settled New England a few years later. But in the absence of direct evidence we may discover among the ideas current in late sixteenth- and early seventeenth-century England some clues to the probable state of mind of the first Virginians, clues to the way they felt about work, whether in the Old World or the New, clues to habits of thinking that may have conditioned their perceptions of what confronted them at Jamestown, clues even to the tangled web of motives that made later Virginians masters of slaves.

Englishmen's ideas about the New World at the opening of the seventeenth century were based on a century of European exploration and settlement. The Spanish, whose exploits surpassed all others, had not attempted to keep their success a secret, and by the middle of the sixteenth century Englishmen interested in America had begun translating Spanish histories and memoirs in an effort to rouse their countrymen to emulation.[8] The land that emerged from these writings was, except in the Arctic regions, an Eden, teeming with gentle and generous people who, before the Spanish conquest, had lived without labor, or with very little, from the fruits of a bountiful nature.[9] There were admittedly some unfriendly exceptions who made a habit of eating their more attractive neighbors; but they were a minority, confined to a few localities, and in spite of their ferocity were scarely a match for Europeans armed with guns.[10] Englishmen who visited the New World confirmed the reports of natural abundance. Arthur Barlowe, for example, reconnoitering the North Carolina coast for Walter Raleigh, observed that "the earth bringeth foorth all things in aboundance, as in the first creation, without toile or labour," while the people were "most gentle, loving, and faithfull, void of all guile, and treason, and such as lived from the manner of the golden age. . . ."[11]

English and European readers may have discounted the more extravagant reports of American abundance, for the same authors who praised the land often gave contradictory accounts of the hardships they had suffered in it. But anyone who doubted that riches were waiting to be plucked from Virginia's trees had reason to expect that a good deal might be plucked from the people of the land. Spanish experience had shown that Europeans could thrive in the New World without undue effort by exploiting the natives. With a mere handful of men the Spanish had conquered an enormous population of Indians in the Caribbean, Mexico, and Peru and had put them to work. In the chronicles of Peter Martyr, Englishmen learned how it was done. Apart from the fact that the Indians were naturally gentle, their division into a multitude of kingdoms, frequently at odds with one another, made it easy to play off one against another. By aiding one group against its enemies the Spaniards had made themselves masters of both.[12]

The story of English plans to imitate and improve on the Spanish strategy is a long one.[13] It begins at least as early as Francis Drake's foray in Panama in 1572–73, when he allied with a band of runaway slaves to rob a Spanish mule train carrying treasure from Peru across the isthmus to Nombre de Dois on the Caribbean.[14] The idea of joining with dissident natives or slaves either against their Spanish masters or against their wicked cannibalistic neighbors became an important ingredient in English plans for colonizing the New World. Martin Frobisher's experiences with the Eskimos in Baffin Land and Ralph Lane's with the Indians at Roanoke[15] should perhaps have disabused the English of their expectations; but they found it difficult to believe that any group of natives, and especially the noble savages of North America, would fail to welcome what they called with honest pride (and some myopia) the "gentle government" of the English.[16] If the savages first encountered by a colonizing expedition proved unfriendly, the thing to do was to make contact with their milder neighbors and rescue them from the tyranny of the unfriendly tribe, who must be their enemies and were probably cannibals to boot.[17]

The settlers at Jamestown tried to follow the strategy, locating their settlement as the plan called for, near the mouth of a navigable river, so that they would have access to the interior tribes if the coastal ones were hostile. But as luck would have it, they picked an area with a more powerful, more extensive, and more effective Indian government than existed anywhere else on the Atlantic Coast, King Powhatan and his enemies, the Monacans of the interior, but he felt no great need of English assistance against them, and he rightly suspected that the English constituted a larger threat to his hegemony than the Monacans did. He submitted with ill grace and no evident comprehension to the coronation ceremony that the Virginia Company arranged for him, and he kept his distance from Jamestown. Those of his warriors who visited the settlement showed no disposition to work for the English. The Monacans, on the other hand, lived too far inland (beyond the falls) to serve as substitute allies, and the English were thus deprived of their anticipated native labor.[18]

They did not, however, give up their expectations of getting it eventually. In 1615 Ralph Hamor still thought the Indians would come around "as they are easily taught and may by lenitie and faire usage . . . be brought, being naturally though ingenious, yet idly given, to be no lesse industrious, nay to exceede our English."[19] Even after the massacre of 1622 Virginians continued to dream of an

Indian labor supply, though there was no longer to be any gentleness in obtaining it. Captain John Martin thought it better to exploit than exterminate the Indians, if only because they could be made to work in the heat of the day, when Englishmen would not. And William Claiborne in 1626 invented a device (whether mechanical or political is not clear) that he claimed would make it possible to keep Indians safely in the settlements and put them to work. The governor and council gave him what looks like the first American patent or copyright, namely a three-year monopoly, to "have holde and enjoy all the benefitt use and profitt of this his project or inventione," and they also assigned him a recently captured Indian, "for his better experience and tryall of his inventione."[20]

English expectations of the New World and its inhabitants died hard. America was supposed to be a land of abundance, peopled by natives who would not only share that abundance with the English but increase it under English direction. Englishmen simply did not envisage a need to work for the mere purpose of staying alive. The problem of survival as they saw it was at best political and at worst military.

Although Englishmen long remained under the illusion that the Indians would eventually become useful English subjects, it became apparent fairly early that Indian labor was not going to sustain the founders of Jamestown. The company in England was convinced by 1609 that the settlers would have to grow at least part of their own food.[21] Yet the settlers themselves had to be driven to that life-saving task. To understand their ineffectiveness in coping with a situation that their pioneering descendants would take in stride, it may be helpful next to inquire into some of the attitudes toward work that these first English pioneers took for granted. How much work and what kind of work did Englishmen at the opening of the seventeenth century consider normal?

The laboring population of England, by law at least, was required to work much harder than the regimen at Jamestown might lead us to expect. The famous Statute of Artificers of 1563 (re-enacting similar provisions from the Statute of Laborers of 1495) required all laborers to work from five in the morning to seven or eight at night from mid-March to mid-September, and during the remaining months of the year from daybreak to night. Time out for eating, drinking, and rest was not to exceed two and a half hours a day.[22] But these were injunctions not descriptions. The Statute of Laborers of 1495 is preceded by the complaint that laborers "waste much part of the day . . . in late coming unto their work, early departing therefrom, long sitting at their breakfast, at their dinner and noon-meat, and long time of sleeping after noon."[23] Whether this statute or that of 1563 (still in effect when Jamestown was founded) corrected the situation is doubtful.[24] The records of local courts show varying efforts to enforce other provisions of the statute of 1563, but they are almost wholly silent about this provision,[25] in spite of the often-expressed despair of masters over their lazy and negligent laborers.[26]

It may be said that complaints of the laziness and irresponsibility of workmen can be met with in any century. Were such complaints in fact justified in sixteenth- and early seventeenth-century England? There is some reason to believe that they were, that life during those years was characterized by a large amount of idleness or underemployment.[27] The outstanding economic fact of the sixteenth and early seventeenth century in England was a rapid and more or less steady rise in prices, followed at some distance by a much smaller rise in wages, both in industry and in agriculture. The price of provisions used by a laborer's family rose faster than wages during the whole period from 1500 to 1640.[28] The government made an effort to narrow the gap by requiring the justices in each county to readjust maximum wages at regular intervals. But the wages established by the justices reflected their own nostalgic notions of what a day's work ought to be worth in money, rather than a realistic estimate of what a man could buy with his wages. In those counties, at least, where records survive, the level of wages set by the justices crept upward very slowly before 1630.[29]

Wages were so inadequate that productivity was probably impaired by malnutrition. From a quarter to a half of the population lived below the level recognized at the time to constitute poverty. Few of the poor could count on regular meals at home, and in years when the wheat crop failed, they were close to starvation.[30] It is not surprising that men living under these conditions showed no great energy for work and that much of the population was, by modern standards, idle much of the time. The health manuals of the day recognized that people normally slept after eating, and the laws even prescribed a siesta for laborers in the summer time.[31] If they slept longer and more often than the laws allowed or the physicians recommended, if they loafed on the job and took unauthorized holidays, if they worked slowly and ineffectively when they did work, it may have been due at least in part to undernourishment and to the variety of chronic diseases that undernourishment brings in its train.[32]

Thus low wages may have begot low productivity that in turn justified low wages.[33] The reaction of employers was to blame the trouble on deficiencies, not of diet or wages, but of character. A prosperous yeoman like Robert Loder, who kept close track of his expenses and profits, was always bemoaning the indolence of his servants. Men who had large amounts of land that they could either rent out or work with hired labor generally preferred to rent because labor was so inefficient and irresponsible.[34]

Even the division of labor, which economists have customarily regarded as a means of increased productivity, could be a source of idleness. Plowing, for example, seems to have been a special skill—a plowman was paid at a higher rate than ordinary farm workers. But the ordinary laborer's work might have to be synchronized with the plowman's, and a whole crew of men might be kept idle by a plowman's failure to get his job done at the appropriate time. It is difficult to say whether this type of idleness, resulting from failure to synchronize the performance of related tasks, was rising or declining; but cheap, inefficient, irresponsible labor would be unlikely to generate pressures for the careful planning of time.

The government, while seeking to discourage idleness through laws requiring long hours of work, also passed laws that inadvertently discouraged industry. A policy that might be characterized as the conservation of employment frustrated those who wanted to do more work than others. English economic policy seems to have rested on the assumption that the total amount of work for which society could pay was strictly limited and must be rationed so that everyone could have a little,[35] and those with family responsibilities could have a little more. It was against the law for a man to practice more than one trade or one craft.[36] And although large numbers of farmers took up some handicraft on the side, this was to be discouraged, because "for one man to be both an husbandman and an Artificer is a gatheringe of divers mens livinges into one mans hand."[37] So as not to take work away from his elders, a man could not independently practice most trades until he had become a master through seven years of apprenticeship. Even then, until he was thirty years old or married, he was supposed to serve some other master of the trade. A typical example is the case of John Pikeman of Barking, Essex, a tailor who was presented by the grand jury because he "being a singleman and not above 25 years of age, does take in work of tailoring and works by himself to the hindrance of other poor occupiers, contrary to the law."[38]

These measures doubtless helped to maintain social stability in the face of a rapid population increase, from under three million in 1500 to a probable four and a half million in 1640 (an increase reflected in the gap between wages and prices).[39] But in its efforts to spread employment so that every able-bodied person would have a means of support, the government in effect discouraged energetic labor and nurtured the workingman's low expectations of himself. By requiring masters to engage apprentices for seven-year terms and servants (in agriculture and in most trades) for the whole year rather than the day, it prevented employers from hiring labor only when there was work to be done and prevented the diligent and effective worker from replacing the ineffective. The intention to spread work is apparent in the observation of the Essex justices that labor by the day caused "the great depauperization of other labourers."[40] But labor by the year meant that work could be strung out to occupy an unnecessary amount of time, because whether or not a master had enough work to occupy his servants they had to stay and he had to keep them. The records show many instances of masters attempting to turn away a servant or apprentice before the stipulated term was up, only to have him sent back by the courts with order that the master "entertain" him for the full period.[41] We even have the extraordinary spectable of the runaway master, the man who illegally fled from his servants and thus evaded his responsibility to employ and support them.[42]

In pursuit of its policy of full employment in the face of an expanding population, the government often had to create jobs in cases where society offered none. Sometimes men were obliged to take on a poor boy as a servant whether they needed him or not. The parish might lighten the burden by paying a fee, but it might also fine a man who refused to take a boy assigned to him.[43] To provide for men and women who could not be foisted off on unwilling employers, the government established houses of correction in every county, where the inmates toiled at turning wool, flax, and hemp into thread or yarn, receiving nothing but their food and lodging for their efforts. By all these means the government probably did succeed in spreading employment. But in the long run its policy, insofar as it was effective, tended to depress wages and to diminish the amount of work expected from any one man.

Above and beyond the idleness and underemployment that we may blame on the lethargy and irresponsibility of underpaid labor, on the failure to synchronize the performance of related tasks, and on the policy of spreading work as thinly as possible, the very nature of the jobs to be done prevented the systematic use of time that characterizes modern industrialized economies. Men could seldom work steadily because they could work only at the tasks that could be done at the moment; and in sixteenth- and seventeenth-century England the tasks to be done often depended on forces beyond human control: on the weather and the seasons, on the winds, on the tides, on the maturing of crops. In the countryside work from dawn to dusk with scarcely an intermission might be normal at harvest time, but there were bound to be times when there was very little to do. When it rained or snowed, most farming operations had to be stopped altogether (and so did some of the stages of cloth manufacture). As late as 1705 John Law, imagining a typical economy established on a newly discovered island assumed that the persons engaged in agriculture would necessarily be idle, for one reason or another, half the time.[44]

To be sure, side by side with idleness and inefficiency, England exhibited the first signs of a rationalized economy. Professor J. U. Nef has described the many large-scale industrial enterprises that were inaugurated in England in the late sixteenth and early seventeenth centuries.[45] And if the development of systematic agricultural production was advancing less rapidly than historians once supposed, the very existence of men like Robert Loder, the very complaints of the idleness and irresponsibility of laborers, the very laws prescribing hours of work all testify to the beginnings of a rationalized economy. But these were beginnings only and not widely felt. The laborer who seemed idle or irresponsible to a Robert Loder probably did not seem so to himself or to his peers. His England was not a machine for producing wool or corn. His England included activities and pleasures and relationships that systematic-minded employers would resent and that modern economists would classify as uneconomic. At the opening of the seventeenth century, England was giving him fewer economic benefits than she had given his grandfathers so that he was often ready to pull up stakes and look for a better life in another county or another country.[46] But a life devoted to more and harder work than he had known at home might not have been his idea of a better life.

Perhaps we may now view Jamestown with somewhat less surprise at the idle and hungry people occupying the place: idleness and hunger were the rule in much of England much of the time; they were facts of life to be taken for granted. And if we next ask what the settlers thought they had come to America to do, what they thought they were up to in Virginia, we can find several English enterprises comparable to their own that may have served as models and that would not have led them to think of hard, continuous disciplined work as a necessary ingredient in their undertaking.

If they thought of themselves as settling a wilderness, they could look for guidance to what was going on in the northern and western parts of England and in the high parts of the south and east.[47] Here were the regions, mostly wooded, where wastelands still abounded, the goal of many in the large migrant population of England. Those who had settled down were scattered widely over the countryside in isolated hovels and hamlets and lived by pasture farming, that is, they cultivated only small plots of ground and ran a few sheep or cattle on the common land. Since the gardens required little attention and the cattle hardly any, they had most of their time to themselves. Some spent their spare hours on handicrafts. In fact, they supplied the labor for most of England's minor industries, which tended to locate in pasture-farming regions, where agriculture made fewer demands on the inhabitants, than in regions devoted to market crops. But the pasture farmers seem to have offered their labor sporadically and reluctantly.[48] They had the reputation of being both idle and independent. They might travel to the richer arable farming regions to pick up a few shillings in field work at harvest time, but their own harvests were small. They did not even grow the wheat or rye for their own bread and made shift to live in hard times from the nuts and berries and herbs that they gathered in the woods.

Jamestown was mostly wooded, like the pasture-farming areas of England and Wales; and since Englishmen used the greater part of their own country for pasture farming, that was the obvious way to use the wasteland of the New World. If this was the Virginians' idea of what they were about, we should expect them to be idle much of the time and to get grain for bread by trading rather than planting (in this case not wheat or rye but maize from the Indians); we should even expect them to get a good deal of their food, as they did, by scouring the woods for nuts and berries.

As the colony developed, a pasture-farming population would have been quite in keeping with the company's expectation of profit from a variety of products. The Spaniards' phenomenal success with raising cattle in the West Indies was well known. And the proposed employment of the settlers of Virginia in a variety of industrial pursuits (iron works, silk works, glass works, shipbuilding) was entirely fitting for a pasture-farming community. The small gardens assigned for cultivation by Governor Dale in 1614 will also make sense: three acres would have been far too small a plot of land to occupy a farmer in the arable regions of England, where a single man could handle thirty acres without assistance.[49] But it would be not at all inappropriate as the garden of a pasture farmer. In Virginia three acres would produce more than enough corn to sustain a man for a year and still leave him with time to make a profit for the company or himself at some other job—if he could be persuaded to work.

Apart from the movement of migrant workers into wastelands, the most obvious English analogy to the Jamestown settlement was that of a military expedition. The settlers may have had in mind not only the expeditions that subdued the Irish[50] but also those dispatched to the European continent in England's wars. The Virginia Company itself seems at first to have envisaged the enterprise as partly military, and the *Lawes Divine, Morall and Martiall* were mostly martial. But the conception carried unfortunate implications for the company's expectations of profit. Military expeditions were staffed from top to bottom with men unlikely to work. The nucleus of sixteenth-century English armies was the nobility and the gangs of genteel ruffians they kept in their service, in wartime to accompany them into the field (or to go in their stead), in peacetime to follow them about as living insignia of their rank.[51] Work was not for the nobility nor for those who wore their livery. According to the keenest student of the aristocracy in this period, "the rich and well-born were idle almost by definition." Moreover they kept "a huge labor force . . . absorbed in slothful and parasitic personal service." Aside from the gentlemen retainers of the nobility and their slothful servants the military expeditions that England sent abroad were filled out by misfits and thieves whom the local constables wished to be rid of. It was, in fact, government policy to keep the able-bodied and upright at home and to send the lame, the halt, the blind, and the criminal abroad.[52]

The combination of gentlemen and ne'er-do-wells of which the leaders at Jamestown complained may well have been the result of the company's using a military model for guidance. The Virginia Company was loaded with noblemen (32 present or future earls, 4 countesses, 3 viscounts, and 19 barons).[53] Is it possible that the large number of Jamestown settlers listed as gentlemen and captains came from among the retainers of these lordly stockholders and that the rest of the settlers included some of the gentlemen's personal servants as well as a group of hapless vagabonds or migratory farm laborers who had been either impressed or lured into the enterprise by tales of the New World's abundance? We are told, at least, that persons designated in the colony's roster as "laborers" were "for most part footmen, and such as they that were Adventures brought to attend them, or such as they could perswade to goe with them, that never did know what a dayes work was."[54]

If these men thought they were engaged in a military expedition, military precedent pointed to idleness, hunger, and death, not to the effective organization of labor. Soldiers on campaign were not expected to grow their own food. On the other hand they *were* expected to go hungry often and to die like flies even if they never saw an enemy. The casualty rates on European expeditions resembled those at Jamestown and probably from the same causes: disease and undernourishment.[55]

But the highest conception of the enterprise, often expressed by the leaders, was that of a new commonwealth on the model of England itself. Yet this, too, while it touched the heart, was not likely to turn men toward hard, effective, and continuous work.[56] The England that Englishmen were saddled with as a model for new commonwealths abroad was a highly complex society in which the governing consideration in accomplishing a particular piece of work was not how to do it efficiently but who had the right or the duty to do it, by custom, law, or privilege. We know that the labor shortage in the New World quickly diminished considerations of custom, privilege, and specialization in the organization of labor. But the English model the settlers carried with them made them think initially of a society like the one at home, in which each of them would perform his own special task and not encroach on the rights of other men to do other tasks. We may grasp some of the assumptions about labor that went into the most intelligent planning of a new commonwealth by considering Richard Hakluyt's recommendation that settlers include both carpenters and joiners, tallow chandlers and wax chandlers, bowyers and fletchers, men to roughhew pike staffs and other men to finish them.[57]

If Jamestown was not actually troubled by this great an excess of specialization, it was not the Virginia Company's fault. The company wanted to establish at once an economy more complex than England's, an economy that would include not only all the trades that catered to ordinary domestic needs of Englishmen but also industries that were unknown or uncommon in England: a list of artisans the company wanted for the colony in 1611 included such specialists as hemp planters and hemp dressers, gun makers and gunstock makers, spinners of pack thread and upholsterers of feathers.[58] Whatever idleness arose from the specialization of labor in English society was multiplied in the New World by the presence of unneeded skills and the absence or shortage of essential skills. Jamestown had an oversupply of glassmakers and not enough carpenters or blacksmiths, an oversupply of gentlemen and not enough plowmen. These were Englishmen temporarily baffled by missing links in the economic structure of their primitive community. The later jack-of-all-trades American frontiersman was as yet unthought of. As late as 618 Governor Argall complained that they lacked the men "to set their Ploughs on worke." Although they had the oxen to pull them, "they wanted men to bring them to labour, and Irons for the Ploughs, and harnesse for the Cattell." And the next year John Rolfe noted that they still needed "Carpenters to build and make Carts and Ploughs, and skilfull men that know how to use them, and traine up our cattell to draw them; which though we indeavour to effect, yet our want of experience brings but little to perfection but planting Tobacco."[59]

Tobacco, as we know, was what they kept on planting. The first shipload of it, sent to England in 1617, brought such high prices that the Virginians stopped bowling in the streets and planted tobacco in them. They did it without benefit of plows, and somehow at the same time they managed to grow corn, probably also without plows. Seventeenth-century Englishmen, it turned out, could adapt themselves to hard and varied work if there was sufficient incentive.

But we may well ask whether the habits and attitudes we have been examining had suddenly expired altogether. Did tobacco really solve the labor problem in Virginia? Did the economy that developed after 1618 represent a totally new set of social and economic attitudes? Did greater opportunities for profit completely erase the old attitudes and furnish the incentives to labor that were needed to make Virginia a success? The study of labor in modern underdeveloped countries should make us pause before we say yes. The mere opportunity to earn high wages has not always proved adequate to recruit labor in underdeveloped countries. Something more in the way of expanded needs or political authority or national consciousness or ethical imperatives has been required.[60] Surely Virginia, in some sense, became a success. But how did it succeed? What kind of success did it have? Without attempting to answer, I should like very diffidently to offer a suggestion, a way of looking ahead at what happened in the years after the settlement of Jamestown.

The founders of Virginia, having discovered in tobacco a substitute for the sugar of the West Indies and the silver of Peru, still felt the lack of a native labor force with which to exploit the new crop. At first they turned to their own overpopulated country for labor, but English indentured servants brought with them the same haphazard habits of work as their masters. Also like their masters, they were apt to be unruly if pressed. And when their terms of servitude expired— if they themselves had not expired in the "seasoning" that carried away most immigrants to Virginia—they could be persuaded to continue working for their betters only at exorbitant rates. Instead they struck out for themselves and joined the ranks of those demanding rather than supplying labor. But there was a way out. The Spanish and Portuguese had already demonstrated what could be done in the New World when a local labor force became inadequate: they brought in the natives of Africa.

For most of the seventeenth century Virginians were unable to compete for the limited supply of slaves hauled across the ocean to man the sugar plantations of the Americas. Sugar was a more profitable way to use slaves than tobacco. Moreover, the heavy mortality of newcomers to Virginia made an investment in Africans bound for a lifetime more risky than the same amount invested in a larger number of Englishmen, bound for a term that was likely to prove longer than a Virginia lifetime.

But Virginians continued to be Englishmen: the more enterprising continued to yearn for a cheaper, more docile, more stable supply of labor while their servants loafed on the job, ran away, and claimed the traditional long lunch hour. As the century wore on, punctuated in Virginia by depression, discontent, and rebellion, Virginia's position in the market for men gradually improved: the price of sugar fell, making it less competitive with tobacco; the heavy mortality in the colony declined, making the initial outlay of capital on slaves less risky; and American and European traders expanded their infamous activities in Africa. The world supply of slaves, which had fallen off in the second quarter of the seventeenth century, rose sharply in the third quarter and continued to rise.[61]

With these developments the Virginians at last were able to acquire substitute natives for their colony and begin, in their own English way, to Hispanize Virginia. By the middle of the eighteenth century Africans constituted the great majority of the colony's entire labor force.[62] This is not to say that plantation slavery in Virginia or elsewhere can be understood simply as a result of inherited attitudes toward work confronting the economic opportunities of the New World. The forces that determined the character of plantation slavery were complex. But perhaps an institution so archaic and at the same time so modern as the plantation cannot be fully understood without taking into consideration the attitudes that helped to starve the first settlers of the colony where the southern plantation began.

NOTES

1. Ralph Hamor, *A True Discourse of the Present State of Virginia* (London, 1615; Richmond, 1957), 26.

2. John Smith, *Travels and Works,* ed. Edward Arber and A. G. Bradley (Edinburgh, 1910), 1: 149; 2: 466.

3. L. B. Wright, ed., *A Voyage to Virginia in 1609* (Charlottesville, 1964), 69–70.

4. *A True Declaration of the Estate of the Colonie in Virginia* (London, 1610), reprinted in Peter Force, ed., *Tracts and Other Papers* (Washington, 1844), 3, no. 1: 20; Smith, *Travels and Works,* 2: 502. Captain Daniel Tucker maintained a similar program in Bermuda in 1616: "according to the Virginia order, hee set every one [that] was with him at Saint Georges, to his taske, to cleere grounds, fell trees, set corne, square timber, plant vines and other fruits brought out of England. These by their taske—Masters by breake a day repaired to the wharfe, from thence to be imployed to the place of their imployment, till nine of the clocke, and then in the after-noone from three till Sunneset." *Ibid.,* 653.

5. *For the Colony in Virginia Brittannia: Lawes Divine, Morall and Martiall* (London, 1612). 61–62.

6. Smith, *Travels and Works,* 2: 487.

7. A much more sophisticated version of this explanation is suggested by Professor Sigmund Diamond in his discussion of the development of social relationships in Virginia, "From Organization to Society: Virginia in the Seventeenth Century," *American Journal of Sociology,* 63 (1958): 457–75; see also his "Values as an Obstacle to Economic Growth: The American Colonies," *Journal of Economic History,* 27 (1967): 561–75.

8. See especially the translation of Peter Martyr, in Richard Eden, *The Decades of the new worlde or west India* (London, 1555); a useful bibliographical history is John Parker, *Books to Build an Empire* (Amsterdam, 1966).

9. Gustav H. Blanke, *Amerika im Englishen Schrifttum Des 16. und 17. Jahrhunderts* Beitrage Zur Englischen Philologie, 46 (Bochum-Langendreer, 1962), 98–104.

10. Since Peter Martyr, the principal Spanish chronicler, identified most Indians who resisted the Spaniards as cannibals, this became the familiar sixteenth-century epithet for unfriendly Indians. It is doubtful that many tribes actually practiced cannibalism, though some certainly did.

11. D. B. Quinn, ed., *The Roanoke Voyages 1584–1590,* Works issued by the Hakluyt Society, 2d ser., 104, 105 (London, 1955), 1: 108.

12. Eden, *Decades, passim.* For English awareness of the Spanish example, see Smith, *Travels and Works,* 2: 578–81, 600–03, 955–56, and Susan M. Kingsbury, ed., *The Records of the Virginia Company of London* (Washington, 1906–35), 558–62.

13. I have dealt with this subject in a work still in progress.

14. Irene A. Wright, ed., *Documents concerning English Voyages to the Spanish Main 1569–1580.* Works issued by the Hakluyt Society, 2d ser., 71 (London, 1932), gives the original sources, both English and Spanish.

15. Richard Collinson, ed., *The Three Voyages of Martin Frobisher,* Works issued by the Hakluyt Society, 1st ser., 38 (London, 1867), 131, 141–42, 145–50, 269, 271, 280–89; Quinn, *Roanoke Voyages,* 1: 275–88.

16. The phrase "gentle government" is the younger Hakluyt's, in a proposal to make use of Drake's Negro allies from Panama for a colony at the Straits of Magellan, E. G. R. Taylor, ed., *The Original Writings and Correspondence of the two Richard Hakluyts,* Works issued by the Hakluyt Society, 2d ser., 76, 77 (London, 1935), 1: 142.

17. *Ibid.,* 121, 2: 241–42, 246–49, 257–65, 275, 318, 342.

18. The secondary literature on the Indians of Virginia is voluminous, but see especially Nancy O. Lurie, "Indian Cultural Adjustment to European Civilization," in J. M. Smith, ed., *Seventeenth-Century America* (Chapel Hill, 1959), 33–60. The most helpful original sources, on which most of our

information is necessarily based, are Smith, *Travels and Works,* and William Strachey, *The Historie of Travell into Virginia Britania* (composed 1612), ed. L. B. Wright and V. Freund, Works issued by the Hakluyt Society, 2d ser., 103 (London, 1953), 53–116.

19. *True Discourse,* 2. See also Strachey *Historie of Travell,* 91–94; Alexander Whitaker, *Good Newes from Virginia* (London, 1613), 40.

20. Susan M. Kingsbury, ed., *The Records of the Virginia Company of London* (Washington, 1906-35), 3: 705–06; H. R. McIlwaine, ed., *Minutes of the Council and General Court of Colonial Virginia* (Richmond, 1924), 111.

21. *Records of the Virginia Company,* 3: 17, 27.

22. R. H. Tawney and Eileen Powers, eds., *Tudor Economic Documents* (London, 1924), 1: 342. For some seventeenth-century prescriptions of long working hours, see Gervase Markham, *A Way to get Wealth* (13th ed.; London, 1676), 115–17; Henry Best, *Rural Economy in Yorkshire in 1641,* Surtees Society, *Publications,* 33 (Durham, 1857), 44. See also L. F. Salzman, *Building in England down to 1540* (Oxford, 1952), 61–65.

23. 11 Henry 7, cap. 22, sec. 4; Douglas Knoop and G. P. Jones, *The Medieval Mason* (Manchester, 1933), 117.

24. Tawney and Power, *Tudor Economic Documents,* 1: 352–63.

25. A minor exception is in J. H. E. Bennett and J. C. Dewhurst, eds., *Quarter Sessions Records . . . for the County Palatine of Chester, 1559-1760,* Publications of the Record Society for the Publication of Original Documents relating to Lancashire and Cheshire, 94 (Chester, 1940), 95–96, where a master alleged that his apprentice, John Dodd, "hath negligently behaved him selfe in his service in idleinge and sleepinge in severalle places where he hath been comanded to work." But sleeping (from eight in the morning till two in the afternoon and beyond) was only one of Dodd's offenses. On the enforcement of other provisions in the statute, see Margaret G. Davies, *The Enforcement of English Apprenticeship . . . 1563-1642* (Cambridge, Mass., 1956); R. K. Kelsall, *Wage Regulation under the Statute of Artificers* (London, 1938); and R. H. Tawney, "The Assessment of Wages in England by Justices of the Peace," *Vierteljahrschrift für Sozial- und Wirtschaftsgeschichte,* 11 (1913): 307–37, 533–64.

26. E. S. Furniss, *The Position of the Laborer in a System of Nationalism* (Boston, 1920), 117–34; E. P. Thompson, "Time, Work Discipline, and Industrial Capitalism," *Past and Present,* no. 38 (1967): 56–97.

27. D. C. Coleman, "Labour in the English Economy of the Sixteenth Century," *Economic History Review,* 2d ser., 8 (1956), reprinted in E. M. Carus Wilson, ed., *Essays in Economic History* (London, 1954–62), 2: 291–308.

28. E. H. Phelps Brown and Sheila V. Hopkins, "Seven Centuries of Building Wages," *Economica,* 2d ser., 22 (1955): 95–206; "Seven Centuries of the Prices of Consumables, compared with Builders' Wage-Rates," *ibid.,* 2d ser., 23 (1956): 296–314; "Wage Rates and Prices: Evidence for Population Pressure in the Sixteenth Century," *ibid.,* 2d ser., 24 (1957): 289–306; H. P. R. Finberg, ed., *The Agrarian History of England and Wales,* 4, *1500-1640,* ed. Joan Thirsk (Cambridge, 1967), 435–57, 531, 583–695.

29. Tawney, "Assessment of Wages," 555–64; Kelsall, *Wage Regulation,* 67–86. Tawney and Kelsall both argue that the enforcement of maximum wages according to the statute of 1563 demonstrates a shortage of labor; but except in a few isolated instances (there may well have been local temporary shortages) the evidence comes from the period after the middle of the seventeenth century.

30. Coleman, "Labour in the English Economy," 295; Peter Laslett adduces figures to show that actual starvation was probably rare among English peasants (*The World We Have Lost* [London, 1965], 107–27), but there can be little doubt that they were frequently close to it and chronically undernourished. See Carl Bridenbaugh, *Vexed and Troubled Englishmen* (New York, 1968), 91–98.

31. Thomas Elyot, *The Castel of Helthe* (London, 1541), fols. 45–46; Thomas Cogan, *The Haven of Health* (London, 1589), 231–39; *The Englishmans Doctor, or The School of Salerne* (orig. pub. London, 1608) (New York, 1920), 77.

32. E. P. Thompson, "Time, Work Discipline, and Industrial Capitalism."

33. On the prevalence of such a vicious circle in pre-industrial countries, see W. F. Moore, *Industrialization and Labor* (Ithaca, 1951), 106–13, 308. But see also E. J. Berg, "Backward-Sloping Labor Supply Functions in Dual Economies—The Africa Case," *Quarterly Journal of Economics,* 75 (1961): 468–92. For a comparison of Tudor and Stuart England with modern underdeveloped countries, see F. J. Fisher. "The Sixteenth and Seventeenth Centuries: The Dark Ages in English Economic History," *Economica,* 2d ser., 24 (1957): 2–18.

34. G. E. Fussell, ed., *Robert Loder's Farm Accounts 1610-1620,* Camden Society, 3d ser., 53 (London, 1936); Lawrence Stone, *The Crisis of the Aristocracy, 1558-1641* (New York, 1965), 295–97; Thirsk, *Agrarian History,* 198.

35. Compare Bert F. Hoselitz, *Sociological Aspects of Economic Growth* (Glencoe, 1960), 33–34.

36. 37 Edward 3, c.6. *A Collection in English of the Statutes now in Force* (London, 1594), fols. 22–23; Calendar of Essex Quarter Session Rolls (microfilm in the University of Wisconsin Library), 4: 228; 17: 124.

37. Tawney and Power, *Tudor Economic Documents*, 1: 353.

38. April 1594. Calendar of Essex Quarter Sessions Rolls, 16: 165. See also the indictment (1589) of four bachelors for taking up the trade of poulterer, which "hindreth other powre men." *Ibid.*, 15:54. While the statute seems to allow single men and women under thirty to set up in trade unless their services are demanded by a master, the courts, in Essex County at least (where the earliest and most extensive records are preserved), required such persons to find themselves a master. Moreover, the court was already issuing such orders before the statute of 1563. See *ibid.*, 1: 85, 116.

39. See note 28.

40. Calendar of Essex Quarter Sessions Rolls, 4: 128.

41. For examples: William LeHardy, ed., *Hertfordshire County Records,* 5 (Hertford, 1928): 191–92, 451; E. H. Bates, ed., *Quarter Sessions Records for the County of Somerset,* 1, Somerset Record Society, 23 (London, 1907), 11–12, 21; B. C. Redwood, ed., *Quarter Sessions Order Book 1642–1649,* Sussex Record Society, 54 (1954), 34, 44, 46, 128, 145–46, 188, 190.

42. For examples: *Hertfordshire County Records,* 5: 376; *Quarter Sessions Records for Somerset, 1: 97, 193, 258, 325.*

43. Bates, *Quarter Sessions . . . Somerset,* 114, 300; Redwood, *Order Book* (Sussex), 96, 146, 194; W. L. Sachse, ed., *Minutes of the Norwich Court of Mayoralty,* Norfolk Record Society, 15 (Norwich, 1942), 78, 216.

44. Coleman, "Labour in the English Economy"; E. P. Thompson, "Time, Work Discipline, and Industrial Capitalism"; Keith Thomas, "Work and Leisure in Pre-Industrial Society," *Past and Present,* no. 29 (1964): 50–66.

45. J. U. Nef, *The Conquest of the Material World* (Chicago, 1964), 121–328.

46. On the geographical mobility of the English population, see E. E. Rich, "The Population of Elizabethan England," *Economic History Review,* 2d ser., 2 (1949–56): 249–65; and Peter Laslett and John Harrison, "Clayworth and Cogenhoe," in H. E. Bell and R. L. Ollards, eds., *Historical Essays 1600–1750 Presented to David Ogg* (New York, 1963), 157–84.

47. This paragraph and the one that follows are based on the excellent chapters by Joan Thirsk and by Alan Everitt, in Thirsk, *Agrarian History.*

48. Thirsk, *Agrarian History,* 417–29; Joan Thirsk, "Industries in the Countryside" in F. J. Fisher, ed., *Essays in the Economic and Social History of Tudor and Stuart England* (London, 1961), 70–88. See also E. L. Jones, "Agricultural Origins of Industry," *Past and Present,* no. 40 (1968): 58–71. Lawrence Stone, "An Elizabethan Coalmine," *Economic History Review,* 2d ser., 3 (1950): 97–106, especially 101–02; Thirsk, *Agrarian History,* xxxv, 111.

49. Hamor, *True Discourse,* 16–17; Peter Bowden, in Thirsk, *Agrarian History,* 652. It is impossible to determine whether the settlers had had direct experience in pasture farming, but the likelihood that they were following familiar pasture-farming procedures and may have been expected to do so by the company is indicated by the kind of cattle they brought with them: swine, goats, neat cattle, and relatively few horses. When they proposed to set plows going, they were to be drawn by oxen as was the custom in pasture-farming areas. In arable farming areas it was more common to use horses. The company's concern to establish substantial herds is evident in the *Lawes Divine, Morall and Martial* in the provisions forbidding slaughter without government permission.

50. See Howard M. Jones, *O Strange New World* (New York, 1964), 167–79; David B. Quinn, "Ireland and Sixteenth Century European Expansion," in *Historical Studies,* ed. T. D. Williams, Papers Read at the Second Conference of Irish Historians (London, 1958); *The Elizabethans and the Irish* (Ithaca, 1966), 106–22. Professor Quinn and Professor Jones have both demonstrated how the subjugation of Ireland served as a model for the colonization of America. Ireland must have been in the minds of many of the settlers at Jamestown.

51. W. H. Dunham, *Lord Hastings' Indentured Retainers 1461–1483,* Connecticut Academy of Arts and Sciences, *Transactions,* 39 (New Haven, 1955); Gladys S. Thompson, *Lords Lieutenants in the Sixteenth Century* (London, 1923); Stone, *Crisis of the Aristocracy,* 199–270.

52. Stone, *Crisis of the Aristocracy,* 331; Lindsay Boynton, *The Elizabethan Militia 1558–1638* (Toronto, 1967); Thompson, *Lords Lieutenants,* 115.

53. Stone, *Crisis of the Aristocracy,* 372. About fifty percent of the other members were gentry. See Theodore K. Rabb, *Enterprise and Empire: Merchant and Gentry Investment in the Expansion of England 1575–1630* (Cambridge, Mass., 1967).

54. Smith, *Travels and Works,* 2: 486–87.

55. The expedition of the Earl of Essex in 1591 to assist Henry IV of France met with only a few skirmishes, but only 800 men out of 3,400 returned. Thompson, *Lords Lieutenants,* 111. Even the naval forces mustered to meet the Armada in 1588 suffered appalling losses from disease. In ten of the largest ships, in spite of heavy replacements, only 2,195 out of the original complement of 3,325 men were on the payroll by September. The total loss was probably equal to the entire original number. Lawrence Stone, "The Armada Campaign of 1588," *History,* 29 (1944): 120-43, especially 137-41.

56. For typical statements implying that Virginia is a new commonwealth on the English model, see the *Lawes Divine, Morall and Martiall,* 47-48; Robert Johnson, *The New Life of Virginia,* in Force, *Tracts,* 1, no. 7: 17-18.

57. Taylor, *Writings of the two Richard Hakluyts,* 2: 323, 327-38.

58. Alexander Brown, *The Genesis of the United States* (Boston, 1890), 1: 469-70.

59. Smith, *Travels and Works,* 2: 538, 541.

60. Moore, *Industralization and Labor,* 14-47; Melville J. Herskovits, "The Problem of Adapting Societies to New Tasks," in Bert F. Hoselitz, *The Progress of Underdeveloped Areas* (Chicago, 1952), especially 91-92. See also William O. Jones, "Labor and Leisure in Traditional African Societies," Social Science Research Council, *Items,* 23 (1968): 1-6.

61. On the last point, see Philip D. Curtin, *The Atlantic Slave Trade: A Census* (Madison, 1969), 119. I hope to deal elsewhere with the other developments that brought slavery to Virginia.

62. In 1755 the total number of white tithables in the colony was 43,329, of black tithables 59,999. Evarts B. Greene and Virginia D. Harrington, *American Population before the Federal Census of 1790* (New York, 1932), 150-51. Tithables were white men and black men and women over sixteen. Black women were tithable because they were made to work like men.

4. Indian Cultural Adjustment to European Civilization: The Case of Powhatan's Confederacy

Nancy Oestreich Lurie

In comparison with other early English adventurers and settlers like the Pilgrims and Puritans, the first Virginians had to establish relations with a politically sophisticated intertribal organization known as Powhatan's Confederacy. At the outset the Confederacy seemed quite interested in forming some type of diplomatic alliance with the Virginians, but that notion evaporated rapidly. Why was the Confederacy of Powhatan peaceful, even friendly and helpful in the early years of Jamestown? And why did that pattern break down, ultimately resulting in two bloody massacres initiated by Powhatan's successors in 1622 and 1644? Cultural anthropologist Nancy Oestreich Lurie (b. 1924), currently serving as Curator of Anthropology at the Milwaukee Public Museum, here offers important answers to these questions, drawing upon anthropological literature and historical materials.

The patterns described by Lurie may seem at variance with those presented by Calvin Martin in the second selection. But are they? Similarities may be more striking, and differences may lie in the relative timing and overall impact of European diseases in the two regions. Is it possible that the Confederacy's tribes had become so weakened by diseases at a point well before the Jamestown landfall that the Confederacy itself grew out of the need for remnant group protection? If the Confederacy could have had more time to mature before the first Virginians arrived, would it have been in a better position to drive the English back into the sea? Whatever the case, full Indian acculturation with whites, whether in Canada, New England, Virginia, or the Caribbean, never developed as a viable alternative. The decimation of groups like the Micmacs and Powhatan's Confederacy stand as examples of what happened over and over again to native American peoples as wave upon wave of white adventurers, traders, and settlers rolled across the American continents.

In 1907, on the 300th anniversary of the beginning of English colonization in America, James Mooney made the brief observation that the Jamestown settlers "landed among a people who already knew and hated whites." In effect, this remark summed up the accepted anthropological explanation for the Indians'

Source: From Nancy Oestreich Lurie, "Indian Cultural Adjustment to European Civilization," in *Seventeenth-Century America: Essays in Colonial History,* ed. James Morton Smith (Chapel Hill: University of North Carolina Press, 1959), p. 33–52, 60. Footnotes omitted. Reprinted by permission of the University of North Carolina Press and the Institute of Early American History and Culture.

unpredictable behavior; it indicated why they alternated elaborate expressions and actions of good will with apparent treachery. Mooney implied that the Indians' attitudes and behavior were more than justified by the demonstrated greed and aggressiveness of the whites.

Little work was done in the succeeding years to explore the complete significance of Mooney's remark or to probe more deeply into underlying motivations for the Indians' actions. This neglect was inevitable, since attention had to be devoted to a more fundamental problem. Before achieving an understanding of Indian reaction to the effects of contact with Europeans, it was necessary to establish a valid and cohesive picture of aboriginal culture. Thanks to the labors of such scholars as Mooney, Frank G. Speck, David I. Bushnell, John R. Swanton, Maurice A. Mook, and others, the fragmentary data relating to native life have been gathered into comprehensive and analytical accounts concerned with such problems as Indian demography, the cultural and linguistic identity of given tribes, tribal locations, and the prehistoric diffusion and changes in Indian cultures.

Likewise, in the past fifty years, general theoretical techniques of ethnological interpretation have been refined through field research in observable situations of culture contact. These acculturational studies, which are an invaluable aid in the interpretation of historical data, have investigated the reasons why some groups lose their cultural identity in a situation of culture contact while other groups continue to preserve ethnic integrity despite widespread alterations of purely native patterns. With this backlog of necessary information and analysis, anthropologists have begun a more intensive consideration of the dynamics of culture contact in ethnohistorical terms.

Turning to Mooney's contention, there is evidence that the Virginia Indians had several opportunities to form opinions about Europeans both in terms of direct experience and of information communicated to them. Direct knowledge of Europeans may have occurred as early as the first quarter of the sixteenth century, when Giovanni de Verrazano and Estevan Gomez are believed to have made observations in the Chesapeake Bay region. Of somewhat greater significance is the alleged founding of a Spanish Jesuit mission on the York River in 1570. According to this theory, the missionaries were killed by Indians under the leadership of a native known as Don Luis de Velasco, who had lived in Spain, where he was educated and converted to Christianity. The Spaniards had hoped that he would act as guide and model in the proselytizing of his people, but it appears that the effects of his early life negated his later training. In 1572 a punitive expedition under Pedro Menendez de Aviles attacked and defeated the Indians responsible for the destruction of the mission; in succeeding years Menendez made other forays into the region. A recent study insists that this area must have been along the Virginia coast.

Whether or not the case for a sixteenth-century mission in Virginia has been proved is problematical. Many details are uncertain: the precise location of the mission on the York River, the tribal affiliations of Don Luis, the extent of his leadership, his age at the time he lived in Spain, and his possible genealogical affiliations with the ruling hierarchy of the Virginia Indians of the seventeenth century. However, historical investigation leaves no doubt of Spanish activity at this time, and these ventures must have occurred between St. Augustine and the Potomac River. The natives of Virginia, who borrowed cultural traits from neighboring tribes along the coast and further inland, could have received news of

European explorations to the south and west by the same routes that carried purely native ideas. Generalized impressions of Europeans were doubtless prevalent in the Virginia area long before 1607.

The Spaniards came to America primarily as adventurers and fortune seekers. Although they attempted to found settlements their efforts usually met with failure. They plundered Indian villages but did not remain long in any one region; they were frequently routed by angry Indians or by their own inability to subsist in a strange terrain. After 1520, raids were conducted along the Gulf and southern Atlantic coast to obtain slaves for shipment to the West Indies. News of these incursions may have reached Virginia via the various coast tribes, and similarly Virginia natives may have heard of De Soto's hapless wanderings to the south and west. Even though the Spaniards later achieved success in colonization in Florida through the use of missionaries, the first hostile impressions had been made.

The French entered the scene to the south of Virginia in 1562. Because of lack of supplies and Spanish aggression, they failed in their attempts to establish a foothold in the region. However, the interests of France as well as of Britain were served by unknown numbers of piratical freebooters from the Caribbean area who touched along the coast of the Carolinas and intrigued with the Indians. Not until 1580 was Spain able to dislodge foreign intruders and punish recalcitrant Indians. Even then, Spanish dominion remained precarious, although the Spanish Franciscans continued to extend their missions up the coast. Finally, in 1597, a general uprising among the Carolina tribes destroyed these religious outposts and forced Spain again to concentrate most of her forces in Florida.

Thus, during much of the sixteenth century Europeans were active in regions immediately adjacent to Virginia and possibly in Virginia itself. Their activity was often associated with violence, and there was sufficient time for rumors concerning them to have reached the Virginia natives before any direct contacts were made. By the time the English attempted to found colonies on the east coast toward the close of the sixteenth century, they encountered difficulties which may have been more than the simple result of European inexperience in developing techniques for survival in the New World. Raleigh's enterprise, for example, may have been singularly ill-timed. A general unrest in Indian-white relationships marked the period from 1577 to 1597 in the Carolina region where Raleigh's followers chose to remain. Pemisipan, a Secotan chief who attempted to organize opposition to the British in 1585, could hardly have been blamed if he saw a curious similarity to accounts he may have heard concerning the Spanish when, for the trifling matter of the theft of a silver cup, the English burned the corn and destroyed the buildings at his village of Aquascogoc.

The later events at Cape Henry, the first landfall of the Jamestown colonists, suggest that the immediate hostility expressed by the Indians was inspired by fear of reprisals for the fate of Raleigh's colony. The Indians who attacked the English belonged to the Chesapeake tribe, immediately adjacent to the tribes with whom Pemisipan conspired. It is also possible, as Mooney implies, that by 1607 the Virginia Indians evaluated any sudden appearance of Europeans as evil and took immediate measures to repel them. However, this view oversimplifies several important factors. Long before any Europeans arrived at Jamestown, the Indians had been fighting over matters of principle important to them, such as possession of land and tribal leadership. If they were aware of the fate of other Indians at the hands of Europeans, there was no reason for them to assume that their fate would be similar; they were not necessarily allied with the beleaguered tribes, nor did they share a sense of racial kinship. Sharp cultural differences and even sharper linguistic differences separated the various Indian societies. While there was reason to fear and hate the Europeans as invaders who made indiscriminate war on all Indians, the fear was only that of being taken unawares and the hate could be modified if the tribes which had fallen victim thus far were strangers or even enemies. If the Indians of Virginia had any knowledge of Europeans, they must have been aware that the white men were fundamentally outnumbered, frequently unable to support themselves in an environment which the Indians found eminently satisfactory, and that European settlements were usually short lived. The appearance of the English was probably far less alarming than 350 years of hindsight indicate ought to have been the case.

This is demonstrated by the fact that the Virginia Indians under the leadership of Powhatan seem to have made their first adjustments to Europeans in terms of existing native conditions. Primary among these conditions were Powhatan's efforts to gain firmer control over his subject tribes and to fight tribes traditionally at enmity with his followers. It was expedient to help the settlers stay alive, for they could be useful allies in his established plans; but at the same time he could not allow them to gain ascendancy. The situation was complicated by factionalism in Powhatan's ranks and lack of accord among the settlers. However, recognition of the fundamental aboriginal situation makes the early events at Jamestown understandable on a rational basis. It offers a logical foundation for subsequent developments in Indian-white relationships and Indian adjustments to European civilization as the result of something more than barbaric cupidity and a thirst for the white man's blood.

Certainly a wary sensitivity to any sign of hostility or treachery characterized the behavior of both whites and Indians at the outset of settlement at Jamestown. The Europeans were still seriously concerned about the probable fate of Raleigh's colony and they had already been attacked by the Indians at Cape Henry. The Indians, in turn, may well have possessed information concerning the alarmingly retributive temperament of Europeans, at least in terms of the incident at nearby Aquascogoc, if not through generalized opinions derived from the history of intermittent European contact along the east coast.

Nevertheless, the party of Europeans that set out on exploration of the country about Jamestown encountered a welcome at the various Indian villages different from the greetings offered at Cape Henry. Except for one cold but not overtly hostile reception in the Weanoc country, the white men were feted, fed, and flattered. At the same time a suggestion of the uncertainty of the next years occurred before the exploring party had even returned to their headquarters—at Jamestown the remaining colonists were attacked by a party of local Indians. Events of this nature as well as the general observations recorded during the first two years at Jamestown are particularly instructive in any attempt to understand Indian motivations and policy regarding the British.

The narratives are difficult to follow because of the variety of orthographies employed for Indian words. Certain features remain speculative because initial communication between whites and Indians was limited to the use of signs and the few native words that could be learned readily. However, it is possible to see native culture in terms of regularities and consistencies which were not obvious to the colonists. Likewise, the apparent inconsistencies on the part of the natives, recounted by the settlers as innate savage treachery, indicate that the aboriginal culture was in a process of growth, elaboration, and internal change. These phases of culture, which included both extensive tendencies of intertribal confederation and divisive reactions expressed by individual tribes, were interrupted and redirected but not initiated by the arrival of Europeans in 1607.

From the viewpoint of the twentieth century, it is difficult to realize that the material differences between the Indians and the European colonists, who lived before the full development of the industrial revolution, were equalled if not outweighed by the similarities of culture. This was especially true in Virginia, where a local fluorescence of culture and a demonstrated ability to prevail over other tribes gave the Indians a sense of strength which blinded them to the enormity of the threat posed by the presence of Europeans. There was actually little in the Europeans' imported bag of tricks which the Indians could not syncretize with their own experience. Metal was not unknown to them: they used native copper, brought in from the West, for decorative purposes. Metal weapons and domestic utensils were simply new and effective forms of familiar objects to accomplish familiar tasks. Even guns were readily mastered after the noise, which evoked astonishment at first, was understood as necessary to their operation. Likewise, fabrics and articles of personal adornment were part of Indian technology. Many utilitarian objects such as nets, weirs, and gardening implements were very similar in both Indian and European culture. European ships were simply larger and different, as was fitting for a people interested in traveling greater distances by open water than the Indians had ever cared to do.

Expansive accounts of the size and permanence of the great European cities could easily have been likened by the natives to the impressive aboriginal developments in the lower Mississippi Valley; archeological evidence suggests that knowledge of this cultural complex was widespread. Even if these Indian models of nascent urbanization are discounted, the statements made by Europeans about their country and king may well have sounded like the exaggerations of outnumbered strangers endeavoring to buttress their weaknesses with talk of powerful but distant brothers. This explanation is admittedly conjectural, although we find ample documentation of the Indians' disinclination to admit any significant superiority in white culture at a somewhat later period. During the early nineteenth century, when the industrial revolution was underway and the eastern United States was heavily populated by whites, Indian visitors were brought from the West in the hope that they would be cowed by the white man's power and cease resistance to the forces of civilization. The Indians remained singularly unimpressed. Furthermore, at the time Jamestown was founded in the seventeenth century, the only knowledge Indians possessed concerning Europeans indicated that Indians were well able to oppose white settlement. Raleigh's ill-fated colony was a clear reminder of the Europeans' mortality.

Although the early accounts tend to take a patronizing view of the Indians, the points on which the Europeans felt superior had little meaning for the aborigines: literacy, different sexual mores, ideas of modesty, good taste in dress and personal adornment, and Christian religious beliefs. The argument of technological superiority at that time was a weak one; despite guns and large ships the Europeans could not wrest a living from a terrain which by Indian standards, supported an exceptionally large population. Scientific knowledge of generally predictable group reactions thus suggests that the degree of ethnocentrism was probably equal on both sides of the contact between Indians and Europeans in Virginia. Recognition of the Indians' self-appraisal is necessary for a clear understanding of their basis of motivation and consequent behavior in relation to Europeans.

Moreover, it was evident to the colonists that they were dealing with a fairly complex society, exhibiting many characteristics of leadership, social classes, occupational specialization, social control, and economic concepts that were eminently comprehensible in European terms. If the exploring parties overstated the case when they translated *weroance* as "king" and likened tribal territories to European kingdoms, they at least had a truer understanding of the nature of things than did the democratic Jefferson, who first designated the Virginia tribes as the "Powhatan Confederacy." Since the term "Confederacy" is so firmly entrenched in the literature, it will be retained here as a matter of convenience; but, in reality, Powhatan was in the process of building something that approximated an empire. By 1607 it was not an accomplished fact, but the outlines were apparent and the process was sufficiently advanced to allow a geographical description of the extent of Powhatan's domain.

Powhatan's influence, if not his undisputed control, extended over some thirty Algonkian-speaking tribes along the entire length of the present Virginia coast, including the Accohannoc and Accomac of the Eastern Shore. The nucleus of his domain consisted of six tribes which were centrally located in the region drained by the James, Pamunkey, and Mattaponi rivers. These tribes were the Powhatan, Arrohattoc, Pamunkey, Youghtanund, Appomattoc, and Mattaponi, with Powhatan's own tribe, the Pamunkey, consistently referred to in the early narratives as the largest and most powerful. The Confederacy was bounded to the north and south by other Algonkian tribes. Except on the basis of their declared political allegiance, the uniformity of language and culture in the region makes it difficult to differentiate between the tribes within the Confederacy and even between the Confederacy and neighboring Maryland and Carolina groups.

It is generally accepted that these Algonkian peoples moved into the lower coastal region from the north. According to their own account this had occurred about three hundred years before Jamestown was settled, although recent archeological investigations suggest a longer occupation. Once arrived, the Algonkians acquired numerous cultural traits from the Southeast culture area and developed many similarities to the interior Muskhogean-speaking groups. Some of these new elements were in turn transferred to the more northerly Algonkians, but they never existed there in the cohesive complexity found in the tidelands.

Powhatan inherited the six central tribes as an already unified intertribal organization and extended his domain by conquest from the south bank of the Potomac to the Norfolk region. The Chesapeake Indians are included in the Confederacy, but this southernmost group was not fully under Powhatan's control at the time the settlers arrived. Their attack on the colonists at Cape Henry gave Powhatan the opportunity to gain favor with the English by swiftly avenging the hostile action. Although some historians have implied that Powhatan destroyed the entire tribe, it is far more likely that he simply killed the leaders and placed trusted kinsmen in these positions.

Powhatan's method of fighting and his policy of expanding political control combined a reasoned plan of action with quick ferocity and a minimum of bloodshed. Indian warfare was generally limited to surprise attacks and sniping from cover. Constant replacements of fighting men kept the enemy occupied and wore down their resistance, while actual casualties were relatively limited in number. Accounts of Powhatan's conquests and the occurrences observed after 1607 point to a carefully devised method of establishing his control over a wide territory. Entire communities might be killed if they proved exceptionally obstinate in rendering homage and paying tribute, but in most cases Powhatan simply defeated groups of questionable loyalty and upon their surrender moved them to areas where he could keep better watch over them. Trusted members of the Confederacy were then sent to occupy the vacated regions, while Powhatan's relatives were distributed throughout the tribes in positions of leadership. Mook's studies indicate that the degree of Powhatan's leadership decreased in almost direct proportion to the increase in geographical distance between the Pamunkey and the location of a given tribe. Throughout the entire region, however, the combination of ample sustenance, effective techniques of production, provident habits of food storage, and distribution of supplies through exchange offset shortcomings in the political framework connecting the tribes and helped to cement social ties and produce a commonality of culture.

Despite certain internal dissensions the Confederacy can be seen as a unified bloc, distinct from neighboring tribes. To the north were numerous small Algonkian-speaking tribes, either friendly or representing no serious danger to Powhatan. They tended to shade off in cultural characteristics toward the more northern Algonkian types to be found along the coast into New England. The best known of these tribes was the Nanticoke in eastern Maryland and Delaware. North of the Potomac lived the Conoy (Piscataway), Tocwough, Ozinie, and others, about whom little is recorded. At a later date the tribes in this region were known collectively as the "Doeg" Indians. Beyond the Conoy and up into the present state of Pennsylvania were the Susquehanna, in Captain John Smith's judgment a powerful and impressive group, distinguished from the Virginia tribes in both language and culture. However, they seem to have felt closer ties of friendship with the Algonkians than they did with their Iroquoian linguistic affiliates to the north. The Nansemond and Chesapeake tribes formed the southern terminus of the Confederacy, and beyond them in the Carolina region were a number of linguistically and culturally similar tribes extending along the coast to the Neuse River. The Roanoke narratives and particularly the illustrations of John White provide somewhat fuller documentation for the southerly neighbors of the Confederacy than is available for the northern Algonkian groups.

The western border, formed by the fall line and paralleling the coast, was characterized by greater cultural and linguistic differences than those observed to the north and south of the Confederacy; it also represented a definite danger area for Powhatan. Virtually all Indian occupation ended somewhat east of the falls, however, allowing a strip of land a mile to ten or twelve miles wide as a safe margin between the Powhatan tribes and their nearest neighbors, who were also their deadliest enemies, the tribes of the Virginia piedmont region. These peoples have long been designated as Siouan-speaking but a recent study casts doubt on this identification. It is now suggested that these groups spoke a highly divergent and extremely old dialect of the basic Algonkian language stock. Except for linguistic distinctiveness little is known about these piedmont people. This is most unfortunate, since they appear to figure as a key to much of Powhatan's policy toward the English and helped to influence the course of Indian adjustment to European settlement. A few of these tribes are known by name, but they are usually considered as having comprised two major confederacies, comparable in some measure to the groupings associated with Powhatan. These were the Manahoac on the upper Rappahannock and surrounding region, and the Monacan along the upper James and its tributary streams. Both were aggressive groups, and their incursions were a constant threat to the tidelands Indians.

Powhatan's desire to subdue these westerly tribes as a matter of protection was underscored by another consideration: copper, highly prized by the Virginia Confederacy, came from the West, and the enemy tribes formed an obstacle to trade for that commodity.

Thus, at the outset of colonization in 1607 Powhatan's policies can best be understood in relation to circumstances antedating the arrival of the Jamestown settlers. Powhatan saw the whites in his territory as potential allies and as a source of new and deadly weapons to be used in furthering his own plans for maintaining control over his Confederacy and protecting the Confederacy as a whole against the threat posed by the alien tribes of the piedmont region. Likewise, existing concepts of intertribal trade in foodstuffs and other commodities were extended to include trade with the newly arrived whites. It is worth noting that European novelties, apart from weapons, were of far less interest to Powhatan than the fact that the British possessed copper, an object vested with traditional native values and heretofore obtained with great difficulty.

In the initial stages of contact between the Indians and the whites, therefore, it is hardly surprising that Powhatan and his people felt at least equal to the English. The chieftain could appreciate the foreigners as allies in the familiar business of warfare and trade, but in general there seemed little to emulate in European culture and much to dislike about the white men. However, even in the most difficult phases of their early relationship, Powhatan did not indulge in a full-scale attack against the settlers. At that time he was still engaged in strengthening his Confederacy and perhaps he could not risk extensive Indian defection to the side of the whites. But there is an equal likelihood that Powhatan's primary motivation was the desire to control and use the whites for his own purposes rather than to annihilate them.

At the time Jamestown was founded, native civilization was enjoying a period of expansion, and Powhatan had ample reason for sometimes considering the English as more an annoyance than a serious danger. The unusually rich natural environment and the security offered by the Confederacy stimulated the growth of social institutions and cultural refinements. In addition, the Virginia Indians were exceptionally powerful and, by aboriginal standards, their population was large: the entire Confederacy numbered some 8,500 to 9,000 people, or a density of approximately one person to every square mile. The Indians lived according to a well-ordered and impressively complex system of government. They dwelled in secure villages, had substantial houses and extensive gardens, and had a notable assemblage of artifacts for utilitarian, religious, and decorative purposes.

The Indians won the grudging respect of the colonists for their advanced technology, but the Europeans were contemptuous of their seemingly hopeless commitment to superstition, while their ceremonialism appeared to the whites a ridiculous presumption of dignity. A typical bias of communication between Europeans and Indians is seen in Smith's account of the Quiyoughcohannock chief who begged the settlers to pray to the Christian God for rain because their own deities had not fulfilled the Indian's requests. Smith asserted that the Indians appealed to the whites because they believed the Europeans' God superior to their own, just as the Europeans' guns were superior to bows and arrows. Yet Smith notes with some wonder that the Quiyoughcohannock chief, despite his cordiality and interest in the Christian deity, could not be prevailed upon to "forsake his false Gods." Actually this chief of one of the lesser tribes of the Confederacy illustrated the common logic of polytheistic people who often have no objection to adding foreign deities to their pantheon if it seems to assure more efficient control of the natural universe. The chief was not interested in changing his religious customs in emulation of the Europeans; he merely wished to improve his own culture by judicious borrowing—a gun at one time, a supernatural being at another.

Nor would the chief have dared respond to a new religion in its entirety, even if such an unlikely idea had occurred to him. The whole structure of tribal life relied upon controlling the mysterious aspects of the world by a traditional body of beliefs which required the use of religious functionaries, temples, idols, and rituals. These were awesome arrangements and not to be treated lightly, although improvement by minor innovations might be permitted.

The geopolitical sophistication of the Virginia tribes is reflected in the secular hierarchy of leadership which extended in orderly and expanding fashion from the villages, through the separate tribes, up to Powhatan as head of the entire Confederacy. A gauge of the complexity of government is the fact that the Confederacy shared with the Europeans such niceties of civilization as capital punishment. In small societies having a precarious economy, indemnities in goods or services are usually preferred to taking the life of a culprit even in crimes as serious as murder. However, where the life of the offender or one of his kinsmen is exacted for the life of the victim, punishment is the concern of the particular families involved; the rest of the group merely signifies approval of the process as a means of restoring social equilibrium after an offense is committed. Powhatan's government, however, was much closer to that of the English than it was to many of the tribes of North America. Punishment was meted out by a designated executioner for an offense against the society as the society was symbolized in the person of the leader.

Nevertheless, despite its elaborate civil structure, the Confederacy exhibited a universal rule of any society: a complex theory of government does not necessarily assure complete success in application. Powhatan not only had unruly subjects to deal with, but entire tribes in his domain could not be trusted. Relations between whites and Indians therefore were always uncertain, largely because of political developments within the Confederacy. When the colonists were supported by Powhatan, they were in mortal danger from those dissatisfied tribes of the Confederacy which had the foresight to realize that the English might one day assist Powhatan to enforce his authority. When Powhatan and his closest associates turned upon the settlers, the less dependable tribes became friendly to the whites.

In view of this morass of political allegiances, it is little wonder that early accounts of the settlers are replete with material which seems to prove the innate treachery of the Indians. Yet the militant phases of Indian activity, as illustrated by the initial attack on Jamestown and Powhatan's vengeance on the offending Chesapeake tribe, must be seen as part of a larger policy involving alternative methods of settling inter-group differences. Although the settlers knew that dissatisfaction among Powhatan's followers offered a means of preventing a coordinated Indian attack, they also discovered that established mechanisms of diplomacy existed among the Indians that could be employed for their benefit. For example, the Jamestown settlement was located in the territory of the Paspehegh tribe, and relations with this tribe frequently became strained. The Powhatan forces represented by the leaders of the Pamunkey, Arrohattoc, Youghtanund, and Mattaponi offered to act as intermediaries in negotiating peace with the Paspehegh and other hostile tribes or, if necessary, to join forces with the settlers in an armed assault on mutual enemies.

If the Europeans found it difficult to live among the Indians, the Europeans seemed equally unpredictable to the Indians. Early in his relationship with the English, Powhatan was promised five hundred men and supplies for a march on the Monacan and Manahoac; but instead of finding wholehearted support among his allies for this campaign, Powhatan discovered that the whites were helpless to support themselves in the New World. As time wore on and they became increasingly desperate for food, the Europeans were less careful in the difficult business of trying to distinguish friends from enemies. They extorted supplies promiscuously, driving hard bargains by the expedient of burning villages and canoes.

It is problematical whether, as Smith implies, Powhatan was actually unable to destroy the handful of English because he could not organize his tribes for a full-scale offensive or whether he was biding his time in the hope of eventually establishing a clear-cut power structure in which the colonists would be allowed to survive but remain subservient to his designs in native warfare. At any rate, after two years of English occupation at Jamestown, Powhatan moved from his traditional home on the Pamunkey River some fifteen miles from the Europeans and settled in a more remote village upstream on the Chickahominy River. Violence flared periodically during these early years: colonists were frequently killed and often captured. Sometimes, being far from united in their allegiance, they fled to the Indian villages, where they were usually well treated. Captives and runaways were exchanged as hostages when one side or the other found it convenient. However, if Powhatan was willing to take advantage of dissident feeling among the whites, he was no fool and he finally put to death two colonists who seemed to be traitors to both sides at the same time. The execution was much to Smith's satisfaction, for it saved him from performing the task and assured a far more brutal punishment than he would have been able to inflict upon the renegades.

Throughout the period from 1607 and 1609, the chronicles include a complexity of half-told tales involving alliances and enmities and mutual suspicions, of Indians living among settlers and settlers living among Indians. Although this interaction was of an individual nature, the two groups learned something of each other; yet each side maintained its own values and traditions as a social entity. The Indians were primarily concerned with obtaining new material goods. By theft, trade, and the occupation of European artisans in their villages, they increased their supply of armaments and mental work. With the use of Indian guides and informants, the settlers became familiar with the geography of the region, and they also learned the secrets of exploiting their new environment through techniques of native gardening. For ther most part, however, conscious efforts to bridge the cultural gap were unavailing. There was one amusing attempt to syncretize concepts of Indian and European monarchy and thereby bring about closer communication, when Powhatan was treated to an elaborate "coronation." The chief *weroance* was only made more vain by the ceremonies; he was by no means transformed into a loyal subject of the English sovereign, as the white settlers had intended.

An increasing number of settlers arrived in Virginia and, with the help of Indians who by this time had ample reason to let the whites perish, managed to weather the hazards of the "starving time." As the whites became more firmly established, competition between Europeans and Indians took on the familiar form of a struggle for land. Armed clashes occurred frequently, but there were no organized hostilities, and the Indians continued to trade with the English. A peace which was formally established in 1614 and lasted until 1622 is often attributed to a refinement of Powhatan's sensibilities because of the marriage of Pocahontas and John Rolfe. Although Pocahontas was indeed the favorite child of Powhatan, it is likely that the chieftain's interest in her marriage was not entirely paternal. This strengthening of the social bond between Indians and Europeans helped solidify Powhatan's power and prestige among the confederated tribes, as he was thus enduringly allied with the whites.

Continuation of harmony between Indians and whites for a period of eight years was doubtless rendered possible because enough land still remained in Virginia for both settlers and Indians to live according to their accustomed habits. The seriousness of the loss of Indian land along the James River was lessened by the existence of a strip of virtually unoccupied territory just east of the fall line which ran the length of the Confederacy's holdings. If properly armed and not disturbed by internal dissensions and skirmishes with the English, the Powhatan tribes could afford to settle at the doorstep of their piedmont neighbors and even hope to expand into enemy territory. Hostilities require weapons, and peaceful trade with the English meant easier access to arms which the Confederacy could turn against the Monacan and Manahoac. It is also possible that by this time Powhatan realized the vast strength of the English across the sea and was persuaded to keep the settlers as friends. Knowledge of Europe would have been available to the chieftain through such Indians as Machumps, described by William Strachey as having spent "somtym in England" as well as moving "to and fro amongst us as he dares and as Powhatan gives him leave."

Whatever were Powhatan's reasons for accepting the peace, it appears that he utilized the lull in hostilities to unify the Confederacy and deal with his traditional enemies. We have no direct evidence of activities against the piedmont tribes, for there is little historical data regarding the western area at this time. However, by the time the fur trade became important in the West the Monacan and Manahoac had lost the power which had once inspired fear among the tribes of the Confederacy. In view of Powhatan's years of scheming and the probable closer proximity of the Confederacy to the piedmont region after 1614, it may be conjectured that the Virginia chieftain and his people took some part in the downfall of the Monacan and Manahoac.

When Powhatan died in 1618, his brother Opechancanough succeeded him as leader of the Confederacy. Opechancanough continued to observe Powhatan's policy of peace for four years, although relations between Indians and Europeans were again degenerating. The Indians' natural resources were threatened as the increasing tobacco crops encroached on land where berries had grown in abundance and game had once been hunted. In the face of European advance, the Indians became restive and complained of the settlers' activities; but these signs went unnoticed by the colonists. Opechancanough was aware that the real danger to the Confederacy arose from neither internal dissensions nor traditional Indian enemies but from the inexorable growth of European society in Virginia. He was apparently able to convince all the member tribes of this fact, if they had not already drawn their own conclusions. The subsequent uprising of 1622 was a well-planned shock to the English; it was alarming not so much for the destruction wrought, since by that time the Europeans could sustain the loss of several hundred people, but for the fact that the Confederacy could now operate as a unified fighting organization. This was a solidarity which Powhatan either had been unable or was disinclined to achieve.

Doubtless Opechancanough expected reprisals, but he was totally unprepared for the unprecedented and utter devastation of his lands and the wholesale slaughter of his people. The tribes were scattered, some far beyond the traditional boundaries of their lands, and several of the smaller groups simply ceased to exist as definable entities. Gradually as the fury of revenge died down, the remnants of the Confederacy regrouped and began to return to their homelands. However, the settlers were no longer complacent about their Indian neighbors. In addition to compaigning against the natives, they erected a string of fortifications between Chesiac and Jamestown, and they tended to settle Virginia in the south rather than toward the north and west. In effect, therefore, Opechancanough accomplished a limited objective; a line was established between Indians and Europeans, but the line was only temporary and the Indians paid a terrible price.

Moreover, the cultural gap widened during the ensuing years. Following the period of reprisals the Indians were left to make a living and manage their affairs as best they could. Many old grievances seemed to be forgotten, and the natives gave the appearance of accepting their defeat for all time. Opechancanough, who had eluded capture immediately after the attack of 1622, remained at large, but the Europeans attempted to win tribes away from his influence rather than hunt him down at the risk of inflaming his followers. Finally, white settlement once more began to spread beyond the safety of concentrated colonial population. Tensions were re-created on the frontier, and there were minor skirmishes; the Indians complained to the English, but they also continued their trading activities. Thus matters continued for more than twenty years until large-scale hostilities again broke out.

The uprising of 1644 was surprisingly effective. It is generally known that in both the 1622 and the 1644 uprisings the percentage of Indians killed in relation to the total Indian population was far greater than the percentage of settlers killed in relation to the total white population. Yet with far fewer Indians to do the fighting, Opechancanough managed to kill at least as many Europeans in the second attack as he had in the first. The uprising is another proof that the Indians' method of adjusting to changes wrought by the Europeans continued to be an attempt to prevail over or remove the source of anxiety—the settlers—rather than to adapt themselves to the foreign culture. Certainly the Indians never felt that their difficulties would be resolved by assimilation among the whites, a solution which the colonists at times hoped to effect through the adoption of Indian children, intermarriage, and Indian servitude.

Hopeless though the uprising appears in retrospect, it was entirely logical within Opechancanough's own cultural frame of reasoning. It is impossible to determine whether the Indians were aware of the futility of their action, nor do we know enough about the psychology of these people to ascribe to them such a grim fatalism that they would prefer a quick and honorable death to the indignities of living in subjection to the whites. But there is something impressive about Opechancanough, an old and enfeebled man, being carried on a litter to the scene of battle. Whatever the outcome his days were numbered. His young warriors, however, knew of the horrible reprisals of 1622 and they understood the cost of being defeated by the white man. Yet they too were willing to risk an all-out attack.

There is little doubt that Opechancanough realized the danger inherent in rebellion. He was a shrewd strategist and a respected leader. It is entirely possible that he hoped for assistance from forces outside the Confederacy. Tension had existed between the whites of Virginia and Maryland for a number of years, and in one instance the Virginians had hoped to incite the Confederacy against their neighbors. Maryland had been settled only ten years before the second uprising, and although hostile incidents between whites and Indians had occurred, her Indian policy had been more just and humane than Virginia's. If Opechanca- nough did expect military assistance from whites for his uprising against whites, he had historical precedent to inspire him. Powhatan had exploited factionalism among the Jamestown settlers, and it may be that the tension between Virginia and Maryland suggested an extension of his policy to Opechancanough. Whatever the motivations behind Opechancanough's design for rebellion, the second upris- ing attested to the strength of the old Confederacy and indicated clearly the stub- born resistance of the Indians to cultural annihilation.

Although the usual revenge followed the attack of 1644, Virginia's Indian policy was beginning to change. The Powhatan tribes were too seriously reduced in numbers to benefit greatly by the progress, but their treatment at the hands of the colonists following the uprising marked a new development in Indian-white relations, one which eventually culminated in the modern reservation system. In 1646 a formal treaty was signed with the Powhatan Confederacy establishing a line between Indian and white lands and promising the Indians certain rights and protection in their holdings. While their movements were to be strictly regulated, the natives were guaranteed recognition for redress of wrongs before the law. There were two particularly important features of the treaty. First, the Indians were to act as scouts and allies against the possibility of outside tribes' invading the colony; this policy was in contrast to the earlier device of attempting to win the friendship of peripheral tribes to enforce order among the local Indians. Second, and consistent with the growing importance of the fur trade in colonial economics, the Indians were to pay a tribute each year in beaver skins. During the following years various legislative acts were adopted to protect the Indians in their rights and establish mutual responsibilities with the tribes. . . .

Although the Virginia Indians were utterly defeated by the close of the seventeenth century, the experience of that period laid the foundations for modern adjustment to the white man's culture. As a result of stubborn opposition to amal- gamation, some tribes have survived into the mid-twentieth century as popula- tional entities, although they had been unable to retain a distinctive culture. Their primary technique of adjustment to European civilization, at least as documented in the Virginia tidelands region, was, with few exceptions, one of rigid resistance to alien ways which held no particular attractions, except for disparate items. Their culture simply disintegrated under the strain of continued pressure placed upon it. In contrast, the tribes further inland, by their more flexible adaptation to Europeans, achieved a social and cultural continuity which is still impressive despite many material innovations from European and American civilization.

SECTION 1: SUGGESTIONS FOR FURTHER READING

Among the most informative textbooks covering the panorama of early American history are D. J. Boorstin, *The Americans: The Colonial Experience* (1958), David Hawke, *The Colonial Experience* (1966), H. M. Jones, *O Strange New World: American Culture, the Formative Years* (1964), L. H. Leder, *America, 1603–1789: Prelude to a Nation* (1972), G. B. Nash, *Red, White, and Black: The Peoples of Early America* (1974), D. B. Rutman, *The Morning of America, 1603–1789* (1970), Carl Ubbelohde, *The American Colonies and the British Empire, 1607–1763* (1968), and C. L. Ver Steeg,

The Formative Years, 1607–1763 (1964). Of these, Hawke's book is by far the most detailed, and all contain numerous insights. Two primary source collections of distinction with excellent annotations are J. P. Greene, ed., *Settlements to Society, 1607–1763: A Documentary History of Colonial America* (1966), and Merrill Jensen, ed., *English Historical Documents, vol. 9: American Colonial Documents 1776* (1955).

The history of Indian cultures and their destruction by white settlers only now is getting the type of thorough attention that it deserves. Introductory works of a general nature include A. M. Josephy, Jr., *The Indian Heritage of America* (1968), anthropologist H. E. Driver, *The Indians of North America* (rev. ed., 1969), W. T. Hagan, *American Indians* (1961), and W. E. Washburn, *The Indian in America* (1975). The Hagan and Washburn volumes are both succinct and incisive. For the colonial period they should be supplemented by A. T. Vaughan, *New England Frontier: Puritans and Indians, 1620–1675* (1965), and D. E. Leach, *Flintlock and Tomahawk: New England in King Philip's War* (1958), both of which now must be set in juxtaposition to Francis Jennings, *The Invasion of America: Indians, Colonialism, and the Cant of Conquest* (1975). Jennings's comments on white rationalizations for removing native Americans from the land may be supplemented in a companion piece to Professor Lurie's essay by W. E. Washburn, "The Moral and Legal Justifications for Dispossessing the Indians," *Seventeenth-Century America: Essays in Colonial History*, ed. J. M. Smith (1959), pp. 15–32. Washburn has expanded substantially upon this essay in *Red Man's Land—White Man's Law: A Study of the Past and Present Status of the American Indian* (1971). Further information about changing white attitudes may be found in R. H. Pearce, *The Savages of America: A Study of the Indian and the Idea of Civilization* (1953), Richard Slotkin, *Regeneration Through Violence: The Mythology of the American Frontier, 1600–1860* (1973), and G. B. Nash, "The Image of the Indian in the Southern Colonial Mind," *William and Mary Quarterly*, 3rd ser., 29 (1972), pp. 197–230.

Anthropological and ecological findings treated historically, as in Calvin Martin's essay, may be pursued in W. R. Jacobs, *Dispossessing the American Indian: Indians and Whites on the Colonial Frontier* (1972), and A. F. C. Wallace, *The Death and Rebirth of the Seneca* (1969). The important debate over how many Indians were living in the Americas on the eve of contact should be traced through James Mooney, *The Aboriginal Population of America North of Mexico* (1928), H. F. Dobyns, "Estimating Aboriginal American Population: An Appraisal of Techniques with a New Hemispheric Estimate," *Current Anthropology*, 7 (1966), pp. 395–416, and A. F. Crosby, *The Columbian Exchange: Biological and Cultural Consequences of 1492* (1972). Although considered too high by some experts, Dobyns's estimate would place the pre-Columbian contact population somewhere between 90,000,000 and 112,000,000.

Students wanting further bibliographical information on Indians and their contact with whites should look at W. N. Fenton, *American Indian and White Relations to 1830: Needs and Opportunities for Study* (1957), B. W. Sheehan, "Indian-White Relations in Early America: A Review Essay," *William and Mary Quarterly*, 3rd ser., 26 (1969), pp. 267–286, and R. F. Berkhofer, Jr., "The Political Context of the New Indian History," *Pacific Historical Review*, 40 (1971), pp. 357–382.

Those wanting to pursue the European explorations should consult J. B. Brebner, *The Explorers of North America, 1492–1806* (1933), J. R. Hale, *Renaissance Exploration* (1968), J. H. Parry, *The Establishment of the European Hegemony, 1415–1715* (1949), and L. B. Wright, *Gold, Glory, and the Gospel* (1970). Standard introductory accounts of the Spanish empire are contained in Charles Gibson, *Spain in America* (1966), and J. H. Parry, *The Spanish Seaborne Empire* (1966). Similarly, W. J. Eccles, *France in America* (1972), is an excellent introduction to the northernmost New World empire of significance. The most rewarding investigation of the voyages of Columbus remains S. E. Morison's *Admiral of the Ocean Sea* (1942). For incisive detail on all of the explorations, Morison's *The European Discovery of America: The Northern Voyages* (1971), and *The European Discovery of America: The Southern Voyages* (1975), cannot be surpassed.

Internal change in early modern England leading to the founding of Anglo-American colonies may be traced in Wallace Notestein, *The English People on the Eve of Colonization, 1603–1630* (1954), Carl Bridenbaugh, *Vexed and Troubled Englishmen, 1590–1642* (1968), and Peter Laslett, *The World We Have Lost: England before the Industrial Age* (2nd ed., 1970). The history of Elizabethan adventurers as well as helpful background material is contained in A. L. Rowse's trilogy, *The England of Elizabeth* (1950), *The Expansion of Elizabethan England* (1955), and *The Elizabethans and America* (1959). Also of significance is D. B. Quinn, *England and the Discovery of America* (1974). For the broader European background, W. C. Abbott's *The Expansion of Europe* (1938), Robert-Henri Bautier's *The Economic Development of Medieval Europe* (1971), and C. M. Cipolla's *Guns, Sails, and Empires: Technological Innovation and the Early Phases of European Expansion, 1400–1700* (1966), are standard treatments.

J. E. Pomfret and F. M. Shumway, *Founding the American Colonies, 1583–1660* (1970), is an excellent summary of Englishmen settling in America, as is the biographical overview provided in A.

T. Vaughan, *American Genesis: Captain John Smith and the Founding of Virginia* (1975). The fate of Virginia's early settlers, as suggested by E. S. Morgan's essay, makes for gruesome reading. Standard secondary works about Virginia's colonization include C. M. Andrews, *The Colonial Period of American History*, vol. 1 (1934), which may be supplemented by W. F. Craven, *The Dissolution of the Virginia Company* (1930), and Craven's more general *The Southern Colonies in the Seventeenth Century* (1949). E. S. Morgan carries his challenging investigation of life in early Virginia forward in *American Slavery—American Freedom: The Ordeal of Colonial Virginia* (1975), which should be compared in its early chapters to Sigmund Diamond, "From Organization to Society: Virginia in the Seventeenth Century," *American Journal of Sociology,* 63 (1958), pp. 457–475. Also suggestive is A. P. Middleton, *Tobacco Coast: A Maritime History of Chesapeake Bay in the Colonial Era* (1953).

The Puritan Experience

SECTION 2

While Virginians were forming a society predicated upon personal economic ambition, another kind of English colonizing enterprise was getting under way to the north along the rugged, inhospitable shores of New England. Pilgrim and Puritan plantations were not based primarily on the profit motive; they arose from the desires of people to construct biblical commonwealths unfettered by Old World religious practices and theology. The Pilgrim Separatists actually represented a minor strain in the populating of colonial New England. Far more prolific were those dedicated Puritan zealots who left England during and after 1630 with the hope of creating an utopian communal society (one built upon their interpretation of biblical injunctions of God) in the area stretching inland from present-day Boston.

The Puritans were Protestants who first voiced their dissent in the reign of Elizabeth, men and women who wanted to purify what they felt were the remaining "popish" practices of the established Church of England. The Anglican Church, to which all Englishmen belonged, was the institution that the Tudor monarch, King Henry VIII (1509–1547), had wrought, in part, out of his frustrations with his first wife, Catherine of Aragon, who failed to produce a male heir. Within England, Henry faced little opposition to his structural reformation of Roman Catholicism. He simply placed himself at the head of the church hierarchy, substituting the personage of the Crown for the pope. Anglican ritual retained many Roman Catholic overtones, practices which growing numbers of Puritans and Separatists of the late sixteenth century found repugnant. Puritan dissenters wanted more than structural modifications; they wanted a theological reformation as well. Several substantive practices of the Church of England infuriated the Puritans. The Anglican Church continued such disturbing rituals as kneeling before crosses and alters. Worse yet, it seemed susceptible to settling ungodly, licentious clergymen in local parishes. Church government also presented a dilemma, since its structure consisted not only of the king or queen but also of bishops and ecclesiastical courts. The Puritans wanted to simplify ritual and to place Church decision making more squarely in the hands of the Saints (or the regenerate). They sought to "purify" away those practices which they viewed as barriers to the redemption of human souls.

The Puritans of late sixteenth-century England were not Separatists, the name given some small splinter groups like the Pilgrims; rather, they worked within the body of the Anglican Church for good reason. In general, Puritans hoped to infuse people with a strong sense of godliness based upon their biblical, quasi-Calvinist theology. They believed that all people were conceived in sin (a result of the fall of Adam), but argued also that some were destined to be raised above the carnal state of sin to that of sanctification in life and glorification in heaven. Regeneration and, ultimately, glorification came through the conversion experience.

Yet not all people, according to the doctrine of predestination, could hope to experience conversion. Some mortals were permanently damned, but that was no reason why individuals should not actively "prepare" themselves for conversion. The practical problem was that the Church of England, being the spiritual congregation of all Englishmen, was not fastidious enough in motivating all citizens to prepare. How could that be achieved with ungodly, unregenerate clergy? Further, the Church was not active enough in ferreting out and excommunicating those souls who would not even obey the basic commandments of God.

The Puritans desired, then, to make the Church of England a closer approximation of the invisible church of God (the congregation of those who had experienced conversion and saving grace—the Saints). In England the first generations of Puritans tried to create from within what the state Church had prevented, a visible church of redeemed Saints who could demonstrate that conversion and saving grace had been achieved in their lives.

Puritan theology thus became the basis of life for thousands of individuals seeking regeneration. As the most astute student of Puritan mind, Perry Miller, has shown, the Puritan divines ordered their theology around covenants, that is contractual agreements involving God and man. Covenants not only governed the actual procedures for seeking the redeemed life (the covenant of grace) but also gave form to social, political, and churchly relationships. If individuals covenanted with God but drifted away from the prescribed standards of behavior as determined by any particular covenant, then God in all his Calvinist wrath would "afflict" saintly communities with such phenomena as droughts, diseases, and plagues until the believers repented, rooted out the sin in their midst, and returned to the righteous path.

The first generation of New England Puritans hoped to found a model, utopian commonwealth based on covenanted relationships. Like the early Virginians, the Puritans came to the New World under the aegis of a joint-stock company, one that received royal approval in 1629. The Massachusetts Bay Company charter was unique in that it did not specify a meeting place for stockholders. Puritans among the original stockholder group gained control of the Company and decided to send the charter to New England along with the first contingent of settlers. That way only Company members in New England would decide the rules and regulations by which settlers, many of whom were not Puritans, lived. The Puritan founders thus had carte blanche to construct the kind of institutions that they wanted, centered in a theology devoted to following the true principles of God, a model society that would shine as a beacon for those souls back in England who were desperately working for the acceptance of Puritan doctrines against the increasing hostility of the king and the Anglican Church.

With Company charter in hand, John Winthrop led an initial group of some one thousand settlers across the Atlantic in 1630. Before the year was out several towns had been planted in semicircular fashion around Boston. And before the decade was over, another ten to twenty thousand immigrants would not only fill up these town plots but also begin many others. By 1640 the first generation of Saints was firmly established and thriving in New England.

It was not easy to construct a communal, utopian society in America and to keep it operating according to covenants with God. Indeed, much of early New England history concerns Puritan divines who laid down and enforced orthodox rules of behavior, separating unorthodox peoples (among them Anne Hutchinson and Roger Williams) from the New England way. It was a society that paid homage to God and honored the regenerate Saint, yet it also tolerated the unregenerate so long as they remained unobtrusive, attended church, and obeyed covenanted rules of behavior. Only those who caused trouble were driven from the land. Purity and orthodoxy simply were necessary for a utopian society with a mission—a mission in serious trouble after 1650 as poignantly described by Perry Miller in the first selection.

It is open to debate how long the first generation sustained its perfectionist ideal of a utopian biblical order, but there is no doubt that the original mission gave out late in the seventeenth century. The questions are only when and whether utopian fervor ever penetrated farther into the society than the small handful of early leaders like the clergy or dominant lay figures like Governor John Winthrop. The second generation was clearly not fired with the enthusiasm of its progenitors. Harmony among the settlers and individual concern with conversion and the saintly life metamorphosed in time into individualism and material lust, or so claimed the clergy. Massachusetts began to experience a pattern of *declension* (drifting away from the original mission and religious ideals); and each year the ministers delivered more *jeremiads* (sermons calling settlers back to the mission). The biblical, perfectionist ideals of the Puritans ultimately went the way of all flesh in the American wilderness, becoming over time a community not that distinct from the other English New World colonies.

But why declension? Must it be the fate of ideological reformers to lose their zeal, their desire to uplift humanity? Why did the original mission, if it was as pervasive as the clergy insisted, lose its power? Was it that the abundance of the American environment somehow turned people toward the pursuit of wealth and away from godly matters? What impact did the abundant environment have upon the Puritan mind or on Puritan relations with the Indians? How did habits and attitudes brought over from old England affect that changing nature of New England society? Were the Puritans justified in excluding deviant individuals from their communities, given that they were escaping from the intolerant religious atmosphere of England? No matter how such questions are answered, the Puritans in the end became the harbingers of Yankee culture, a vital force in the dawning Euramerican civilization.

5. Errand into the Wilderness

Perry Miller

No person writing in the twentieth century has had a more profound impact upon our understanding of Puritanism than Perry Miller (1905–1963), late Professor of American Thought and Literature at Harvard University. The depth of Miller's comprehension of the Puritan mind is spellbinding for all those who behold it. To Miller, who first wrote in the days when scholars and laymen alike debunked the Puritans as dour enemies of pleasure, Puritan thought represented much more. The Puritan mentality embodied a way of life lived according to the mind; it represented an articulate, ordered, rational system of thought enunciated by Puritan intellectuals (ministers and certain lay leaders) and absorbed by Puritan listeners. It was the Puritan mind that gave form, character, and meaning to the early New England experience. Puritanism was a mode of vital religious thought upon which men modelled their lives.

Miller, in the following selection, summarizes his conceptual framework with regard to the decline of the Puritan mission. Note in particular the words of Governor John Winthrop spoken aboard the *Arbella* in 1630: "For we must Consider that we shall be as a City upon a Hill, the eyes of all people are upon us." These words suggest that New England's Puritans were on an "errand." They wanted to construct a model religious society to guide those who were watching in the Old World. But something went wrong. Explaining why, through the eyes of Puritan thinkers, is the task that Miller accomplishes.

But we must also consider how representative such thoughts were of all settlers in New England. Do the ideas of the articulate few (of the collective mind of the community as presented by Miller) necessarily reflect the goals and aspirations of the inarticulate many? Was the errand something that motivated only a few people, and was this the reason that the mission gave out?

It was a happy inspiration that led the staff of the John Carter Brown Library to choose as the title of its New England exhibition of 1952 a phrase from Samuel Danforth's election sermon, delivered on May 11, 1670: *A Brief Recognition of New England's Errand into the Wilderness.* It was of course an inspiration, if not of genius at least of talent, for Danforth to invent his title in the first place. But all the election sermons of this period—that is to say, the major expressions of the second generation, which, delivered on these forensic occasions, were in the fullest

Source: From Perry Miller, *Errand into the Wilderness* (Cambridge, Mass.: Harvard University Press, Belknap Press, 1956), pp. 2–15. Copyright 1956 by the President and Fellows of Harvard College. Reprinted by permission of Harvard University Press.

sense community expression—have interesting titles; a mere listing tells the story of what was happening to the minds and emotions of the New England people: John Higginson's *The Cause of God and His People In New-England* in 1663, William Stoughton's *New England's True Interest, Not to Lie* in 1668, Thomas Shepard's *Eye-Salve* in 1672, Urian Oakes's *New England Pleaded With* in 1673, and, climactically and most explicitly, Increase Mather's *A Discourse Concerning the Danger of Apostasy* in 1677.

All of these show by their title pages alone—and, as those who have looked into them know, infinitely more by their contents—a deep disquietude. They are troubled utterances, worried, fearful. Something has gone wrong. As in 1662 Wigglesworth already was saying in verse, God has a controversy with New England; He has cause to be angry and to punish it because of its innumerable defections. They say, unanimously, that New England was sent on an errand, and that it has failed.

To our ears these lamentations of the second generation sound strange indeed. We think of the founders as heroic men—of the towering stature of Bradford, Winthrop, and Thomas Hooker—who braved the ocean and the wilderness, who conquered both, and left to their children a goodly heritage. Why then this whimpering?

Some historians suggest that the second and third generations suffered a failure of nerve; they weren't the men their fathers had been, and they knew it. Where the founders could range over the vast body of theology and ecclesiastical polity and produce profound works like the treatises of John Cotton or the subtle psychological analyses of Hooker, or even such a gusty though wrongheaded book as Nathaniel Ward's *Simple Cobler,* let alone such lofty and rightheaded pleas as Roger Williams' *Bloudy Tenent,* all these children could do was tell each other that they were on probation and that their chances of making good did not seem very promising.

Since Puritan intellectuals were thoroughly grounded in grammar and rhetoric, we may be certain that Danforth was fully aware of the ambiguity concealed in his word "errand." It already had taken on the double meaning which it still carries with us. Originally, as the word first took form in English, it meant exclusively a short journey on which an inferior is sent to convey a message or to perform a service for his superior. In that sense we today speak of an "errand boy"; or the husband says that while in town on his lunch hour, he must run an errand for his wife. But by the end of the Middle Ages, errand developed another connotation: it came to mean the actual business on which the actor goes, the purpose itself, the conscious intention in his mind. In this signification, the runner of the errand is working for himself, is his own boss; the wife, while the husband is away at the office, runs her own errands. Now in the 1660's the problem was this: which had New England originally been—an errand boy or a doer of errands? In which sense had it failed? Had it been despatched for a further purpose, or was it an end in itself? Or had it fallen short not only in one or the other, but in both of the meanings? If so, it was indeed a tragedy, in the primitive sense of a fall from a mighty designation.

If the children were in grave doubt about which had been the original errand—if, in fact, those of the founders who lived into the later period and who might have set their progeny to rights found themselves wondering and confused—there is little chance of our answering clearly. Of course, there is no problem about Plymouth Colony. That is the charm about Plymouth: its clarity. The Pilgrims, as we have learned to call them, were reluctant voyagers; they had never wanted to leave England, but had been obliged to depart because the authorities made life impossible for Separatists. They could, naturally, have stayed at home had they given up being Separatists, but that idea simply did not occur to them. Yet they did not go to Holland as though on an errand; neither can we extract the notion of a mission out of the reasons which, as Bradford tells us, persuaded them to leave Leyden for "Virginia." The war with Spain was about to be resumed, and the economic threat was ominous; their migration was not so much an errand as a shrewd forecast, a plan to get out while the getting was good, lest, should they stay, they would be "intrapped or surrounded by their enemies, so as they should neither be able to fight nor flie." True, once the decision was taken, they congratulated themselves that they might become a means for propagating the gospel in remote parts of the world, and thus of serving as steppingstones to others in the performance of his great work; nevertheless, the substance of their decision was that they "thought it better to dislodge betimes to some place of better advantage and less danger, if any such could be found." The great hymn that Bradford, looking back in his old age, chanted about the landfall is one of the greatest passages, if not the very greatest, in all New England's literature; yet it does not resound with the sense of a mission accomplished—instead, it vibrates with the sorrow and exultation of suffering, the sheer endurance, the pain and the anguish, with the somberness of death faced unflinchingly:

> May not and ought not the children of these fathers rightly say: Our fathers were Englishmen which came over this great ocean, and were ready to perish in this wilderness; but they cried unto the Lord, and he heard their voyce, and looked on their adversitie. . . .

We are bound, I think, to see in Bradford's account the prototype of the vast majority of subsequent immigrants—of those Oscar Handlin calls "The Uprooted": They came for better advantage and for less danger, and to give their posterity the opportunity of success.

The Great Migration of 1630 is an entirely other story. True, among the reasons John Winthrop drew up in 1629 to persuade himself and his colleagues that they should commit themselves to the enterprise, the economic motive frankly figures. Wise men thought that England was overpopulated and that the poor would have a better chance in the new land. But Massachusetts Bay was not just an organization of immigrants seeking advantage and opportunity. It had a positive sense of mission—either it was sent on an errand or it had its own intention, but in either case the deed was deliberate. It was an act of will, perhaps of willfulness. These Puritans were not driven out of England (thousands of their fellows stayed and fought the Cavaliers)—they went of their own accord.

So, concerning them, we ask the question, why? If we are not altogether clear about precisely how we should phrase the answer, this is not because they themselves were reticent. They spoke as fully as they knew how, and none more magnificently or cogently than John Winthrop in the midst of the passage itself, when he delivered a lay sermon aboard the flagship *Arbella* and called it "A Modell of Christian Charity." It distinguishes the motives of this great enterprise from those of Bradford's forlorn retreat, and especially from those of the masses who later have come in quest of advancement. Hence, for the student of New England and of America, it is a fact demanding incessant brooding that John

Winthrop selected as the "doctrine" of his discourse, and so as the basic proposition to which, it then seemed to him, the errand was committed, the thesis that God had disposed mankind in a hierarchy of social classes, so that "in all times some must be rich, some poor, some highe and eminent in power and dignitie; others mean and in subjeccion." It is as though, preternaturally sensing what the promise of America might come to signify for the rank and file, Winthrop took the precaution to drive out of their heads any notion that in the wilderness the poor and the mean were ever so to improve themselves as to mount above the rich or the eminent in dignity. Were there any who had signed up under the mistaken impression that such was the purpose of their errand, Winthrop told them that, although other peoples, lesser breeds, might come for wealth or pelf, this migration was specifically dedicated to an avowed end that had nothing to do with incomes. We have entered into an explicit covenant with God, "we haue professed to enterprise these Accions vpon these and these ends"; we have drawn up indentures with the Almighty, wherefore if we succeed and do not let ourselves get diverted into making money, He will reward us. Whereas if we fail, if we "fall to embrace this present world and prosecute our carnall intencions, seekeing greate things for our selves and our posterity, the Lord will surely breake out in wrathe against us be revenged of such a periured people and make us knowe the price of the breache of such a Covenant."

Well, what terms were agreed upon in this covenant? Winthrop could say precisely—"It is by a mutuall consent through a specially overruleing providence, and a more than ordinary approbation of the Churches of Christ to seeke out a place of Cohabitation and Consorteshipp under a due forme of Government both civill and ecclesiasticall." If it could be said thus concretely, why should there be any ambiguity? There was no doubt whatsoever about what Winthrop meant by a due form of ecclesiastical government: he meant the pure Biblical polity set forth in full detail by the New Testament, that method which later generations, in the days of increasing confusion, would settle down to calling Congregational, but which for Winthrop was no denominational peculiarity but the very essence of organized Christianity. What a due form of civil government meant, therefore, became crystal clear: a political regime, possessing power, which would consider its main function to be the erecting, protecting, and preserving of this form of polity. This due form would have, at the very beginning of its list of responsibilities, the duty of suppressing heresy, of subduing or somehow getting rid of dissenters—of being, in short, deliberately, vigorously, and consistently intolerant.

Regarded in this light, the Massachusetts Bay Company came on an errand in the second and later sense of the word: it was, so to speak, on its own business. What it set out to do was the sufficient reason for its setting out. About this Winthrop seems to be perfectly certain, as he declares specifically what the due forms will be attempting: the end is to improve our lives to do more service to the Lord, to increase the body of Christ, and to preserve our posterity from the corruptions of this evil world, so that they in turn shall work out their salvation under the purity and power of Biblical ordinances. Because the errand was so definable in advance, certain conclusions about the method of conducting it were equally evident: one, obviously, was that those sworn to the covenant should not be allowed to turn aside in a lust for mere physical rewards; but another was, in Winthrop's simple but splendid words, "we must be knit together in this worke as one man, wee must entertaine each other in brotherly affection." We must actually delight in each other, "always having before our eyes our Commission and community in the worke, our community as members of the same body." This was to say, were the great purpose kept steadily in mind, if all gazed only at it and strove only for it, then social solidarity (within a scheme of fixed and unalterable class distinctions) would be an automatic consequence. A society despatched upon an errand that is its own reward would want no other rewards: it could go forth to possess a land without ever becoming possessed by it; social gradations would remain eternally what God had originally appointed; there would be no internal contention among groups or interests, and though there would be hard work for everybody, prosperity would be bestowed not as a consequence of labor but as a sign of approval upon the mission itself. For once in the history of humanity (with all its sins), there would be a society so dedicated to a holy cause that success would prove innocent and triumph not raise up sinful pride or arrogant dissension.

Or, at least, this would come about if the people did not deal falsely with God, if they would live up to the articles of their bond. If we do not perform these terms, Winthrop warned, we may expect immediate manifestations of divine wrath; we shall perish out of the land we are crossing the sea to possess. And here in the 1660's and 1670's, all the jeremiads (of which Danforth's is one of the most poignant) are castigations of the people for having defaulted on precisely these articles. They recite the long list of afflictions an angry god had rained upon them, surely enough to prove how abysmally they had deserted the covenant: crop failures, epidemics, grasshoppers, caterpillars, torrid summers, arctic winters, Indian wars, hurricanes, shipwrecks, accidents, and (most grievous of all) unsatisfactory children. The solemn work of the election day, said Stoughton in 1668, is "Foundation-work"—not, that is, to lay a new one, "but to continue, and strengthen, and beautifie, and build upon that which has been laid." It had been laid in the covenant before even a foot was set ashore, and thereon New England should rest. Hence the terms of survival, let alone of prosperity, remained what had first been propounded:

> If we should so frustrate and deceive the Lords Expectations, that his Covenant-interest in us, and the Workings of his Salvation be made to cease, then All were lost indeed; Ruine upon Ruine, Destruction upon Destruction would come, until one stone were not left upon another.

Since so much of the literature after 1660—in fact, just about all of it—dwells on this theme of declension and apostasy, would not the story of New England seem to be simply that of the failure of a mission? Winthrop's dread was realized: posterity had not found their salvation and pure ordinances but had, despite the ordinances, yielded to the seductions of the good land. Hence distresses were being piled upon them, the slaughter of King Philip's War and now the attack of a profligate king upon the sacred charter. By about 1680, it did in truth seem that shortly no stone would be left upon another, that history would record of New England that the founders had been great men, but that their children and grandchildren progressively deteriorated.

This would certainly seem to be the impression conveyed by the assembled clergy and lay elders who, in 1679, met at Boston in a formal synod, under the leadership of Increase Mather, and there prepared a report on why the land suffered. The result of their deliberation, published under the title *The Necessity of Reformation,* was the first in what has proved to be a distressingly long succession of investigations into the civic health of Americans, and it is probably the most pessimistic. The land was afflicted, it said, because corruption had proceeded apace; assuredly, if the people did not quickly reform, the last blow would fall and nothing but desolation be left. Into what a moral quagmire this dedicated community had sunk, the synod did not leave to imagination; it published a long and detailed inventory of sins, crimes, misdemeanors, and nasty habits, which makes, to say the least, interesting reading.

We hear much talk nowadays about corruption, most of it couched in generalized terms. If we ask our current Jeremiahs to descend to particulars, they tell us that the republic is going on the rocks, or to the dogs, because the wives of politicians aspire to wear mink coats and their husbands take a moderate five per cent cut on certain deals to pay for the garments. The Puritans were devotees of logic, and the verb "methodize" ruled their thinking. When the synod went to work, it had before it a succession of sermons, such as that of Danforth and the other election-day or fast-day orators, as well as such works as Increase Mather's *A Brief History of the Warr With the Indians,* wherein the decimating conflict with Philip was presented as a revenge upon the people for their transgressions. When the synod felt obliged to enumerate the enormities of the land so that the people could recognize just how far short of their errand they had fallen, it did not, in the modern manner, assume that regeneration would be accomplished at the next election by turning the rascals out, but it digested this body of literature; it reduced the contents to method. The result is a staggering compendium of iniquity, organized into twelve headings.

First, there was a great and visible decay of godliness. Second, there were several manifestations of pride—contention in the churches, insubordination of inferiors toward superiors, particularly of those inferiors who had, unaccountably, acquired more wealth than their betters, and, astonishingly, a shocking extravagance in attire, especially on the part of these of the meaner sort, who persisted in dressing beyond their means. Third, there were heretics, especially Quakers and Anabaptists. Fourth, a notable increase in swearing and a spreading disposition to sleep at sermons (these two phenomena seemed basically connected). Fifth, the Sabbath was wantonly violated. Sixth, family government had decayed, and fathers no longer kept their sons and daughters from prowling at night. Seventh, instead of people being knit together as one man in mutual love, they were full of contention, so that lawsuits were on the increase and lawyers were thriving. Under the eighth head, the synod described the sins of sex and alcohol, thus producing some of the juiciest prose of the period: militia days had become orgies, taverns were crowded; women threw temptation in the way of befuddled men by wearing false locks and displaying naked necks and arms "or, which is more abominable, naked Breasts"; there were "mixed Dancings," along with light behavior and "Company-keeping" with vain persons, wherefore the bastardy rate was rising. In 1672, there was actually an attempt to supply Boston with a brothel (it was suppressed, but the synod was bearish about the future). Ninth, New Englanders were betraying a marked disposition to tell lies, especially when selling anything. In the tenth place, the business morality of even the most righteous left everything to be desired: the wealthy speculated in land and raised prices excessively; "Day-Labourers and Mechanicks are unreasonable in their demands." In the eleventh place, the people showed no disposition to reform, and in the twelfth, they seemed utterly destitute of civic spirit.

"The things here insisted on," said the synod, "have been oftentimes mentioned and inculcated by those whom the Lord hath set as Watchmen to the house of Israel." Indeed they had been, and thereafter they continued to be even more inculcated. At the end of the century, the synod's report was serving as a kind of handbook for preachers: they would take some verse of Isaiah or Jeremiah, set up the doctrine that God avenges the iniquities of a chosen people, and then run down the twelve heads, merely bringing the list up to date by inserting the new and still more depraved practices an ingenious people kept on devising. I suppose that in the whole literature of the world, including the satirists of imperial Rome, there is hardly such another uninhibited and unrelenting documentation of a people's descent into corruption.

I have elsewhere endeavored to argue[1] that, while the social or economic historian may read this literature for its contents—and so construct from the expanding catalogue of denunciations a record of social progress—the cultural anthropologist will look slightly askance at these jeremiads; he will exercise a methodological caution about taking them at face value. If you read them all through, the total effect, curiously enough, is not at all depressing: you come to the paradoxical realization that they do not bespeak a despairing frame of mind. There is something of a ritualistic incantation about them; whatever they may signify in the realm of theology, in that of psychology they are purgations of soul; they do not discourage but actually encourage the community to persist in its heinous conduct. The exhortation to a reformation which never materializes serves as a token payment upon the obligation, and so liberates the debtors. Changes there had to be: adaptations to environment, expansion of the frontier, mansions constructed, commercial adventures undertaken. These activities were not specifically nominated in the bond Winthrop had framed. They were thrust upon the society by American experience; because they were not only works of necessity but of excitement, they proved irresistible—whether making money, haunting taverns, or committing fornication. Land speculation meant not only wealth but dispersion of the people, and what was to stop the march of settlement? The covenant doctrine preached on the *Arbella* had been formulated in England, where land was not to be had for the taking; its adherents had been utterly oblivious of what the fact of a frontier would do for an imported order, let alone for a European mentality. Hence I suggest that under the guise of this mounting wail of sinfulness, this incessant and never successful cry for repentance, the Puritans launched themselves upon the process of Americanization.

However, there are still more pertinent or more analytical things to be said of this body of expression. If you compare it with the great productions of the founders, you will be struck by the fact that the second and third generations had become oriented toward the social, and only the social, problem; herein they were deeply and profoundly different from their fathers. The finest creations of the founders—the disquisitions of Hooker, Shepard, and Cotton—were written in Europe, or else, if actually penned in the colonies, proceeded from a thoroughly European mentality, upon which the American scene made no impression whatsoever. The most striking example of this imperviousness is the poetry of Anne Bradstreet: she came to Massachusetts at the age of eighteen, already two years married to Simon Bradstreet; there, she says, "I found a new world and new manners, at which my heart rose" in rebellion, but soon convincing herself that it was the way of God, she submitted and joined the church. She bore Simon eight children, and loved him sincerely, as her most charming poem, addressed to him, reveals:

If ever two were one, then surely we:
If ever man were loved by wife, then thee.

After the house burned, she wrote a lament about how her pleasant things in ashes lay and how no more the merriment of guests would sound in the hall; but there is nothing in the poem to suggest that the house stood in North Andover or that the things so tragically consumed were doubly precious because they had been transported across the ocean and were utterly irreplaceable in the wilderness. In between rearing children and keeping house she wrote her poetry; her brother-in-law carried the manuscript to London, and there published it in 1650 under the ambitious title, *The Tenth Muse Lately Sprung Up in America.* But the title is the only thing about the volume which shows any sense of America, and that little merely in order to prove that the plantations had something in the way of European wit and learning, that they had not receded into barbarism. Anne's flowers are English flowers, the birds, English birds, and the landscape is Lincolnshire. So also with the productions of immigrant scholarship: such a learned and acute work as Hooker's *Survey of the Summe of Church Discipline,* which is specifically about the regime set up in America, is written entirely within the logical patterns, and out of the religious experience, of Europe; it makes no concession to new and peculiar circumstances.

The titles alone of productions in the next generation show how concentrated have become emotion and attention upon the interest of New England, and none is more revealing than Samuel Danforth's conception of an errand into the wilderness. Instead of being able to compose abstract treatises like those of Hooker upon the soul's preparation, humiliation, or exultation, or such a collection of wisdom and theology as John Cotton's *The Way of Life* or Shepard's *The Sound Believer,* these later saints must, over and over again, dwell upon the specific sins of New England, and the more they denounce, the more they must narrow their focus to the provincial problem. If they write upon anything else, it must be about the halfway covenant and its manifold consequences—a development enacted wholly in this country—or else upon their wars with the Indians. Their range is sadly constricted, but every effort, no matter how brief, is addressed to the persistent question: what is the meaning of this society in the wilderness? If it does not mean what Winthrop said it must mean, what under Heaven is it? Who, they are forever asking themselves, who are we?—and sometimes they are on the verge of saying, who the Devil are we, anyway?

This brings us back to the fundamental ambiguity concealed in the word "errand," that *double entente* of which I am certain Danforth was aware when he published the words that give point to the exhibition. While it was true that in 1630, the covenant philosophy of a special and peculiar bond lifted the migration out of the oridinary realm of nature, provided it with a definite mission which might in the secondary sense be called its errand, there was always present in Puritan thinking the suspicion that God's saints are at best inferiors, despatched by their Superior upon particular assignments. Anyone who has run errands for other people, particularly for people of great importance with many things on their minds, such as army commanders, knows how real is the peril that, by the time he returns with the report of a message delivered or a bridge blown up, the Superior may be interested in something else; the situation at headquarters may be entirely changed, and the gallant errand boy, or the husband who desperately remembered to buy the ribbon, may be told that he is too late. This tragic pattern appears again and again in modern warfare: an agent is dropped by parachute and, after immense hardships, comes back to find that, in the shifting tactical or strategic situations, his contribution is no longer of value. If he gets home in time and his service proves useful, he receives a medal; otherwise, no matter what prodigies he has performed, he may not even be thanked. He has been sent, as the devastating phrase has it, upon a fool's errand, than which there can be a no more shattering blow to self-esteem.

The Great Migration of 1630 felt insured against such treatment from on high by the covenant; nevertheless, the God of the covenant always remained an unpredictable Jehovah, a *Deus Absconditus*. When God promises to abide by stated terms, His word, of course, is to be trusted; but then, what is man that he dare accuse Omnipotence of tergiversation? But if any such apprehension was in Winthrop's mind as he spoke on the *Arbella,* or in the minds of other apologists for the enterprise, they kept it far back and allowed it no utterance. They could stifle the thought, not only because Winthrop and his colleagues believed fully in the covenant, but because they could see in the pattern of history that their errand was not a mere scouting expedition: it was an essential maneuver in the drama of Christendom. The Bay Company was not a battered remnant of suffering Separatists thrown up on a rocky shore; it was an organized task force of Christians, executing a flank attack on the corruptions of Christendom. These Puritans did not flee to America; they went in order to work out that complete reformation which was not yet accomplished in England and Europe, but which would quickly be accomplished if only the saints back there had a working model to guide them. It is impossible to say that any who sailed from Southampton really expected to lay his bones in the new world; were it to come about—as all in their heart of hearts anticipated—that the forces of righteousness should prevail against Laud and Wentworth, that England after all should turn toward reformation, where else would the distracted country look for leadership except to those who in New England had perfected the ideal polity and who would know how to administer it? This was the large unspoken assumption in the errand of 1630: if the conscious intention were realized, not only would a federated Jehovah bless the new land, but He would bring back these temporary colonials to govern England.

In this respect, therefore, we may say that the migration was running an errand in the earlier and more primitive sense of the word—performing a job not so much for Jehovah as for history, which was the wisdom of Jehovah expressed through time. Winthrop was aware of this aspect of the mission—fully conscious of it. "For wee must Consider that wee shall be as a Citty upon a Hill, the eies of all people are uppon us." More was at stake than just one little colony. If we deal fasely with God, not only will He descend upon us in wrath, but even more terribly, He will make us "a story and a by-word through the world, wee shall open the mouthes of enemies to speake evill of the wayes of god and all professours for Gods sake." No less than John Milton was New England to justify God's ways to man, though not, like him, in the agony and confusion of defeat but in the confidence of approaching triumph. This errand was being run for the sake of Reformed Christianity; and while the first aim was indeed to realize in America the due form of government, both civil and ecclesiastical, the aim behind that aim was to vindicate the most rigorous ideal of the Reformation, so that ultimately all Europe would imitate New England. If we succeed, Winthrop told his audience, men will say of later plantations, "the lord make it like that of New England." There was an elementary prudence to be observed: Winthrop said that the prayer would arise from subsequent plantations; yet what was England itself but one of God's plantations? In America, he promised, we shall see, or may see, more of God's wisdom, power, and truth "then formerly we have beene acquainted with." The situation was such that, for the moment, the model had no chance to be exhibited in England; Puritans could talk about it, theorize upon it, but they could not display it, could not prove that it would actually work. But if they had it set up in America—in a bare land, devoid of already established (and corrupt) institutions, empty of bishops and courtiers, where they could start *de novo*, and the eyes of the world were upon it—and if then it performed just as the saints had predicted of it, the Calvinist internationale would know exactly how to go about completing the already begun but temporarily stalled revolution in Europe.[2]

When we look upon the enterprise from this point of view, the psychology of the second and third generations becomes more comprehensible. We realize that the migration was not sent upon its errand in order to found the United States of America, nor even the New England conscience. Actually, it would not perform its errand even when the colonists did erect a due form of government in church and state: what was further required in order for this mission to be a success was that the eyes of the world be kept fixed upon it in rapt attention. If the rest of the world, or at least of Protestantism, looked elsewhere, or turned to another model, or simply got distracted and forgot about New England, if the new land was left with a polity nobody in the great world of Europe wanted—then every success in fulfilling the terms of the covenant would become a diabolical measure of failure. If the due form of government were not everywhere to be saluted, what would New England have upon its hands? How give it a name, this victory nobody could utilize? How provide an identity for something conceived under misapprehensions? How could a universal which turned out to be nothing but a provincial particular be called anything but a blunder or an abortion?

If an actor, playing the leading role in the greatest dramatic spectacle of the century, were to attire himself and put on his make-up, rehearse his lines, take a deep breath, and stride onto the stage, only to find the theater dark and empty, no spotlight working, and himself entirely alone, he would feel as did New England around 1650 or 1660. For in the 1640's, during the Civil Wars, the colonies, so to speak, lost their audience. First of all, there proved to be, deep in the Puritan movement, an irreconcilable split between the Presbyterian and Independent wings, wherefore no one system could be imposed upon England, and so the New England model was unserviceable. Secondly—most horrible to relate—the Independents, who in polity were carrying New England's banner and were supposed, in the schedule of history, to lead England into imitation of the colonial order, betrayed the sacred cause by yielding to the heresy of toleration. They actually welcomed Roger Williams, whom the leaders of the model had kicked out of Massachusetts so that his nonsense about liberty of conscience would not spoil the administrations of charity.

In other words, New England did not lie, did not falter; it made good everything Winthrop demanded—wonderfully good—and then found that its lesson was rejected by those choice spirits for whom the exertion had been made. By casting out Williams, Anne Hutchinson, and the Antinomians, along with an assortment of Gortonists and Anabaptists, into that cesspool then becoming known as Rhode Island, Winthrop, Dudley, and the clerical leaders showed Oliver Cromwell how he should go about governing England. Instead, he developed the utterly absurd theory that so long as a man made a good soldier in the New

Model Army, it did not matter whether he was a Calvinist, an Antinomian, an Arminian, an Anabaptist or even—horror of horrors—a Socinian! Year after year, as the circus tours this country, crowds howl with laughter, no matter how many times they have seen the stunt, at the bustle that walks by itself: the clown comes out dressed in a large skirt with a bustle behind; he turns sharply to the left, and the bustle continues blindly and obstinately straight ahead, on the original course. It is funny in a circus, but not in history. There is nothing but tragedy in the realization that one was in the main path of events, and now is sidetracked and disregarded. One is always able, of course, to stand firm on his first resolution, and to condemn the clown of history for taking the wrong turning: yet this is a desolating sort of stoicism, because it always carries with it the recognition that history will never come back to the predicted path, and that with one's own demise, righteousness must die out of the world.

The most humiliating element in the experience was the way the English brethren turned upon the colonials for precisely their greatest achievement. It must have seemed, for those who came with Winthrop in 1630 and who remembered the clarity and brilliance with which he set forth the conditions of their errand, that the world was turned upside down and inside out when, in June 1645, thirteen leading Independent divines—such men as Goodwin, Owen, Nye, Burroughs, formerly friends and allies of Hooker and Davenport, men who might easily have come to New England and helped extirpate heretics—wrote the General Court that the colony's law banishing Anabaptists was an embarrassment to the Independent cause in England. Opponents were declaring, said these worthies, "that persons of our way, principall and spirit cannot beare with Dissentors from them, but Doe correct, fine, imprison and banish them wherever they have power soe to Doe." There were indeed people in England who admired the severities of Massachusetts, but we assure you, said the Independents, these "are utterly your enemyes and Doe seek your extirpation from the face of the earth: those who now in power are your friends are quite otherwise minded, and doe professe they are much offended with your proceedings." Thus early commenced that chronic weakness in the foreign policy of Americans, an inability to recognize who in truth constitute their best friends abroad.

We have lately accustomed ourselves to the fact that there does exist a mentality which will take advantage of the liberties allowed by society in order to conspire for the ultimate suppression of those same privileges. The government of Charles I and Archbishop Laud had not, where that danger was concerned, been liberal, but it had been conspicuously inefficient; hence, it did not liquidate the Puritans (although it made halfhearted efforts), nor did it herd them into prison camps. Instead, it generously, even lavishly, gave a group of them a charter to Massachusetts Bay, and obligingly left out the standard clause requiring that the document remain in London, that the grantees keep their office within reach of Whitehall. Winthrop's revolutionaries availed themselves of this liberty to get the charter overseas, and thus to set up a regime dedicated to the worship of God in the manner they desired—which meant allowing nobody else to worship any other way, especially adherents of Laud and King Charles. All this was perfectly logical and consistent. But what happened to the thought processes of their fellows in England made no sense whatsoever. Out of the New Model Army came the fantastic notion that a party struggling for power should proclaim that, once it captured the state, it would recognize the right of dissenters to disagree and to have their own worship, to hold their own opinions. Oliver Cromwell was so far gone in this idiocy as to become a dictator, in order to impose toleration by force! Amid this shambles, the errand of New England collapsed. There was nobody left at headquarters to whom reports could be sent.

Many a man has done a brave deed, been hailed as a public hero, had honors and ticker tape heaped upon him—and then had to live, day after day, in the ordinary routine, eating breakfast and brushing his teeth, in what seems protracted anticlimax. A couple may win their way to each other across insuperable obstacles, elope in a blaze of passion and glory—and then have to learn that life is a matter of buying the groceries and getting the laundry done. This sense of the meaning having gone out of life, that all adventures are over, that no great days and no heroism lie ahead, is particularly galling when it falls upon a son whose father once was the public hero or the great lover. He has to put up with the daily routine without ever having known as first hand the thrill of danger or the ecstasy of passion. True, he has his own hardships—clearly rocky pastures, hauling in the cod during a storm, fighting Indians in a swamp—but what are these compared with the magnificence of leading an exodus of saints to found a city on a hill, for the eyes of all the world to behold? He might wage a stout fight against the Indians, and one out of ten of his fellows might perish in the struggle, but the world was no longer interested. He would be reduced to writing accounts of himself and scheming to get a publisher in London, in a desperate effort to tell a heedless world, "Look, I exist!"

His greatest difficulty would be not the stones, storms, and Indians, but the problem of his identity. In something of this sort, I should like to suggest, consists the anxiety and torment that inform productions of the late seventeenth and early eighteenth centuries—and should I say, some thereafter? It appears most clearly in *Magnalia Christi Americana,* the work of that soul most tortured by the problem, Cotton Mather: "I write the Wonders of the Christian Religion, flying from the Depravations of Europe, to the American Strand." Thus he proudly begins, and at once trips over the acknowledgment that the founders had not simply fled from depraved Europe but had intended to redeem it. And so the book is full of lamentations over the declension of the children, who appear, page after page, in contrast to their mighty progenitors, about as profligate a lot as ever squandered a great inheritance.

And yet, the *Magnalia* is not an abject book; neither are the election sermons abject, nor is the inventory of sins offered by the synod of 1679. There is bewilderment, confusion, chagrin, but there is no surrender. A task has been assigned upon which the populace are in fact intensely engaged. But they are not sure any more for just whom they are working; they know they are moving, but they do not know where they are going. They seem still to be on an errand, but if they are no longer inferiors sent by the superior forces of the Reformation, to whom they should report, then their errand must be wholly of the second sort, something with a purpose and an intention sufficient unto itself. If so, what is it? If it be not the due form of government, civil and ecclesiastical, that they brought into being, how otherwise can it be described?

The literature of self-condemnation must be read for meanings far below the surface, for meanings of which, we may be so rash as to surmise, the authors were not fully conscious, but by which they were troubled and goaded. They looked in vain to history for an explanation of themselves; more and more it appeared that the meaning was not to be found in theology, even with the help of the convenantal dialectic. Thereupon, these citizens found that they had no other place to search but within themselves—even though, at first sight, that repository appeared to be nothing but a sink of iniquity. Their errand having failed in the first sense of the term, they were left with the second, and required to fill it with meaning by themselves and out of themselves. Having failed to rivet the eyes of the world upon their city on the hill, they were left alone with America.

NOTES

1. See *The New England Mind: From Colony to Province* (1952), Chapter II.

2. See the perceptive analysis of Alan Heimert (*The New England Quarterly,* XXVI, September 1953) of the ingredients that ultimately went into the Puritans' metaphor of the "wilderness," all the more striking a concoction because they attached no significance a priori to their wilderness destination. To begin with, it was simply a void.

6.The Puritans and Sex

Edmund S. Morgan

If Perry Miller liberated our conception of the Puritan mind from a host of debilitating stereotypes, then Professor Edmund S. Morgan performed the same function for our idea of the Puritan body. Early in his academic career, Morgan argued that Puritan settlers were anything but prudes. Indeed, Puritan ministers and magistrates acknowledged that sexual relationships were a normal and necessary function of life, especially if they were properly channeled through marriage. Turning to ministerial tracts and to local court records, Professor Morgan discovered that somewhere between the supposed moral repressiveness of Puritanism and the actual sexual conduct of settlers the Puritans found a middle ground of understanding. Ministers and magistrates presumed that people were likely to depart from a strict code; they felt that illicit sexual behavior, within limits, should be tolerated. After all, the Puritans believed that human beings, tainted by the fall of Adam, were bound to be less than perfect in behavior. Therefore, ministers stressed the necessity of sexual intercourse in marriage, and magistrates were not as harsh in punishing sexual offenders as modern stereotypes about the Puritans would suggest.

Morgan's findings in the realm of social behavior have implications in other areas of Puritan life. They indicate that Bay Colony leaders strove for a definable ideal in human relationships, but that they also recognized that people could not attain perfection in life. How wide was the gap, then, between the ideal of corporate biblical communalism and the social reality of life in New England towns? May we conclude that Puritans maintained a flexible range of tolerance toward unwanted behavior within the larger context of communal subordination of the self to the larger aims of the society?

Henry Adams once observed that Americans have "ostentatiously ignored" sex. He could think of only two American writers who touched upon the subject with any degree of boldness—Walt Whitman and Bret Harte. Since the time when Adams made this penetrating observation, American writers have been making up for lost time in a way that would make Bret Harte, if not Whitman, blush. And yet there is still more truth than falsehood in Adams's statement. Americans, by comparison with Europeans or Asiatics, are squeamish when confronted with

Source: Edmund S. Morgan, "The Puritans and Sex," *New England Quarterly,* 15 (1942), pp. 591–607. Footnotes omitted. Reprinted by permission of Edmund S. Morgan and the *New England Quarterly.*

the facts of life. My purpose is not to account for this squeamishness, but simply to point out that the Puritans, those bogeymen of the modern intellectual, are not responsible for it.

At the outset, consider the Puritans' attitude toward marriage and the role of sex in marriage. The popular assumption might be that the Puritans frowned on marriage and tried to hush up the physical aspect of it as much as possible, but listen to what they themselves had to say. Samuel Willard, minister of the Old South Church in the latter part of the seventeenth century and author of the most complete textbook of Puritan divinity, more than once expressed his horror at "that Popish conceit of the Excellency of Virginity." Another minister, John Cotton, wrote that

> Women are Creatures without which there is no comfortable Living for man: it is true of them what is wont to be said of Governments, *That bad ones are better than none:* They are a sort of Blasphemers then who dispise and decry them, and call them a *necessary Evil,* for they are *a necessary Good.*

These sentiments did not arise from an interpretation of marriage as a spiritual partnership, in which sexual intercourse was a minor or incidental matter. Cotton gave his opinion of "Platonic love" when he recalled the case of

> one who immediately upon marriage, without ever approaching the *Nuptial Bed,* indented with the *Bride,* that by mutual consent they might both live such a life, and according did sequestring themselves according to the custom of those times, from the rest of mankind, the afterwards from one another too, in their retired Cells, giving themselves up to a Contemplative life; and this is recorded as an instance of no little or ordinary Vertue; but I must be pardoned in it, if I can account it no other than an effort of blind zeal, for they are the dictates of a blind mind they follow therein, and not of that Holy Spirit, which saith *It is not good that man should be alone.*

Here is as healthy an attitude as one could hope to find anywhere. Cotton certainly cannot be accused of ignoring human nature. Nor was he an isolated example among the Puritans. Another minister stated plainly that "the Use of the Marriage Bed" is "founded in mans Nature," and that consequently any withdrawal from sexual intercourse upon the part of husband or wife "Denies all reliefe in Wedlock vnto Human necessity: and sends it for supply vnto Beastiality when God gives not the gift of Continency." In other words, sexual intercourse was a human necessity and marriage the only proper supply for it. These were the views of the New England clergy, the acknowledged leaders of the community, the most Puritanical of the Puritans. As proof that their congregations concurred with them, one may cite the case in which the members of the First Church of Boston expelled James Mattock because, among other offenses, "he denyed Coniugall fellowship vnto his wife for the space of 2 years together vpon pretense of taking Revenge upon himself for his abusing of her before marryage." So strongly did the Puritans insist upon the sexual character of marriage that one New Englander considered himself slandered when it was reported, "that he Brock his deceased wife's hart with Greife, that he wold be absent from her 3 weeks together when he was at home, and wold never come nere her, and such Like."

There was just one limitation which the Puritans placed upon sexual relations in marriage: sex must not interfere with religion. Man's chief end was to glorify

God, and all earthly delights must promote that end, not hinder it. Love for a wife was carried too far when it led a man to neglect his God:

> . . . sometimes a man hath a good affection to Religion, but the love of his wife carries him away, a man may bee so transported to his wife, that hee dare not bee forward in Religion, lest hee displease his wife, and so the wife, lest shee displease her husband, and this is an inordinate love, when it exceeds measure.

Sexual pleasures, in this respect, were treated like other kinds of pleasure. On a day of fast, when all comforts were supposed to be foregone in behalf of religious contemplation, not only were tasty food and drink to be abandoned but sexual intercourse, too. On other occasions, when food, drink, and recreation were allowable, sexual intercourse was allowable too, though of course only between persons who were married to each other. The Puritans were not ascetics; they never wished to prevent the enjoyment of earthly delights. They merely demanded that the pleasures of the flesh be subordinated to the greater glory of God: husband and wife must not become "so transported with affection that they look at no higher end than marriage it self." "Let such as have wives," said the ministers, "look at them not for their own ends, but to be fitted for Gods service, and bring them nearer to God."

Toward sexual intercourse outside marriage the Puritans were as frankly hostile as they were favorable to it in marriage. They passed laws to punish adultery with death, and fornication with whipping. Yet they had no misconceptions as to the capacity of human beings to obey such laws. Although the laws were commands of God, it was only natural—since the fall of Adam—for human beings to break them. Breaches must be punished lest the community suffer the wrath of God, but no offense, sexual or otherwise, could be occasion for surprise or for hushed tones of voice. How calmly the inhabitants of seventeenth-century New England could contemplate rape or attempted rape is evident in the following testimony offered before the Middlesex County Court of Massachusetts:

> The examination of Edward Wire taken the 7th of october and alsoe Zachery Johnson. who sayeth that Edward Wires mayd being sent in the towne about busenes meeting with a man that dogd hir from about Joseph Kettles house to goody marches. She came into William Johnsones and desired Zachery Johnson to goe home with her for that the man dogd hir. accordingly he went with her and being then as far as Samuell Phips his house the man over tooke them. which man caled himselfe by the name of peter grant would have led the mayd but she oposed itt three times: and coming to Edward Wires house the said grant would have kist hir but she refused itt: wire being at prayer grant dragd the mayd between the said wiers and Nathanill frothinghams house. hee then flung the mayd downe in the streete and got atop hir; Johnson seeing it hee caled vppon the fellow to be sivill and not abuse the mayd then Edward wire came forth and ran to the said grant and took hold of him asking him what he did to his mayd, the said grant asked whether she was his wife for he did nothing to his wife: the said grant swearing he would be the death of the said wire. when he came of the mayd; he swore he would bring ten men to pul down his house and soe ran away and they followed him as far as good[y] phipses house where they mett with John Terry and George Chin with clubs in there hands and soe they went away together. Zachy Johnson going to Constable Heamans, and wire going home. there came John Terry to his house to ask for beer and grant was in the streete but afterward departed

into the towne, both Johnson and Wire both aferme that when grant was vppon the mayd she cryed out severall times.

Deborah hadlocke being examined sayth that she mett with the man that cals himselfe peeter grant about good prichards that he dogd hir and followed hir to hir masters and there threw hir downe and lay vppon hir but had not the use of hir body but swore several othes that he would ly with hir and gett hir with child before she got home.

Grant being present denys all saying he was drunk and did not know what he did.

The Puritans became inured to sexual offenses, because there were so many. The impression which one gets from reading the records of seventeenth-century New England courts is that illicit sexual intercourse was fairly common. The testimony given in cases of fornication and adultery—by far the most numerous class of criminal cases in the records—suggests that many of the early New Englanders possessed a high degree of virility and very few inhibitions. Besides the case of Peter Grant, take the testimony of Elizabeth Knight about the manner of Richard Nevars's advances toward her:

The last publique day of ,Thanksgiving (in the year 1674) in the evening as I was milking Richard Nevars came to me, and offered me abuse in putting his hand, under my coates, but I turning aside with much adoe, saved my self, and when I was settled to milking he agen took me by the shoulder and pulled me backward almost, but I clapped one hand on the Ground and held fast the Cows teatt with the other hand, and cryed out, and then came to mee Jonathan Abbot one of my Masters Servants, whome the said Never asked wherefore he came, the said Abbot said to look after you, what you doe unto the Maid, but the said Never bid Abbot goe about his business but I bade the lad to stay.

One reason for the abundance of sexual offenses was the number of men in the colonies who were unable to grafity their sexual desires in marriage. Many of the first settlers had wives in England. They had come to the new world to make a fortune, expecting either to bring their families after them or to return to England with some of the riches of America. Although these men left their wives behind, they brought their sexual appetites with them; and in spite of laws which required them to return to their families, they continued to stay, and more continued to arrive, as indictments against them throughout the seventeenth century clearly indicate.

Servants formed another group of men, and of women too, who could not ordinarily find supply for human necessity within the bounds of marriage. Most servants lived in the homes of their masters and could not marry without their consent, a consent which was not likely to be given unless the prospective husband or wife also belonged to the master's household. This situation will be better understood if it is recalled that most servants at this time were engaged by contract for a stated period. They were, in the language of the time, "covenant servants," who had agreed to stay with their masters for a number of years in return for a specified recompense, such as transportation to New England or education in some trade (the latter, of course, were known more specifically as apprentices). Even hired servants who worked for wages were usually single, for as soon as a man had enough money to buy or build a house of his own and to get married, he would set up in farming or trade for himself. It must be emphasized, however, that anyone who was not in business for himself was necessarily a servant. The economic organization of seventeenth-century New England had no place for the independent proletarian workman with a family of his own. All production was carried on in the household by the master of the family and his servants, so that most men were either servants or masters of servants; and the former, of course, were more numerous than the latter. Probably most of the inhabitants of Puritan New England could remember a time when they had been servants.

Theoretically no servant had a right to a private life. His time, day or night, belonged to his master, and both religion and law required that he obey his master scrupulously. But neither religion nor law could restrain the sexual impulses of youth, and if those impulses could not be expressed in marriage, they had to be given vent outside marriage. Servants had little difficulty in finding the occasions. Though they might be kept at work all day, it was easy enough to slip away at night. Once out of the house, there were several ways of meeting with a maid. The simplest way was to go to her bedchamber, if she was so fortunate as to have a private one of her own. Thus Jock, Mr. Solomon Phipps's Negro man, confessed in court.

> that on the sixteenth day of May 1682, in the morning, betweene 12 and one of the clock, he did force open the back doores of the House of Laurence Hammond in Charlestowne, and came in to the House, and went up into the garret to Marie the Negro.
>
> He doth likewise acknowledge that one night the last week he forced into the House the same way, and sent up to the Negro Woman Marie and that the like he hath done at several other times before.

Joshua Fletcher took a more romantic way of visiting his lady:

> Joshua Fletcher . . . doth confesse and acknowledge that three severall nights, after bedtime, he went into Mr Fiskes Dwelling house at Chelmsford, at an open window by a ladder that he brought with him. the said windo opening into a chamber, whose was the lodging place of Gresill Juell servant to mr. Fiske. and there he kept company with the said mayd. she sometimes having her cloathes on, and one time he found her in her bed.

Sometimes a maidservant might entertain callers in the parlor while the family were sleeping upstairs. John Knight described what was perhaps a common experience for masters. The crying of his child awakened him in the middle of the night, and he called to his maid, one Sarah Crouch, who was supposed to be sleeping with the child. Receiving no answer, he arose and

> went downe the stayres, and at the stair foot, the latch of doore was pulled in. I called severall times and at the last said if shee would not open the dore, I would breake it open, and when she opened the doore shee was all undressed and Sarah Largin with her undressed, also the said Sarah went out of doores and Dropped some of her clothes as shee went out. I enquired of Sarch Crouch what men they were, which was with them. Shee made mee no answer for some space of time, but at last shee told me Peeter Brigs was with them, I asked her whether Thomas Jones was not there, but shee would give mee no answer.

In the temperate climate of New England it was not always necessary to seek out a maid at her home. Rachel Smith was seduced in an open field "about nine of the clock at night, being darke, neither moone nor starrs shineing." She was walking through the field when she met a man who

> asked her where shee lived, and what her name was and shee told him. and then shee asked his name, and he told her Saijing that he as old Good-man Shepards man. Also shee saith he gave her strong liquors, and told her that it was not the first time he had been with maydes after his master was in bed.

Sometimes, of course, it was not necessary for a servant to go outside his master's house in order to satisfy his sexual urges. Many cases of fornication are on record between servants living in the same house. Even where servants had no private bedroom, even where the whole family slept in a single room, it was not impossible to make love. In fact many love affairs must have had their consummation upon a bed in which other people were sleeping. Take for example the case of Sarah Lepingwell. When Sarah was brought into court for having an illegitimate child, she related that one night when her master's brother, Thomas Hawes, was visiting the family, she went to bed early. Later, after Hawes had gone to bed, he called to her to get him a pipe of tobacco. After refusing for some time,

> at the last I arose and did lite his pipe and cam and lay doune one my one bead and smoaked about half the pip and siting vp in my bead to giue him his pip my bead being a trundell bead at the sid of his bead he reached beyond the pip and Cauth me by the wrist and pulled me on the side of his bead but I biding him let me goe he bid me hold my peas the folks wold here me if it be replyed come why did you not call out I Ansar I was posesed with fear of my mastar least my master shold think I did it only to bring a scandall on his brothar and thinking thay wold all beare witnes agaynst me but the thing is true that he did then begete me with child at that tim and the Child is Thomas Hauses and noe mans but his.

In his defense Hawes offered the testimony of another man who was sleeping "on the same side of the bed," but the jury nevertheless accepted Sarah's story.

The fact that Sarah was intimidated by her master's brother suggests that maidservants may have been subject to sexual abuse by their masters. The records show that sometimes masters did take advantage of their position to force unwanted attentions upon their female servants. The case of Elizabeth Dickerman is a good example. She complained to the Middlesex County Court,

> against her master John Harris senior for profiring abus to her by way of forsing her to be naught with him: . . . he has tould her that if she tould her dame: what cariag he did show to her shee had as good be hanged and shee replyed then shee would run away and he sayd run the way is befor you: . . . she says if she should liwe ther she shall be in fear of her lif.

The court accepted Elizabeth's complaint and ordered her master to be whipped twenty stripes.

So numerous did cases of fornication and adultery become in seventeenth-century New England that the problem of caring for the children of extramarital unions was a serious one. The Puritans solved it, but in such a way as to increase rather than decrease the temptation to sin. In 1668 the General Court of Massachusetts ordered:

that where any man is legally convicted to be the Father of a Bastard childe, he shall be at the care and charge to maintain and bring up the same, by such assistance of the Mother as nature requireth, and as the Court from time to time (according to circumstances) shall see meet to Order: and in case the Father of a Bastard, by confession or other manifest proof, upon trial of the case, do not appear to the Courts satisfaction, then the Man charged by the Woman to be the Father, shee holding constant in it, (especially being put upon the real discovery of the truth of it in the time of her Travail) shall be the reputed Father, and accordingly be liable to the charge of maintenance as aforesaid (though not to other punishment) notwithstanding his denial, unless the circumstances of the case and pleas be such, on the behalf of the man charged, as that the Court that have the cognizance thereon shall see reason to acquit him, and otherwise dispose of the Childe and education thereof.

As a result of this law a girl could give way to temptation without the fear of having to care for an illegitimate child by herself. Furthermore, she could, by a little simple lying, spare her lover the expense of supporting the child. When Elizabeth Wells bore a child, less than a year after this statute was passed, she laid it to James Tufts, her master's son. Goodman Tufts affirmed that Andrew Robinson, servant to Goodman Dexter, was the real father, and he brought the following testimony as evidence:

> Wee Elizabeth Jefts aged 15 ears and Mary tufts aged 14 ears doe testyfie that their being one at our hous sumtime the last winter who sayed that thear was a new law made concerning bastards that If aney man wear aqused with a bastard and the woman which had aqused him did stand vnto it in her labor that he should bee the reputed father of it and should mayntaine it Elizabeth Wells hearing of the sayd law she sayed vnto vs that If shee should bee with Child shee would bee sure to lay it vn to won who was rich enough abell to mayntayne it wheather it wear his or no and shee farder sayed Elizabeth Jefts would not you doe so likewise If it weare your case and I sayed no by no means for right must tacke place: and the sayd Elizabeth wells sayed If it wear my Càus I think I should doe so.

A tragic unsigned letter than somehow found its way into the files of the Middlesex County Court gives more direct evidence of the practice which Elizabeth Wells professed:

> der loue i remember my loue to you hoping your welfar and i hop to imbras the but now i rit to you to let you nowe that i am a child by you and i wil ether kil it or lay it to an other and you shal have no blame at al for I haue had many children and none have none of them. . . . [*i.e.,* none of their fathers is supporting any of them.]

In face of the wholesale violation of the sexual codes to which all these cases give testimony, the Puritans could not maintain the severe penalties which their laws provided. Although cases of adultery occurred every year, the death penalty is not known to have been applied more than three times. The usual punishment was a whipping or a fine, or both, and perhaps a branding, combined with a symbolical execution in the form of standing on the gallows for an hour with a rope about the neck. Fornication met with a lighter whipping or a lighter fine, while rape was treated in the same way as adultery. Though the Puritans established a code of laws which demanded perfection—which demanded, in other words, strict obedience to the will of God, they nevertheless knew that frail human beings could never live up to the code. When fornication, adultery, rape, or even buggery and sodomy appeared, they were not surprised, nor were they so severe with the offenders as their codes of law would lead one to believe. Sodomy, to be sure, they usually punished with death; but rape, adultery, and fornication they regarded as pardonable human weaknesses, all the more likely to appear in a religious community, where the normal course of sin was stopped by wholesome laws. Governor Bradford, in recounting the details of an epidemic of sexual misdemeanors in Plymouth, wrote resignedly:

> it may be in this case as it is with waters when their streames are stopped or damned up, when they gett passage they flow with more violence, and make more noys and disturbance, then when they are suffered to rune quietly in their owne chanels. So wickednes being here more stopped by strict laws, and the same more nerly looked unto, so as it cannot rune in a comone road of liberty as it would, and is inclined, it searches every wher, and at last breaks out wher it getts vente.

The estimate of human capacities here expressed led the Puritans not only to deal leniently with sexual offenses but also to take every precaution to prevent such offenses, rather than wait for the necessity of punishment. One precaution was to see that children got married as soon as possible. The wrong way to promote virtue, the Puritans thought, was to "ensnare" children in vows of virginity, as the Catholics did. As a result of such vows, children, "not being able to contain," would be guilty of "unnatural pollutions, and other filthy practices in secret: and too oft of horrid Murthers of the fruit of their bodies," said Thomas Cobbett. The way to avoid fornication and perversion was for parents to provide suitable husbands and wives for their children:

> Lot was to blame that looked not out seasonably for some fit matches for his two daughters, which had formerly minded marriage (witness the contract between them and two men in *Sodom,* called therfore for his Sons in Law, which had married his daughters, Gen. 19. 14.) for they seeing no man like to come into them in a conjugall way . . . then they plotted that incestuous course, whereby their Father was so highly dishonoured. . . .

As marriage was the way to prevent fornication, successful marriage was the way to prevent adultery. The Puritans did not wait for adultery to appear; instead, they took every means possible to make husbands and wives live together and respect each other. If a husband deserted his wife and remained within the jurisdiction of a Puritan government, he was promptly sent back to her. Where the wife had been left in England, the offense did not always come to light until the wayward husband had committed fornication or bigamy, and of course there must have been many offenses which never came to light. But where both husband and wife lived in New England, neither had much chance of leaving the other without being returned by order of the county court at its next sitting. When John Smith of Medfield left his wife and went to live with Patience Rawlins, he was sent home poorer by ten pounds and richer by thirty stripes. Similarly Mary Drury, who deserted her husband on the pretense that he was impotent, failed to convince the court that he actually was so, and had to return to him as well as to pay a fine of five pounds. The wife of Phillip Pointing receiving lighter treatment: when the court thought that she had overstayed her leave in Boston, they simply ordered her "to depart the Towne and goe to Tanton to her husband." The courts, moreover, were not satisfied with mere cohabitation; they insisted that it be peaceful cohabitation. Husbands and wives were forbidden by law to strike one another, and the law was enforced on numerous occasions. But the courts did not stop there. Henry Flood was required to give bond for good behavior because he had abused his wife simply by "ill words calling her whore and cursing of her." The wife of Christopher Collins was presented for railing at her husband and calling him "Gurley gutted divill." Apparently in this case the court thought that Mistress Collins was right, for although the fact was proved by two witnesses, she was discharged. On another occasion the court favored the husband: Jacob Pudeator, fined for striking and kicking his wife, had the sentence moderated when the court was informed that she was a woman "of great provocation."

Wherever there was strong suspicion that an illicit relation might arise between two persons, the authorities removed the temptation by forbidding the two to come together. As early as November, 1630, the Court of Assistants of Massachusetts prohibited a Mr. Clark from "cohabitacion and frequent keepeing company with Mrs. Freeman, vnder paine of such punishment as the Court shall thinke meete to inflict." Mr. Clark and Mr. Freeman were both bound "in XX £ apeece that Mr. Clearke shall make his personall appearance att the nexte Court to be holden in March nexte, and in the meane tyme to carry himselfe in good behavior towards all people and espetially towards Mrs. Freeman, concerneing whome there is stronge suspicion of incontinency." Forty-five years later the Suffolk County Court took the same kind of measure to protect the husbands of Dorchester from the temptations offered by the daughter of Robert Spurr. Spurr was presented by the grand jury.

> for entertaining persons at his house at unseasonable times both by day and night to the greife of theire wives and Relations &c The Court having heard what was alleaged and testified against him do Sentence him to bee admonish't and to pay Fees of Court and charge him upon his perill not to entertain any married men to keepe company with his daughter especially James Minott and Joseph Belcher.

In like manner Walter Hickson was forbidden to keep company with Mary Bedwell, "And if at any time hereafter hee bee taken in company of the saide Mary Bedwell without other company to bee forthwith apprehended by the Constable and to be whip't with ten stripes." Elizabeth Wheeler and Joanna Peirce were admonished "for theire disorderly carriage in the house of Thomas Watts being married women and founde sitting in other mens Laps with theire Armes about theire Necks." How little confidence the Puritans had in human nature is even more clearly displayed by another case, in which Edmond Maddock and his wife were brought to court "to answere to all such matters as shalbe objected against them concerning Haarkwoody and Ezekiell Euerells being at their house at unseasonable tyme of the night and her being up with them after her husband was gone to bed." Haarkwoody and Everell had been found "by the Constable Henry Bridghame about tenn of the Clock at night sitting by the fyre at the house of Edmond Maddocks with his wyfe a suspicious weoman her husband being on sleepe [*sic*] on the bedd." A similar distrust of human ability to resist temptation is evidence in the following order of the Connecticut Particular Court:

> James Hallett is to returne from the Correction house to his master Barclyt, who is to keepe him to hard labor, and course dyet during the pleasure of the Court provided

that Barclet is first to remove his daughter from his family, before the sayd James enter therein.

These precautions, as we have already seen, did not eliminate fornication, adultery, or other sexual offenses, but they doubtless reduced the number from what it would otherwise have been.

In sum, the Puritan attitude toward sex, though directed by a belief in absolute, God-given moral values, never neglected human nature. The rules of conduct which the Puritans regarded as divinely ordained had been formulated for men, not for angels and not for beasts. God had created mankind in two sexes; He had ordained marriage as desirable for all, and sexual intercourse as essential to marriage. On the other hand, He had forbidden sexual intercourse outside of marriage. These were the moral principles which the Puritans sought to enforce in New England. But in their enforcement they took cognizance of human nature. They knew well enough that human beings since the fall of Adam were incapable of obeying perfectly the laws of God. Consequently, in the endeavor to enforce those laws they treated offenders with patience and understanding, and concentrated their efforts on prevention more than on punishment. The result was not a society in which most of us would care to live, for the methods of prevention often caused serious interference with personal liberty. It must nevertheless be admitted that in matters of sex the Puritans showed none of the blind zeal or narrow-minded bigotry which is too often supposed to have been characteristic of them. The more one learns about these people, the less do they appear to have resembled the sad and sour .portraits which their modern critics have drawn of them.

7. Family Structure in Seventeenth-Century Andover, Massachusetts

Philip J. Greven, Jr.

While Professors Miller and Morgan utilized surviving literary records to get at an understanding of the Puritan world, a number of younger scholars in recent years have been reconstructing the behavior and values of individuals in early New England by using the techniques of demographic analysis. One of these is Philip J. Greven, Jr. (b. 1935) of Rutgers University. Professor Greven's point of departure in demographic study is family structure and what family arrangements reveal about patterns of human existence. Greven, in the selection below, subjects to inquiry the first two generations of settlers who located in the town of Andover, north of Boston. In this relatively homogeneous farming community, he discovered a pattern of late marriages among second-generation sons and daughters, reflecting an apparent reluctance on the part of first-generation fathers to transfer family lands to their sons when the latter reached adulthood. Andover sons, as a consequence, remained economically dependent upon their fathers well into their adult years. Greven's conclusion was that the Andover community was strongly patriarchal in family organization.

Indeed, one senses from Professor Greven's materials that early settlers in communities like Andover may not have driven with all of their bodily energy toward the goal of personal economic fulfillment. Could it be that the community ascribed higher value to spiritual growth and familial harmony than to acquiring land and economic independence? Or did delays in transferring land from the first to the second generation reflect more directly the deeply rooted standards of family behavior brought to New England from English communities? What might Greven's analysis suggest about the possible pervasiveness of the Puritan mission and Perry Miller's investigation of the lost errand?

Surprisingly little is known at present about family life and family structure in the seventeenth-century American colonies. The generalizations about colonial family life embedded in textbooks are seldom the result of studies of the extant source materials, which historians until recently have tended to ignore. Genealogists long have been using records preserved in county archives, town halls, churches, and graveyards as well as personal documents to compile detailed

Source: Philip J. Greven, Jr., "Family Structure in Seventeenth-Century Andover, Massachusetts," William and Mary Quarterly, 3rd ser., 23 (1966), pp. 234–256. Footnotes omitted. Reprinted by permission of Philip J. Greven, Jr. and the William and Mary Quarterly. Note: This article, in a revised form, appears in the author's book, Four Generations: Populations, Land, and Family in Colonial Andover, Massachusetts (Ithaca: Cornell University Press, 1970).

information on successive generations of early American families. In addition to the work of local genealogists, many communities possess probate records and deeds for the colonial period. A study of these last testaments and deeds together with the vital statistics of family genealogies can prove the answers to such questions as how many children people had, how long people lived, at what ages did they marry, how much control did fathers have over their children, and to what extent and under what conditions did children remain in their parents' community. The answers to such questions enable an historian to reconstruct to some extent the basic characteristics of family life for specific families in specific communities. This essay is a study of a single seventeenth-century New England town, Andover, Massachusetts, during the lifetimes of its first and second generations—the pioneers who carved the community out of the wilderness, and their children who settled upon the lands which their fathers had acquired. A consideration of their births, marriages, and deaths, together with the disposition of land and property within the town from one generation to the next reveals some of the most important aspects of family life and family structure in early Andover.

The development of a particular type of family structure in seventeenth-century Andover was dependent in part upon the economic development of the community during the same period. Andover, settled by a group of about eighteen men during the early 1640's and incorporated in 1646, was patterned at the outset after the English open field villages familiar to many of the early settlers. The inhabitants resided on house lots adjacent to each other in the village center, with their individual holdings of land being distributed in small plots within two large fields beyond the village center. House lots ranged in size from four to twenty acres, and subsequent divisions of land within the two were proportionate to the size of the house lots. By the early 1660's, about forty-two men had arrived to settle in Andover, of whom thirty-six became permanent residents. During the first decade and a half, four major divisions of the arable land in the town were granted. The first two divisions established two open fields, in which land was granted to the inhabitants on the basis of one acre of land for each acre of house lot. The third division, which provided four acres of land for each acre of house lot, evidently did not form another open field, but was scattered about the town. The fourth and final division of land during the seventeenth century occurred in 1662, and gave land to the householders at the rate of twenty acres for each acre of their house lots. Each householder thus obtained a minimum division allotment of about eighty acres and a maximum allotment of about four hundred acres. Cumulatively, these four successive divisions of town land, together with additional divisions of meadow and swampland, provided each of the inhabitants with at least one hundred acres of land for farming, and as much as six hundred acres. During the years following these substantial grants of land, many of the families in the town removed their habitations from the house lots in the town center onto their distant, and extensive, farm lands, thus altering the character of the community through the establishment of independent family farms and scattered residences. By the 1680's, more than half the families in Andover lived outside the original center of the town on their own ample farms. The transformation of the earlier open field village effectively recast the basis for family life within the community.

An examination of the number of children whose births are recorded in the Andover town records between 1651 and 1699 reveals a steady increase in the number of children being born throughout the period. (See Table 1.) Between

TABLE 1 The Number of Sons and Daughters Living
at the Age of 21 in Twenty-nine First Generation Families

Sons	0	1	2	3	4	5	6	7	8	9	10
Families	1	2	7	1	6	6	3	3	0	0	0
Daughters	0	1	2	3	4	5	6	7	8	9	10
Families	0	2	7	6	11	2	0	0	0	1	0

1651 and 1654, 28 births are recorded, followed by 32 between 1655 and 1659, 43 between 1660 and 1664, 44 between 1665 and 1669, 78 between 1670 and 1674, and 90 between 1675 and 1679. After 1680, the figures rise to more than one hundred births every five years.

The entire picture of population growth in Andover, however, cannot be formed from a study of the town records alone since these records do not reflect the pattern of generations within the town. Looked at from the point of view of the births of the children of the first generation of settlers who arrived in Andover between the first settlement in the mid-1640's and 1660, a very different picture emerges, hidden within the entries of the town records and genealogies. The majority of the second-generation children were born during the two decades of the 1650's and the 1660's. The births of 159 second-generation children were distributed in decades as follows: 10 were born during the 1630's, either in England or in the towns along the Massachusetts' coast where their parents first settled; 28 were born during the 1640's; 49 were born during the 1650's; 43 were born during the 1660's; declining to 21 during the 1670's, and falling to only 8 during the 1680's. Because of this pattern of births, the second generation of Andover children, born largely during the 1650's and the 1660's, would mature during the late 1670's and the 1680's. Many of the developments of the second half of the seventeenth century in Andover, both within the town itself and within the families residing there, were the result of the problems posed by a maturing second generation.

From the records which remain, it is not possible to determine the size of the first-generation family with complete accuracy, since a number of children were undoubtedly stillborn, or died almost immediately after birth without ever being recorded in the town records. It is possible, however, to determine the number of children surviving childhood and adolescence with considerable accuracy, in part because of the greater likelihood of their names being recorded among the children born in the town, and in part because other records, such as church records, marriage records, tax lists, and wills, also note their presence. Evidence from all of these sources indicates that the families of Andover's first settlers were large, even without taking into account the numbers of children who may have been born but died unrecorded. An examination of the families of twenty-nine men who settled in Andover between 1645 and 1660 reveals that a total of 247 children are known to have been born to these particular families. Of these 247 children whose births may be ascertained, thirty-nine, or 15.7 per cent, are known to have died before reaching the age of 21 years. A total of 208 children or 84.3 per cent of the number of children known to be born thus reached the age of 21 years, having survived the hazards both of infancy and of adolescence. This suggests that the number of deaths among children and adolescents during the middle of the seventeenth century in Andover was lower than might have been expected.

In terms of their actual sizes, the twenty-nine first-generation families varied considerably, as one might expect. Ten of these twenty-nine families had between 0 and 3 sons who survived to the age of 21 years; twelve families had either 4 or 5 sons surviving, and six families had either 6 or 7 sons living to be 21. Eighteen of these families thus had four or more sons to provide with land or a trade when they reached maturity and wished to marry, a fact of considerable significance in terms of the development of family life in Andover during the years prior to 1690. Fewer of these twenty-nine families had large numbers of daughters. Fifteen families had between 0 and 3 daughters who reached adulthood, eleven families had 4 daughters surviving, and three families had 5 or more daughters reaching the age of 21. In terms of the total number of their children born and surviving to the age 21 or more, four of these twenty-nine first-generation families had between 2 and 4 children (13.8 per cent), eleven families had between 5 and 7 children (37.9 per cent), and fourteen families had between 8 and 11 children (48.3 per cent). Well over half of the first-generation families thus had 6 or more children who are known to have survived adolescence and to have reached the age of 21. The average number of children known to have been born to these twenty-nine first-generation families was 8.5, with an average of 7.2 children in these families being known to have reached the age of 21 years. The size of the family, and particularly the number of sons who survived adolescence, was a matter of great importance in terms of the problems which would arise later over the settlement of the second generation upon land in Andover and the division of the estates of the first generation among their surviving children. The development of a particular type of family structure within Andover during the first two generations depended in part upon the number of children born and surviving in particular families.

Longevity was a second factor of considerable importance in the development of the family in Andover. For the first forty years following the settlement of the town in 1645, relatively few deaths were recorded among the inhabitants of the town. Unlike Boston, which evidently suffered from smallpox epidemics throughout the seventeenth century, there is no evidence to suggest the presence of smallpox or other epidemical diseases in Andover prior to 1690. With relatively few people, many of whom by the 1670's were scattered about the town upon their own farms, Andover appears to have been a remarkably healthy community during its early years. Lacking virulent epidemics, the principal hazards to health and to life were birth, accidents, non-epidemical diseases, and Indians. Death, consequently, visited relatively few of Andover's inhabitants during the first four decades following its settlement. This is evidence in the fact that the first generation of Andover's settlers was very long lived. Prior to 1680, only five of the original settlers who came to Andover before 1660 and established permanent residence there had died; in 1690, fifteen of the first settlers (more than half of the original group) were still alive, forty-five years after the establishment of their town. The age at death of thirty men who settled in Andover prior to 1660 can be determined with a relative degree of accuracy. Their average age at the time of their deaths was 71.8 years. Six of the thirty settlers died while in their fifties, 11 in their sixties, 3 in their seventies, 6 in their eighties, 3 in their nineties, and 1 at the advanced age of 106 years. The longevity of the first-generation fathers was to have great influence on the lives of their children, for the authority of the first generation was maintained far longer than would have been possible if death had struck them down at an early age. The second generation, in turn, was almost as long lived as the first generation had been. The average age of 138 second-genera-

TABLE 2 Second-generation Ages at Death

	Males		Females	
Ages	NUMBERS	PERCENTAGES	NUMBERS	PERCENTAGES
20–29	10	7.3	4	6.1
30–39	9	6.5	4	6.1
40–49	6	4.3	6	9.1
50–59	16	11.5	10	15.2
60–69	26	18.8	13	19.7
70–79	42	30.4	16	24.2
80–89	25	18.1	8	12.1
90–99	4	3.1	5	7.5
Total	138	100.0%	66	100.0%

tion men at the time of their deaths was 65.2 years, and the average age of sixty-six second-generation women at the time of their deaths was 64.0 years. (See Table 2.) Of the 138 second-generation men who reached the age of 21 years and whose lifespan is known, only twenty-five or 18.1 per cent, died between the ages of 20 and 49. Forty-two (30.3 per cent) of these 138 men died between the ages of 50 and 69; seventy-one (51.6 per cent) died after reaching the age of 70. Twenty-five second-generation men died in their eighties, and four died in their nineties. Longevity was characteristic of men living in seventeenth-century Andover.

The age of marriage often provides significant clues to circumstances affecting family life and to patterns of family relationships which might otherwise remain elusive. Since marriages throughout the seventeenth century and the early part of the eighteenth century were rarely fortuitous, parental authority and concern, family interests, and economic considerations played into the decisions determining when particular men and women could and would marry for the first time. And during the seventeenth century in Andover, factors such as these frequently dictated delays of appreciable duration before young men, especially, might marry. The age of marriage both of men and of women in the second generation proved to be much higher than most historians hitherto have suspected.

Traditionally in America women have married younger than men, and this was generally true for the second generation in Andover. Although the assertion is sometimes made that daughters of colonial families frequently married while in their early teens, the average age of sixty-six second-generation daughters of Andover families at the time of their first marriage was 22.8 years. (See Table 3.) Only two girls are known to have married at 14 years, none at 15, and two more at 16. Four married at the age of 17, with a total of twenty-two of the sixty-six girls marrying before attaining the age of 21 years (33.3 per cent). The largest percentage of women married between the ages of 21 and 24, with twenty-four or 36.4 per cent being married during these years, making a total of 69.7 per cent of the second-generation daughters married before reaching the age of 25. Between the ages of 25 and 29 years, fourteen women (21.2 per cent) married, with six others marrying at the age of 30 or more (9.1 per cent). Relatively few second-generation women thus married before the age of 17, and nearly 70 per cent married before the age of 25. They were not as young in most instances as one might have expected if very early marriages had prevailed, but they were relatively young nonetheless.

TABLE 3 Second-generation Female Marriage Ages

Age	Numbers	Percentages	
under 21	22	33.3	24 & under = 69.7%
21–24	24	36.4	25 & over = 30.3%
25–29	14	21.2	29 & under = 90.9%
30–34	4	6.1	30 & over = 9.1%
35–39	1	1.5	
40 & over	1	1.5	
	66	100.0%	Average age = 22.8 years

The age of marriage for second-generation men reveals a very different picture, for instead of marrying young, as they so often are said to have done, they frequently married quite late. (See Table 4.) The average age for ninety-four second-generation sons of Andover families at the time of their first marriages was 27.1 years. No son is known to have married before the age of 18, and only one actually married then. None of the ninety-four second-generation men whose marriage ages could be determined married at the age of 19, and only three married at the age of 20. The contrast with the marriages of the women of the same generation is evident, since only 4.3 per cent of the men married before the age of 21 compared to 33.3 per cent of the women. The majority of second-generation men married while in their twenties, with thirty-three of the ninety-four men marrying between the ages of 21 and 24 (35.1 per cent), and thirty-four men marrying between the ages of 25 and 29 (36.2 per cent). Nearly one quarter of the second-generation men married at the age of 30 or later, however, since twenty-three men or 24.4 per cent delayed their marriages until after their thirtieth year. In sharp contrast with the women of this generation, an appreciable majority of the second-generation men married at the age of 25 or more, with 60.6 per cent marrying after that age. This tendency to delay marriages by men until after the age of 25, with the average age being about 27 years, proved to be characteristic of male marriage ages in Andover throughout the seventeenth century.

Averages can sometimes obscure significant variations in patterns of behavior, and it is worth noting that in the second generation the age at which particular sons might marry depended in part upon which son was being married. Eldest sons tended to marry earlier than younger sons in many families, which suggests variations in their roles within their families, and differences in the attitudes of their fathers towards them compared to their younger brothers. For twenty-six eldest second-generation sons, the average age at their first marriage was 25.6 years. Second sons in the family often met with greater difficulties and married at an average age of 27.5 years, roughly two years later than their elder brothers. Youngest sons tended to marry later still, with the average age of twenty-two youngest sons being 27.9 years. In their marriages as in their inheritances, eldest sons often proved to be favored by their families; and family interests and paternal wishes were major factors in deciding which son should marry and when. More often than not, a son's marriage depended upon the willingness of his father to allow it and the ability of his father to provide the means for the couple's economic independence. Until a second-generation son had been given the means to support a wife—which in Andover during the seventeenth century generally meant land—marriage was virtually impossible.

TABLE 4 Second-generation Male Marriage Ages

Age	Numbers	Percentages	
Under 21	4	4.3	24 & under = 39.4%
21–24	33	35.1	25 & over = 60.6%
25–29	34	36.2	
30–34	16	17.2	29 & under = 75.6%
35–39	4	4.3	30 & over = 24.4%
40 & over	3	2.9	
	94	100.0%	Average age = 27.1 years

Marriage negotiations between the parents of couples proposing marriage and the frequent agreement by the father of a suitor to provide a house and land for the settlement of his son and new bride are familiar facts. But the significance of this seventeenth-century custom is much greater than is sometimes realized. It generally meant that the marriages of the second generation were dependent upon their fathers' willingness to let them leave their families and to establish themselves in separate households elsewhere. The late age at which so many sons married during this period indicates that the majority of first-generation parents were unwilling to see their sons married and settled in their own families until long after they had passed the age of 21. The usual age of adulthood, marked by marriage and the establishment of another family, was often 24 or later. Since 60 per cent of the second-generation sons were 25 or over at the time of their marriage and nearly one quarter of them were 30 or over, one wonders what made the first generation so reluctant to part with its sons?

At least part of the answer seems to lie in the fact that Andover was largely a farming community during the seventeenth century, structured, by the time that the second generation was maturing, around the family farm which stood isolated from its neighbors and which functioned independently. The family farm required all the labor it could obtain from its own members, and the sons evidently were expected to assist their fathers on their family farms as long as their fathers felt that it was necessary for them to provide their labor. In return for this essential, but prolonged, contribution to their family's economic security, the sons must have been promised land by their fathers when they married, established their own families, and wished to begin their own farms. But this meant that the sons were fully dependent upon their fathers as long as they remained at home. Even if they wanted to leave, they still needed paternal assistance and money in order to purchase land elsewhere. The delayed marriages of second-generation men thus indicates their prolonged attachment to their families, and the continuation of paternal authority over second-generation sons until they had reached their mid-twenties, at least. In effect, it appears, the maturity of this generation was appreciably later than has been suspected hitherto. The psychological consequences of this prolonged dependence of sons are difficult to assess, but they must have been significant.

Even more significant of the type of family relationships emerging with the maturing of the second generation than their late age of marriage is the fact that paternal authority over sons did not cease with marriage. In this community, at least, paternal authority was exercised by the first generation not only prior to their sons' marriages, while the second generation continued to reside under the same roof with their parents and to work on the family farm, and not only at the time of marriage, when fathers generally provided the economic means for their sons' establishment in separate households, but also *after* marriage, by the further step of the father's withholding legal control of the land from the sons who had settled upon it. The majority of first-generation fathers continued to own the land which they settled their sons upon from the time the older men received it from the town to the day of their deaths. All of the first-generation fathers were willing to allow their sons to build houses upon their land, and to live apart from the paternal house after their marriage, but few were willing to permit their sons to become fully independent as long as they were still alive. By withholding deeds to the land which they had settled their sons upon, and which presumably would be theirs to inherit someday, the first generation successfully assured the continuity of their authority over their families long after their sons had become adults and had gained a nominal independence. Since the second generation with a few exceptions, lacked clear legal titles to the land which they lived upon and farmed, they were prohibited from selling the land which their fathers had settled them upon, or from alienating the land in any other way without the consent of their fathers, who continued to own it. Being unable to sell the land which they expected to inherit, second-generation sons could not even depart from Andover without their fathers' consent, since few had sufficient capital of their own with which to purchase land for themselves outside of Andover. The family thus was held together not only by settling sons upon family land in Andover, but also by refusing to relinquish control of the land until long after the second generation had established its nominal independence following their marriages and the establishment of separate households. In a majority of cases, the dependence of the second-generation sons continued until the deaths of their fathers. And most of the first generation of settlers was very long lived.

The first generations' reluctance to hand over the control of their property to their second-generation sons is evident in their actions. Only three first-generation fathers divided their land among all of their sons before their deaths and gave them deeds of gift for their portions of the paternal estate. All three, however, waited until late in their lives to give their sons legal title to their portions of the family lands. Eleven first-generation fathers settled all of their sons upon their family estates in Andover, but gave a deed of gift for the land to only one of their sons; the rest of their sons had to await their fathers' deaths before inheriting the land which they had been settled upon. Ten of the settlers retained the title to all of their land until their deaths, handing over control to their sons only by means of their last wills and testaments. For the great majority of the second generation inheritances constituted the principal means of transferring the ownership of land from one generation to the next. The use of partible inheritances in Andover is evident in the division of the estates of the first generation. Twenty-one of twenty-two first-generation families which had two or more sons divided all of their land among all of their surviving sons. Out of seventy-seven sons who were alive at the time their fathers either wrote their wills or gave them deeds to the land, seventy-two sons received some land from their fathers. Out of a total of sixty-six sons whose inheritances can be determined from their fathers' wills, sixty-one or 92.4 per cent received land from their fathers' estates in Andover. Often the land bequeathed to them by will was already in their possession, but without legal conveyances having been given. Thus although the great majority of second-generation sons were settled upon their fathers' lands while their fathers were still alive, few actually owned the land which they lived upon until after their fathers' deaths. With their inheritances came ownership; and with ownership came independence. Many waited a long time.

The characteristic delays in the handing over of control of the land from the first to the second generation may be illustrated by the lives and actions of several Andover families. Like most of the men who wrested their farms and their community from the wilderness, William Ballard was reluctant to part with the control over his land. When Ballard died intestate in 1689, aged about 72 years, his three sons, Joseph, William, and John, agreed to divide their father's estate among themselves "as Equally as they could." They also agreed to give their elderly mother, Grace Ballard, a room in their father's house and to care for her as long as she remained a widow, thus adhering voluntarily to a common practice for the provision of the widow. The eldest son, Joseph, had married in 1665/6, almost certainly a rather young man, whereas his two brothers did not marry until the early 1680's, when their father was in his mid-sixties. William, Jr., must have been well over 30 by then, and John was 28. Both Joseph and William received as part of their division of their father's estate in Andover the land where their houses already stood, as well as more than 75 acres of land apiece. The youngest son, John, got all the housing, land, and meadow "his father lived upon except the land and meadow his father gave William Blunt upon the marriage with his daughter," which had taken place in 1668. It is unclear whether John lived with his wife and their four children in the same house as his parents, but there is a strong likelihood that this was the case in view of his assuming control of it after his father's death. His two older brothers had been given land to build upon by their father before his death, but no deeds of gift had been granted to them, thus preventing their full independence so long as he remained alive. Their family remained closely knit both by their establishment of residences near their paternal home on family land and by the prolonged control by William Ballard over the land he had received as one of the first settlers in Andover. It was a pattern repeated in many families.

There were variations, however, such as those exemplified by the Holt family, one of the most prominent in Andover during the seventeenth century. Nicholas Holt, originally a tanner by trade, had settled in Newbury, Massachusetts, for nearly a decade before joining the group of men planting the new town of Andover during the 1640's. Once established in the wilderness community, Holt ranked third among the householders, with an estate which eventually included at least 400 acres of land in Andover as a result of successive divisions of the common land. At some time prior to 1675, he removed his family from the village, where all the original house lots had been located, and built a dwelling house on his third division of land. Although a small portion of his land still lay to the north and west of the old village center, the greatest part of his estate lay in a reasonably compact farm south of his new house. Holt owned no land outside of Andover, and he acquired very little besides the original division grants from the town. It was upon this land that he eventually settled all his sons. In 1662, however, when Nicholas Holt received the fourth division grant of 300 acres from the town, his eldest son, Samuel, was 21 years old, and his three other sons were 18, 15, and 11. The fifth son was yet unborn. His four sons were thus still adolescents, and at ages at which they could provide the physical labor needed to cultivate the land already cleared about the house, and to clear and break up the land which their father had just received. The family probably provided most of the labor, since there is no evidence to indicate that servants or hired laborers were numerous in Andover at the time. With the exception of two daughters who married in the late 1650's, the Holt family remained together on their farm until 1669, when the two oldest sons and the eldest daughter married.

By 1669, when Holt's eldest son, Samuel, finally married at the age of 28, the only possible means of obtaining land to settle upon from the town was to purchase one of the twenty-acre lots which were offered for sale. House-lot grants with accommodation land had long since been abandoned by the town, and Samuel's marriage and independence therefore depended upon his father's willingness to provide him with sufficient land to build upon and to farm for himself. Evidently his father had proved unwilling for many years, but when Samuel did at last marry, he was allowed to build a house for himself and his wife upon his father's "Three-score Acres of upland," known otherwise as his third division. Soon afterwards, his second brother, Henry, married and also was given land to build upon in the third division. Neither Samuel nor Henry was given a deed to their land by their father at the time they settled upon it. Their marriages and their establishment of separate households left their three younger brothers still living with their aging father and stepmother. Five years passed before the next son married. James, the fourth of the five sons, married in 1675, at the age of 24, whereupon he, too, was provided with a part of his father's farm to build a house upon. The third son, Nicholas Jr., continued to live with his father, waiting until 1680 to marry at the late age of 32. His willingness to delay even a token independence so long suggests that personal factors must have played an important part in his continued assistance to his father, who was then about 77 years old. John Holt, the youngest of the sons, married at the age of 21, shortly before his father's death.

For Nicholas Holt's four oldest sons, full economic independence was delayed for many years. Although all had withdrawn from their father's house and had established separate residences of their own, they nonetheless were settled upon their father's land not too far distant from their family homestead, and none had yet been given a legal title to the land where they lived. Until Nicholas Holt was willing to give his sons deeds of gift for the lands where he had allowed them to build and to farm, he retained all legal rights to his estate and could still dispose of it in any way he chose. Without his consent, therefore, none of his sons could sell or mortgage the land where they lived since none of them owned it. In the Holt family, paternal authority rested upon firm economic foundations, a situation characteristic of the majority of Andover families of this period and these two generations.

Eventually, Nicholas Holt decided to relinquish his control over his Andover property by giving to his sons, after many years, legal titles to the lands which they lived upon. In a deed of gift, dated February 14, 1680/1, he conveyed to his eldest son, Samuel, who had been married almost twelve years, one half of his third division land, "the Said land on which the said Samuels House now Stands," which had the land of his brother, Henry, adjoining on the west, as well as an additional 130 acres of upland from the fourth division of land, several parcels of meadow, and all privileges accompanying these grants of land. In return for this gift, Samuel, then forty years old, promised to pay his father for his maintenance so long as his "natural life Shall Continue," the sum of twenty shillings a year. Ten months later, December 15, 1681, Nicholas Holt conveyed almost exactly the same amount of land to his second son, Henry, and also obligated him to pay twenty shillings yearly for his maintenance. Prior to his gift, Nicholas had given his fourth son, James, his portion, which consisted of one-third part of "my farme" including "the land where his house now stands," some upland, a third of the great meadow, and other small parcels. In return, James promised to pay his father three pounds a year for life (three times the sum his two elder brothers were to pay), and to pay his mother-in-law forty shillings a year when she should become a widow. The farm which James received was shared by his two other brothers, Nicholas and John, as well. Nicholas, in a deed of June 16, 1682, received "one third part of the farme where he now dwells," some meadow, and, most importantly, his father's own dwelling house, including the cellar, orchard, and barn, which constituted the principal homestead and house of Nicholas Holt, Sr. In "consideration of this my fathers gift . . . to me his sone," Nicholas, Junior, wrote, "I doe promise and engage to pay yearly" the sum of three pounds for his father's maintenance. Thus Nicholas, Junior, in return for his labors and sacrifices as a son who stayed with his father until the age of 32, received not only a share in the family farm equal to that of his two younger brothers, but in addition received the paternal house and homestead. The youngest of the five Holt sons, John, was the only one to receive his inheritance from his father by deed prior to his marriage. On June 19, 1685, Nicholas Holt, Sr., at the age of 83, gave his "Lovinge" son a parcel of land lying on the easterly side of "my now Dwelling house," some meadow, and fifteen acres of upland "as yett unlaid out." One month later, John married, having already built himself a house upon the land which his father promised to give him. Unlike his older brothers, John Holt thus gained his complete independence as an exceptionally young man. His brothers, however, still were not completely free from obligations to their father since each had agreed to the yearly payment of money to their father in return for full ownership of their farms. Not until Nicholas Holt's death at the end of Janary 1685/6 could his sons consider themselves fully independent of their aged father. He must have died content in the knowledge that all of his sons had been established on farms fashioned out of his own ample estate in Andover, all enjoying as a result of his patriarchal hand the rewards of his venture into the wilderness.

Some Andover families were less reluctant than Nicholas Holt to let their sons marry early and to establish separate households, althouth the control of the land in most instances still rested in the father's hands. The Lovejoy family, with seven sons, enabled the four oldest sons to marry at the ages of 22 and 23. John Lovejoy, Sr., who originally emigrated from England as a young indentured servant, acquired a seven-acre house lot after his settlement in Andover during the mid-1640's, and eventually possessed an estate of over 200 acres in the town. At his death in 1690, at the age of 68, he left an estate worth a total of £327.11.6, with housing and land valued at £260.00.0, a substantial sum at the time. Although he himself had waited until the age of 29 to marry, his sons married earlier. His eldest son, John, Jr., married on March 23, 1677/8, aged 22, and built a house and began to raise crops on land which his father gave him for that purpose. He did not receive a deed of gift for his land, however; his inventory, taken in 1680 after his premature death, showed his major possessions to consist of "one house and a crope of corn" worth only twenty pounds. His entire estate, both real and personal, was valued at only £45.15.0, and was encumbered with £29.14.7 in debts. Three years later, on April 6, 1683, the land which he had farmed without owning was given to his three year old son by his father, John Lovejoy, Sr. In a deed of gift, the elder Lovejoy gave his grandson, as a token of the love and affection he felt for his deceased son, the land which John, Junior, had had, consisting of fifty acres of upland, a piece of meadow, and a small parcel of another meadow, all of which lay in Andover. Of the surviving Lovejoy sons only the second, William, received a deed of gift from the elder Lovejoy for the land which he had given them. The others had to await their inheritances to come into full possession of their land. In his will dated September 1, 1690, shortly before his death, Lovejoy distributed his estate among his five surviving sons: Christopher received thirty acres together with other unstated amounts of land, and Nathaniel received the land which his father had originally intended to give to his brother, Benjamin, who had been killed in 1689. Benjamin was 25 years old and unmarried at the time of his death, and left an estate worth only £1.02.8, his wages as a soldier. Without their father's land, sons were penniless. The youngest of the Lovejoy sons, Ebenezer, received his father's homestead, with the house and lands, in return for fulfilling his father's wish that his mother should "be made comfortable while she Continues in this world." His mother inherited the east end of the house, and elaborate provisions in the will ensured her comfort. With all the surviving sons settled upon their father's land in Andover, with the residence of the widow in the son's house, and with the fact that only one of the sons actually received a deed for his land during their father's lifetime, the Lovejoys also epitomized some of the principal characteristics of family life in seventeenth-century Andover.

Exceptions to the general pattern of prolonged paternal control over sons were rare. The actions taken by Edmund Faulkner to settle his eldest son in Andover are instructive precisely because they were so exceptional. The first sign that Faulkner was planning ahead for his son came with his purchase of a twenty-acre lot from the town at the annual town meeting of March 22, 1669/70. He was the only first-generation settler to purchase such a lot, all of the other purchasers being either second-generation sons or newcomers, and it was evident that he did not buy it for himself since he already had a six-acre house lot and more than one hundred acres of land in Andover. The town voted that "in case the said Edmond shall at any time put such to live upon it as the town shall approve, or have no just matter against them, he is to be admitted to be a townsman." The eldest of his two sons, Francis, was then a youth of about nineteen years. Five years later, January 4, 1674/5, Francis was admitted as a townsman of Andover "upon the account of the land he now enjoyeth," almost certainly his father's twenty acres. The following October, aged about 24, Francis married the minister's daughter. A year and a half later, in a deed dated February 1, 1676/7, Edmund Faulkner freely gave his eldest son "one halfe of my Living here at home" to be "Equally Divided between us both." Francis was to pay the town rates on his half, and was to have half the barn, half the orchard, and half the land about his father's house, and both he and his father were to divide the meadows. Significantly, Edmund added that "all my Sixscore acres over Shawshinne river I wholly give unto him," thus handing over, at the relatively young age of 52, most of his upland and half of the remainder of his estate to his eldest son. The control of most of his estate thereby was transferred legally and completely from the first to the second generation, Edmund's second and youngest son, John, was still unmarried at the time Francis received his gift, and waited until 1682 before marrying at the age of 28. Eventually he received some land by his father's will, but his inheritance was small compared to his brother's. Edmund Faulkner's eagerness to hand over the control of his estate of his eldest son is notable for its rarity and accentuates the fact that almost none of his friends and neighbors chose to do likewise. It is just possible that Faulkner, himself a younger son of an English gentry family, sought to preserve most of his Andover estate intact by giving it to his eldest son. If so, it would only emphasize his distinctiveness from his neighbors. For the great majority of the first-generation settlers in Andover, partible inheritances and delayed control by the first generation over the land were the rule. Faulkner was the exception which proved it.

Embedded in the reconstructions of particular family histories is a general pattern of family structure unlike any which are known or suspected to have existed either in England or its American colonies during the seventeenth century. It is evident that the family structure which developed during the lifetimes of the first two generations in Andover cannot be classified satisfactorily according to any of the more recent definitions applied to types of family life in the seventeenth century. It was not simply a "patrilineal group of extended kinship gathered into a single household," nor was it simply a "nuclear independent family, that is man, wife, and children living apart from relatives." The characteristic family structure which emerged in Andover with the maturing of the second generation during the 1670's and 1680's was a combination of both the classical extended family and the nuclear family. This distinctive form of family structure is best described as a *modified extended family*—defined as a kinship group of two or more generations living within a single community in which the dependence of the children upon their parents continues after the children have married and are living under a separate roof. This family structure is a *modified* extended family because all members of the family are not "gathered into a single household," but it is still an *extended* family because the newly created conjugal unit of husband and wife live in separate households in close proximity to their parents and siblings and continue to be economically dependent in some respects upon their parents. And because of the continuing dependence of the second generation upon their first-generation fathers, who continued to own most of the family land throughout the better part of their lives, the family in seventeenth-century Andover was *partriarchal* as well. The men who first settled the town long remained the dominant figures both in their families and their community. It was their decisions and their actions which produced the family characteristic of seventeenth-century Andover.

One of the most significant consequences of the development of the modified extended family characteristic of Andover during this period was the fact that remarkably few second-generation sons moved away from their families and their community. More than four fifths of the second-generation sons lived their entire lives in the town which their fathers had wrested from the wilderness. The first generation evidently was intent upon guaranteeing the future of the community and of their families within it through the settlement of all of their sons upon the lands originally granted to them by the town. Since it was quite true that the second generation could not expect to acquire as much land by staying in Andover as their fathers had by undergoing the perils of founding a new town on the frontier, it is quite possible that their reluctance to hand over the control of the land to their sons when young is not only a reflection of their patriarchalism, justified both by custom and by theology, but also of the fact that they could not be sure that their sons would stay, given a free choice. Through a series of delays, however, particularly those involving marriages and economic independence, the second generation continued to be closely tied to their paternal families. By keeping their sons in positions of prolonged dependence, the first generation success-fully managed to keep them in Andover during those years in which their youth and energy might have led them to seek their fortunes elsewhere. Later genera-tions achieved their independence earlier and moved more. It remains to be seen to what extent the family life characteristic of seventeenth-century Andover was the exception or the rule in the American colonies.

8. Puritans, Indians, and the Deed Game

Francis Jennings

While the Spanish seized upon readily extractable New World riches in the form of gold and silver, Englishmen had no such luck. As a long-term substitute, though, land became the basis for status, even wealth, among English settlers. But the land clearly belonged to various Eastern Woodland Indian nations. Thus Englishmen like the Puritans went through a series of legalistic claims in defining ways to dispossess native Americans of the land. According to Francis Jennings (b. 1918), faculty member at Cedar Crest College in Pennsylvania, the issue must be conceptualized in terms of "sovereignty," "property," and "expediency." From the author's stridently revisionist point of view, the Puritans simply stole the land from the native population. Crucial questions are only how and why.

Professor Jennings's presentation includes words which may not be a standard part of vocabularies, such as "Amerindians" and "Euramericans," but the definitions and meanings should be obvious. One of the central arguments of *The Invasion of America,* the source of this selection, is that Europeans ruthlessly resettled the New World by force, seizing territory which was extensively populated with peoples whose numbers and morale had been seriously undermined by white diseases. Thus the Puritans were a small part of that European invasion force. They wanted land, as a potential source of personal sustenance and profit, and they took it any way they could.

Jennings's perspective on the Puritans, then, is quite different from that of Miller, Morgan, and even Greven. What does the author's approach suggest in terms of critiquing the preceding three essays? Has Jennings perhaps overstated his own case in turning John Winthrop and other Bay Colony leaders into narrow-minded bigots? What is the most satisfying context for evaluating the Puritans and Puritanism as a source of Anglo-American culture?

During the whole of the "colonial" period Amerindians and Euramericans lived as neighbors in the long strip of country between the Appalachians and the Atlantic. Necessarily they adjusted to each other's presence by arrangements to share the land, generally in separate communities under separate governments. The ultimate effect of those arrangements was to dispossess the Indians, depriving

Source: From Francis Jennings, *The Invasion of America: Indians, Colonialism, and the Cant of Conquest* (Chapel Hill: University of North Carolina Press, 1975), pp. 128–146. Footnotes omitted. Reprinted by permission of the University of North Carolina Press and the Institute of Early American History and Culture.

them simultaneously of government over persons and ownership in land. In legal terms they lost both sovereignty and property.

The distinction must be closely attended to. Conquest by Europeans of other Europeans, though resulting in transfer of sovereignty, did not necessarily imply depriving the vanquished of their property. When, for example, the duke of York conquered New Netherland, he left Dutch landholders in full possession of their own, requiring only that they transfer allegiance from the Netherlands to himself. York's conquest destroyed the political entity of New Netherland, but he recreated former property rights under the laws of New York.

Abstractly property is a legal right derivative from the sovereignty that recognizes and enforces it. When an old sovereign power departs, its laws and institutions go with it. The new sovereignty creates its own laws. Although they may be word for word the same as formerly, their source of authority and enforcement is the new sovereign. So also with property: it does not legally exist until recognized by the new sovereign. Prior possession may be generally accepted as a moral right, but legal sanction is required to create property right.

It follows that the acquisition of landed property by Euramericans from Amerindians was a function of relationships between their respective governments as well as the result of negotiations between buyer and seller. Loose talk of the "conquest" of the Indians has obscured the fact that Indians relinquished much jurisdictional territory by negotiated voluntary cession appearing in the form of the sale of property.

My phrasing uses terms of European law. Warner F. Gookin has given an Indian formulation: "The 'sale' in the Indian's mind meant the admission of the white man to a Sachem's rights within the area specified." I would add, however, that the European not only was admitted to the rights of the sachem; he was substituted for the sachem in the enjoyment of those rights.

Thus it was not possible for a free Indian, living under his independent tribal government, to sell only his property, unencumbered by jurisdictional ties, to a Euramerican living under a colonial government. Such a transaction was impossible in law. The Euramerican would not accept the sanctions of the tribe; when he bought, he intended to put his land under the jurisdiction of his own colonial government and to secure recognition from *that* government of his property right. Neither was it possible for an Indian to enjoy property under colonial law while he refused to subject his person to colonial jurisdiction. There was a sort of legal valve controlling the conveyance of land so that it always moved from Indian to Englishman and never reversed direction. This situation was peculiar to colonialism; it did not apply between the subjects of different European nations. A Frenchman, for instance, might buy an English estate while still preserving his French nationality and allegiance, and his property right would be recognized and protected by English law.

The Indian tribe gave up jurisdiction simultaneously as the Indian landlord quitted his property (whatever that may have been). From the Indian side the transaction was therefore absolute and final unless an easement had been reserved, as frequently happened, to permit the Indian grantor to hunt and fish and perhaps to maintain a residence and cultivate a garden in one corner of his former estate. But what the English purchaser got depended on his status. It was impossible for a private person to acquire governmental jurisdiction by purchase, and there could be no property where there was no jurisdiction to sanction it. The land covered by a deed to a private person therefore legally became no-man's-land until an English government assumed jurisdiction. The bulk of Indian territory was conveyed in large cessions to purchasing or conquering governments, which then parceled out the land by means of patents of property to private individuals. Strictly speaking, then, an Indian "deed" was not a deed at all as that term is understood in Anglo-American law. When it was written in favor of an English government it was a deed of cession, and when it was written in favor of a private person it was a quit-claim rather than a conveyance.

These complicated readjustments often appear in highly ambiguous forms, and each transaction must be interpreted according to the circumstances then prevailing. Sooner or later, all colonial governments outlawed the purchase of Indian land by private persons, because the practice had led to circumvention of laws regarding the distribution of property. Privately purchased "Indian titles" frequently conflicted with governmental intentions and also led to endless litigation over purchase of fraudulent titles. At certain times and places private purchases of the same land were made by persons subject to different colonial governments, whereupon their property claims became the basis for competition over jurisdiction. As Joseph Henry Smith has remarked, the crown came to recognize "some sort of status in the tribes . . . for the safeguard of the crown's own property rights."

It took some while for all these possibilities to appear in practice. Each colony experimented in its own way and at its own rate of progress. In the earliest years of English colonization, purchases from Indians were mere expedients without valid legal significance in English eyes. When John Smith and other Virginians gave goods for land, they were merely pacifying the natives. Thus they did not bother to make records of the transactions, because the records would have served no useful purpose. The Virginians' problem with the natives was only to get them to remove with the least possible trouble. They did not get property from the natives; they got it from the Virginia Company.

When the Pilgrims landed in New Plymouth, their problem appeared in a different form, because they had no charter and therefore no legally sanctioned claim to territory. They made a mutual assistance pact with the Wampanoag Indians, which they chose to regard as a deed of cession legitimizing their seizure of unspecified acreage. The Wampanoags tolerated their intrusion as a matter of political realism. The land in question had no Indian residents, having been depopulated by an exterminating epidemic, and the weakened tribe was not eager to launch itself against English weaponry. Plymouth also offered protection for the Wampanoags against the encroachments of the nearby Narragansett tribe. Although this protection quickly established a patron-client relationship, the Wampanoags retained formal independence until 1671. In the meantime New Plymouth adopted the practice of territorial purchase under circumstances to be discussed below.

Two events transformed Euramerican attitudes and practices in confusingly opposed ways. As already noticed . . . , the Indian rising of 1622 in Virginia helped inspire rationalizations about virgin land, free for the taking. In contrast, the Dutch West India Company entered colonial competition and, for its own reasons, decided to recognize Indian jurisdictions at just the historical moment that the English were determining to ignore them. The Dutch company had been chartered as a commerical monopoly with semisovereign powers but without a grant of territory. It could not appeal to papal donation or first discovery to support its jurisdictional claims, and it proposed to colonize in lands where England had established prior claims. Like New Plymouth, the Dutch were obliged to create a new rationalization to validate their presence.

Out of prior experience in competition with England halfway around the world, the Dutch devised a strategy. In the Spice Islands of the East Indies, they and the English had invoked against each other the vague law-of-nations doctrines that heathens and their territories belonged by right to that Christian prince whose subjects had made first discovery or conquest. In practice these doctrines had proved inconclusive. In 1580 the English government had propounded "possession" instead of just "discovery" as the basis of Christian right, and in 1619 the East Indies companies of England and the Netherlands temporarily abated their conflict in the Moluccas by stipulating that each should keep the areas it already possessed. The Dutch perceived possibilities in this formula: "possession" did not have to coincide fully with habitation. A few Dutchmen living in one town could "possess" the region or country surrounding the town. Legal possession could be created out of material such as natural rights by the simple process of manufacturing legal forms. Therefore the Dutch West India Company instructed its resident director of New Netherland in 1625 that Indian claims to land should be extinguished by persuasion or purchase, "a contract being made thereof and signed by them [the Indians] in their manner, *since such contracts upon other occasions may be very useful to the Company.*" The point is unmistakable, because the legitimacy of a contract in Indian eyes did not depend on its being in written form. The "other occasions" foreseen by the Dutch were their approaching clashes in America with other European—especially English—claimants. When the Dutch became embroiled in the Delaware and Connecticut valleys with Swedes and assorted English provincials, they pulled out their deeds.

The issue actually arose first in Europe early in 1632 when port officials of Plymouth, England, seized the Dutch ship *Eendracht* while it sheltered in their harbor with a rich cargo of furs from New Netherland. Ambassadors from the Dutch States General immediately protested the seizure on the formal grounds that no potentate could "prevent the subjects of another to trade in countries whereof his people have not taken, nor obtained actual possession from the right owners, either by contract or purchase." This was especially true in the instant case, they said, when Dutch subjects, rather than Englishmen, had "acquired the property, partly by confederation with the owners of the lands, and partly by purchase." To this argument the English crown entered a flat denial that Indians could be considered legal possessors of lands, having a bona fide right "to dispose of them either by sale or donation," and the wrangle went on. But the Dutch had taken the high ground, and subsequent events demonstrated that their technical advantage had impressed their equally legalistic English adversaries. English colonials began to strengthen their territorial claims by acquiring written Indian deeds like the Dutchmen's, and in due course they adapted and adopted the Dutch rationale.

But not everywhere, all at once. New Plymouth, in its charterless state, was quick to seize on the device. Massachusetts Bay, however, had been founded in 1630 with a charter of ample authority for jurisdiction over a bounded grant of territory, and so its leaders made no move to buy from Indians until opportunity tempted them beyond chartered bounds.

Plymouth traders competed with the Dutch at various points, struggling to keep from being overwhelmed by the Dutch commercial colossus. Each party attempted to build permanent trading posts at key points and to establish regular trading relationships with the surrounding Indians. One such key point lay in the upper Connecticut Valley where canoe-borne peltry from the northern interior could be intercepted before it got within the reach of coastwise traders. Dutchmen and Englishmen alike understood the strategic value of controlling the Connecticut trade. On June 8, 1633, the New Netherland Dutch purchased a tract of land for a trading post where Hartford, Connecticut, now stands. They bought from the grand sachem of the Pequot Indians with the consent of the Pequots' tributaries resident at the place. In so doing, the Dutch created the first deed of sale of Indian territory in the region of lower New England. Plymouth's traders, having no other weapons, fought back with the Dutchmen's own.

Breaking with their own nonpurchasing precedents, Plymouth's traders acknowledged Indian tenure rights in principle in order to turn the principle against the Dutch. They neatly accomplished this feat by recognizing and purchasing the right of a different Indian than the one from whom the Dutch had bought—an Indian who had earlier been defeated in battle by the Pequots and had been driven from his former territory. Plymouth's men, although strong advocates of the rights of conquest when it suited their purposes, now contended that their client Indian had not lost his true rights through the Pequot conquest and solemnly set up their own deed against the Dutch deed. Similar transactions later occurred in a wide variety of circumstances, but one general principle underlay them all: Euramericans competing for Indian lands—whether governments, companies, or individuals—legitimized their claims by recognizing or inventing whatever purported rights might be severally available to them.

Massachusetts Bay did not soon follow Plymouth's example on purchasing Indian land. Although Massachusetts' parent company in England had issued instructions in 1629 for the colonists to make "reasonable composition" with the native landowners so as to be free of any "scruple of intrusion," this directive was not carried out. John Endecott, who received the instruction at Salem, showed no interest in Indian purchases. His replacement as governor in 1630 was John Winthrop, a lawyer who held views about Indian property rights that were thoroughly inconsistent with the company's instruction, and Winthrop escaped the authority of the English company's directors by taking the colony's royal patent to America.

Before migrating, Winthrop had adopted Samuel Purchas's dictum about the virginity of American land. Lawyer that he was, Winthrop declared that most land in America was *vacuum domicilium*—i.e., legally "waste"—because the Indians had not "subdued" it by methods recognized in English law and therefore had no "natural" right to it; the alternative of "civil" right was impossible for Indians because they did not have civil government. In operational terms civil government meant European government.

Morally and pragmatically Winthrop's Puritans were obliged to leave individual Indians in possession of tracts actually under tillage, for such small plots of cultivated land obviously qualified as "subdued," but legally they recognized as real property only those lands whose claimants could show deeds from grants made by the Massachusetts Bay Company. Inherent in this doctrine was the notion that no Indian government was sovereign over any domain claimed by the English crown, and therefore no legal sanction could exist for Indian tenure of real estate except as derived, directly or indirectly, from the crown. Since the Puritan magistrates interpreted their royal patent as having delegated the crown's rights and powers to themselves, their doctrine meant in practice that there could be no property in the territorial jurisdiction of Massachusetts except what Massachusetts law created. Regardless of habitation by living persons, Indian lands were *legally* vacant.

Winthrop's logic chopping cut more than one way. In creating a magisterial monopoly on the creation of property in land, he not only denied Indian rights but also forestalled the possibility to private colonists creating property for themselves out of Indian rights. This was a living issue in early Massachusetts. . . .

Lesser men than Winthrop interpreted Indian sanctions over the land quite differently. Early seventeenth-century English observers had quickly concluded that New England's Indians held land among themselves under customs not very different from the relationships prescribed by English law and custom. Explicit testimony exists for the Wampanoag, Narragansett, and Mohegan "nations," and circumstantial evidence implies like customs among the Massachuset and Pequot "nations," to the following effect. The grand sachem of each Indian nation held a jurisdictional right, like that of eminent domain, over all the territory of the nation. Subordinate sachems held property rights in hunting tracts and fishing stations within the national territory. Early data indicate that cropland was held as commons, the sachem assigning annually the land to be tilled by each family; however, as native institutions adjusted to English practices, croplands seem to have become fixed in the possession of their cultivators.

Epidemics preceding and accompanying English colonization catastrophically reduced Indian populations without effecting concomitant reduction of customary rights and claims. Property rights were bequeathed to surviving heirs, and the jurisdictional rights of the grand sachems remained theoretically intact. The land that was *vacuum domicilium,* or "waste," in English eyes, was completely covered by Indians with property and jurisdictional rights. Generally when Englishmen were willing to recognize these customary rights, Indians were willing enough to sell functionally surplus lands. Some students have doubted that Indians understood how they were dispossessing themselves by sale of land to Europeans. Perhaps that was so in the earliest transactions, but Indian sophistication grew rapidly. European power soon drove home the lesson that a land sale involved full and final alienation of right.

A conveyance of land to an Englishman necessarily implied its removal from the domain governed by the tribe's paramount sachem. For such a transaction to be legitimate in Indian eyes it had to be approved by the grand sachem, just as European cessions of territory from one sovereignty to another could only be legitimized by the sovereign power itself. The proper procedure, therefore, was for English purchases from free Indians to be made directly from their grand sachem, with compensation being given also to the particular Indian who had held personal tenure.

Evidence for these inferences exists in both personal and official sources. Roger Williams's comment is deservedly well known: "The law and tenor of the natives, (I take it) in all New England and America, viz.: that the inferior Sachems and subjects shall plant and remove at the pleasure of the highest and supreme Sachems." Less famous than Williams, Francis Brinley arrived in America via Newport in 1652 and took up residence in the midst of what he estimated to be thirty thousand Indians. He remarked: "To these [Chief] Sachems belongs the power of disposall of Lands, to which their people Subject themselves, as a power due to them, Some gratuity being usually bestowed upon the possessors by the Purchasers to make them the more free to remove and depart." The formula of the deed to Shawomet, Rhode Island, dated January 12, 1643, is expressed as the chief sachem selling "with the Free and joint consent of the present inhabitants, being natives." The pattern outlined by these remarks is confirmed by two quite diverse official agencies—the Royal Commissioners of Charles II and the General Court of New Plymouth.

Such data seem to lend credence to the often-repeated assertion that all of New England's territory was purchased at one time or another from Indian landholders. Regardless of the merits of that claim in its fullness, the matter now at issue is exactly when the purported transactions are supposed to have occurred. No deeds exist today for any purchases before the 1633 Plymouth acquisition on the Connecticut, simply because none were written. Numerous extant deeds from post-1633 purport to be "confirmations" of transactions supposed to have occurred at earlier dates, but, closely examined, each of these turns into an effort to meet a later political crisis. Most notably, Sir Edmund Andros's assumption of government over the Dominion of New England in 1686 sent people scurrying for these "confirmations." George Edward Ellis as tartly suggested that the deed to Boston's site "was shrewdly contrived by the astute authorities of the town, as they were trembling over the royal challenging of their Colony Charter, the fall of which might render worthless all grants of parcels of territory that depended upon legislation under it."

John Winthrop's behavior has provided one source of confusion about the interpretation of New England's Indian deeds. Although Winthrop never renounced his doctrine of *vacuum domicilium* or explicated an alternative, in 1642 he bought 1,260 Indian-held acres on the Concord River, being careful to take and register a deed for them. Few acres have ever been bought more cheaply— Winthrop paid only his proportion of a joint purchase price amounting to about one pound in money—but the point is that he acted in direct contradiction to his earlier-stated principle. Winthrop's change of heart is all the more curious because, when in the mid-1630s the principle had been challenged by dissenters, he had reaffirmed it vigorously. To see how and why he later abandoned the principle requires close attention to a series of detailed events.

The Indian-right principle first showed itself in Massachusetts as a threat not only to Winthrop's ideas but to the power of the whole ruling oligarchy among whom Winthrop stood out. The source of this danger lay in the town of Salem, where both leaders and commonalty struggled against the assumption of superior jurisdiction by the magistrates at Boston.

The situation is best understood in the perspective of a few years. The community of Salem consisted of a mixed lot of people who had come to America at various times preceding Winthrop's great fleet of 1630 and who were therefore self-consciously "Old Planters." Besides the feeling of privilege and status naturally deriving from such identification, these Old Planters held other peculiar distinctions. Among them were Church of England adherents faithful to the very doctrines regarded as odious by the Puritans. Even the dissenters at Salem differed from the dissenters who had come with Winthrop: the Salem church was established on such purely Separatist principles that Roger Williams could accept the post of minister there after having rejected membership in the Boston church. Williams first went to Salem, however, only as an assistant to the minister, and he was not long permitted to stay there. Pressure from Governor Winthrop and his associates achieved Williams's removal to Plymouth, outside Massachusett's jurisdiction. Besides its religious distinctiveness, Salem also preserved remembrance of its political independence under Governor John Endecott prior to Winthrop's arrival and his supersession of Endecott. The demoted Endecott held aloof from the newcomers. Salem sought to maintain as much autonomy as possible under the new regime, clinging to the name "General Court" for its own town meeting.

For a time Salem's effort to go its own way was aided by members of other towns, all seeking to wrest some degree of autonomy from the supreme power asserted by the magistrates at Boston. These rebels shared the demand that each town control the allotment of land to its own inhabitants. Implied in this demand, also was the claim that each should have the power to enlarge its bounds of its own volition. The magistrates yielded so far as to permit towns to control distribution of lands within their established limits but held fast to their final authority to set the territorial limits. Their authority, said the magistrates, was vested in their central government by its royal patent, which had granted the soil of Massachusetts Bay. It was this final line of defense of magisterial prerogative that Roger Williams assaulted when he wrote a treatise, while still at Plymouth, affirming that the royal patent could not lawfully convey rights to the soil. Title to the land, said Williams, rested in the aboriginal owners, the Indians, and could be lawfully acquired only by purchase from them. What seemed to turn this essentially legal argument into a theological dispute was Williams's characteristic designation of the magistrates' reliance on their patent as sinful. We do not know what else Williams said in his "large treatise," but his argument plainly implied that any town or any person could go directly to the Indians to buy any quantity of land without prior authority from king or magistrate; in fact, he had done just that, albeit discreetly outside the chartered limits of Massachusetts.

In August 1633 Williams returned to Salem to resume his assistance to the town's minister, much to the disturbance of the magistrates. The action represented defiance on two counts: though Williams's position was not a formal office of government, his acceptance by the church was a reversal of Salem's previous compliance with the magistrates' wishes in regard to Williams's church status, and it also seemed to constitute an endorsement of his views opposing the magistrates' patent-derived authority. If Williams were to be allowed to preach as the Word of God that the very foundation of the magistrates' authority was invalid, how long could it be before Salem seceded entirely to set itself up in competition with the Bay? The General Court responded with a series of new laws, the first of which banned the purchase of Indian lands *except* when such purchase had the Court's prior approval.

The General Court also ordered a survey and registry of all lands and meaningfully stipulated that no agency other than itself might "dispose of land, viz., to give and confirm proprietyes." Joined to the latter order was the enactment of an oath to be required of all free men that in effect transferred allegiance from the English crown to the government of Massachusetts Bay. What has been less noticed by historians is that the oath also destroyed all possibility of transcendent allegiance to autonomous towns within the territory claimed by Massachusetts.

Sorting out parties and sides in the confusion is not easy, but it seems clear that Salem and Roger Williams were steadily losing ground, both in metaphor and in actuality. Salem had claimed jurisdiction over the tract of territory called Marblehead Neck, which the General Court refused to recognize. In May 1635 the Court ordered a new "Plantation" and required Salem's inhabitants to sell their Marblehead lands to the new planters at cost. Williams then rose in Salem's pulpit to denounce the authorities, "teaching publickly against the king's patent" and against the magistrates' "great sin in claiming right thereby to this country." The General Court responded in September 1635 by appointing a commission "to sett out the bounds of all townes not yet sett out, or in difference betwixte any towne, provided that the committees of those townes where the difference is shall have noe vote in that particular," and Salem's claim to Marblehead was overborne. It is also noteworthy that Salem's "General Court" was here casually reduced to the rank of a "committee."

Tension mounted as Williams and many of his supporters refused the Bay government's oath of allegiance and pitted Salem church against the doctrine that magistrates should have power to punish heresy. In the midst of the quarrels Salem church formally elevated Williams from his assistantship to the post of minister. Magistrates and orthodox clerics alike were outraged by the town that wanted autonomy and the minister who wanted liberty. Clergy thundered their wrath and called it God's, thus defining Williams as the sort of heretic that magistrates had power to punish. Salem's deputies were expelled from the General Court, and Williams was brought to trial and sentenced to banishment explictly because he had "broached and dyvulged dyvers newe and dangerous opinions, against the aucthoritie of magistrates, as also writt lettres of defamation, both of the magistrates and church *here* . . . and yet mainetaineth the same without retraction." As the Reverend William Hubbard would later remark, "Mr. Williams did lay his axe at the very root of the magistratical power in matters of the first table [i.e., the first four of the Ten Commandments]."

In the historical controversy that has been waged over precisely which issue dominated the magistrates' minds, S. H. Brockunier's judgment seems best: "Heresy and sedition in Massachusetts were inextricably joined." For present purposes it may be observed that, despite the gravity of other charges, much of the trial court's time was spent on Williams's ideas about Indian rights. Williams reaffirmed his belief that it was "a National sinne" to claim right to Indian lands by virtue of the royal patent "and a Nationall duty to renounce the Patent," which, the magistrates thought "to have done, had subverted the fundamentall State and Government of the Countrey." They were correct, of course. Only a quite different sort of government could have functioned on Williams's principles.

In the management of power these magistrates were wholly rational. Having expelled Williams and having briefly punished John Endecott for abetting him, they accepted Salem's and Endecott's submissions. Salem's deputies were restored to the General Court, and in March 1636, Salem, meek and penitent, even received the Marblehead lands that had been denied to Salem, proud and challenging—though perhaps not as much land as had been claimed. There was no longer any question about who held final authority; Salem had obtained that land only on the terms of the General Court. A few years later, when tension again mounted, the Court again asserted its ascendancy. In March 1640 Salem appointed a "Mr. Sharpe" to keep the records of town lands, but in October the General Court overrode the town by installing Winthrop's brother-in-law Emanuel Downing in that office. The nature of the controversy is suggested by the fact that the last entries of Elder Sharpe, who had been one of Roger Williams's strongest supporters, are missing from the record. Downing's substitutions for them provided that Marblehead's inhabitants could have only such lands "as have not been formerly granted to other men," leaving no doubt of the Court's revocation of at least some of the claims of the Salem-Marblehead people.

No Indian purchase sullied the Court's supreme prerogative at the time, and

none was made until half a century later when Massachusetts Bay was incorporated into the Dominion of New England. The extinction then of the old
government raised a specter of possible invalidation of land titles acquired
irregularly, and Salem men hastened to buttress their possessions with an Indian
quitclaim. Dated October 11, 1686, this stipulates on the part of its Indian sellers
that *"untill the ensealing and delivery of these presents,* they [the Indians] and
their ancestors were the true, sole and lawfull owners of all the afore bargained
premises, and were lawfully seized of and in the same, and every part thereof in
their own proper right." Thus Salem fended off a review of its land titles by the
new royal governor, Sir Edmund Andros, whose known rule was that title could
not be fully valid while Indian claims existed.

But this all happened long after Roger Williams's tilt with the Massachusetts
General Court. In the 1630s the magistrates alternated between assertions of principle and acts of expedience. By overriding Salem they temporarily silenced arguments that Indian purchases were legally prerequisite to good land titles, but they
acted to forestall future difficulties of a like nature by ordering a series of purchases
to be made from Indian landowners along the coast between Boston and Ipswich.
This was done for convenience, without rationalization or concession of right, and
no specific fuss was made about it.

When a new situation arose that gave an appearance of advantage for Massachusetts in Williams's rejected principle of Indian right, the magistrates suddenly
abandoned their old hostility and laid a loving clutch upon the former anathema.
John Winthrop's startling change of heart (and the other magistrates' also) occurred in 1641 when an opportunity arose for Massachusetts to gain an opening
onto Narragansett Bay. Pursuing the chance, Winthrop mounted an invasion of a
small nonchartered colony already existing at Narragansett, doing so with an
elaborately concocted formal justification in terms of Indian rights. Besides, "the
place was likely to be of use to us," he noted succinctly. . . . The point there is
simply that Winthrop and the other Massachusetts magistrates were very ready to
abandon their early theses about Indian land being free for the taking when the
takers were people other than themselves.

Further study of deed games will shed light on the complex maneuvers of
interprovincial aggression through which the early colonists established their
boundary lines. Generalizations will not suffice. Each situation requires attention
to its own circumstances, because official acceptance of Indian property right did
not guarantee ethical practices in Englishmen's acquisition of those rights.

Within the limits of a jurisdiction, as well as across boundary lines, colonials
everywhere used numerous identifiable devices (and doubtless others) to seize
Indian property with some show of legality. One method was to allow livestock to
roam into an Indian's crops until he despaired and removed. Even when the
Indian uncharacteristically fenced his cropland, he found that there was something
nocturnally mysterious that did not love an Indian's wall. The Indian who dared
to kill an Englishman's marauding animals was promptly hauled into a hostile
court. A second method was for Englishmen to get the Indian drunk and have him
sign a deed that he could not read. A third method was to recognize a claim by a
corrupt Indian who was not the legitimate landlord and then to "buy" the land
from him. A fourth method, highly reminiscent of feudal Europe, was a simple
threat of violence. A timorous Indian—there were many—would turn over his
property for no other reason than the "love and goodwill" he bore the man behind
the gun; he was then permitted to remain as a tenant on a corner of the land he

formerly had owned. A fifth method, which seems to have been a favorite in New England, was the imposition of fines for a wide variety of offenses, the Indian's lands becoming forfeit if the fines were not paid by their due date. The offenses ranged from unauthorized riding of an Englishman's horses to conspiracy against English rule. Small or great, the offense was likely to incur a fine larger than the offender could probably pay. An Englishman would "rescue" him from his straits, paying his fine for a short-term mortgage on his land and later foreclosing.

These were devices to put a fair face on fraud. When taken at face value, they present a rosy picture of upright, fair-minded Euramericans giving value for value in honest business transactions. Only when surrounding circumstances are taken into account is the fraud revealed.

Fraud was widespread though not universal, but even when the Indian was dealt with fairly, as also happened, the cession of his land was traumatic for himself and his society. Whether negotiated by diplomatic treaty or commercial contract, the effect of systematic dispossession cannot be overestimated. The selling Indians had only two choices: to retreat into the interior with the hope of being accepted as guests in other tribes' jurisdictions or to accept subjection and exploitation in the lands of their former freedom.

Peaceful purchase of Indian territory was more drastic in its consequences than many armed conquests of one European power by another. It was a *double* conquest in which Indians lost not only sovereignty but also commons and severalty, and it established the harshest possible terms for the Indians who might hope to assimilate into "civilization." Property and liberty were synonyms in the seventeenth and eighteenth centuries. When the Indian was dispossessed of his land, he lost all hope of finding any niche in the society called civilized, except that of servant or slave.

SECTION 2: SUGGESTIONS FOR FURTHER READING

There is no more vital area of scholarly inquiry about early American history today than Puritan studies. The breadth and depth of recent writings has been covered in Michael McGiffert, "American Puritan Studies in the 1960's," *William and Mary Quarterly*, 3rd ser., 27 (1970), pp. 36–67, J. M. Murrin, "Review Essay," *History and Theory*, 11 (1972), pp. 226–275, and T. H. Breen, "Persistent Localism: English Social Change and the Shaping of New England Institutions," *William and Mary Quarterly*, 3rd ser., 32 (1975), pp. 3–28.

Earlier in the twentieth century scholars perceived Puritanism as a repressive roadblock standing in the way of the creation of a democratic America. Representative studies include those ot J. T. Adams, *The Founding of New England* (1921), and V. L. Parrington, *Main Currents in American Thought, vol. 1: The Colonial Mind, 1620–1800* (1927). A later general treatment with similar overtones is T. J. Wertenbaker, *The Puritan Oligarchy: The Founding of American Civilization* (1947), representing a point of view that, from a different perspective, has beeen reemphasized after several years' lapse in Francis Jennings, *The Invasion of America* (1975), and Neal Salisbury, "Red Puritans: The 'Praying Indians' of Massachusetts Bay and John Eliot," *William and Mary Quarterly*, 3rd ser., 31 (1974), pp. 27–54.

A major turnaround in interpretive emphasis began during the 1920s and 1930s when a group of Harvard University scholars argued that debunking the Puritans made it impossible to understand them on their own terms. First appeared K. B. Murdock's *Increase Mather: Foremost American Puritan* (1925), followed a few years later by S. E. Morison's wider-ranging *Builders of the Bay Colony* (1930). Both men profoundly influenced Perry Miller in the writing of his three-volume delineation of the Puritan mind, contained in *Orthodoxy in Massachusetts, 1630–1650* (1933), *The New England Mind: The Seventeenth Century* (1939), and *The New England Mind: From Colony to Province* (1953). The findings of Miller now must be supplemented by those of D. D. Hall, *The Faithful Shepherd: A History of the New England Ministry in the Seventeenth Century* (1972), and Robert Middlekauff, *The Mathers: Three Generations of Puritan Intellectuals, 1596–1728* (1971). Other basic works within Miller's framework are Bernard Bailyn's *The New England Merchants in the Seventeenth Century* (1955), and E. S. Morgan's *The Puritan Family: Religion and Domestic Relations in Seventeenth-Century New England* (rev. ed., 1966), *Visible Saints: The History of a Puritan Idea* (1963), and *The Puritan Dilemma: The Story of John Winthrop* (1958).

While the latter volume remains the most readable introduction to the first two decades of Puritan life in America, a number of studies provide additional insight about Puritan social mores, attitudes, habits, and cultural values. R. G. Pope, *The Half-Way Covenant: Church Membership in Puritan New England* (1969), takes a quantitative look at the pattern of declension in the Puritans' strivings for conversion and regeneration. K. T. Erikson, *Wayward Puritans: A Study in the Sociology of Deviance* (1966), D. H. Flaherty, *Privacy in Colonial New England* (1972), and Stephen Foster, *Their Solitary Way: The Puritan Social Ethic in the First Century of Settlement in New England* (1971), must also be consulted. The most sweeping chronological overview in terms of values in contact with New World realities is Larzer Ziff, *Puritanism in America: New Culture in a New World* (1973).

Beginning in the 1960s many students of New England history started to employ the techniques of quantitative and demographic analysis, producing a host of valuable community studies. The assumption was that the ideals and aspirations of all citizens, rather than just the thoughts of political and intellectual leaders, could be reconstructed through surviving local records—tax lists, probated wills, court documents, church records, and land deeds. Such quantifiable materials would permit the full investigation of the values and economic and social relationships of all citizens. Pioneering community studies included C. S. Grant, *Democracy in the Connecticut Frontier Town to Kent* (1961), S. C. Powell, *Puritan Village: The Formation of a New England Town* [Sudbury] (1963), and D. B. Rutman, *Winthrop's Boston: Portrait of a Puritan Town, 1630–1649* (1965).

Rutman's book specifically challenged Perry Miller's assumption about a Puritan blueprint for the creation of a biblical communal order in the New World. Yet Rutman's conclusion about rampant individualism from the outset in Boston, regardless of the leaders' enunciated ideals, has not been supported in three noteworthy quantitative studies, those of John Demos, *A Little Commonwealth: Family Life in Plymouth Colony* (1970), P. J. Greven Jr., *Four Generations: Population, Land, and Family in Colonial Andover, Massachusetts* (1970), and K. E. Lockridge, *A New England Town: The First Hundred Years* [Dedham] (1970). Differing conclusions about the Puritans' relative early success in establishing stable community relationships in New England may be compared in J. J. Waters, Jr., "Hingham, Massachusetts, 1631–1661: An East Anglian Oligarchy in the New World," *Journal of Social History,* 1 (1967–1968), pp. 351–370, T. H. Breen and Stephen Foster, "The Puritans' Greatest Achievement: A Study of Social Cohesion in Seventeenth-Century Massachusetts," *Journal of American History,* 60 (1973), pp. 5–22, L. A. Bissell, "From One Generation to Another: Mobility in Seventeenth-Century Windsor, Connecticut," *William and Mary Quarterly,* 3rd ser., 31 (1974), pp. 79–110, R. P. Gildrie, *Salem, Massachusetts, 1626–1683: A Covenant Community* (1975), and P. R. Lucas, *Valley of Discord: Church and Society along the Connecticut River, 1636–1725* (1976). Stifling communal harmony carried over well into the eighteenth century according to Michael Zuckerman, *Peaceable Kingdoms: New England Towns in the Eighteenth Century* (1970), but the evidence presented by Greven and Lockridge suggests no such pattern of conformist stability.

Students desiring a succinct introductory assessment of Puritan life in the New World beyond Morgan's *Puritan Dilemma* should consult D. B. Rutman's *American Puritanism: Faith and Practice* (1970), and F. J. Bremer, *The Puritan Experiment: New England Society from Bradford to Edwards* (1976). Those wanting further information about Puritan political thought and practices should look at T. H. Breen, *The Character of a Good Ruler: Puritan Political Ideas in New England, 1630–1730* (1970), R. E. Wall, Jr., *Massachusetts Bay: The Crucial Decade, 1640–1650* (1972), and E. S. Morgan, ed., *Puritan Political Ideas, 1558–1794* (1965). Serious disagreements among leaders in the early years may be explored in Perry Miller, *Roger Williams: His Contribution to the American Tradition* (1962), E. S. Morgan, *Roger Williams: The Church and the State* (1967), Emery Battis, *Saints and Sectaries: Anne Hutchinson and the Antinomian Controversy in Massachusetts Bay Colony* (1962), and Lyle Koehler, "The Case of the American Jezebels: Anne Hutchinson and Female Agitation during the Years of Antinomian Turmoil, 1636–1640," *Williams and Mary Quarterly* 3rd ser., 31 (1974), pp. 55–78. An excellent primary source collection on the last-named internal crisis has been edited by D. D. Hall, *The Antinomian Controversy, 1636–1638: A Documentary History* (1968).

More on New England's general economy and settlement patterns may be found in C. F. Carroll, *The Timber Economy of Puritan New England* (1974), and C. E. Clark, *The Eastern Frontier: The Settlement of Northern New England, 1610–1763* (1970). Essential for understanding the goals and aspirations of the Pilgrims, as compared to the Puritans, are G. D. Langdon, Jr., *Pilgrim Colony: A History of New Plymouth, 1620–1691* (1966), and D. B. Rutman, *Husbandmen of Plymouth: Farms and Villages in the Old Colony, 1620–1692* (1967).

Indentured Servitude and Slavery

SECTION 3

Populating the English colonies in North America was no easy task. One hundred adventurers established the first foothold at Jamestown in 1607, for example, yet within two years all but a few of them were dead. The Virginia Company claimed in the early 1620s that some six thousand people had been sent out to work on stockholder lands, but only two thousand were still alive and resident in Virginia at that time. Mortality rates varied from region to region and, generally, were much higher in the southern colonies, where diseases took an awesome toll, than in northern areas. Yet personal travail, suffering, and death were present everywhere among the thousands upon thousands of people who attempted or were forced into passage to the New World. After a century of struggle only an estimated quarter of a million inhabitants lived in the scattered plantations stretching from Maine to the Carolinas. No one knows how many men and women lost their lives in making that token force of settlers possible.

For those hardy and lucky souls who survived, who gained titles to land tracts, who had children, and who prospered, their greatest need, given a marginally increasing population base, was human muscle power to use (and in many cases abuse) in wresting not only a bare sustenance but also a profit from so much fertile land. The Virginia Company set the tone in the insatiable quest for laborers as a source of profits. Out of desperation it contracted with vagrants, criminals, and poor but honest people in England, usually for seven-year terms, to work for the Company in Virginia. At the end of their terms these laborers gained small land parcels and their first opportunity to fend for themselves as free agents. Before 1620 the Company was establishing other precedents by offering "headrights" of 50 acres of land per person for all those who would settle in the James River area. The only problem confronting those who wanted to emigrate as free pesons was the necessary passage money. If the funds could be found, then abundant new opportunity in the form of fertile land awaited those who survived the Atlantic crossing.

Virginia planters, especially after tobacco cultivation had begun, sought out laborers to perform the time-consuming and delicate tasks of tobacco production. A vast supply of human labor was available in England. New World necessities, then, led almost inexorably to the emergence of indentured servitude, modeled on the English apprenticeship system. Men and women in old England sold their labor for a given number of years in return for passage money. The planter who ultimately paid for individual crossings received the labor. For those who signed indentured contracts, there were deferred rewards. After submitting to temporary bondage, servants gained "freedom dues" in the form of clothing, farming implements, perhaps even land parcels (there were local variations on this pattern), and the opportunity to strike out for themselves unfettered by legal contracts.

One must ask what kinds of people in England would sell themselves into temporary servitude and why. A small percentage were vagrants and criminals who had nothing to lose. Some were peasants and tenant farmers driven from their homes by landlords who were enclosing lands to raise sheep for the sprawling woolens industry. Many were yeoman farmers caught up in unstable economic conditions. The early seventeenth-century English economy was suffering from rapid inflation (caused primarily by the influx of Spanish gold and silver from America into European markets) and unsteady labor needs (the woolens industry faced a serious depression because of warfare on the Continent and the consequent disruption of European consumer demand). England seemed to be overcrowded and overpopulated. Clearly the economy was not generating enough work for the growing numbers of unemployed laborers. Thus, whether they were peasants, yeomen, or ne'er-do-wells, the individuals who signed indentures represented what might be called unneeded or unwanted population in England, and they became a major source of *labor* and of *population* in the Anglo-American colonies (except for New England). One estimate has it that three out of every four residents in Virginia during the 1660s were then or had been indentured servants.

Yet, whether because of the brutality or despite the advantages of the indenture system, it was declining in significance by the end of the seventeenth century. Its demise was directly related to the formulation and legalization of a more cruel, inhumane labor-producing system—chattel slavery. Slavery developed in the colonies over several decades following the introduction of Africans into the colonial labor force. The first forced black emigrants arrived in 1619 when a Dutch trading vessel sold twenty Africans to some Jamestown planters. Surviving evidence indicates that these Africans and the others who followed in the next few years were not formally considered slaves. Many early Africans were treated as indentured servants. Confusion about the status of Afro-Americans reflected the fact that no legal definition for human slavery existed in English law. Nor was it before midcentury that Virginia legislators began to formalize their "peculiar institution." (How many blacks fell victim to de facto slavery before this time, of course, is open to debate.) As defined over time in Virginia law, slavery came to mean permanent, inheritable servitude, not temporary service. Slavery implied the lowest form of human debasement in the loss of all personal rights and privileges before the law. It converted men and women into human property, to be done with as owners saw fit.

At least two critical questions present themselves at this juncture. Why did the indentured servitude system decline while chattel slavery became more firmly fixed as the years passed? Why were blacks subjected to permanent, inheritable servitude when whites were not? Historians have gone full circle in attempting to formulate a satisfactory answer to the latter question (as can be seen in the selections by Carl N. Degler and Winthrop D. Jordan in this section). In terms of the first question, however, a partial explanation as background information should be outlined here.

Virginians and Marylanders, first of all, were excessive in their zeal for tobacco cultivation from the start. Their yearly crop yields increased by fantastic proportions, from a few thousand pounds per year in the late 1610s to nearly thirty million pounds a year at the end of the seventeenth century. The supply of tobacco rose far beyond market demands—so far that prices became quite unstable after midcentury.

Tobacco planters, rather than diversifying their interests, clung in loyal allegiance to tobacco as the primary cash crop. They attempted to make up for price declines by still higher levels of production, only leading in turn to further saturation of the marketplace and more downward spiraling of prices. The only other choice for planters trying to maintain a solvent financial footing was to hold down on the fixed costs of production. Here was the economic advantage of chattel slavery. A slave's labor was a permanent commodity, and slavery lasted through the generations. By the end of the century tobacco magnates turned with increasing frequency to Africans as the primary source of plantation labor. When rice and then indigo (both, like tobacco, involving time-consuming cultivation) developed into dominant cash crops in South Carolina, the institution of slavery became even more firmly fixed there. By the mid-eighteenth century more than 30 percent of the population south of Pennsylvania (plus a scattering in the North) was both slave and black. The two qualities had become inseparable.

A number of related factors abetted the growing transition from indentured to slave labor. In England economic conditions began to improve markedly during the second half of the century. Fewer Englishmen, as a result, felt so pressed to sign indenture contracts and flee from economic deprivation and personal hardship. Mortality rates, at the same time, declined significantly in the South (they were not a significant factor in the North) as settlements became more firmly rooted. Both whites and blacks were showing greater resistance to diseases and to other elements which had so adversely affected longevity among first-generation settlers. This phenomenon increased the likelihood that laborers would survive into old age. Economically, it meant that more whites would live through contracted terms of indentured service and claim freedom dues, raising the actual costs of that form of labor. By comparison, the investment return on the greater initial price of slaves would be more secure, reducing long-run expenses for labor, especially if the numbers of female slaves increased and produced children.

These trends help to explain why more and more traders entered the marketplace for slaves in the late seventeenth- and early eighteenth-centuries. They first challenged the English monopoly over the slave trade which the Royal African Company held between 1672 and 1698. Responding to New World labor demands, they forced their way into this profitable form of commerce, bartering independently with coastal tribes in Africa and buying up the victims of tribal warfare in return for liquor and other merchandise.

Still, any set of explanations about the declining importance of indentured servitude and the rising importance of chattel slavery does nothing to unravel the reasons why only black Africans became victims of that latter institution. No matter what the origins of slavery, we must keep in mind that some set of factors dictated the difference. Did those factors center on racial prejudice? If they did, then what were the sources of prejudice and how did they affect the conditions faced by those Africans forced to migrate to the New World? How did blacks who survived the middle passage adjust to their status as human property? And what methods did they employ in resisting the oppression which engulfed them? The readings that follow consider these vital questions in the history of indentured servants and black slaves in early America.

9. The Servant in the Plantations

Abbot Emerson Smith

One of the enduring myths of early American history is that great plantation houses, cultured masters, and large numbers of black slaves somehow instantaneously appeared on the seventeenth-century southern landscape. No myth could be more misleading. In the early years the term "plantation" simply referred to the location of a settlement or a farm, no matter how rude and unrefined. The dominant type of unfree laboring person, furthermore, was not a black slave but a white indentured servant, who worked and often died in the hope of achieving freeman planter status comparable to that of his temporary owner.

In the following selection Abbot E. Smith (b. 1906) recounts in exemplary fashion the experiences of numberless indentured servants living in English colonies on the mainland and in the Caribbean area. In sketching out the interaction between those men and women who sold their labor for New World passage and the individuals who purchased it, Smith maintains that no consistent patterns of treatment emerged. Important variables were the attitudes of masters, the strictness of local statutes, and the willingness of the servants themselves to work. For some in temporary bondage the system was anything but humanly destructive—perhaps it was even pleasant—but many others suffered cruelty, mistreatment, and death. We need to ask, then, what was daily existence like for the indentured servant? Did the people who signed indentures have any legal or de facto rights, any allowances for privacy, or any guarantees of normal relationships involving sex and marriage?

Smith does not make specific comparisons between the lot of whites in temporary and blacks in permanent bondage. Readers may develop that comparative dimension by relating the author's findings to those of Professors Degler, Jordan, and Wood ahead.

Accounts rendered by contemporaries of the life and labor of white servants are extraordinarily inharmonious. Having read a letter from Barbados saying that they were used as if hell had already commenced for them, one may turn to Dalby Thomas, who declared at about the same time that they lived much easier than in England, or to John Wilmore, who reported that in Jamaica none of them worked as hard as they would at home. "I thought no head had been able to hold so much

Source: From Abbot Emerson Smith, *Colonists in Bondage: White Servitude and Convict Labor in America, 1607-1776* (Chapel Hill: University of North Carolina Press, 1947), pp. 253-279. Footnotes omitted. Reprinted by permission of the University of North Carolina Press and the Institute of Early American History and Culture.

water as hath and doth daily flow from mine eyes," wrote a servant from Virginia in 1623, but John Hammond announced some years later that none had gone to that colony without commending the place in letters to their friends, and urging others to come. The Maryland court records show that a significant number of servants committed suicide under their burdens, but a Scot in New Jersey declared in 1684 that they worked not a third as hard as in Britain, and had much better food. William Eddis wrote that servants in Maryland groaned beneath a worse than Egyptian bondage; a visitor to Jamaica in 1739 reported that some of them dined as well as their masters, and wore as good clothes, while all were better off than at home. Gottlieb Mittelberger, after filling the air with denunciations of life in Pennsylvania, himself went on to write that "an English servant-woman, especially in Philadelphia, is as elegantly dressed as an aristocratic lady in Germany."

Such conflicting testimonies, of which these are only a few examples, are to be expected from observers of various sentiments concerning any diversified society. It would not be difficult to subject them to criticism, based on the known predilections of the authors, and thus to whittle away the important differences until they came to a fairly common and colorless agreement. The same result, however, may be reached more instructively by other means.

Of all those things which caused misery to white servants, the first and most important was not the temper of their masters nor the unfairness of magistrates, but simply the climate of the country in which they landed. Men and women of menial status were accustomed to obey masters in England, and often to suffer grievous cruelties from them, but they were not accustomed to the heat and glare of tropical countries, nor even to the milder temperatures of Virginia. The English, masters as well as servants, had to learn about such countries, and their knowledge was gained at the price of the lives and happiness of many thousands from both classes. In early days mortality from fevers and pestilences was very high indeed; Governor Berkeley reported in 1671 that in previous years four out of five servants had died of disease soon after their landing. If the unfortunate immigrant did not perish of the "bloody flux," he was apt to be taken off by the "dry gripes," while malaria, until the use of "bark" began to be understood, wrought havoc among all. A period of one year was supposed to "season" the new arrivals, and servants thus partially immunized to the climate sometimes brought a higher price than newly imported ones.

It was learned, eventually that people should be landed towards the beginning of the winter season, but though this became the rule for ships from Rotterdam it does not appear that British and Irish emigrants were particularly favored in this way. They fared better as conditions in the colonies themselves became more stable, and as intelligent masters provided against the worst effects of the climate. Colonel Walrond, of Barbados, about 1650, provided his servants with a change of clothes when they came in wet from the fields, and not content with this he sent to England for rugs to cover them while sleeping, supplying them also with hammocks so that they should not rest on the ground. He was rewarded both by their better health and by their greater regard for his service. Hours of labor, furthermore, had to be suited somewhat to climatic conditions. The instructions given Gates when he went to Virginia in 1609 directed that the men have three hours' rest at noon in summer and two in winter. Ligon says of Barbados:

> They are rung out with a bell to work, at six o'clock in the morning, with a severe Overseer to command them, till the Bell ring again, which is at eleven o'clock, and then

they return, and are set to dinner. . . . At one o'clock they are rung out again to the field, there to work till six, and then home again. . . .

These hours were by no means excessive according to English standards, but they eventually proved too long for white men in Barbados. Hammond declared that the servants in Virginia had five hours of rest in the heat of the day; a statement which seems scarcely credible. Three hours was the rule in Maryland. Saturday afternoons and Sundays were free from labor in all colonies, and in Maryland at least masters were haled into court for working their servants on the Sabbath. Though doubtless these regulations were for religious rather than humanitarian reasons they were none the less necessary if white men were to survive at all.

Servants commonly lived in huts or cabins which they built for themselves; apparently they never lived with the Negroes, though the two races worked side by side in the fields. Food in early years consisted largely of a mess called "loblolly," made from ground Indian corn; in Barbados servants drank a liquid brewed from potatoes called "mobbie," or a concoction of spring water, orange juice, and sugar. With one accord Englishmen complained if they did not eat meat three or four times a week, and by the time Ligon left Barbados they were getting it. From New Jersey it was written in 1684 that servants had "beef, pork, bacon, pudding, milk, butter and good beer and cyder for drink," fare of which no one could complain. In Maryland, during the 1660's, a group of servants went on strike because they were given no meat, and complained bitterly to the Provincial Court that their master made them live on bread and beans. The court was unsympathetic, particularly when their master explained that this was a temporary shortage and that he had been utterly unable to buy any meat. The servants were condemned to thirty lashes, but this punishment was remitted and they returned amiably to work.

Of the various kinds of plantation labor which servants had to perform one was certainly more difficult and exhausting than commonly fell to the lot of English workers; this was the preparing of new land for planting. Trees had to be felled, trimmed, and dragged away, brush had to be cleared, and the soil turned for the first time without benefit of good plows and sometimes even without draft animals. However long this might be postponed by expedients learned from the Indians it had eventually to be done on every respectable property, and immigrants groaned under the unaccustomed burden. The skilled American axeman was a colonial product, not a European importation, and he learned his art painfully. Once this had been done, however, there is no reason to believe that the regular processes of colonial agriculture were more toilsome than those of Europe. The cultivation of tobacco and sugar called for a somewhat different technique, to be sure, and the harvesting, curing, and refining of these products was a matter for new and special skills, but the physical labor involved was not impossibly arduous.

It is plain that work in the fields was generally required of all servants. This was what they were primarily wanted for, at least until the Negroes came, and even artisans were employed in this fashion unless their indentures specifically released them from the obligation. There were a few schoolmasters, clerks, and accountants, but it was written of Virginia that men who could chop logs were more valuable than those who could chop logic, and Jeaffreson said that one who could handle a pen rarely got as much as an artisan, for such were in fact more plentiful. The court records show that servants attempted to escape the burden of field work, often in a manner shown by the following typical entry from Lancaster County, Virginia, in 1667:

> Robert Clark servaunt to Robert Beverley, appeareing at this Court is willing to serve his master one yere longer than hee came in for provided his said master will during all his tyme free him from workeing in the ground, carryeing, or fetching of railes or loggs or the like things and beateing at the morter , and keepe hym to his trade either at home or abroad, which the said Beverley doth promise. All which the Court doth order to bee entred upon record.

Servants who made their indentures before leaving England were oftentimes careful to include a provision that they should work only at their proper trades or crafts. In 1741 the Chester County Court of Pennsylvania ordered a certain master to keep his servant to the trade of a weaver "according to the Tenour of his Indenture," and not to employ him at field labor under penalty of having the servant set free. Such cases also are frequent in the records, but it appears that the servant had to have a clear statement in his indenture in order to liberate him from toil "in the ground."

These facts provide a basis for understanding the true difficulties of the servant population. Contemporaries, observing their shorter hours of labor and other advantages, compared them with agricultural workers at home and found them well off. Those who wrote thus generally were interested in giving a favorable account, and they ignored the important fact that a large proportion of servants were not bred to agricultural labor, and hence found it extremely burdensome. The honest English farmer or German countryman found no great hardship in his tasks in the new world, but it was far otherwise for the tailor, or shoemaker, or weaver who was forced into the tobacco fields. Perhaps it was worst of all for the idle rogues, the thieves, pickpockets, and miscellaneous vagrants who were thus transplanted to unwonted toil; they suffered grievously, and few wasted sympathy on them. Put broadly, the fundamental human problem in colonization was simply that of adaptation, and the white servants did not come from the most adaptable levels of society. Men who had been idle had to work; men whose occupations had been sedentary found themselves tilling the soil. They had to go without fresh meat; they had to eat Indian corn instead of wheat and rye; they had to wear cotton or linen instead of wool, and sleep in hammocks instead of beds; probably for the most part they had to drink water. It was these things that made life painful for so many servants. For these reasons we can understand that while hours of labor might be shorter in the colonies than in Britain, and rewards for diligence might be greater, the servant unable to adapt his habits to colonial conditions and his muscles to physical labor could be said, without gross exaggeration, to be in bondage worse than Egyptian.

Probably the women servants had slightly less extraordinary burdens to bear than the men. They were not worked in the fields in Barbados, and Hammond claimed that they were not in Virginia, at least unless they were "nasty, beastly, and not fit" for other services. They cooked and cleaned and wove and mended, like women in Europe, and indeed any plantation with a considerable number of menservants required several women to look after their clothing and food. Some evidences indicate that they took a hand in tobacco cultivation; certainly there are several examples of women appearing before the Virginia courts and promising extra service in exchange for freedom from this heavy toil.

The labor of servants was supervised by overseers on the larger plantations who were not apt to be men notable for Christian charity. It was unfortunate and tragic that so much should depend not only upon the servant's own character and adaptability but also upon the temper of his immediate superiors. "I have seen an Overseer beat a Servant with a cane about the head, till the blood has followed," wrote Ligon, "for a fault that is not worth the speaking of; and yet he must have patience, or worse will follow." The greatest cruelties occurred in the earlier years, for colonial enterprises had to be put under way by the hardest types of adventurers and pioneers, men who bore tremendous difficulties themselves, extended small mercy to shiftless or weak servants, and punished them excessively when they fainted at their labors. Ligon noted that as time went on "discreeter and better natur'd men" took control of affairs, and there was a marked improvement in the treatment of laborers. Hammond and Alsop, as might be expected, give a favorable report of the relations between servants and masters. A traveller to Jamaica in 1739, after describing how handsomely good servants were treated, goes on to say that stupid and roguish ones were hardly used, set in the stocks, and beaten. "Their salt Provisions are weighed out, and they have nothing but what the Law obliges the Master to give." Ligon remarked that "as for the usage of the Servants it is much as the Master is; merciful or cruel."

On three or four occasions there was an attempt at concerted rebellion among the servants in a small locality, but information about these is too scanty to permit much description. Father John White, accompanying the first voyage to Maryland, landed in Barbados on Janary 3, 1634, and found a full-fledged conspiracy of servants in process of being put down. Their idea was, according to White, to kill all their masters, take the first ship which arrived thereafter, and put to sea, presumably as pirates. One of the plotters gave the scheme away, and on the very day that White landed, eight hundred men were in arms to oppose the design. This indicates that the danger must have been formidable, but since only one ringleader was punished, though the nature of men at Barbados in those days was not mild, it may well be that the conspiracy was exaggerated. Ligon reports that in 1649 just before he left the island there was a rebellion worse than any before. Some leading spirits among the servants, unable to endure their sufferings longer, resolved to break through their slavery or die in the attempt. This project was communicated among the servants, and a day appointed to fall on their masters and cut their throats. On the eve of this attempt it was given away by one of the servants involved, and the affair was crushed. This time eighteen of the leaders were executed, and the assembly appointed an annual day of thanksgiving for the deliverance of the islanders from such a peril. It was probably in this rising that Colonel Guy Molesworth was suspected of being a ringleader; he was deported, and returned in 1661 to petition for reinstatement, charging that although the servants had been tortured with lighted matches between their fingers they had refused actually to implicate him. No doubt there were political as well as class interests involved.

A disposition to general rebellion seems scarcely to have existed among servants on the continent, perhaps because the chance of success was negligible as compared with that on a relatively small island. A curious affair occurred in York County, Virginia, in 1661, when a certain William Clutton told the servants they were not getting the food that ought to be given them. One Isaac Friend proposed that they "get a matter of Forty of them together, & get Armes & he would be the first & have them cry as they went along, 'who would be for Liberty, and free from bondage,' & that there would enough come to them & they would goe through the Countrey and kill those that made any opposition." This valorous scheme petered out, to be followed two years later by a more serious conspiracy in Gloucester County. A general rising was said to be contemplated, and the servants intended to demand of the governor that they be released from a year's servitude, or perhaps be given full freedom. One of their number gave the plan away; the legislature felt that it had escaped from a "horrid plot," and resolved that the servant who revealed it should have his freedom and 5000 pounds of tobacco. Many of the planters believed this rebellion to have been schemed by transported convicts, and it formed one argument against allowing more of them in the colony.

Far more significant are the speculations which were sometimes indulged as to whether servants would join and assist a foreign invader. Sir Henry Colt, visiting St. Christopher in 1631 and commenting on the possibility of defending it, said that it would be easy if the servants would fight, but that generally they preferred the Spanish to win in order that they might be free. This idea was often repeated and was given some support during the later wars, when Irish Catholics joined the French and attacked the English from the rear. Some of these were doubtless servants, but in these instances nationality and religion were stronger forces than class. Nothing indicates that in the many vicissitudes of the island wars servants as a class ever assisted the invader. During the eighteenth century the colonies of Pennsylvania, Maryland, and even Virginia were much alarmed by the number of foreign and Catholic servants and other inhabitants who might lean in sympathy towards their French Catholic brethren. Again there is no evidence that they had any real desire to do so, but since French troops never got near enough to many servants to tempt them we cannot say that the idea was groundless. In 1765, after the war was over, a French traveller declared that if any foreign power invaded and promised freedom to those under indenture, they would certainly give every assistance. Later on representatives of the French government reported that servants were ripe for rebellion against England.

The most ambitious plans for this sort of thing were drawn up by the Anglican clergyman Jonathan Boucher, who returned to England in high dudgeon just before the Revolution. He addressed a letter on the subject to an English official, and after explaining what servants were, continued:

> It appears to me to be worth while to send Troops thither, if for no other Purpose than the enlisting of these men whom, I cannot but think peculiarly fit for the American Service. They will bring with Them an ill Humour & Prejudice against the Country which it will not be unuseful to have propagated amongst those with whom they may be incorporated; They have some Knowledge of the country . . . &, above all, They have been seasoned to the Climate.

Boucher, reported that a gentleman of Baltimore, "not addicted to random Declarations," was positive that five hundred could be enrolled in that city and its environs; "it is certain," wrote Boucher, "the richest Harvest of Them may be gleaned there, at Elk-Ridge, the Iron Works & Annapolis." He recommended that plans be carefully drawn for dispatching at one and the same time parties in armed vessels to the heads of rivers in Pennsylvania, Maryland, and Virginia, so that notice could be spread "to the back Settlements, where most of these People have been carried." Many servants, he said, had already run away to join the king's army in Boston.

So far as we know the parson's detailed plans were not followed, nor did the servants manifest any united determination to turn the Revolution to their own ends. Boucher's opinion of their willingness to rise against their masters deserves credit, for he was in a position to know. Yet the situation was surely far more complicated than he represented it; it would scarcely have been a politic move, for example, to seduce away the servants of good Loyalists, nor would it have been easy to avoid doing so if a general campaign to enlist servants had been started. Furthermore, a great proportion of persons under indenture in those years were serious redemptioners, unlikely to be turned aside from their purposes by political adventures. The sentiments of servants during the war were determined by the same fortuitous circumstances that established other people's opinions.

We may conclude that the indentured servants and redemptioners, who certainly formed a distinct social and economic class in all the colonial communities, were practically never "class-conscious" to the point of seriously threatening the order of society, either by rebellions of their own or by joining the forces of an invader. It is nevertheless significant that the idea occurred to men like Sir Henry Colt and Jonathan Boucher. There was always a vague fear that servants might join with Negroes in a servile rising, but the West Indian islands, where this danger was most real, soon became convinced that white men would stick together, and looked upon the importation of more servants as adding to the general security rather than imperilling it.

Though the servants were not much disposed to engage in organized conspiracies, they were very prone to individual misdoing. Colonial laws concerning servants are mainly devoted to fixing penalties for their usual crimes and misdemeanors, and the proceedings of county courts are full of judgments respecting them. We have already seen that the masters were expected to discipline their servants by various means, including mild physical punishments, for smaller departures from grace or for laziness and carelessness in work. But just as certainly masters were forbidden to take into their own hands punishment for major crimes. Since the only penalties which could be inflicted on an indentured servant were physical ones, such as whipping or setting in the stocks and the prolongation of the period of servitude, it was necessary that these penalties be administered only by legal authority or gross injustices would have been the rule.

The most common misdoing was that of running away, and the statute books are full of prescriptions against it, while the records show that this was the most frequent cause for the appearance of servants before the magistrates. The natural desire of the planters to retain their laborers was reinforced, especially in earlier years, by a lively fear that servants would join with Negroes or Indians to overcome the small number of masters. Hence the extraordinary harshness of early laws, the worst being that of Maryland in 1639, which enacted that a servant convicted of running away should be executed. There is no evidence that this drastic punishment was ever actually inflicted. Legislation on runaways began in Virginia in 1642/3, when they were condemned to serve double the time they had been absent, after the time of the original indenture should expire. For a second offense they were to be branded on the cheek or shoulder with the letter R, and were to be deemed incorrigible rogues. In 1658/9 it was provided that the hair of returned runaways should be clipped, for easier identification in case they resumed their wanderings. The penalty in Barbados in 1652 was an extra month's service for every two hours' absence, and in 1661 an extra day for every two hours, but the total extension of time was not to be more than three years.

From the confusion of early laws and procedures on the subject of runaways several definite problems and solutions gradually appear. We may distinguish first preventive measures, designed to make running away difficult. Most important of these was the provision in all colonies from very early times that all persons travelling had to have a pass, and that no person should be hired as a servant or harbored as a guest without presenting a certificate from competent authority showing that he was free. Presumably such laws were administered with some discretion, for there seem to be few cases of the prosecution of innocent men for travelling without a pass. Servants would occasionally forge such a certificate, and in one instance a very enterprising convict forged a pass for himself under an assumed name, to travel about Maryland searching for himself under his real name. In addition to these provisions for certificates and passes there were stringent laws in all colonies against the "harboring" of runaways. Any persons receiving and keeping individuals who had no pass or certificate were subject to fines, the amount of which varied greatly from colony to colony, but which were levied at so many pounds of tobacco or sugar per hour, or per twenty-four hours, that the fugitive was sheltered. It is plain that one of the principal motives for these laws was that of preventing servants who stole their masters' goods from taking them to free confederates and dividing the spoils. Lastly, all the southern colonies, and especially the islands, had severe laws regulating the keeping of boats and wherries, and providing that before any persons left the colony their intention to depart should be public posted for a certain number of days. Often ship captains were put under bond not to take away any persons not thus posted. Such regulations were directed as much against free debtors as against servants.

The most difficult problem was to get a servant back after he had run away. Early laws provided for the pursuit of such servants by hue and cry, thus depending upon the ancient obligations of Anglo-Saxons to insure recovery. Since in every colony this proved inadequate, new acts directed the public officials to pursue at public expense, pressing into service men, boats, and whatever assistance might be necessary. But the most effective method was simply that of offering a reward to anyone who brought such a servant back, or lodged him in a jail whence he could be procured by his master. Sheriffs were granted so much a mile for bringing back absconding servants, and in the eighteenth century rewards to those taking up runaways eventually became fixed amounts: twenty shillings in South Carolina, 200 pounds of tobacco in Virginia and Maryland, fifteen shillings in Jersey, and so on. Some colonies provided that runaways, once caught, should be returned by passing them from constable to constable until they reached home, as was done in England with rogues. When a servant was picked up by the authorities for travelling without a pass and refused to tell who his master was, the sheriff might take him to jail and keep him there for a definite time until the master claimed him; if no master appeared the sheriff was authorized after a suitable time to sell the servant at auction to pay his jail fees. On several occasions a runaway servant was incarcerated and his master refused to take him back, whereupon the magistrates usually instructed the sheriff to sell him.

Last come the penalties inflicted upon the servant. These were dual in purpose; first to reimburse the master for his expense and trouble incurred in recovering the runaway and for the days of labor which were lost, and second to punish the servant for his misdoing. The punishment was clearly set forth in the statutes, though it varied greatly from colony to colony: for each day absent the servant was to serve two days extra in New Jersey, Virginia, North Carolina, and St. Christopher; five days in Pennsylvania, ten in Maryland, and seven in South Carolina. In a few colonies the scales of extra service to be enforced for reimbursement of expense are also provided by law; thus Virginia specifies one and a half months' extra service for every 100 pounds of tobacco paid out, but in general this matter was left to the discretion of the justices.

By the eighteenth century the considerable numbers of runaway cases which came before the local courts were being adjusted in a perfectly cut and dried fashion. A sample entry from the Chester County, Pennsylvania, records will show what happened:

> Ephraim Jackson having Petitioned this Court prays Relief for sundry Charges Occasioned by the Runing away of his servant Paul Whitton amounting in the whole to [£3.2.0] with Eight days run away time which the Court allows of and adjudges the said servant to serve his master or his assigns Forty days for Runaway Time after the Expiration of his former servitude and to pay his said master [£3.2.0] Expended in Costs and Charges in Retaking of him after the Expiration of his former servitude or serve his said master or assigns nine months in Liew thereof.

The same procedure was followed in Maryland and Virginia, with the changes made necessary by different laws. It may be remarked that the Maryland act allowed the magistrates some discretion in adjudging ten days of service for each day absent, but they seem nevertheless to have generally prescribed the full penalty, unless the servant had been away so long that his time was thereby hopelessly extended.

The courts seem always to have accepted the word of the master as to the length of time the servant had been absent, though the servant was present in court, and the entries occasionally indicate that he "had nothing to say for himself." Usually the unhappy victim was silent, and I have never come across a successful protest by a servant against one of these judgments. There must have been many abuses. A case from the Anne Arundel records illustrates a highly unpleasant mode of procedure. Here a maidservant was brought to court in March, 1719, with 133 days of absence claimed against her, beginning with four days in 1714. What had happened was that her master had kept an account, as the years went by, of various short absences, and as she approached the end of her five-year term he brought her to court, produced a tabulation of all these small delinquencies, and was actually awarded 1330 days of extra service. The unfortunate woman stood in the court, and "sayes she has nothing to say against the said account." It may have been a true account, but obviously she would have had an almost impossible task to prove that it was not, and with her habits being what they apparently were she had small chance of ever becoming free, unless the courts became more merciful than Maryland courts generally were.

Procedure respecting runaways was more irregular in the seventeenth century, but it followed the same principles, and has been so often described that there is no need for further elaboration here. A few cases illustrating the situation in Barbados may nevertheless be of interest. In August, 1654, one Thomas Carter was given permission by his master to visit some friends for the day. Being "overtaken in drink" he stayed out an extra day, and was haled by his master before John Colleton, Esq., who ordered that he serve an extra year. Governor

Searle and his council heard the evidence, however, and reversed Colleton's decision, freeing the servant from his outrageous penalty. Similarly, when some Scottish servants absented themselves from their master "upon a pretence of freedom," the whole party, masters and servants, appeared before the Council and the masters agreed to take no advantage of the statute, while the servants promised to return peaceably to their labors.

Probably the majority of runaways got successfully away. Governor Stede wrote in 1688 that many escaped even from the island of Barbados, by joining together in groups and seizing fishing boats; John Urmstone of North Carolina went so far as to declare that most servants never completed their times, but ran away and could not be recovered. Scharf calculated that there was an average of 150 advertisements for different runaways, including Negroes, each year in the *Maryland Gazette;* certainly there was not more than four or five cases of recovered servants each year in any of the county court records, and usually the number was even less. Complaints were heard in early years that servants escaped into the Dutch colonies, and also that they went north into Connecticut, where there were no laws by which they might be recovered. In general, however, they were returned from one colony to another whenever found without undue formality, and the newspapers of Pennsylvania carried large numbers of advertisements for servants who had escaped from Maryland.

The institutions of indentured servitude appear at their worst in this matter of runaways, and there is little to distinguish a servant from a slave. Obviously the penalties of extra service were imposed principally for the enrichment of masters; there can be no possible reason for the Maryland law with a punishment five times as severe as that of Virginia except that the planters of that colony more openly pursued their own advantage. Newspaper advertisements for absconding servants make painful reading; often the fugitives are described as having iron collars about their necks, and the whole spectacle was a degrading one. Nevertheless, it has received a disproportionate amount of treatment from writers on colonial labor; as compared with the total number of indentured servants the number who ran away was probably not great, and certainly the number brought back and condemned to extended servitude was almost insignificant. It is the plentiful evidence rather than the actual importance of runaways that makes their history so well known.

Scarcely less conspicuous in the court records than the offense of running away was that of fornication, and the begetting of bastard children. The moral delinquency involved was expiated in all colonies by a ceremonial whipping, usually of twenty-one lashes, and commonly applied to both man and woman. But colonists took rather more seriously the economic consequences, which consisted of the loss of time by maidservants having children, and the expense involved in bringing up the child. This latter by English practice fell upon the county, and the laws provided that the father of an illegitimate should be discovered by the oath of the mother, and a sum exacted from him sufficient to bear the cost of supporting the child until it could be bound out to work. Such a sum could rarely be got from a manservant, and hence would either be paid by his master, in which case the court judged extra service, or would be temporarily borne by the county and the servant taken by the sheriff after his time was up and sold again for the amount necessary. As for the maidservant, some colonies prescribed a year's extra service to make up for her lost time, while others left the period to the discretion of magistrates, who rarely gave less than a year. In fact a good deal depended on her master's story; if he had expended any considerable amount of trouble and money when the child was born the length of service judged to repay him would be greater. In many cases a master paid a fine, usually of thirty shillings, for his maidservant rather than having her subjected to the prescribed whipping; he was of course reimbursed by several months of extra service, properly adjudged by the court. Once again it is plain that the maidservant generally served far more extra time than she can possibly have lost through her misdeeds; sentences of two and even three years are quite common, though childbirth can rarely have incapacitated a woman for more than a month or six weeks.

Legal marriage between servants without the consent of masters was always forbidden; Pennsylvania held such marriages invalid in 1682 and provided that they were to be proceeded against as for adultery or fornication, and children were to be accounted bastards. Penalties were always heavy, and as usual were in the form of extra service. We may cite one case in illustration: James Hall and Margaret Ryan ran away from their master in Chester County, stayed thirteen days, got married, and were eventually brought back at a cost to the master of £9. The court judged each to serve thirty extra days for their runaway time, five months for the £9, and one year for marrying. Penalties in other colonies were generally one year's extra service, though Barbados and the other West Indian islands in 1661 required an additional four years of any manservant who secretly married.

When a freeman got a maidservant with child he merely had to satisfy the county for the child's maintenance in most cases, though a few colonies made him pay a fine to the woman's master. In all cases he suffered the usual penalty for fornication, a whipping or sometimes a fine of thirty shillings. More serious were instances in which a master got his own maidservant with child; the court might be forced to decide between her word and his, and though it was the rule in such cases to accept the statement of the woman, made when the child was born, the court could not always discover that such a statement had been made, and so was forced to hear evidence which was apt to be rather colorful. If the case was proved, the maidservant was generally taken away from her master and sold elsewhere, but not set free. The heaviest penalties was reserved for those white women who bore mulatto bastards; long periods of extra service, extending to seven years, were inflicted, usually in addition to a sound whipping.

The fact is that one of the most troublesome and least satisfactory aspects of the whole system was that of sex relations among the servants. The early trade brought to America many more men than women; practically all of them were unmarried, and a very large proportion were of bad character. The prohibition of marriage tended to encourage illicit relations between servants who might under other conditions have lived in conventional fashion. It is true that masters sometimes made generous arrangements for their servants who wished to marry, and that the eighteenth-century redemptioners often had families before beginning their service. Nevertheless the average servant found his chances of marriage reduced below those of persons of similar economic status in England, and the consequences were not healthy. To illustrate one of the less obvious possibilities we may quote the following pathetic plea of a certain Sarsh West to the Baltimore County Court:

> Humbly Sheweth That your Petitioner having now the Misfortune of an Illegitimate Child, Which I am very sorry for and by Gods Grace I hope I shall never be Guilty of

the like again I Doe Declare to your Worships in this Petition the Father of my Child which I hope will be sufficient without publication to any Persons Else (I Do Desire that Favour of your Worships) the Father of my Child is John Michael my Fathers Servant Man. I must beg your Worships to take my Obligation for my fine for I Cannot Gett Security Noe neither have I any Ready Tobacco or Money this year to pay but I have sold three head of Cattle this Spring for Tobacco to pay you this Ensueing year. I hope your Worships will take this unto your Grave and Wise Consideration to Use me kindly. I must stand up to your Worships Clemency.

The justices spared Sarah a whipping but required her to come to the next court and swear publicly as to the father of her child, and to give security for payment of the fine and for any expense to the county from the child. These were given by Robert West, presumably Sarah's father. As for John Michael, he escaped with ten lashes.

It may be that the newspaper writer who claimed that the convicts, besides their other crimes, "pox'd" the daughters of the colonists, was guilty of exaggeration. Yet the number of illegitimates begotten by servants was large, and since many of the lower grade of servants remained in the colonies only as long as their period of service or of transportation lasted, it may well be that they left behind memorials of their character which were more enduring than their own careers in the new world. One's estimate of the importance of this factor will be influenced by his views on the relative importance of heredity and environment, and in any case the proportion of such baseborn elements in the population was not large; yet this is an aspect of the servant trade which cannot altogether be neglected.

Women servants, besides doing a great deal of domestic and some field labor in the southern colonies, contributed much to make life a bit more tolerable by becoming the wives and mistresses of settlers, or even by merely existing as amiable parts of society. This last function may be thought harmless enough, but the island of Nevis found it becoming a problem, and faced the situation boldly in an act entitled "Women Servants Inveagled." This recited that complaints had been made by masters of families that their women servants had been "inveagled" by idle persons under pretense of marriage or freedom, and had therefore been careless and neglectful in their work. It enacted that any man, free or servant, who should "keepe often company with such women servants, and thereby allure them soe that they neglect their dutyes, or entice them under the afforesaid pretenses of marriage or freedome, without knowledge or consent of their said masters," should be subject to penalties. Life on the island of Nevis in the 1670's had few enough amenities, and it was a pity that free men should be deprived of the right of enticing, alluring, and inveigling women servants, to say nothing of the pleasure this must have given the women. We know nothing about the enforcement of this decree, but its text suggests a good deal concerning life and servitude on the islands.

Of the other misdoings of servants little need be said. Most colonies provided by law that those committing theft should forfeit double the amount stolen, which meant, of course, extra service. Those who spent time in jail had to serve extra time for their fees and for the days lost from their masters' work. All colonies prescribed extra service of six months or a year for servants who resisted their masters, or struck them. Other misdemeanors, which if committed by a freeman were punished with a fine, were in the case of servants punished by whipping, South Carolina providing that nine lashes be given for every twenty shillings ordinarily levied. Otherwise they were treated by the courts just as other inhabitants of the colony were. In the records of the sessions held in Chester County, Pennsylvania, for example, one may read long lists of cases in which no mention is made of the status of person involved, though many of them can be recognized as servants because they appear as such in some other entry.

One who attempts a comparative summary of colonial penal codes concerning servants may perhaps first be struck by the similarities and relationships among them. We have already described how the Barbados statute of 1661 spread to Jamaica and in its principles through all the islands. The continental colonies found it necessary to deal with most of the same special problems by special enactments. Thus in every colony from Barbados to New York there was erected substantially the same mechanism for pursuing and returning runaway servants; the same sorts of penalties were applied to the recovered wanderer by extending his service, the same complicated enactments punishing those who "harbored" runaways were found necessary. Likewise, every colony found it desirable to pass laws concerning servants having bastard children, servants striking their masters, servants stealing from their masters, servants trading with freemen or with natives. Everywhere it was necessary eventually to provide by statute that a servant should not be whipped "naked" save by order of a magistrate. Above all, everywhere the same familiar penalty appears again and again: an extension of the culprit's servitude, usually for a time apparently out of all proportion to the magnitude of this offense. These regulations, together with those concerning freedom dues and customary times of servitude, constitute a body of statue law peculiarly colonial in its nature, though in some respects derived from older English practice. In some cases, as for instance when the Barbados law of 1661 was adopted in Jamaica, we know that there was conscious and deliberate copying of these codes among the colonies, but in most instances we should probably be right in supposing that similarities originally arose merely because the same problems were being met in the same way, under the compulsion of colonial circumstances. No doubt there was much conscious imitation later, as for instance when South Carolina in 1717 enacted freedom dues for women in the same words used by Maryland in 1692.

But after observing these relationships one would probably next be impressed by the considerable differences in detail among the colonies. Many of these have already been mentioned, and it has been pointed out that most of them seem impossible of rational explanation. Why, for example, should the laws of Maryland in general have been so much more harsh than those of her neighbors, and this before the wholesale introduction of convicts gave her some excuse for severity? Why should a runaway serve ten days for one in Maryland, and only two for one in Virginia? Why should a person who harbored a runaway forfeit five hundred pounds of tobacco for every night in Maryland, and only sixty pounds in Virginia? And most remarkable of all, why, when most colonies progressively made their penal codes milder, should Maryland after abandoning her original death penalty for runaways and substituting double service, progressively make her code more severe? I know of no answer to these questions, except to assume that the planters of Maryland were a harsher breed than those of Virginia and Pennsylvania. This assumption appears foolish, but one certainly gains the impression from reading court records that not only the laws but also the magistrates of that colony were less merciful.

Year after year the courts from Pennsylvania southward found a considerable proportion of their time taken up by the troubles and the misdoings of indentured servants. Most of our information about servants comes in fact from these court records, and indeed it is difficult not to draw all conclusions about them from the evidences of their clashes with the law or with their masters. Perhaps this section had best be ended, therefore, with a summary view of the relations between the servant and the authorities in one typical locality, by which they may appear more nearly in their true proportions. Lancaster County, in the "Northern Neck" of Virginia, was neither so old and rich as those counties on the lower James River, nor so new and raw as those in the Piedmont. In the year 1665 one hundred and eighty-one persons in the county made returns of 965 "tithables," from which we may guess that there were about 500 white servants. During that year the county court judged the age of eleven young servants, heard the cases of four runaways, of three maidservants having bastards, of four servants applying for their freedom, and of four others appearing for miscellaneous reasons.

In 1698 Lancaster County having been split into two, returned 708 tithables, 257 persons making the returns, and there may have been three hundred white servants. That year there were seventeen judgments of age, one case of bastardy, and one registration of an indenture. The year was hardly typical in not producing any runaways. In 1725 there were 1,249 tithables, but since Negroes were coming in we had best not assume that there were more than about 500 white servants. Four runaways appeared before the court, one maidservant on a charge of having a bastard, and six servants for various reason, two of them for misdemeanors. In 1740, with 1,579 tithables and perhaps still about 500 servants, there were seven runaways, five cases of bastardy, and four miscellaneous affairs involving servants. In 1757 there were no servant cases, nor in 1764, from which it may be inferred that slaves had practically replaced white servants, and that individual magistrates attended to whatever small disputes may have arisen over those who were left.

These figures are fairly typical, as far as I can discover, of any colonial county in those regions. Even if the numbers of white servants have been overestimated it is still plain that only a very small proportion of them appear in court records. The vast majority of them worked out their time without suffering excessive cruelty or want, received their freedom dues without suing for them, and left no evidences from which to tell the stories of their careers. These points need to be emphasized, for nearly all accounts of white servitude are principally based on the records of courts of justice.

For the most part, American colonists succeeded in treating their indentured servants as private property. They bought and sold them, sued each other for possession of them, and set up engines of law for the protection of their rights in them. Though on occasion the state took a servant away from a cruel master without providing due compensation, this was certainly avoided as often as possible, and many cruel masters, though losing their servants, received the sum procured by selling them elsewhere. To be sure, the servant had rights, but while he was in servitude these rarely conflicted with the conception of him as property.

10. Slavery and the Genesis of American Race Prejudice

Carl N. Degler

Professor Carl N. Degler (b. 1921) of Stanford University wrote the article appearing here in direct reaction to an earlier thesis propounded by Oscar and Mary Handlin of Harvard University. The Handlins asserted that racial prejudice became a force of great consequence in American historical development after chattel slavery was legalized in the colonies. Before that time Africans were neither thought of in perjorative terms, nor were they treated necessarily as inferior beings.

"Not true," was Degler's rejoinder. The slow evolution of colonial statutes defining permanent and inheritable slave status for blacks involved the legalization of what had already become pervasive in the minds and actions of the whites. How else could one explain the institutionalization of slavery? How could it be possible for the peculiar institution to affect only one group in society unless racial prejudice already existed in the minds of whites?

Since Professor Degler unearthed impressive individual examples of de facto slavery long before legalization occurred, we must also then ask about the sources of prejudice. And we need to consider whether the law is merely a reflection of or a creator of social conditions and relationships. How has Degler's analysis allowed us to more clearly perceive the evolution of chattel slavery as an English institution in the New World? But how do we explain the prejudice shown by white Virginians?

Over a century ago, Tocqueville named slavery as the source of the American prejudice against the Negro. Contrary to the situation in antiquity, he remarked: "Among the moderns the abstract and transient fact of slavery is fatally united with the physical and permanent fact of color." Furthermore, he wrote, though "slavery recedes" in some portions of the United States, "the prejudice to which it has given birth is immovable."[1] More modern observers of the American past have also stressed this causal connection between the institution of slavery and the color prejudice of Americans.[2] Moreover, it is patent to anyone conversant with the nature of American slavery, particularly as it functioned in the nineteenth century, that the impress of bondage upon the character and future of the Negro in the United States has been both deep and enduring.

But if one examines other societies which the Negro entered as a slave, it is

Source: Carl N. Degler, "Slavery and the Genesis of American Race Prejudice," *Comparative Studies in Society and History,* 2 (1959), pp. 49–66. Reprinted by permission of the Cambridge University Press.

apparent that the consequences of slavery have not always been those attributed to the American form. Ten years ago, for example, Frank Tannenbaum demonstrated that in the Spanish and Portuguese colonies in South America, slavery did not leave upon the freed Negro anything like the prejudicial mark which it did in the United States.[3] He and others[4] have shown that once the status of slavery was left behind, the Negro in the lands south of the Rio Grande was accorded a remarkable degree of social equality with the whites. In the light of such differing consequences, the role of slavery in the development of the American prejudice against the Negro needs to be reexamined, with particular attention paid to the historical details of origins.

I

Tannenbaum showed that in the Portuguese and Spanish colonies there were at least three historical forces or traditions which tended to prevent the attribution of inferiority to the Negro aside from the legal one of slavery. One was the continuance of the Roman law of slavery in the Iberian countries, another was the influence of the Roman Catholic Church, and the third was the long history—by Anglo-American standards—of contacts with darker-skinned peoples in the course of the Reconquest and the African explorations of the fifteenth and sixteenth centuries. Roman law, at least in its later forms, viewed slavery as a mere accident, of which anyone could be the victim. As such it tended to forestall the identification of the black man with slavery, thus permitting the Negro to escape from the stigma of his degraded status once he ceased to be a slave. The same end, Tannenbaum showed, was served by the Roman Church's insistence upon the equality of all Christians and by the long familiarity of the Iberians with Negroes and Moors.

In North America, of course, none of these forces was operative—a fact which partly explains the differing type of slavery and status for Negroes in the two places. But this cannot be the whole explanation since it is only negative. We know, in effect, what were the forces which permitted the slave and the Negro in South America to be treated as a human being, but other than the negative fact that these forces did not obtain in the North American colonies, we know little as to why the Negro as slave or freedman, occupied a degraded position compared with that of any white man. A more positive explanation is to be found in an examination of the early history of the Negro in North America.

It has long been recognized that the appearance of legal slavery in the laws of the English colonies was remarkably slow. The first mention does not occur until after 1660—some forty years after the arrival of the first Negroes. Lest we think that slavery existed in fact before it did in law, two historians have assured us recently that such was not the case. "The status of Negroes was that of servants," Oscar and Mary Handlin have written, "and so they were identified and treated down to the 1660's."[5] This late, or at least, slow development of slavery[6] complicates our problem. For if there was no slavery in the beginning, then we must account for its coming into being some forty years after the introduction of the Negro. There was no such problem in the history of slavery in the Iberian colonies, where the legal institution of slavery came in the ships with the first settlers.

The Handlins' attempt to answer the question as to why slavery was slow in appearing in the statutes is, to me, not convincing. Essentially their explanation is that by the 1660's, for a number of reasons which do not have to be discussed here, the position of the white servant was improving, while that of the Negroes was sinking to slavery. In this manner, the Handlins contend, Negro and white servants, heretofore treated alike, attained different status. There are at least two major objections to this argument. First of all, their explanation, by depending upon the improving position of white servants as it does, cannot apply to New England, where servants were of minor importance. Yet the New England colonies, like the Southern, developed a system of slavery for the Negro that fixed him in a position of permanent inferiority. The greatest weakness of the Handlins' case is the difficulty in showing that the white servant's position was improving during and immediately after the 1660's.

Without attempting to go into any great detail on the matter, several acts of the Maryland and Virginia legislatures during the 1660's and 1670's can be cited to indicate that an improving status for white servants was at best doubtful. In 1662, Maryland restricted a servant's travel without a pass to two miles beyond his master's house;[7] in 1671 the same colony lengthened the time of servants who arrived without indenture from four to five years.[8] Virginia in 1668 provided that a runaway could be corporally punished and also have additional time exacted from him.[9] If, as these instances suggest, the white servant's status was not improving, then we are left without an explanation for the differing status accorded white and Negro servants after 1660.

Actually, by asking why slavery developed late in the English colonies we are setting ourselves a problem which obscures rather than clarifies the primary question of why slavery in North America seemed to leave a different mark on the Negro than it did in South America. To ask why slavery in the English colonies produced discrimination against Negroes after 1660 is to make the tacit assumption that prior to the establishment of slavery there was none. If, instead, the question is put, "Which appeared first, slavery or discrimination?" then no prejudgment is made. Indeed, it now opens a possibility for answering the question as to why the slavery in the English colonies, unlike that in the Spanish and Portuguese, led to a caste position for Negroes, whether free or slave. In short, the recent work of the Handlins and the fact that slavery first appeared in the statutes of the English colonies forty years after the Negro's arrival, have tended to obscure the real possibility that the Negro was actually *never* treated as an equal of the white man, servant or free.

It is true that when Negroes were first imported into the English colonies there was no law of slavery and therefore whatever status they were to have would be the work of the future. This absence of a status for black men, which, it will be remembered was not true for the Spanish and Portuguese colonies, made it possible for almost any kind of status to be worked out. It was conceivable that they would be accorded the same status as white servants, as the Handlins have argued; it was also possible that they would not. It all depended upon the reactions of the people who received the Negroes.

It is the argument of this paper that the status of the Negro in the English colonies was worked out within a framework of discrimination; that from the outset, as far as the available evidence tells us, the Negro was treated as an inferior to the white man, servant or free. If this be true, then it would follow that as slavery evolved as a legal status, it reflected and included as a part of its essence, this same discrimination which white men had practised against the Negro all along and before any statutes decreed it. It was in its evolution, then, that American colonial slavery differed from Iberian, since in the colonies of Spain and

Portugal, the legal status of the slave was fixed before the Negro came to the Americas. Moreover, in South America there were at least three major traditional safeguards which tended to protect the free Negro against being treated as an inferior. In summary, the peculiar character of slavery in the English colonies as compared with that in the Iberian, was the result of two circumstances. One, that there was no law of slavery at all in the beginning, and two, that discrimination against the Negro antedated the legal status of slavery. As a result, slavery, when it developed in the English colonies, could not help but be infused with the social attitude which had prevailed from the beginning, namely, that Negroes were inferior.

II

It is indeed true as the Handlins in their article have emphasized that before the seventeenth century the Negro was rarely called a slave. But this fact should not overshadow the historical evidence which points to the institution without employing the name. Because no discriminatory title is placed upon the Negro we must not think that he was being treated like a white servant; for there is too much evidence to the contrary. Although the growth of a fully developed slave law was slow, unsteady and often unarticulated in surviving records, this is what one would expect when an institution is first being worked out.[10] It is not the same, however, as saying that no slavery or discrimination against the Negro existed in the first decades of the Negro's history in America.

As will appear from the evidence which follows, the kinds of discrimination visited upon Negroes varied immensely. In the early 1640's it sometimes stopped short of lifetime servitude or inheritable status—the two attributes of true slavery—in other instances it included both. But regardless of the form of discrimination, the important point is that from the 1630's up until slavery clearly appeared in the statutes in the 1660's, the Negroes were being set apart and discriminated against as compared with the treatment accorded Englishmen, whether servants or free.

The colonists of the early seventeenth century were well aware of a distinction between indentured servitude and slavery.[11] This is quite clear from the evidence in the very early years of the century. The most obvious means the English colonists had for learning of a different treatment for Negroes from that for white servants was the slave trade[12] and the slave systems of the Spanish and Portuguese colonies. As early as 1623, a voyager's book published in London indicated that Englishmen knew of the Negro as a slave in the South American colonies of Spain. The book told of the trade in "blacke people" who were "sold unto the Spaniard for him to carry into the West Indies, to remaine as slaves, either in their Mines or in any other servile uses, they in those countries put them to."[13] In the phrase "remaine as slaves" is the element of unlimited service.

The Englishmen's treatment of another dark-skinned, non-Christian people—the Indians—further supports the argument that a special and inferior status was accorded the Negro virtually from the first arrival. Indian slavery was practiced in all of the English settlements almost from the beginning[14] and, though it received its impetus from the perennial wars between the races, the fact that an inferior and onerous service was established for the Indian makes it plausible to suppose that a similar status would be reserved for the equally different and pagan Negro.

The continental English could also draw upon other models of a differentiated status for Negroes. The earliest English colony to experiment with large numbers of Negroes in its midst was the shortlived settlement of Providence island, situated in the western Caribbean, just off the Mosquito Coast. By 1637, long before Barbados and the other British sugar islands utilized great numbers of Negroes, almost half of the population of this Puritan venture was black. Such a disproportion of races caused great alarm among the directors of the Company in London and repeated efforts were made to restrict the influx of blacks.[15] Partly because of its large numbers of Negroes, Old Providence became well known to the mainland colonies of Virginia and New England.[16] A. P. Newton has said that Old Providence

> forms the connecting link between almost every English colonising enterprise in the first half of the seventeenth century from Virginia and Bermuda to New England and Jamaica, and thus it is of much greater importance than its actual accomplishments would justify.[17]

Under such circumstances, it was to be expected that knowledge of the status accorded Negroes by these Englishmen would be transmitted to those on the mainland with whom they had such close and frequent contact.

Though the word "slave" is never applied to the Negroes on Providence, and only rarely the word "Servant," "Negroes," which was the term used, were obviously *sui generis;* they were people apart from the English. The Company, for example, distrusted them. "Association [Tortuga island] was deserted thro' their mutinous conduct," the Company told the Governor of Old Providence in 1637. "Further trade for them prohibited, with exceptions, until Providence be furnished with English."[18] In another communication the Company again alluded to the dangers of "too great a number" of Negroes on the island and promised to send 200 English servants over to be exchanged for as many Negroes.[19] A clearer suggestion of the difference in status between an English servant and a Negro is contained in the Company's letter announcing the forwarding of the 200 servants. As a further precaution against being overwhelmed by Negroes, it was ordered that a "family of fourteen"—which would include servants—was not to have more than six Negroes. "The surplusage may be sold to the poor men who have served their apprenticeship."[20] But the Negroes, apparently, were serving for life.

Other British island colonies in the seventeenth century also provide evidence which is suggestive of this same development of a differing status for Negroes, even though the word "slave" was not always employed. Though apparently the first Negroes were only brought to Bermuda in 1617,[21] as early as 1623 the Assembly passed an "Act to restrayne the insolencies of Negroes." The blacks were accused of stealing and of carrying "secretly cudgels, and other weapons and working tools." Such weapons, it was said, were "very dangerous and not meete to be suffered to be carried by such Vassals. . . ." Already, in other words, Negroes were treated as a class apart. To reinforce this, Negroes were forbidden to "weare any weapon in the daytyme" and they were not to be outside or off their master's land during "any undue hours in the night tyme. . . ."[22]

During the 1630's there were other indications that Negroes were treated as inferiors. As early as 1630 some Negroes' servitude was already slavery in that it was for life and inheritable. One Lew Forde possessed a Negro man, while the company owned his wife; the couple had two children. Forde desired "to know which of the said children properly belong to himself and which to the Company." The Council gave him the older child and the Company received the other.[23] A letter of Roger Wood in 1634 suggests that Negroes were already serving for life, for he asked to have a Negro, named Sambo, given to him, so that through the Negro "I or myne may *ever* be able" to carry on an old feud with an enemy who owned Sambo's wife.[24]

There is further evidence of discrimination against Negroes in later years. A grand jury in 1652 cited one Henry Gaunt as being "suspected of being unnecessarily conversant with negro women"—he had been giving them presents. The presentment added that "if he hath not left his familiarity with such creatures, it is desired that such abominations be inquired into, least the land mourne for them."[25] The discrimination reached a high point in 1656 when the Governor proclaimed that "any Englishman" who discovered a Negro walking about at night without a pass, was empowered to "kill him then and theire without mercye." The proclamation further ordered that all free Negroes "shall be banished from these Islands, never to return eyther by purchase of any man, or otherwise. . . ."[26] When some Negroes asked the Governor for their freedom in 1669, he denied they had any such claim, saying that they had been "purchased by" their masters "without condition or limitation. It being likewise soe practised in these American plantations and other parts of the world."[27]

In Barbados Negroes were already slaves when Richard Ligon lived there in 1647–50. "The Iland," he later wrote, "is divided into three sorts of men, viz: Masters, servants, and slaves. The slaves and their posterity, being subject to their masters for ever," in contrast to the servants who are owned "but for five years. . . ."[28] On that island as at Bermuda it was reported that Negroes were not permitted "to touch or handle any weapons."[29]

On Jamaica, as on the other two islands, a clear distinction was made between the status of the Negro and that of the English servant. In 1656 one resident of the island wrote the Protector in England urging the importation of African Negroes because then, he said, "the planters would have to pay for them," and therefore "they would have an interest in preserving their lives, *which was* wanting in the case of bond servants. . . ."[30]

It is apparent, then, that the colonists on the mainland had ample opportunity before 1660 to learn of a different status for black men from that for Englishmen, whether servants or free.

III

From the evidence available it would seem that the Englishmen in Virginia and Maryland learned their lesson well. This is true even though the sources available on the Negro's position in these colonies in the early years are not as abundant as we would like. It seems quite evident that the black man was set apart from the white on the continent just as he was being set apart in the island colonies. For example, in Virginia in 1630, one Hugh Davis was "soundly whipped before an Assembly of Negroes and others for abusing himself to the dishonor of God and the shame of Christians, by defiling his body in lying with a negro."[31] The unChristian-like character of such behavior was emphasized ten years later when Robert Sweet was ordered to do penance in Church for "getting a negro woman with child."[32] An act passed in the Maryland legislature in 1639 indicated that at that early date the word "slave" was being applied to non-Englishmen. The act was an enumeration of the rights of "all Christian inhabitants (slaves excepted)."[33] The slaves referred to could have been only Indians or Negroes,[34] since all white servants were Christians. It is also significant of the differing treatment of the two races that though Maryland and Virginia very early in their history enacted laws fixing limits to the terms for servants who entered without written contracts, Negroes were never included in such protective provisions.[35] The first of such laws were placed upon the books in 1639 in Maryland and 1643 in Virginia; in the Maryland statute, it was explicitly stated: "Slaves excepted."[36]

In yet another way, Negroes and slaves were singled out for special status in the years before 1650. A Virginia law of 1640 provided that "all masters" should try to furnish arms to themselves and "all those of their families which shall be capable of arms"—which would include servants—"(excepting negros)."[37] Not until 1648 did Maryland get around to such a prohibition, when it was provided that no guns should be given to "any Pagan for killing meate or to any other use," upon pain of a heavy fine.[38] At no time were white servants denied the right to bear arms; indeed, as these statutes inform us, they were enjoined to possess weapons.[39]

One other class of discriminatory acts against Negroes in Virginia and Maryland before 1660 also deserves to be noticed. Three different times before 1660— in 1643, 1644 and 1658—the Virginia assembly (and in 1654, the Maryland legislature) included Negro and Indian women among the "tithables." But white servant women were never placed in such a category,[40] inasmuch as they were not expected to work in the fields. From the beginning, it would seem, Negro women, whether free or bond, were treated by the law differently from white women servants.[41]

It is not until the 1640's that evidence of a status for Negroes akin to slavery, and, therefore, something more than mere discrimination begins to appear in the sources. Two cases of punishment for runaway servants in 1640 throw some light on the working out of a differentiated status for Negroes. The first case concerned three runaways, of whom two were white men and the third a Negro. All three were given thirty lashes, with the white men having the terms owed their masters extended a year, at the completion of which they were to work for the colony for three more years. The other, "being a Negro named John Punch shall serve his said master or his assigns for the time of his natural Life here or elsewhere."[42] Not only was the Negro's punishment the most severe, and for no apparent reason, but he was, in effect, reduced to slavery. It is also clear, however, that up until the issuing of the sentence, he must have had the status of a servant.

The second case, also of 1640, suggests that by that date some Negroes were already slaves. Six white men and a Negro were implicated in a plot to run away. The punishments meted out varied, but Christopher Miller "a dutchman" (a prime agent in the business) "was given the harshest treatment of all: thirty stripes, burning with an "R" on the cheek, a shackle placed on his leg for a year "and longer if said master shall see cause" and seven years of service for the colony upon completion of his time due his master. The only other one of the seven plotters to receive the stripes, the shackle and the "R" was the Negro Emanuel, but, significantly, he did not receive any sentence of work for the colony. Presumably he was already serving his master for a lifetime—*i.e.,* he was a slave.[43] About this time in Maryland it does not seem to have been unusual to speak of Negroes as slaves, for in 1642 one "John Skinner mariner" agreed "to deliver unto . . . Leonard Calvert, fourteen negro-men-slaves and three women-slaves."[44]

From a proceeding before the House of Burgesses in 1666 it appears that as early as 1644 that body was being called upon to determine who was a slave. The Journal of the House for 1666 reports that in 1644 a certain "mulata" bought "as a slave for Ever" was adjudged by the Assembly "no slave and but to serve as other Christian servants do and was freed in September 1665."[45]

Though no reason was given for the verdict, from the words "other Christian servants" it is possible that he was a Christian, for it was believed in the early years of the English colonies that baptism rendered a slave free. In any case, the Assembly uttered no prohibition of slavery as such as the owner was sufficiently surprised and aggrieved by the decision to appeal for recompense from the Assembly, even though the Negro's service was twenty-one years, an unheard of term for a "Christian servant."[46]

In early seventeenth century inventories of estates, there are two distinctions which appear in the reckoning of the value of servants and Negroes. Uniformly, the Negroes were more valuable, even as children, than any white servant. Secondly, the naming of a servant is usually followed by the number of years yet remaining to his service; for the Negroes no such notation appears. Thus in an inventory in Virginia in 1643, a 22-year old white servant, with eight years still to serve, was valued at 1,000 pounds of tobacco, while a "negro boy" was rated at 3,000 pounds and a white boy with seven years to serve was listed as worth 700 pounds. An eight-year old Negro girl was calculated to be worth 2,000 pounds. On another inventory in 1655, two good men servants with four years to serve were rated at 1,300 pounds of tobacco, and a woman servant with only two years to go was valued at 800 pounds. Two Negro boys, however, who had no limit set to their terms, were evaluated at 4,100 pounds apiece, and a Negro girl was said to be worth 5,500 pounds.[47]

These great differences in valuation of Negro and white "servants" strongly suggest, as does the failure to indicate term of service for the Negroes, that the latter were slaves at least in regard to life-time service. Beyond a question, there was some service which these blacks were rendering which enhanced their value—a service, moreover, which was not or could not be exacted from the whites. Furthermore, a Maryland deed of 1649 adumbrated slave status not only of life-time term, but of inheritance of status. Three Negroes "and all their issue both male and female" were deeded.[48]

Russell and Ames culled from the Virginia court records of the 1640's and 1650's several instances of Negroes held in a status that can be called true slavery. For example, in 1646 a Negro woman and a Negro boy were sold to Stephen Charlton to be of use to him and his "heyers etc. for ever." A Negro girl was sold in 1652 "with her Issue and produce . . . and their services forever." Two years later a Negro girl was sold to one Armsteadinger "and his heyers . . . forever with all her increase both male and female."[49] For March 12, 1655 the minutes of the Council and General Court of Virginia contain the entry, "Mulatto held to be a slave and appeal taken."[50] Yet this is five years before Negro slavery is even implied in the statutes and fifteen before it is declared. An early case of what appears to be true slavery was found by Miss Ames on the Virginia eastern shore. In 1635 two Negroes were brought to the area; over twenty years later, in 1656, the widow of the master was bequeathing the child of one of the original Negroes and the other Negro and her children.[51] This was much more than mere servitude—the term was longer than twenty years and apparently the status was inheritable.

Wesley Frank Craven, in his study of the seventeenth-century Southern colonies, has concluded that in the treatment of the Negro "the trend from the first was toward a sharp distinction between him and the white servant."[52] In view of the evidence presented here, this seems a reasonable conclusion.

Concurrently with these examples of onerous service or actual slavery of Negroes, there were of course other members of the race who did gain their freedom.[53] But the presence of Negroes rising out of servitude to freedom[54] does not destroy the evidence that others were sinking into slavery; it merely underscores the unsteady evolution of a slave status. The supposition that the practice of slavery long antedated the law is strengthened by the tangential manner in which recognition of Negro slavery first appeared in the Virginia statutes.[55] It occurred in 1660 in a law dealing with punishments for runaway servants, where casual reference was made to those "negroes who are in-capable of making satisfaction by addition of time,"[56] since they were already serving for life.

Soon thereafter, as various legal questions regarding the status of Negroes came to the fore, the institution was further defined by statute law. In 1662 Virginia provided that the status of the offspring of a white man and a Negro would follow that of the mother—an interesting and unexplained departure from the common law and a reversion to Roman law. The same law stated that "any christian" fornicating "with a negro man or woman . . . shall pay double the fines imposed by the former act." Two years later Maryland prescribed service for Negroes "durante vita" and provided for hereditary status to descend through the father. Any free white woman who married a slave was to serve her husband's master for the duration of the slave's life, and her children would serve the master until they were thirty years of age. Presumably, no penalty was to be exacted of a free white man who married a Negro slave.[57]

As early as 1669 the Virginia law virtually washed its hands of protecting the Negro held as a slave. It allowed punishment of refractory slaves up to and including accidental death, relieving the master, explicitly, of any fear of prosecution, on the assumption that no man would "destroy his owne estate."[58]

In fact by 1680 the law of Virginia had erected a high wall around the Negro. One discerns in the phrase "any negro or other slave" how the word "negro" had taken on the meaning of slave. Moreover, in the act of 1680 one begins to see the lineaments of the later slave codes. No Negro may carry any weapon of any kind, nor leave his master's grounds without a pass, nor shall "any negroe or other slave . . . presume to lift his hand in opposition against any christian," and if a Negro runs away and resists recapture it "shalbe lawful for such person or persons to kill said negroe or slave. . . ."[59]

Yet it would be a quarter of a century before Negroes would comprise even a fifth of the population of Virginia. Thus long before slavery or black labor became an important part of the Southern economy, a special and inferior status had been worked out for the Negroes who came to the English colonies. Unquestionably it was a demand for labor which dragged the Negro to American shores, but the status which he acquired here cannot be explained by reference to that economic motive. Long before black labor was as economically important as unfree white labor, the Negro had been consigned to a special discriminatory status which mirrored the social discrimination Englishmen practised against him.[60]

IV

In the course of the seventeenth century New Englanders, like Southerners, developed a system of slavery which seemed permanently to fasten its stigma upon the Negro race. But because of the small number of Negroes in the northern provinces, the development of a form of slavery, which left a caste in its wake, cannot be attributed to pressure from increasing numbers of blacks, or even from an insistent demand for cheap labor. Rather it seems clearly to be the consequence of the general social discrimination against the Negro. For in the northern region, as in the southern, discrimination against the Negro preceded the evolution of a slave status and by that fact helped to shape the form that institution would assume.

References to the status of the Negroes in New England in this period are scattered, but, as was true of the Southern provinces, those references which are available suggest that from the earliest years a lowly, differential status, if not slavery itself, "was reserved and recognized for the Negro—and the Indian, it might be added. The earliest date asserted in the sources for the existence of Negro slavery in Massachusetts is that of 1639. John Josselyn tells of a Negro woman held on Noddles Island in Boston harbor. Her master sought to mate her with another Negro, Josselyn says, but she kicked her prospective lover out of the bed, saying that such behavior was "beyond her slavery. . . ."[61] Though the first legal code of Massachusetts, the Body of Liberties of 1641, prohibited "bond-slavery" for the inhabitants, it clearly permitted enslavement of those who are "sold to us,"[62] which would include Negroes brought in by the international slave trade.[63]

Such use of Negroes was neither unknown nor undesirable to the Puritans. Emanuel Downing wrote to John Winthrop in 1645 about the desirability of a war against the Indians so that captives might be taken who, in turn, could be exchanged

> for Moores, which wilbe more gayneful pilladge for us then [*sic*] wee conceive, for I doe not see how wee can thrive until wee gett into a stock of slaves sufficient to doe all our busines, for our children's children will hardly see this great Continent filled with people, soe that our servants will still desire freedome for themselves, and not stay but for verie great wages. And I suppose you know verie well how we shall maynteyne 20 Moores cheaper than one English servant.[64]

The following year the Commissioners of the United Colonies recommended that in order to spare the colonies the cost of imprisoning contumacious Indians they should be given over to the Englishmen whom they had damaged or "be shipped out and exchanged for Negroes as the cause will justly serve."[65] Negroes were here being equated with Indians who were being bound out as prisoners: this was treatment decidedly a cut lower than that visited upon white servants.[66] That enslavement of Negroes was well known in New England by the middle of the century at the latest is revealed by the preamble to an act of Warwick and Providence colonies in 1652. It was said that it "is a common course practised amongst Englishmen to buy negers, to that end they may have them for service or slaves forever. . . ."[67]

By mid-century, Negroes were appearing in the inventories of estates and, significantly, the valuation placed upon them was very close to that found in Virginia inventories of the same period. Their worth is always much more than that of a white servant. Thus in 1650 "a neager Maide" was valued at £25; in 1657 the well-known merchant, Robert Keayne left "2 negroes and a negro child" estimated to be worth £30. "A negro boy servant" was set at £20 in an estate of 1661.[68] A further indication of the property character of Negroes was the attachment by the constable of Salem in 1670 of a Negro boy "Seasar" as the "proper goods of the said Powell."[69]

Despite the small numbers of Negroes in New England in this early period, the colonies of that region followed the example of the Southern and insular provinces in denying arms to the blacks in their midst—a discrimination which was never visited upon the English servant. In 1652 Massachusetts provided that Indians and Negroes could train in the militia the same as whites, but this apparently caused friction. The law was countermanded in 1656 by the statement "henceforth no negroes or Indians, altho servants of the English, shalbe armed or permitted to trayne."[70] Although as late as 1680 it was officially reported to London that there were no more than thirty "slaves" in Connecticut, that colony in 1660 excluded Indians and "negar servants" from the militia and "Watch and Ward."[71]

Edward Randolph in 1676 reported that there were a few indentured servants in Massachusetts "and not above two hundred slaves," by which he meant Negroes, for he said "they were brought from Guinea and Madagascar."[72] But it was not until 1698 that the phrase "Negro slave" actually appeared in the Massachusetts statutes.[73] The practice of slavery was preceding the law in Massachusetts precisely as it had in the South. Though an official report to London in 1680 distinguished between Negro slaves and servants in Connecticut,[74] the law of that colony did not bother to define the institution of slavery. Indeed, as late as 1704, the Governor gave it as his opinion that all children born of "negro bond-women are themselves in like condition, i.e., born in servitude," though he admitted that there was no statute which said so. His contention was, however, that such legislation was "needless, because of the constant practice by which they are held as such. . . ."[75]

During the last years of the seventeenth century, laws of Connecticut and Massachusetts continued to speak of Negroes as "servants," but it was very clear that the Negro's status was not being equated with that of the white servant. The General Court of Connecticut observed in 1690 that "many persons of this Colony doe . . . purchase negroe servants" and, since these servants run away, precautions have to be taken against such eventualities. It was therefore laid down that all "negroe or negroes shall" be required to have a pass in order to be outside the town bounds. Any inhabitant could stop a Negroe, free or slave, and have him brought before a magistrate if the black man were found to be without such a pass. Moreover, all ferrymen, upon pain of fine, were to deny access to their ferries to all Negroes who could not produce a pass.[76] Massachusetts in 1698 forbade trade with "any Indian, or negro servant or slave, or other known dissolute, lewd, and disorderly person, of whom there is just cause of suspicion."[77]

By the early years of the eighteenth century, the laws of Connecticut and Massachusetts had pretty well defined the Negro's subordinate position in society. Massachusetts acted to restrict the manumission of slaves by providing in 1703 that "molatto or negro slaves" could be freed only if security was given that they would not be chargeable upon the community. Another law set a curfew upon Indians, mulattoes and Negroes for nine o'clock each night. In 1705 Massachusetts became the only New England province to prohibit sexual relations between Negroes and mulattoes and Englishmen or those of "any other Christian nation."[78] Moreover, "any negro or mulatto" presuming to "smite or strike" an English person or any of another Christian nation would be "severely whipped."[79] In 1717 Negroes were barred from holding land in Connecticut.[80]

Thus, like the colonists to the South, the New Englanders enacted into law, in the absence of any prior English law of slavery, their recognition of the Negroes as different and inferior. This was the way of the seventeenth century; only with a later conception of the brotherhood of all men would such legal discrimination begin to recede; but by then, generations of close association between the degraded status of slavery and black color would leave the same prejudice against the Negro in the North that it did in the South.

It would seem, then, that instead of slavery being the root of the discrimination visited upon the Negro in America, slavery was itself molded by the early colonists' discrimination against the outlander. In the absence of any law of slavery or commandments of the Church to the contrary—as was true of Brazil and Spanish-America—the institution of slavery into which the African was placed in the English colonies inevitably mirrored that discrimination and, in so doing, perpetuated it.

Once the English embodied their discrimination against the Negro in slave law, the logic of the law took over. Through the early eighteenth century, judges and legislatures in all the colonies elaborated the law along the discriminatory lines laid down in the amorphous beginnings. In doing so, of course, especially in the South, they had the added incentive of perpetuating and securing a labor system which by then had become indispensable to the economy. The cleavage between the races was in that manner deepened and hardened into the shape which became quite familiar by the nineteenth century. In due time, particularly in the South, the correspondence between the black man and slavery would appear so perfect that it would be difficult to believe that the Negro was fitted for anything other than the degraded status in which he was almost always found. It would also be forgotten that the discrimination had begun long before slavery had come upon the scene.

NOTES

1. *Democracy in America* (New York, 1948), I, 358–60.

2. Most recently, Oscar and Mary Handlin, "The Origins of the Southern Labor System", *William and Mary Quarterly*, 3rd series, (April, 1950), 188–222.

3. *Slave and Citizen; The Negro in the Americas* (New York, 1947).

4. Gilberto Freyre, *Brazil: An Interpretation* (New York, 1945), pp. 96–101; Donald Pierson, *Negroes in Brazil* (Chicago, 1942), pp. 330–6.

5. Handlin, "Origins of Southern Labor", p. 203.

6. Virtually all historians of the institution agree on this. See U. B. Phillips, *American Negro Slavery* (New York, 1933), pp. 74–77; J. C. Ballagh, *History of Slavery in Virginia* (Baltimore, 1902), pp. 28–35. More recently, however, Susie Ames, *Studies of the Virginia Eastern Shore in the Seventeenth Century* (Richmond, 1940), pp. 101–10 and W. F. Craven, *Southern Colonies in the Seventeenth Century, 1607–1689* (Baton Rouge, 1949), pp. 217–9 have more than suggested that it is possible that slavery existed in Virginia almost from the very beginning of the Negro's history in America.

7. *Maryland Archives,* I, 451.

8. *Ibid.,* II, 335.

9. W. W. Hening, *Statutes at Large; being a Collection of all the Laws of Virginia. . .* (Richmond, 1809), II, 266.

10. John C. Hurd, *Law of Freedom and Bondage in the United States* (Boston, 1858–61), I, 163, points out that the trade "in negroes as merchandise was. . . recognized as legitimate by European governments, without any direct sanction from positive legislation, but rested on the general customs among nations, known both in municipal and international private law." Furthermore, he reported that none of the colonies ever found it necessary to pass laws legalizing slavery. He quotes from the Connecticut Code of 1821: "Slavery was never directly established by statute; but has been indirectly sanctioned by various statutes and frequently recognized by courts, so that it may be said to have been established by law." I, 212 n.

11. The Handlins, "Origins of Southern Labor," pp. 203–4, have argued that in the early years

slavery meant nothing more than a low form of labor and that it had no basis in law. This is true insofar as statute law is concerned, but, as will appear later, in practice quite a different situation obtained.

12. The Handlins, "Origins of Southern Labor," pp. 203–4, argue that the continental colonies could not have learned about a different status for Negroes from that of white servants from the slave trade because, they say, "the company of Royal Adventurers referred to their cargo as 'Negers,' 'Negro-servants,' 'Servants . . . from Africa,' or 'Negro Persons' but rarely as slaves." They overlook, however, abundant references to Negro slaves in the correspondence of the contemporary Royal African Company. Thus in 1663 a warrant for that company refers to "negro slaves" as a part of its monopoly. *Calendar of State Papers, Colonial,* V, 121; see also p. 204. In that same year the Privy Council wrote that the Spanish were "seeking to trade with our island of Barbada for a supply of Negro Slaves. . . ." And then the letter referred to a "supply of Negro Servants," and later still "for every Negro Person a Slave" and then "all such Negro Slaves." K. Donnan, *Documents Illustrative of the History of the Slave Trade,* (Washington, 1930), I, 161–2.

13. Quoted in Donnan, *Slave Trade,* I, 125.

14. See particularly, Almon Lauber, *Indian Slavery in Colonial Times Within the Present Limits of the United States* (New York, 1913), Chap. IV.

15. A. P. Newton, *The Colonising Activities of the English Puritans* (New Haven, 1914), p. 258.

16. *Ibid.,* p. 260.

17. A. P. Newton, *The European Nations in the West Indies, 1493–1688* (London, 1933), pp. 173–4.

18. *Calendar of State Papers, Colonial,* I, 249.

19. *Ibid.,* pp. 277–8.

20. *Ibid.,* pp. 278–9.

21. J. H. Lefroy, *Memorials of the Discovery and Early Settlement of the Bermudas or Somers Islands, 1515–1685* (London, 1877), I, 127.

22. *Ibid.,* I, 308–9.

23. *Ibid.,* I, 505. Cases in 1676 and 1685 indicate that this practice of dividing the children became the standard practice under slavery in a colony where the parcels of slaves were so small that few masters could have a spouse on their plantations for each of his adult Negroes. *Ibid.,* II, 427, 547–8.

24. *Ibid.,* I, 539. Emphasis added.

25. *Ibid.,* II, 30.

26. *Ibid.,* II, 95–6.

27. *Ibid.,* II, 293. As late as 1662 the perpetual character of slavery for Negroes was being obscured by their serving for ninety-nine years. See *Ibid.,* II, 166, 184.

28. Richard Ligon, *A True and Exact History of the Island of Barbados* (London, 1657), p. 43.

29. *Ibid.,* p. 46.

30. Quoted in Richard B. Morris, *Government and Labor in Early America* (New York, 1946), p. 499. As early as 1633, on the island of Tortuga, the separation of whites, servants or no, from Negroes was in evidence. At a time of anarchy on the island, "The eighty-odd Englishmen in the island had formed a council among themselves for the government of the colony and to keep in subjection the one hundred and fifty negroes, twenty-seven of whom were the company's property." Newton, *Colonising Activities,* p. 214.

31. Hening, *Statutes,* I, 146.

32. *Ibid.,* I, 552.

33. *Maryland Archives,* I, 80.

34. It is not known whether there were any Negroes in Maryland at that date. J. R. Brackett, *The Negro in Maryland* (Baltimore, 1889), p. 26 found no evidence of Negroes before 1642.

35. Handlin, "Origins of Southern Labor," p. 210; Hening, *Statutes,* I, 411, 539. This is not to say that some Negroes were not indentured servants, for there is evidence to show that limited service was enjoyed by some black men. This was true even during the period after the recognition of slavery in the statutes. In October, 1673, for instance, the Council and General Court of Virginia ordered that "Andrew Moore A Servant Negro," who asserted he was to serve only five years, and who had the support of several "oathes," was declared free. Moreover, his erstwhile master was compelled to "pay him Corne and Clothes According to the custome of the country" and 400 pounds of tobacco and cask for the Negro's service since his time expired and to "pay costs." *Minutes of the Council and General Court of Colonial Virginia,* edited by H. R. McIlwaine (Richmond, 1924), p. 354.

36. Hening, *Statutes,* I, 257; *Maryland Archives,* I, 80.

37. *William and Mary Quarterly,* Second Series, IV (July, 1924), 147.

38. *Maryland Archives,* I, 233.

39. Handlin, "Origins of Southern Labor," p. 209, implies that these early restrictions were later

repealed. "Until the 1660's," the Handlins write, "the statutes on the Negroes were not at all unique. Nor did they add up to a decided trend." In substantiation of this point they instance the "fluctuations" in the Negro's right to bear arms. Their cited evidence, however, does not sustain this generalization. Four references to the statutes of Virginia are made; of these four, only two deal with arms bearing. The first one, that referred to in the text above, indicates that Negroes were not to be armed. The other reference is at best an ambiguous statement about who is taxable and which of the taxables are to serve in the militia. It in no wise constitutes either a repeal or even a contradiction of the earlier statute, which, therefore, must be presumed to be controlling. Their evidence for "fluctuations" in the right of Indians to bear arms suffers from the same weakness of sources. The two statutes they cite merely confirm the right to certain Indians to possess guns and deny them to other Indians. No "fluctuation" in rights is involved.

40. Hening, *Statutes*, I, 242, 292, 455; *Maryland Archives*, I, 342. The statement in Handlin, "Origins of Southern Labor," p. 217 n, that the "first sign of discrimination was in 1668 when white but not Negro women were exempt," is therefore erroneous.

41. In his well-known emigrant pamphlet, *Leah and Rachel* (London, 1656), p. 12, John Hammond casts some interesting light on contemporary opinion regarding women who worked in the fields in Virginia. "The Women are not (as is reported) put into the ground to work, but occupie such domestique imployments and housewifery as in England . . . yet some wenches that are nasty, beastly and not fit to be so imployed are put into the ground. . . ."

42. *Minutes of the Council*, p. 466.

43. *Ibid.*, p. 467.

44. Catterall, *Judicial Cases*, I, 57 n. Mrs. Catterall does not think any Negroes came under this agreement, but the language itself testifies to an accepted special status for Negroes at that time.

45. *Journals of the House of Burgesses of Virginia*, edited by H. R. McIlwaine (Richmond, 1914), II, 34.

46. *Ibid.*, II, 34–5. His plea, however, was turned down, the Assembly not knowing "any Reason why the Publick should be answerable for the inadvertency of the Buyer. . . ."

47. John H. Russell, *The Free Negro in Virginia, 1619–1865* (Baltimore, 1913), p. 36. Russell concludes from his survey of inventories of estates for this early period that Negroes were valued from 20 to 30 pounds sterling, "while white servants of the longest term . . . receive a valuation of not more than £15 sterling". *Ibid.*, p. 35. Catterall, *Judicial Cases*, I, 58 n, upon concluding her investigation of inventories of estates, picked 1644 as the date at which "'servant' standing alone, had generally become synonymous with 'white servant' and 'negro' with 'negro slave'. . . ."

48. Catterall, *Judicial Cases*, IV, 9.

49. Russell, *Free Negro in Virginia*, pp. 34–5. He also reports the instance of a Negro by the name of John Casor who was claimed, in 1655, as a "Negro for his life," but he was rescued from such a status by two witnesses testifying that he had an indenture. *Ibid.*, pp. 32–3.

50. *Minutes of the Council*, p. 504. Handlin, "Origins of Southern Labor," p. 216, in arguing the late development of a different status for Negroes as compared with whites in Virginia, says: "As late as the 1660's the law had not even a word to describe the children of mixed marriages. But two decades later, the term mulatto is used. . . ." Such a statement is obviously misleading, for though the Handlins presumably mean statute law, the decisions of the General Court were also "law." The *Oxford English Dictionary* cites references for the word "mulatto" for 1595, 1613 and 1657.

51. Ames, *Eastern Shore*, p. 105.

52. Craven, *Southern Colonies*, p. 219.

53. See especially Russell, *Free Negro in Virginia*, pp. 36–9. See also Brackett, *Negro in Maryland*, p. 37.

54. An indication that even freedom for the Negro carried certain disabilities is afforded by an instance reported by Ames, *Eastern Shore*, p. 107 from the Northampton County court records of 1654. For contempt of authority and abuse of certain persons, Anthony Longoe, a Negro, was ordered, almost twenty years after his release from service, to receive "thirty lashes now applied, and tomorrow morning thirty lashes more."

55. A year earlier, 1659/60, a statute dealing with trade with the Dutch promised remission of a ten shilling tax if "the said Dutch or other forreiners shall import any negro slaves. . . ." This is the first reference in the Virginia statutes to Negroes as slaves. Hening, *Statutes*, I, 540.

56. Hening, *Statutes*, II, 26. The equivalent Maryland statute (1663) referred to "Negroes and other Slaves, who are incapeable of making Stisfaction [sic] by Addition of Tyme. . . ." *Maryland Archives*, I, 489.

57. Hening, *Statutes*, II, 170: *Maryland Archives*, I, 533–4. Handlin. "Origins of Southern Labor," p. 215 sees the genesis of these prohibitions in concern over status rather than in objection to racial intermarriage. This seems to be true for Maryland. But in speaking of the Virginia circum-

stances they write: "It was to guard against the complications of status that the laws after 1691 forbade 'spurious' or illegitimate mixed marriages of the slave and the free. . . ." Actually, however, the Virginia statute of 1691 (Hening, *Statutes,* III, 87) clearly aimed at the prevention of "abominable mixture and spurious issue" by forbidding marriage of "English or other white man or woman being free" with "a negro, mulatto or Indian man or woman *bond or free.*" (Emphasis added.)

58. Hening, *Statutes,* II, 270. The working out of the exact legal status of slave property, however, was a slow one. A Virginia law of 1705 (Hening, *Statutes,* III, 333–4), declared "Negro, Mulatto and Indian Slaves . . . to be real estate," but there were a number of exceptions which suggest the later chattel nature of property in slaves. In South Carolina slaves were decreed to be real estate in 1690 and not until 1740 were they said to be legally chattels. Hurd, *Law of Freedom,* I, 297, 303.

59. Hening, *Statutes,* II, 481–2.

60. Like Virginia, Maryland developed its slave law and status long before the Negroes had become an important aspect of the labor force. As late as 1712, Negroes made up only slightly more than 20 per cent of the population. Brackett, *Negro in Maryland,* pp. 38–9. If Virginia was slow in bringing her slave practices out into the open air of the statute books, the same could not be said of Carolina. In the Fundamental Constitutions, drawn up in 1669, it is stated in article CX that "Every freeman of Carolina shall have absolute power and authority over his negro slaves, of what opinion or religion so ever."

61. Massachusetts Historical Society, *Collections,* Third Series, III, 231. There is no doubt that there were Negroes at this time in Massachusetts, for in 1638 Winthrop reported that Capt. Peirce brought back from Old Providence "some cotton, and tobacco and negroes. . . ." John Winthrop, *History of New England,* James Savage, ed. (Boston, 1853), I, 305.

62. Some events of 1645 indicate that those few words were of crucial importance to the Puritans. That year some Negroes were brought to Massachusetts by a Captain Smith and they were ordered by the General Court to be returned to Africa on the ground that their importation constituted "the hainous and crying sinn of man-stealing". But this was man-stealing only because Smith and his men had captured the Negroes in a raid, instead of buying them from traders. *Records of Massachusetts,* III, 48, 58, 84.

63. Very early in New England history the concept of perpetual servitude—one of the distinguishing marks of slavery—appears in the records. In 1637 Roger Williams, in pleading for the lives of the captured Indians during the Pequot War, alludes to "perpetuall slaverie" as an alternative to their execution. Massachusetts Historical Society, *Collections,* Fourth Series, VI, 214. The will of John Winthrop, written in 1639, deeded to his son Adam "my island" and "also my Indians there and my boat and such household as is there." Robert C. Winthrop, *Life and Letters of John Winthrop* (Boston, 1869), II, 252. Though at least three white men were sentenced to "slavery" in Massachusetts in the early years, in at least two cases this did not, in fact, amount to perpetuity, for they appear to have been released in a short time. The use of the word as a special form of service, however, is most interesting. *Records of Massachusetts,* I, 246, 310, 269.

64. Massachusetts Historical Society, *Collections,* Fourth Series, VI, 65.

65. *Records of the Colony of Plymouth* (Boston, 1859), IX, 71.

66. John Cotton in 1651 clearly distinguished between slavery and servitude. He wrote Cromwell in that year in regard to the Scottish prisoners sent to New England, that "we have been desirous . . . to make their yoke easy. . . . They have not been sold for slaves to perpetuall servitude, but for 6, or 7 yeares, as we do our owne," Quoted in George H. Moore, *Notes on the History of Slavery in Massachusetts* (New York, 1866), p. 17 n.

67. *Records of the Colony of Rhode Island . . .* (Providence, 1856), I, 243.

68. Quoted in William B. Weeden, *Economic and Social History of New England* (Boston, 1891), p. 149 n. It was officially reported in 1680 by Connecticut colony that three or four "Blacks" were imported each year from the Barbados, and that they usually sold for £22 apiece. This was much more than the going price for servants. *Public Records of the Colony of Connecticut* (Hartford, 1850–90), III, 298.

69. Quoted in Lorenzo Greene, *The Negro in Colonial New England, 1620–1776* (New York, 1942), p. 172.

70. *Records of Massachusetts,* III, 268, 397.

71. *Records of Connecticut,* III, 298, I, 349.

72. Quoted in Palfrey, *History of New England,* III, 298.

73. Hurd, *Law of Freedom,* I, 262. Greene, *Negro in New England,* pp. 65–6, says that in 1670 slavery in Massachusetts became legally inheritable, for in that year the word "strangers" was dropped from the Body of Liberties as a description of those who might be enslaved.

74. *Records of Connecticut,* III, 298.

75. Quoted in Bernard C. Steiner, *History of Slavery in Connecticut* (Baltimore, 1893), p. 18.

76. *Records of Connecticut,* IV, 40.

77. Hurd, *Law of Freedom,* I, 262–3.

78. *Ibid.,* I, 263, Massachusetts had prohibited marriages between whites and Negroes, mulattoes and Indians in 1692. Lauber, *Indian Slavery,* p. 253.

79. Hurd, *Law of Freedom,* I, 263. Rhode Island, too, in 1728, provided that before a Negro or mulatto could be manumitted, security had to be given that he would not become a public charge. Hurd, *Law of Freedom,* I, 276.

80. Greene, *Negro in New England,* p. 312.

II. Unthinking Decision: Enslavement of Negroes in America to 1700

Winthrop D. Jordan

Whether slavery caused prejudice or prejudice slavery has been an important question for historians, but to Winthrop D. Jordon (b. 1931), who teaches at the Berkeley campus of the University of California, the problem is more complex and significant than that. The Handlin-Degler debate did not clarify the reasons why Englishmen held prejudicial attitudes toward Africans, attitudes that led to a system of chattel slavery for blacks, but not for whites. Searching through the fragmentary literature, Professor Jordan found that certain key words and phrases expressed and even explained the negative frame of mind. The African was distinct (and set apart) in the English mind not only because he was black, but also because he was thought to be both heathen and savage, the antithesis of the Christian, civilized, white Englishman. Therefore, Africans did not fall within the protective boundaries of expanding English notions about liberty of person.

Professor Jordan also points out that other variables were working to produce degradation for blacks in the English North American colonies. Englishmen were familiar with the Spanish model of subjecting blacks to slavery. Spanish practices abetted the rapid installation of chattel slavery on the English islands in the West Indies. But Virginians and Marylanders, who did not have much contact with the Caribbean settlements, were slow to legalize what had become common social practice by the mid-seventeenth century. Despite the lag between law and practice in those two tobacco colonies, the debasement of blacks had become the norm in all colonies by the end of the century.

May we conclude, then, that the origins of slavery for blacks in the English colonies stemmed from a certain peculiar set of attitudes long fixed in the minds of whites? What similarities were there between attitudes toward Indians as compared to blacks? What other factors may account for the origins of prejudice and its institutionalization through the law in the Anglo-American provinces?

FREEDOM AND BONDAGE IN THE ENGLISH TRADITION

Thinking about freedom and bondage in Tudor England was confused and self-contradictory. In a period of social dislocation there was considerable disagreement among contemporary observers as to what actually was going on and even as to what ought to be. Ideas about personal freedom tended to run both

Source: From Winthrop D. Jordan, *White Over Black: American Attitudes toward the Negro, 1550–1812* (Chapel Hill: University of North Carolina Press, 1968), pp. 48–50, 51–53, 54–58, 60, 61, 63–66, 71–75, 76–78, 79–81, 82–86, 87–98. Footnotes omitted. Reprinted by permission of the University of North Carolina Press and the Institute of Early American History and Culture.

ahead of and behind actual social conditions. Both statute and common law were sometimes considerably more than a century out of phase with actual practice and with commonly held notions about servitude. Finally, ideas and practices were changing rapidly. It is possible, however, to identify certain important tenets of social thought that served as anchor points amid this chaos.

Englishmen lacked accurate methods of ascertaining what actually was happening to their social institutions, but they were not wrong in supposing that villenage, or "bondage" as they more often called it, had virtually disappeared in England. William Harrison put the matter most strenuously in 1577: "As for slaves and bondmen we have none, naie such is the privilege of our countrie by the especiall grace of God, and bountie of our princes, that if anie come hither from other realms, so soone as they set foot on land they become so free of condition as their masters, whereby all note of servile bondage is utterlie remooved from them." Other observers were of the (correct) opinion that a few lingering vestiges—bondmen whom the progress of freedom had passed by—might still be found in the crannies of the decayed manorial system, but everyone agreed that such vestiges were anachronistic. In fact there were English men and women who were still "bond" in the midsixteenth century, but they were few in number and their status was much more a technicality than a condition. In the middle ages, being a villein had meant dependence upon the will of a feudal lord but by no means deprivation of all social and legal rights. In the thirteenth and fourteenth centuries villenage had decayed markedly, and it may be said not to have existed as a viable social institution in the second half of the sixteenth century. Personal freedom had become the normal status of Englishmen. Most contemporaries welcomed this fact; indeed it was after about 1550 that there began to develop in England that preening consciousness of the peculiar glories of English liberties.

How had it all happened? Among those observers who tried to explain, there was agreement that Christianity was primarily responsible. They thought of villenage as a mitigation of ancient bond slavery and that the continuing trend to liberty was animated, as Sir Thomas Smith said in a famous passage, by the "perswasion . . . of Christians not to make nor keepe his brother in Christ, servile, bond and underling for ever unto him, as a beast rather than as a man." They agreed also that the trend had been forwarded by the common law, in which the disposition was always, as the phrase went, *in favorem libertatis,* "in favor of liberty. . . ."

Some experiments in compulsion ran counter to the trend toward personal liberty. In 1547, shortly after the death of Henry VIII, a parliamentary statute provided that any able-bodied person adjudged a vagabond upon presentment to two justices of the peace should be branded with a "V" on the chest and made a "slave" for two years to the presenter who was urged to give "the saide Slave breade and water or small dryoucke and such refuse of meate as he shall thincke mete [and] cause the said Slave to worke by beating cheyninge or otherwise in such worke and Labor how vyle so ever it be." Masters could "putt a rynge of Iron about his Necke Arme or his Legge for a more knowledge and suretie of the keepinge of him." A runaway "slave" convicted by a court was to be branded on the cheek or forehead and adjudged "to be the saide Masters Slave for ever." These provisions reflected desperation. Fully as significant as their passage was their repeal three years later by a statute which frankly asserted in the preamble that their "extremitie" had "byn occation that they have not ben putt in ure [use]."

Englishmen generally were unwilling to submit or subscribe to such debasement. Despite a brief statutory experiment with banishment "beyond the Seas" and with judgment "perpetually to the Gallyes of this Realme" in 1598, Tudor authorities gradually hammered out the legal framework of a labor system which permitted compulsion but which did not permit so total a loss of freedom as lifetime hereditary slavery. Apprenticeship seemed to them the ideal status, for apprenticeship provided a means of regulating the economy and of guiding youth into acceptable paths of honest industry. By 1600, many writers had come to think of other kinds of bound labor as inferior forms of apprenticeship, involving less of an educative function, less permanence, and a less rigidly contractual basis. This tendency to reason from apprenticeship downward, rather than from penal service up, had the important effect of imparting some of the very strong contractualism in the master-apprentice relationship to less formal varieties of servitude. There were "indentured" servants in England prior to English settlement in America. Their written "indentures" gave visible evidence of the strong element of mutual obligation between master and servant: each retained a copy of the contract which was "indented" at the top so as to match the other.

As things turned out, it was indentured servitude which best met the requirements for settling in America. Of course there were other forms of bound labor which contributed to the process of settlement: many convicts were sent and many children abducted. Yet among all the numerous varieties and degrees of non-freedom which existed in England, there was none which could have served as a well-formed model for the chattel slavery which developed in America. This is not to say, though, that slavery was an unheard-of novelty in Tudor England. On the contrary, "bond slavery" was a memory trace of long standing. Vague and confused as the concept of slavery was in the minds of Englishmen, it possessed certain fairly consistent connotations which were to help shape English perceptions of the way Europeans should properly treat the newly discovered peoples overseas.

THE CONCEPT OF SLAVERY

At first glance, one is likely to see merely a fog of inconsistency and vagueness enveloping the terms *servant* and *slave* as they were used both in England and in seventeenth-century America. When Hamlet declaims "O what a rogue and peasant slave am I," the term seems to have a certain elasticity. When Peter Heylyn defines it in 1627 as "that ignominious word, *Slave*; whereby we use to call ignoble fellowes, and the more base sort of people," the term seems useless as a key to a specific social status. And when we find in the American colonies a reference in 1665 to "Jacob a negro slave and servant to Nathaniel Utye," it is tempting to regard slavery as having been in the first half of the seventeenth century merely a not very elevated sort of servitude.

In one sense it was, since the concept embodied in the terms *servitude, service,* and *servant* was widely embracive. *Servant* was more a generic term than *slave*. Slaves could be "servants"—as they were eventually and ironically to become in the ante-bellum South—but servants *should not* be "slaves." This injunction, which was common in England, suggests a measure of precision in the concept of slavery. In fact there was a large measure which merits closer inspection. . . .

So much was slavery a complete loss of liberty that it seemed to Englishmen somehow akin to loss of humanity. No theme was more persistent than the claim that to treat a man as a slave was to treat him as a beast. Almost half a century after Sir Thomas Smith had made this connection a Puritan divine was condemning masters who used "their servants as slaves, or rather as beasts" while Captain John Smith was moaning about being captured by the Turks and "all sold for slaves, like beasts in a market-place." No analogy could have better demonstrated how strongly Englishmen felt about total loss of personal freedom.

Certain prevalent assumptions about the origins of slavery paralleled this analogy at a different level of intellectual construction. Lawyers and divines alike assumed that slavery was impossible before the Fall, that it violated natural law, that it was instituted by positive human laws, and, more generally, that in various ways it was connected with sin. These ideas were as old as the church fathers and the Roman writers on natural law. In the social atmosphere of pre-Restoration England it was virtually inevitable that they should have been capsulated in the story of Ham. The Reverend Jeremy Taylor (an opponent of the Puritans) explained what it was "that brought servitude or slavery into the world": God had "consigned a sad example that for ever children should be afraid to dishonour their parents, and discover their nakedness, or reveal their turpitude, their follies and dishonours." Sir Edward Coke (himself scarcely a Puritan) declared, "This is assured, That Bondage or Servitude was first inflicted for dishonouring of Parents: For Cham the Father of Canaan . . . seeing the Nakedness of his Father Noah, and shewing it in Derision to his Brethren, was therefore punished in his Son Canaan with Bondage."

The great jurist wrote this in earnest, but at least he did offer another description of slavery's genesis. In it he established what was perhaps the most important and widely acknowledged attribute of slavery: at the time of the Flood "all Things were common to all," but afterward, with the emergence of private property, there "arose battles"; "then it was ordained by Constitution of Nations . . . that he that was taken in Battle should remain Bond to his taker for ever, and he to do with him, all that should come of him, his Will and Pleasure, as with his Beast, or any other Cattle, to give, or to sell, or to kill." This final power, Coke noted, had since been taken away (owing to "the Cruelty of some Lords") and placed in the hands only of kings. The animating rationale here was that captivity in war meant an end to a person's claim to life as a human being; by sparing the captive's life, the captor acquired virtually absolute power over the life of the man who had lost the power to control his own.

More than any other single quality, *captivity* differentiated slavery from servitude. Although there were other, subsidiary ways of becoming a slave, such as being born of slave parents, selling oneself into slavery, or being adjudged to slavery for crime, none of these were considered to explain the way slavery had originated. Slavery was a power relationship; servitude was a relationship of service. Men were "slaves" to the devil but "servants" of God. Men were "galley-slaves," not galley servants. Bondage had never existed in the county of Kent because Kent was "never vanquished by [William] the Conquerour, but yeelded it selfe by composition."

This tendency to equate slavery with captivity had important ramifications. Warfare was usually waged against another people; captives were usually foreigners—"strangers" as they were termed. Until the emergence of nation-states in Europe, by far the most important category of strangers was the non-Christian. International warfare seemed above all a ceaseless struggle between Christians and Turks. Slavery, therefore, frequently appeared to rest upon the "perpetual enmity" which existed between Christians on the one hand and "infidels" and "pagans" on the other. In the sixteenth and seventeenth centuries Englishmen at home could read scores of accounts concerning the miserable fate of Englishmen and other Christians taken into "captivity" by Turks and Moors and oppressed by the "verie worst manner of bondmanship and slaverie." Clearly slavery was tinged by the religious disjunction.

Just as many commentators thought that the spirit of Christianity was responsible for the demise of bondage in England, many divines distinguished between ownership of Christian and of non-Christian servants. The Reverend William Gouge referred to "such servants as being strangers were bond-slaves, over whom masters had a more absolute power than others." The Reverend Henry Smith declared, "He which counteth his servant a slave, is in error: for there is difference between beleeving servants and infidell servants." Implicit in every clerical discourse was the assumption that common brotherhood in Christ imparted a special quality to the master-servant relationship.

Slavery did not possess that quality, which made it fortunate that Englishmen did not enslave one another. As we have seen, however, Englishmen did possess a *concept* of slavery, formed by the clustering of several rough but not illogical equations. The slave was treated like a beast. Slavery was inseparable from the evil in men; it was God's punishment upon Ham's prurient disobedience. Enslavement was captivity, the loser's lot in a contest of power. Slaves were infidels or heathens.

On every count, Negroes qualified.

THE PRACTICES OF PORTINGALS AND SPANYARDS

Which is not to say that Englishmen were casting about for a people to enslave. What happened was that they found thrust before them not only instances of Negroes being taken into slavery but attractive opportunities for joining in that business. Englishmen actually were rather slow to seize these opportunities; on most of the sixteenth-century English voyages to West Africa there was no dealing in slaves. The notion that it was appropriate to do so seems to have been drawn chiefly from the example set by the Spanish and Portuguese.

Without inquiring into the reasons, it can be said that slavery had persisted since ancient times in the Iberian peninsula, that prior to the discoveries it was primarily a function of the religious wars against the Moors, that Portuguese explorers pressing down the coast in the fifteenth century captured thousands of Negroes whom they carried back to Portugal as slaves, and that after 1500, Portuguese ships began supplying the Spanish and Portuguese settlements in America with Negro slaves. By 1550 European enslavement of Negroes was more than a century old, and Negro slavery had become a fixture of the New World.

For present purposes there is no need to inquire into the precise nature of this slavery except to point out that in actual practice it did fit the English concept of bond slavery. The question which needs answering pertains to contemporary English knowledge of what was going on. And the answer may be given concisely: Englishmen had easily at hand a great deal of not very precise information.

The news that Negroes were being carried off to forced labor in America was broadcast across the pages of the Hakluyt and Purchas collections. While only one account stated explicitly that Negroes "be their slaves during their life," it was clear that the Portuguese and Spaniards treated Negroes and frequently the Indians as "slaves." This was the term customarily used by English voyagers and by translators of foreign accounts and documents. Readers of a lament about the treatment of Indians in Brazil by an unnamed Portuguese could hardly mistake learning that slavery there was a clearly defined condition: Indians held "a title of free" but were treated as "slaves, all their lives," and when masters died the poor Indians "remaine in their wils with the name of free, but bound to serve their children perpetually . . . as if they were lawful slaves." The same author objected to unjust wars mounted against Indians in "the hope of the profit that is offered them, of getting of slaves . . . to serve themselves perpetually." Repeatedly the language employed in these widely read books gave clear indication of how the Negro was involved. William Towrson was told by a Negro in 1556 "that the Portingals were bad men, and that they made them slaves, if they could take them, and would put yrons upon their legges." There were "rich trades" on that coast in Negroes "which be caried continually to the West Indies." The Portuguese in the Congo "have divers rich Commodities from this Kingdome, but the most important is every yeere about five thousand Slaves, which they transport from thence, and sell them at good round prices in . . . the West Indies." In the New World the Spaniards "buy many slaves to follow their husbandry" and had "Negros to worke in the mynes." As for the Negroes, according to an Englishman they "doe daily lie in waite to practice their deliverance out of that thraldome and bondage, that the Spaniards do keepe them in"; according to a Spanish official, "there is no trust nor confidence in any of these Negroes, and therefore we must take heede and beware of them, for they are our mortall enemies." By 1600 the European demand for slaves in Africa had altered the character of West African slavery, which for the most part had been a household institution very different from the chattel slavery practiced in America. A description of Guinea by an unnamed Dutchman explained that "in this Warre whosoever is taken Prisoner they make him a slave all his life long"; the "Kings of the Townes have many Slaves, which they buy and sell, and get much by them; and to be briefe, in those Countries there are no men to be hired to worke or goe of any errand for money, but such as are Slaves and Captives, which are to spend their dayes in slaverie. . . ."

By the end of the first quarter of the seventeenth century it had become abundantly evident in England that Negroes were being enslaved on an international scale. A century before, Leo Africanus had referred frequently to "Negro-slaves" in North Africa. By 1589 Negroes had become so preeminently "slaves" that Richard Hakluyt gratuitously referred to five Africans brought temporarily to England as "black slaves." Readers of Hakluyt, Purchas, and other popular accounts were informed that the Dutch had "Blacks (which are Slaves)" in the East Indies; that Greeks ventured "into Arabia to steale Negroes"; that the blacks of Mozambique" were frequently taken as "slaves" to India, and, according to George Sandys, that near Cairo merchants purchased "Negroes" (for "slavery") who came from the upper Nile and were "descended of *Chus,* the Sonne of cursed *Cham;* as are all of that complexion."

As suggested by Sandys's remark, an equation had developed between African Negroes and slavery. Primarily, the associations were with the Portuguese and Spanish, with captivity, with buying and selling in Guinea and in America. While the Negro's exact status in America was not entirely clear, neither was it conceived as an off-brand of apprenticeship or servitude: Hawkins assumed as his crest a "demi-Moor" (plainly Negroid) "captive and bound. . . ."

When they came to settle in America, Englishmen found that things happened to liberty, some favorable, some not. Negroes became slaves, partly because there were social and economic necessities in America which called for some sort of bound, controlled labor. The Portuguese and Spanish had set an example, which, however rough in outline, proved to be, at very least, suggestive to Englishmen. It would be surprising if there had been a clear-cut line of influence from Latin to English slavery. Elizabethans were not in the business of modeling themselves after Spaniards. Yet from about 1550, Englishmen were in such continual contact with the Spanish that they could hardly have failed to acquire the notion that Negroes could be enslaved. Precisely what slavery *meant*, of course, was a matter of English preconceptions patterning the information from overseas, but from the first, Englishmen tended to associate, in a diffuse way, Negroes with the Portuguese and Spanish. The term *negro* itself was incorporated into English from the Hispanic languages in mid-sixteenth century and *mulatto* a half century later. This is the more striking because a perfectly adequate term, identical in meaning to *negro,* already existed in English; of course *black* was used also, though not so commonly in the sixteenth century as later. . . .

ENSLAVEMENT: THE WEST INDIES

The Englishmen who settled the Caribbean colonies were not very different from those who went to Virginia, Bermuda, Maryland, or even New England. Their experience in the islands, however, was very different indeed. By 1640 there were roughly as many English in the little islands as on the American continent. A half century after the first settlements were established in the 1620's, the major islands—Barbados, St. Kitts and the other Leeward Islands—were overcrowded. Thousands of whites who had been squeezed off the land by burgeoning sugar plantations migrated to other English colonies, including much larger Jamaica which had been captured from the Spanish in 1655. Their places were taken by Negro slaves who had been shipped to the islands, particularly after 1640, to meet an insatiable demand for labor which was cheap to maintain, easy to dragoon, and simple to replace when worked to death. Negroes outnumbered whites in Barbados as early as 1660. This rapid and thorough commitment to slavery placed white settlers under an ever-present danger of slave rebellion (the first rising came in 1638 on Providence Island), and whereas in the very early years authorities had rightly been fearful of white servant revolt, by the 1670's they were casting about desperately for means to attract white servants as protection against foreign and servile attack. Negro slavery matured hothouse fashion in the islands.

This compression of development was most clearly evident in the Puritan colony on the tiny island of Providence 150 miles off the coast of Central America, first settled in 1629 though not a going concern for several years. During the brief period before the Spanish snuffed out the colony in 1641 the settlers bought so many Negroes that white men were nearly outnumbered, and in England the Providence Company, apprehensive over possible Negro uprisings (with good reason as it turned out), drew up regulations for restricting the ratio of slaves to white men, "well knowing that if all men be left at Libty to buy as they please no man will take of English servants." Not only were Negroes cheaper to maintain but it was felt that they could legitimately be treated in a different way from Englishmen—they could be held to service for life. At least this was the impression prevailing among officials of the Providence Company in London, for in 1638 they wrote Governor Nathaniel Butler and the Council, "We also think it reasonable that whereas the English servants are to answer XX [pounds of tobacco] per head the Negros being procured at Cheaper rates more easily kept as perpetuall servants should answer 40 [pounds of tobacco] per head. And the rather that the desire of English bodyes may be kept, we are depending upon them for the defense of the Island. We shall also except that Negroes performe service in the publique works in double proporcon to the English."

In Barbados this helpful idea that Negroes served for life seems to have existed even before they were purchased in large numbers. In 1627 the ship bearing the first eighty settlers captured a prize from which ten Negroes were seized, so white men and Negroes settled the island together. Any doubt which may have existed as to the appropriate status of Negroes was dispelled in 1636 when Governor Henry Hawley and the Council resolved "that *Negroes* and *Indians,* that came here to be sold, should serve for Life, unless a Contract was before made to the contrary." Europeans were not treated in this manner: in 1643 Governor Philip Bell set at liberty fifty Portuguese who had been captured in Brazil and then offered for sale to Barbadians by a Dutch ship. The Governor seems to have been shocked by the proposed sale of Christian white men. In the 1650's several observers referred to the lifetime slavery of Negroes as if it were a matter of common knowledge. "Its the Custome for a Christian servant to serve foure yeares," one wrote at the beginning of the decade, "and then enjoy his freedome; and (which hee hath dearly earned) 10£ Ster. or the value of it in goods if his Master bee soe honest as to pay it; the Negros and Indians (of which latter there are but few here) they and the generation are Slaves to their owners to perpetuity." The widely read Richard Ligon wrote in 1657: "The Iland is divided into three sorts of men, *viz*. Masters, Servants, and slaves. The slaves and their posterity, being subject to their Masters for ever, are kept and preserv'd with greater care then the servants, who are theirs but for five yeers, according to the law of the Iland." Finally, one Henry Whistler described the people of the island delightfully in 1655:

The genterey heare doth live far better than ours doue in England: thay have most of them 100 or 2 or 3 of slaves apes whou they command as they pleas: hear they may say what they have is thayer oune: and they have that Libertie of contienc which wee soe long have in England foght for: But they doue abus it. This Island is inhabited with all sortes: with English, french, Duch, Scotes, Irish, Spaniards thay being Jues: with Ingones and miserabell Negors borne to perpetuall slavery thay and thayer seed: these Negors they doue alow as many wifes as thay will have, sume will have 3 or 4, according as they find thayer bodie abell: our English heare doth think a negor child the first day it is born to be worth 05, they cost them noething the bringing up, they goe all ways naked: some planters will have 30 more or les about 4 or 5 years ould: they sele them from one to the other as we doue shepe. This Illand is the Dunghill wharone England doth cast forth its rubidg: Rodgs and hors and such like peopel are those which are genneraly Broght heare.

Dunghill or no dunghill, Barbados was treating her Negroes as slaves for life.

The rapid introduction of Negro slavery into the English islands was accomplished without leaving any permanent trace of hesitation or misgivings. This was not the case in many of the continental colonies, both because different geographic and economic conditions prevailed there and because these conditions permitted a more complete and successful transplantation of English ways and values. . . .

ENSLAVEMENT: VIRGINIA AND MARYLAND

In Virginia and Maryland the development of Negro slavery followed a very different course, for several reasons. Most obviously, geographic conditions and the intentions of the settlers quickly combined to produce a successful agricultural staple. The deep tidal rivers, the long growing season, the fertile soil, and the absence of strong communal spirit among the settlers opened the way. Ten years after settlers first landed at Jamestown they were on the way to proving, in the face of assertions to the contrary, that it was possible "to found an empire upon smoke." More than the miscellaneous productions of New England, tobacco required labor which was cheap but not temporary, mobile but not independent, and tireless rather than skilled. In the Chesapeake area more than anywhere to the northward, the shortage of labor and the abundance of land—the "frontier"— placed a premium on involuntary labor.

This need for labor played more directly upon these settlers' ideas about freedom and bondage than it did either in the West Indies or in New England. Perhaps it would be more accurate to say that settlers in Virginia (and in Maryland after settlement in 1634) made their decisions concerning Negroes while relatively virginal, relatively free from external influences and from firm preconceptions. Of all the important early English settlements, Virginia had the least contact with the Spanish, Portuguese, Dutch, and other English colonies. At the same time, the settlers of Virginia did not possess either the legal or Scriptural learning of the New England Puritans whose conception of the just war had opened the way to the enslavement of Indians. Slavery in the tobacco colonies did not begin as an adjunct of captivity; in marked contrast to the Puritan response to the Pequot War the settlers of Virginia did *not* generally react to the Indian massacre of 1622 with propositions for taking captives and selling them as "slaves." It was perhaps a correct measure of the conceptual atmosphere in Virginia that there was only one such proposition after the 1622 disaster and that that one was defective in precision as to how exactly one treated captive Indians.

In the absence, then, of these influences which obtained in other English colonies, slavery as it developed in Virginia and Maryland assumes a special interest and importance over and above the fact that Negro slavery was to become a vitally important institution there and, later, to the southwards. In the tobacco colonies it is possible to watch Negro slavery *develop,* not pop up full-grown overnight, and it is therefore possible to trace, very imperfectly, the development of the shadowy, unexamined rationale which supported it. The concept of Negro slavery there was neither borrowed from foreigners, nor extracted from books, nor invented out of whole cloth, nor extrapolated from servitude, nor generated by English reaction to Negroes as such, nor necessitated by the exigencies of the New World. Not any one of these made the Negro a slave, but all.

In rough outline, slavery's development in the tobacco colonies seems to have undergone three stages. Negroes first arrived in 1619, only a few days late for the meeting of the first representative assembly in America. John Rolfe described the event with the utmost unconcern: "About the last of August came in a dutch man of warre that sold us twenty Negars." Negroes continued to trickle in slowly for the next half century; one report in 1649 estimated that there were three hundred among Virginia's population of fifteen thousand—about 2 per cent. Long before there were more appreciable numbers, the development of slavery had, so far as we can tell, shifted gears. Prior to about 1640, there is very little evidence to show

how Negroes were treated—though we will need to return to those first twenty years in a moment. After 1640 there is mounting evidence that some Negroes were in fact being treated as slaves, at least that they were being held in hereditary lifetime service. This is to say that the twin essences of slavery—the two kinds of perpetuity—first become evident during the twenty years prior to the beginning of legal formulation. After 1660 slavery was written into statute law. Negroes began to flood into the two colonies at the end of the seventeenth century. In 1705 Virginia produced a codification of laws applying to slaves.

Concerning the first of these stages, there is only one major historical certainty, and unfortunately it is the sort which historians find hardest to bear. There simply is not enough evidence to indicate with any certainty whether Negroes were treated like white servants or not. At least we can be confident, therefore, that the two most common assertions about the first Negroes—that they were slaves and that they were servants—are *unfounded,* though not necessarily incorrect. And what of the positive evidence?

Some of the first group bore Spanish names and presumably had been baptized, which would mean they were at least nominally Christian, though of the Papist sort. They had been "sold" to the English; so had other Englishmen but not by the Dutch. Certainly these Negroes were not fully free, but many Englishmen were not. It can be said, though, that from the first in Virginia Negroes were set apart from white men by the word *Negroes.* The earliest Virginia census reports plainly distinguished Negroes from white men, often giving Negroes no personal name. in 1629 every commander of the several plantations was ordered to "take a generall muster of all the inhabitants men woemen and Children as well *Englishe* as Negroes." A distinct name is not attached to a group unless it is regarded as distinct. It seems logical to suppose that this perception of the Negro as being distinct from the Englishman must have operated to debase his status rather than to raise it, for in the absence of countervailing social factors, the need for labor in the colonies usually told in the direction of non-freedom. There were few countervailing factors present, surely, in such instances as in 1629 when a group of Negroes were brought to Virginia freshly captured from a Portuguese vessel which had snatched them from Angola a few weeks earlier. Given the context of English thought and experience sketched in this chapter, it seems probable that the Negro's status was not ever the same as that accorded the white servant. But we do not know for sure.

When the first fragmentary evidence appears about 1640 it becomes clear that *some* Negroes in both Virginia and Maryland were serving for life and some Negro children inheriting the same obligation. Not all Negroes, certainly, for Nathaniel Littleton had released a Negro named Anthony Longoe from all service whatsoever in 1635, and after the mid-1640's the court records show that other Negroes were incontestably free and were accumulating property of their own. At least one Negro freeman, Anthony Johnson, himself owned a Negro. Some Negroes served only terms of usual length, but others were held for terms far longer than custom and statute permitted with white servants. The first fairly clear indication that slavery was practiced in the tobacco colonies appears in 1639, when a Maryland statute declared that "all the Inhabitants of this Province being Christians (Slaves excepted) Shall have and enjoy all such rights liberties immunities priviledges and free customs within this Province as any naturall born subject of England." Another Maryland law passed the same year provided that "all persons being Christians (Slaves excepted)" over eighteen who were imported without indentures would serve for four years. These laws make very little sense unless the term *slaves* meant Negroes and perhaps Indians. . . .

Further evidence that some Negroes were serving for life in this period lies in the prices paid for them. In many instances the valuations placed on Negroes (in estate inventories and bills of sale) were far higher than for white servants, even those servants with full terms yet to serve. Higher prices must have meant that Negroes were more highly valued because of their greater length of service. Negro women may have been especially prized, moreover, because their progeny could also be held perpetually. In 1643, for example, William Burdett's inventory listed eight servants, with the time each had still to serve, at valuations ranging from 400 to 1,100 pounds of tobacco, while a "very anntient" Negro was valued at 3,000 and an eight-year-old Negro girl at 2,000 pounds, with no time remaining indicated for either. In the late 1650's an inventory of Thomas Ludlow's estate evaluated a white servant with six years to serve at less than an elderly Negro man and only one half of a Negro woman. Similarly, the labor owned by James Stone in 1648 was evaluated as follows:

	LB. TOBO
Thomas Groves, 4 yeares to serve	1300
Francis Bomley for 6 yeares	1500
John Thackstone for 3 yeares	1300
Susan Davis for 3 yeares	1000
Emaniell a Negro man	2000
Roger Stone 3 yeares	1300
Mingo a Negro man	2000

The 1655 inventory of Argoll Yeardley's estate provides clear evidence of a distinction between perpetual and limited service for Negroes. Under the heading "Servants" were listed "Towe Negro men, towe Negro women (their wifes) one Negro girle aged 15 yeares, Item One Negro girle aged about teen yeares and one Negro child aged about sixe moneths," valued at 12,000 pounds, and under the heading "Corne" were "Servants, towe men their tyme three months," valued at 300 pounds, and "one Negro boye ["about three yeares old"] (which by witness of his godfather) is to bee free att twenty foure yeares of age and then to have towe cowes given him," valued at 600 pounds. Besides setting a higher value on Negroes, these inventories failed to indicate the number of years they had still to serve, presumably because their service was for an unlimited time.

Where Negro women were involved, higher valuations probably reflected the facts that their issue was valuable and that they could be used for field work while white women generally were not. This latter discrimination between Negro and white women did not necessarily involve perpetual service, but it meant that Negroes were set apart in a way clearly not to their advantage. This was not the only instance in which Negroes were subjected to degrading distinctions not immediately and necessarily attached to the concept of slavery. Negroes were singled out for special treatment in several ways which suggest a generalized debasement of Negroes as a group. Significantly, the first indications of this debasement appeared at about the same time as the first indications of actual enslavement.

The distinction concerning field work is a case in point. It first appears on the written record in 1643, when Virginia almost pointedly endorsed it in a tax law. Previously, in 1629, tithable persons had been defined as "all those that worke in the ground of what qualitie or condition soever." The new law provided that *all* adult men were tithable and, in addition, *Negro* women. The same distinction was made twice again before 1660. Maryland adopted a similar policy beginning in 1654. This official discrimination between Negro and other women was made by men who were accustomed to thinking of field work as being ordinarily the work of men rather than women. As John Hammond wrote in a 1656 tract defending the tobacco colonies, servant women were not put to work in the fields but in domestic employments, "Yet som wenches that are nasty, and beastly and not fit to be so employed are put into the ground." The essentially racial character of this discrimination stood out clearly in a law passed in 1668 at the time slavery was taking shape in the statute books:

> Whereas some doubts, have arisen whether negro women set free were still to be accompted tithable according to a former act, *It is declared by this grand assembly* that negro women, though permitted to enjoy their Freedome yet ought not in all respects to be admitted to a full fruition of the exemptions and impunities of the English, and are still lyable to payment of taxes.

Virginia law set Negroes apart from all other groups in a second way by denying them the important right and obligation to bear arms. Few restraints could indicate more clearly the denial to Negroes of membership in the white community. This first foreshadowing of the slave codes came in 1640, at just the time when other indications first appeared that Negroes were subject to special treatment.

Finally, an even more compelling sense of the separateness of Negroes was revealed in early reactions to sexual union between the races. Prior to 1660 the evidence concerning these reactions is equivocal, and it is not possible to tell whether repugnance for intermixture preceded legislative enactment of slavery . . . . In the early 1660's when slavery was gaining statutory recognition, the assemblies acted with full-throated indignation against miscegenation. These acts aimed at more than merely avoiding confusion of status. In 1662 Virginia declared that "if any christian shall commit Fornication with a negro man or woman, hee or shee soe offending" should pay double the usual fine. (The next year Bermuda prohibited all sexual relations between whites and Negroes.) Two years later Maryland banned interracial marriages: "forasmuch as divers freeborne English women forgetfull of their free Condicion and to the disgrace of our Nation doe intermarry with Negro Slaves by which alsoe divers suites may arise touching the Issue of such woemen and a great damage doth befall the Masters of such Negros for prevention whereof for deterring such freeborne women from such shamefull Matches," strong language indeed if "divers suites" had been the only problem. A Maryland act of 1681 described marriages of white women with Negroes as, among other things, "always to the Satisfaccion of theire Lascivious and Lustfull desires, and to the disgrace not only of the English butt allso of many other Christian Nations." When Virginia finally prohibited all interracial liaisons in 1691, the Assembly vigorously denounced miscegenation and its fruits as "that abominable mixture and spurious issue."

From the surviving evidence, it appears that outright enslavement and these other forms of debasement appeared at about the same time in Maryland and Virginia. Indications of perpetual service, the very nub of slavery, coincided with indications that English settlers discriminated against Negro women, withheld arms from Negroes, and—though the timing is far less certain—reacted unfavorably to interracial sexual union. The coincidence suggests a mutual relationship between slavery and unfavorable assessment of Negroes. Rather than slavery causing "prejudice," or vice versa, they seem rather to have generated each other. Both were, after all, twin aspects of a general debasement of the Negro. Slavery and "prejudice" may have been equally cause and effect, continuously reacting upon each other, dynamically joining hands to hustle the Negro down the road to complete degradation. Much more than with the other English colonies, where the enslavement of Negroes was to some extent a borrowed practice, the available evidence for Maryland and Virginia points to less borrowing and to this kind of process: a mutually interactive growth of slavery and unfavorable assessment, with no cause for either which did not cause the other as well. If slavery caused prejudice, then invidious distinctions concerning working in the fields, bearing arms, and sexual union should have appeared *after* slavery's firm establishment. If prejudice caused slavery, then one would expect to find these lesser discriminations preceding the greater discrimination of outright enslavement. Taken as a whole, the evidence reveals a process of debasement of which hereditary lifetime service was an important but not the only part.

White servants did not suffer this debasement. Rather, their position improved, partly for the reason that they were not Negroes. By the early 1660's white men were loudly protesting against being made "slaves" in terms which strongly suggest that they considered slavery not as wrong but as inapplicable to themselves. The father of a Maryland apprentice petitioned in 1663 that "he Craves that his daughter may not be made a Slave a tearme soe Scandalous that if admitted to be the Condicon or tytle of the Apprentices in this Province will be soe distructive as noe free borne Christians will ever be induced to come over servants." An Irish youth complained to a Maryland court in 1661 that he had been kidnapped and forced to sign for fifteen years, that he had already served six and a half years and was now twenty-one, and that eight and a half more years of service was "contrary to the lawes of God and man that a Christian Subject should be made a Slave." (The jury blandly compromised the dispute by deciding that he should serve only until age twenty-one, but that he was now only nineteen). Free Negro servants were generally increasingly less able to defend themselves against this insidious kind of encroachment. Increasingly, white men were more clearly free because Negroes had become so clearly slave.

Certainly it was the case in Maryland and Virginia that the legal enactment of Negro slavery followed social practice, rather than vice versa, and also that the assemblies were slower than in other English colonies to declare how Negroes could or should be treated. These two patterns in themselves suggest that slavery was less a matter of previous conception or external example in Maryland and Virginia than elsewhere. . . .

By about 1700 the slave ships began spilling forth their black cargoes in greater and greater numbers. By that time, racial slavery and the necessary police powers had been written into law. By that time, too, slavery had lost all resemblance to a perpetual and hereditary version of English servitude, though service for life still seemed to contemporaries its most essential feature. In the last quarter of the seventeenth century the trend was to treat Negroes more like property and less like men, to send them to the fields at younger ages, to deny them automatic existence as inherent members of the community, to tighten the bonds on their personal and civil freedom, and correspondingly to loosen the traditional restraints on the master's freedom to deal with his human property as he saw fit. In 1705 Virginia gathered up the random statutes of a whole generation and baled them into a "slave code" which would not have been out of place in the nineteenth century.

ENSLAVEMENT: NEW YORK AND THE CAROLINAS

While the development of Negro slavery followed a different pattern in the tobacco colonies than in New England, and while, indeed, there was distinctive patterns of development in each of the English colonies, there were also factors which made for an underlying similarity in the slavery which emerged. The universal need for labor, the common cultural background and acceptance of English law, and the increasing contacts among the various colonies all worked eventually to make Negro slavery a roughly similar institution from one colony to the next, especially where economic and demographic conditions did not differ markedly. In each of the colonies which England acquired after the Restoration of Charles II, slavery developed in a distinctive fashion, yet by 1700 New York's slavery was much like New England's and Carolina's much like Virginia's.

In 1664, at about the time slavery was being written into law in the tobacco colonies, the English took over a Dutch colony which had been in existence for over forty years. New York was already a hodgepodge of nationalities—Dutch, English, Walloons, French, Negroes and others. The status of Negroes under Dutch rule lies enshrouded in the same sort of fog which envelops the English colonies. It is clear, however, that the early and extensive Dutch experience in the international slave trade must have had some influence on the treatment of Negroes in New Amsterdam. There were Negroes in the colony as early as 1628. In that year (perhaps by coincidence) came the colony's first minister, the Reverend Jonas Michaëlius, who had previously been on the West African coast. Yet the first clearly indicated status of any Negroes was freedom, in the 1640's; indeed it remains possible that Negroes were not slaves in New Netherland until the 1650's. In 1650 two sparring pamphleteers disagreed as to whether some Negroes were actually slaves. Within a very few years, though, the records show indisputably that certain colonists were actively interested in the African slave trade. Possibly this interest may have been stimulated by Jacob Steendam, a poet who had resided at a Dutch fort in Guinea before coming to New Amsterdam about 1652.

So far as their response to Negroes is concerned, the cultural background of Dutchmen was not very different from Englishmen. They shared a similar commercial orientation and large portions of religious and intellectual heritage. One of Steendam's poems, addressed to his legitimate mulatto son in Africa, lamented (in translation):

Since two bloods course within your veins,
Both Ham's and Japhet's intermingling;
One race forever doomed to serve,
The other bearing freedom's likeness.

Certainly there is no evidence of friction concerning slave-owning when Englishmen took over the Dutch colony in 1664. The first English code (the "Duke's Laws"), adopted in 1665 by an assemblage composed largely of New

Englanders who had migrated to Long Island and presided over by the newly appointed English governor, specifically recognized the practice of service for life in a proviso patterned after the Massachusetts Bay law of 1641. During the remaining years of the century Negro slavery flourished, and New York eventually came to have a higher proportion of Negroes than any other colony north of Delaware. In New York more than anywhere else, Negro slavery seems to have grown Topsy fashion.

By contrast, in the Carolinas Negro slavery was deliberately planted and cultivated. In the 1660's a group of enterprising gentlemen in Barbados, well acquainted with perpetual slavery, proposed removal with some Negroes to the new mainland colony; their agreement with the proprietors in England clearly distinguished between white servants and Negro slaves. Barbadian influence remained strong in South Carolina throughout the seventeenth century. The establishment of slavery in the Carolinas was the more easily accomplished because after 1660 traditional controls over master-servant relations were breaking down rapidly in England itself. Since the state in England was abdicating some of its traditional responsibilities for overseeing the relationship between landlords and tenants at home, it felt little solicitude for the relations between planters and Negroes in far-off plantations. Besides, a good supply of sugar was enough to bury any questions about its production. It was a telling measure of how far this process had advanced in the English-speaking world that the famous Fundamental Constitutions of Carolina (1669) should have granted each freeman of the colony "absolute power and authority over his negro slaves, of what opinion or religion soever." English civil authorities offered little or no resistance to the growth of this new idea of uncontrolled personal dominion in the colonies; they knew perfectly well what was going on and were inclined to welcome it, for, as the Council for Foreign Plantations exclaimed happily in 1664, "Blacks [are] the most useful appurtenances of a Plantation and perpetual servants." For their part, the planters demanded that their legislative assemblies regulate Negro slavery, but what they wanted and got was unfettering of their personal power over their slaves and the force of the state to back it up. In the 1690's the South Carolina Assembly borrowed from the already mature slave code of Barbados in an effort to maintain control over the growing masses of slaves. Negroes were given virtually none of the protections accorded white servants, protections which were in fact designed to encourage immigration of white men to counterbalance the influx of Negroes. A requirement that "all slaves shall have convenient clothes, once every year," the only right accorded slaves by an act of 1690, was dropped in 1696. Perhaps it would have comforted slaves had they known that anyone killing a slave "cruelly or willfully" (death or dismemberment during punishment specifically expected) was liable to a fine of five hundred pounds. By the end of the seventeenth century the development of rice plantations and the Barbadian example had combined to yield in South Carolina the most rigorous deprivation of freedom to exist in institutionalized form anywhere in the English continental colonies.

THE UN-ENGLISH: SCOTS, IRISH, AND INDIANS

In the minds of overseas Englishmen, slavery, the new tyranny, did not apply to any Europeans. Something about Negroes, and to lesser extent Indians, set them apart for drastic exploitation, oppression, and degradation. In order to discover why, it is useful to turn the problem inside out, to inquire why Englishmen in America did not treat any other peoples like Negroes. It is especially revealing to see how English settlers looked upon the Scotch (as they frequently called them) and the Irish, whom they often had opportunity and "reason" to enslave, and upon the Indians, whom they enslaved, though only, as it were, casually.

In the early years Englishmen treated the increasingly numerous settlers from other European countries, especially Scottish and Irish servants, with condescension and frequently with exploitive brutality. Englishmen seemed to regard their colonies as exclusively *English* preserves and to wish to protect English persons especially from the exploitation which inevitably accompanied settlement in the New World. In Barbados, for example, the assembly in 1661 denounced the kidnapping of youngsters for service in the colony in a law which applied only to "Children of the *English* Nation." In 1650 Connecticut provided that debtors were not to "bee sould to any but of the English Nation. . . ."

As time went on Englishmen began to absorb the idea that their settlements in America were not going to remain exclusively English preserves. In 1671 Virginia began encouraging naturalization of legal aliens, so that they might enjoy "all such liberties, priviledges, immunities whatsoever, as a naturall borne Englishman is capable of," and Maryland accomplished the same end with private naturalization acts that frequently included a potpourri of French, Dutch, Swiss, Swedes, and so forth.

The necessity of peopling the colonies transformed the long-standing urge to discriminate among non-English peoples into a necessity. Which of the non-English were sufficiently different and foreign to warrant treating as "perpetual servants"? The need to answer this question did not mean, of course, that upon arrival in America the colonists immediately jettisoned their sense of distance from those persons they did not actually enslave. They discriminated against Welshmen and Scotsmen who, while admittedly "the best servants," were typically the servants of Englishmen. There was a considerably stronger tendency to discriminate against Papist Irishmen, those "worst" servants, but never to make slaves of them. And here lay the crucial difference. Even the Scottish prisoners taken by Cromwell at Worcester and Dunbar—captives in a just war!—were never treated as slaves in England or the colonies. Certainly the lot of those sent to Barbados was miserable, but it was a different lot from the African slave's. In New England they were quickly accommodated to the prevailing labor system, which was servitude. As the Reverend Mr. Cotton of the Massachusetts Bay described the situation to Oliver Cromwell in 1651,

> The Scots, whom God delivered into you hand at Dunbarre, and whereof sundry were sent hither, we have been desirous (as we could) to make their yoke easy. Such as were sick of the scurvy or other diseases have not wanted physick and chyrurgery. They have not been sold for slaves to perpetuall servitude, but for 6 or 7 or 8 yeares, as we do our owne; and he that bought the most of them (I heare) buildeth houses for them, for every 4 an house, layeth some acres of ground thereto, which he giveth them as their owne, requiring 3 dayes in the weeke to worke for him (by turnes) and 4 days for themselves, and promisteth, as soone as they can repay him the money he layed out for them, he will set them at liberty.

Here was the nub: captive Scots were men "as our owne." Negroes were not. They were almost hopelessly far from being of the English nation. As the Bermuda legislature proclaimed in 1663, even such Negroes "as count themselves

Free because no p.ticler masters claymeth their services, in our judgments are not Free to all nationall privileges."

Indians too seemed radically different from Englishmen, far more so than any Europeans. They were enslaved, like Negroes, and so fell on the losing side of a crucial dividing line. It is easy to see why: whether considered in terms of complexion, religion, nationality, savagery, bestiality, or geographical location, Indians were more like Negroes than like Englishmen. Given this resemblance the essential problem becomes why Indian slavery never became an important institution in the colonies. Why did Indian slavery remain numerically insignificant and typically incidental in character? Why were Indian slaves valued at much lower prices than Negroes? Why were Indians, as a kind of people, treated like Negroes and yet at the same time very differently?

Certain obvious factors made for important differentiations in the minds of the English colonists. As was the case with first confrontations in America and Africa, the different contexts of confrontation made Englishmen more interested in converting and civilizing Indians than Negroes. That this campaign in America too frequently degenerated into military campaigns of extermination did nothing to eradicate the initial distinction. Entirely apart from English intentions, the culture of the American Indians probably meant that they were less readily enslavable than Africans. By comparison, they were less used to settled agriculture, and their own variety of slavery was probably even less similar to the chattel slavery which Englishmen practiced in America than was the domestic and political slavery of the West African cultures. But it was the transformation of English intentions in the wilderness which counted most heavily in the long run. The Bible and the treaty so often gave way to the clash of flintlock and tomahawk. The colonists' perceptions of the Indians came to be organized not only in pulpits and printshops but at the bloody cutting edge of the English thrust into the Indians' lands. Thus the most pressing and mundane circumstances worked to make Indians seem very different from Negroes. In the early years especially, Indians were in a position to mount murderous reprisals upon the English settlers, while the few scattered Negroes were not. When English-Indian relations did not turn upon sheer power they rested on diplomacy. In many instances the colonists took assiduous precautions to prevent abuse of Indians belonging to friendly tribes. Most of the Indians enslaved by the English had their own tribal enemies to thank. It became a common practice to ship Indian slaves to the West Indies where they could be exchanged for slaves who had no compatriots lurking on the outskirts of English settlements. In contrast, Negroes presented much less of a threat—at first.

Equally important, Negroes had to be dealt with as individuals—with supremely impartial anonymity, to be sure—rather than as nations. Englishmen wanted and had to live with their Negroes, as it were, side by side. Accordingly their impressions of Negroes were forged in the heat of continual, inescapable personal contacts. There were few pressures urging Englishmen to treat Indians as integral constituents in their society, which Negroes were whether Englishmen liked or not. At a distance the Indian could be viewed with greater detachment and his characteristics acknowledged and approached more coolly and more rationally. At a distance too, Indians could retain the quality of nationality, a quality which Englishmen admired in themselves and expected in other peoples. Under contrasting circumstances in America, the Negro nations tended to become Negro people.

Here lay the rudiments of certain shadowy but persistent themes in what turned out to be a multi-racial nation. Americans came to impute to the braves of the Indian "nations" an ungovernable individuality (which was perhaps not merited in such exaggerated degree) and at the same time to impart to Negroes all the qualities of an eminently governable sub-nation, in which African tribal distinctions were assumed to be of no consequence and individuality unaspired to. More immediately, the two more primitive peoples rapidly came to serve as two fixed points from which English setlers could triangulate their own position in America; the separate meanings of *Indian* and *Negro* helped define the meaning of living in America. The Indian became for Americans a symbol of their American experience; it was no mere luck of the toss that placed the profile of an American Indian rather than an American Negro on the famous old five-cent piece. Confronting the Indian in America was a testing experience, common to all the colonies. Conquering the Indian symbolized and personified the conquest of the American difficulties, the surmounting of the wilderness. To push back the Indian was to prove the worth of one's own mission, to make straight in the desert a highway for civilization. With the Negro it was utterly different.

RACIAL SLAVERY: FROM REASONS TO RATIONALE

And *difference,* surely, was the indispensable key to the degradation of Negroes in English America. In scanning the problem of *why* Negroes were enslaved in America, certain constant elements in a complex situation can be readily, if roughly, identified. It may be taken as given that there would have been no enslavement without economic need, that is, without persistent demand for labor in underpopulated colonies. Of crucial importance, too, was the fact that for cultural reasons Negroes were relatively helpless in the face of European aggressiveness and technology. In themselves, however, these two elements will not explain the enslavement of Indians and Negroes. The pressing exigency in America was labor, and Irish and English servants were available. Most of them would have been helpless to ward off outright enslavement if their masters had thought themselves privileged and able to enslave them. As a group, though, masters did not think themselves so empowered. Only with Indians and Negroes did Englishmen attempt so radical a deprivation of liberty—which brings the matter abruptly to the most difficult and imponderable question of all: what was it about Indians and Negroes which set them apart, which rendered them *different* from Englishmen, which made them special candidates for degradation?

To ask such questions is to inquire into the *content* of English attitudes, and unfortunately there is little evidence with which to build an answer. It may be said, however, that the heathen condition of the Negroes seemed of considerable importance to English settlers in America—more so than to English voyagers upon the coasts of Africa—and that heathenism was associated in some settlers' minds with the condition of slavery. This is not to say that the colonists enslaved Negroes because they were heathens. The most clear-cut positive trace of such reasoning was probably unique and certainly far from being a forceful statement: in 1660 John Hathorne declared, before a Massachusetts court in partial support of his contention that an Indian girl should not be compelled to return to her master, that "first the law is undeniable that the indian may have the same distribusion of Justice with our selves: ther is as I humbly conceive not the same argument as amongst the negroes[,] for the light of the gospell is a begineing to appeare amongst them—that is the indians."

The importance and persistence of the tradition which attached slavery to heathenism did not become evident in any positive assertions that heathens might be enslaved. It was not until the period of legal establishment of slavery after 1660 that the tradition became manifest at all, and even then there was no effort to place heathenism and slavery on a one-for-one relationship. Virginia's second statutory definition of a slave (1682), for example, awkwardly attempted to rest enslavement on religious difference while excluding from possible enslavement all heathens who were not Indian or Negro. Despite such logical difficulties, the old European equation of slavery and religious difference did not rapidly vanish in America, for it cropped up repeatedly after 1660 in assertions that slaves by becoming Christian did not automatically become free. By about the end of the seventeenth century, Maryland, New York, Virginia, North and South Carolina, and New Jersey had all passed laws reassuring masters that conversion of their slaves did not necessitate manumission. These acts were passed in response to occasional pleas that Christianity created a claim to freedom and to much more frequent assertions by men interested in converting Negroes that nothing could be accomplished if masters thought their slaves were about to be snatched from them by meddling missionaries. This decision that the slave's religious condition had no relevance to his status as a slave (the only one possible if an already valuable economic institution was to be retained) strongly suggests that heathenism was an important component in the colonists' initial reaction to Negroes early in the century.

Yet its importance can easily be overstressed. For one thing, some of the first Negroes in Virginia had been baptized before arrival. In the early years others were baptized in various colonies and became more than nominally Christian; a Negro woman joined the church in Dorchester, Massachusetts, as a full member in 1641. With some Negroes becoming Christian and others not, there might have developed a caste differentiation along religious lines, yet there is no evidence to suggest that the colonists distinguished consistently between the Negroes they converted and those they did not. It was racial, not religious, slavery which developed in America.

Still, in the early years, the English settlers most frequently contrasted themselves with Negroes by the term *Christian,* though they also sometimes described themselves as *English;* here the explicit religious distinction would seem to have lain at the core of English reaction. Yet the concept embodied by the term *Christian* embraced so much more meaning than was contained in specific doctrinal affirmations that it is scarcely possible to assume on the basis of this linguistic contrast that the colonists set Negroes apart because they were heathen. The historical experience of the English people in the sixteenth century had made for fusion of religion and nationality; the qualities of being English and Christian had become so inseparably blended that it seemed perfectly consistent to the Virginia Assembly in 1670 to declare that "noe negroe or Indian though baptised and enjoyned their owne Freedome shall be capable of any such purchase of christians, but yet not debarred from buying any of their owne nation." Similarly, an order of the Virginia Assembly in 1662 revealed a well-knit sense of self-identity of which Englishness and Christianity were interrelated parts: "METAPPIN a Powhatan Indian being sold for life time to one Elizabeth Short by the king of Wainoake Indians who had no power to sell him being of another nation, *it is ordered* that the said Indian be free, he speaking perfectly the English tongue and desiring baptism."

From the first, then, vis-à-vis the Negro the concept embedded in the term

Christian seems to have conveyed much of the idea and feeling of *we* as against *they:* to be Christian was to be civilized rather than barbarous, English rather than African, white rather than black. The term *Christian* itself proved to have remarkable elasticity, for by the end of the seventeenth century it was being used to define a species of slavery which had altogether lost any connection with explicit religious difference. In the Virginia code of 1705, for example, the term sounded much more like a definition of race than of religion: "And for a further christian care and usage of all christian servants, *Be it also enacted, by the authority aforesaid, and it is hereby enacted.* That no negroes, mulattos, or Indians, although christians, or Jews, Moors, Mahometans, or other infidels, shall, at any time, purchase any christian servant, nor any other, except of their own complexion, or such as are declared slaves by this act." By this time "Christianity" had somehow become intimately and explicitly linked with "complexion." The 1705 statute declared "That all servants imported and brought into this country, by sea or land, who were not christians in their native country, (except Turks and Moors in amity with her majesty, and others that can make due proof of their being free in England, or any other christian country, before they were shipped, in order to transportation hither) shall be accounted and be slaves, and as such be here bought and sold notwithstanding a conversion to christianity afterwards." As late as 1753 the Virginia slave code anachronistically defined slavery in terms of religion when everyone knew that slavery had for generations been based on the racial and not the religious difference.

It is worth making still closer scrutiny of the terminology which Englishmen employed when referring both to themselves and to the two peoples they enslaved, for this terminology affords the best single means of probing the content of their sense of difference. The terms *Indian* and *Negro* were both borrowed from the Hispanic languages, the one originally deriving from (mistaken) geographical locality and the other from human complexion. When referring to the Indians the English colonists either used that proper name or called them *savages,* a term which reflected primarily their view of Indians as uncivilized, or occasionally (in Maryland especially) *pagans,* which gave more explicit expression to the missionary urge. When they had reference to Indians the colonists occasionally spoke of themselves as *Christians* but after the early years almost always as *English.*

In significant contrast, the colonists referred to *Negroes* and by the eighteenth century to *blacks* and to *Africans,* but almost never to Negro *heathens* or *pagans* or *savages.* Most suggestive of all, there seems to have been something of a shift during the seventeenth century in the terminology which Englishmen in the colonies applied to themselves. From the initially most common term *Christian,* at mid-century there was a marked drift toward *English* and *free.* After about 1680, taking the colonies as a whole, a new term appeared—*white.*

So far as the weight of analysis may be imposed upon such terms, diminishing reliance upon *Christian* suggests a gradual muting of the specifically religious element in the Christian-Negro disjunction in favor of secular nationality: Negroes were, in 1667, "not in all respects to be admitted to a full fruition of the exemptions and impunities of the English." As time went on, as some Negroes became assimilated to the English colonial culture, as more "raw Africans" arrived, and as increasing numbers of non-English Europeans were attracted to the colonies, the colonists turned increasingly to the striking physiognomic difference. By 1676 it was possible in Virginia to assail a man for "eclipsing" himself in the "darke imbraces of a Blackamoore" as if "Buty consisted all together in the Antiphety of Complections." In Maryland a revised law prohibiting miscegenation (1692) retained *white* and *English* but dropped the term *Christian*—a symptomatic modification. As early as 1664 a Bermuda statute (aimed, ironically, at protecting Negroes from brutal abandonment) required that the "last Master" of senile Negroes "provide for them such accomodations as shall be convenient for Creatures of that hue and colour until their death." By the end of the seventeenth century dark complexion had become an independent rationale for enslavement: in 1709 Samuel Sewall noted in his diary that a "Spaniard" had petitioned the Massachusetts Council for freedom but that "Capt. Teat alledg'd that all of that Color were Slaves." Here was a barrier between "we" and "they" which was visible and permanent: the Negro could not become a white man. Not, at least, as yet.

What had occurred was not a change in the justification of slavery from religion to race. No such justifications were made. There seems to have been, within the unarticulated concept of the Negro as a different sort of person, a subtle but highly significant shift in emphasis. Consciousness of the Negro's heathenism remained through the eighteenth and into the nineteenth and even the twentieth century, and an awarenss, at very least, of his different appearance was present from the beginning. The shift was an alteration in emphasis within a single concept of difference rather than a development of a novel conceptualization. The amorphousness and subtlety of such a change is evident, for instance, in the famous tract, *The Negro's and Indians Advocate,* published in 1680 by the Reverend Morgan Godwyn. Baffled and frustrated by the disinterest of planters in converting their slaves, Godwyn declared at one point that "their *Complexion,* which being most obvious to the sight, by which the *Notion* of things doth seem to be most certainly conveyed to the Understanding, is apt to make no *slight* impressions upon rude Minds, already prepared to admit of any thing for *Truth* which shall make for Interest." Altering his emphasis a few pages later, Godwyn complained that "these two words, *Negro* and *Slave*" are "by custom grown Homogeneous and Convertible; even as *Negro* and *Christian, Englishman* and *Heathen,* are by the like corrupt Custom and Partiality made Opposites." Most arresting of all, throughout the colonies the terms *Christian, free, English,* and *white* were for many years employed indiscriminately as metonyms. A Maryland law of 1681 used all four terms in one short paragraph!

Whatever the limitations of terminology as an index to thought and feeling, it seems likely that the colonists' initial sense of difference from the Negro was founded not on a single characteristic but on a congeries of qualities which, taken as a whole, seemed to set the Negro apart. Virtually every quality in the Negro invited pejorative feelings. What may have been his two most striking characteristics, his heathenism and his appearance, were probably prerequisite to his complete debasement. His heathensim alone could never have led to permanent enslavement since conversion easily wiped out that failing. If his appearance, his racial characteristics, meant nothing to the English settlers, it is difficult to see how slavery based on race ever emerged, how the concept of complexion as the mark of slavery ever entered the colonists' minds. Even if the colonists were most unfavorably struck by the Negro's color, though, blackness itself did not urge the complete debasement of slavery. Other qualities—the utter strangeness of his language, gestures, eating habits, and so on—certainly must have contributed to the colonists' sense that he was very different, perhaps disturbingly so. In Africa these qualities had for Englishmen added up to *savagery;* they were major components in that sense of *difference* which provided the mental margin absolutely requisite for placing the European on the deck of the slave ship and the Negro in the hold.

The available evidence (what little there is) suggests that for Englishmen settling in America, the specific religious difference was initially of greater importance than color, certainly of much greater relative importance than for the Englishmen who confronted Negroes in their African homeland. Perhaps Englishmen in Virginia, living uncomfortably close to nature under a hot sun and in almost daily contact with tawny Indians, found the Negro's color less arresting than they might have in other circumstances. Perhaps, too, these first Virginians sensed how inadequately they had reconstructed the institutions and practices of Christian piety in the wilderness; they would perhaps appear less as failures to themselves in this respect if compared to persons who as Christians were *totally* defective. In this connection they may be compared to their brethren in New England, where godliness appeared (at first) triumphantly to hold full sway; in New England there was distinctly less contrasting of Negroes on the basis of the religious disjunction and much more militant discussion of just wars. Perhaps, though, the Jamestown settlers were told in 1619 by the Dutch shipmaster that these "negars" were heathens and could be treated as such. We do not know. The available data will not bear all the weight that the really crucial questions impose.

Of course once the cycle of degradation was fully under way, once slavery and racial discrimination were completely linked together, once the engine of oppression was in full operation, then there is no need to plead *ignoramus*. By the end of the seventeenth century in all the colonies of the English empire there was chattel racial slavery of a kind which would have seemed familiar to men living in the nineteenth century. No Elizabethan Englishman would have found it familiar, though certain strands of thought and feeling in Elizabethan England had intertwined with reports about the Spanish and Portuguese to engender a willingness on the part of English settlers in the New World to treat some men as suitable for private exploitation. During the seventeenth century New World conditions had exploited this predisposition and vastly enlarged it, so much so that English colonials of the eighteenth century were faced with full-blown slavery—something they thought of not as an institution but as a host of ever-present problems, dangers, and opportunities.

12. Black Resistance: The Stono Uprising and Its Consequences

Peter H. Wood

Surprisingly, it has only been in the last few decades that historians have tried to assess the ways in which black Americans adjusted and responded to the institution of chattel slavery. No one has more ably performed that task for the colonial period than Peter H. Wood (b. 1943) of Duke University. In his study of blacks in prerevolutionary South Carolina, he carefully pieces together the fragmentary evidence for a full-scale portrait of the adjustment and resistance process. Pointing out that neither docile nor rebellious behavior—the "Sambo" and "Nat" literary images of nineteenth-century authors—will explain the full range of responses, Wood suggests that each slave reacted in a variety of fashions, depending upon particular circumstances. As a result, it is possible to posit a full continuum of slave behavior.

South Carolina appeared as a New World English colony somewhat later in time than Virginia or Maryland. From shaky beginnings in the 1660s and 1670s, it developed rapidly after 1700 because of booming rice and indigo production. In this selection from *Black Majority,* Professor Wood concentrates on the period after 1700 when white planters imported huge numbers of Africans, numbers which quickly outdistanced the white population. Especially heavy importations during the 1730s helped to set the stage for the Stono Uprising, an example of the most feared form of slave resistance. What does the Stono Uprising tell us about the overall nature and forms of black resistance? What factors, including population demographics and dates of arrival of black Carolinians, were most important in precipitating the crisis? What were the effects? How might the effects further explain, beyond attitudes of prejudice, the process of degradation for black Americans in colonial times?

It is by no means paradoxical that increasingly overt white controls met with increasingly forceful black resistance. The stakes for Negroes were simply rising higher and the choices becoming more hopelessly difficult. As the individual and collective tensions felt by black slaves mounted, they continued to confront the immediate daily questions of whether to accept or deny, submit or resist, remain or flee. Given their diversity of background and experience, it is not surprising that slaves responded to these pressures in a wide variety of ways. To separate

Source: From Peter H. Wood, *Black Majority: Negroes in South Carolina from 1670 through the Stono Rebellion* (New York: Alfred A. Knopf, Inc., 1974), pp. 285–288, 301–304, 308–326. Footnotes omitted. Reprinted by permission of Random House, Inc.

their reactions into docility on the one hand and rebellion on the other, as has occasionally been done, is to underestimate the complex nature of the contradictions each Negro felt in the face of new provocations and new penalties. It is more realistic to think in terms of a spectrum of response, ranging from complete submission to total resistance, along which any given individual could be located at a given time.

As in any situation overladen with contradictory pulls, there were those few persons who could not be located on such a spectrum at all; that is, their personalities "dis-integrated" in the face of conflicting pressures—internal and external—and their responses became unpredictable even to themselves. The Negro Act of 1751 made provision for local parishes to relieve poorer masters of the cost of confining and maintaining "slaves that may become lunatic." This category of individuals is not easy to define, for mental illness, like physical illness, became an element in the incessant game of deception developing between masters and slaves; Negroes pretended outright insanity upon occasion, and owners readily called such bluffs, perhaps more frequently than they occurred. Deception aside, it is no easy matter to define rational behavior within an arbitrary social system. Certain acts of resistance . . ., such as appropriating goods and running away, usually involved prior calculation by their very nature, as did poisoning, arson, and conspiracy. . . . Many other actions represented impromptu responses to trying situations, but even reactions which seemed most irrational in terms of straightforward appearances and consequences rested upon a rational appraisal of the slave environment.

At one end of the spectrum of individual resistance were the extreme incidents of physical violence. There are examples of slaves who, out of desperation, fury, or premeditation, lashed out against a white despite the consequences. Jemmy, a slave of Capt. Elias Ball, was sentenced to death in 1724 "for striking and wounding one Andrew Songster." The master salvaged the slave's life and his own investment by promising to deport Jemmy forever within two months. For others who vented individual aggression there was no such reprieve. In August 1733 the *Gazette* reported tersely: "a Negro Man belonging to Thomas Fleming of Charlestown, took an Opportunity, and kill'd the Overseer with an Axe. He was hang'd for the same yesterday." An issue during 1742 noted: "Thursday last a Negro Fellow belonging to Mr. Chessman, was brought to Town, tried, condemn'd and hang'd, for attempting to murder a white lad."

Such explosions of rage were almost always suicidal, and the mass of the Negro population cultivated strict internal constraints as a means of preservation against external white controls. (The fact that whites accepted so thoroughly the image of a carefree and heedless black personality is in part a testimony to the degree to which black slaves learned the necessity of holding other emotional responses in outward check.) This essential lesson of control, passed on from one generation to the next, was learned by early immigrants through a painful process of trial and error. Those newcomers whose resistance was most overt were perceived to be the least likely to survive, so there ensued a process of conscious or unconscious experimentation (called "seasoning" or "breaking" by the whites) in which Africans calculated the forms and degrees of resistance which were most possible.

Under constant testing, patterns of slave resistance evolved rapidly, and many of the most effective means were found to fall at the low (or invisible) end of the spectrum. For example, for those who spoke English, in whatever dialect, verbal insolence became a consistent means of resistance. Cleverly handled, it allowed slaves a way to assert themselves and downgrade their masters without committing a crime. All parties were aware of the subversive potential of words (along with styles of dress and bearing), as the thrust of the traditional term "uppity" implies, and it may be that both the black use of this approach and the white perception of it increased as tensions grew. In 1737 the Assembly debated whether the patrols should have the right "to kill any resisting or saucy Slave," and in 1741 the Clerk of the Market proposed that "if any Slave should in Time of Market behave him or herself in any insolent abusive Manner, he or she should be sent to the Work-house, and there suffer corporal Punishment."

At the same time traits of slowness, carelessness, and literalmindedness were artfully cultivated, helping to disguise countless acts of willful subterfuge as inadvertent mistakes. To the benefit of the slave and the frustration of the historian, such subversion was always difficult to assess, yet considerable thought has now been given to these subtle forms of opposition. Three other patterns of resistance—poisoning, arson, and conspiracy—were less subtle and more damaging, and each tactic aroused white fears which sometimes far exceeded the actual threat. . . .

The thought that newcomers from Africa were the slaves most likely to rebel does not appear to have been idle speculation, for the late 1730s, a time of conspicuous unrest, was also a time of massive importation. In fact, at no earlier or later date did recently arrived Africans (whom we might arbitrarily define as all those slave immigrants who had been in the colony less than a decade) comprise such a large proportion of South Carolina's Negro population. By 1740 the black inhabitants of the colony numbered roughly 39,000. During the preceding decade more than 20,000 slaves had been imported from Africa. Since there is little evidence that mortality was disproportionately high among newcomers, this means that by the end of the 1730s fully half of the colony's Negroes had lived in the New World less than ten years. The proportion had been growing steadily. In 1720 fewer than 5 per cent of black adults had been there less than a decade (and many of these had spent time in the West Indies); by 1730 roughly 40 per cent were such recent arrivals. Heavy importation and low natural increase sent the figure over 50 per cent by 1740, but it dropped sharply during the nearly total embargo of the next decade, and after that point the established black population was large enough so that the percentage of newcomers never rose so high again.

Each of the lowland parishes must have reflected this shift in the same way. In St. Paul's, for example, where the Stono Uprising originated, there were only 1,634 slaves in 1720, the large majority of whom had been born in the province or brought there long before. By contrast, in 1742 the parish's new Anglican minister listed 3,829 "heathens and infidels" in his cure, well over 3,000 of whom must have been slaves. Of these, perhaps as many as 1,500 had been purchased in Charlestown since 1730. A predominant number of the Africans reaching the colony between 1735 and 1739 have been shown to have come from Angola, so it is likely that at the time of the Stono Uprising there were close to 1,000 residents of St. Paul's Parish who had lived in the Congo-Angola region of Africa less than ten years before. While this figure is only an estimate, it lends support to the assertion in one contemporary source that most of the conspirators in the 1739 incident were Angolans. The suggestion seems not only plausible, but even probable.

European settlers contemplating the prospects of rebellion, however, seem to have been more concerned with contacts the slaves might establish in the future than with experience that came from their past. White colonists were already beginning to subscribe to the belief that most Negro unrest was necessarily traceable to outside agitators. Like most shibboleths of the slave culture, this idea contained a kernel of truth, and it is one of the difficult tasks in considering the records of the 1730s and 1740s to separate the unreasonable fears of white Carolinians from their very justifiable concerns.

Numerous anxieties were intertwined. It was all too clear, for example, that internal and external threats to white security were likely to coincide and reinforce each other, if for no other reason than that the militia with its dual responsibilities for defense and control was divided and thereby weakened in times of trouble. Even if not linked beforehand, hostile elements inside and outside the colony could be expected to join forces during any alarm, so Europeans were as anxious about foreign infiltration as domestic conspiracy. For this reason Indians often appeared to be the slaves' likeliest allies. For example, suspicion of a Negro plot had scarcely died in 1733, when an Indian slave was brought before the Assembly. He testified "that an Indian Woman had told him that all the Indians on the Continent design'd to rise and make War, against the English." Had such word contained any substance it might have triggered slave impulses to rise against the English as well, but this particular rumor apparently lacked foundation, and the informant was dismissed.

The following spring the Assembly sent a memorial to the king, outlining the threats posed by the Indians, Spanish, and French and asking assistance in defense. This document from 1734 stressed that white colonists faced "many intestine Dangers from the great Number of Negroes" and went on to observe, "Insurrections against us have been often attempted, and would at any time prove very fatal if the French should instigate them by artfully giving them [the Negroes] an Expectation of Freedom." The next ten years were filled with enough dangers—real and imagined—from these various quarters to keep the English in a constant state of agitation. In 1748 James Glen, thinking back to this period, summarized the sea of anxieties which had beset white Carolinians:

> Sometime ago the People of this Province were Annually alarmed with accounts of intended Invasions, & even in time of profound Peace they were made believe that the Spaniards had prepared Embarkations for that purpose at St. Augustine & the Havanna, or that the French were marching by Land from Louisiana with more Men than ever were in that Country to drive us into the Sea. Sometimes the Negroes were to rise & cut their Masters Throats at other times the Indians were confederating to destroy us. . . .

In September 1739 South Carolina was shaken by an incident which became known as the Stono Uprising. A group of slaves struck a violent but abortive blow for liberation which resulted in the deaths of more than sixty people. Fewer than twenty-five white lives were taken, and property damage was localized, but the episode represented a new dimension in overt resistance. Free colonists, whose anxieties about controlling slaves had been growing for some time, saw their fears of open violence realized, and this in turn generated new fears.

According to a report written several years later, the events at Stono "awakened the Attention of the most Unthinking" among the white minority; "Every one that had any Relation, any Tie of Nature; every one that had a Life to lose were in the most sensible Manner shocked at such Danger daily hanging over their Heads." The episode, if hardly major in its own right, seemed to symbolize the critical impasse in which Carolina's English colonists now found themselves. "With Regret we bewailed our peculiar Case," the same report continued, "that we could not enjoy the Benefits of Peace like the rest of Mankind and that our own Industry should be the Means of taking from us all the Sweets of Life and of rendering us Liable to the Loss of our Lives and Fortunes."

The Stono Uprising can also be seen as a turning point in the history of South Carolina's black population. . . . This episode was preceded by a series of projected insurrections, any one of which could have assumed significant proportions. Taken together, all these incidents represent a brief but serious groundswell of resistance to slavery, which had diverse and lasting repercussions. The slave system in the British mainland colonies withstood this tremor, and never again faced a period of such serious unrest. For Negroes in South Carolina the era represented the first time in which steady resistance to the system showed a prospect of becoming something more than random hostility. But the odds against successful assertion were overwhelming; it was slightly too late, or far too soon, for realistic thoughts of freedom among black Americans.

The year 1739 did not begin auspiciously for the settlement. The smallpox epidemic which had plagued the town in the previous autumn was still lingering on when the council and commons convened in Charlestown in January. Therefore, Lt. Gov. William Bull, in his opening remarks to the initial session, recommended that the legislature consider "only what is absolutely necessary to be dispatched for the Service of the Province." The primary issue confronting them, Bull suggested, was the desertion of their slaves, who represented such a huge proportion of the investments of white colonists. The Assembly agreed that the matter was urgent, and a committee was immediately established to consider what measures should be taken in response to "the Encouragement lately given by the Spaniards for the Desertion of Negroes from this Government to the Garrison of St. Augustine."

Even as the legislators deliberated, the indications of unrest multiplied. In Georgia William Stephens, the secretary for the trustees of that colony, recorded on February 8, 1739, "what we heard told us by several newly come from Carolina, was not to be disregarded, viz. that a Conspiracy was formed by the Negroes in Carolina, to rise and forcibly make their Way out of the Province" in an effort to reach the protection of the Spanish. It has been learned, Stephens wrote in his journal, that this plot was first discovered in Winyaw in the northern part of the province, "from whence, as they were to bend their Course South, it argued, that the other Parts of the Province must be privy to it, and that the Rising was to be universal; whereupon the whole Province were all upon their Guard." If there were rumblings in the northernmost counties, Granville County on the southern edge of the province probably faced a greater prospect of disorder. Stephens' journal for February 20 reports word of a conspiracy among the slaves on the Montaigut and de Beaufain plantations bordering on the Savannah River just below the town of Purrysburg. Two days later the Upper House in Charlestown passed on to the Assembly a petition and several affidavits from "Inhabitants of Granville County relating to the Desertion of their Slaves to the Castle of St. Augustine."

That same week the commons expressed its distress over information that several runaways heading for St. Augustine had been taken up but then suffered to go at large without questioning. An inquiry was ordered, but it was not until early April that the Assembly heard concrete recommendations upon the problem of desertions. The first suggestion was for a petition to the English king requesting relief and assistance in this matter. Secondly, since many felt that the dozens of slaves escaping in November had eluded authorities because of a lack of scout boats, it was voted to employ two boats of eight men each in patrolling the southern coastal passages for the next nine months. Finally, to cut off Negroes escaping by land, large bounties were recommended for slaves taken up in the all-white colony of Georgia. Men, women, and children under twelve were to bring £40, £25, and £10, respectively, if brought back from beyond the Savannah River, and each adult scalp "with the two Ears" would command £20.

In the midst of these deliberations, four slaves, apparently good riders who knew the terrain through hunting stray cattle, stole some horses and headed for Florida, accompanied by an Irish Catholic servant. Since they killed one white and wounded another in making their escape, a large posse was organized which pursued them unsuccessfully. Indian allies succeeded in killing one of the runaways, but the rest reached St. Augustine, where they were warmly received. Spurred by such an incident, the Assembly completed work April 11 on legislation undertaken the previous month to prevent slave insurrections. The next day a public display was made of the punishment of two captured runaways, convicted of attempting to leave the province in the company of several other Negroes. One man was whipped and the other, after a contrite speech before the assembled slaves, "was executed at the usual Place, and afterwards hung in Chains at Hangman's Point opposite to this Town, in sight of all Negroes passing and repassing by Water."

The reactions of colonial officials mirrored the desperate feelings spreading among the white population. On May 18 the Rev. Lewis Jones observed in a letter that the desertion of more than a score of slaves from his parish of St. Helena the previous fall, in response to the Spanish proclamation, seemed to "Considerably Encrease the Prejudice of Planters agst the Negroes, and Occasion a Strict hand, to be kept over them by their Several Owners, those that Deserted having been Much Indulg'd." But concern continued among English colonists as to whether even the harshest reprisals could protect their investments and preserve their safety.

A letter the same month from Lt. Gov. Bull to the Duke of Newcastle, summarizing the situation, reflected the anxiety of the white populace:

> My Lord,
> I beg to lay before Your Grace an Affair, which may greatly distress if not entirely ruin this His Majesty's Province of South Carolina.
> His Catholick Majesty's Edict having been published at St. Augustine declaring Freedom to all Negroes, and other slaves, that shall Desert from the English Colonies, Has occasioned several Parties to desert from this Province both by Land and Water, which notwithstanding They were pursued by the People of Carolina as well as the Indians, & People in Georgia, by General Oglethorpes Directions, have been able to make their escape.

Bull repeated the blunt refusal which the Spanish governor had given to deputies visiting St. Augustine to seek the return of fugitives, and he reported that "This Answer has occasioned great disatisfaction & Concern to the Inhabitants of this

Province, to find their property now become so very precarious and uncertain." There was a growing awareness among whites, Bull concluded, "that their Negroes which were their chief support may in little time become their Enemies, if not their Masters, and that this Government is unable to withstand or prevent it."

Developments during the summer months did little to lessen tensions. In July the *Gazette* printed an account from Jamaica of the truce which the English governor there had felt compelled to negotiate with an armed and independent force of runaways. During the same month a Spanish Captain of the Horse from St. Augustine named Don Piedro sailed into Charlestown in a launch with twenty or thirty men, supposedly to deliver a letter to Gen. Oglethorpe. Since Oglethorpe was residing in Frederica far down the coast, the visit seemed suspicious, and it was later recalled, in the wake of the Stono incident, that there had been a Negro aboard who spoke excellent English and that the vessel had put into numerous inlets south of Charlestown while making its return. Whether men were sent ashore was unclear, but in September the Georgians took into custody a priest thought to be "employed by the Spaniards to procure a general Insurrection of the Negroes."

Another enemy, yellow fever, reappeared in Charlestown during the late summer for the first time since 1732. The epidemic "destroyed many, who had got thro' the Small-pox" of the previous year, and as usual it was remarked to be "very fatal to Strangers & Europeans especially." September proved a particularly sultry month. A series of philosophical lectures was discontinued "by Reason of the Sickness and Heat"; a school to teach embroidery, lacework, and French to young ladies was closed down; and the *Gazette* ceased publication for a month when the printer fell sick. Lt. Gov. Bull, citing "the Sickness with which it hath pleased God to visit this Province," prorogued the Assembly which attempted to convene on September 12. The session was postponed again on October 18 and did not get under way until October 30. By then cool weather had killed the mosquitoes which carried the disease, and the contagion had subsided, but it had taken the lives of the chief justice, the judge of the Vice-Admiralty Court, the surveyor of customs, the clerk of the Assembly, and the clerk of the Court of Admiralty, along with scores of other residents.

The confusion created by this sickness in Charlestown, where residents were dying at a rate of more than half a dozen per day, may have been a factor in the timing of the Stono Rebellion, but calculations might also have been influenced by the newspaper publication, in mid-August, of the Security Act which required all white men to carry firearms to church on Sunday or submit to a stiff fine, beginning on September 29. It has long been recognized that the free hours at the end of the week afforded the slaves their best opportunity for cabals, particularly when whites were engaged in communal activities of their own. In 1724 Gov. Nicholson had expressed to the Lords of Trade his hope that new legislation would "Cause people to Travel better Armed in Times of Publick meetings when Negroes might take the better opportunity against Great Numbers of Unarmed men." Later the same year the Assembly had complained that the recent statute requiring white men "to ride Arm'd on every Sunday" had not been announced sufficiently to be effective, and in 1727 the Committee of Grievances had objected that "the Law w^{ch}: obliged people to go arm'd to Church & ^{ca}: wants strengthening." Ten years later the presentments of the Grand Jury in Charlestown stressed the fact that Negroes were still permitted to cabal together during the hours of divine service, "which if not timely prevented may be of fatal Consequence to this Province." Since the Stono Uprising, which caught planters at church, occurred only weeks before the published statute of 1739 went into effect, slaves may have considered that within the near future their masters would be even more heavily armed on Sundays.

One other factor seems to be more than coincidental to the timing of the insurrection. Official word of hostilities between England and Spain, which both whites and blacks in the colony had been anticipating for some time, appears to have reached Charlestown the very weekend that the uprising began. Such news would have been a logical trigger for rebellion. If it did furnish the sudden spark, this would help explain how the Stono scheme, unlike so many others, was put into immediate execution without hesitancy or betrayal, and why the rebels marched southward toward Spanish St. Augustine with an air of particular confidence.

During the early hours of Sunday, September 9, 1739, some twenty slaves gathered near the western branch of Stono River in St. Paul's Parish, within twenty miles of Charlestown. Many of the conspirators were Angolans, and their acknowledged leader was a slave named Jemmy. The group proceeded to Stono Bridge and broke into Hutchenson's store, where small arms and powder were on sale. The storekeepers, Robert Bathurst and Mr. Gibbs, were executed and their heads left upon the front steps.

Equipped with guns, the band moved on to the house of Mr. Godfrey, which they plundered and burned, killing the owner and his son and daughter. They then turned southward along the main road to Georgia and St. Augustine and reached Wallace's Tavern before dawn. The innkeeper was spared, "for he was a good man and kind to his slaves," but a neighbor, Mr. Lemy, was killed with his wife and child and his house was sacked. "They burnt Colonel Hext's house and killed his Overseer and his Wife. They then burnt Mr Sprye's house, then Mr Sacheverell's, and then Mr Nash's house all lying upon the Pons Pons Road, and killed all the white People they found in them." A man named Bullock eluded the rebels, but they burned his house. When they advanced upon the home of Thomas Rose with the intention of killing him, several of his slaves succeeded in hiding him, for which they were later rewarded. But by now reluctant slaves were being forced to join the company to keep the alarm from being spread. Others were joining voluntarily, and as the numbers grew, confidence rose and discipline diminished. Two drums appeared; a standard was raised; and there were shouts of "Liberty!" from the marchers. The few whites whom they encountered were pursued and killed.

By extreme coincidence, Lt. Gov. Bull was returning northward from Granville County to Charlestown at this time for the beginning of the legislative session. At about eleven in the morning, riding in the company of four other men, Bull came directly in view of the rebel troop, which must have numbered more than fifty by then. Comprehending the situation, he wheeled about, "and with much difficulty escaped & raised the Countrey." The same account states that Bull "was pursued," and it seems clear that if the lieutenant governor had not been on horseback he might never have escaped alive. Bull's death or capture would have had incalculable psychological and tactical significance. As it was, the rebels probably never knew the identity of the fleeing horseman or sensed the crucial nature of this chance encounter. Instead they proceeded through the Ponpon district, terrorizing and recruiting. According to a contemporary account, their numbers were being "increased every minute by new Negroes coming to them, so that they were above Sixty, some say a hundred, on which they halted in a field and set to dancing, Singing and beating Drums to draw more Negroes to them."

The decision to halt came late on Sunday afternoon. Having marched more than ten miles without opposition, the troop drew up in a field on the north side of the road, not far from the site of the Jacksonburough ferry. Some of the recruits were undoubtedly tired or uncertain; others were said to be intoxicated on stolen liquor. Many must have felt unduly confident over the fact that they had already struck a more successful overt blow for resistance than any previous group of slaves in the colony, and as their ranks grew, the likelihood of a successful exodus increased. It has been suggested that the additional confidence needed to make such a large group of slaves pause in an open field in broad daylight may have been derived from the colors which they displayed before them. Whatever the validity of this suggestion, the main reason for not crossing the Edisto River was probably the realistic expectation that by remaining stationary after such an initial show of force, enough other slaves could join them to make their troop nearly invincible by morning.

But such was not to be the case, for by Sunday noon some of the nearest white colonists had been alerted. Whether Bull himself was the first to raise the alarm is unclear. According to one tradition Rev. Stobo's Presbyterian congregation at Wiltown on the east bank of the Edisto was summoned directly from church, and since this would have been the first community which Bull and his fellow riders could reach, the detail is probably valid. By about four in the afternoon a contingent of armed and mounted planters, variously numbered from twenty to one hundred, moved in upon the rebels' location (long after known as "the battlefield").

Caught off guard, the Negroes hesitated as to whether to attack or flee. Those with weapons fired two quick but ineffective rounds; they were described later in white reports as having "behaved boldly." Seeing that some slaves were loading their guns and others were escaping, a number of whites dismounted and fired a volley into the group, killing or wounding at least fourteen. Other rebels were surrounded, questioned briefly, and then shot.

White sources considered it notable that the planters "did not torture one Negroe, but only put them to an easy death," and several slaves who proved they had been forced to join the band were actually released. Those who sought to return to their plantations, hoping they had not yet been missed, were seized and shot, and one account claimed that the planters "Cutt off their heads and set them up at every Mile Post they came to." Whether the riders used drink to fortify their courage or to celebrate their victory, a bill of more than £90 was drawn up the next day for "Liquors &c" which had been consumed by the local militia company.

Although secondary accounts have suggested that the Stono Uprising was suppressed by nightfall, contemporary sources reveal a decidedly different story. By Sunday evening more than twenty white settlers had already been killed. Initial messages from the area put the number twice as high and reported "the Country thereabout was full of Flames." The fact that black deaths scarcely exceeded white during the first twenty-four hours was not likely to reassure the planters or intimidate the slave majority. Moreover, at least thirty Negroes (or roughly one third of the rebel force) were known to have escaped from Sunday's skirmish in several groups, and their presence in the countryside provided an invitation to wider rebellion. Roughly as many more had scattered individually, hoping to rejoin the rebels or return to their plantations as conditions dictated.

During the ensuing days, therefore, a desperate and intensive manhunt was staged. The entire white colony was ordered under arms, and guards were posted at key ferry passages, The Ashley River militia company, its ranks thinned by yellow fever, set out from Charlestown in pursuit. Some of the militia captains turned out Indian recruits as well, who, if paid in cash, were willing to serve as slavecatchers. A white resident wrote several weeks later that within the first two days these forces "kill'd twenty odd more, and took about 40; who were immediately some shot, some hang'd, and some Gibbeted alive. A Number came in and were seized and discharged." Even if these executions were as numerous, rapid, and brutal as claimed, the prospect of a sustained insurrection continued. It was not until the following Saturday, almost a week after the initial violence, that a white militia company caught up with the largest remnant of the rebel force. This band, undoubtedly short on provisions and arms, had made its way thirty miles closer to the colony's southern border. A pitched battle ensued, and at length (according to a note sent the following January) "ye Rebels [were] So entirely defeated & dispersed y^t there never were Seen above 6 or 7 together Since."

It was not until a full month later, however, that a correspondent in South Carolina could report that "the Rebellious Negroes are quite stopt from doing any further Mischief, many of them having been put to the most cruel Death." And even then, white fears were by no means allayed. The Purrysburg militia company had remained on guard at the southern edge of the colony, and in Georgia Gen. Oglethorpe, upon receiving Lt. Gov. Bull's report of the insurrection, had called out rangers and Indians and issued a proclamation, "cautioning all Persons in this Province, to have a watchful Eye upon any Negroes, who might attempt to set a Foot in it." He had also garrisoned soldiers at Palachicolas, the abandoned fort which guarded the only point for almost one hundred miles where horses could swim the Savannah River and where Negro fugitives had previously crossed. Security in South Carolina itself was made tight enough, however, so that few if any rebels reached Georgia. But this only increased the anxiety of whites in the neighborhood of the uprising.

In November several planters around Stono deserted their homes and moved their wives and children in with other families, "at particular Places, for their better Security and Defence against those Negroes which were concerned in that Insurrection who were not yet taken." And in January the minister of St. Paul's Parish protested that some of his leading parishioners, "being apprehensive of Danger from ye Rebels Still outstanding," had "carried their Families to Town for Safety, & if y Humour of moving continues a little longer, I shall have but a Small Congregation at Church." The Assembly placed a special patrol on duty along the Stono River and expended more than £1,500 on rewards for Negroes and Indians who had acted in the white interest during the insurrection. Outlying fugitives were still being brought in for execution the following spring, and one ringleader remained at large for three full years. He was finally taken up in a swamp by two Negro runaways hopeful of a reward, tried by authorities at Stono, and immediately hanged.

It is possible to emphasize the small scale and ultimate failure of the uprising at Stono or to stress, on the other hand, its large potential and near success. Either approach means little except in the wider context of slave resistance during these years. Certain elements of the insurrection—total surprise, ruthless killing, considerable property damage, armed engagements, protracted aftermath—are singular in South Carolina's early history. Yet it remains only one swell in the tide of rebellious schemes which characterize these years. In retrospect, its initial success appears a high-water mark, and its ruthless suppression represents a significant turning of the tide. But the troubled waters of resistance did not subside any more abruptly than they had risen. For several years after the outbreak in St. Paul's Parish, the safety of the white minority, and the viability of their entire plantation system, hung in serious doubt for the first time since the Yamasee War.

Rebels from Stono were still at large in late November 1739 when rumors of new threats began. The Assembly requested of Bull that special precautions be taken for the upcoming Christmas holidays, and on December 7 Assemblyman Joseph Izard departed for a week in order to raise the local militia and pursue "several runaway Negroes belonging to Mrs. Middleton that kept about Dorchester who had committed a great many Robberies in those Parts." Four days later the council, in a message outlining the critical situation of the white inhabitants, explained that "we have already felt the unhappy Effects of an Insurrection of our Slaves . . . (an intestine Enemy the most dreadful of Enemies) which we have just Grounds to imagine will be repeated." The council continued, "it is well known to us, that . . . if the present Session of Assembly be determined with the same unhappy Conclusion as the last," then "many of our [white] Inhabitants are determined to remove themselves and their Effects, out of this Province; insomuch, that upon the whole the Country seemed to be at Stake."

Such fears were apparently well founded. Two days after Christmas Robert Pringle the Charlestown merchant, wrote to his brother:

> We have been fatigued for this Week past keeping Guard in Town, on acco^t of a Conspiracy that has been detected to have been Carrying on by some of our Negroes in Town but has been discovered before it came to any maturity. We shall Live very Uneasie with our Negroes, while the Spaniards continue to keep Possession of St. Augustine & it is pity our Goverm^t at home did not incourage the disslodging of them from thence.

In response to a special order of the lieutenant governor and council, the attorney general "spent a great Deal of Time" on an investigation and trial, but the Assembly had to be reminded in May that it had forgotten to repay this officer for "his Trouble and Attendance in prosecuting the Negroes concerned in the intended Insurrection last Christmass." In March, Assembly members had rejected a £60 bill from the five constables of Charlestown for their attendance at the six-day examination of "certain Negroes who were apprehended on Suspicion of a Conspiracy," probably the same one investigated by the attorney general.

The legislature had scarcely adjourned when another potential uprising was revealed during the first week of June 1740. According to first reports among whites, this conspiracy had "the Appearance of greater Danger than any of the former." It originated somewhere between the Ashley and Cooper rivers "in the very Heart of the Settlements." Its focus was apparently on the western edge of St. John's Parish, Berkeley County, near the rice-growing district of Goose Creek. This time between 150 and 200 slaves "got together in defiance." These rebels lacked weapons, and they must also have had the failure of the Stono scheme fresh in their minds. For these reasons, nearby Charlestown, rather than the southern border, became their immediate objective. "As they had no prospect of escaping through the Province of Georgia, their design was to break open a store-house, and supply themselves, and those who would join them, with arms."

How carefully such a strike had been planned and how close it came to execution cannot be determined. It appears that the conspirators' large numbers, which must have provided the confidence for so direct and desperate a plan as the seizure of Charlestown, also proved the source of their undoing. The hope for secrecy was destroyed, in this instance by a slave of Maj. Cordes named Peter, and white forces had time to prepare a suitable ambush for the rebels. Therefore, according to an account reaching Georgia, "when they appeared the next day fifty of them were seized, and these were hanged, ten in a day, to intimidate the other negroes." All told, some sixty-seven slaves were brought to trial, and their betrayer, Peter, appeared personally before the legislature to receive thanks in the form of a new wardrobe and £20 in cash. Robert Pringle summarized the incident in a letter to his wife in Boston at the end of the summer: "We had a Report in June last of some Negroes Intending to make an Insurrection, but [it] was timely Discovered and the Ring Leaders punished."

Further hints of slave resistance would follow. Acts of arson were suspected, and the great Charlestown fire that November did little to ease tensions. The spring of 1741 brought lurid tales of slave resistance in northern colonies, and during the winter of 1742 the Assembly was obliged to investigate reports of "frequent Meetings of great Numbers of Slaves in the Parish of St. Helena" which were still striking "Terror" into local Europeans. But by 1740 the implications of growing rebelliousness among slaves had already become unavoidable for the white majority. One Englishman, reflecting back upon Stono and other incidents, wrote:

> Such dreadful Work, it is to be feared, we may hear more of in Time, in case they come to breaking open Stores to find Arms, as they did the last Year; and are able to keep the Field, with Plenty of Corn and Potatoes every where; and above all, if it is considered how vastly disproportionate the Number of white Men is to theirs: So that at best, the Inhabitants cannot live without perpetually guarding their own Safety, now become so precarious.

The Europeans' response to this "precarious" situation was desperate and effectual. Confronting at last the actual possibility of widespread revolution, bickering factions were able to cooperate in ways which maintained the English slave colony and determined many aspects of Negro existence for generations to come. Their actions constitute the beginning of a new chapter in the history of South Carolina and therefore lie outside the scope of this study, but they also signify the end of an era for the Negro in the colony, so it is fitting to cite them briefly in conclusion.

One thrust of the white response involved efforts to reduce provocations for rebellion. Besides waging war on the Spanish in St. Augustine, whose proximity was considered a perpetual incitement, the colonial government laid down penalties for masters who imposed such excessive work or such brutal punishments that the likelihood of revolt was enhanced. Efforts to extend Negro dependence were also undertaken: it was at this time that a Negro school was started in Charlestown on the assumption that a few slaves might be trained to teach other slaves certain carefully selected doctrines of the Christian faith, such as submissiveness and obedience. (The school persisted for several decades, though its impact on the total Negro population was negligible.)

These gestures of calculated benevolence were overshadowed by far more intensive efforts to control and to divide the slaves. The comprehensive Negro Act, which had been in the works for several years but about which white legislators had been unable to agree in less threatening times, was passed into law and stringently enforced. This elaborate statute, which would serve as the core of South Carolina's slave code for more than a century to come, rested firmly upon prior enactments. At the same time, however, it did more than any other single piece of legislation in the colony's history to curtail *de facto* personal liberties, which slaves had been able to cling to against formidable odds during the first three generations of settlement. Freedom of movement and freedom of assembly, freedom to raise food, to earn money, to learn to read English—none of these rights had ever been assured to Negroes and most had already been legislated against, but always the open conditions of life in a young and strugging colony had kept vestiges of these meager liberties alive. Now the noose was being tightened: there would be heavier surveillance of Negro activity and stiffer fines for masters who failed to keep their slaves in line. Even more than before, slaves were rewarded for informing against each other in ways which were considered "loyal" by the white minority (and "disloyal" by many blacks). The ultimate reward of manumission was now taken out of the hands of individual planters and turned over to the legislature, and further steps were taken to discourage the presence of free Negroes.

Finally, and most significantly, authorities took concrete steps to alter the uneven ratio between blacks and whites which was seen to underlie the colony's problems as well as its prosperity. Since the economy by now was highly dependent upon rice exports, and since the Europeans in South Carolina were dependent upon African labor at every stage of rice production, there was talk of developing laborsaving machinery and of importing white hands to take on some of the jobs which could not be mechanized. A law was passed reiterating the requirement for at least one white man to be present for every ten blacks on any plantation, and the fines collected from violators were to be used to strengthen the patrols. The most dramatic move was the imposition of a prohibitive duty upon new slaves arriving from Africa and the West Indies. While Negroes had arrived at a rate of well over one thousand per year during the 1730s, slave importations were cut to nearly one tenth this size during the 1740s, and the duties collected were used toward encouraging immigration from Europe. Before 1750 the slave trade was resuming its previous proportions, but this interim of nearly a decade meant that newly imported slaves would never again constitute so high a proportion of the colony's total population as they had in the late 1730s.

Among all these simultaneous efforts by whites to reassert their hold over black Carolinians, no single tactic was entirely successful. There is little to suggest that treatment became notably less brutal among masters or that doctrines of submissive Christianity were accepted rapidly among slaves. Despite the Negro Act of 1740, slaves continued to exercise clandestinely and at great cost the freedoms which the white minority sought to suppress. Those who wished to travel or to congregate, those who wished to grow food, hunt game, practice a trade, or study a newspaper learned increasingly to do these things secretly, and since informants were well rewarded, it was necessary to be as covert among other blacks as among whites. The result was not stricter obedience but deeper mistrust; a shroud of secrecy was being drawn over an increasing portion of Negro life.

Nor could white dependency on Negro workers be effectively reduced. The technique of periodically flooding the rice fields to remove weeds without the use of slave labor (which came into practice sometime around mid-century) may have originated in part to serve this end. But machines which could supplant the slaves who pounded rice every autumn made little headway until after the Revolution. Moreover, the recruitment of European settlers never burgeoned, despite offers of free land on the frontier. Therefore, in spite of the reduced import of slaves in the 1740s, the black-white ratio in the colony did not alter markedly.

If no one of these efforts succeeded fully enough to alter the nature of the colony, the combined effects were nevertheless clearly felt. The Negro majority, through persistent and varied resistance to the constraints of the slave system, brought South Carolina closer to the edge of upheaval than historians have been willing to concede. But in the process the slaves inspired a concerted counterattack from their anxious and outnumbered masters. The new social equilibrium which emerged in the generation before the Revolution was based upon a heightened degree of white repression and a reduced amount of black autonomy. By the time Europeans in America were prepared to throw off the yoke of slavery under which they felt themselves laboring as the subjects of the English king, the enslaved Negroes in South Carolina were in no position to take advantage of the libertarian rhetoric. Though they still constituted the bulk of South Carolina's population, too many had been reduced too soon into too thorough a state of submission. Had the earlier pervasive efforts at black resistance in South Carolina been less abortive, the subsequent history of the new nation might well have followed an unpredictably different path.

SECTION 3: SUGGESTIONS FOR FURTHER READING

There are only a few studies now in print detailing the role of indentured servants in early America. That subject is ripe for further research. One must still depend upon the excellent works of T. J. Wertenbaker, *The Planters of Colonial Virginia* (1922), M. W. Jernegan, *Laboring and Dependent Classes in Colonial America, 1607–1763* (1931), A. E. Smith, *Colonists in Bondage: White Servitude and Convict Labor in America, 1607–1776* (1947), a portion of which has been reprinted here, and R. B. Morris, *Government and Labor in Early America* (1946). R. R. Menard, "From Servant to Freeholder: Status Mobility and Property Accumulation in Seventeenth-Century Maryland," *William and Mary Quarterly,* 3rd ser., 30 (1973), pp. 37–64, confirms in many facets Wertenbaker's quantitative materials. W. P. Sears, Jr., "Indentured Servants in Colonial America," *Dalhousie Review,* 37 (1957), pp. 121–140, provides a convenient overview, while W. B. Smith, *White Servitude in Colonial South Carolina* (1961), and L. W. Towner, "A Fondness for Freedom: Servant Protest in Puritan Society," *William and Mary Quarterly,* 3rd ser., 19 (1962), pp. 201–219, are suggestive case studies. An analysis stressing the yeoman backgrounds of many indentured servants is Mildred Campbell, "Social Origins of Some Early Americans," *Seventeenth-Century America: Essays in Colonial History,* ed. J. M. Smith (1959), pp. 63–89.

The secondary literature on slavery is mountainous in comparison to that on indentured servants, although most studies focus on postrevolutionary aspects of the system. Valuable general introductions include J. H. Franklin, *From Slavery to Freedom: A History of Negro Americans* (3rd ed., 1967), and August Meier and Elliott Rudwick, *From Plantation to Ghetto: An Interpretive History of American Negroes* (3rd ed., 1976). Basil Davidson, *The Africans Genius: An Introduction to African Social and Cultural History* (1969), is an essential starting point on the African background.

A number of studies have focused on the origins of slavery in North America and its evolution toward a closed, dehumanizing system. A logical starting point is with Oscar and Mary Handlin, "The Origins of the Southern Labor System," *William and Mary Quarterly,* 3rd ser., 7 (1950), pp. 199–222, which should be read in conjunction with the essay by Carl N. Degler reprinted here. The essentials of what is currently known about the subject are contained in two complementary studies of

176 / INDENTURED SERVITUDE AND SLAVERY

superior quality by D. B. Davis, *The Problem of Slavery in Western Culture* (1966), and W. D. Jordan, *White Over Black: American Attitudes toward the Negro, 1550–1812* (1968). Additional insight may be found in J. L. Alpert, "The Origin of Slavery in the United States: The Maryland Precedent," *American Journal of Legal History*, 14 (1970), pp. 189–221, W. F. Craven, *White, Red, and Black: The Seventeenth-Century Virginian* (1971), and E. S. Morgan, *American Slavery— American Freedom: The Ordeal of Colonial Virginia* (1975).

By and large, American historians have been reluctant to immerse themselves in comparative analysis, but the field of slavery studies, a definite exception, has yielded many useful insights by juxtaposing slave societies in Spanish, Portuguese, Dutch, and English American colonies. The pioneering effort was Frank Tannenbaum, *Slave and Citizen: The Negro in the Americas* (1947), which stressed the harsh reality of North American slavery. Tannenbaum pointed to the absence of institutional barriers, such as Roman law and the Roman Catholic Church, existing in Latin America and tempering the normal brutality of slavery. S. M. Elkins built upon and expanded the Tannenbaum hypothesis in his controversial *Slavery: A Problem in American Institutional and Intellectual Life* (3rd ed., 1976). H. S. Klein, *Slavery in the Americas: A Comparative Study of Virginia and Cuba* (1967), generally confirms Tannenbaum's and Elkins's findings, but C. N. Degler, *Neither Black Nor White: Slavery and Race Relations in Brazil and the United States* (1971), disagrees, given the continuance of extraordinarily high mortality rates among South American slaves. In this context P. D. Curtin's *The Atlantic Slave Trade: A Census* (1969), should be consulted.

Besides Curtin's book, D. P. Mannix and Malcolm Cowley, *Black Cargoes: The Story of the Atlantic Slave Trade, 1518–1865* (1962), James Pope-Hennessy, *Sins of the Fathers: A Study of the Atlantic Slave Traders, 1441–1807* (1968), and Elizabeth Donnan, ed., *Documents Illustrative of the History of the Slave Trade to America* (4 vols., 1930–1935), are valuable on that subject. Investigations which link slavery to broader commercial and industrial trends include Eric Williams, *Capitalism and Slavery* (1944), M. W. Jernegan, "Slavery and the Beginnings of Industrialism in the American Colonies," *American Historical Review*, 25 (1920), pp. 220–240, and C. R. Haywood, "Mercantilism and Colonial Slave Labor, 1700–1763," *Journal of Southern History*, 23 (1957), pp. 454–469.

Dealing with psychology and personality theory, S. M. Elkins suggested in *Slavery*, cited above, that the middle passage experience was so traumatic that docile, "Sambo-like" personalities resulted among transported, enslaved black Americans. His arguments have been challenged on many counts, perhaps best summarized in J. W. Blassingame, *The Slave Community: Plantation Life in the Antebellum South* (1972). If all slaves had been passive, then resistance in its various forms would have been impossible. In this context see Herbert Aptheker, *American Negro Slave Revolts* (1943), F. M. Szasz, "The New York Slave Revolt of 1741: A Re-Examination," *New York History*, 48 (1967), pp. 215–230, T. J. Davis, "The New York Slave Conspiracy of 1741 as Black Protest," *Journal of Negro History*, 56 (1971), pp. 17–30, D. D. Wax, "Negro Resistance to the Early American Slave Trade," *Journal of Negro History*, 51 (1966), pp. 1–15, G. W. Mullin, *Flight and Rebellion: Slave Resistance in Eighteenth-Century Virginia* (1972), and P. H. Wood, *Black Majority: Negroes in South Carolina from 1670 through the Stono Rebellion* (1974), the source of the last selection.

In other sections of his book Wood investigates African contributions to South Carolina's socioeconomic makeup and the beginnings of a distinct, cohesive Afro-American culture among slaves, despite planters' restrictions. On the latter point see also Roger Bastide, *African Civilizations in the New World* (1971), R. R. Menard, "The Maryland Slave Population, 1658 to 1730: A Demographic Profile of Blacks in Four Counties," *William and Mary Quarterly*, 3rd ser., 32 (1975), pp. 29–54, G. B. Nash, "Slaves and Slaveholders in Colonial Philadelphia," *William and Mary Quarterly*, 3rd ser., 30 (1973), pp. 223–256, and H. G. Gutman, *The Black Family in Slavery and Freedom, 1750–1925* (1976). The bulk of scholarship on black culture and values among slaves focuses on the nineteenth century, and the most comprehensive analysis is Eugene Genovese, *Roll, Jordan, Roll: The World the Slaves Made* (1975).

A number of fine regional and local studies exist and should be investigated by those seeking greater detail about the nature and development of slavery in particular areas. Important investigations include L. J. Greene, *The Negro in Colonial New England, 1620–1776* (1942), R. C. Twombly and R. H. Moore, "Black Puritan: The Negro in Seventeenth-Century Massachusetts," *William and Mary Quarterly*, 3rd ser., 24 (1967), pp. 224–242, E. J. McManus, *Black Bondage in the North* (1973), T. W. Tate, Jr., *The Negro in Eighteenth-Century Williamsburg* (1965), M. E. Sirmans, "The Legal Status of the Slave in South Carolina, 1670–1740," *Journal of Southern History*, 28 (1962), pp. 462–473, J. M. Clifton, "A Half-Century of a Georgia Rice Plantation," *North Carolina Historical Review*, 47 (1970), pp. 368–415, D. D. Wax, "Georgia and the Negro Before the American Revolution," *Georgia Historical Quarterly*, 51 (1967), pp. 63–77, and R. S. Dunn, *Sugar and Slaves: The Rise of the Planter Class in the British West Indies, 1624–1713* (1972).

Those interested in carrying the history of slavery into the Revolutionary period, including the early emancipation efforts, should begin with three standard volumes, including D. B. Davis, *The Problem of Slavery in the Age of Revolution, 1770–1823* (1975) D. L. Robinson, *Slavery in the Structure of American Politics, 1765–1820* (1971), and Arthur Zilversmit, *The First Emancipation: The Abolition of Slavery in the North* (1967).

Emerging Empire
and Colonial Rebellions

SECTION 4

Even with an improving economy, the second half of the seventeenth century was an era of heightened political instability for all Englishmen. The decade of the 1640s witnessed the bloody Puritan Revolution in which Oliver Cromwell and his New Model army swept before them the forces of the absolutist Stuart monarch Charles I (1625–1649). The culmination of revolution came in 1649 when a high court sanctioned by the ascendant Puritan Parliament sentenced King Charles to death. The ensuing years of Puritan rule were less than satisfying, and by the end of another decade, Englishmen welcomed the Restoration government of Charles II (1660–1685). The son of the beheaded Charles I worked feverishly to recapture the shattered prestige of the monarchy and to stabilize his personal power. Among other ways he built loyalty among courtly followers by awarding some of them vast tracts in America, including the proprietary grants to New York, New Jersey, the Carolinas, Pennsylvania, and Delaware.

Even though tending toward Roman Catholicism, Charles was intelligent enough to suppress his spiritual tastes until near his death, but his younger brother James, the Duke of York, who was an open Catholic, threw all caution aside when he acceded to the Crown in 1685 and pursued an entirely anti-Protestant policy. When his Catholic wife produced a male heir, parliamentary leaders, faced with the prospect of a long line of Catholic kings and increasing insensitivity to Parliament's rights, ousted James. They sent him fleeing from the country and called James's Protestant daughter Mary and her Dutch husband William of Orange to the empty throne. The Glorious Revolution of 1688–1689 was the second time in the span of a normal lifetime that Parliament had overthrown a Stuart monarch.

Even though political life in England was turbulent under the absolutist Stuart monarchs, it would be erroneous to suppose that the royal ministers lost sight of the American colonies. During the second half of the seventeenth century, leaders in England were conceptualizing and implementing rudimentary notions of empire. Their economic ideas have been lumped together in the term "mercantilism." The basic tenet of the mercantile system was self-sufficiency, or not having to depend upon other nations for vital raw materials. Self-sufficiency implied a favorable balance of trade: the value of exports outweighing the value of imports and the difference being made up in a flow of bullion into England, in balancing payments for the exports. Thus the homeland would not be caught short of precious trading metals, considered then to be the most reliable measure of national strength.

In the mercantilist scheme of things the colonies were to serve as the source of valued raw materials. The parent country, in turn, would supply its overseas provinces with manufactured goods, thereby promoting imperial economic growth and stability. England would enhance its own economic and political strength in relation to other powerful European nations in the process of building up such trading connections in the empire. The parent state, moreover, would never find itself in the position of being cut off from critical resources needed to carry on warfare with European powers, when confrontations developed, as it was expected they would.

It was early, inchoate mercantilist reasoning that led the Puritan Parliament to endorse the first of the Navigation Acts in 1650 and 1651. Cromwell's followers were striking a blow at the mighty Dutch carrying trade, which dominated too much of the Anglo-American colonial commerce at that time. The Acts specified that foreign ships were not to be involved in trading with English colonists. All goods brought to England or to the colonies had to be carried in English or colonial vessels. (The one exception was that European goods could be sent to England in ships of the country of origin.)

The Navigation Acts directly resulted in the first of three short wars with the Dutch, but the threat of warfare did not deter the Restoration Parliament from refining and extending the scope of navigation legislation. In three acts (1660, 1663, and 1673) Parliament made it law that commerce passing between the mother country and the colonies had to be handled by English ships (defined as English owned, including colonists, with the captain and three-fourths of the crew being English), that certain vital provincial "enumerated" commodities had to be transported only to English or other colonial markets, and that European trading goods destined for the colonies had to pass through England. Foreign carriers, such as the Dutch, were to be cut off from imperial commerce; England was to serve as the entrepot of the empire; and the colonies, in theory at least, were to produce the basic raw materials for England's manufacturing, for its defense, and for general imperial consumption.

From the perspective of English merchants, shippers, and government officials, implementing the navigation system and with it a formal imperial structure had untold advantages, but from the colonists' perspective in America the picture had mixed qualities. Tobacco, for instance, was one of the original enumerated commodities. It had to be transported directly to England. Yet the home market, even though reserved as a monopoly for the colonial product, was not elastic enough to absorb the ever-increasing supply. According to the trading rules, enumerated goods could be reshipped to European markets; but the various fees incurred in unloading, storing, and reloading in England drove tobacco prices up to the point where the American brand could not always compete favorably with Spanish tobacco. Some of the instability in tobacco prices, then, resulted from the market limitations of the Navigation Acts. A few disloyal colonists resorted to trading covertly with the Dutch. Yet most obeyed the Navigation laws in the face of mounting economic insecurity. Falling tobacco prices, in fact, may be posited as one of several factors causing the 1676 uprising against royal authority and Governor Sir William Berkeley in Virginia, led by the young, impetuous nobleman Nathaniel Bacon; still, as Bernard Bailyn insists in the next selection,

Bacon's Rebellion was also symptomatic of far more profound sources of Anglo-American strain.

Bacon's 1676 Rebellion reflected directly upon the growing amounts of colonial ill-feeling about the thrust of imperial policies and royalist administrators. It was only the first in a great wave of provincial-based insurrections occurring in the latter part of the century. Colonial discontent actually reached its climax in 1689 with the local coup against Sir Edmund Andros and the Dominion of New England in Massachusetts, with Jacob Leisler's Rebellion in New York, and with the uprising of John Coode's Protestant Association against proprietary officials in Maryland, all three events being a part of the American reaction to the Glorious Revolution in England and the dethroning of James II.

Part of the explanation of serious tensions, especially in the southern colonies, does lie in unstable economic conditions. Yet much more than economic security and material prosperity was at stake. The Stuart monarchs, notorious for their arbitrariness, were often indifferent to colonial political rights. New Yorkers, living under the proprietary regime of James, Duke of York, clamored for a representative assembly, but they did not have their demands fully recognized until after Leisler's Rebellion. The King's ministers forced independent-minded Massachusetts Puritans to give up their valued trading company charter (the legal basis of their government) in 1684. That action resulted from the pleas of new imperial administrators in the colonies, such as Edward Randolph, who was sent to America by the Lords of Trade, after that body was organized in 1675, to watch over colonial affairs. Randolph insisted upon greater centralization of imperial authority as the only way to get full provincial adherence to the Navigation Acts. When James became King he approved plans for the Dominion of New England, a vast territorial and administrative entity that was to supersede all the older governments from Maine to Pennsylvania. The Dominion wiped out local autonomy and placed a few men, such as the exacting Sir Edmund Andros and his advisers, in charge of all political decision making. Finally, certain Bostonians, tired of Andros's arbitrariness, rose up in April 1689 after news reached them that James II had fallen from power, as analyzed by Richard S. Dunn in a selection ahead. The Boston revolt in turn touched off the New York and Maryland insurrections.

Local leaders in the colonies thus were striving to establish a range of political rights within the emerging context of empire. The colonists wanted guarantees that they too would have the known rights and privileges of Englishmen and be able to express themselves through representative assemblies. One way of characterizing their aims is to say that they were searching for equality of standing in an age when imperial administrators were attempting to force them into a subordinate position—certainly subordination was implicit in the Navigation Acts and the Dominion of New England. London officials in the Cromwellian and Restoration eras were hardly sensitive to colonial rights when they implemented imperial plans. Hence in trying to bring order, unity, and central direction to the disparate colonial settlements, the home leaders planted seeds that would sprout from the ground as insurrections. The causes of the various uprisings were numerous, and they reflected local conditions as much as negative reactions to imperial programs. Yet the colonists were asking for a definition of their rights and privileges as Anglo-Americans. Were they to be equals or subordinates? If they were to be in the latter status, then how low were they to be? Who was to lead in America, imperial administrators or local men of wealth and standing? Were colonists to have economic security or insecurity? Were they to have the known rights of Englishmen? The various colonial rebellions failed to provide a clear-cut answer, but a long standing truce was established after 1689. The truce lasted for three-quarters of a century until another sequence of events raising these and other questions produced the American Revolution.

13. Politics and Social Structure in Virginia

Bernard Bailyn

Historians once presumed that Bacon's Rebellion in Virginia represented an outpouring of popular democratic sentiment against the arbitrary and high-handed tactics of Governor William Berkeley. The common citizens rose up in defiance because of their pent-up frustrations about faltering tobacco prices, heavy local taxes, and the failure of Berkeley's government to protect white settlers from chronic Indian depredations. However, Bernard Bailyn (b. 1922), a member of the history faculty at Harvard University, has called such accounts into question. He asserts that the Bacon insurrection was really the final culmination of clashing interests among members of an emerging Virginia social and political aristocracy.

Reflecting upon seventeenth-century attitudes about who should rule in state and society and relating those attitudes to the formation of leadership groups in early Virginia, Professor Bailyn claims that it was not until the 1650s that a socioeconomic elite capable of sustaining political authority appeared in the colony. Yet something happened to disintegrate that elite into two factions, something relating to the new imperial programs of the Restoration era. Explaining what happened, how it affected the coming of Bacon's Rebellion, and its long-term significance in terms of colonial political development forms the central thrust of Bailyn's presentation.

According to Professor Bailyn, the Rebellion spilled over from tensions arising out of an evolving social and political structure. Does he suggest that Virginia's structure, more fluid than its English model, was the source of continuing but formative political instability in the decades to come? What did instability portend for the future? How does Virginia's situation compare with New England's, where the traditional Puritan ruling elite was being threatened on all sides by aggrandizing local merchants and imperial administrators?

By the end of the seventeenth century the American colonists faced an array of disturbing problems in the conduct of public affairs. Settlers from England and Holland, reconstructing familiar institutions on American shores, had become participants in what would appear to have been a wave of civil disobedience. Constituted authority was confronted with repeated challenges. Indeed, a veritable anarchy seems to have prevailed at the center of colonial society, erupting in a

Source: Bernard Bailyn, "Politics and Social Structure in Virginia," in *Seventeenth-Century America: Essays in Colonial History,* ed. James Morton Smith (Chapel Hill: University of North Carolina Press, 1959), pp. 90–115. Footnotes omitted. Reprinted by permission of the University of North Carolina Press and the Institute of Early American History and Culture.

series of insurrections that began as early as 1635 with the "thrusting out" of Governor Harvey in Virginia. Culpeper's Rebellion in Carolina, the Protestant Association in Maryland, Bacon's Rebellion in Virginia, Leisler's seizure of power in New York, the resistance to and finally the overthrow of Andros in New England—every colony was affected.

These outbursts were not merely isolated local affairs. Although their immediate causes were rooted in the particular circumstances of the separate colonies, they nevertheless had common characteristics. They were, in fact, symptomatic of a profound disorganization of European society in its American setting. Seen in a broad view, they reveal a new configuration of forces which shaped the origins of American politics.

In a letter written from Virginia in 1623, George Sandys, the resident treasurer, reported despondently on the character and condition of the leading settlers. Some of the councilors were "no more than Ciphers," he wrote; others were "miserablie poore"; and the few substantial planters lived apart, taking no responsibility for public concerns. There was, in fact, among all those "worthie the mencioninge" only one person deserving of full approval. Lieutenant William Peirce "refuses no labour, nor sticks at anie expences that may aduantage the publique." Indeed, Sandys added, Peirce was "of a Capacitie that is not to bee expected in a man of his breedinge."

The afterthought was penetrating. It cut below the usual complaints of the time that many of the settlers were lazy malcontents hardly to be preferred to the Italian glassworkers, than whom, Sandys wrote, "a more damned crew hell never vomited." What lay behind Sandys' remark was not so much that wretched specimens are arriving in the shipments of servants nor even that the quality of public leadership was declining but that the social foundations of political power were being strangely altered.

All of the settlers in whatever colony presumed a fundamental relationship between social structure and political authority. Drawing on a common medieval heritage, continuing to conceive of society as a hierarchical unit, its parts justly and naturally separated into inferior and superior levels, they assumed that superiority was indivisible; there was not one hierarchy for political matters, another for social purposes. John Winthrop's famous explanation of God's intent that "in all times some must be rich some poore, some highe and eminent in power and dignitie; others meane and in subieccion" could not have been more carefully worded. Riches, dignity, and power were properly placed in apposition; they pertained to the same individuals.

So closely related were social leadership and political leadership that experience if not theory justified an identification between state and society. To the average English colonist that state was not an abstraction existing above men's lives, justifying itself in its own terms, taking occasional human embodiment. However glorified in monarchy, the state in ordinary form was indistinguishable from a more general social authority; it was woven into the texture of everyday life. It was the same squire or manorial lord who in his various capacities collated to the benefice, set the rents, and enforced the statutes of Parliament and the royal decrees. Nothing could have been more alien to the settlers than the idea that competition for political leadership should be open to all levels of society or that obscure social origins or technical skills should be considered valuable qualifications for office. The proper response to new technical demands on public servants was not to give power to the skilled but to give skills to the powerful. The English gentry and landed aristocracy remained politically adaptable and hence politically competent, assuming when necessary new public functions, eliminating the need for a professional state bureaucracy. By their amateur competence they made possible a continuing identification between political and social authority.

In the first years of settlement no one had reason to expect that this characteristic of public life would fail to transfer itself to the colonies. For at least a decade and a half after its founding there had been in the Jamestown settlement a small group of leaders drawn from the higher echelons of English society. Besides well-born soldiers of fortune like George Percy, son of the Earl of Northumberland, there were among them four sons of the West family—children of Lord de la Warr and his wife, a second cousin of Queen Elizabeth. In Virginia the West brothers held appropriately high positions; three of them served as governors. Christopher Davison, the colony's secretary, was the son of Queen Elizabeth's secretary William Davison, M.P. and Privy Councilor. The troublesome John Martin, of Martin's Brandon, was the son of Sir Richard Martin, twice Lord Mayor of London, and also the brother-in-law of Sir Julius Caesar, Master of the Rolls and Privy Councilor. Sir Francis and Haute Wyatt were sons of substantial Kent gentry and grandsons of the Sir Thomas Wyatt who led the rebellion of 1554 against Queen Mary. George Sandys' father was the archbishop of York; of his three older brothers, all knights and M.P.'s, two were eminent country gentlemen, and the third, Edwin, of Virginia Company fame, was a man of great influence in the city. George Thorpe was a former M.P. and Gentleman of the Privy Chamber.

More impressive than such positions and relationships was the cultural level represented. For until the very end of the Company period, Virginia remained to the literary and scientific an exotic attraction, its settlement an important moment in Christian history. Its original magnetism for those in touch with intellectual currents affected the early immigration. Of the twenty councilors of 1621, eight had been educated at Oxford, Cambridge, or the Inns of Court. Davison, like Martin trained in the law, was a poet in a family of poets. Thorpe was a "student of Indian views on religion and astronomy." Francis Wyatt wrote verses and was something of a student of political theory. Alexander Whitaker, M.A., author of *Good Newes from Virginia,* was the worthy heir "of a good part of the learning of his renowned father," the master of St. John's College and Regius Professor of Divinity at Cambridge, John Pory, known to history mainly as the speaker of the first representative assembly in America, was a Master of Arts, "protege and disciple of Hakluyt," diplomat, scholar, and traveler, whose writings from and about America have a rightful place in literary history. Above all there was George Sandys, "poet, traveller, and scholar," a member of Lord Falkland's literary circle; while in Jamestown he continued as a matter of course to work on his notable translation of Ovid's *Metamorphoses.*

There was, in other words, during the first years of settlement a direct transference to Virginia of the upper levels of the English social hierarchy as well as of the lower. If the great majority of the settlers were recruited from the yeoman class and below, there was nevertheless a reasonable representation from those upper groups acknowledged to be the rightful rulers of society.

It is a fact of some importance, however, that this governing elite did not survive a single generation, at least in its original form. By the thirties their number had declined to insignificance. Percy, for example, left in 1612. Whitaker drowned in 1617. Sandys and Francis Wyatt arrived only in 1621, but their enthusiasm cooled quickly; they were both gone by 1626. Of the Wests, only John was alive and resident in the colony a decade after the collapse of the Company. Davison, who returned to England in 1622 after only a year's stay, was sent back in 1623 but died within a year of his return. Thorpe was one of the six councilors slain in the massacre of 1622. Pory left for England in 1622; his return as investigating commissioner in 1624 was temporary, lasting only a few months. And the cantankerous Martin graced the Virginia scene by his absence after 1625; he is last heard from in the early 1630's petitioning for release from a London debtor's prison.

To be sure, a few representatives of important English families, like John West and Edmund Scarborough, remained. There were also one or two additions from the same social level. But there were few indeed of such individuals, and the basis of their authority had changed. The group of gentlemen and illuminati that had dominated the scene during the Company era had been dispersed. Their disappearance created a political void which was filled soon enough, but from a different area of recruitment, from below, from the toughest and most fortunate of the surviving planters whose eminence by the end of the thirties had very little to do with the transplantation of social status.

The position of the new leaders rested on their ability to wring material gain from the wilderness. Some, like Samuel Mathews, started with large initial advantages, but more typical were George Menefie and John Utie, who began as independent landowners by right of transporting themselves and only one or two servants. Abraham Wood, famous for his explorations and like Menefie and Utie the future possessor of large estates and important offices, appears first as a servant boy on Mathews' plantation. Adam Thoroughgood, the son of a country vicar, also started in Virginia as a servant, aged fourteen. William Spencer is first recorded as a yeoman farmer without servants.

Such men as these—Spencer, Wood, Menefie, Utie, Mathews—were the most important figures in Virginia politics up to the Restoration, engrossing large tracts of land, dominating the Council, unseating Sir John Harvey from the governorship. But in no traditional sense were they a ruling class. They lacked the attributes of social authority, and their political dominance was a continuous achievement. Only with the greatest difficulty, if at all, could distinction be expressed in a genteel style of life, for existence in this generation was necessarily crude. Mathews may have created a flourishing estate and Menefie had splendid fruit gardens, but the great tracts of land such men claimed were almost entirely raw wilderness. They had risen to their positions, with few exceptions, by brute labor and shrewd manipulation; they had personally shared the burdens of settlement. They succeeded not because of, but despite, whatever gentility they may have had. William Claiborne may have been educated at the Middle Temple; Peirce could not sign his name; but what counted was their common capacity to survive and flourish in frontier settlements. They were tough, unsentimental, quick-tempered, crudely ambitious men concerned with profits and increased landholdings, not the grace of life. They roared curses, drank exuberantly, and gambled (at least according to deVries) for their servants when other commodities were lacking. If the worst of Governor Harvey's offenses had been to knock out the teeth of an offending councilor with a cudgel, as he did on one occasion, no one would have questioned his right to the governorship. Rank had its privileges, and these men were the first to claim then, but rank itself was unstable and the lines of class or status were fluid. There was no insulation for even the most elevated from the rude impact of frontier life.

As in style of life so in politics, these leaders of the first permanently settled generation did not re-create the characteristics of a stable gentry. They had had little opportunity to acquire the sense of public responsibility that rests on deep identification with the land and its people. They performed in some manner the duties expected of leaders, but often public office was found simply burdensome. Reports such as Sandys' that Yeardley, the councilor and former governor, was wholly absorbed in his private affairs and scarcely glanced at public matters and that Mathews "will rather hazard the payment of fforfeitures than performe our Injunctions" were echoed by Harvey throughout his tenure of office. Charles Harmar, justice of the peace on the Eastern Shore, attended the court once in eight years, and Claiborne's record was only slightly better. Attendance to public duties had to be specifically enjoined, and privileges were of necessity accorded provincial officeholders. The members of the Council were particularly favored by the gift of tax exemption.

The private interests of this group, which had assumed control of public office by virtue not of inherited status but of newly achieved and strenuously maintained economic eminence, were pursued with little interference from the traditional restraints imposed on a responsible ruling class. Engaged in an effort to establish themselves in the land, they sought as specific ends: autonomous local jurisdiction, an aggressive expansion of settlement and trading enterprises, unrestricted access to land, and, at every stage, the legal endorsement of acquisitions. Most of the major public events for thirty years after the dissolution of the Company—and especially the overthrow of Harvey—were incidents in the pursuit of these goals.

From his first appearance in Virginia, Sir John Harvey threatened the interests of this emerging planter group. While still in England he had identified himself with the faction that had successfully sought the collapse of the Company, and thus his mere presence in Virginia was a threat to the legal basis of land grants made under the Company's charter. His demands for the return as public property of goods that had once belonged to the Company specifically jeopardized the planters' holdings. His insistence that the governorship was more than a mere chairmanship of the Council tended to undermine local autonomy. His conservative Indian policy not only weakened the settlers' hand in what already seemed an irreconcilable enmity with the natives but also restricted the expansion of settlement. His opposition to Claiborne's claim to Kent Island threatened to kill off the lucrative Chesapeake Bay trade, and his attempt to ban the Dutch ships from the colony endangered commerce more generally. His support of the official policy of economic diversification, together with his endorsement of the English schemes of tobacco monopoly, alienated him finally and completely from the Council group.

Within a few months of his assuming the governorship, Harvey wrote home with indignation of the "waywardnes and oppositions" of the councilors and condemned them for factiously seeking "rather for their owne endes then either seekinge the generall good or doinge right to particuler men." Before a year was out the antagonisms had become so intense that a formal peace treaty had to be drawn up between Harvey and the Council. But both sides were adamant, and conflict was inescapable. It exploded in 1635 amid comic opera scenes of "extreame coller and passion" complete with dark references to Richard the Third and musketeers "running with their peices presented." The conclusion was Harvey's enraged arrest of George Menefie "of suspicion of Treason to his Majestie"; Utie's response, "And wee the like to you sir"; and the governor's forced return to England.

Behind these richly heroic "passings and repassings to and fro" lies not a victory of democracy or representative institutions or anything of the sort. Democracy, in fact, was identified in the Virginians' minds with the "popular and tumultuary government" that had prevailed in the old Company's quarter courts, and they wanted none of it; the Assembly as a representative institution was neither greatly sought after nor hotly resisted. The victory of 1635 was that of resolute leaders of settlement stubbornly fighting for individual establishment. With the reappointment of Sir Francis Wyatt as governor, their victory was assured and in the Commonwealth period it was completely realized. By 1658, when Mathews was elected governor, effective interference from outside had disappeared and the supreme authority had been assumed by an Assembly which was in effect a league of local magnates secure in their control of county institutions.

One might at that point have projected the situation forward into a picture of dominant county families dating from the 1620's and 1630's, growing in identification with the land and people, ruling with increasing responsibility from increasingly eminent positions. But such a projection would be false. The fact is that with a few notable exceptions like the Scarboroughs and the Wormeleys, these struggling planters of the first generation failed to perpetuate their leadership into the second generation. Such families as the Woods, the Uties, and Mathews, and the Peirces faded from dominant positions of authority after the deaths of their founders. To some extent this was the result of the general insecurity of life that created odds against the physical survival in the male line of any given family. But even if male heirs had remained in these families after the death of the first generation, undisputed eminence would not. For a new emigration had begun in the forties, continuing for close to thirty years, from which was drawn a new ruling group that had greater possibilities for permanent dominance than Harvey's opponents had had. These newcomers absorbed and subordinated the older group, forming the basis of the most celebrated oligarchy in American history.

Most of Virginia's great eighteenth-century names, such as Bland, Burwell, Byrd, Carter, Digges, Ludwell, and Mason, appear in the colony for the first time within ten years either side of 1655. These progenitors of the eighteenth-century aristocracy arrived in remarkably similar circumstances. The most important of these immigrants were younger sons of substantial families well connected in London business and governmental circles and long associated with Virginia; family claims to land in the colony or inherited shares of the original Company stock were now brought forward as a basis for establishment in the New World.

Thus the Bland family interests in Virginia date from a 1618 investment in the Virginia Company by the London merchant John Bland, supplemented in 1622 by another in Martin's Hundred. The merchant never touched foot in America, but three of his sons did come to Virginia in the forties and fifties to exploit these investments. The Burwell fortunes derive from the early subscription to the Company of Edward Burwell, which was inherited in the late forties by his son, Lewis I. The first William Byrd arrived about 1670 to assume the Virginia properties of his mother's family, the Steggs, which dated back to the early days of the Company. The Digges's interests in Virginia stem from the original investments of Sir Dudley Digges and two of his sons in the Company, but it was a third son,

Edward, who emigrated in 1650 and established the American branch of the family. Similarly, the Masons had been financially interested in Virginia thirty-two years before 1652, when the first immigrant of that family appeared in the colony. The Culpeper clan, whose private affairs enclose much of the history of the South in the second half of the seventeenth century, was first represented in Virginia by Thomas Culpeper, who arrived in 1649; but the family interests in Virginia had been established a full generation earlier: Thomas' father, uncle, and cousin had all been members of the original Virginia Company and their shares had descended in the family. Even Governor Berkeley fits the pattern. There is no mystery about his sudden exchange in 1642 of the life of a dilettante courtier for that of a colonial administrator and estate manager. He was a younger son without prospects, and his family's interests in Virginia, dating from investments in the Company made twenty years earlier, as well as his appointment held out the promise of an independent establishment in America.

Claims on the colony such as these were only one, though the most important, of a variety of forms of capital that might provide the basis for secure family fortunes. One might simply bring over enough of a merchant family's resources to begin immediately building up an imposing estate, as, presumably, did that ambitious draper's son, William Fitzhugh. The benefits that accrued from such advantages were quickly translated into landholdings in the development of which these settlers were favored by the chronology of their arrival. For though they extended the area of cultivation in developing their landholdings, they were not obliged to initiate settlement. They fell heirs to large areas of the tidewater region that had already been brought under cultivation. "Westover" was not the creation of William Byrd; it had originally been part of the De la Warr estate, passing, with improvements, to Captain Thomas Pawlett, thence to Theodorick Bland, and finally to Byrd. Lewis Burwell inherited not only his father's land, but also the developed estate of his stepfather, Wingate. Some of the Carters' lands may be traced back through John Utie to a John Jefferson, who left Virginia as early as 1628. Abraham Wood's entire Fort Henry property ended in the hands of the Jones family. The Blands' estate in Charles City County, which later became the Harrisons' "Berkeley" plantation, was cleared for settlement in 1619 by servants of the "particular" plantation of Berkeley's Hundred.

Favored thus by circumstance, a small group within the second generation migration moved toward setting itself off in a permanent way as a ruling landed gentry. That they succeeded was due not only to their material advantages but also to the force of their motivation. For these individuals were in social origins just close enough to establishment in gentility to feel the pangs of deprivation most acutely. It is not the totally but the partially dispossessed who build up the most propulsive aspirations, and behind the zestful lunging at propriety and status of a William Fitzhugh lay not the narcotic yearnings of the disinherited but the pent-up ambitions of the gentleman *manque*. These were neither hardhanded pioneers nor dilettante romantics, but ambitious younger sons of middle-class families who knew well enough what gentility was and sought it as a specific objective.

The establishment of this group was rapid. Within a decade of their arrival they could claim, together with a fortunate few of the first generation, a marked social eminence and full political authority at the county level. But their rise was not uniform. Indeed, by the seventies a new circumstance had introduced an effective principle of social differentiation among the colony's leaders. A hierarchy of position within the newly risen gentry was created by the Restoration government's efforts to extend its control more effectively over its mercantile empire. Demanding of its colonial executives and their advisors closer supervision over the external aspects of the economy, it offered a measure of patronage necessary for enforcement. Public offices dealing with matters that profoundly affected the basis of economic life—tax collection, customs regulation, and the bestowal of land grants—fell within the gift of the governor and tended to form an inner circle of privilege. One can note in Berkeley's administration the growing importance of this barrier of officialdom. Around its privileges there formed the "Green Spring" faction, named after Berkeley's plantation near Jamestown, a group bound to be governor not by royalist sympathies so much as by ties of kinship and partronage.

Thus Colonel Henry Norwood, related to Berkeley by a "near affinity in blood," was given the treasurership of the colony in 1650, which he held for more than two decades. During this time Thomas Ludwell, a cousin and Somerset neighbor of the governor, was secretary of state, in which post he was succeeded in 1678 by his brother Philip, who shortly thereafter married Berkeley's widow. This Lady Berkeley, it should be noted, was the daughter of Thomas Culpeper, the immigrant of 1649 and a cousin of Thomas Lord Culpeper who became governor in 1680. Immediately after her marriage to Berkeley, her brother Alexander requested and received from the governor the nomination to the surveyor-generalship of Virginia, a post he filled for twenty-three years while resident in England, appointing as successive deputies the brothers Ludwell, to whom by 1680 he was twice related by marriage. Lady Berkeley was also related through her mother to William Byrd's wife, a fact that explains much about Byrd's prolific office-holding.

The growing distinctiveness of provincial officialdom within the landed gentry may also be traced in the transformation of the Council. Originally, this body had been expected to comprise the entire effective government, central and local; councilors were to serve, individually or in committees, as local magistrates. But the spread of settlement upset this expectation, and at the same time as the local offices were falling into the hands of autonomous local powers representing leading county families, the Council, appointed by the governor and hence associated with official patronage, increasingly realized the separate, lucrative privileges available to it.

As the distinction between local and central authority became clear, the county magistrates sought their own distinct voice in the management of the colony, and they found it in developing the possibilities of burgess representation. In the beginning there was no House of Burgesses; representation from the burghs and hundreds was conceived of not as a branch of government separate from the Council but as a periodic supplement to it. Until the fifties the burgesses, meeting in the Assemblies with the councilors, felt little need to form themselves into a separate house, for until that decade there was little evidence of a conflict of interests between the two groups. But when, after the Restoration, the privileged status of the Council became unmistakable and the county magnates found control of the increasingly important provincial administration pre-empted by this body, the burgess part of the Assembly took on a new meaning in contrast to that of the Council. Burgess representation now became vital to the county leaders if they were to share in any consistent way in affairs larger than those of the counties. They looked to the franchise, hitherto broad not by design but by neglect, introducing qualifications that would ensure their control of the Assembly. Their interest in provincial government could not longer be expressed in the conglomerate Assembly, and at least by 1663 the House of Burgesses began to meet separately as a distinct body voicing interests potentially in conflict with those of the Council.

Thus by the eighth decade the ruling class in Virginia was broadly based on leading county families and dominated at the provincial level by a privileged officialdom. But this social and political structure was too new, too lacking in the sanctions of time and custom, its leaders too close to humbler origins and as yet too undistinguished in style of life, to be accepted without a struggle. A period of adjustment was necessary, of which Bacon's Rebellion was the climactic episode.

Bacon's Rebellion began as an unauthorized frontier war against the Indians and ended as an upheaval that threatened the entire basis of social and political authority. Its immediate causes have to do with race relations and settlement policy, but behind these issues lay deeper elements related to resistance against the maturing shape of a new social order. These elements explain the dimensions the conflict reached.

There was, first, resistance by substantial planters to the privileges and policies of the inner provincial clique led by Berkely and composed of those directly dependent on his patronage. These dissidents, among whom were the leaders of the Rebellion, represented neither the downtrodden masses nor a principle of opposition to privilege as such. Their discontent stemmed to a large extent from their own exclusion from privileges they sought. Most often their grievances were based on personal rebuffs they had received as they reached for entry into provincial officialdom. Thus—to speak of the leaders of the Rebellion—Giles Bland arrived in Virginia in 1671 to take over the agency of his late uncle in the management of his father's extensive landholdings, assuming at the same time the lucrative position of customs collector which he had obtained in London. But, amid angry cries of *"pittyfull fellow, puppy* and *Sonn of a Whore,"* he fell out first with Berkeley's cousin and favorite, Thomas Ludwell, and finally with the governor himself; for his "Barbarous and Insolent Behaviors" Bland was fined, arrested, and finally removed from the collectorship. Of the two "chiefe Incendiarys," William Drummond and Richard Lawrence, the former had been quarreling with Berkeley since 1664, first over land claims in Carolina, then over a contract for building a fort near James City, and repeatedly over lesser issues in the General Court; Lawrence "some Years before . . . had been partially treated at Law, for a considerable Estate on behalfe of a Corrupt favorite." Giles Brent, for his depredations against the Indians in violation of official policy, had not only been severely fined but barred from public office. Bacon himself could not have appeared under more favorable circumstances. A cousin both of Lady Berkeley and of the councilor Nathaniel Bacon, Sr., and by general agreement "a Gent: man of a Liberall education" if of a somewhat tarnished reputation, he had quickly staked out land for himself and had been elevated, for reasons "best known to the Governour," to the Council. But being "of a most imperious and dangerous hidden Pride of heart . . . very ambitious and arrogant," he wanted more, and quickly. His alienation from and violent opposition to Berkeley were wound in among the animosities created by the Indian problem and were further complicated by his own unstable personality; they were related also to the fact that Berkeley finally turned down the secret offer Bacon and Byrd made in 1675 for the purchase from the governor of a monopoly of the Indian trade.

These specific disputes have a more general aspect. It was three decades since Berkeley had assumed the governorship and begun rallying a favored group, and it was over a decade since the Restoration had given this group unconfined sway over the provincial government. In those years much of the choice tidewater land as well as the choice offices had been spoken for, and the tendency of the highly placed was to hold firm. Berkeley's Indian policy—one of stabilizing the borders between Indians and whites and protecting the natives from depredation by land-hungry settlers—although a sincere attempt to deal with an extremely difficult problem, was also conservative, favoring the established. Newcomers like Bacon and Bland and particularly landholders on the frontier felt victimized by a stabilization of the situation or by a controlled expansion that maintained on an extended basis the existing power structure. They were logically drawn to aggressive positions. In an atmosphere charged with violence, their interests constituted a challenge to provincial authority. Bacon's primary appeal in his "Manifesto" played up the threat of this challenge:

> Let us trace these men in Authority and Favour to whose hands the dispensation of the Countries wealth has been commited; let us observe the sudden Rise of their Estates [compared] with the Quality in wch they first entered this Country . . . And lett us see wither their extractions and Education have not bin vile, And by what pretence of learning and vertue they could [enter] soe soon into Imployments of so great Trust and consequence, let us . . . see what spounges have suckt up the Publique Treasure and wither it hath not bin privately contrived away by unworthy Favourites and juggling Parasites whose tottering Fortunes have bin repaired and supported at the Publique chardg.

Such a threat to the basis of authority was not lost on Berkeley or his followers. Bacon's merits, a contemporary wrote, "thretned an eclips to there riseing gloryes. . . . (if he should continue in the Governours favour) of Seniours they might becom juniours, while there younger Brother . . . might steale away that blessing, which they accounted there owne by birthright."

But these challengers were themselves challenged, for another main element in the upheaval was the discontent among the ordinary settlers at the local privileges of the same newly risen county magnates who assailed the privileges of the Green Spring faction. The specific Charles City County grievances were directed as much at the locally dominant family, the Hills, as they were at Berkeley and his clique. Similarly, Surry County complained of its county court's highhanded and secretive manner of levying taxes on "the poore people" and of setting the sheriffs' and clerks' fees; they petitioned for the removal of these abuses and for the right to elect the vestry and to limit the tenure of the sheriffs. At all levels the Rebellion challenged the stability of newly secured authority.

It is this double aspect of discontent behind the violence of the Rebellion that explains the legislation passed in June, 1676, by the so-called "Bacon's Assembly." At first glance these laws seem difficult to interpret because they express disparate if not contradictory interests. But they yield readily to analysis if they are seen not as the reforms of a single group but as efforts to express the desires of two levels of discontent with the way the political and social hierarchy was becoming stabilized. On the one hand, the laws include measures designed by the numerically predominant ordinary settlers throughout the colony as protests against the recently acquired superiority of the leading county families. These were popular protests and they relate not to provincial affairs but to the situation within the local areas of jurisdiction. Thus the statute restricting the franchise to freeholders was repealed; freemen were given the right to elect the parish vestrymen; and the county courts were supplemented by elected freemen to serve with the regularly appointed county magistrates.

On the other hand, there was a large number of measures expressing the dissatisfactions not so much of the ordinary planter but of the local leaders against the prerogatives recently acquired by the provincial elite, prerogatives linked to officialdom and centered in the Council. Thus the law barring officeholding to newcomers of less than three years' residence struck at the arbitrary elevation of the governor's favorites, including Bacon; and the acts forbidding councilors to join the county courts, outlawing the governor's appointment of sheriffs and tax collectors, and nullifying tax exemption for councilors all voiced objections of the local chieftains to privileges enjoyed by others. From both levels there was objection to profiteering in public office.

Thus the wave of rebellion broke and spread. But why did it subside? One might have expected that the momentary flood would have become a steady tide, its rhythms governed by a fixed political constellation. But in fact it did not; stable political alignments did not result. The conclusion to this controversy was characteristic of all the insurrections. The attempted purges and counterpurges by the leaders of the two sides were followed by a rapid submerging of factional identity. Occasional references were later made to the episode, and there were individuals who found an interest in keeping its memory alive. Also, the specific grievances behind certain of the attempted legal reforms of 1676 were later revived. But of stable parties or factions around these issues there were none.

It was not merely that in the late years of the century no more than in the early was there to be found a justification for permanently organized political opposition or party machinery, that persistent, organized dissent was still indistinguishable from sedition; more important was the fact that at the end of the century as in 1630 there was agreement that some must be "highe and eminent in power and dignitie; others meane and in subieccion." Protests and upheaval had resulted from the discomforts of discovering who was, in fact, which, and what the particular consequences of "power and dignitie" were.

But by the end of the century the most difficult period of adjustment had passed and there was an acceptance of the fact that certain families were distinguished from others in riches, in dignity, and in access to political authority. The establishment of these families marks the emergence of Virginia's colonial aristocracy.

It was a remarkable governing group. Its members were soberly responsible, alive to the implications of power; they performed their public obligations with notable skill. Indeed, the glare of their accomplishments is so bright as occasionally to blind us to the conditions that limited them. As a ruling class the Virginian aristocracy of the eighteenth century was unlike other contemporary nobilities or aristocracies, including the English. The differences, bound up with the special characteristics of the society it ruled, had become clear at the turn of the seventeenth century.

Certain of these characteristics are elusive, difficult to grasp and analyze. The leaders of early eighteenth-century Virginia were, for example, in a particular sense, cultural provincials. They were provincial not in the way of Polish *szlachta* isolated on their estates by poverty and impassable roads, nor in the way of sunken *seigneurs* grown rustic and old-fashioned in lonely Norman chateaux. The Virginians were far from uninformed or unaware of the greater world; they were in fact deeply and continuously involved in the cultural life of the Atlantic community. But they knew themselves to be provincials in the sense that their culture was not self-contained; its sources and superior expressions were to be found elsewhere than in their own land. They must seek it from afar; it must be acquired, and once acquired be maintained according to standards externally imposed, in the creation of which they had not participated. The most cultivated of them read much, purposefully, with a diligence the opposite of that essential requisite of aristocracy, uncontending ease. William Byrd's diary with its daily records of stints of study is a stolid testimonial to the virtues of regularity and effort in maintaining standards of civilization set abroad.

In more evident ways also the Virginia planters were denied an uncontending ease of life. They were not *rentiers*. Tenancy, when it appeared late in the colonial period, was useful to the landowners mainly as a cheap way of improving lands held in reserve for future development. The Virginia aristocrat was an active manager of his estate, drawn continuously into the most intimate contacts with the soil and its cultivation. This circumstance limited his ease, one might even say bound him to the soil, but it also strengthened his identity with the land and its problems and saved him from the temptation to create of his privileges an artificial world of self-indulgence.

But more important in distinguishing the emerging aristocracy of Virginia from other contemporary social and political elites were two very specific circumstances. The first concerns the relationship between the integrity of the family unit and the descent of real property. "The English political family," Sir Lewis Namier writes with particular reference to the eighteenth-century aristocracy,

> is a compound of "blood," name, and estate, this last . . . being the most important of the three. . . . The name is a weighty symbol, but liable to variations. . . . the estate . . . is, in the long run, the most potent factor in securing continuity through identification. . . . Primogeniture and entails psychically preserve the family in that they tend to fix its position through the successive generations, and thereby favour conscious identification.

The descent of landed estates in eighteenth-century England was controlled by the complicated device known as the strict settlement which provided that the heir at his marriage received the estate as a life tenant, entailing its descent to his unborn eldest son and specifying the limitations of the encumbrances upon the land that might be made in behalf of his daughters and younger sons.

If was the strict settlement, in which in the eighteenth century perhaps half the land of England was bound, that provided continuity over generations for the landed aristocracy. This permanent identification of the family with a specific estate and with the status and offices that pertained to it was achieved at the cost of sacrificing the younger sons. It was a single stem of the family only that retained its superiority; it alone controlled the material basis for political dominance.

This basic condition of aristocratic governance in England was never present in the American colonies, and not for lack of familiarity with legal forms. The economic necessity that had prompted the widespread adoption of the strict settlement in England was absent in the colonies. Land was cheap and easily available, the more so as one rose on the social and political ladder. There was no need to deprive the younger sons or even daughters of landed inheritances in order to keep the original family estate intact. Provision could be made for endowing each of them with plantations, and they in turn could provide similarly for their children. Moreover, to confine the stem family's fortune to a single plot of land, however extensive, was in the Virginia economy to condemn it to swift decline. Since the land was quickly worn out and since it was cheaper to acquire new land than to rejuvenate the worked soil by careful husbandry, geographical mobility, not stability, was the key to prosperity. Finally, since land was only as valuable as the labor available to work it, a great estate was worth passing intact from generation to generation only if it had annexed to it a sufficient population of slaves. Yet this condition imposed severe rigidities in a plantation's economy—for a labor force bound to a particular plot was immobilized—besides creating bewildering confusions in law.

The result, evident before the end of the seventeenth century, was a particular relationship between the family and the descent of property. There was in the beginning no intent on the part of the Virginians to alter the traditional forms; the continued vitality of the ancient statutes specifying primogeniture in certain cases was assumed. The first clear indication of a new trend came in the third quarter of the century, when the leading gentry, rapidly accumulating large estates, faced for the first time the problem of the transfer of property. The result was the subdivision of the great holdings and the multiplication of smaller plots while the net amount of land held by the leading families continued to rise.

This trend continued. Primogeniture neither at the end of the seventeenth century nor after prevailed in Virginia. It was never popular even among the most heavily endowed of the tidewater families. The most common form of bequest was a grant to the eldest son of the undivided home plantation and gifts of other tracts outside the home county to the younger sons and daughters. Thus by his will of 1686 Robert Beverley, Sr., bequeathed to his eldest son, Peter, all his land in Gloucester County lying between "Chiescake" and "Hoccadey's" creeks (an unspecified acreage); to Robert, the second son, another portion of the Gloucester lands amounting to 920 acres; to Harry, 1,600 acres in Rappahannock County; to John, 3,000 acres in the same county; to William, two plantations in Middlesex County; to Thomas, 3,000 acres in Rappahannock and New Kent counties; to his wife, three plantations including those "whereon I now live" for use during her lifetime, after which they were to descend to his daughter Catherine, who was also to receive £200 sterling; to his daughter Mary, £150 sterling; to "the childe that my wife goeth with, be it male or female," all the rest of his real property; and the residue of his personal property was "to be divided and disposed in equall part & portion betwix my wife and children." Among the bequests of Ralph Wormeley, Jr., in 1700 was an estate of 1,500 acres to his daughter Judith as well as separate plantations to his two sons.

Entail proved no more popular than primogeniture. Only a small minority of estates, even in the tidewater region, were ever entailed. In fact, despite the extension of developed land in the course of the eighteenth century, more tidewater estates were docked of entails than were newly entailed.

Every indication points to continuous and increasing difficulty in reproducing even pale replicas of the strict settlement. In 1705 a law was passed requiring a special act of the Assembly to break an entail; the law stood, but between 1711 and 1776 no fewer than 125 such private acts were passed, and in 1734 estates of under £200 were exempted from the law altogether. The labor problem alone was an insuperable barrier to perpetuating the traditional forms. A statute of 1727, clarifying the confused legislation of earlier years, had attempted to ensure a labor force on entailed land by classifying slaves as real property and permitting them to be bound together with land into bequests. But by 1748 this stipulation had resulted in such bewildering "doubts, variety of opinions, and confusions" that it was repealed. The repeal was disallowed in London, and in the course of a defense of its action the Assembly made vividly clear the utter impracticality of entailment in Virginia's economy. Slaves, the Assembly explained, were essential to the success of a plantation, but "slaves could not be kept on the lands to which they were annexed without manifest prejudice to the tenant in tail. . . . often the tenant was the proprietor of fee simple land much fitter for cultivation than his intailed lands, where he could work his slaves to a much greater advantage." On the other hand, if a plantation owner did send entailed slaves where they might be employed most economically the result was equally disastrous:

> the frequent removing and settling them on other lands in other counties and parts of the colony far distant from the county court where the deeds or wills which annexed them were recorded and the intail lands lay; the confusion occasioned by their mixture with fee simple slaves of the same name and sex and belonging to the same owner; the uncertainty of distinguishing one from another after several generations, no register of their genealogy being kept and none of them having surnames, were great mischiefs to purchasers, strangers, and creditors, who were often unavoidably deceived in their purchases and hindered in the recovery of their just debts. It also lessened the credit of the country; it being dangerous for the merchants of Great Britain to trust possessors of many slaves for fear the slaves might be intailed.

A mobile labor force free from legal entanglements and a rapid turnover of lands, not a permanent hereditary estate, were prerequisites of family prosperity. This condition greatly influenced social and political life. Since younger sons and even daughters inherited extensive landed properties, equal often to those of the eldest son, concentration of authority in the stem family was precluded. Third generation collateral descendants of the original immigrant were as important in their own right as the eldest son's eldest son. Great clans like the Carters and the Lees, though they may have acknowledged a central family seat, were scattered throughout the province on estates of equal influence. The four male Carters of the third generation were identified by contemporaries by the names of their separate estates, and, indistinguishable in style of life, they had an equal access to political power.

Since material wealth was the basis of the status which made one eligible for public office, there was a notable diffusion of political influence throughout a broadening group of leading families. No one son was predestined to represent the family interest in politics, but as many as birth and temperament might provide. In the 1750's there were no fewer than seven Lees of the same generation sitting together in the Virginia Assembly; in the Burgesses they spoke for five separate counties. To the eldest, Philip Ludwell Lee, they conceded a certain social superiority that made it natural for him to sit in the Council. But he did not speak alone for the family; by virtue of inheritance he had no unique authority over his brothers and cousins.

The leveling at the top of the social and political hierarchy, creating an evenness of status and influence, was intensified by continuous intermarriage within the group. The unpruned branches of these flourishing family trees, growing freely, met and intertwined until by the Revolution the aristocracy appeared to be one great tangled cousinry.

As political power became increasingly diffused throughout the upper stratum of society, the Council, still at the end of the seventeenth century a repository of unique privileges, lost its effective superiority. Increasingly through the successive decades its authority had to be exerted through alignments with the Burgesses— alignments made easier as well as more necessary by the criss-crossing network of kinship that united the two houses. Increasingly the Council's distinctions became social and ceremonial.

The contours of Virginia's political hierarchy were also affected by a second main conditioning element, besides the manner of descent of family property. Not only was the structure unusually level and broad at the top, but it was incomplete in itself. Its apex, the ultimate source of legal decision and control, lay in the quite different society of England, amid the distant embroilments of London, the court, and Parliament. The levers of control in that realm were for the most part hidden from the planters; yet the powers that ruled this remote region could impose an arbitrary authority directly into the midst of Virginia's affairs.

One consequence was the introduction of instabilities in the tenure and transfer of the highest offices. Tenure could be arbitrarily interrupted, and the transfer to kin of such positions at death or resignation—uncertain in any case because of the diffusion of family authority—could be quite difficult or even impossible. Thus William Byrd II returned from England at the death of his father in 1704 to take over the family properties, but though he was the sole heir he did not automatically or completely succeed to the elder Byrd's provincial offices. He did, indeed, become auditor of Virginia after his father, but only because he had carefully arranged for the succession while still in London; his father's Council seat went to someone else, and it took three years of patient maneuvering through his main London contact, Micajah Perry, to secure another; he never did take over the receivership. Even such power as "King" Carter, the reputed owner at his death of 300,000 acres and 1,000 slaves, was rebuffed by the resident deputy governor and had to deploy forces in England in order to transfer a Virginia naval office post from one of his sons to another. There was family continuity in public office, but at the highest level it was uncertain, the result of place-hunting rather than of the absolute prerogative of birth.

Instability resulted not only from the difficulty of securing and transferring high appointive positions but also and more immediately from the presence in Virginia of total strangers to the scene, particularly governors and their deputies, armed with extensive jurisdiction and powers of enforcement. The dangers of this element in public life became clear only after Berkeley's return to England in 1677, for after thirty-five years of residence in the colony Sir William had become a leader in the land independent of his royal authority. But Howard, Andros, and Nicholson were governors with full legal powers but with at best only slight connections with local society. In them, social leadership and political leadership had ceased to be identical.

In the generation that followed Berkeley's departure, this separation between the two spheres created the bitterest of political controversies. Firmly entrenched behind their control of the colony's government, the leading families battled with every weapon available to reduce the power of the executives and thus to eliminate what appeared to be an external and arbitrary authority. Repeated complaints by the governors of the intractable opposition of a league of local oligarchs marked the Virginians' success. Efforts by the executives to discipline the indigenous leaders could only be mildly successful. Patronage was a useful weapon, but its effectiveness diminished steadily, ground down between a resistant Assembly and an office-hungry bureaucracy in England. The possibility of exploiting divisions among the resident powers also declined as kinship lines bound the leading families closer together and as group interests became clearer with the passage of time. No faction built around the gubernatorial power could survive independently; ultimately its adherents would fall away and it would weaken. It was a clear logic of the situation that led the same individuals who had promoted Nicholson as a replacement for Andros to work against him once he assumed office.

Stability could be reached only by the complete identification of external and internal authority through permanent commitment by the appointees to local interests. Commissary Blair's extraordinary success in Virginia politics was based not only on his excellent connections in England but also on his marriage into the Harrison family, which gave him the support of an influential kinship faction. There was more than hurt pride and thwarted affection behind Nicholson's reported insane range at being spurned by the highly marriageable Lucy Burwell; and later the astute Sportswood, for all his success in imposing official policy, fully quieted the controversies of his administration only by succumbing completely and joining as a resident Virginia landowner the powers aligned against him.

But there was more involved than instability and conflict in the discontinuity between social and political organization at the topmost level. The state itself had changed its meaning. To a Virginia planter of the early eighteenth century the highest public authority was no longer merely one expression of a general social authority. It had become something abstract, external to his life and society, an ultimate power whose purposes were obscure, whose direction could neither be consistently influenced nor accurately plotted, and whose human embodiments were alien and antagonistic.

The native gentry of the early eighteenth century had neither the need nor the ability to fashion a new political theory to comprehend their experience, but their successors would find in the writings of John Locke on state and society not merely a reasonable theoretical position but a statement of self-evident fact.

I have spoken exclusively of Virginia, but though the histories of each of the colonies in the seventeenth century are different, they exhibit common characteristics. These features one might least have expected to find present in Virginia, and their presence there is, consequently, most worth indicating.

In all of the colonies the original transference of an ordered European society was succeeded by the rise to authority of resident settlers whose influence was rooted in their ability to deal with the problems of life in wilderness settlements. These individuals attempted to stabilize their positions, but in each case they were challenged by others arriving after the initial settlements, seeking to exploit certain advantages of position, wealth, or influence. These newcomers, securing after the Restoration governmental appointments in the colonies and drawn together by personal ties, especially those of kinship and patronage, came to constitute colonial officialdom. This group introduced a new principle of social organization; it also gave rise to new instabilities in a society in which the traditional forms of authority were already being subjected to severe pressures. By the eighth decade of the seventeenth century the social basis of public life had become uncertain and insecure, its stability delicate and sensitive to disturbance. Indian warfare, personal quarrels, and particularly the temporary confusion in external control caused by the Glorious Revolution became the occasions for violent challenges to constituted authority.

By the end of the century a degree of harmony had been achieved, but the divergence between political and social leadership at the topmost level created an area of permanent conflict. The political and social structures that emerged were by European standards strangely shaped. Everywhere as the bonds of empire drew tighter the meaning of the state was changing. Herein lay the origins of a new political system.

14. The Dominion of New England

Richard S. Dunn

Sir Edmund Andros arrived in Boston at the end of 1686 prepared to give the recalcitrant Puritans a strong dose of Stuart absolutism. Andros was an efficient if not a brilliant administrator with a military background—certainly he was prepared to be overbearing. To his dismay he discovered in April 1689 that ostensibly loyal followers had turned against him and the type of militarist-authoritarian imperial thinking he represented. But why? Professor Richard S. Dunn (b. 1928), who teaches at the University of Pennsylvania, suggests one answer in recording the political fortunes of some Massachusetts leaders during the Andros regime. Among those men of "moderate" persuasion were Fitz Winthrop (1638–1707) and his brother Wait (1642–1717), grandsons of the first Bay Colony governor, John Winthrop. Unlike their grandfather, these "two cavaliers in Israel," as Professor Dunn labels them, were rather exclusively dedicated to worldly gain in the form of personal wealth and political perquisites. They, like many other Massachusetts men, had drifted far away from the colony's original missionary goal and the concern with conversion, saving grace, and eternal salvation. The grandsons of John Winthrop were part of a world where religious values were losing out to secular interests.

The Dominion of New England personified that shift, emphasizing loyalty to the commercial goals of the developing empire above all else. The grand question for New Englanders living during the 1680s was whether to subordinate their spiritual commitments to the demands of imperial administrators. Andros perhaps went too far in an authoritarian direction, yet, paradoxically, even after he was removed Massachusetts Bay did not return to the ways of John Winthrop's generation. Acquisitive men like Fitz and Wait Winthrop had more political authority than ever in the years after the fall of the Dominion. What do these patterns suggest? What seemed to cause the shift in values? Was de facto imperial standardization still taking place, despite all the local uprisings, because of broader forces that were impinging on life everywhere in the provinces?

There is an extraordinary parallel between the course of events in England and New England between 1685 and 1689. On opposite shores of the Atlantic, James II and his deputy Sir Edmund Andros governed in such a highhanded and

Source: From Richard S. Dunn, *Puritans and Yankees: The Winthrop Dynasty of New England, 1630–1717* (Princeton: Princeton University Press, 1962), pp. 229–257. Footnotes omitted. Copyright © 1962 by Princeton University Press and reprinted by permission.

authoritarian fashion as to alienate their subjects, particularly those persons in the upper level of society who were used to sharing political power. The Dominion of New England had all the unpopular features of James' home government. Just as the King broke with Parliament in England, so he abolished representative institutions in New England. While James II whipped up religious hysteria in England by appointing Catholics to high offices, Sir Edmund was fostering the Anglican service in Boston, which in Puritan eyes was little better than the Whore of Rome. Andros was buttressed by a troop of redcoats in Boston, equivalent to James' standing army at Houslow Heath. In England, seven Anglican bishops were prosecuted for challenging the government's religious policy; in New England, Master John Wise and others were prosecuted for challenging the government's tax policy. Even Harvard College felt her independence threatened, as did Oxford and Cambridge.

Nor does the parallel end here. On both sides of the Atlantic this unpopular government was overthrown by revolution: November 1688 in the mother country, and April 1689 in America. Neither revolt was spontaneous. Both were precipitated by external circumstances; the landing of William of Orange galvanized the English rebels, and the news of William's landing spurred on the colonists. James II and Sir Edmund Andros were both unseated easily and without bloodshed. There was no popular or social upheaval. The revolution was carefully managed by those with the greatest stake in society, the great aristocratic landholders in England, merchants and clergymen in New England, who were not so much fighting for a noble cause as for their personal entrenchment. Finally, on both sides of the Atlantic a number of the principal actors engaged in double-dealing. Lord John Churchill, for instance, the future Duke of Marlborough, pledged himself to both James and William and slipped over to William's side only at the last minute when he was sure that James would lose. Similarly, in the far smaller world of Boston, Wait Winthrop remained a member of Andros' Dominion Council until the day the revolt broke out, when he abruptly became a member of the Council of Safety, which directed the rebellion, arrested Andros, and took over the government.

The Winthrop brothers' participation in and last-minute revulsion against the Dominion of New England marked the great turning point of both their careers. The momentous events of the 1680's taught them a hard lesson: the danger of dependence on the home government. Despite all the parallels between the situation in England and New England, the revolutionary crisis forced Fitz and Wait Winthrop to identify themselves as either Britons or colonials, to decide whether their prime loyalty was to the imperial service or to their local society. The Winthrop brothers decided that they were New Englanders.

The atmosphere was peculiar in Boston when the new royal government supplanted the old charter government in May 1686. The defeated orthodox party was bitterly unhappy. Magistrate Samuel Sewall tells in his *Diary* how the last session of the Bay court was closed "by the Weeping Marshal-Generall. Many Tears Shed in Prayer and at parting." But the jubilation of Randolph's circle was oddly muted. Month after month had passed without the arrival of either royal frigates or royal governor. Everyone was straining for news. In March, Wait wrote to Fitz: "Here is little new since my last to you, only . . . a coppye of the commission for the Government of this Collony, the Province of Maine, New Hampsheir, and Kings Province or Narrogansett country. . . . The commission is to Mr Dudly, as President till the chiefe Governor come, and to the rest named as of Counsell, whereof you are one, who are . . . to do all things with respect to the Government of the forenamed places as the commission largly directs." Wait did not bother to mention that he also was named to Dudley's council. Another month passed, and Wharton wrote Fitz that Boston was in an uproar: "some pray for Kirke, & some for Dudley, and as many curse both." At last on May 14 Edward Randolph debarked from the frigate *Rose* and took a coach for Joseph Dudley's house in Roxbury to present him with the Commission for the President and Council of New England. Three days later, as secretary of the council, Randolph curtly informed Fitz of his appointment and pressed him to come to Boston as quickly as possible.

Dudley's provisional government held office from May to December 1686. There was a distinctly new atmosphere in Boston, but by no means a wholesale transformation of Massachusetts society or institutions. By firmly refusing to dicker with members of the defunct charter government, Joseph Dudley was able to supplant them with a minimum of friction. His council was installed on May 25. When the new officers took their oaths before a public assembly in the Boston Town House, Dudley established the tone for the administration in his inaugural address. It was every colonist's duty to support the King's aim, which he defined as "the happy increase and advance of these Provinces, by their more immediate dependence upon the Crown of England." Obviously ruffled by his personal unpopularity, Dudley endeavored to meet his critics half-way, by promising that the transition from old government to new would be "as plain and easie as is possible."

The transition was suspiciously easy. With ten days of hard work, the council fulfilled its instructions to reorganize local government, the judicial system, and the militia. Many of the old officeholders were reappointed. Only a handful of men were haled before the council for contempt; one man was imprisoned and fined for speaking sedition. Samuel Sewall, whose sensitivity to innovations was exceptionally delicate, did complain about the new regime in his *Diary* but only on religious grounds. Sewall was upset by Anglican services in the Town House, by several Prayer Book marriages and burials, and by the insidious reappearance of the popish St. George's cross in the colony flags. Chiefly he was scandalized by the uninhibited behavior of Samuel Shrimpton and other nonpuritan Boston gentlemen, who seized the opportunity to "drink Healths, curse, swear, talk profanely and baudily to the great disturbance of the Town and grief of good people. Such high-handed wickedness has hardly been heard of before in Boston." Sewall had not seen anything yet.

Ironically, by the time Dudley's council had held office for a few weeks, Edward Randolph was more critical of the new regime than was Samuel Sewall. Randolph speedily discovered that his colleagues were more interested in the perquisites of office than in fundamental reform programs. After only four council meetings, he was finding that his supposed ally, Richard Wharton, "has carried himselfe very odly," thwarting the appointment of Randolph's nominee as Captain of Castle Island in Boston harbor. Instead, Wharton secured this strategic post for his brother-in-law. "The Castle of Boston," explained the council to the Lords of Trade on June 1, "a place of great importance to this Country, is now put under the care and Command of Captaine Wait Winthrop, a person of known Loyalty." When Randolph saw that the council was unwilling to foster the Church of England actively, and that most of the councilors, being merchants, would only pay lip service to the Navigation Acts, he felt horribly cheated. New Moderate was but Old Faction writ large.

Week by week, Randolph's frustration mounted. Initially merely complaining that Dudley had outmaneuvered him in the division of spoils, he was soon wildly slandering the President as "a man of base, servile and antimonarchial principle." Wharton he found not merely an engrosser of great land tracts and a smuggler, but a seditionary, for Wharton "did openly declare that his Majesty, in appointing me his Secretary and Register, intended to inthrall this people in vassalage." Writing home in August, Randolph summed up his predicament: "I am attack'd from every part: the Ministers quarrell for my bringing in the Common prayer, the old magistrates and freemen for vacating their charter: the mobile are troubled that the Lawes of England are in force; & the Merchants for putting the acts of trade in full execution: by which they have lost severall ships & large quantityes of Goods. . . . such is their implacable malice, the Oliver the late Tyrant was not more ingrateful to the Royalists then I am to the most of the people. . . ." Randolph called for a sweeping counterattack. An English governor general must be immediately dispatched who could displace uncooperative council members and "hold the raines of Government in his hands & restrain the liberty of Conscience which they now grosly abuse."

Too drastic for Sewall, not drastic enough for Randolph, Dudley's council offered no real policy because it had no real power. Not daring to levy direct taxes without an assembly, it had almost no funds. The councilors, who were unsalaried, resented having to neglect their personal affairs in order to meet at Boston. After the initial burst of activity, meetings were held only about once a week and often lacked the prescribed quorum of eight members. According to Randolph, the councilors were jealous of Dudley's powers and fought passionately among themselves. "Wee have very seldome Councills and then little done besides quarrelling: and agree in nothing but Sharing the Country amongst themselves and laying out Larg tracts of lands. . . . I am forcd to say little," he added, "in regard wee have but a very thin Councill . . . and I feare they will throw all up." As usual, Randolph was exaggerating. Yet Dudley's caretaker government was manifestly incapable of handling any emergency. Left indefinitely to its own devices, the council might have disintegrated completely.

Of the two Winthrop brothers, Wait was much more active in Dudley's council. Like a number of his colleagues, Fitz lived so far from Boston that his membership was perfunctory. He came up from New London for the organizational meetings of the council, May 25 to June 3, 1686, and then went home again. Wait, being a Boston resident, was one of the half-dozen most faithful councilors and missed only six of the forty-four meetings. In addition to his appointment as Captain of the Castle, Wait served on a number of committees. He was not aggressive enough, however, to benefit from the council's pleasant habit of voting land, commercial privileges, and cash rewards to its members. Wait missed the opportunity to confirm the title to his father's lead mines because he did not have the deeds and Fitz did not send him attested copies. Among the core of councilors Wait was clearly a less forceful personage than either President Dudley, Deputy-President Stoughton, or Richard Wharton. Randolph never bothered to insult him in his letters home.

The Winthrop brothers were particularly concerned in the council's handling of the perennial Narragansett Country problem. Inevitably, with the Winthrops and several of their fellow councilors being Narragansett proprietors, the council determined to enforce Cranfield's 1683 judgment in their favor. On June 23, Dudley, Fitz Winthrop, Randolph, and Wharton held court at Kingston and reorganized the whole Narragansett Country government. They announced that anyone settling without permission on the Narragansett proprietors' lands must make prompt composition by purchase or rent. Fitz presided over a second Narragansett court session in October. The Rhode Island government did not dare to contest this action because Randolph had a writ of *quo warranto* against their charter. By cooperating with the council, they hoped to avoid complete surrender. The proprietors, losing no time in turning their land to advantage, contracted to sell to a group of French Protestant refugees a tract near Kingston at £20 per 100 acres, for the plantation of a new town. In fact, the proprietors were pushing too far too fast. When dispute arose over the eastern limits of the Narragansett Country, their inveterate enemy John Greene of Warwick took ship for England and petitioned the King that the proprietors were unsurping royal land. The question of the Narragansett land title was fatally left open for Sir Edmund Andros to decide.

In 1686 the Winthrop brothers also figured in the council's efforts to annex Connecticut to the Dominion of New England. There were strong arguments for ending Connecticut's political autonomy. With the collapse of John Winthrop, Jr.'s 1662 plan to make the Long Island Sound area an economic unit, the colony was an agrarian backwater. Some Connecticut planters were actively criticizing the existing charter government, in the manner of Randolph's circle of Boston moderates. Two men close to Fitz and Wait, their brother-in-law Edward Palmes of New London, and Fitz's hunting and fishing partner Samuel Willys, of Hartford, especially resented being excluded from the Connecticut council. Palmes, who had been unsuccessfully nominated for the magistracy a number of times, petitioned in 1685 against the arbitrary irregularity of the colony's judicial system. Willys, dropped from the magistracy in 1685, complained to Fitz that Connecticut was ruled contrary to English law. Undoubtedly Sir Edmund Andros "hath a sense of my sufferings," said Willys.

Edward Randolph and Wait Winthrop tried in different ways to make the Connecticut government surrender, and with equal lack of success. Randolph's technique was bullying, if not dishonest. He had two writs of *quo warranto* against the Connecticut charter, and one against Rhode Island, but by the time he reached Boston in May 1686 all these writs were invalid, because their time of return had lapsed. Randolph wrote Governor Treat that if Connecticut were so foolish as to resist the *quo warranto* proceedings, she would be punished by being partitioned between New England and New York. But Treat played off New York against Boston. He hinted to Governor Dongan that if he could offer better terms than Randolph, Connecticut might ask to be joined to New York. The Connecticut General Court met on July 6, and petitioned the King to recall his attack upon their charter. Now Randolph was forced to come to Hartford, on July 20, and deliver his worthless writs. Treat told his visitor how he honored all representatives from the imperial crown, and raised Randolph's hopes for a humble surrender. Actually, Randolph's visit stirred the Connecticut government into looking for an English agent to defend the charter at law.

Randolph claimed that Dudley's council was secretly advising the Connecticut leaders to stall, in order to delay or prevent the coming of a permanent governor general. He was probably correct. For Dudley's council was trying to arrange an alliance with the Connecticut government, which was certainly somewhat contrary to Randolph's purpose. On July 21, while Randolph was safely off in Connecticut, the council decided to send three of its members, Wait and Fitz Winthrop and John Pynchon, on a separate mission to Hartford. These three missionaries bore instructions to dwell on Connecticut's New England heritage of religion and liberty, as well as her economic ties with Massachusetts. They were to urge that Connecticut petition the King, requesting that in case the charter was annulled, she would like to join Massachusetts rather than New York. The trump card was to propose sending a joint Massachusetts-Connecticut agent or agents to England, probably Richard Wharton and Fitz Winthrop, for both men were talking of sailing to England in the fall. Surely the main aim of such an agency would be to persuade the home government to continue the Dudley government indefinitely, with a few salutary modifications such as the reestablishment of a legislature and the removal of Edward Randolph.

The trouble with the councilors' plan was that they had nothing attractive to offer Connecticut. Wait Winthrop and Pynchon went to Hartford without Fitz, who became violently ill while setting out from New London. Fitz wrote Wait that he would welcome "any expedient, that might conduce to the continuance of the hapiness, and prosperity, of this good Collony; whose welfare wee are obliged to intend, haveing our intrest wrapped up with them in all Respects." However, he suggested no expedients. On August 3 Wait and Pynchon were politely received at Hartford, but came away with neither an alliance nor an agreement on a joint agent. "We must tell you we love our own things, if we may injoy them," the Connecticut magistrates wrote pointedly to Dudley, "but if we be deprived of them, . . . the will of the Lord be done." Treat and his colleagues were almost as suspicious of Dudley as of Randolph, and they knew that the tenure of his government was extremely uncertain. Not that they intended to ally with New York. Instead they commissioned a London merchant, William Whiting (who had been John Winthrop, Jr.'s landlord in 1661–1663), as their agent, and petitioned the King once more to recall his attack. In the instructions to Whiting, however, they did take one agonized glance into the future; if Whiting could not defend their charter, they wanted Connecticut joined to the royal government of New England, rather than to New York.

On August 25, 1686, just as the Connecticut government was drafting its instructions to Whiting, Randolph jubilantly wrote to Fitz, "I send you for a cordiall the good newes that Sir Edmund Andros is appointed our gouvernor." He expected Andros to reach Boston in a fifty-gun frigate sometime in November. Wait, less enthusiastic than Randolph, told his brother that Andros' commission "differs not much from that which is here already, the same councill, Pemaquid and Plimouth added. . . . The procedure against Conecticutt and Rode Island to be this next terme. Quo waranntose out against Pensillvania, East and West Jarsey, Carolina, &c. . . . It will be best to be prepared to be here at the first notice after Sir Edmond comes." Wait's letters in late 1686 plainly revealed his awe of Sir Edmund. He could see that however similar Andros' commission was to Dudley's in form, it was quite different in spirit. The new appointment signalized the home government's decision to rely on trusted royal servants to carry through a new policy of tight, unified control over all the colonies. The Dudley council's talk of sending an agency to England had abruptly become irrelevant. After waiting nearly four months for their new master, Wait and some of his colleagues went out to Nantasket on December 19 to greet Sir Edmund's incoming ship. "He inquired for you as soon as I came on bord," Wait told Fitz, "and sayes you must come, being of the Councill. I told him I expected you this week; therefore hope if this finds you not on the roade you will make all the hast you can after you receive this." The salad days were over.

Andros' administration lasted just over two years, from December 1686 to April 1689. Despite this brief period of power, Sir Edmund's regime has fascinated historians, and properly so. It represents a forceful effort to reconstruct, radically and quickly, an established social order. Sir Edmund's break with New England's past was more radical than James II's parallel innovations at home, but because New England was a smaller society, her local traditions less virile, and Andros an abler man, he was able to accomplish more positive and lasting results.

Unlike Dudley, whose policy had been to make the transition from old to new government as easy and slight as possible, Andros made a grand entrance, marching in a laced scarlet coat through an honor guard of militia to the Boston Town House, escorted by the local dignitaries and merchants, while the rest of the populace huzzaed. Every action was masterful. He immediately asserted his superiority over his councilors by standing with his hat on when they took their oaths. He threw the congregational clergy, his chief potential source of opposition, on the defensive by coolly demanding that the Anglicans be given one of their three Boston meetinghouses. Perhaps Andros thought back to his first reception by New Englanders, at Saybrook in July 1675. He had not changed much since then. Always Andros' greatest strength and greatest weakness was his extreme self-confidence. With his knighthood, court connections, and two companies of English soldiers, he cut a far more imposing figure than had Dudley. he had no need for Randolph's supercharged self-pity. Andros' letters to the Lords of Trade breathed crisp efficiency. He told briskly of how he was carrying out the Lords' plans, and he minimized his difficulties. Andros was not trying to deceive the Lords of Trade; he was deceiving himself.

Andros' greatest success came in the opening year of his administration, when his energy and decision made the Dominion of New England for the first time a reality. Plymouth and Rhode Island were quietly annexed. Andros shrewdly capitalized on the divisions within his unwieldy council, Puritans against Quakers, landowners against merchants, to ram through a program favorable to the prerogative, tackling issues upon which Dudley's Council had temporized. The New England court system was made conformable to English practice, the Anglican Church was protected and encouraged, the Navigation Acts were enforced, the printing presses were censored, and most crucial of all, revenue was provided by a direct land tax and increased import duties. This produced an estimated rise in revenue from £2,466 to £3,846 per annum. To be sure, most of the towns in Essex County tried to resist this taxation without representation, but Andros quickly silenced opposition in his most famous display of arbitrary power; he imprisoned the ringleaders, secured their conviction, and fined them heavily. As he explained to Fitz, the Essex people soon paid their taxes, with "all persons well disposed & satisfied." Sir Edmund, being a soldier first and foremost, was less upset by the colonists' refractoriness than by their feeble defenses against French attack. In the fall of 1687 the militia was mobilized to construct a palisade fort at the south end of Boston, on Fort Hill, commanding both the sea and land approaches to the town. Stronger batteries at Castle Island were also built. As it turned out, Andros' energies were here misapplied, for the French in America did not have the resources to mount direct attacks on English seaports and instead harried the inland frontier, where Andros' defensive forts offered little protection.

The diarist Sewall tells how he called at Wait Winthrop's house on January 7, 1687, and found Governor Andros there. "Capt. Winthrop had me up to him, so I thankfully acknowledged the protection and peace we enjoyed under his Excellencie's Government." Sewall felt less thankful when Andros decided to hold Anglican services in Sewall's South Meetinghouse until an Anglican church could be built. South Meetinghouse became a busy place every Sunday. The Anglicans and Congregationalists both held morning and afternoon meetings, and each group regularly accused the other of violating the agreed time limits.

Edward Randolph had more cause than Sewall to acknowledge gratitude, and indeed Randolph did admit that Andros "is ready att all tymes to favour me and is very solicitous on my behalfe." But he was still unhappy. With its trade decaying as a result of the enforcement of the Navigation Laws, New England seemed unable to support Andros' ambitious military program. The golden spoils of office were likewise illusory. Randolph raised the schedule of fees for work done by his secretary's office but still failed to make money and soon leased out the secretary's post. Meanwhile he saw almost all the councilors continuing clandestinely to undermine the Dominion. Randolph could only sadly conclude that "His Excellency has to do with a perverse people."

Fitz Winthrop, a long-standing disciple of Andros, played a larger role in his council than he had in Dudley's. As before, Fitz lived too far from Boston to attend council meetings regularly. He was at most of the important organizational meetings, between December 31, 1686, and March 12, 1687, and joined in the work of collecting and revising the laws of the former New England governments and in reorganizing the militia. Sir Edmund was genuinely fond of Fitz, probably more so than of any other New Englander. In recognition of his military experience, he named Fitz in January 1687 as colonel of the Rhode Island and Narrangansett Country militia, the most responsible office Fitz had yet held. In April Fitz exercised his troops, and was warmly thanked by the Governor "for your going by Roode Island & setling things as you did."

Fitz did useful work for Andros in trying to bring Connecticut into the Dominion. The Hartford leaders had no loving memory of Sir Edmund, and continued to procrastinate. After receiving a third (and valid) writ of *quo warranto,* they wrote to Secretary of State Sunderland in January 1687 that, if necessary, they would submit to Andros' government. As a result of this letter, the home authorities did not bother to pursue the legal forfeiture of their charter. Yet when Andros wrote four separate invitations to submit and finally sent Randolph to Hartford in June 1687, Connecticut's answer was invariably that she would continue in her present station until she received new directions from the King. Resistance was cracking, however. Secretary John Allyn asked Fitz to provide him with ammunition to convert the General Court. In reply, January 13, 1687, Fitz indicated his disappointment at Connecticut's intransigence. The colony was going to have to surrender, "it being his Majesties pleasure to make some alteration in all his governments in America; and it will be pitty that many of yourselves should not be continued in place of trust." Connecticut's behavior might provoke Andros into refusing to give the present colony leaders positions on the Dominion council, so that "many persons possibly may be imposed upon you that your selves may not think suitable." Fitz praised the generous constitution of the Dominion:

"All things that will really conduce to the growth and prosperety of the people . . . will readely be granted by his Excellence." On March 30, Allyn and two other magistrates publicly declared their desire for immediate submission, but the majority in the General Court remained blind to Fitz's arguments. Allyn could only ask Fitz to be patient, and to explain Connecticut's conduct to Andros as favorably as possible.

Diplomacy having failed, Andros went to Hartford in October 1687 and seized the Connecticut government. The situation had indeed become unseemly; Governor Dongan was insisting to the Lords of Trade that New York needed the province more badly than did Massachusetts. He, too, had been writing the Connecticut Governor and General Court and had even sent three councilors to drum up sentiment for surrendering to him rather than to Andros. On October 18 Andros received instructions from home to annex Connecticut, and the next day, before discussing the matter with his council or notifying Governor Treat, he wrote Fitz at New London to be ready to join him in Hartford. Precisely what happened to Andros' arrival, the evening of October 31 at Hartford meetinghouse, it shrouded in legend. He failed to confiscate the Connecticut charter; it was placed before him (so the story goes), but the candles were suddenly blown out and the precious document spirited away by Joseph Wadsworth to a hollow oak tree in Samuel Willys' yard. This story ignores the lack of contemporary substantiation, or the fact that Willys was one of Andros' warmest admirers. Otherwise, the Hartford status quo was much less disturbed than in Boston in 1686. Fitz attended the two council meetings in Hartford at which Treat and Allyn were sworn in as his colleagues, and all the other former magistrates made justices of the peace. Andros did, however, appoint as justices several other men who had been at odds with the old government, most notably Fitz's brother-in-law Edward Palmes, and the former minister of his New London church, Gershom Bulkeley.

With Andros' annexation of Connecticut, Fitz Winthrop gained new power and prestige. The Governor and his suite toured the principal Connecticut towns, establishing local courts, militia, and customs officers for the Dominion government. In New London on November 10 Andros gave Fitz command of the militia in Connecticut in addition to Rhode Island and the Narragansett Country, and promoted him to Major General. Fitz was (after the Governor himself) the highest military officer in New England, in charge of 3,800 men. John Allyn thanked Fitz for securing him Andros' patronage, and William Jones, a magistrate of long standing in the old Connecticut government, asked the Winthrops' favor in obtaining the probation and registry of wills for one of several counties. As a New York friend noted in congratulating Fitz on "the new honour which your meritts have acquired you in his Majesties service, . . . The times are well alter'd in the reception of Sir Edmund Andros in those parts now, to what they were formerly."

In contrast to Fitz, Wait Winthrop found that the change in administration took away much of the responsibility he had had under Dudley and placed him in an increasingly awkward position. One of Andros' first acts was to order Wait to deliver Castle Island to Captain Nicholson, commander of his bodyguard. The new Governor pointedly observed that the Castle was in wretched repair. Wait continued to be one of the most diligent councilors, attending sixty-three of the seventy-nine recorded meetings in 1687. But he was no longer given special committee assignments, and he was unhappily conscious of becoming a cipher.

In 1690, safely after Andros' overthrow, Wait joined four other Dominion councilors, William Stoughton, Thomas Hinckley, Bartholomew Gedney, and Samuel Shrimpton, in *A Narrative of the Proceedings of Sir Edmond Androsse and his Complices*. The authors complained that Andros had habitually overruled or side-stepped council debate, that important bills were privately drafted and unexpectedly presented for discussion, that the Governor listened only to a small clique of outsiders and ignored the majority of his council. In Wait's case, there is more justification than with last-minute converts like Stoughton or Shrimpton for reading back into 1687 the complaints voiced in 1690. The *Narrative* condemns Andros' restriction of local self-government, permitting only one town meeting per year, and it is interesting to find that Wait attended the annual Boston town meetings in 1687 and 1688, the only councilor to do so. Again, the *Narrative* objects to the way Andros rammed through his tax legislation, as well as his technique of bypassing local courts in order to bring critics of his regime to trial before the council at Boston, so it is interesting to find that Wait did not attend the council meetings or the special Boston court of oyer and terminer which punished the leading Essex County rebels. Perhaps it was not accidental that he chose this time to visit New London. If Wait felt troubled by Andros' policy, he also found himself uncomfortably identified as Andros' creature by the man in the street. He complained to Fitz in 1687 of never getting news from Connecticut, since "no body has the manners to come nere me unless I mete with them accidentally."

Unquestionably, Wait's greatest grievance against Andros was the royal Governor's land policy. At first, the issue was simply that Sir Edmund halted the Dudley councilors' practice of feathering their own nests. A case in point was his crushing rejection of the Narragansett proprietors' title to their land. Andros sifted the rival claims to the area, including Wharton's plea for the proprietors, and then recommended to the Lords of Trade that all unimproved land titles should be dismissed. In thus reversing the Cranfield judgment of 1683, Andros argued (no doubt correctly) that the settlement of the Narragansett Country had been hindered by the proprietors' speculative claims. Wharton got a patent for only 1,700 acres of Narrangansett land, which was under cultivation, on payment of an annual quitrent of ten shillings. The Winthrops got nothing.

Andros' rebuff of the Narrangansett proprietary, together with his hostility toward Wharton's similar scheme for developing a vast tract of Pejepscot in Maine, drove Wharton to England in June 1687 in the hope of persuading the home government to reverse Sir Edmund's land policy. Wharton began playing a double game, superficially a cordial colleague of Andros and Randolph, yet trying to ambush them at Whitehall. The man who had been more conspicuously enthusiastic about the Dominion than any other New Englander in 1686 was the first colonist to take positive measures to circumvent it. When Wharton reached England, he sent Wait a copy of Andros' report on the Narrangansett claims, which he believed "may prove more to our advantage than was intended. My Lord Culpepper promises to make the best on t." Culpeper joined Wharton in petitioning the King that Andros be instructed to grant the proprietors patents for 60,000 acres of Narrangansett land. The Lords of Trade actually drafted a letter to this effect on April 10, 1688. But by this time Wharton told Wait, "I dispair of bringing [the Narrangansett business] to any good head," and for some unexplained reason his scheme was stalled.

Wharton, however, had become engrossed in a grander venture, which also concerned the Winthrops. This was the creation of a joint-stock company, to be chartered by the King and generously capitalized by subscribers on both sides of the Atlantic, to develop New England's mines and naval stores. Wharton exhibited specimen ores and resins in London, and Wait supplied him with an optimistic report on ore found at Woburn. Money was no problem, for Wharton had the promise of £25,000 from English investors, a far larger opening stock that John Winthrop, Jr., had been able to raise for his ironworks. Wharton told Wait, in March 1688, "I have subscribed £200 for you in the new company, and shall give you my vote for president. You will have roome to subscribe £1,600 more when the patten comes out, if you please. Pray faile not to satisfy yourselfe as privately as you can what the Wooborne oare will yield. . . . indeed, if you . . . have had a cheat put upon you, as I am something fearfull, I shall suffer much in my reputacion heer, and great discouragement will fall upon the undertakeing." Wharton petitioned for incorporation in February 1688, and the Lords of Trade ordered a patent to be drafted, August 10, 1688. At the point of success, Wharton's scheme again stalled, this time probably because of the impending revolutionary crisis in England.

Meanwhile, back in New England Governor Andros was encountering increasing difficulties during 1688. His wife died in the middle of her first Boston winter. His most powerful Puritan adversary, Increase Mather, the pastor of Boston North Church, escaped surveillance and fled to England. Edward Randolph was getting thoroughly jealous of Andros' New York favorites, John West, John Palmer, and James Graham, and he complained to England that "now the Governor is safe in his New Yorke confidents, all others being strangers to his councill." A more fundamental problem was that Andros was being given too much work for any one man. Hardly had he finished inspecting his most northerly territories in New Hampshire and Maine, in the spring of 1688, than his jurisdiction was greatly extended southward by the addition of New York and the Jerseys to his Dominion. These territories he proceeded to annex and reorganize in August and September, with much the same pomp and circumstance as in Connecticut the year before, though with less tranquillity, since there was no love lost between Dongan, the supplanted New York governor, and Andros. On the top of everything else, Sir Edmund had to guard his sprawling Dominion against the mounting threat of attack from the French in Canada and their Indian allies. In 1688 trouble was brewing at all points along the English frontier where the raiders from the North could most easily strike—in Maine, the Connecticut Valley, and the Hudson Valley.

Fitz continued to be active in Andros' service. The two men corresponded on how to train the militia and how to manage the Indians. In all his extant letters to Andros during 1688, Fitz harped on a single theme: his gratitude over Andros' paternal care for New England, "& those designes your Excellency layes to settle a lasting hapines to the posterety of this country." Andros called for Fitz at New London on his way to New York in August 1688, and for the next two months Fitz travelled in the Governor's party. He joined in parleys with the chiefs of the Five Nations at Albany and in less ceremonious parleys with Dongan, who wanted the Dominion government to reimburse him for the £6,482 which he claimed to have spent in New York's defense. The high point of Fitz's stay in New York came with the news of the birth of the Prince of Wales, the event which triggered revolutionary preparations in England. Sir Edmund stood in Fort James amid his councilors and local dignitaries, and when he proposed the new Prince's health, the guns in the fort were fired, the soldiers volleyed, and all the ships in the harbor echoed their guns in salute. Then followed general feasting, bonfires, "and nothing but God blesse the prince and drinking his health and loud acclamations were heard that night." The scene was a little different in Boston, where none of the Congregational churches chose to observe the absent Governor's proclamation for a day of public thanksgiving.

The touchstone to New England's temper on the eve of the Glorious Revolution was her reaction to Andros' land policy, the most authoritarian aspect of his general program. The Dominion had been designed to be financed largely from quitrents, thus calling for a profound change in New England land tenure. At first Andros applied this system only when he was asked (as by the Narrangansett proprietors) to grant titles for vacant or disputed lands. By 1688 he was calling into question all property titles issued under the old charter governments, many of which he asserted to be defective. If landholders wanted secure titles, they must petition for new patents at a uniform quitrent of 2s. 6d. per hundred acres. Only about two hundred persons in the whole Dominion actually did petition for such patents during Andros' administration. These included Edward Randolph, whose petitions for commons land belong to the towns of Lynn, Watertown, and Cambridge were naturally not very popular, and Joseph Dudley, whose petition that his estate be repatented "for his own benifitt, and for a good Example to others, But he would not have his lands Surveied," was concisely judged by his enemies: "Oh the poyson of a Serpent is deadly."

Another petitioner was Fitz Winthrop. In an undated letter he asked Andros to confirm the whole Winthrop estate, since "tis his Majestyes grace to give renewed title to all our possessions." This letter marks the peak of Fitz's subservience to Andros and to the home authorities, and it suggests other things as well: Fitz's thinly veiled greed for land, his frustration at falling behind pushing entrepreneurs such as his brother Wharton in the race for power and wealth, and, in general, the long distance travelled between the first and third generations of his family. As Fitz states the case to Andros, the present Winthrop property is at best a poor reward "for the waste of that plentifull estate which my predecessors joyfully layde downe to begin the growth & prosperity of this country. . . . I am not myselfe sollicitous for the sweete of this world; but, being now ready to leave it, and haveing two nephewes, the hopes of our family, I would gladly leave a settled and sure title of such accommodations at I have. . . . It will be great in your Excellency to build up the ruines of our family, whose decay was one of the greatest supplyes that gave life to the beginning and growth of these plantations, since tis soe much in your power, whose generous hand is allwayes ready to doe good. . . . [May it] please the King to continue you a shield to the people under your Government. I beg your Excellency will not please to let me fall. . . ."

In his desire to have Andros build up the ruins of the Winthrop family, Fitz was even out of step with his own brother. Wait Winthrop saw that if the reconfirmation of land titles enabled Sir Edmund to build up, it also enabled him to tear down. The Winthrop property was peculiarly vulnerable to demolition. Many of the family's extensive claims were to unimproved, unsurveyed lands which had been vaguely deeded to John Winthrop, Jr., many years before by Indians. Wait was more aware than his brother seems to have been that rival speculators in eastern Connecticut lands, such as James Fitch of Norwich or their own brother Palmes, were being given a golden opportunity by Andros to secure confirmation of properties which the Winthrops also claimed. In July 1688, Wait explained to Fitz why he was delaying coming down from Boston to New

London: "J.F. [James Fitch] is here, but I beleive is scared with the charge of taking patents. he is not going home yet, and I am willing to se him gon before I goe. I am very desireous to se some ships from England also before I come. My last letters from thence give me grate hope of a generall confirmation from his Majesty of all lands according to former useage."

During 1688 New England landholders of every political shade began banding together in opposition to Andros' repatenting program, and Wait Winthrop was among them. In July Andros tried to force a general application for new titles by instituting test cases of eviction against properties held by Samuel Sewall and Samuel Shrimpton, prototypes respectively of the old psalm-singing orthodoxy and the new swash-buckling, episcopalian, mercantile aristrocracy. The result was decisive. Sewall petitioned for a new title, but he immediately wrote to Wharton in London for help, offering to subscribe £50 or £100, and in November he was sailing himself for England. Shrimpton refused to petition for a new title, and announced that he would carry his appeal to the King if necessary. Sewall and Shrimpton even dined together, and in company with Cotton Mather "Had Sturgeon, Wine, Punch, Musick." The property issue likewise produced a coalition among diverse New Englanders in London. Wharton dropped his Narragansett and mining projects to join Increase Mather in attendance on James II, and together they beseeched the King to deliver New England from oppression. Optimistic as always, Wharton wrote Wait on October 18, 1688, the day before William of Orange's fleet set sail for England, by which time James II was making desperate concessions and "hath often assured us our propertyes shall be continued and confirmed." Wharton felt sure that Andros' arbitrary rule would be investigated by Court or Parliament, but he and Mather would need at least £ 2,000 in subscriptions from New Englanders to support their agency. "If other men of estate," he told Wait, "would give the same assurance you have done to contribute, wee would find creditt heer. . . ." Wait Winthrop was now actively enrolled in the attack upon the Dominion.

Men as dissimilar as Wait Winthrop and Increase Mather were drawn together on the property issue not merely because they disliked a new tax nor because they feared that their dubious land titles would be exposed, important as both these considerations undoubtedly were. Wait and his fellow councilors, in their *Narrative,* later summed up their objections to Andros' policy: "The purchasing of the Natives Right, was made nothing of, and next to a Ridicule. The Enjoyment and Improvement of Lands not inclosed, and especially if lying in common amongst many was denied to be possession; . . . Many were Solicited, and Encouraged to Petition for other mens Lands, and had a shameful Example set them by some of the chief Contrivers of all this Mischief. When some men have Petitioned for a confirmation of their own Lands, a part of these only was offered to be granted to them, and another part denied. Nor could any mans own Land be confirmed to him, without a particular Survey of every part and parcel of them first made, the great charges whereof, and of other Fees to be taken would have been to most men Insupportable." In short, Andros' land policy created a state of war between the government and each individual property holder. Wait Winthrop can hardly be blamed for concluding that such a situation was intolerable.

In April 1689 Wait Winthrop actively participated in overthrowing the Dominion of New England. Fitz Winthrop passively accepted the turn of events. As in any revolutionary episode, there are a number of mysteries about this

Boston coup d'état, but the Winthrop brothers' role in the affair is reasonably clear. It is certain that Wait's and Fitz's desertion of Andros marked the watershed in both brothers' lives.

In a sense, it was Fitz who inaugurated the revolution. In October 1688 came the Dominion's first and only serious military test, when Indian outrages began multiplying alarmingly along the frontier settlements in the Connecticut Valley and in Maine. Andros called an emergency session of his council in Boston, at which it was agreed to send 300 militia immediately to the eastern frontier. Andros offered the command of this expedition "upon very good terms" to Fitz. According to Randolph, Fitz "at first assented but afterwards declined it wholly"; no other councilor being willing, the Governor accepted their advice to take command himself. Why did Fitz back out? The official reason is that he fell sick. Fitz frequently fell sick on such occasions. Certainly he was not very sick this time. He was able to travel back to New London in mid-November, just as Andros was heading up to Maine, and in his correspondence with Wait in the next few weeks the most urgent topic was his selection of a new winter coat and waistcoat. Fitz's refusal forced Andros to depart into the Maine woods on a four-month winter campaign, at the critical time when rumors of William of Orange's successful invasion of England were stirring up the dicontented colonists. Fitz's behavior also demonstrated that there was now almost no New Englander whom Andros could depend upon. As Randolph said, "his Excellence discharges all offices: from Generall to Sutler."

Wait Winthrop was later accused of plotting with the Congregational ministry to strike against Andros as early as January. The anonymous author of *New England's Faction Discovered* notes meaningfully that the warrant for public observance of the martyrdom of Charles I on January 30 "was called in and suppressed by Captain *Waite Winthrop,* one of the Council, who in the Commotion appeared the chief Man and Head of the Faction against the Government, which he twice swore to maintain. . . ." Wait's extant letters from the winter of 1688–1689, however, indicate that he was not engaged in long-range plots with Cotton Mather and the old charter party, though they do confirm his estrangement from Andros. He wrote tartly to Fitz on the inconclusiveness of Andros' Indian campaign. "If you had gon," he said, "it would have bin counted ill conduct if all the enemys had not bin destroyed before this between us and the north star." He gave no hint of believing, as the more credulous Puritans did, that Andros was betraying the militia to the popish French. Wait quoted approvingly from Wharton's letter of the previous October, reporting progress in the New England agents' campaign against Andros, and by mid-December he was getting the first stories of William of Orange's invasion. Yet he told Fitz, "tis generally feared the Duch are landed in England before this," as though the invasion was bad news. On January 28 he reported that Andros was embargoing all ships for England, "which I understand the meaneing of no more than of many other things. . . . He has communicated nothing which came by the last ships to any of the councill here that I know of." Wait's prevailing tone of helpless mystification is inappropriate to a conspirator.

Like most rebellions, the Boston outbreak was precipitated by the increasingly nervous behavior of an administration which knew it was losing effective power. Andros' efforts to embargo news from England and to punish William of Orange's partisans for sedition completed the fatal division between colonials and outsiders and turned his government into a naked army of occupation amid a potential mob.

New England was saturated with rumors. "We have no certainty of any thing," John Allyn wrote Wait on April 15, "but great talkes there is that things will be as sometimes they have bin by reason of a proclamation made by his Majestie October last that restores charters; but when it will be I know not, & what new changes ther may be I canot tell, & wither that proclamation reacheth us I know not. . . ." Allyn had not heard about the latest sensation, that a copy of the Prince of Orange's Declaration, even more exhilarating than James II's restoration of charters since it instructed unjustly expelled magistrates to resume their offices, had been smuggled into Boston on April 4. Andros, who had returned to Boston from the frontier in late March, sensed that trouble was brewing. "There's a general buzzing among the people, great with expectation of their old charter, or they know not what," he wrote just two days before the revolt. In a desperate effort to restore authority, he decided to try Cotton Mather at a special council meeting, April 18, on the charge of preaching sedition.

The revolt that cut short Andros' plan was effected by a combination of spontaneity and planning. There was no dominant rebel leader. Wait Winthrop and the other dissident Dominion councilors drew up plans with a few of the old charter leaders for the management of a coup d'état. Cotton Mather tells us in his *Magnalia* that "some of the Principal Gentlemen in *Boston* consulting what was to be done in this Extraordinary Juncture," they agreed that if it proved necessary "to prevent the shedding of *Blood* by ungoverned *Mobile,* some of the Gentlemen present should appear at the Head of the *Action* with a *Declaration* accordingly prepared." Undoubtedly the "Principal Gentlemen" played a more active hand than Mather cared to admit. Their problem was how to make Andros' two garrisons at Fort Hill and Castle Island and the frigate *Rose* capitulate without bloodshed. To prevent the *Rose's* escape, the first step in the coup was the seizure of her commander, Captain George, as he came ashore about eight o'clock on the morning of April 18. Over a thousand Bostonians rushed to arms by beat of drum and formed themselves into companies. Militia from the neighboring towns streamed in with suspicious alacrity. According to a hostile reporter, Wait Winthrop was designated as the commander of this army, and "had bin with the conspirators of the North end [of town] very early that Morning. . . ." When he saw the armed mob come "to his house requesting Him to bee their Commander and lead them, with abundance of Modesty and no less hypochrisy refused to offer. But at length pretending he was wearied with their importunity's, and to doe the Governour a signall kindness, he condescended to accept of the office, and walk'd before them." Boston was thus easily occupied, though Randolph, West, Graham, and Palmer had managed to reach Fort Hill, where they found Andros with a garrison of fourteen soldiers.

The mob and its leaders gathered at the Town House and listened to Cotton Mather's windy Declaration, which announced that the colonists, in imitation of the Prince of Orange and the English people, were resolved to seize "the Persons of those few *Ill Men* which have been (next to our Sins) the grand Authors of our Miseries; resolving to Secure them, for what Justice, Orders from his Highness, with the *English Parliament* shall direct. . . ." Thus had new England's revolutionary credo been transmuted since the 1630's. In the council chamber, Wait joined a carefully balanced panel of fifteen men (five Dominion councilors, five charter magistrates, and five merchants who had never held office), the fruition of the anti-Andros coalition which had been uniting almost all New Englanders during the past year. These men drew up a letter summoning Andros to surrender, arguing disingenuously that the mob action had totally surprised them, that the mob was prepared to storm Fort Hill, but that they could promise security to Andros' party if he delivered up his government and fortifications. Sir Edmund tried to escape to the *Rose,* but when the colonials chased his handful of redcoats inside the palisade and trained the shore batteries on it, he led his loyal councilors to the Town House, where they were made prisoners and harangued by their former colleagues. None of the contemporary narratives tell whether Wait supervised the investment of Fort Hill, nor whether he joined in insulting the captive governor. The next day, Castle Island and the *Rose* also surrendered, and the bloodless revolution had been achieved.

The establishment of a new government over the excited Massachusetts populace promised to be a harder job than the overthrow of Andros. On April 20 Wait and the other gentlemen who had managed the coup styled themselves a provisional Council for the Safety of the People and Conservation of the Peace. They invited "such other of the old Magistrates Or such other Gentlemen as they shall judge meet" to join the council, enlarging their membership to thirty-seven and retaining the balance between old and new enemies of Andros. Former Governor Simon Bradstreet, eighty-seven years old, was chosen president, and Wait Winthrop was appointed commander of the militia. The composition of this Council of Safety was extremely significant. It heralded Massachusetts' new ruling class, the combination of former charter magistrates, former Dominion councilors and heretofore private citizens who would hold power under the new charter of 1691. Nine of the fifteen men who summoned Andros to surrender, for instance, would sit on the Bay council in 1692, and ten of them in 1696. The only prominent Massachusetts man to be conspicuously excluded from the Council of Safety was Joseph Dudley. He had been out of town when the revolt occurred, but was caught and carried to the Boston common jail, where he was kept for over nine months until he was shipped to England with Andros and the other prisoners. He was the one "moderate" who had irretrievably committed himself to English over colonial interests. Dudley never forgot his bitter humiliation, and the remainder of his career may be seen as a calculated revenge on the Massahcusetts rebels. But for the moment the Council of Safety had the triumph. On May 20 an address to William and Mary was prepared. It explained how the Bostonians had risen "as one Man" in emulation of their Highnesses' "late glorious Enterprise," though happily the people were "so Overruled by the Interposition, and prudence of some Gentlemen upon the place; that the thing was Effected without the least Bloodshed or Plunder." The council asked for the restoration of Massachusetts' charter and English liberties. Meanwhile, Edward Randolph joined Dudley in Boston jail. He gave his address to correspondents as "the Common Gaol in New Algiers."

The Council of Safety itself lasted only five weeks. Lacking instruction from England, the council sought to imitate the Prince of Orange's Convention of January 1689 by calling a similar assembly of representatives from forty-four towns at Boston on May 9. Here the English parallel ends, for the great majority of the towns wanted immediate resumption of the old charter government. This naturally displeased most of the councilors such as Wait, who were nonfreemen or at least had not held office under the charter. A vocal minority of the towns wanted to continue the Council of Safety. The anti-Andros coalition seemed to dissolve completely when Bradstreet and the charter magistrates of 1686 agreed on May 24 to resume administration under the old form. However, Wait Winthrop,

Samuel Shrimpton, and nine other excluded councilors signed a Declaration to the charter party, May 25, pledging to support their administration "in this dangerous conjuncture," and promising to try "to pacifie the dissatisfied in our regards, and promote the publick tranquility as far as in us lies." For a week Wait retired from the council. Then a new Convention of deputies from the towns made a modest concession by choosing Winthrop, Shrimpton, and three others to join the 1686 panel of charter magistrates. Wait was not yet a freeman, and he did not become one until 1690. Still, on June 7, 1689, he took his oath as an Assistant in the charter government and as Major General of the Massachusetts militia.

Indeed, it was only in the aftermath of the Boston revolt that Wait became a first-class citizen of his colony. The Reverend John Higginson renewed his former plea that Wait follow Christ's command, as well as the example of his grandfather and father, and "joyn your self in full communion with Mr Willard's church (where you do constantly attend)." Three weeks later, on August 25, 1689, he was admitted to South Church. As he read the humble thanks of another clerical correspondent, Samuel Stow, that "the Lord . . . raised up your noble heart to do worthyly for his poor people in the spring," Wait might be pardoned for thinking that in Massachusetts life begins at forty-five. At last he was securely launched as a popular public man, the role he would play for the rest of his life. Wait's performance in 1689 illustrates how the overthrow of the Dominion, while much in character with the Glorious Revolution at home, had insensibly widened again the transatlantic gap. The old orthodoxy and the new moderates of Boston, by learning to submerge their differences in common cause against Andros, were solidifying the instinct for local self-determination within their provincial society.

15. The Glorious Revolution and the Pattern of Imperial Relationships

Lawrence H. Leder

Professor Lawrence H. Leder (b. 1927) of Lehigh University, who has written extensively about the impact of imperial policies upon colonial political development, here summarizes his thoughts on the consequences of the Glorious Revolution for Anglo-American colonists. Leder suggests that certain formative patterns emerged out of the wave of colonial insurrections, pointing toward greater local autonomy for provincial leaders who supported imperial policies. The Crown would not attempt again the disastrous experiment of authoritarian rule as embodied in the Dominion, thereby confirming the colonists in the rights of Englishmen, when taken in conjunction with the full establishment of representative assemblies.

Yet Crown-appointed governors and imperial administrators still arrived in the colonies, charged with doing the Crown's bidding; and questions were bound to arise concerning the nature and extent of provincial rights within royal frameworks of government. How much authority were representative assemblies to have relative to royal officials? Since Parliament was emerging as the supreme lawmaking body in England as a result of the Glorious Revolution there, why should American assemblies, which thought of themselves as "little Parliaments," remain subordinate to royal governors and other Crown officials when the converse formed the political reality in England? The contours of political debate, then, took on a new dimension. How did local contests over royal prerogatives affect the nature of Anglo-American politics after 1689? Was a serious confrontation simply being delayed?

For students of British and British-American history, the year 1689 is of major importance. To Englishmen it stands for the Glorious Revolution and the triumph of parliamentary authority over Stuart absolutism; to Americans it signifies the end of one period and the beginning of another, although precisely what ended and what began has never been clearly defined. Certain it is that Americans for a generation reverently referred to "the late happy revolution" as a touchstone in their political arguments. Perhaps our own lack of understanding stems from too close an inspection of the events in each colony with their diverse local experiences and a failure to see in the Glorious Revolution the blending of these

Source: Lawrence H. Leder, "The Glorious Revolution and the Pattern of Imperial Relationships," *New York History,* 46 (1965), pp. 203–211. Footnotes omitted. Reprinted by permission of the New York State Historical Association, Cooperstown, New York.

events into a common pattern, into the imperial structure of the eighteenth century.

The year 1689 marks the attainment of a level of maturity by certain mainland colonies, and with it the accumulation of problems, tensions and frustrations, all of which were unleashed by William of Orange's invasion of his father-in-law's kingdom. Five of the mainland colonies celebrated their sixtieth anniversaries within a few years of 1689—Massachusetts, New York, Maryland, Connecticut, and Rhode Island—and only the latter two passed that anniversary peacefully. They could do so because, thanks to the actions of their neighbors, they fell heir to a peaceful solution to their problems.

Massachusetts, New York, and Maryland were not as lucky, and the overthrow of James II triggered the violence built up within the structure of each colony. Indeed, they might well have undergone violent upheavals whether or not James' throne was challenged, for the causes of the rebellions in each of these colonies had little to do with the Glorious Revolution, although the consequences for each were clearly shaped by it. Each had accumulated a backlog of perplexing problems or had posed against it insuperable obstacles. In all three colonies, those discontented for whatever reason flocked to the banner of William of Orange, hailed his revolution as "glorious," and promptly identified their local causes with his. The only question unanswered was whether William of Orange, or more properly William III, would concur in those identifications.

Bostonians by 1689 were still battling to determine who would rule the erstwhile Bible Commonwealth—the old-line Puritan leadership or the Crown. This was not a religious struggle, but a political one, although all controversies in New England seemed to be couched in theological terms. It was a constitutional problem of the nature of the empire. The Bay Colony, with the passage of years, had become increasingly independent of royal authority; by 1660 it was practically a self-governing commonwealth. After the restoration of Charles II, this independence was challenged—first by a royal commission sent in 1664 to compel the colony to acknowledge the Crown's authority, and second by Edward Randolph who appeared on the scene in 1676 as a sort of avenging angel to force conformity to the Navigation Acts. Neither effort met with much success.

As the conflict between the Crown and the Puritan leadership deepened in the 1680's, many in the colony whose interests were more commercial than theological began to ponder the consequences of this dispute. The Bay Colony depended for its livelihood on trade, and the possible results of the colony's obstinacy were frightening to the merchants. They were forced to take action, but their decision came too late. By the time they had turned to the idea of supporting conversion of Massachusetts to royal status in the mid-1680's, the Crown had already determined upon more than mere surrender. The Charter was dissolved, the government assumed by the Crown, and the imperial bureaucracy began to fashion a new approach to imperial organization.

Massachusetts was remodeled by its absorption into the Dominion of New England, the elimination of any representative legislature, repression of town meetings, attacks upon the validity of the colonists' land titles, and introduction under royal protection of the detested Church of England. These measures inflamed the populace and made the merchants rue their decision to surrender to royal authority. The rebellion was ready to move; all that it lacked was the spark. The news of William of Orange's landing at Torbay provided that, and the people of the Bay Colony re-opened the questions of colonial self-government and imperial relationships.

Little similarity existed between the Massachusetts and New York situations even though both were incorporated into the Dominion of New England. The former Dutch territory had different problems: first, the underlying tension created by the transformation of a Dutch trading company outpost into a ducal proprietary and then into a royal colony; second, the imposition of a rigid governmental framework which destroyed the flexibility essential in any growing society by eliminating the channels through which one group can strive peacefully to displace another in the continuing struggle for power.

The quarter century following the English conquest of 1664 was clearly a transitional period in New York. As things English gradually supplanted those of Dutch origins, there were bound to be points of dispute and areas of discontent, and these were accentuated by the economic decline that began in the 1670's and continued throughout the period. Colonial authorities ascribed the depression to various causes and sought to alleviate it by the creation of monopolies and the tranmission of appeals to London, but without any noticeable improvement in the colony's economy.

The desire of the proprietor, the Duke of York, heir presumptive to the throne, to make his colony financially self-supporting if not profitable complicated the colony's economic distress. His goal became less attainable by the mid-1680's as Anglo-French hostilities erupted, but the Duke's fiscal hopes continued unabated. He finally authorized a legislative assembly solely in the hope that the people would assume a greater financial share of maintaining the colony.

These rapid alterations and these uncertainties made for a fluid situation in which a group of shrewd politicians gained power, governmental offices, and prestige. But their rise was challenged by another group standing on a slightly lower rung of the ladder, and these potential aristocrats forced the Duke's hand in the matter of a legislative assembly. To them, it offered a logical path for advancement. But once the Duke of York became James II of England in 1685, he no longer needed the colony's financial aid. The Assembly was abolished and the colony was incorporated into the Dominion. Those already in power found themselves confirmed in their places, but those still seeking recognition were blocked. The path to preferment no longer lay in local agencies of government, but in the autocratic machinery of the Dominion at best, or in the complex bureaucracy of Whitehall at worst.

The question in New York was not one of self-government versus Crown authority, but rather who would rule under the King's aegis. The repressed ambitions of a number of New Yorkers determined the leadership of the rebellion once William of Orange made his fateful decision, and once the Bostonians took the initiative by shattering the Dominion. New Yorkers hailed the Glorious Revolution and nursed the hope that the new monarch would extend the rights of Englishmen to this distant corner of the empire.

Further southward in the proprietary of Maryland another set of problems evoked different responses. The crucial complaint was the Charter granted to the first proprietor in the 1630's which created a reservoir of anachronistic feudal privileges. The Council served as the bulwark for protecting the proprietor's legal rights against the assaults of the Assembly which sought to win the same parliamentary rights for itself that had been wrested from unwilling English monarchs in the earlier seventeenth century. Moreover, the vast majority of

Protestants resented the extensive power of the small minority of Catholics, and this gave a unique religious flavor to the Maryland situation.

Maryland differed from Massachusetts and New York, too, in that the discontented oftentimes allied themselves with royal officials and supported royal policy as a tool with which to bludgeon the proprietor. This alliance, albeit an uneasy one, would soon prove too powerful for the Baltimores. When word reached Maryland of the overthrow of James II, and when the proprietor seemingly failed to provide for the colony's formal acceptance of the new monarchs, the rebels immediately seized their opportunity to cast the proprietor into the same role as the deposed King, overthrow proprietary rule, and align themselves fully with the imperial bureaucracy.

The different backgrounds and problems of each colony resulted in sharply different immediate results, but a remarkable uniformity developed as the final revolutionary settlement. The rebel leadership in all three colonies had thrown themselves wholeheartedly behind William's cause and urgently prayed that he accept their particular causes as his own. To each situation the monarch and his bureaucrats reacted differently.

The rebel leaders of Massachusetts divided into two overlapping camps, the merchants and the old oligarchy. The religious group fervently hoped for a restoration of the colony's former charter and favored immediate resumption of the old governmental forms as though the Dominion had been nothing more than a passing nightmare. They prepared indictments of the Governor-General, Sir Edmund Andros, and the other royal officials, and prepared to return them to England for trial.

The merchant leaders of the Bay Colony cooperated half-heartedly with these plans. They also wanted self-government, but not in the hands of the religious oligarchy. They understood the need to accommodate the colony to the plans of the imperial bureaucracy, but they hoped at the same time to moderate those plans and to salvage some control for themselves. When the revolutionary settlement was forged in Whitehall by the same imperial authorities who had earlier created and managed the Dominion, it was a compromise effected along the lines of the merchants' hopes. The colony had a representative legislature, but one elected on property rather than religious qualifications; it had a governor, but one appointed by the Crown rather than elected, and he had a veto power over the election of the council. The monopoly of the righteous had been broken, and the colony would veer in the future more and more toward a mercantile entrepot rather than a Godly City on a Hill.

New York's problems were resolved with much less felicity. The avowed aim of the rebel leaders had been to break the power monopoly held by a handful of the aristocracy. During the rebellion itself, they seized the chance to wreak their vengeance upon former officeholders for past insults, thereby creating bitter animosities which colored New York's politics for decades. The old leadership, temporarily displaced, utilized its contacts with the imperial authorities and insured its eventual return to power. When the new royal Governor, Henry Sloughter, arrived, he immediately imprisoned the rebel leaders, tried them for treason and murder, and executed the two most important, Jacob Leisler and his son-in-law Jacob Milborne, before royal clemency could be sought.

The New York rebels met with no sympathy in London because their plans did not mesh with those of the imperial bureaucracy. Unless the old guard leadership in the colonies had opposed or interfered with plans for enhancing royal control, there was no reason to abandon them. In Massachusetts the Puritans had committed this sin and were dropped in favor of the new merchant oligarchy; in New York the old leadership had been complaisant, had gone along with the Dominion, and were now willing to support whatever scheme was concocted in Whitehall. Thus there was no transfer of power in New York to a new class or generation, and the New York rebellion failed.

The only significant accomplishment in New York—and this was not a direct consequence of the rebels' actions—was the re-establishment of a legislative assembly. This would later permit a more conventional challenge to the authority of the old guard and a gradual, peaceful transfer of power. But until that happened, the fight within the colony would be hard, bitter, and long. New York's split into two warring camps permitted the Governors sent from England to use the situation for their personal benefit during the next two decades. Not until Robert Hunter's arrival in 1710 did the colony acquire a Governor strong, honest, and shrewd enough to place the colony's welfare foremost, break with the old patterns, and end the factional bickering.

In Maryland, the consequences of the revolution differed dramatically from that in either Massachusetts or New York. The primary ambition in the Bay Colony had been to restore self-government, in New York to transfer power to a new group, but in Maryland it was to destroy the proprietary power. To accomplish this, the Maryland rebels sought a closer unity with the Crown as the lesser of two evils and, as a consequence, that colony came closest to meeting the desires of the imperial authority. It was the only colony in which the revolution successfully achieved all its goals.

When the Maryland rebels petitioned the Crown to recognize their coup, eliminate proprietary authority, and convert the colony into a royal one, their wishes became royal commands. The Attorney-General of England began proceedings to deprive Baltimore of his charter, and the Crown assumed governmental authority in the colony, leaving the land title vested in the proprietor. Within the colony, the assembly made a clean sweep of the statute books, eliminating objectionable laws, established a more harmonious relationship with the Indians, and attacked the financial practices of the proprietary group. This shift in power resulted from Whitehall's recognition that the rebels' ambitions coincided at the moment with the Crown's policy of centralization. The consequent harmony was short-lived, for in the eighteenth century the Marylanders split with royal authority over financial matters and imperial restrictions, but for the moment the alliance held and the rebels were triumphant.

Out of the maelstrom of revolutions emerged several lessons for imperial administrators. The Dominion was dead as a device to curb the individuality of the colonies, and future schemes for imperial unification met with chilled responses from Whitehall. Colonial cooperation replaced imperial coercion as the established goal in the first half of the eighteenth century. Moreover, the imperial authorities recognized the inadvisability of imposing alien forms upon British subjects. From 1689 on each royal colony—and conversion of colonies to royal status became a fixed principle of policy—had a standard set of governmental institutions: a royal governor, an appointed council, and an elected assembly. This uniformity of institutional organization carried with it the premise that the rights of Englishmen followed the flag to the far corners of the empire. And future arguments over governmental power and imperial relations would be predicated upon the implications of this touchstone of political faith.

Neither of these lessons, of course, affected the substance of bureaucratic thinking about the role and nature of empire. No change took place on this score from the days of Charles II and James II except for agreement that the methods of those monarchs were wrong. The passage of the Navigation Act and the creation by royal warrant of the Board of Trade and Plantations, both in 1696, spelled out imperial policy anew. These were among the most important political and administrative decisions to emerge from the glorious Revolution because they enhanced royal authority in the colonies at the same time that parliamentary authority within England was greatly expanded.

A dichotomy developed, one which created a little difficulty until the 1760's when Parliament sought to correct its oversight by extending its control to the colonies more directly. This would shatter the revolutionary settlement of 1689, it would wrench apart the pattern of empire created by the Glorious Revolution. The events of 1689 defined the rights and relationships of the members of the eighteenth-century empire, and Americans had accepted and even revered that definition. Suddenly in the 1760's it was assaulted and the empire as the Americans understood it was in jeopardy.

16. Army and Empire: English Garrison Government in Britain and America, 1569-1763

Stephen Saunders Webb

Unlike Professors Dunn and Leder, Stephen Saunders Webb (b. 1937), a faculty member at Syracuse University, does not attach as much formative significance to the specific years of internal upheaval and the Glorious Revolution in America. Rather Professor Webb puts greater emphasis upon the types of individuals who from the beginning became royal officials in America as well as upon the principles governing thinking in England about what function the colonists were to have as contributing members of the empire. An earlier generation of historians, weaned on Charles M. Andrews's distinction between a mercantilist (commercial) and imperial (military) conception of empire, believed that the latter type did not become important in British policymakers' minds until the years immediately prior to the American Revolution.

Webb, on the other hand, challenges that distinction in the important essay appearing here. Rather he asserts the presence of the imperial-military model from the outset. In this context students might profitably recheck the essay by E. S. Morgan in the first section of this volume in evaluating Webb's position relative to Dunn's and Leder's findings. If Webb's revisionist approach has validity, then how will it alter our conceptualization of Anglo-American relations in the setting of the intentions and goals of seventeenth-century English officials? Would the concept of liberty mean more or less to the first generations of colonists than heretofore presented by historians? In turn, given Webb's thesis, how do we explain the timing of the provincial insurrections of the late seventeenth century and, perhaps even more important, the timing of the coming of the American Revolution? Does the author's analysis indicate that historians should assign greater or lesser significance to the first wave of internal rebellions in the context of emerging empire?

Since 1924 Charles M. Andrews's essay, "Conditions Leading to the Revolt of the Colonies," has exercised a controlling influence over historians' understanding of the origins of the American Revolution. In this essay Andrews declared:

> The year 1763 has always and rightly been considered a great turning point in the history of America's relations with the mother country. . . . [B]y her victory over France,

Source: Stephen Saunders Webb, "Army and Empire: English Garrison Government in Britain and America, 1569 to 1763," *William and Mary Quarterly*, 3rd ser., 34 (1977), pp. 1–31. Some footnotes omitted. Reprinted by permission of Stephen Saunders Webb and the *William and Mary Quarterly*.

Great Britain obtained peace and a securely established imperial status. . . . In the past men had spoken of "empire," meaning the self-sufficient empire of the mercantilists rather than a thing of territory, centralization, maintenance, and authority. After 1763, however, territorial empire came into real and visible existence, and writers, both British and colonial, became aware that "imperialism" meant something more than commerce and colonies and that the colonial problem, with which they were familiar only in its mercantile aspects, had taken on a distinctly territorial and political form.

Andrews pointed out that this "new and untried policy of imperialism" had "autocratic" and "paternal" elements. Its promoters "advocated the use of force or the employment of a policy of coercion." After 1763, therefore, "British statesmen affronted in one way or another the colonies in America, because they were thinking in terms, not of accepted mercantilism but in those of the new imperialism."[1]

Reinforcing the orthodoxy of his pioneering historical generation, Andrews persuaded virtually all subsequent historians of early America that "imperialism and not mercantilism was the first cause of the eventual rupture"; that imperialism was inaugurated after 1763; and that it was not in accord with "the principles or methods of the old British colonial policy." Indeed, in his final statement on the subject, published in 1938, Andrews asserted that, in the classic sense of rule and control by a state over dependencies, "'imperial' and 'imperialism' have no place in the vocabulary of our early history." Although historians have since challenged the significance of 1763 as a turning point in British policy toward America, and although they have debated the degree of change that occurred during and after "the great war for the empire," they have acquiesced nonetheless in the dictum that, before the war, England's had been a "commercial and colonial policy" which was altered to a military and metropolitan policy, with revolutionary results. Thus historians have gone on assessing the Anglo-American empire in a commercial framework, one laden with whig political assumptions and late nineteenth-century economic concepts. The result has been to obscure both the political and the economic realities of Anglo-American history, as well as to unduly restrict the study of the causes of the Revolution.[2]

From its beginning, English colonization was as much imperial as it was mercantile, and English colonial policy was as much military as it was commercial. Of course, English attitudes toward the colonists (and vice versa) were also shaped by the ties of family and place, by Christian and classical ideologies, and by the growth of the state. All of these influences, however, tended to promote Anglo-American empire at least as much as they enhanced transatlantic commerce. The forces fostering imperialism were most clearly summarized in the political role of the English army and in the administrative careers of its officers commanding colonies, the governors-general. Their imperial influence was coeval with colonization itself. The empire that they organized originated almost two centuries before the onset of the American Revolution in 1763. It achieved constitutional definition a century prior to its dissolution in 1783. In Anglo-America commercial considerations, while always present, were dominant only occasionally. More often the imperial ethos prevailed in English thinking about the provinces, and imperialism had economic as well as bureaucratic and military bases. The coexistence of these policy extremes, and their continual competition for political influence, provide the terms of analysis for Anglo-American relationships. It is time to end the "commercial and colonial" monopoly of interpretation. In reassessing Anglo-America, historians must recognize the fact of empire embodied in the governors-general and applied through garrison government.[3]

The present essay sets forth some themes of this reassessment. First, it reexamines the Tudor military foundations of English empire. The essential element in the definition of empire is the imposition of state control on dependent peoples by force. The instrument of that imposition is the army. There are no empires without armies. Second, this reinterpretation notes the development of "garrison government"—that is, militarized and centralized provincial administration—particularly during the English Civil Wars and the Interregnum. Third, the essay observes that throughout the Protectorate, and during most of the Restoration, paramilitary power relationships were applied over ever-widening territorial areas, first in the British Isles and then in England's overseas provinces.

The Anglo-American empire thus created was formalized by 1681. At this early date, a century before the winning of independence by thirteen of the continental colonies, Anglo-American relations were already dominated by an imperial system whose principal agents were the governors-general—officers of the English army who constituted nine-tenths of the royal provincial governors during the adolescence of the "old Empire," 1660–1727. By 1727, however, the imperial militarization finally impressed upon England's colonies by Marlborough's subordinates was being overlaid, if not undone, by the commercial and colonial policies long advocated by "country" politicians and "city" merchants, and finally effected by the Walpole regime. The renewal of imperial war at the close of the era of "salutary neglect" opened the penultimate phase in the struggle of armed imperial authority with commercial motivation and colonial autonomy. "The great war for the empire" at last realized the imperial ambitions of two centuries, but at the price of provoking the resistance of the colonial elites and the revenge of imperial rivals which combined as the American Revolution.

The political and administrative usefulness of military men had been impressed on English sovereigns during their long obsession with the conquest of France. Continental experience had endowed the monarchy with an imperial title, an imperial ambition, and an imperial instrument. By the reign of Henry VIII, military governors, assisted by councils of military, fiscal, and secretarial officers, controlled the European possessions of "the imperial crown of England." "Governors"—the English title is of Tudor coinage—commanded garrisons in provincial capitals. Their troops marched out from urban citadels to enforce the orders the governor received from the crown and to collect the taxes he levied for the crown. English soldier-administrators used the forceful methods they had learned in France to subject England itself to royal authority. This process was concluded at Naworth in 1569, when the governor of the Berwick citadel and the soldiers of his garrison shot down the feudal followers of the northern earls. The crisis of the Elizabethan regime was thus decided in favor of royal, central government.

In 1585 Tudor governors and garrisons sailed overseas once more as Spain replaced France in English enmity. Holding fortified commercial towns in the formerly Spanish Netherlands, the English soldier-administrators discovered that wealth followed the flag—that Spain, and through her all of Europe, was enriched by the spoil of conquered kingdoms in America. English officers observed that imperial rivalry would make them the agents of an English authority extended over England's neighbors and overseas, as well as the instruments of crown control over England itself.

To the army's domestic police function and its American ambition, the reconquest and colonization of Ireland between 1550 and 1622 added agrarian and societal duties. The Irish "first phases of modern English imperialism" led to the implementation of the classic colonial model: by 1609 "the custom of plantation in colonies, whereby the Roman plant was removed into the soil of other nations," was imposed in Munster and in Ulster as a central component of English imperialism. Plantation government was defined on the Roman model, modified by the European conciliar tradition: "For Government, let it be in the Hands of one, assisted with some Counsell: and let them have Commission, to exercise Martiall Lawes, with some limitation." Governor, council, and martial law—such was the prescription for English empire in America in the coming century.

In their memories and in their orders, English army officers carried imperial ideas across the Atlantic. Trained in arms and administration in the cities and citadels of France and in the Netherlands, experienced in Irish conquest and plantation, these officers came to command the palisaded plantations of Jamestown and Henrico; St. Mary's, Sagadahoc, and Saybrook; Plymouth and Piscataqua; Charlestown and Cambridge—all in North America—and the even more embattled outposts in the West Indies; Providence, St. Kitts, and Barbados. As scattered settlements grew, touched, and required governmental organization, military units helped define political jurisdictions. In Virginia local squads gave way to plantation companies, and these were subsequently amalgamated into country commands. The association of township militia companies in regiments was fundamental to county definition in Massachusetts. And all around the Atlantic circuit of the English empire, town government reflected Netherlands garrison practices and obeyed the orders of Netherlands veterans.

The model was established not only at Jamestown, the capital of a dominion in the making, with its triple bastions and uniformed guards, but also at tiny Plymouth, ordered within its palisade, lying down the hill beneath its fort, with "pateroes" pointing from the guard post at the town intersection, its men organized by Captain Standish, mustering by squads for guard duty, fire fighting, and religious worship. This simple model was easily duplicated in Captain Graves's Charlestown, Captain Dudley's Cambridge, Captain Endecott's Salem, Captain Gardiner's Saybrook, Captain Mason's Hartford. Each of these towns was defined by "watch and ward." Each was a militarized node of English conquest and colonization in America. The governmental institutions of England's colonies, whether in Ireland, the West Indies, or North America, thus were shaped by military men, intent on establishing security and imposing social order within their jurisdictions, and determined to spread crusading Christianity and English authority over conquered territories and "native" peoples. Here were elements of empire.

On the American continent, Virginia was from the first what it would continue to be, the bellwether of English empire. It was the continental colony that contributed most to the development of an imperial constitution, and prior to the outbreak of the English Civil Wars it especially exemplified the effect, and the limits, of military ideas and institutions in the early English colonies. Virginia's beginnings suggest a general Anglo-American pattern. With a heroism reminiscent of archaic eras, Capt. John Smith, soldier, adventurer, imperialist, played out in Virginia a socially significant scene from the militant drama of his life. His ideas were institutionalized, and the colony's society stabilized, by a quartet of Netherlands veterans who subjected Virginia to the continent's first English and imperial code, the "Lawes Divine, Morall and Martiall." Subsequent testimony about Virginia by soldier-advisors and military officials illustrated the influence of army administrators over the "plantations," the "natives," and the "colonists" (all terms that these officers derived from Irish conquest and colonization, and applied to the definition of early American experience). The soldier-statesmen of Virginia also defined the fundamental and perennial divisions of English expansionist thought by strongly contrasting their imperial and authoritarian programs for Virginia with more legislative, legalistic, civilian, commercial, and oligarchical colonial concepts.

Captain Smith militarized Virgina government. Nothing else could be expected of a man whose experience had led him to equate social order with army discipline. In 1596, aged sixteen, Smith had run away from his merchant master and apprenticed himself to war. "When France and Netherlands had taught him to use his Armes," he came home to camp in the fields of his native Lincolnshire, run courses with his lance, and read Machiavelli and Marcus Aurelius on the interrelations of force, morality, and empire. The year 1601 found him fighting for the German empire against the Turkish empire, and for Christianity against Islam. In the siege, storm, and defense of central European citadels, and by cultivating their governors and serving in their garrisons, Smith—and many other English cavaliers—learned the socially stabilizing use of the garrisoned government center. Such a fortified central place, he observed, "could bee of no great strength, yet it keepes all them barbarous Countreyes about it in admiration and subjection."

Eager to help found an English empire in which he might serve, and desiring a capital to command, Smith first visited Ireland and then, in December 1606, sailed for Virginia as a member of the first American colonial council. At Jamestown factionalism, starvation, and Indian war produced a reaction toward absolutism among the colonists whom Smith addressed as "Fellow Soldiers." Taking command, the captain forced the adoption of the military plantation model of society which had been developed by the English conquerors of Ireland from their European garrison experience: "The Church was repaired; the Store-house recovered; buildings prepared for the Supplyes we expected; the Fort reduced to a five-square forme; the order of the watch renewed; the squadrons . . . trained; the whole Company every Saturday exercised," both to awe the natives and to discipline the English. So Smith pioneered in America the pattern of imperial settlement: "the effect of a Cittadell, or the true modell of a Plantation."

The survival of citadels and plantations depended on the military ability of their commanders or "governors." "What is requisite to be in a Gouvernour of a plantation?" Smith was asked. Aggressiveness, he answered. In a world of warring empires, on American seas and Dutch battlefields, "many hundreds of brave English Souldiers, Captaines and Gentlemen" had found that "peace was onely but an empty name," and security was better won by war than purchased by tribute. Brains as well as bravery were essential in governors, Smith contended, for "there is no misery worse than [to] be conducted by a foole, or commanded by a coward." Leader and led were subordinate parts of an imperial whole, "obedient to government and their Soveraigne, as duty required." To promote the cause of disciplined national expansion, Smith concluded, England's military governors should emulate the Spanish conquistadors "that advanced themselves from poore Souldiers to great Captaines, their posterity to great Lords, and their King to be one of the greatest potentates on earth, and the fruits of their labours his greatest glory, power, and renowne."

Before Captain Smith's imperial dream could be realized, much social building would be required of the English empire's "hammerors and rough masons . . . I mean our old soldiers trained up in the Netherlands." Smith's executive model was officially adopted for Virginia government in 1609, and he himself was succeeded by three Netherlands veterans, each of whom had been knighted in battle, had captained a garrisoned town, and had served in Ireland. These three—Virginia's "Lord Governour and Captaine General," Sir Thomas West (Lord de la Warr); the lieutenant general, Sir Thomas Gates; and the provost marshal and deputy governor, Sir Thomas Dale—carried Virginia from Smith's garrisoned beginnings to plantation permanency. Their political principles and social definitions were expressed in the code "For The Colony In Virginea Brittannia Lawes Divine, Morall and Martiall, etc." This code the veterans compiled with the aid of another Netherlands officer, William Strachey, secretary of the colony, from the marital law of the English army in the Netherlands and from Sir Thomas Smythe's regulations for the Ulster military plantation.

Determined to "proceede by martial lawe according to your commission as of most despatch and terror and fittest for this government," the military administrators of Virginia made themselves absolute by defining all adult males as soldiers. The soldier's oath bound each armed settler "to serve his Prince, and obey his officers: for the true order of warre is fitly resembled to true religion ordeined of God, which bindeth the souldier to observe justice, loyaltie, faith, constancie, patience, silence, and above all, obedience." As religion enforced every soldier's obedience to "his Colonel or Governor," so that commander (like his king) pictured himself as a Biblical patriarch. Responsible to God, "as knowing assuredly that all the crimes and trespasses of his people under him shall be exacted at his hands," the military governor enforced the "Lawes Divine, Morall and Martiall" that made it death to criticize his sacred person. His authority was restricted only by his own military oath—to "perform [in] all Integrity [and] uprightnesse, justice and sincere administration of the discipline and Lawes in all causes and cases, for the good of the Colony or Colonies . . ."—and by the physical limits of his power. These two factors compelled every governor-general to rely primarily on his own example—"a lively pattern of industry, order and comliness"—to secure the public good, while reserving for emergencies "the power and Sword of Justice and authority."

By 1618, after four years of local peace, amidst the first flush of tobacco prosperity and during control of the Virginia Company by partisans of parliamentary authority, the "Lawes Divine, Morall and Martiall" had been displaced. There ensued that degraded command, unregulated settlement, and concentration on individual economic aggrandizement at the cost of order, community, and security, that led to the massacre of 1622. "The cause of the massacre was the want of marshall discipline," John Smith told a royal commission of enquiry. Deficiencies of "marshall discipline," the captain explained, included a variety of social and political elements: dispersed settlement compounded the shortage of soldiers, and there were too many councilors and counsels, both in England and Virginia. Their number exacerbated the destabilizing, discordant results of overfrequent changes of executive. Moreover, the councilors' disunity reemphasized the Virginia executive's lack of military authority.

Even those English observers of Virginia's plight who did not share Smith's conviction that the crown should institute direct royal rule in Virginia and restore a military governor and government, backed by a regular garrison, nonetheless repeated the martial commonplaces of the age, which Smith from the first had applied to the colony. In a deathbed letter to his son—Sir Francis Wyatt, governor of Virginia—George Wyatt recalled that Virginia had begun as a combination of Roman "colony" and English "plantation." It was designed to force "Barbarians to Civilitie and Christianitie." A settlement among savages, Wyatt concluded, should have continued to concentrate on "Soldgership, afore better deservinge wel, now more to be respected[,] which neclected hathe cost you so deare."

The elder Wyatt was a veteran of the contest with Spain in the Netherlands. To direct observation of the Spaniards' European military practice he added reading about their American colonial experience. Both supported his call for compact, socially graduated, militarily ordered, fortified settlements in Virginia. These were to be connected, protected, and dominated by three garrisoned cities. The whole colony should be ruled, Wyatt suggested, by a well-guarded, loyally counseled governor-general, commanding armed forces modeled on the Greek phalanx and the Roman legion. These formations, the old soldier observed, had "spreade their branches even over the world": they were the shade trees of empire. In advocating the "feedfight" and by applying Xenophon's hunting techniques to guerrilla war against the natives, as well as by recommending that firearms be substituted for polearms (most useful against cavalry which the natives did not have; unwieldy in the forests where they dwelt), Wyatt adapted classic tactics to Virginia. His prescriptions for well-garrisoned urban places, for legionary-type entrenchments, and for elaborate drill, however, all required far greater resources than those which his son commanded in the colony.

Francis Wyatt did revive military plantation practices after the massacre of 1622, but they continually conflicted with commercial and localist drives, as Capt. George Donne reported in 1638. Having fought for the Protestants in France and against the Spaniards in the West Indies, Donne was commissioned muster-master general and provost marshal of Virginia in 1637. In the following year he presented to Charles I "two Consideracions without which this sound limbe of your confirmed Empire cannott bee fast joynted to the full bodie." The first was a "Serious Strict observation" of those laws and rules especially suited to colonies. The second was "ready Instruction in the use of armes." Both should be required in a colonial constitution, "An Injunction by Authority imposed," to which colonial assent need not be secured by the crown. Armed authority would both enforce colonial order and accomplish the conquest of neighbors and natives, for domestic peace and foreign conquest had been "the chiefe Glorye and firmity of the Roman Empire."

Military government, Donne asserted in terms that had become imperialist commonplaces, would check the "search for growing rich to soone" which was producing unsuitable political ambition in colonial and commercial elites, leading to contention with executive authority and "a Competition with a Governor for Superiority." Unwise dependence on "the Wills and counsailes of Men of Trade," had produced oligarchic license and conciliar pretensions. Monarchical and military political prescriptions of the sort the king wished to revive at home and overseas in the later 1630s, therefore, "disquieted the Composition of some Mynds in Virginia and of too many (as it appears) in England." Anglo-American opposition to the executive had other springs also. The provost marshal told the king that, as in old England so in New England, religious dissent had induced political treason. Thus this imperial officer anticipated that social aspiration, political ambition, and religious enthusiasm would excite civil war.

Within three years Donne's fears became fact: a civil war, inimical alike to monarchy, army, and empire, destroyed the authority of the English executive in America. By forcing the development of autonomous colonial elites and institutions, and by providing a republican ideology, the Civil Wars became the essential precondition of American independence. For example, Sir William Berkeley was recommissioned governor of Virginia in 1641 by a monarch suffering from a reaction against his absolutism, and recommissioned by an exiled prince in 1650. He was stripped of the military authority possessed by his veteran predecessors. He was reduced to being merely first among equals in the colony's council. He lost the institutional model which a strong English executive provided the dependencies, and he was deprived as well of monarchical support for his provincial government. Concurrent with the abasement of executive authority throughout the empire by civil war, provincial autonomy was enhanced by the political aggression of acquisitive elites. They took control of the now-dominant local institutions of the provincial council and the county courts, and their outport commercial connections with England were as antimetropolitan as their politics. Anglo-American republicanism—oligarchic, localist, autarchic alike in religion and commerce—successfully challenged monarchical centralization of politics and imperial uniformity in church and commerce during the imperial civil wars of the 1640s and of the 1770s and 1780s.

While executive authority shrank overseas, a centralizing reaction against the social disintegration and political factionalization of civil war strengthened the institutions of garrison government in England. There, during the 1640s, both royalist and parliamentary military governors sought to pacify their commands by establishing the authority of one or the other of the competing central governments. They thereby introduced a metropolitan focus into local politics. The governors made "court" and "country" partisanships the polarities of English provincial politics by forcing local leaders either to defend local autonomy or to support state sovereignty. Thus they forecast the shape of Anglo-American politics as well. In Nottingham from 1644 to 1646, as in Virginia from 1676 to 1681, local partisanships were sublimated in the struggle to determine the dimensions of metropolitan authority in provincial life. Established elites saw the continuation of their sway in the maintenance of local autonomy. Aspirant outgroups tied their ascent to an expansion of the central government's local role. Appeals to London to resolve the contest for local power produced gubernatorial commissions that divided authority between the executive and elements of the local elite organized as a council. In these commissions, consultative and judicial roles were always reserved to the councilors, but the preponderance of power was held by the governor in the form of extensive military authority.

The governors used their military authority to patronize their supporters. They not only personified but also developed a professional administrative class—

governmental "men of business"—and they helped to organize an alternative elite to the traditional governing class by paying particular attention to "the middling sort" of people. These were the heart of the governors' militias, the friends of public order. Their approval of executive authority contrasted with the arrogance and independence of the provincial elites and the anarchism of the poor. The governors' social rebalancing, political reorganization, and paramilitary administration were financed in part by local requisitions and taxes, collected by the governor for the state and spent by him for military purposes. Further support for prerogative politics came from central government grants to localities. These were disbursed by the governor largely to pay himself, his staff, his garrison, and their local suppliers. Increased governmental revenue and expenditure provided politically directed economic alternatives in agriculture, clothing, processing, shipping, and finance. These new economic opportunities tended to be monopolized by the growing official "interest" of officers, administrators, court-connected merchants, and farmer-suppliers. Garrison government, whether of nation, province, town, or colony, required the recruitment and organization of masses of men and money, supplies and food, that laid the economic basis of prerogative politics. Merchant-bankers, clothiers, manufacturers, recruiters, and farmers all stood to profit from garrison government.

Twenty-six veterans carried the Civil War institutions of garrison government to ten different colonies, seven in America and in the West Indies, and one each in Europe, North Africa, and India. These officers had governed a dozen different English cities, towns, and citadels. They subsequently served thirty terms in governorships overseas. Among New World colonies, Jamaica, Barbados, New York, and Virginia were especially influenced by the administration of these civil warriors.

In the British Isles, the Celtic kingdoms felt the rough hand of English paramilitary rulers after 1649, as Oliver Cromwell extended the priciples and practices of garrison government from England to the conquest, pacification, and development of Ireland and Scotland. His officers then transferred experiences of military government, widened and intensified by Irish and Scottish application, to the overseas units of the empire. So the forceful local administrations of the English Civil Wars were transmuted into an Anglo-American imperial system by royalist and parliamentary officers alike, and by the military executives of the Commonwealth and of the Protectorate.

Basing empire in conquest, Cromwell's legions had massacred Irish urban garrisons and "pacified" the Irish countryside with fire and sword. More constructively, they renewed urban garrison government and agricultural military plantation. Together, these operations supported an army of occupation and administration. As frontier police, militia cadres, and seaport patrols, English soldiers redistributed land, regulated political activity, and collected customs. Officer-executives were regularly shifted from Irish posts to provincial service elsewhere in the British Isles and in Dunkirk, Tangier, Jamaica, Barbados, Massachusetts, New York, and Maryland as well. Repeated Irish revolts insured that Ireland continued to employ the English army's largest reserve as a garrison. So Ireland educated both governors-general and an increasing variety of other officer-administrators, down to the American Revolution. Five officers, who afterwards commanded Jamaica, New York, and Tangier, had served in Ireland before 1660. During the Restoration they were succeeded in Ireland by six officer-executives who later went out to govern New York, New England, and the

Leeward Islands. Between 1689 and 1727 fifteen or more veterans of William III's Irish war also served as royal governors in Virginia, Gibraltar, Minorca, Jamaica, Barbados, the Leeward Islands, Nova Scotia and Newfoundland, and New York and Pennsylvania.

The first of these classes of Irish military administrators, trained as much in social as in military discipline under Cromwell, Monck, and Jones, had gone on to complete their unification of the British Isles by the conquest of Scotland. They were suspicious of merchant motivations, and the public order they imposed on the Scots was biased in favor of yeomen and tradesmen. It was distinguished, even among garrison governments, by its high degree of centralization and militarization. In the period 1654–1658 officer-governors carried the paternalist, regulatory, and coercive tendencies, developed in Scotland, to Jamaica, where they survived to find expression in the imperial constitutional formulations of 1681. After 1688, Williamite repression in Scotland trained seven soldiers who subsequently ruled Virginia, New York, Barbados, and Jamaica. The Union of 1707 refreshed the flow of army administrators from Scotland to the American provinces (and vice versa). Therefore another half-dozen or more veterans of Scottish garrisons, several of whom were themselves Scots, were commissioned as governors-general in America before 1727. Whether in expanding the frontier westward, as did Col. Alexander Spotswood, or in interrelating provincial and metropolitan political groups, as the earl of Orkney did, Scots officers had an especially marked influence on Virginia in the early eighteenth century.

While this routine transfer of officers from governments in the three British kingdoms to the empire's American provinces continued until the American Revolution, it had begun much earlier, with the Commonwealth's punitive expeditions to Barbados in 1651 and to Virginia in 1652. Next the Protectorate tried to unite the British Isles and every English colony into a single transatlantic state, directed by its military executive to the reduction of the Spanish empire. This "Western Design" was planned by a Barbadian, Thomas Modyford. It was directed by a commissioner from the New English Plymouth, Edward Winslow. Its settlers were recruited by a Massachusetts officer, Daniel Gookin. The governors of Irish plantations and Scottish citadels, Robert Venables and William Brayne, commanded expeditionary regiments drawn from London and the Leeward Islands. The widespread residences of its officers and men attest to the geographic scope of the Protector's imperial vision. It produced the massive expedition of 1654 that attacked Hispaniola, conquered Jamaica, and so revived and intensified military plantation and garrison government in America after the imperially decadent era of the early Stuarts and the disintegrative period of the Civil Wars. The imperialists of the Restoration would force a reluctant Charles II to recognize the political and administrative necessity of adopting the Cromwellian system of territorial control and political administration. Thus they would keep provincial government, in Britain and overseas, a military preserve.

As this decision was especially apparent in colonial government, so it was an especially contentious issue in colonial policy. From the outset of English colonization, military-imperial and civilian-commercial elements had competed for domination of English expansion overseas; but never was that struggle more severe than in the first fifteen years of the Restoration. Control of colonial policy, and of overseas investment and direction of money and men, fluctuated between the devotees of the Tudor-Cromwellian imperial tradition and those who sought to negate the militarist and statist outcome of the Interregnum and to reaffirm instead commercial freedom and local autonomy. From the eve of the Restoration, Anthony Ashley Cooper, afterwards earl of Shaftesbury, headed those who wished to ally particularist "country" politicians with the anti-governmentalists among the "city" merchants and with the clients of both groups among the colonial oligarchs. By 1674 Shaftesbury had defined the proto-whig commercial and colonial program, most notably restated twenty-five years later by his secretary, John Locke, and finally realized by the Walpoles after 1722.

That whig and commercial dominance was so long delayed, however, only emphasizes the profundity of the monarchical and imperial triumph of 1675. The fall of Shaftesbury, and the dissolution of the council of foreign plantations of which he was president, opened imperial administration to the reformed, revitalized, and royalist committee of the Privy Council for the plantations (the so-called "Lords of Trade and Plantations"). This committee was chaired on occasion by the duke of York, afterwards James II, always the personification of unbending monarchy, militarism, and empire. It was influenced by the earl of Danby, who tied an administration aggressive overseas and absolutist at home to a vision of English national achievement. The Privy Council committee was informed, and so directed, by a secretariat first drawn from council, customs, treasury, and the army by Sir Robert Southwell and afterwards developed by William Blathwayt, the imperial fixer. The imperialists' achievement in the six years after 1675 was summarized by the constitution for the empire which they formalized in 1681.

That accomplishment primarily depended upon the work of three generations of governors-general in defining and establishing English military and imperial authority, both in the British Isles and overseas. Between the restoration of Charles II in 1660 and the death of George I in 1727, the crown commissioned 206 commanders-in-chief of royal provinces overseas. Almost nine in every ten (87.5 percent) of these appointees were English army officers prior to their promotion to the command of colonies. The commissions carried the rank of colonel in the royal army and local rank as general. The prior military service of the governors-general was not nominal, nor was it merely the attribute of social status. These officers had served an average of ten years as captains, or at higher rank, before being promoted to governorships. About 65 percent of the veterans who became governors-general had already had extensive garrison service in the British Isles, and often in England's possessions as well. In the royal garrisons they acquired the administrative skills, worked out the social policies, and practiced the paramilitary, prerogative politics that had helped stabilize England itself, the most turbulent society of seventeenth-century Europe, and that made these veterans of garrison government effective agents of imperialism.

Through these officers the English executive shaped an empire between 1654 and 1681. Its principles were territorial conquest and plantation, political coercion and centralization. Ever-expanding territories were seized from imperial rivals or were reclaimed by the state either from private proprietors or from those local oligarchies that claimed royal sanction for their rule but refused to obey the crown's commands. The conquest of Jamaica in 1655 and of New York in 1664, the subsequent reversion of Barbados and the Leeward Islands from proprietary to royal rule, and the royalization of Virginia government are Restoration cases in point. With cumulative and lasting effect on provincial polities, both in the British Isles and in America and the West Indies, the English executive sought to impose a classic, avowedly Roman, imperial system on its dependencies.

Proconsular government of provinces in the interest of the "imperial princes" of England played upon the regional, cultural, and familial ties between Englishmen at home and overseas; and the provincial executives also made political and social use of the mercantile acts designed to define the relationships between the merchants of the metropolis and their colonial correspondents. Thus the military cousinage of the Moncks and the Modyfords, and the government service connection of the Nicholas and D'Oyley families, were powerful in Jamaica. In Virginia the influence of the military, banking, and factoring house of Jeffreys had imperial political results equaled only by the Anglican Morrisons or the Gloucestershire Norwoods and Berkeleys.

The political interplay of family, fortune, and profession produced a transatlantic imperial interest, premised on the crown's ability to patronize, protect, and direct its provincial officers (most of whom were both military and economic leaders in their communities) and to require their obedience to royal orders. This primitive "military-industrial complex" meant that arms and munitions for provincial forts and militias were the most common subject of solicitation at court by colonial agents in the seventeenth century. The crown's provision of military supplies, together with the military salaries it paid the army officers commanding colonies, was the largest fiscal cost of empire. Royal commissions reiterated the military bias of empire by directing the governors-general to give the largest share of their attention to militia discipline, drill, and command. The social policy enjoined by these commissions opposed land engrossment and poll taxes. Instead, the governors-general were ordered to favor food crops and excise taxes. The dispersion of population caused by unproductive, speculative landholding and by commercial agriculture, and the penalty placed on the poor and on families by poll taxes, were opposed by the governors-general in order to encourage farm families to settle closely in self-sustaining settlements, Such settlements could support a numerous militia, capable of self-defense and subject to garrison government discipline.

Other military institutions than the provincial militias expressed the imperialists' agrarian, authoritarian, paramilitary social policy. The regimental plantations of Cromwellian soldiers defined the settlement patterns of Jamaica and so shaped the island's social structure. In Virginia a regiment of Charles II's Guards, elements of which stayed in the colony for seven years, helped a succession of governors-general displace Berkeleyan oligarchs and repress Baconian rebels, clearing a social middle ground for aspirant, but obedient, planter-militiamen. Regular troops in three New York garrisons, and garrisons in Nova Scotia and Newfoundland, repeatedly essayed soldier-colonization on the Roman model from 1696 until the eve of the Revolution. Such units manifested the army's social, political, and profoundly imperial influence in colonial America.

"Force gives the rule to law." The laws of trade, of politics, of religion, unquestionably important as they were to the shape of empire, received the color of authority from the palette of physical force. Symbolically as well as actually, the army supported executive authority everywhere in the empire. Whether in Carlisle, England, or in Port Royal, Jamaica, the earl of Carlisle took coach to church surrounded by his life guard of cavalry. He took his seat in a canopied chair of state, the altar at his left hand the redcoated files of his garrison at his right. He heard a sermon on the holy duty of obedience to governors preached by the garrison chaplain. Carlisle's garrison governments thus manifested the authoritarian marriage of the military and the ministry in the service of the state. In Portsmouth or New York, Col. Richard Nicolls found little fighting for his soldiers, but they enforced the embargoes by which he kept wheat in the port in famine times. They manned patrol boats and (rather roughly) collected the customs duties from merchants. Even by their impact on the local labor supply Nicolls's garrisons helped show how much the economic authority of the English government was a function of force. The corporation of York and the council of Virginia both suffered as Col. Herbert Jeffreys turned from a civil war career of fighting English and French rebels against royal authority to a peacetime occupation of punishing English and American opponents of the crown's control. The elements of the royal Guards which composed Jeffreys's garrisons chopped up defiant Yorkshiremen and hanged Baconians. Hearing of the obduracy of some Virginia councilors, rather more provincial-minded than the rest, the Guards asked leave of the colonel to hang them too. The ultimate identity of military force and monarchical—imperial—politics was apparent to all.

There are questions about the efficacy of English soldiers as the physical basis of garrison government in America. The garrisons were diseased, dispersed, and undisciplined, and their numbers were small. In the seventeenth century there were seldom more than one thousand regular soldiers on the North American continent. Often there were no more than three hundred. Both numbers were doubled in the English West Indies. These deficiencies, however, were at least partly offset by the physical debility and the small numbers of the colonists themselves. In proportion to population the garrisons were larger than the armies commanded by present-day authoritarian regimes. Moreover, the garrisons' domestic effect was multiplied many times, both in British and American provinces, by the militarily weak but politically puissant select militias. The garrisons' greatest reinforcement was psychological. A widespread desire for local peace and social order placed much of the populace of almost every province on the side of the armed agents of imperial authority. In addition, when provincials felt exposed to the attacks of hostile natives or alien empires, as was often the case in much of the Atlantic world, the exchange of popular acquiescence, and often ready obedience, to royal rule in return for the protection of garrison government or the leadership offered by the governors-general was especially easy and natural.

Fear of alien attack and desire for domestic order produced provincial political successes for the party of monarchical and military authority, while arousing metropolitan criticism. The crown's crippling of the Jamaica and Virginia assemblies, for example, helped alert English parliamentary enemies of executive power to the menace that garrison government posed to legislative and statutory rule. American elites' apprehensions that "we shall be governed as an army," rather than by legislature and law, were validated in English opinion as the crown enhanced its influence by regarrisoning Cromwellian citadels and "reforming" corporate charters. Their power enhanced physically and politically, the local governors grew increasingly aggressive in England as well as overseas.

As the imperial executive verged on absolutism, political moderates or "trimmers" such as the earl of Halifax moved to strengthen their position midway between monarchical militarism and legislative republicanism. Rejecting the exclusion from the royal succession of James, duke of York, and accepting the argument that James's supporters in Ireland, Scotland, "and the Plantations" would react to exclusion with civil war, Halifax joined the garrison government elements that upheld the crown—"Well, if it come to a war," he said to the governor of York, "you and I must go together"—and denounced the "popular" program of Shaftesbury and the Commons majority.

Halifax's forum was as much the Privy Council as it was the House of Lords, and he was as much concerned for the survival of colonial representative assemblies as he was to preserve an effective executive for the empire. The imperial debate of 1680–1681 was a part of the Exclusion Crisis. That debate shaped the constitution of the English empire to, and indeed far beyond, the American Revolution. Its decisive moment occurred in two dramatic Privy Council sessions. There the earl of Halifax helped persuade Charles II to partially re-empower provincial legislatures and to excuse the leaders of their opposition parties from prosecution as enemies of the crown. The royal return of the power of legislative initiative and amendment to the assemblies of Jamaica and Virginia was soon followed by the duke of York's grant of a representative body to New York. Excusing political opposition and confirming assembly authority (once the assemblies agreed to raise revenues for royal use) was a victory for political moderation. These acts went far to establish the governmental structure of the empire and also helped to define the conduct of Anglo-American politics for a century to come.

Resolution of the imperial crisis was facilitated by an available and proven compromise between the extreme opinions of "court" and "country." Lord Culpeper had worked out such a compromise while in command of Virginia. He had actually preserved the colonial legislature's powers of initiative and amendment, despite royal orders to the contrary. But in return Culpeper had exacted a high price in prerogative power: the Virginia assembly accepted a bill, written in the Privy Council, that provided for a permanent provincial tax to support imperial authority. Equally important to the reduction of local autonomy and to the increase of imperial influence was the acquiescence of the Virginia burgesses in the division of legislative authority among the governor, the council, and themselves. Unwillingly, the lower house had also adopted parliamentary practices and public records, both of which opened legislative proceedings to pre-rogative influence, and accepted regular royal review, revision, and rejection of provincial laws. Finally, and most important, the assembly formally acknowledged as law the absolute military authority of the king's governor-general.

Utilizing the Virginia model, Charles II quickly extended the constitutional settlement of 1681 to all the crown colonies. Limited local legislative authority, provincial taxes for imperial use, and an unfettered military prerogative characterized the 1681 settlement. This imposition on American provinces of the Civil War formula of governor, council, and martial law testified to the great growth of executive authority in the empire in the generation after 1653, while the survival of the provincial assemblies and courts preserved elements of corporate privilege, provincial autonomy, and individual liberty. The imperial balance struck in 1681 between metropolis and provinces, coercion and consultation, military-imperial executive and civilian-localist legislature endured for the greater part of a century as the constitution of the first English empire. Thus Anglo-American relations were not shaped by an exclusively "commercial and colonial system," in which the strongest political element was "colonial self-government." Rather, they were predominantly directed by a military and provincial system the strongest political element of which was Anglo-American *imperial* government.

Imperialism and its leader, James Stuart, prevailed in 1681 only because of the support of such moderates as Halifax, many of them powerfully placed in the army and in James's own household, where, as members of his "shadow cabinet," they greatly influenced imperial administration. The moderates had not dared let James, the personification of monarchical order and social stability, fall before the levelling, republican, and localist forces led by Shaftesbury. So, too, in the garrisoned provinces of Britain and America the party of authority had succeeded with the aid of imperially ambitious, but not authoritarian, councilor-administrators.

The character and authority of the councilors themselves had been, and would continue to be, a precise measure of the influence of the "court" or of the "country" in each royal colony. Acting on their garrison government principles, the governors-general regarded their colonial councils as advisory and executive groups of subordinate officers. In this view each of the councilors, if only as colonel of the royal militia, was bound by marital law, first to advise the provincial captain general and governor-in-chief and then "to express his obedience to his *General,* although it be a service that corresponded not with his own opinion at the first." Opposite expectations of the council model and the councilors' role were held by "country" politicians. When in 1674 Shaftesbury and Locke sought to limit the governors' power to suspend councilors and to declare martial law without council consent, they made their social and political purposes plain. Councilors were to be chosen by Shaftesbury and his "city" merchant allies from colonial candidates who combined "country" principles with wealth. The councilors were to possess freedom to debate and to oppose governors' proposals. The governors' colonial councils were to be remodeled on the king's Privy Council, as it was idealized in "country" opinion. That is, the council was to represent the various elements of oligarchy in the provincial society. So composed, it would check the authority of the royal executive.

By the mid-1680s the upshot of the struggle to shape the colonial councils was not so much a compromise between the opposed views as it was a division of each royal council into two parties. The majority was composed of men powerful in their communities, possessed of administrative talent, and loyal to the prerogative. The minority was made up of oligarchs who devoted their personal force, economic advantage, and "country" opinions to the leadership of legislative and localist opposition to the executive and to imperialism. Combined in the colonial councils, these opposed elements both effectively administered prerogative programs and criticized executive excesses, either directly or, more commonly, through their English correspondents.

These correspondents were increasingly sympathetic to complaints of absolutism. During the seven years after 1681, metropolitan as well as provincial moderates slowly and reluctantly were driven to join James Stuart's opponents as he pushed autocratic government (and religious change) to counterproductive extremes. He executed the leading whigs in 1683; massacred the Monmouth rebels in 1685; subverted both the most and the least imperial of the colonial constitutions, those of Jamaica and New England, in 1686; and in 1687 attacked the status of that sanctuary of social order, the Church of England. The antagonisms thus accumulated gave social and ideological focus to the army's dislike of stricter discipline and the admission of Irish and Catholics to military service. There followed the military coup (called "the Glorious Revolution") against James in 1688 and against his governors-general in America in 1689. By

1692, William III, the soldier-king who displaced James, had rebuffed whig-commercialist efforts to return to the status quo ante 1675 and, instead, had restored the 1681 imperial settlement, which balanced military, imperial, and executive dictates with civilian, localist, and legislative demands.

The reestablished imperial constitution proved its worth in inspiring and organizing provincial defenses as far apart as Newfoundland and Jamaica during the first round of England's war with France for Atlantic empire. The truce in that conflict, from 1697 to 1702, offered whigs and commercialists a chance to reassert the Shaftesbury-Locke program of 1674. In England they forced William III to constitute a board of trade and to appoint John Locke to it. In America they tried to re-enfranchise the colonial elites in council and assembly, to reinforce the rule of law in the provinces, and to reduce the imperial authority of the governors-general, especially by attacking their military power. By 1705 this whig effort had failed, for further war with France had once again mandated executive authority and military discipline throughout the empire.

The North American colonies soon shared more directly than ever before in the political as well as the military outcome of England's conflict with her European rivals. During the five years after the battle of Blenheim, from 1705 to 1710, officers who had trained under England's greatest general and chief minister, John Churchill, duke of Marlborough, went out to govern Virginia, New York, Massachusetts, Newfoundland and Nova Scotia, Jamaica, and the Leeward Islands. The decade that followed marked the acme of the "old empire." Two thousand regular troops in North America and large garrisons in the West Indies carried out the orders of professional officers deeply imbued with the precepts of garrison government. Marlborough's governors-general gave a momentum to imperial administration and to shape to provincial politics and society that were not overtly challenged until the mid-1760s, when an overdecisive imperial victory permitted and inspired the Revolutionary generation to enter politics.

Yet, in their own eyes, the imperialists suffered decisive defeat as early as 1722. In the previous year the Board of Trade (headed by a colonel whose particular qualification for imperial office seems to have been his translation of Caesar's *Commentaries* into English and its dedication to the duke of Marlborough) had urged on the king-in-council a program of American government prepared by Marlborough's governors-general. This plan proposed the coordination of American commands under a captain-general. It would set limits to the colonies, and defend them against France, by fortifying and garrisoning the inland frontiers. Eight additional regiments would control the Atlantic coast and its population centers. But this summary of imperial aspirations was filed away for a generation when the entire imperialist leadership—Marlborough, Sunderland, and Stanhope—died in 1722.

In their places the whiggish and commercialist Walpole regime came to power. That regime—the partisans of merchants and aristocrats—took advantage of an abnormally peaceful period to debase the administration of the empire into an uncoordinated assortment of patronage posts, reserved for the well-connected and the unqualified. Peace reduced the imperatives of authoritarian politics and substituted the politics of autonomy. Provincial societies became far more concerned with civil profit than with military security. The government of the increasingly autonomous dependencies was gradually assumed by enriched provincial elites, venial English placemen, and, after 1736, aggrandizing assemblies. At last Shaftesbury's alliance of the ambitious classes in the "country," the "city," and the colonies was fully realized. Commonwealthmen, commercialists, and colonists dominated Anglo-American relations as they had not since the 1640s.

The return of war to English America in the decade 1739–1748 meant that, on much evener terms than had prevailed before 1722, the ancient debate between armed authority and moneyed autonomy was resumed. War made its inevitable demands for forcefulness and order even on the most pacifist and oligarchical of English administrations. Indeed, on the frontiers of empire, in South Carolina, Georgia, Nova Scotia, and in Maroon-menaced Jamaica, the physical imperatives of empire produced a doubling of regular forces and the appointment of militant governors-general by 1748. By that date, however, despite the imperialist resurgence, it appeared that the administrative excellence, the political assurance, and the social relevance of the governors-general during the first century of English colonization would not be equaled again. Instead, the anti-imperial forces of acquisitive capitalism, individual liberty, provincial autonomy, and Anglo-American oligarchy had won an irreducible social and political status for their beneficiaries, the eventual authors of the American Revolution.

The final confrontation of empire with autonomy began when four imperial regiments were destroyed or captured on the Ohio and Ontario frontiers in 1754. "The great war for the empire" poured thirty thousand regulars into England's American provinces by 1759. Conquering vast territories, subjugating both natives and planters to England (a subjugation symbolized by American service in the English army and by colonial taxes for the army's support), the army achieved at last the imperial ambition coeval with colonization itself.

Undersecretary William Knox's memorandum of February 1763 has been called the fullest expression of the "new" imperialism. Knox anticipated that protection would be offered and obedience enforced by frontier and urban garrisons, "to secure the Dependence of the Colonys on Great Britain." This was imperialism, but it was not new. The Knox memorandum of 1763 marked the return to Anglo-American political preeminence of coerciveness and power-hunger, paternalism and militarism. These forces had woven an imperial pattern throughout the fabric we habitually call "the colonial period of American history," but which was really the period of Anglo-American empire.

NOTES

1. Charles M. Andrews, *The Colonial Background of the American Revolution,* rev. ed. (New Haven, Conn., 1931), 122, 123, 126–127, 128.

2. *Ibid.,* 129; Charles M. Andrews, *The Colonial Period of American History* (New Haven, Conn., 1934–1938), IV: *England's Commercial and Colonial Policy,* 7, n. 1. Here (pp. 5, 7) we also find the decisive statements: "England's interest in these colonies was not political but commercial" and "colonies were not looked upon as the stuff out of which an empire was to be made, but rather as the source of raw materials. . . . No one at this time took any other view." The view which Andrews summarized was earlier expressed by George Louis Beer, *The Old Colonial System, 1660–1754,* Pt. I: *The Establishment of the System, 1660–1688* (New York, 1913), vii. Beer defined "colonial system" as "that complex system of regulations whose fundamental aim was to create a self-sufficient empire of mutually complementary economic parts." For the continued dominance of the "commercial and colonial" interpretation of Anglo-American history see such recent and well-regarded studies as Michael Kammen, *Empire and Interest: The American Colonies and the Politics of Mercantilism* (Philadelphia, 1970), esp. chap. 1; Alison Gilbert Olson and Richard Maxwell Brown, eds., *Anglo-American Political Relations, 1675–1775* (New Brunswick, N.J., 1970), esp. fig. 2; and Thomas C. Barrow, *Trade and Empire: The British Customs Service in Colonial America, 1660–1775* (Cambridge, Mass., 1967), esp. 1–3. Andrews had not gone unchallenged, at least in private: "James

Truslow Adams, in a long correspondence [1922], demonstrated that the word and the concept [of "empire"] had been extensively used prior to that year [1763], in contemporary literature, and that no latter-day misreading of England's colonial relations was being committed by speaking of 'empire' during that period." A. S. Eisenstadt, *Charles McLean Andrews: A Study in American Historical Writing* (New York, 1956), 127. As Andrews's subsequent publications and those of his students show, he was not convinced.

3. Evidence for this reassessment appears at large in Stephen Saunders Webb, *The Governors-General: The English Army and the Definition of the Empire, 1569–1681* (Chapel Hill, N.C., 1977).

SECTION 4: SUGGESTIONS FOR FURTHER READING

Students interested in the development of the Navigation Acts as well as other general aspects of mercantile and imperial policies should begin with S. S. Webb, *The Governors-General: The English Army and the Definition of the Empire, 1569–1681* (1977), M. G. Kammen, *Empire and Interest: The American Colonies and the Politics of Mercantilism* (1970), T. C. Barrow, *Trade and Empire: The British Customs Service in Colonial America, 1660–1775* (1967), C. M. Andrews, *The Colonial Period of American History*, vol. 4 (1938), and G. L. Beer, *The Old Colonial System, 1660–1754* (2 vols., 1912). Webb specifically challenges the heretofore accepted formulations of C. M. Andrews's *The Colonial Background of the American Revolution* (rev. ed., 1931), as explained in the preceding selection. Perhaps the fullest explication of the system may be found in L. H. Gipson's first volumes of *The British Empire before the American Revolution* (15 vols., 1936–1970), a magisterial work. O. M. Dickerson, *The Navigation Acts and the American Revolution* (1951), argues that the system had salubrious effects, but L. A. Harper, *The English Navigation Laws* (1939), maintains the opposite. A balanced theoretical statement, taking a middle position, is R. P. Thomas, "A Quantitative Approach to the Study of the Effects of British Imperial Policy upon Colonial Welfare: Some Preliminary Findings," *Journal of Economic History*, 25 (1965), pp. 615–638.

Two excellent primary source introductions to the years of colonial insurrections are C. M. Andrews, ed., *Narratives of the Insurrections, 1675–1690* (1915), and M. G. Hall et al., eds., *The Glorious Revolution in America: Documents on the Colonial Crisis of 1689* (1964). There has been little agreement about the proper way to interpret Bacon's Rebellion. The insurrection is dealt with from a pro-Bacon perspective in two volumes by T. J. Wertenbaker, *Virginia under the Stuarts, 1607–1688* (1914), and *Torchbearer of the Revolution: The Story of Bacon's Rebellion and Its Leader* (1940). W. E. Washburn, *The Governor and the Rebel: A History of Bacon's Rebellion in Virginia* (1957), by comparison, takes a pro-Berkeley approach. The Washburn volume is particularly strong on white-Indian relations as a precipitating factor, and his findings should be compared with those of E. S. Morgan in the middle chapters of *American Slavery—American Freedom: The Ordeal of Colonial Virginia* (1975). The Rebellion as seen from the point of view of a search for the rights and privileges of Englishmen is presented in D. S. Lovejoy, "Virginia's Charter and Bacon's Rebellion, 1675–1676," *Anglo-American Political Relations, 1675–1775*, ed. A. G. Olson and R. M. Brown (1970), pp. 31–51. This volume contains a number of incisive essays about emerging patterns of empire and the role of the colonists in the imperial framework. In particular R. M. Brown's introductory essay is especially suggestive.

Over the decades a series of valuable books and essays have appeared which explain the years of turmoil in the context of the beginnings of empire. The best general introductions are W. F. Craven, *The Colonies in Transition, 1660–1713* (1968), and M. G. Hall, *Edward Randolph and the American Colonies, 1676–1703* (1960). Until recently no one book covered the years and events of the American phase of the Glorious Revolution in detail. D. S. Lovejoy, *The Glorious Revolution in America* (1972), has admirably filled that gap.

Regional studies of note include V. F. Barnes, *The Dominion of New England: A Study of British Colonial Policy* (1923), containing an assessment of Sir Edmund Andros which must be compared to S. S. Webb, "The Trials of Sir Edmund Andros," *The Human Dimensions of Nation Making: Essays on Colonial and Revolutionary America*, ed. J. K. Martin (1976), pp. 23–53. R. S. Dunn, *Puritans and Yankees: The Winthrop Dynasty of New England, 1630–1717* (1962), and Bernard Bailyn, *The New England Merchants in the the Seventeenth Century* (1955), are also valuable on the Massachusetts uprising. J. R. Reich, *Leisler's Rebellion: A Study of Democracy in New York, 1664–1720* (1953), now must be treated in conjunction with L. H. Leder, *Robert Livingston, 1654–1728, and the Politics of Colonial New York* (1961), and two quantitative presentations by T. J. Archdeacon, "The Age of Leisler—New York City, 1689–1710: A Social and Demographic Interpretation," *Aspects of Early New York Society and Politics*, ed. Jacob Judd and I. H. Polishook (1974), pp. 63–82, and *New York City, 1664–1710: Conquest and Change* (1976), in evaluating Leisler's upheaval as part of New York's participation in the Glorious Revolution. M. G. Kammen, "The Causes of the Maryland Revolution of 1689," *Maryland Historical Magazine,* 55 (1960), pp. 293–333, and L. G. Carr and D. W. Jordan, *Maryland's Revolution of Government, 1689–1692* (1974), are model studies on Maryland's rebellion. P. S. Haffenden, *New England in the English Nation, 1689–1713* (1974), analyzes the long-term effects of the turmoil on the northern region.

For those seeking more information on the fundamental conflict in England between Stuart monarchs and Parliament, and on the resolution of that conflict through the Glorious Revolution and resulting trends, the essential starting point is J. H. Plumb, *The Growth of Political Stability in England, 1675–1725* (1967). Important supplements to Plumb's succinct, perceptive analysis are G. N. Clark, *The Later Stuarts, 1660–1714* (2nd ed., 1955), John Miller, *Popery and Politics in England, 1660–1688* (1973), J. R. Western, *Monarchy and Revolution: The English State in the 1680s* (1972), and J. R. Jones, *The Revolution of 1688 in England* (1972). Ministerial conceptions leading to the creation of the Dominion of New England as part of a centralizing thrust in Stuart government are traced in P. S. Haffenden, "The Crown and the Colonial Charter, 1675–88," *William and Mary Quarterly,* 3rd ser., 15 (1958), pp. 297–311, 452–466. Of particular value in linking political developments in England and America within the context of empire and party development before and after 1689 are S. S. Webb, "Brave Men and Servants to His Royal Highness: The Household of James Stuart in the Evolution of English Imperialism," *Perspectives in American History,* 8 (1974), pp. 55–80, A. G. Olson, *Anglo-American Politics, 1660–1775: The Relationship between Parties in England and Colonial America* (1973), I. K. Steele, *The Politics of Colonial Policy: The Board of Trade in Colonial Administration, 1696–1720* (1968), and J. A. Henretta, *"Salutary Neglect": Colonial Administration under the Duke of Newcastle* (1972).

It is possible to argue that the Salem witchcraft trials of 1692 represented a culminating, purgating incident in colonial reactions to attempted imperial restraints. Important works on that much-studied subject include M. L. Starkey, *The Devil in Massachusetts* (1949), Chadwick Hansen, *Witchcraft at Salem* (1969), John Demos, "Underlying Themes in the Witchcraft of Seventeenth-Century New England," *American Historical Review,* 75 (1970), pp. 1311–1326, and Paul Boyer and Stephen Nissenbaum, *Salem Possessed: The Social Origins of Witchcraft* (1974), all of which make for engaging reading.

The Maturing American Provinces— The Eighteenth Century

PART TWO

Economic Opportunity and the Structure of Society
SECTION 5

Historians generally agree that the range of economic opportunity and social mobility in provincial America was greater than in Europe or Old England. In the mother country the supply of land was fixed, and estates were tied by primogeniture and entail to the passing generations of first sons born into aristocratic families. Inherited social distinctions such as gentry and peerage status set the well-born few apart from the mass of commoners. Seventeenth-century Englishmen lacking in land or family breeding could rarely rise to more than middling social standing, no matter how economically successful. The chief means of economic mobility for ambitious commoners was commercial enterprise; yet even aspiring mercantile leaders who had earned great personal wealth somehow had to acquire land and/or marry into a titled family to insure upper-class social status for themselves and their descendants.

Despite the relative inflexibility of English class lines and the desire of many early settlers to reconstruct an ordered, hierarchical social milieu in the colonies, typifying English patterns, the vast open space of the American environment made it difficult at the outset to recreate fixed class distinctions. Severe labor shortages tended to produce high wages for all those who did not have to sell themselves into bondage in emigrating from England to the New World. As a result, free persons coming to America as well as former indentured servants surviving that system could charge dearly for their labor, acquire reservoirs of working capital, invest their earnings in land, begin planting operations, and thus gain their economic independence. By the end of the seventeenth century, landholding in modest amounts (usually 50 acres) carried with it freemanship status and political privileges like voting rights, as well as middle-class social standing. Hence abundant land and scarce labor often resulted in rapid upward mobility for immigrants leaving behind the fixed social classes of the Old World.

Yet we must keep in mind that a discussion limited to land and labor alone will result in a static conception of varying rates of opportunity for economic and social mobility in provincial America. No simple portrait of the bucolic freehold farmer can encompass the reality of the evolving colonial socioeconomic structure as the seventeenth century gave way to the eighteenth. We must consider four additional and related variables—population expansion, the emergence of urban centers, the growth of commerce, and overcrowding in the older settlements—if we are to be in a position to comprehend the full evolution of the provincials' economy and society.

The eighteenth century, first of all, witnessed a population explosion in America. Natural increase and high fertility rates in combination with large-scale immigration of such groups as Germans, Scots-Irish, and Africans resulted in a sevenfold expansion in population between 1700 and 1760. There were 250,000 men and women in the English North American colonies as the new century dawned, and that population mushroomed to nearly 1,600,000 (including over 300,000 black slaves) by 1760. Fifteen years later the total population stood at 2,500,000 as the Revolution became reality.

Rapid expansion stimulated economic growth. Inhabitants moved westward to new frontiers, where they produced foodstuffs for waiting eastern and imperial markets; and in many cases these inhabitants prospered. Primary (coastal) and secondary (inland) trading centers grew up in handling the flow of goods, and a few exploded in size. Philadelphia, for example, became almost overnight a major center of population and trade. Besides serving as the main debarking point for German and Scots-Irish settlers who began filling the interior regions running west and even as far south as the new colony of Georgia, Philadelphia became a collection and transhipment point for agricultural produce raised in the surrounding Pennsylvania countryside. Yet Philadelphia with a 1760 population of 23,750 did not stand alone. Boston (15,600), New York City (18,000), and Charleston (8,000) were serving similar economic functions in their regions; they too were emerging commercial and cultural capitals in the New World.

The growth in population helped to stimulate the production of goods and the beginnings of urbanization, patterns that could not be missed by royal administrators wanting a dynamic imperial economy. Administrators encouraged production, so long as provincial goods did not compete with home manufactures. And only on occasion did a clash of interests over such items as finished iron and fur hats occur. By and large the colonists (more Yankee than Puritan in the eighteenth century) confined themselves to the production of agricultural staples, fish, furs, naval stores and other wood products, tobacco, rice, and indigo, exchanged in the imperial marketplace for such "luxury" items as linens, silks, spices, glass, wine, tea, and even books. On the whole it was a happy partnership.

Yet there were also internal problems associated with rapid population growth. Overcrowding caused distress in many older seaboard settlements, especially those of New England. As successive generations split up family land on the principle of equal estate division among children (partible inheritance), the sons and daughters of the second and third generations were simply not inheriting enough land to sustain themselves and their children above minimum subsistence levels. Thus the grandchildren and the great-grandchildren of the earliest inhabitants often had to sell their meager plots and face the disconcerting process of moving out onto frontier areas and beginning the rhythm of life again. It was either the psychological trauma of leaving behind all that was familiar, or facing poverty—a growing problem for eighteenth-century Americans. In older seaboard settlements, moreover, those who were fiscally solvent could buy up oversubdivided family plots and enhance their own socioeconomic standing relative to families having just enough land for survival. It seems obvious, then, that economic distance among individuals was increasing rather than declining in the more established settlements. High levels of opportunity and vertical rather than horizontal (geographic) mobility for individuals was often a function of a community's age, the numbers of children in each generation, and the magnitude of the population relative to local land supplies. While some individuals might prosper anew and rise in economic status after having moved to frontier settlements and having reestablished themselves, many others in older communities of three generations or more struggled harder each day to get by rather than give up the security of life in a familiar setting. No one pattern, it seems, will explain all the possibilities confronting individuals.

Thus the portrait of opportunity in the maturing provinces can be etched in a variety of hues, depending upon the location one chooses for the drawing. What was constant among all the varying factors was the heightened commercial ethos, which had the effect of accentuating wealth as the basis for distinguishing the first families from everyday citizens. In the absence of traditional Old World measures (family name, breeding, and inheritance) of a person's social importance, personal wealth had became the provincial standard of success and status. And with increased commercialization of economic activity, property and wealth meant even more in setting people apart. For example, a Philadelphia merchant involved in overseas trading commanded higher community esteem than did a ship's carpenter, a teamster, a shoemaker, a dock worker, or a common seaman. A Maryland tobacco planter or a South Carolina rice-producer who owned hundreds if not thousands of acres, who worked the fields with teams of slaves, and who lived in a newly built manor house held greater respect than the struggling freehold farmer who grew a small parcel of wheat for market but who concentrated his energies upon raising enough food to sustain his family and livestock through long, harsh winter months. Monied and propertied elite families were appearing all over the landscape in the eighteenth century, while on the lower end of the socioeconomic hierarchy poverty was a phenomenon of broadening significance. It was a gap of haunting contrasts.

It is in this general context that we need to consider what kind of socioeconomic arrangements were developing in the maturing provinces. Was economic opportunity and the ability to get ahead in the socioeconomic structure uniformly prevalent as some contemporaries suggested, or were those provincial spokesmen somehow creating a myth? How fluid and open were institutions? Did property and income become more or less evenly distributed through time? If the economy was as buoyant as has been suggested, then how do we account for the growing poverty problem? In terms of social values and ideals, were the provinces becoming more directly a reflection of the parent state, rather than the opposite? What is the most accurate way to portray American society on the eve of revolution, and how might patterns in socioeconomic arrangements help to explain the coming of the American Revolution? Clearly the concept of fixed and hardened class lines did not have as much cogency in provincial America, when compared with the Old World. But does that mean that the British North American provinces of the eighteenth century were maturing as classless, equalitarian, democratic societies?

17. Economic Democracy

Robert E. Brown

Robert E. Brown (b. 1907) of Michigan State University often has joined forces with his wife B. Katherine Brown in attempting to refute decades of historical thinking about the nature of society in eighteenth-century America. The Browns argue that the prerevolutionary world was almost an utopian democracy, much more democratic in fact than America has been since that time. Studying extensively the socioeconomic and political cultures of provincial Massachusetts and Virginia, the Browns continue to insist that all those scholars who have seen American society moving in stages toward greater equalitarianism, culminating in the Age of Andrew Jackson, simply have the whole process backwards. The selection below outlines Robert Brown's position about "middle-class democracy" in provincial America as it pertains to landholding opportunities, income distribution, and social structure in Massachusetts. Showing that property holding was widespread and that high percentages of prerevolutionary free white adult males had voting rights, the author assumes that income distribution remained relatively constant through time. Moreover, he claims that the colonists did not conceive of themselves in class terms.

Despite Professor Brown's conclusions, basic methodological questions need to be aired. May we be sure from the author's unsystematic use of literary sources and random sampling of quantitative data that other source materials would support the author's position? Has the author only presented evidence that specifically fits his thesis? Even if provincial society was more open to personal achievement than the hierarchical European social order, does that mean that opportunity in the colonies represented the opposite extreme of rampant equalitarianism?

The term "democracy" has come to mean many things to many people. In common usage, Lincoln's definition—government of the people, by the people, and for the people—expresses the accepted idea of political democracy. But "democracy" can also mean the right to choose one's religion freely, a chance for all to be educated, and an opportunity to participate in the material benefits of the community.

In colonial days, as is so well known, there was a close connection between political democracy and what, for want of a better term, we might call "economic

Source: From Robert E. Brown, *Middle-Class Democracy and the Revolution in Massachusetts, 1691–1780* (Ithaca: Cornell University Press, 1955), pp. 1–20. Footnotes omitted. Copyright 1955 by the American Historical Association. Reprinted by permission of Cornell University Press.

democracy," that is, the opportunity which the average man had to acquire property and to get ahead in society. This connection was close because there were property qualifications for voting, which meant that if a man could not acquire property he would never be entitled to political rights.

Therefore, any understanding of colonial democracy must of necessity be prefaced by a discussion of some of the economic aspects of Massachusetts society. Since the right to vote depended on the possession of worldly goods, we would want to know how much property was required, what part of the population possessed property, how much property men had, and what opportunity existed for the acquisition of property by those who did not have it. Was there a political aristocracy which rested on the existence of an economic aristocracy, or was there much economic opportunity, that is, economic democracy, so that the average man could acquire property? Was the "common man" excluded from political life because he lacked the opportunity to acquire sufficient property, or could he easily become a property holder and therefore a voter?

Some of the available information on economic conditions in colonial America deals with the colonies in general. The inference is that there was not much difference in the colonies and that what applied to one applied to all. Until the evidence proves otherwise, we can assume that references to the colonies included Massachusetts.

Contrary to the accepted interpretation, one thing on which both foreign observers and contemporary Americans concurred was the vast difference between European and American societies. There was little doubt in their minds that the people who came here from Europe had not simply transplanted their old-country class structure to the New World. In fact, observers agreed that a unique social order had developed in the American colonies.

One of the best known of the European observers, and one who was particularly struck by the contrast between Europe and America, was the French immigrant, Michel-Guillaume Jean de Crèvecoeur. Unlike Europe, said Crèvecoeur, America did not have a few great lords who possessed everything and a herd of people who had nothing. There were no aristocratical families, no courts, no kings, no bishops, no great manufacturers employing thousands of workers, and no great refinements of luxury. There was not the wide gulf between the rich and the poor that existed in Europe. In the rural districts the traveler did not see, as he did in Europe, the hostile castle and haughty mansion in contrast with the clay hut or miserable cabin, where men and animals lived together in meanness and indigence, keeping each other warm. America had no princes for whom to toil, starve, and bleed. The poor of Europe had come to America because Europe offered them neither bread nor land—nothing but penury, starvation, and the abuse of the rich. Europe, in short, contained few distinctions but lords and tenants, rich and poor.

What, then, were the characteristics of this American society which differed so markedly from that of Europe? Crèvecoeur called it a country of fair cities, substantial villages, and extensive fields, filled with decent houses, good roads, orchards, meadows, and bridges. The immigrant found a society differing from what he had seen. Except for the inhabitants of a few towns, the people from Nova Scotia to West Florida were farmers. They were motivated by a spirit of industry which was unfettered and unrestrained because each person worked for himself, not for others. There was a pleasing uniformity of decent competence throughout the country, with the poorest log cabin a dry and comfortable habitation. Lawyer, merchant, or farmer were the only titles in a country where the dictionary was short on words of dignity or honor. Among the Sunday congregation of respectable farmers and their wives there was not an esquire except the unlettered magistrate, and even the minister himself was a simple farmer who did not live in luxury on the labor of others. America, said Crèvecoeur, was the most perfect society then in existence, where men were as free as they ought to be—a predominantly middle-class, equalitarian society.

The reason for this, continued Crèvecoeur, was the abundance of economic opportunity. Immigrants received ample compensation for their labor, and this in turn enabled them to procure land. Their labor was founded on self-interest, the fruits of which were not claimed by despotic princes, rich abbots, or mighty lords. Their land gave them the rank of independent freeholders, which in turn conferred all the political honors in the society. Europe had no such class as this. It was in America that the idle were employed, the useless became useful, and the poor became rich—rich not in terms of gold and silver, but in cleared lands, cattle, good houses, and good clothes. The immigrant did not find a crowded society as in Europe, but one in which there was room for everyone. If he were a laborer, he would soon be hired, well fed at the table of his employer, and paid four or five times as much as he could get in Europe. If he wanted uncultivated lands, there were thousands of acres from which to make a cheap purchase. Not everyone would become rich in a short time, but industry would procure an easy, decent maintenance. The rich stayed in Europe; only the middle class and poor migrated. For laborers or men of middle stations, Crèvecoeur concluded, Europe with all its pomp was not to be compared with America.

Another observer who had firsthand knowledge of the differences between European and American societies was Benjamin Franklin. Franklin pointed out that the population rate in any country was directly proportional to the prevailing economic opportunity. In Europe, all the land was occupied, forcing some men to work for others; labor was plentiful, which meant low wages; and the result was a slow increase in population. But conditions in America were just the opposite. Land was plentiful and so cheap that a laboring man could soon save enough money to buy a farm, raise a family, and be assured that cheap land would provide economic opportunity for his children. Economic opportunity meant that in America there were twice as many marriages and twice as many children per marriage in proportion to the population as there were in Europe, so that the population in America doubled about every twenty years. Even so, land was so easy to obtain and so plentiful that conditions in Europe would not be duplicated in this country for many ages. Labor would never be cheap in America, for no man continued to work for others very long; either he acquired a farm or, if he were an artisan, went out to a new settlement to set up for himself.

Later Franklin, like Crèvecoeur, advised Europeans that this country particularly offered opportunities for people of the middle and lower income groups who had to work for a living. America, he said, was predominantly middle class—few were as miserable as the poor of Europe, but also very few were rich. A general happy mediocrity prevailed. There were few great proprietors of land and few tenants; most people cultivated their own lands or were merchants or artisans. Not many men were rich enough to live on their rents or incomes, and there were no offices of profit for the rich or well born. A title was valuable in Europe, but it was a commodity that could not be carried to a worse market than America. People there did not ask a man what he was but what he could do. The test was a man's usefulness. Farmers and mechanics were respected because of this quality. In short, America was what Franklin called "the land of labour," a land in which an "almost general mediocrity of fortune" prevailed among the people.

Given this middle-class society, who should migrate to America? Franklin declared that a young man who understood farming could easily establish himself there, for land was cheap and he could obtain a hundred acres of fertile soil near the frontier for eight or ten guineas. If he did not have money, a little saved from the good wages he received while working for others would enable him to buy land and start his own farm. Many people, who would have remained poor in Europe, had thus become wealthy farmers in a few years. The rapid increase in population also created a continual demand for artisans, who would easily find employment and be well paid. If they were poor they started as servants or journeymen, but if they were frugal and industrious, they could soon establish their own business. America was no place for large-scale manufacturing: labor was too expensive and too difficult to keep, for either the worker wanted to be a master, or cheap land lured him away from a trade and into agriculture. Factories required poor laborers who would work for small wages, such as Europe had, but these poor workers would not be found in America until all the land had been occupied. Persons of moderate fortune could also secure estates for themselves and their posterity in America. Franklin said he had known several instances of land purchased on the frontier for ten pounds a hundred acres which increased in value in twenty years to three hundred pounds, without any improvement and simply because of the expanding settlement.

Franklin then compared the apprentice systems in Europe and America as further evidence of the economic opportunity which the latter offered. In Europe the arts, trades, professions, and farms were all so crowded that a poor man experienced difficulty in placing his children where they could earn a living. Artisans there, fearing future competition, refused to take apprentices unless they were well paid, which poor parents could not afford to do, so children were forced to become soldiers, servants, or thieves. The rapid increase of population in America, on the other hand, removed the fear of competition. Artisans not only accepted apprentices willingly, but would even pay for the opportunity. Many poor parents had thus raised enough money to buy land and establish themselves in agriculture. Then having served his apprenticeship, the artisan could establish himself in business in some new settlement.

Still another observer who stressed the economic opportunity in America compared with that of Europe was a customs official, Comptroller Weare. Like Franklin, Weare pointed out that the tremendous growth of population was due to the fact that the means of gaining a livelihood were so easily obtained in America that no one avoided marriage because of the expense of a family. Moderate labor gained a plentiful subsistence, he said, while industry and economy often resulted in opulence. Under democratic colonial governments, all mortifying distinctions of rank were lost in common equality, and the way to wealth and preferment was alike open to all men. When they discovered these things, Weare said, the poor of Europe would leave their necessitous and servile condition for independence in America, where the lowest orders lived better than journeymen artificers did in London, and corresponding classes all lived better than did their prototypes in England.

In England government officials sometimes stressed the differences between England and the colonies as bases for certain colonial policies. For instance, when

Parliament considered a proposal for using the British Mutiny Act on colonial soldiers, the objection was made that British and American soldiers represented different economic and social classes, and would therefore have to be treated differently. Members of Parliament maintained that British soldiers came from the lowest classes and needed strict discipline, but American soldiers were gentlemen, freeholders, farmers, and master tradesmen—men who were economically independent, who could not be forced to serve in the army and who would not volunteer if they thought they were subjecting themselves to the same kind of treatment given to British regulars. In a letter to Lord Shelburne during the Revolution, one James Anderson said that migration from Scotland and Ireland to America had reached such alarming proportions that the government would be forced to take action to prevent it and would have to consider the problem after the war was over. Declared Anderson: "The disease evidently originated from an idea prevailing of the comparative advantages that British subjects in America enjoyed above those in Europe."

These three discussions described all the colonies in general. Of particular concern here, however, is whether they applied equally well to Massachusetts.

Among Crèvecoeur's many observations was his remark that New Englanders held a special place in the American scene. They, too, came in for a great share in the pleasing perspective displayed in the thirteen colonies, he said, for there never was a people situated as they were who had done so much with such ungrateful soil. A presumption might be that if there was economic democracy in New England, and in Massachusetts in particular, there was probably as much or more in the other colonies.

In spite of its ungrateful soil, however, even New England seems to have been something of a promised land compared with Europe. Franklin noted the contrast on a tour he made through Ireland and Scotland:

> In those countries a small part of society are landlords, great noblemen, and gentlemen, extreamly [*sic*] opulent, living in the highest affluence and magnificence: The bulk of the people tenants, extreamly poor, living in the most sordid wretchedness, in dirty hovels of mud and straw, and cloathed only in rags.
>
> I thought often of the happiness of New England, where every man is a freeholder, has a vote in public affairs, lives in a tidy, warm house, has plenty of good food and fewel [*sic*], with whole cloaths from head to foot, the manufacture perhaps of his own family. . . .
>
> . . . Had I never been in the American colonies, but was to form my judgment of civil society by what I have lately seen, I should never advise a nation of savages to submit to civilization: For I assure you, that, in the possession and enjoyment of the various comforts of life, compar'd to those people every Indian is a gentleman. And the effect of this kind of civil society seems only to be, the depressing multitudes below the savage state that a few may be rais'd above it.

As for Massachusetts, there is ample evidence that the social order there was also relatively equalitarian rather than sharply divided into classes. The Massachusetts agent in England, William Bollan, argued against extension of the Mutiny Act to the colonies on the ground that the people of Massachusetts were freeholders and persons of some property or business, not the class of men who became professional soldiers. John Adams spoke of the "equality of knowledge, wealth, and power" which prevailed, maintaining that this equality was fostered by a colonial law for the distribution of interstate estates which resulted in frequent divisions of landed property and prevented monopolies of land. On another occasion he declared that the land was divided among the common people in every state so that nineteen-twentieths of the property was in their hands. The Boston merchant-politician Andrew Oliver also explained to an English friend that land did not descend to the eldest son or heir as in England, but that the law provided for an equal distribution of all property, real and personal, among all the children except for a double portion for the eldest son. And Thomas Hutchinson, merchant, legislator, judge, historian, and colonial governor, wrote as follows: "Property is more equally distributed in the colonies, especially those to the northward of Maryland than in any nation in Europe. In some towns you see scarce a man destitute of a competency to make him easy."

Travelers in particular were impressed by the middle-class, equalitarian society of colonial Massachusetts. A British officer said the country around Boston was rough and stony, yet it produced all kinds of English grains and roots "in plenty and perfection." He said he never saw such quantities of apple and pear trees—all the roads were lined with them, and "the poorest farmer, or rather proprietor" had one or more orchards and drank cider as common beverage. He expressed surprise at finding such respectable names as Howard, Wentworth, Pelham, Dudley, and others among the common people. The reason, he said, was that the "levelling principle here, everywhere operates strongly, and takes the lead, everybody has property, & everybody knows it." He also remarked that at dances, "every girl who has a pretty face and good clothes, is free to come, and is well received at public places there, where there is no sort of distinction of persons." Another traveler noted that in spite of the hilly land and great abundance of rocks and stones, the countryside looked prosperous. The land was well cultivated, and neat and substantial farmhouses with their leaded windows were thickly settled on the land, there was an abundance of fine large cattle, and the people looked hale and hearty. Near Marblehead, the land looked "as bare, rocky & uncomfortable" as could be imagined, yet the houses were "as thick seated" and looked as well as any he ever saw in the most fertile country. He said he mentioned this because it did "so much honour to the incomparable industry of the inhabitants."

As both Crèvecoeur and Franklin emphasized, one reason for the prevailing economic democracy was the favorable conditions for workers and for ordinary people in America. John Woolman recorded in his *Journal* in 1772 that workingmen near London received 10*d*. a day and had to provide their own food. During harvest, they received 1*s*. a day and food. In Massachusetts, towns paid about 1*s*.8*d*. to 2*s*. a day for work on the highways during the winter months and about 3*s*. in the summer. One writer claimed that manufacturing failed in Massachusetts because workers there would not take less than 2*s*. a day and that they could not hope to compete with English workers who received 6*d*. or 8*d*. a day. This, of course, was also what Franklin had said. At the same time that wages were higher in the colony than in England, provisions were much lower. Woolman reported that wheat was 8*s*. and rye 5*s*. sterling a bushel in England. Colonial prices were 4*s*. for wheat and 3*s*. for rye, Massachusetts money, which would make the price of grain in England about double the colonial price. Ann Hulton, English sister of a customs official, complained of the lack of servants in Boston. No one would call anyone else master, she said, and the reason was that there were "no distinctions, scarsly" in the society there.

Two examples illustrate Franklin's contention that artisans could easily set up for themselves in new settlements and that economic opportunity resulted in rapid population growth. The Massachusetts town of Stockbridge, for instance, not only offered Stephen Nash the opportunity of establishing his blacksmith business there, but actually granted him fifty acres of land as an inducement to do so. David Chapman, a Northampton blacksmith, paid neither poll nor estate tax in 1771, paid a poll tax only in 1772, was rated one poll and £9.8.0 estate in 1773, and eleven years later, 1784, had a house, seven acres of improved land, twenty-two acres unimproved, and a family of thirteen. If, as Franklin said, the increase of population was directly proportional to economic opportunity, Chapman's family of eleven children within twelve years after he started paying poll taxes ought to be indicative.

Another contributing factor, and perhaps even more important to colonial economic democracy than opportunity for workers, was the availability of free or cheap land. Franklin, Crèvecoeur, Weare, and others emphasized this for the colonies as a whole, but they could have done the same for Massachusetts in particular. In 1755, the general court declared that the colony was a new country with so much land to be given away or sold for a trifling consideration that the means of subsistence were easily obtained. As a result, said the court, every young man who was so inclined could start a family without venturing a farthing—something that could not be done in the old countries of Europe. Nash and Chapman were examples of this. During the French and Indian War, proprietors of land in Maine offered 200 acres to any settler who would begin to build a house within a year after the end of the war, clear five acres within three years, and live on the land seven years. In 1765, this same area had only 1,500 families scattered over 6,000 square miles of land (one family for each four square miles) and though it was a poor frontier community then, the minister who described it said the soil was rich and that future prospects looked good.

Even in Massachusetts proper, there was still much uncultivated land for expansion. Often only a small part of a man's land would actually be improved. For example, in Northampton, one man had but five of his eighty acres improved, and in Westhampton, the ratio for another man was twenty-seven out of 187 acres. David Chapman had improved only seven of his twenty-nine acres. In 1763, Stockbridge voters whose right to vote had been challenged and who were called "young men," "labourers," and "way fareing men," turned out to have up to £100 sterling in wild lands recently granted by the General Court or purchased from others. As the General Court said, a young man could easily acquire land and start a family if he so desired.

It cannot be overemphasized that with land cheap and plentiful, the great majority of the people were independent, property-owning farmers, in Massachusetts as in the other colonies. As already noted, Crèvecoeur said that, a few towns excepted, the people from Nova Scotia to West Florida were tillers of the soil. Franklin confirmed this view. He said that the great business of America was agriculture, and that for every merchant or artisan he supposed there were at least a hundred farmers, by far the greatest part cultivators of their own fertile lands. On another occasion he characterized Americans as cultivators of land, with few engaged in fishing and commerce compared with the body of the people. In his examination before Commons on repeal of the Stamp Act, he said that the merchants of Boston were a small number compared with the body of the people, and when asked what the body of the people were, he said they were farmers, husbandmen, or planters.

Except for those in the few seaport towns in Massachusetts, even the artisans and laborers generally combined farming with a trade, so that it was difficult to say exactly what they were. Blacksmiths David Chapman and Stephen Nash, as well as the "labourers" in Stockbridge were examples. Josiah Burrage of Lynn, heelmaker, glazier, and joiner, also had a house and thirty-nine acres of land, and a half interest in another house and barn. One Consider Leeds, Dorchester cordwainer, had a house and barn and 102 acres of land. Nathan Bailey, Andover cordwainer, possessed a farm of fifty-six acres with some livestock and husbandry tools; and Skipper Lunt, Newbury joiner, had thirteen acres of land with buildings. Henry Pain, Marblehead shipwright, owned a house, barn, and land worth £240 and a separate piece of land worth £76. Edward Webber, Wenham "yeoman" with a house, barn, and nine acres, was obviously also a jack-of-all-trades, for his estate included "joynery ware," cooper's ware, spinning wheels, and farm tools. Most artisans in the seaport towns owned only their homes and perhaps a shop, or the shop was in the home, but Caleb Parker, Boston blacksmith, owned twelve or fifteen acres of land in Braintree in addition to his house and land in Boston.

Thomas Hutchinson gave a rather graphic description of colonial society in an essay written in 1764, characterizing colonial economic democracy as follows:

> I must observe to you that but few farms in the colonies are in the hands of tenants. . . .
>
> In all the colonies upon the continent but the northermost more especially the inhabitants are generally freeholders where there is one farm in the hands of a tenant I suppose there are fifty occupied by him who has the fee of it. This is the ruling passion to be a freeholder. Most men as soon as their sons grow up endeavour to procure tracts in some new township where all except the eldest go out one after another with a wife a yoke of oxen a horse a cow or two & maybe a few goats and husbandry tools a small hut is built and the man and his family fare hard for a few.

Here the essay ended, but the implication was that after a few years the young farmer eventually found himself in better circumstances. Hutchinson later wrote to Governor Wentworth of New Hampshire that he had written the essay at Wentworth's request, but he was sure that Wentworth was acquainted with all the information in it.

Almost any Massachusetts town would demonstrate the generalizations made thus far, but the available records make Northampton a particularly good example. The tax lists show that almost all the people were property owners, that the spread in the amount of property owned was not wide, and that the vast majority of men were farmers. Furthermore, a comparison of tax lists for different years shows that practically all men increased their holdings over a period of years. A list of shops in Northampton in 1773 reveals that workers other than farmers were not day laborers who worked for wages, but skilled artisans who worked for themselves—blacksmiths, goldsmiths, joiners, tanners, weavers, tailors, clothiers, traders, shoemakers, barbers, sadlers, coopers, and hatters. Furthermore, the fact that most of them owned substantial amounts of real estate indicates that they were both farmers and artisans. In fact, the wealthiest man in town, Seth Pomeroy, was listed as a blacksmith. Most of these artisans were town proprietors, that is, men who owned a share in the common lands, and many were town officials, including some who were not proprietors.

Although not as new as many Massachusetts towns, Northampton was still an area with plenty of room for expansion. There were unincorporated sections such as Westhampton, Southampton, Easthampton, Pascommack, Bartlett's Mill, and Nashawamuck where land was still available. A tax list for Pascommack, Bartlett's Mill, and Nashawamuck in 1769 lists twenty-nine persons who were not proprietors of Northampton yet most of whom owned substantial farms. A Westhampton list of nonresidents of Westhampton, taken in 1778 before the town was incorporated, shows that many men had done what Hutchinson said they did—acquired land in some unsettled township. Some were substantial property owners in Northampton, but fifteen of the thirty-nine were not town proprietors of Northampton. Their holdings were 50, 80, 40, 160, 187, 80, 90, 150, 105, 120, 30, 12, 40, 260, and 140 acres respectively, an indication that land was available in sizable amounts for others besides town proprietors even in relatively settled areas.

Strange as it might seem, even the poorhouses confirm the generalization that American society was an equalitarian, middle-class society. Jefferson made the statement that from Portsmouth to Savannah one seldom met a beggar, and then only in the larger towns, but these were usually foreigners who had never obtained a settlement in any parish. Jefferson said he never saw a native American begging in the streets or highways, for a subsistence was easily gained here. The Boston poorhouse, by far the largest in Massachusetts, contained twenty-nine people in 1768. There were eight children, twelve women, and nine men, most of them immigrants from England, Ireland, Scotland, and France. Most of the adults were listed as distracted, blind, weakly, lame, infirm, subject to fits, or aged. None was capable of working to earn a living. So the poorhouse served the multiple purpose of a children's home, hospital, mental hospital, old folks' home, and poorhouse, not a place for people who were on charity because they could not find employment.

I am not contending that the people of Massachusetts were all equal economically, but only that there was relative equality compared, for example, with Europe at that time or America today. The probate records show that a few men had little property when they died, particularly sailors and fishermen in towns such as Boston, Salem, and Marblehead, but these were few compared with those who were property owners. At the other extreme there were a few well-to-do. Thomas Hutchinson estimated the Apthorp estate between £20,000 and £30,000 sterling, which he called "a large property." Andrew Oliver's estate was valued at £9,121, and Thomas Gerry, father of Elbridge Gerry, had property worth £7,919. But between these extremes was the vast majority of the population, men of middling property, farmers whose farms were not only their homes but also their capital stock. These farms generally averaged from 75 to 150 acres, with a value of from £300 to £1,200. For example, a farm of 86 acres was worth £702, one of 98 acres was worth £854, one of 123 acres was worth £920, and one of 170 acres was worth £1,395 for the land alone. The Adams' homestead in Braintree (Quincy), consisting of buildings and 53 acres of land, would have been considered a small farm in colonial times, yet the land and buildings alone were worth £440. So while there was a spread of ten or fifteen to one between the estates of Andrew Oliver or Thomas Gerry and that of an average farmer, this difference is small indeed compared with the difference in the estates of men in similar circumstances today.

It is difficult to tell what such titles as esquire or gentlemen meant, but in

Massachusetts they were certainly not marks of economic class distinction. In Boston, William Tailer, John Neal, William Sheaffe, and Francis Bernard, Jr., son of Governor Francis Bernard, were all distinguished by the title "Esquire," yet they were worth respectively £68, £91, £233, and £27. Three of them had less than the "labourers" out in Stockbridge. Richard Reith, "Gentleman" of Marblehead, was insolvent, and Charles Pierce, "Gentleman" of Newbury, had only £281. Stephen Bartlett of Almsburg, "Capt. and Gentleman," possessed £709, an amount that hundreds of farmers in the colony could have matched.

Even slavery, which might be considered a barometer of class society, did not serve that function in Massachusetts. Joseph Coolidge, Boston gunsmith, had no real estate, a total estate of only £122, yet owned a Negro boy worth £33. Caleb Parker, Boston blacksmith, counted a Negro man in his total estate of £256. Captain Robert Erskine, probably of Boston, had no real estate in his total estate of but £244, yet he owned three Negro men worth £120. John Mellony, Boston mariner, had two tenements (£160), a Negro woman (£40), and total property of £234. And Cord Cordis, Boston liquor merchant who was bankrupt in 1758, possessed £489 including two Negroes when he died. Needless to say, economic democracy did not exist for slaves, but ownership of slaves was not a mark of wealth.

When we interpret the society of Massachusetts which produced the American Revolution and the Constitution, we need to remember that, economically speaking, it was a relatively equalitarian, middle-class society in which there was a great deal of economic opportunity. Land was cheap and easy to acquire, and most men acquired some; wages were high, so that a worker could save money to buy land; apprentices could easily become masters and owners of their own small business in some new community; few men could be called day laborers, of if they were, few remained day laborers for long; most "workers" were self-employed artisans, not day laborers. Even men who were designated "laborers" were nevertheless owners of considerable land. More than 90 per cent of the people were farmers, most of whom owned their own farms. In fact, a vastly greater part of the population owned property then than now, and there was a much smaller gap between the wealthy and the ordinary people. These are some of the factors we need to keep in mind when we consider the problem of political democracy.

18. Economic Base and Social Structure: The Northern Chesapeake in the Eighteenth Century

Aubrey C. Land

If the arguments of the Browns have convinced many historians of eighteenth-century America that property holding opportunities were widespread, there are also others who insist that samplings of quantitative data and qualitative sources have to be subjected to more rigorous analysis before drawing firm conclusions. One such exponent of quantitative precision is Professor Aubrey C. Land (b. 1912) of the faculty of the University of Georgia. Professor Land devoted several years of arduous research to an investigation of the surviving probate court records of provincial Maryland and Virginia. He hoped to establish a profile through time of the property holdings of all probated citizens. For the Chesapeake Bay region Land uncovered a pattern that was very different from an emerging middle-class society. Over 90 percent of the Bay citizenry remained in the two lowest property holding categories well into the eighteenth century. The pattern of wealth distribution and economic achievement, then, was more static than dynamic. Relatively speaking, though, all citizens benefited from a general rise in the standard of living.

Professor Land's presentation confirms the impression that the gulf between a few wealthy planters who diversified their economic interests and the masses of citizens who lived barely above a subsistence level continued to characterize Chesapeake society from the 1690s to the 1740s. Can probate records by themselves, however, insure an accurate rendering of long-term patterns in wealth distribution? Are an individual's property holdings at the time of death a necessary reflection of the income earned from land and labor during prime adult years? Data limitations aside, Professor Land's analysis stands in sharp juxtaposition to the conclusions of the Browns. How do we reconcile the two explanations?

The *Maryland Gazette* for 18 October 1749 carried an obituary of more than common interest:

> On the Eleventh Instant Died, at his Seat on Wye River in Queen Anne's County, Richard Bennett, Esq. in the Eighty-third Year of his Age, generally lamented by all that knew him. As his great fortune enabled him to do much good, so (happily for many) his Inclination was equal to his Ability, to relieve the indigent and distressed, which he did very liberally, without regarding of what Party, Religion or Country,

Source: Aubrey C. Land, "Economic Base and Social Structure: The Northern Chesapeake in the Eighteenth Century," *Journal of Economic History,* 25 (1965), pp. 639–654. Footnotes omitted. Reprinted by permission of Aubrey C. Land and the *Journal of Economic History.*

they were. As he was the greatest Trader in this Province, so great Numbers fell in his Debt, and a more merciful Creditor could not be, having never deprived the Widows or Orphans of his Debtors of a Support; and when what the Debtors left, was not sufficient for that purpose, frequently supply'd the deficiency. His long Experience and great Knowledge in Business, as well as his known Candor and generosity, occasion'd many to apply to him for Advice and Assistance, and none were ever disappointed of what was in his Power, and several by his means, extricated out of great Difficulties. . . .

A later issue adds some particulars:

On Wednesday last was solemnized the Funeral of Richard Bennett, Esq. of Wye River, in a very handsome and decent Manner, by the Direction of his sole executor, the Hon. Col. Edward Lloyd. Mr. Bennett, by his Will, has forgiven above one hundred and fifty of his poor Debtors, and has made Provision for the Maintainance of many of his Overseers, and other poor Dependents, and settled a Sum of Money to be paid annually to the Poor of a Parish in Virginia: and done many other Acts of Charity and Munificence. He was supposed to be the Richest Man on the Continent. . . .

Bennett's obvious virtues as a Christian gentleman need no underscoring, but two comments of the eulogist should be noted: his great wealth and his calling as a "trader." Perhaps the enthusiastic editor went beyond the exact truth in estimating Bennett's fortune, though probably not much. The field certainly included a few other candidates for the richest man. A neighbor across the Bay, Charles Carroll, counted his total worth at something like a hundred thousand pounds sterling, including £30,000 loaned at 6 per cent interest. Robert Carter, south of the Potomac in Virginia, could reckon himself worth nearly as much. The second William Byrd had left an impressive heritage which his son of the same name had already begun to dissipate. Even by the standards of London these were wealthy men.

All three alternate possibilites for the title of richest man are better known than Bennett, because they have had biographies, or because they played important political roles, or both. They belong to what has been variously called the aristocracy, the ruling oligarchy, or the squirearchy. The pejorative connotations of all three terms incline me toward a label suggested by a profound student of early American social and cultural history, "the southern agrarian leaders." We can understand them in a sense as leaders of an agrarian area. But when we inquire about the economic milieu in which they flourished or seek the mechanisms by which they acquired their dominant positions, we are faced with some difficulties.

The traditional historiography has leaned heavily on literary evidence, and when it does not ignore these questions often gives impressions that are positively misleading. As sources, personal letters, travel accounts, and memoirs have the great merit of being relatively easy to put into context and ideal to paraphrase. A few dozen up to a few thousand items of this kind can be quilted into interesting and convincing patterns. The procedure has the limitations of the sources. Even the most acute observer focuses on objects of high visibility. The high tor eclipses the molehill in the landscape until the king falls to his death because of the "little gentleman in black velvet."

In the eighteenth-century Chesapeake, the "great planters" were the element of high visibility. They held slaves, owned vast estates, and built magnificent houses that have survived as showpieces. Visitors came under the spell of these gracious livers and left charming accounts of their balls, their tables, and their luxury. Planters themselves contributed to the effect. They wrote letters and a few left diaries that have survived along with their great houses. Viewed through these sources they cut large figures and play the star roles in the arrangements that the people of the Chesapeake made for themselves in that period. These personages are accurately enough drawn, but they are a detail, though an important one, in the total production. Unfortunately the supporting cast and stage hands that made the production possible receive next to no attention, sometimes not even the courtesy of a billing. Just as *Hamlet* cannot be successfully staged without Hamlet, there can hardly be a play with Hamlet alone.

Not much literary evidence for the minor figures has come down; but another kind does exist and, even though bristling with difficulties and overawing in bulk, it can be compelled to yield some data for a fuller view. This body of material has been brought together in two depositories, the Maryland Hall of Records and the Virginia State Archives, and properly canvassed will fill in some gaps in our knowledge of Chesapeake affairs. It consists of inventories and accounts of the estates in personalty of all free men at the time of their death. The argument in this paper applies only to Maryland, for which a statistical analysis has been completed. The Virginia counties that have been analyzed give me the clear impression that differences between the areas north and south of the Potomac are not very great in respect of the basic contention here. Both were a part of a single economic region which political boundaries could not split asunder and were treated as a unit in contemporary British commercial records.

To obtain from the voluminous Maryland records a sample that faithfully reflects conditions in the northern Chesapeake, some of the usual economies are not possible. Geographical sampling by selected counties is ruled out. The process of carving new counties out of large older counties went on continuously from 1690 to the Revolution. Consequently the county of one decade is not necessarily the same unit in a later decade. Accordingly, all counties of the province are included. Over the entire eighty-year period 1690–1770 for which the records are reasonably complete the alternate decades from 1690–1699 to 1750–1759 have been tabulated. If it can be assumed that these sizable samples reflect with reasonable accuracy the spectrum of planters' estates, then we have some basis for understanding an otherwise shadowy aspect of the Chesapeake economy.

The profile of estates in the decade January 1, 1690, to December 31, 1699, shows an unexpected imbalance. Three quarters of these estates (74.6 per cent, to be precise) are of the magnitude £100 sterling or less. In the next bracket, £100 to £200, the percentage drops to 12.1, and in suceeding hundred-pound brackets to 5.5 per cent, 2.7 per cent, 1.4 per cent, 1.3 per cent, 0.6 per cent, and 0.3 per cent. After a break in the distribution, a meager 1.5 per cent at the top are valued at £1,000 sterling or greater.

Beyond the obvious fact that the less affluent far outnumber the better off, this analysis tells us little. The estates, small or great, are all those of planters—a handful of physicians, mariners, and clergymen specifically excepted. "Planter," then, simply describes an occupation without indicating economic status of the individual. To get at what this distribution means in terms of wordly goods, standard of living, and possibly social status, it is necessary to look at particulars in the inventories themselves. Here impressions become vivid.

The planters at the bottom of the scale, those with estates of £100 or less, have at best a "country living": a saddle horse or two, half a dozen or fewer cows, a few swine to furnish fresh or salt meat for the table according to the season, a modest assortment of household utensils—sometimes nothing more than a cooking pot or skillet, a few tools and agricultural implements. Many essentials of a household—for instance, plates and cups—are missing in fully half the inventories, an omission indicating that makeshifts such as wooden bowls and gourds took the place of these articles. The appraisers of estates overlooked no article, not even a cracked cup without a handle or a single glass bottle. In brief the standard of living might be described as rude sufficiency. The self-styled poet laureate of Maryland, Eben Cooke, calls planters at this level "cockerouses."

The inventories also speak to the productivity of these small planters. In those inventories made during the autumn and winter after the tobacco had been cut the appraisers carefully estimated the size of the deceased's crop. Crop entries range from twelve hundred pounds, a trifle over two hogsheads, up to three thousand pounds, or about six hogsheads. This represented the producer's cash crop, almost his entire annual income, excepting possibly the occasional sale of a heifer, a pig, or a few bushels of corn to a neighbor or local trader. Reckoning the price of tobacco at ten shillings a hundred, these small producers could count their disposable incomes at a figure between £6 and £15 a year.

Even taking into account the small planter's self-sufficiency in fresh vegetables from the kitchen garden, cereals from whatever field crops he grew besides tobacco, and meat from his own farm animals, an income of this size imposed iron limitations on him. Between investment and consumption he had no choice. Such necessities as thread, needles, powder and shot, coarse fabrics for clothing or featherbeds, and an occasional tool or a household utensil strained his credit at the country store until his crop was sold. For the small planter, provincial quitrents, church tithes, and taxes represented a real burden. He cast his ballot for a representative who could resist the blandishments of governors and hold public expenses to the barest minimum. In good part the pressures from men of his kind kept investment in the public sector to lowest dimensions, whether the object was a county courthouse, a lighthouse, or a governor's mansion. As a private person he could not invest from savings because he had none. With tobacco crops barely sufficient to cover his debt to the country merchant, a disastrous year could prostrate him. A lawsuit, the death of cattle in a winter freeze, or a fire in house or barn forced him to contract debts which had often not been paid at the time of his death and which ate up his entire personal estate, leaving his heirs without a penny. Not infrequently his administrator actually overpaid his estate in order to save trifling family heirlooms more precious than their valuation in the inventory. Investment in a slave or indentured servant to increase his productivity, though not completely out of the question, was very difficult.

The small planter clearly was not the beneficiary of the planting society of the Chesapeake. He bred his increase and added to the growing population that filled up vacant land from the shoreline to the mountains before the Revolution. In the language of the courts he qualified as a planter. Considering the circumstances of his life, it would stretch the usual meaning of the term to call him a yeoman, particularly if he fell in the lower half of his group.

In the brackets above £100, different characteristics of the estates immediately strike the eye. Sumptuary standards of planters above this line were obviously higher. Kitchens had ampler stocks of utensils; and for dining, earthenware and china replaced the gourds and wooden makeshifts that apparently were the rule on tables of families in the lowest economic bracket. Ticking stuffed with flock gave way to bedsteads and bedding. Even more striking is the prevalence of bond labor, both indentured servants and slaves, in this higher stratum. The transition comes abruptly. In estates below £100, servants or slaves rarely appear and then only in those within a few pounds of the line. In the estates at £100 to £200, the inventories of eight out of ten estates list bond labor—a higher percentage, actually, than in any of the succeeding £100 brackets up to £500.

In fact, these estates falling between £100 and £500 form a relatively homogeneous group. Altogether they comprise 21.7 per cent of all estates. Though existence for the planter is less frugal, his wordly goods show few signs of real luxury. Not a single estate was debt free, though fewer than a tenth had debts amounting to more than half the value of the inventory. The number of slaves in single estates does not run high: from one to five in 90 per cent of the estates that had them at all. Yet even this small number represented between half and two thirds of the appraised valuation. Reflecting the additional hands for husbandry, tobacco crops ran higher roughly in proportion to the number of slaves or indentured servants. Crops ranged from twelve hundred pounds (planters with no bond labor) up to nearly twenty thousand pounds, or from a little over two up to forty hogsheads. Again using ten shillings per hundred for transforming tobacco values to sterling, we can put the incomes from tobacco production alone between £6 and £100 a year. Other sources of income for families with bond labor should not be ruled out. Doubtless off-season occupations such as riving staves or shingles, sawing plank, and making cereal crops occupied some productive time. Unfortunately only occasional data on this type of product appear, enough to call for acknowledgment but insufficient for measurement.

Nevertheless, with annual incomes of these dimensions from their tobacco crops, planters in this group had alternatives not open to the lowest income group. As respectable citizens with community obligations to act as overseers of roads, appraisers of estates and similar duties, they might choose to lay by something to see their sons and daughters decently started in turn as planters or wives of planters. Or they might within the limitations of their estates live the good life, balancing consumption against income. Social pressure must have urged them in this direction, to a round of activities that included local politics and such country entertainments as dances, horseracing, and cockfights, occasionally punctuated with drinking brawls complete with eye-gougings and other practices not usually associated with the genteel life of the planter. Whatever the choice it is difficult to see how the planter in these circumstances could add appreciably to his estate in a short period of years, or even in a lifetime.

Still further up the scale, the estates appraised at sums above £500 form an even smaller percentage of the total. The five £100 brackets between £500 and £1,000 include altogether 2.2 per cent of all estates. At first glance this small group appears to be a plusher version of the preceding: somewhat more slaves, larger tobacco crops, more personal goods including some luxury items. These are planters of substance, much closer to the stereotype, as the character and contents of their inventories show. And in their activities they moved on a higher plane. One had represented his county for a term in the General Assembly and another had served on the county court as a justice of the peace. In the matter of indebtedness, however, some interesting differences appear. Just over half the inventories list debts owed to the estate among the major assets. In a few cases the portion of total assets in the form of debts owed the estate runs to half or more.

What I think we see here is an emerging business or entrepreneurial element, a small group of planters with sources of income other than planting alone. All were planters in the sense that they, or their bond labor, produced tobacco crops. But the appreciable number in the creditor category have other concerns. The nature of these concerns appears more clearly in the most affluent element, whose members can be studied individually as cases.

This element includes all persons with estates inventoried at more than £1,000 sterling. In the decade 1690–1699, they represent 1.6 per cent of the total. They were the "great planters" of the day.

The smallest estate in personalty, that of Nicholas Gassaway of Anne Arundel County, was inventoried at £1,017 14s. 11½d. sterling; the largest, that of Henry Coursey of Talbot County, at £1,667 17s. 1¼d. Perhaps estates of this size would have cut a mean figure beside those of the sugar planters of the West Indies. In the northern Chesapeake of the closing years of the seventeenth century, they loom high.

The composition of these largest estates varies a bit from what we might expect of the great planter's holdings. Slaves comprise less than a quarter of the assets and, in several, less than a fifth. It should be remembered that this decade lies in the transition period when slaves were displacing indentured servants as field labor. Even so, the numbers seem unimpressive–often no greater than slave holdings in estates a third as large. By contrast, the number and the amount of assets in the form of debts owed the estate are striking. Altogether they comprised between a quarter and a half of the assets in individual estates. In one of the largest estates, debts owed the deceased came to 78 per cent of the total assets.

The inventories themselves give some clues as to how these large planters had become creditors. Occasionally an industrious appraiser included information on how the debtor had incurred his obligation: for a pipe of wine, for a parcel of steers, for corn, for rent of a certain property, for goods. In short, the great planter had also become a "trader." Frequently a portion of the inventory is simply labeled "in the store" and the contents of that room or building listed under this heading. Then the origin of the debts becomes clear. Sometimes they ran well over a hundred major items and were carefully listed under captions "separate debts" and "desperate debts."

Putting this cross section or sample against the general outlines of the Chesapeake economy, I suggest the hypothesis that the men of first fortune belonged functionally to a class whose success stemmed from entrepreneurial activities as much as, or even more than, from their direct operations as producers of tobacco. The Chesapeake closely resembles pioneer economies of other times and places. It was a region with a relatively low ratio of population to resources and an equally low ratio of capital to resources. External commerce was characterized by heavy staple exports and high capital imports. Internally this flow created a current of high capital investment, full employment, profit inflation, and rising property values. The tobacco staple did not lend itself to bonanza agriculture, as did sugar in the West India islands where fortunes could be made in a decade. Consequently the Chesapeake planters did not go "back home" to dazzle the populace with their wealth. Their returns derived in the first instance from tobacco production, which afforded a competence, and secondly from enterprise, which gave greater rewards. As entrepreneurs, they gave the Chesapeake economy both organization and direction. They took the risks, made the decisions, and reaped the rewards or paid the penalties. And they worked unremittingly at these tasks, which could not be performed in their absence by the small planter or by overseers.

It is not easy to analyze the activities of this economic elite into neat categories. They were at once planters, political leaders, and businessmen. The first two roles tend to obscure the last. Their role in politics is a textbook commonplace. As planters they lived in the great tradition, some even ostentatiously. On this point testimony is abundant and unambiguous. Had they depended solely on the produce of their tobacco fields, they doubtless would have lived up to or beyond current income. And some did. But in fact many among them increased their fortunes substantially and a few spectacularly, while still maintaining their reputations as good livers. During the early years of the eighteenth century, when the tobacco trade was far from booming, some of the first families of the Chesapeake established themselves as permanent fixtures. Several had come to the first rank, or very near it, both in politics and wealth by 1700: the Taskers, the Catholic Carrolls, the Lloyds, and the Trumans. Others, less well known but eventually architects of equal or greater fortunes, were rising in the scale within another decade: the Bordleys, the Chews, the Garretts, the Dulanys, the Bennetts, and the Protestant Carrolls. The secret of their success was business enterprise, though almost to a man they lived as planters separated from the kind of urban community in which their more conspicuously entrepreneurial counterparts to the north had their residences and places of business. An examination of the chief forms of enterprise discloses the mechanisms by which they came to the top of the heap.

One of the most profitable enterprises and one most commonly associated with the great planters of the Chesapeake, land speculation, appears early in the eighteenth century in both Virginia and Maryland. The Virginia Rent Roll of 1704, admitted as imperfect but the best that could be done at the time, shows half a dozen holdings that suggest speculative intent. After these tentative beginnings, speculators moved quite aggressively during the administration of Spotswood and his successors, when huge grants in the vacant back country became commonplace events for privileged insiders, with the governors themselves sharing the spoils of His Majesty's bounty. In the more carefully regulated land system of Maryland, agents of the Lords Baltimore made a few large grants to favored persons like Charles Carroll the Settler in the first two decades of the century. During the same decades other wary speculators took up occasional large grants. The Maryland system compelled speculators to be cautious, because it exacted some money for the patents and made evasion of quitrents nearly impossible. But by the 1730's, eager speculators had glimpsed a vision of the possible returns and kept the land office busy issuing warrants for unpatented areas. For a relatively modest outlay a small number of Marylanders obtained assets with which they experimented for years before discovering the last trick in turning them to account.

Speculators capitalized their assets in two chief ways, both enormously profitable. First, as landlords of the wild lands, they leased to tenants who paid rents and at the same time improved their leaseholds by clearing, planting orchards, and erecting houses, barns, and fences. Almost exclusively long-term leases, either for years (commonly twenty-one) or for lives, these instruments specified the improvements to be made. Tenants who could not save from current income thus under compulsion contributed their bit to capital formation to the ultimate benefit of the landlord. Literary sources give the impression that tenancy was not very widespread, but the records tell another story. Something over a third of the planters in the lowest £100 bracket in Maryland leased their land. Secondly, the large landholder sold off plantation-size parcels as settlement enveloped his holdings and brought values to the desired level. Not content to leave this movement to chance, many speculators hastened the process by encouraging immigration and by directing the movement of settlers toward their own properties. Jonathan Hagar in Maryland and William Byrd in Virginia are two among many who attempted to enhance the value of their properties in this way. It is difficult to determine profits even for single speculators except for short periods. Experience must have varied widely, and undoubtedly some speculators failed. But some of the successful ones made incredible gains in a relatively short span of years.

Even more ubiquitous than the planter-speculator was the planter-merchant. The inventories and accounts contain much evidence on the organization of commerce in the tobacco counties of the Chesapeake. Hardly a parish lacked one or more country stores, often no more than a tiny hut or part of a building on the grounds of a planter who could supply, usually on credit, the basic needs of neighboring small producers—drygoods, hoes and other small implements, salt, sugar, spices, tea, and almost always liquor. Inventories show some small stores with a mere handful of those articles in constant demand. Others had elaborate stocks of women's hats, mirrors, mourning gloves, ribbons, patent medicines, and luxury goods. The names of several great families are associated with country stores, particularly in the earlier generations of the line. Frequently, store-keeping duties fell to a trusted servant or to a younger member of the family as a part of his training. Occasionally, an apprentice from one of the county families came to learn the mysteries of trade by measuring out fabrics or liquors and keeping the accounts.

As with land speculation, determining profits of merchants is next to impossible. Consumers complained bitterly of high markups, and a few storekeepers boasted of them. Even so, the country merchant's profits were not limited to sale of goods alone. He stood to gain on another transaction. He took his payment in tobacco, the crops of the two- to six-hogshead producers. The small planter participated directly in the consignment system of the early eighteenth century only to a limited extent. His petty wants and his small crop hardly justified the London merchant's time and trouble in maintaining him as a separate account. His nexus to the overseas market was the provincial merchant, who took tobacco at prices that allowed at least a small profit to himself on every hogshead.

Closely allied to merchandising, moneylending presents almost as great problems of analysis. The Chesapeake economy operated on an elaborate network of credit arrangements. Jefferson's famous remark that Virginia planters were a species of property attached to certain great British merchant houses may have been true of some planters, as it was of Jefferson himself. But the observation has created a mischievous view of credit relations between England and the tobacco colonies and does not describe the debt pattern within the area at all accurately. A full account awaits the onslaught of an industrious graduate student armed with electronic tapes and computers. Meanwhile the accounts can tell us something. Country merchants had to be prepared to extend credit beyond that for goods purchased by their customers. They paid for some of their customers at least the church tithes, the tax levies, and the freedom dues of indentured servants who had served their terms. These petty book debts could be collected with interest in any county court. Loans to artisans—the shoemakers, tanners, and blacksmiths who multiplied in number toward mid century—were of a different order. For working capital, the artisan in need of £5 to £20 and upward turned to men of means, the "traders." Far from abating, the demand for capital increased as the century wore on.

Investment opportunities were never lacking for planters with ready money or with credit in England. As lenders, they squarely faced the conflict of the law and the profits. By law they could take interest at 6 per cent for money loans and 8 per cent for tobacco loans. One wonders why the Carrolls chose to loan their £30,000 sterling at 6 per cent, even on impeccable securities. Could the answer be in part that returns at this rate equaled those from further investment in planting? At any rate they did choose to lend, following the example of Bennett and a dozen or so others.

Far more profitable as an investment opportunity, manufacturing exercised an enduring fascination on imaginative men of the Chesapeake. During Virginia Company days, before the first settlement of Maryland, glass and iron had figured among the projects launched under Company stimulus. Although these had come to ruin in the massacre of 1622, Virginians never gave up hope of producing iron. Their success was limited; but in the upper reaches of the Bay a combination of easily worked ore, limitless forests for charcoal, oyster shell, and water transportation from the furnace site invited exploitation. British syndicates moved first to establish the Principio Works and later the Nottingham and Lancashire works. These remained in British hands until the Revolutionary confiscations. Last of the big four, the Baltimore Iron Works (1733) became the largest producer and the biggest money-maker. Five Maryland investors subscribed the initial capital of £3,500 sterling. The Baltimore enterprise was a triumph for native capital, though technicians and technology were both imported from Britain. After the first three years of operation the partners received handsome dividends but always plowed a substantial part of the profits back into the enterprise. By the early 1760's the share of each partner was valued at £6,000 sterling. The five partners were among the first fortunes in Maryland.

Beyond iron making, other forms of enterprise (mostly small-scale manufacturing or processing) attracted investment capital. In nearly all areas of the Chesapeake some shipbuilding, cooperage, and milling establishments provided essential local services or commodities. None of these required either the capital outlay or the organization of an ironworks. Consequently, as enterprises they were attractive to investors with modest capital but large ambitions. In the area of Baltimore, flour milling developed major proportions after mid century, as the upper counties of Maryland found grain more profitable than tobacco as a field crop.

An astonishing percentage of the personal fortunes of the northern Chesapeake had their roots in law practice. While not entrepreneurial in a technical sense, the rewards went to the enterprising. During the seventeenth century lawyers were neither numerous nor always in good odor. Private persons attended to their own legal business in the courts. By 1700, the fashion had changed as the courts insisted on greater formality in pleading and as the cumbersome machinery of the common law compelled the uninstructed to turn to the professional. Pleading "by his attorney" swiftly replaced appearances *in propria persona*. Still the legal profession remained trammeled. Laws strictly regulated fees attorneys could take and kept these at levels low enough that the ablest members of the Maryland bar went on strike in the 1720's. What lawyers lacked in size of fees they made up in number of cases. An attorney might, and frequently did, bring thirty or forty cases to trial in a three- or four-day session of a county court. Had these been litigation over land, an impression widely held by students who use the *Virginia Reports* and the *Maryland Reports,* attorneys might have spent their entire time in title searches, examining witnesses, and preparing their cases. The court proceedings at large, however, show fifty cases of debt collection for every case over land; and sometimes the ratio runs as high as a hundred to one. One traveler to the Chesapeake, remarking on the "litigious spirit," wryly concluded that this spectacle of everybody suing everybody else was a kind of sport peculiar to the area. In fact, the numbers of suits grew out of the very arrangements—a tissue of book debts, bills of exchange, and promissory notes—that kept the mechanism operating.

In this milieu the lawyer had an enviable position. From his practice he derived a steady income freed from direct dependence on returns from the annual tobacco fleet. In a phrase, he had ready money the year 'round. Furthermore, he had an intimate knowledge of the resources and dependability of the planters in the country—and, indeed, throughout the province if he also practiced at the bar of the superior courts. Consequently he could take advantage of opportunities on the spot, whether they were bargains in land, sales of goods or produce, or tenants seeking leases. He could besides avoid the costs of litigation that inevitably arose as he involved himself in land speculation, lending, or merchandising, as many did. As a rule the lawyers did well, and the most enterprising moved into the highest brackets of wealth. Perhaps the most spectacular example, Thomas Bordley, a younger son of a Yorkshire schoolmaster, came from an impecunious immigrant apprentice in a Maryland law office to distinction in the law, in politics, and in Maryland society within the span of a short lifetime. After his premature death in 1726 his executors brought to probate the largest estate in the history of the province to that time.

Quite commonly, lawyers added a minor dimension to their income from office holding. A fair percentage of Maryland offices were sinecures that could be executed by deputies for a fraction of the fees. Most carried modest stipends, but a few eagerly sought prizes paid handsomely. Baltimore's provincial secretary received £1,000 per annum.

This is not the place to argue the returns from planting, pure and simple. Many planters did well without other sources of income. But impressive fortunes went to those who, in addition, put their talents to work in some of the ways described above. A few engaged in all. The list is finite, for we are referring here to a small percentage of planters, those with estates above £1,000: in the decade 1690–1699 to 1.6 per cent, in 1710–1719 to 2.2 per cent, in 1730–1739 to 3.6 per cent, and in 1750–1759 to 3.9 per cent. When tabulated and examined for group characteristics, they resemble functionally a type that could easily come under that comprehensive eighteenth-century term, merchant. They look very unlike the planter of the moonlight-and-magnolias variety. It is a commentary on the prosperity of the northern Chesapeake that, as this favored category increased in percentage and in absolute numbers, so did the magnitude of its members' individual fortunes. The sample taken just before the turn of the century shows top fortunes between £1,000 and £2,000, with none above. The sample decade 1730–1739 includes an appreciable number over £2,000. The two largest were those of Samuel Chew (£9,937) and Amos Garrett (£11,508), both merchants. Even these did not match the fortunes left by Dr. Charles Carroll and Daniel Dulany the Elder in the decade 1750–1759, nor that of Benjamin Tasker in the next.

The poor were not excluded, individually or as a group, from the general prosperity of the Chesapeake. Four individuals—Thomas Macnemara, Thomas Bordley, Daniel Dulany, and Dr. Charles Carroll—moved up the scale from nothing to the top bracket of wealth, two of them from indentured servitude. These were extraordinary men, but their careers indicate the avenues open to their combination of talents for the law, land speculation, moneylending, merchandising, and manufacturing in which they engaged. Of course all were planters as well.

But for the mass, advance was by comparison glacial. The composition of the base on which such performances took place changed more slowly. In the fourth decade of the eighteenth century the percentage of planters in the lowest economic group, those with estates of £100 or less, had fallen to 54.7 per cent, in marked contrast to the 74.6 per cent of the decade 1690–1699. Between the same two sample decades the percentage in the next higher category of estates (£100 to £500) had increased to 35.7 per cent from 21.7 per cent. If this means that the poor were getting richer, it also means for the great majority that they were doing so by short and slow steps. Together, these two lowest categories still made up 90.4 percent of the planting families in 1730–1739, as compared with 96.3 per cent in the last decade of the seventeenth century. Nonetheless, the shift toward a higher standard of living within this huge mass of lesser planters is quite as important a commentary on the economic well-being of the Chesapeake as is the growth in numbers and magnitude of the great fortunes.

It is never easy to know just how much to claim for statistical evidence. Perhaps there is enough here to raise doubts about the descriptive accuracy of reports from Chesapeake planters themselves. These sound like a protracted wail of hard times, rising occasionally in crescendo to prophesies of impending ruin. Yet even during the early and least prosperous decades, the northern Chesapeake experienced some growth. During the second quarter of the century and on into the following decades the samples made for this study indicate a quickened rate. The results worked no magic change in the way of life or economic station for the small planter, the mass of Maryland. These were always the overwhelming percentage of the producers. As a social group they come in for little notice. Their lives lack the glitter and incident that has made the great planter the focus of all eyes. By the standards of the affluent society theirs was a drab, rather humdrum, existence bound to the annual rhythm of the field crop. The highest rewards were for those who could transcend the routine of producing tobacco and develop the gainful activities that kept the economy functioning.

19. The Economic Development of the Thirteen Continental Colonies, 1720 to 1775

Marc Egnal

Robert E. Brown has postulated an open-ended range of economic opportunity for provincial Americans while Aubrey C. Land has presented a far more mixed evaluation. One way to test these diverging findings is to look at the general economy and its growth and development during the prerevolutionary years. In the essay that follows, Professor Marc Egnal (b. 1943) of York University in Toronto, Canada, analyzes the contours of the provincial economy and the reasons for its steady growth. At the outset, Egnal points out that growth was related to two important factors: first, rapid population expansion and, second, a measurable average increase in per capita income and the standard of living. On the surface Egnal's materials seem to bear out a picture of widespread prosperity.

But is that what he is suggesting? Professor Egnal stresses that prosperity was not necessarily uniform in touching all ranks of citizens, nor was general economic growth neatly linear or always upward. Rather the author proposes that two major periods of overall growth occurred in the years between 1720 and 1775, marked by definite expansion and stagnation cycles. Moreover, in establishing an average annual per capita income growth rate, Egnal in no way implies that each citizen shared equally in the percentage increase. In fact, the average figure may have reflected more directly on the ability of wealthy socioeconomic leaders to gain far more from their investment efforts than everyday citizens could.

Generally, though, the pattern was that of an expanding, developing economy within the imperial context at least before 1760. Yet, if the quality of economic life was improving in aggregate terms, then how do we account for the mounting dilemmas of transiency and poverty, as discussed in the next selection by Douglas Lamar Jones? Assuming general prosperity, why would some colonists be increasingly disenchanted, especially after the end of the French and Indian War in the early 1760s, with imperial restrictions on their economic activity? What are the key relationships among the presentations by Egnal, Land, and Brown in terms of understanding the economy, prosperity, and the growing imperial rift?

The last decade has been marked by a quiet renaissance in early American economic history. Numerous articles and several books have reexamined the colonial period with an approach that emphasizes the use of quantitative data and

Source: Marc Egnal, "The Economic Development of the Thirteen Continental Colonies, 1720 to 1775," *William and Mary Quarterly,* 3rd ser., 32 (1975), pp. 191–222. Some footnotes omitted. Reprinted by permission of Marc Egnal and the *William and Mary Quarterly.*

modern theory. One important topic, however, remains little explored: economic development. Much of the writing of this question has been avowedly impressionistic and serves to underscore Ralph Andreano's pronouncement about American colonial growth that "no period of our national development remains as untouched by testable generalizations as does this one."[1] Several descriptive essays, while listing such valid reasons for growth as abundant land and a rapidly growing population, shed little light on variations in the pace of expansion or on the relationship between the thirteen colonies and the Atlantic economy.[2] At a methodological extreme from such survey articles is a recent econometric model of colonial growth. But his construct is highly abstract and not closely related to the evidence available for the colonial period; the authors confess that "it is not a theory to be tested in this book."[3] A detailed examination of colonial economic development is, however, a feasible undertaking. There exists a surprising amount of quantitative and qualitative data, as well as demographic and regional studies, on which to base a synthesis.

Any discussion of colonial economic development inevitably will be read in the context of another question, that hardy perennial, "Were the Navigation Acts a Burden to the Thirteen Colonies?" Much has been written on this issue, generally in the framework of "counterfactual analysis." This approach compares the total income of the colonies in a given year, say 1770, to an income computed for the same year with the assumption that the Acts of Trade did not exist.[4] But such analysis is mired in difficulties, and ultimately does not elucidate the basic issue—the impact of membership in the British Empire on the colonies. The selection of a proper counterfactual is one problem. The derivation of statistics to show how the international economy would function under hypothetical circumstances is another. And a static emphasis—a focus on a single year rather than on long-term growth—is a further difficulty. Ultimately, figures computed for the cost of routing exports through Britain or for the net gain from bounty payments provide only limited information about the situation the colonists faced. The present discussion of colonial growth suggests a new approach: only by examining the process of development and only by focusing on a lengthy span of years can the effects of the linkages with Britain be judged fully.

This article offers a broad framework for analyzing the economic development of the thirteen colonies between 1720 and 1775. Growth took place because of two related sets of conditions. One was the increase in population and the accompanying expansion of total output; the other was the rise in per capita income or, equivalently, in per capita product or in the standard of living. This second category is often referred to simply as economic growth. The data suggest that colonial growth—both of population and of per capita income—was neither smooth nor uniform. Rather, two periods or "long swings" emerge, one lasting from 1720 to 1745, and the other from 1745 to 1775.[5] The first period was marked by growth during the 1720s and early 1730s, with stagnation apparent by the 1740s. The second period was characterized by expansion from 1745 to 1760, with a gradual slowdown after 1760. The increase in population was slightly more vigorous during the first long swing than during the second, but the rise in the standard of living was more notable in the years following 1745.

An emphasis on long swings is not meant to deny the role played by short-run fluctuations in the well-being of the colonies. King George's War, the French and Indian War, and the nonimportation agreements of 1766 and 1769–1770 were among the events that had an important, immediate impact on economic life in

North America. More generally, the colonists were affected by recurrent periods of prosperity and depression. In analyzing economic development, these year-to-year changes have not been ignored, but have been incorporated into a larger picture. Wherever possible, averages based on a five-year period, for example, 1758–1762, have been used in identifying a trend, and reliance on a single year, such as 1760, has been avoided. Wartime booms, postwar slumps, and non-importation agreements at times reinforced and at times retarded broader developments. These short-run changes, however, must be set in a larger context if the process of growth is to be understood.[6]

The growth of population, which provided the basis for the increased output of the colonies, was rapid. Although the available statistics are estimates, they are derived from a broad variety of sources and may be relied upon to indicate orders of magnitude. Between 1720 and Independence the number of colonists rose about 35 percent a decade, or roughly 3.0 percent a year. The total population, black and white, grew from 466,000 to about 2,500,000.

For the white population, natural increase was more important than immigration. Natural increase involves the interaction of two components—the birth rate and the death rate. Writers frequently commented on the high American birth rate. Peter Kalm, who visited the northern colonies at mid-century, recorded in his journal under the heading "Large Families": "It does not seem difficult to find out the reasons why the people multiply faster here than in Europe. As soon as a person is old enough he may marry in these provinces without any fear of poverty. There is such an amount of good land yet uncultivated that a newly married man can, without difficulty, get a spot of ground where he may comfortably subsist with his wife and children." Although firm data are lacking for the colonial birth rate, the magnitude and trend of later statistics suggest an unusually high level in the eighteenth century. Between 1800 and 1940 the United States birth rate declined steadily, beginning with about 50 births per 1,000 population in 1800. The reasons commonly set forth for the high American birth rate in the nineteenth century—a large and prosperous portion of the population engaged in farming and a relative lack of urbanization—suggest that the colonial birth rate was equal to or greater than that of 1800. A rate of over 55 per 1,000 is unlikely, however; this figure is close to the observed limit of reproduction in any large group.

Estimates of the death rate for the white population must be conjectural. Again the trend of statistics for subsequent periods sheds light on the colonial era. Between the 1790s and the end of the nineteenth century the mortality rate in the United States fell gradually from roughly 25 deaths per 1,000 population to about 19 per 1,000. Demographic studies of several colonial communities suggest that the death rate was only slightly higher between 1720 and 1775 than in the 1790s; in the computations below a figure of 27 deaths per 1,000 is used. This rate is plausible when viewed in a world context. It means that colonial America had roughly the same mortality rate as Scandinavia, a relationship between the two areas that held true in the late eighteenth and nineteenth centuries.

As for the immigration of white settlers, only a rough estimate of its magnitude is possible. Colonial governments kept few records of new arrivals, and the early tabulations that survive are fraught with uncertainties. Net immigration may be computed indirectly, however, by determining the difference between natural increase and the overall growth of colonial population. Assuming a rate of natural increase of 23 per 1,000 population (that is, a birth rate of 50 and a death rate of

TABLE 1 Average Annual Percentage Increase in White Population, 1720 to 1775

Period	Northern Colonies	Upper South	Lower South	All Colonies
1720–1735	3.89	3.96	6.18	4.04
1735–1745	3.39	1.98	5.38	3.13
1745–1760	3.47	2.83	4.88	3.42
1760–1775	3.07	2.66	6.66	3.43

Source: U.S. Bureau of the Census, *Historical Statistics of the United States, Colonial Times to 1957* (Washington, D.C., 1960), 756. The figures exclude trans-Appalachian population. Midpoints between decennial years are computed with the assumption that 0.46 of the incremental population had arrived by the fifth year.

27), computations based on Stella Sutherland's population data suggest that between 1720 and 1770 roughly 270,000 settlers arrived. The actual number could well have been 10 percent larger or smaller. Immigrants accounted for perhaps 20 percent of the growth of white population. Of course, new arrivals made a greater contribution to some regions than to others. New England and the upper South recorded only moderate net gains from immigration, while the middle colonies and the lower South received large numbers of new settlers.

Fluctuations in white immigration to the thirteen colonies map out a pattern that seems closely related to the pace of economic growth. The statistics underlying any investigation of new arrivals are admittedly imprecise. But only the broad ebb and flow of immigration is important here—whether, for example, more settlers arrived during the 1750s or 1760s. With reservation, we may examine the evidence on this question. Assuming a constant rate of natural increase, figures for changes in the size of the population may be read as indicators of fluctuations in the number of new arrivals (see Table 1). Based on these data, the two long swings for each of the regions may be set forth as follows: (1) brisk immigration between 1720 and 1735, with fewer settlers arriving from 1735 to 1745; (2) a marked influx between 1745 and 1760, slackening after 1760. This pattern is in accord with the growth of per capita income discussed below. The figures thus suggest that in the eighteenth century, just as (according to recent studies) in the nineteenth, the "pull" of favorable conditions in the host country played a more significant role in stimulating immigration than the "push" of adverse conditions in the donor land. An exception reinforces the rule. The lower South was the one area in which white population grew more rapidly after 1760 than between 1745 and 1760. As will be discussed below, this was the only region to experience stronger economic growth in the decade and one-half before Independence than in the 1750s.

The black population expanded at an even higher rate than the white population. In 1720 blacks constituted 15 percent of colonial inhabitants, in 1770, 21 percent. Most blacks lived in the southern colonies; in 1770 only 11 percent were in the provinces north of Maryland. In the lower South the importation of slaves made a greater contribution to black population growth than did natural increase. The slow growth of the native-born slave population reflected the high mortality rate suffered by slaves engaged in rice planting. In the upper South slaves were healthier, and natural increase was more important. The arrival of new slaves, however, accounted for roughly 40 percent of black population growth in the tobacco colonies between 1720 and 1770.

Like long swings in white immigration, fluctuations in the importation of slaves and in the increase of black population appears to have been in accord with the pace of economic growth. In the northern colonies, the expansion of black population followed the broad changes in per capita income, at least after 1745. Moreover, the distinct pattern of economic growth exhibited by the lower South— strong growth between 1720 and 1735, which slowed between 1735 and 1745, and more rapid expansion after 1760 than between 1745 and 1760—was true for the growth of slave population as well as for white. Fluctuations in the importation of blacks into the upper South are less easily correlated with changes in that region's economy. After 1750 the black population grew more slowly, and the number of new arrivals declined. This did not reflect the retardation of per capita growth in the region. The standard of living in Virginia and Maryland rose markedly during the 1750s (although there was little further progress in the 1760s). Rather, declining slave imports after mid-century mirrored the comparatively slow growth of tobacco production in a regional economy where the cultivation of foodstuffs became ever more important.

A growing population, both black and white, made possible a remarkable growth in the total output of the colonies. The availability of abundant, rich land meant that each new settler could hope to become an independent producer. The total output of the colonies rose rapidly. Between 1730 and 1750 the number of inhabitants in Pennsylvania, for example, increased by about 130 percent and the volume of flour, bread, and wheat exported from Philadelphia grew roughly 120 percent. Total output also increased remarkably in the southern colonies. The increase, however, cannot be judged fully by the expansion of staple exports. Between 1730 and 1750 the population of Virginia and Maryland increased by over 80 percent, while that of South Carolina more than doubled. At the same time, shipments of tobacco rose only 52 percent, and those of rice about 80 percent. But these cash crops are only partial indicators of the growth of total output. Many agriculturalists, especially as settlement in the backcountry increased, raised little rice or tobacco, but much wheat, corn, and other foodstuffs. Most of these crops never reached the ports and so are unnoticed in British customs records. If James Lemon's data for Pennsylvania are applicable to other colonies, the typical family on a small grain farm consumed 60 percent of the foodstuffs it raised. In the southern colonies a significant portion of the marketable surplus, rather than entering the export trade, went to feed those who lived on the plantations.

Between 1720 and 1775 the growth of population was the most important reason for the increasing total output of the colonies. The rise in per capita product, which will be examined in the remainder of this article, made a comparable contribution to total output only between 1745 and 1760.

Per capita income increased between 1720 and 1775 for several reasons. Three developments had a particularly important, positive impact on the colonial standard of living. First, new techniques enhanced productivity and made the effort of individual laborers more rewarding. Second, the market value of the goods the colonists produced climbed more than the cost of the wares they bought. Third, the amount of capital available to each white colonist increased, making greater investments and higher levels of income possible. The second and third developments were by far the more significant and underlay the period of most rapid

TABLE 2 Rate of Annual Growth of Per Capita Income in the Thirteen Continental Colonies, 1720 to 1775 (Growth Rate as a Percentage)

Period	Northern Colonies	Upper South	Lower South	Thirteen Colonies
1720–1735	0	−2.0 to 0	+5.0	0
1735–1745	−2.0 to 0	+1.0	−4.0 to −3.0	−1.0
1745–1760	+3.0 to +5.0	+2.0 to +3.0	+1.0 to +2.5	+3.0
1760–1775	−1.0 to +1.0	−3.0 to −1.0	+1.5 to +3.0	−1.0 to 0
1720–1775				+0.5

Sources: These figures are estimates based on changes in per capita exports and per capita imports. For imports see U.S. Bureau of the Census, *Historical Statistics of the United States, Colonial Times to 1957* (Washington, D.C., 1960), 757; Customs 14, P.R.O.; and David Macpherson, *Annals of Commerce . . .* , III (London, 1805), 339–599. For exports see *Historical Statistics,* 757–772; Jacob M. Price, *France and the Chesapeake: A History of the French Tobacco Monopoly, 1674–1791, and of Its Relationship to the British and American Tobacco Trades* (Ann Arbor, Mich., 1973), II, 843–844, 852; James F. Shepherd and Gary M. Walton, *Shipping, Maritime Trade, and the Economic Development of Colonial North America* (Cambridge, 1972), 168–171; William S. Sachs, "The Business Outlook in the Northern Colonies, 1750–1775" (Ph.D. diss., Columbia University, 1957), 174–175, 271–276; Helen L. Klopfer, "Statistics of Foreign Trade of Philadelphia, 1700–1860" (Ph.D. diss., University of Pennsylvania, 1936), 173–207; and Marc Egnal, "The Pennsylvania Economy, 1748–1762: An Analysis of Short-Run Fluctuations in the Context of Long-Run Changes in the Atlantic Trading Community" (Ph.D. diss., University of Wisconsin, 1974), appendixes. Relevant price data are presented in the above sources and in Arthur Harrison Cole, *Wholesale Commodity Prices in the United States, 1700–1861: Statistical Supplement* (Cambridge, Mass., 1938). For population see *Historical Statistics,* 756.

growth—1745 to 1760. Between 1760 and 1775 changes in import and export prices and increases in capital invested per capita were of a lesser magnitude and had less influence on the economy. New forces making for per capita growth, however, became evident during the decade and one-half before Independence. These new developments, which collectively had only a moderate effect on the economy, will be considered at the end of this article.

Before examining these reasons for expansion in more detail, statistics suggesting the size of the "growth rate" (the annual change in per capita income or product) may be set forth (see Table 2). These data serve as an introduction to and summary of the discussion that follows. Colonial growth rates must of necessity be conjectural; information about total income or product is lacking. The numbers presented in Table 2 are no more than estimates that comport with the data discussed in the text and notes. In addition to rates covering shorter periods, a figure for average annual growth between 1720 and 1775 is presented: 0.5 percent. This figure is in accord with statistics indicating long-term changes in individual income (for example, British imports per capita) as well as with statistics suggesting long-term changes in individual product (for exmple, per capita value of major staple exports). Such data make clear that the growth rate in the half-century before Independence was well below the pace of 1.6 percent per year which the United States economy averaged between 1840 and 1960.

The introduction of new or improved techniques made a noticeable, if minor, contribution to per capita income. Farming was the most important colonial occupation, and was the chief employment of between 80 and 90 percent of the working population. Agriculturists in the northern colonies and southern backcountry cultivated grains and raised livestock. Fragmentary evidence suggests that in these areas there was an increased use of horsepower. There was also some improvement in hand tools. The introduction of the "cradle" scythe at mid-century allowed the farmer to reap his grain more efficiently. Irrigation was used more widely. But despite certain improvements, basic methods remained more or less unchanged between 1720 and 1775. Throughout these years husbandmen depleted rich soils, made little use of fertilizers, and implemented only rudimentary schemes of crop rotation. The quantity of foodstuffs produced per acre and the number of acres worked by the individual farmer in the 1770s were probably only slightly greater than in the 1720s.

In southern plantation agriculture, new techniques had a somewhat greater impact on output. The most important advances in agricultural productivity occurred in the lower South. Although conclusions must be tentative, the quantity of rice produced per slave appears to have risen markedly between 1720 and 1775 as a result of improvements in irrigation and the migration of the crop from comparatively elevated ground to tidal and river swamplands. The wasteful methods of tobacco cultivation, however, appear to have changed little during the period. Scattered figures for pounds of tobacco produced per slave suggest that there was no increase during the eighteenth century, and perhaps even a decline from the levels reached just before the turn of the century.

The effects of innovation on colonial industries varied. Some enterprises were little affected. Among these was household manufacture of textiles and implements, which was probably the colonies' most important industrial activity. In the northern colonies and southern backcountry virtually every farm family produced woolen or linen cloth and made simple tools. Although the organization of cloth and footwear production changed during the late colonial period (and will be discussed later), technological improvement in home industry was slight. Ranked by value of product, shipping and shipbuilding were probably the second colonial industry, employing thousands of sailors, carpenters, and kindred laborers. Unit costs and methods of building vessels seem to have changed little during the period. Some gains were recorded in the productivity of shipping as a result of the use of increasingly larger vessels and the reduction of the average time spent idle in port, but the largest advances came before 1720, because of efforts to eliminate piracy, and after 1775, because of faster vessels and better market organization.

Other industries benefited more significantly from new techniques. Milling became more efficient, especially near the end of the colonial period. By 1775 the flour mills in Pennsylvania, Delaware, and Maryland were probably among the most advanced in the world. Innovations, such as the mechanical elevation of wheat and new methods of cleaning the grain, increased the capacity of mills and reduced manpower. Price data suggest the timing of these gains in productivity. The unit cost of converting wheat into flour, as reflected by the price of the raw material (wheat) and the finished product (flour), fluctuated with no trend between 1720 and the early 1760s, and then declined markedly in the decade before Independence. The productivity of sawmills also rose. Such laborsaving techniques as mechanical log carriers were American in origin. Information on rum distilling suggests few increases in efficiency. Analysis of molasses and rum prices, which are available for the Boston area between 1750 and 1775, indicates no reduction in processing costs. The production of naval stores and pig iron appears to have changed little. In sum, new or improved techniques had only a minor impact on the colonial economy.

A far more important stimulus for economic growth came from two other developments: the price of the goods the colonists sold rose more than the cost of the wares they bought, and more capital was made available to planters, merchants, and small farmers. Both developments involved America's economic relations with Great Britain, and both were much affected by the mother country's rapid expansion after 1745. Thus an analysis of the pace of colonial development requires a brief examination of the reasons for and the nature of Great Britain's growth between 1720 and 1775.

During the eighteenth century, the British economy grew in two long swings—one lasting from 1720 to 1745, and the next from 1745 to 1783. The first cycle was characterized by slow growth. The second was marked by strong expansion. The growth phase of the second cycle stretched from 1745 to 1760; after 1760 growth gradually was dampened.

Agriculture played a pivotal role in Britain's growth. Although overseas demand was important for England's and Scotland's manufactures, the home market—a free trade area encompassing over 7,000,000 people at mid-century—was even more significant. In large part, the level of consumer demand depended on conditions in the countryside. Between 1720 and 1745 Britain's farm economy was depressed because of overproduction. Various techniques had increased output, while at the same time population grew slowly. Exports of foodstuffs to Europe provided some, but not sufficient, relief. As a result, agricultural prices fell, and the disposable income of individual farmers decreased. After 1745 rural depression yielded to recovery and then prosperity. Landowners benefited from the rise in population. In the 1740s the death rate began to fall, possibly because of improved midwifery and the establishment of lying-in hospitals. Although farm output continued to rise, demands from a growing population pushed up prices and brought new wealth to husbandmen and landowners. As a result of increased domestic consumption of foodstuffs, Britain's agricultural exports to overseas markets, which had reached record levels at mid-century, gradually declined. By the 1760s the growth of agricultural output had slowed, and Britain became a net importer of certain foodstuffs such as wheat.

Britain's industries responded to these changes in rural conditions. Between 1720 and 1745 agricultural depression circumscribed the expansion of manufacturing. Overseas demand (especially European) for the products of Britain's mines and manufactures, it is true, exhibited moderate growth, particularly in the 1720s and early 1730s. This provided a stimulus for some industries (such as tin mining and the production of wrought iron), but not an impetus for general growth. Between 1745 and 1760 British industry expanded rapidly in response to strong demand from the agricultural sector and from foreign (particularly colonial) markets. The rise in both home and overseas consumption of manufactures, as will be discussed below, was not coincidental; one was closely tied to the other. A broad spectrum of industries in England and Scotland increased their output during this period. After 1760 the continued rise of food prices and the slower growth of the agricultural sector helped brake industrial expansion. Only in the 1780s would the economy surge ahead as new industries such as cotton textiles and ferrous metals provided an impetus for growth.

This analysis of the British economy helps us to understand a second reason for colonial economic growth: the price of many of the agricultural commodities that Americans exported rose more rapidly than the cost of the manufactures that they purchased from abroad. These price movements produced a significant increase in the standard of living. For example, where the 100 bushels of wheat produced by a small farm in the mid-1740s could command 150 yards of woolen cloth, the same 100 bushels could be traded for over 250 yards of cloth in the early 1760s.

These price movements were closely connected to the growth of the mother country, both as a supplier of finished goods and as a market for raw materials. Overwhelmingly, the manufactures that the colonists bought from overseas were made in Britain. The Navigation Acts prohibited the direct importation of finished wares from the continent of Europe, and these strictures generally were obeyed. Furthermore, most of the goods shipped by British exporters were of British origin. For example, between 1751 and 1774 only 21 percent of New York's imports from England were manufactures that had been made in other European countries. The colonists were fortunate in their links with an industrializing nation. Because of improvements in technology and business organization, British manufacturers were able to increase output (particularly after 1745) and maintain low prices. Price data for the years between 1720 and 1745, although sparse, suggest that the market price of finished goods remained level or declined slightly. Information for the period between 1745 and 1775 is fuller and indicates that the cost of important manufactured commodities, while fluctuating widely, rose only slightly—about 10 percent.

In its capacity as a market, the expanding British economy helped raise the prices of certain North American exports. The commercial ties between Britain and the northern provinces, however, differed from those between Britain and the southern colonies. The provinces from Pennsylvania north sent only a small portion of their commodities "home," because the Caribbean was always the most important destination and absorbed well over one-half the total value shipped to overseas markets. The southern colonies directed most of their commodities to England and Scotland. Despite seemingly closer links between the South and Great Britain, the North was more affected by increases in British demand.

The West Indies provided the nexus which linked the growth of the northern colonies with that of Britain and which helps explain the trend of northern export prices before and after 1745. Between 1720 and 1745 the English economy grew slowly, English demand for sugar and rum increased only slightly, and the British islands in the Caribbean suffered a prolonged depression. The quantity of tropical produce sent from the sugar islands to England increased before 1745, but the growth of trade reflected lower rum and sugar prices, not strengthened British purchasing power. Depression in the British Caribbean meant that West Indian demand for northern foodstuffs grew slowly. The price of the commodities, such as flour and meat, that North Americans sold to the islanders did not rise between 1720 and 1745. The French plantations, which expanded more rapidly than the English during these years, provided some impetus for northern growth. But the English islands were the more valuable customers even though by mid-century the French plantations were the more important suppliers of tropical produce. As a consequence of hard times in the West Indies, economic growth in the northern colonies lagged. Per capita consumption of British goods, one rough indication of individual prosperity, fell in value steadily between 1725 and 1745 (see Figure 1).

From 1745 to 1760 the Caribbean provided the stimulus for rising northern export prices and hence for improvement in the standard of living. During these years the British economy grew rapidly, British demand for rum and sugar

Figure 1. *Northern Colonies: Per Capita Imports from Great Britain.*

Source: U.S. Bureau of the Census, *Historical Statistics of the United States, Colonial Times to 1957* (Washington, D.C., 1960), 756–757, 766, 768; Customs 14, P.R.O.; David Macpherson, *Annals of Commerce . . . , III* (London, 1805), 339–599. *Imports from Scotland before 1955 are extrapolated based on colonial exports.*

soared, and production in the English sugar plantations, largely based on the spread of cane culture in Jamaica, expanded. The French Antilles experienced a similar surge of growth. Expansion in the islands meant new calls for North American grain, lumber, meat, and fish; the result was a strong rise in the prices of those staples. These higher prices helped produce a significant increase in per capita income in the northern colonies. Although the worth of rum and sugar rose markedly at this time, the cost of English manufactures increased only slightly. Consequently, per capita consumption of imported manufactures in the northern colonies rose steadily, climbing from an annual average of £0.65 sterling per person in 1743–1747 to £1.49 in 1758–1762 (see Figure 1).

After 1760 West Indian growth slackened, reflecting weakened British demand, and the prices of most northern exports leveled off or declined. Per capita consumption of British goods fell slightly. Of the traditional northern exports, only the prices of wheat, bread, and flour soared to new heights in the late colonial period. The rise in grain prices was the result not of additional West Indian purchases, but of England's transition from grain exporter to grain importer and of new calls from markets, particularly Portugal, which Britain had traditionally supplied.

While British growth after 1745 helped raise prices and the standard of living in the northern colonies, the impact of British growth on southern prices and per capita income was less pronounced. The chief southern exports—tobacco, rice, and indigo—were sent directly to the mother country. But these staples, excepting indigo which was the least valuable, were only in part destined for British consumers. Over 70 percent of the tobacco and rice sent "home" was reexported to the European continent. Trends in these continental markets and their effect on southern prices and standard of living may be briefly outlined.

The value of rice, the chief export of the lower South, was linked closely to the European market. Between 1720 and 1740 European demand was strong and rice production in South Carolina boomed. The quantity shipped more than doubled each decade. Permission to send rice directly to southern Europe, which Parliament granted in 1730, provided a further stimulus. (Less than one-fourth of the crop, however, was sent directly to Portugal and the Mediterranean lands, while more than one-half usually was shipped to Britain for reexport.) South Carolina

Figure 2. *Lower South: Per Capita Imports from Great Britain.*

Source: U.S. Bureau of the Census, *Historical Statistics of the United States, Colonial Times to 1957* (Washington, D.C., 1960), 756–757, 766, 768; Customs 14, P.R.O.; David Macpherson, *Annals of Commerce . . . ,* III (London, 1805), 339–599. Imports from Scotland before 1955 are extrapolated based on colonial exports.

prices, expressed in sterling, rose to ten shillings for a hundredweight of rice in the 1730s, from a low of about five shillings in the early 1720s. Prosperity in the Carolinas during the 1720s and 1730s was reflected by a sharp rise in per capita imports of British goods (see Figure 2). The War of the Austrian Succession, which stretched from 1740 to 1748, disrupted trade with the European continent, sent the value of rice tumbling to below two shillings a hundredweight, and plunged Carolina into depression. Per capita imports fell. Sales recovered during the 1750s, but notable upward movement in prices and volume of exports was not apparent until the 1760s. By the early 1770s prices were over eleven shillings a hundredweight. Changes in the standard of living appear to have mirrored the success of rice production. The lower South, alone of the colonial regions, experienced a larger increase in per capita imports during the 1760s than during the 1750s.

Indigo was the second most valuable export of the lower South and the only one of the leading southern staples whose prices reflected the pull of the British market. The plant was used to make a blue dye for textiles, and its cultivation was tied to the strong growth of British industry after 1745. Indigo was virtually uncultivated before 1745; after that date production and prices quickly soared. South Carolina's exports of indigo increased over sixfold between 1747–1749 and 1757–1759. A bounty of sixpence sterling per pound (on a product that sold in the 1750s for about four shillings a pound) provided a strong stimulus. Paralleling developments in Britain, prices declined and the expansion of indigo cultivation was markedly slower after 1760, but compared to the rice crop, changes in the profitability of indigo cultivation appear to have had only a minor effect on the standard of living in the lower South.

The price of tobacco, the chief crop of the upper South and the most valuable colonial export, was affected not only by fluctuations in European demand but also by important changes in British marketing arrangements. Demand for this weed expanded steadily, if moderately, during the eighteenth century. Between

1720 and 1775 colonial shipments to Britain increased an average of roughly 25 percent a decade. Little of the crop was destined for consumers in the realm; British merchants generally reexported between 80 and 90 percent of the hogsheads they received. World prices, which had been unusually high during the first decades of the century, dropped sharply during the 1720s. Tobacco quotations also fell in the upper South at this time, and this drop most likely underlay the decline in Virginia's and Maryland's per capita imports of British goods between 1720 and 1730. By the late 1720s the decline in world tobacco prices had ceased, and the market value of tobacco, while fluctuating, was marked by a level trend. Both in Europe and in the Chesapeake, prices varied about an unchanged mean between 1730 and 1745. Although tobacco cultivation spread in the upper South during this period, there seem to have been only small gains in per capita income.

Between 1745 and 1770 the trends of tobacco prices in Europe and the upper South diverged: European prices continued to exhibit a level trend, while the value of the weed in Virginia and Maryland gradually rose. According to available evidence, between 1740–1744 and 1760–1764 colonial prices for tobacco increased 34 percent. These higher valuations appear to have been the product of a new, more efficient marketing structure, and of increased competition among British houses. Prior to 1745 English merchants and the consignment system dominated the purchase and reshipment of tobacco. The planter directed his produce to a particular London house, and the English firm marketed the hogsheads and advanced credit to finance cultivation of the following crop. This system catered to the larger planters who could assemble a consignment of several dozen hogsheads and who could readily secure a "London credit." Frequently, these wealthy landowners also handled the output of their less affluent neighbors. Consignments persisted after 1745, but a new method of marketing, based on direct purchases by local factors, became increasingly important and helped raise Chesapeake prices. The parent firms for most of these factors were in Glasgow, and the growth of direct purchasing reflected the strong expansion of the Scottish economy after 1745. The factors could offer higher prices because they made more efficient use of shipping (factors were able to load vessels more rapidly than could the consigning planters; the vogage to Glasgow was quicker than that to London) and because they dealt directly with the region's numerous small planters and eliminated the large planter as a middleman. Moreover, vigorous competition among British tobacco houses meant that economies were passed along to planters in the form of higher prices.

Rising tobacco prices had their most significant impact on per capita income in the upper South between 1745 and 1760. Higher quotations increased individual purchasing power and helped raise the level of per capita imports of British manufactures (see Figure 3). But these advances must not be overstated. The rise in tobacco prices was less than the gains recorded by foodstuffs sent to the Caribbean. Between 1740–1744 and 1760–1764, the value of tobacco rose 34 percent, but wheat prices increased 59 percent, flour 54 percent, and pork 48 percent. During this period, the market for produce expanded more vigorously. The quantity of flour shipped from Philadelphia increased about 200 percent while Chesapeake tobacco exports rose less than 50 percent.

Tobacco prices continued to move upward between 1760 and 1775, but higher quotations did not readily translate into an improved standard of living. While the rise in prices between 1745 and 1760 seems to have been the product of genuine

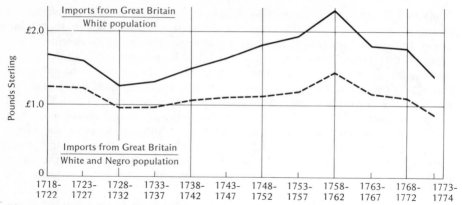

Figure 3. *Upper South: Per Capita Imports from Great Britain.*

Source: U.S. Bureau of the Census, *Historical Statistics of the United States, Colonial Times to 1957* (Washington, D.C., 1960), 756–757, 766, 768; Customs 14, P.R.O.; David Macpherson, *Annals of Commerce . . .* , III (London, 1805), 339–599. Imports from Scotland before 1955 are extrapolated based on colonial exports.

gains in the efficiency of marketing and of vigorous competition among British buyers, the price rise after 1760 was more the result of a run of short crops and of brief spurts of speculative buying. Between 1763 and 1769, the quantity of tobacco shipped from the Chesapeake to Britain declined from 98,000,000 pounds to about 70,000,000 pounds, limiting the gains that might have resulted from higher quotations. During 1770, 1771, and 1772 planters enjoyed favorable crops and high prices as a wave of speculative purchasing increased the worth of tobacco. This wave of buying was halted abruptly, however, and prices plummeted when financial crisis shook the British economy and particularly the tobacco houses. As a result of short crops, the vicissitudes of speculative purchases, and the trouble that planters had in obtaining capital after 1760 (a problem that is examined below), higher tobacco prices between 1760 and 1775 did not mean prosperity for planters. One indication of the problems planters faced was the sharp decline in per capita imports of British wares after 1760 (see Figure 3).

Because of only moderate growth in the demand for and price of tobacco between 1745 and 1775, planters explored the possibility of raising other crops that would allow them to benefit from the post-1745 expansion of the British economy. A slump in tobacco sales in the mid-1750s spurred experimentation. Some planters diverted resources to hemp production. Others made a trial of indigo, although this was short-lived. Most notable was the spread of Indian corn and wheat production in the upper South. The region had always produced significant amounts of these crops, but only after 1745 did output increase sharply. Between 1745 and 1760 the expansion of corn and wheat production and the strong rise in the price of these commodities helped boost the region's per capita income. After 1760 the market value of wheat continued to rise, chiefly because of the growth of the southern European market, but the price of corn, which was less affected by Iberian demand, recorded no further gains after the early 1760s. Moderate corn prices tended to limit increases in per capita income.

In sum, and excepting the lower South, the economic growth stimulated by higher export prices was most notable between 1745 and 1760, and was much less pronounced between 1760 and 1775.

Per capita income rose for a third reason: the amount of capital available to each white settler increased. Those wishing to borrow funds found them easier to obtain. This enabled the colonists to enjoy a higher standard of living. For example, planters found the acquisition of slaves easier, merchants could expand their sphere of activities, and small farmers found local shopkeepers more liberal in selling dry goods or farm implements. The chief source of capital was the increasing amount of credit which Britain extended to the colonies. The growth of colonial capital resources, like changes in export and import prices, was tied closely to the expansion of the British economy. By the late colonial period the value of colonial indebtedness to Britain was sizable. Barlow Trecothick, a leading London "North American" merchant, reported to the House of Commons in 1766:

The Committee of the Merchants of London trading to North America . . . do unanimously authorize me to give it as their opinion, that at the lowest compilation there is due the merchants of London only	£2,900,000
The agent for the merchants in Bristol authorizes in the same manner to say that there is due that town	800,000
Ditto from Glasgow (Virginia and Maryland only)	500,000
Ditto from Liverpool	150,000
Ditto from Manchester	100,000
	£4,450,000

Besides sums due to Lancaster, Whitehaven, Birmingham, Sheffield, Leeds, Norwich, Wakefield, Halifax, and other manufacturing towns, which must considerably augment the balance due from North America.

The extension of British credit to the American colonies may be most usefully examined with a twofold division: those areas where British funds were channeled through the coastal merchants (that is, the northern colonies and lower South); and that area where British houses or their factors dealt directly with the colonists (that is, the upper South).

The value of English capital extended to the merchants in the northern colonies and lower South increased remarkably, especially between 1745 and 1760. Easier credit for the colonies was closely tied to the growth of the mother country's economy. The English shipper relied on various financial intermediaries. As the British economy expanded after 1745 and the banking structure improved, exporting houses could offer more generous credit terms. One manifestation of the increased liberality of credit between 1745 and 1760 was the gradual extension of the credit period. In the mid-1740s goods were shipped typically on six months' credit. Gradually this interval lengthened, so that in 1760 a Philadelphia trader could state firmly: "From London we have twelve months' credit for our goods." A second indication of the increased flow of funds to the New World was the willingness of English houses to grant credit to more individuals within each port city. Shopkeepers and vendue-masters, traditionally excluded from direct dealings with overseas houses, now found themselves beset by offers from London and Bristol. While this development angered the established American merchants, it meant that more individuals in each colonial port city could extend credit to local shopkeepers, who in turn could credit farmers and city dwellers.

After 1760 the growth of the English economy slackened and English exporters became more wary of extending capital to colonial merchants. The credit period, which had reached one year by 1760, was not extended further. Indeed, several English houses discussed the possibility of returning to a shorter period. The practice of offering credit to shopkeepers and vendue-masters was less evident after 1760. Only during a brief upswing in the English economy in the early 1770s did colonial merchants complain about these problems. Rather, traders in the colonial port cities were troubled by a series of credit contractions during the 1760s and during 1772 and 1773. The steps that British exporters took to draw in their affairs were soon felt up and down the chain of credit. Farmers and artisans found imported manufactures more difficult to obtain, and this helped check the rise in the colonial standard of living.

The increased flow of British capital to the New World also helped increase per capita income in the upper South. As in those areas served by port cities, improvement was most apparent between 1745 and 1760. The rise of the Scots factors in Virginia and Maryland after 1745 was accompanied not only by intense competition for the tobacco crop but also by a great expansion of credit. The benefits of the credit expansion were felt particularly by the small tobacco planters. Before 1745, English funds had been available only to the large planters and planter/merchants. Individuals who held less than three hundred acres and one or two slaves had been excluded from direct dealings with the London houses. These smaller planters became the chief debtors of the Scottish firms. The average sum owed to two large Glasgow houses in the late colonial period was £29, and 94 percent of those indebted owed less than £100. By contrast, the amount due six English firms averaged £664, and one-half the debts were over £100. Although the average amount loaned by the Scots was small, aggregate indebtedness was large. Competition among British firms also meant that credit terms became increasingly generous. Overdue debts rarely led immediately to lawsuits. More commonly, the factor allowed the debt to be bonded, or accepted a mortgage as surety. Consequently, a portion of the short-term debt formally became long-term indebtedness and was an important addition to the colonists' working capital.

Between 1760 and 1775 the pace of growth of the British economy slowed and British creditors were more reluctant to extend credit to the tobacco colonies. Although there were periods when British houses were willing or even eager to enlarge their affairs in the Chesapeake, as during the late 1760s and in 1770 and 1771, these houses evinced greater caution than between 1745 and 1760. Twice, in 1762, and again in 1772–1773, British firms contracted their affairs sharply, calling in old debts and causing the planters much hardship. Virginians and Marylanders were forced to redirect funds from purchases to the reduction of indebtedness. As in the northern colonies and lower South, this credit contraction worked to retard improvement in the standard of living.

Although new dimensions to the economy became evident after 1760, they did not compensate for the slowdown in the upward movement of export prices or for the reduced influx of British capital. The other reason for economic growth discussed above—increases in productivity brought about by new techniques—was evident after 1760 as before, but made only a minor contribution to improving the colonial standard of living.

New forces for economic growth, although too weak to assure an increase in per capita income, offered encouragement to colonists between 1760 and 1775.

One stimulus was the growing demand of southern Europe for American grain. The other reasons related to the domestic economy and foreshadowed later patterns of American development—the strengthening of the home market, the expansion of textile and shoe production, and the acquisition and exploitation of western lands. These four developments, their strengths and limitations, may be examined in turn.

First, southern European demand for colonial grain expanded rapidly in the mid-1760s, helping to raise the price of wheat, bread, and flour, and consequently the standard of living in the wheat-growing colonies. The growth of this market reflected the disappearance of Britain's grain surpluses and the need of Iberian importers to seek another source of supply. Although this expanded commerce was important for the middle colonies, and particularly for Pennsylvania, its general impact on the North American economy was less noteworthy. Between 1768 and 1772, when shipments to southern Europe were most significant, only 15 percent of colonial exports were directed to that market.

Second, and more portentous for the future growth of per capita income, was the gathering strength of intercolonial trade and the increasing importance of the market within the thirteen colonies. In terms set down by Adam Smith, a larger market allowed increased specialization and tended to make every individual more productive. Trade statistics suggest the magnitude of intercolonial exchanges and the growing importance of local consumption. Between 1768 and 1772, 54 percent of the tonnage clearing Boston was destined for other mainland ports. The comparable figure for New York was 35 percent, for Philadelphia, 30 percent, and for Charleston, 16 percent. Tonnage figures drawn from the years between 1720 and 1759 indicate that these percentages marked not only significant absolute gains, but also (with the exception of New York) notable increases in the portion of shipping involved in the coasting trade. New England rum and fish, bread and flour from the middle colonies, corn from the upper South, and Carolina rice found a growing market in other colonies. Yet despite its importance, such trade was not yet large enough or rich enough to sustain growth. Each province still relied more heavily on earnings from foreign commerce and, except for Pennsylvania's grain exports and the rice shipments of the lower South, these were slack after 1760.

Third, the rise of textile and shoe production provided another stimulus for economic growth after 1760. An increase in the percentage of the work force engaged in manufactures meant not only the diversification of the colonial economy, but also a significant gain in product per capita. Studies of early nineteenth-century craft industries show that the value added by each industrial worker was substantially greater than the value added by each agricultural worker. If these findings hold for the colonial period—and the activities involved are similar—then any shift in the labor force from agriculture to industry meant a rise in the average standard of living.

An increasing number of people became involved in textile production both in the countryside and in the towns after 1760. Spinning and weaving expanded in rural areas for several reasons. Farmers responded to patriotic appeals for domestic manufactures; the post-1760 credit contraction and the nonimportation agreements made the purchase of imported goods more difficult; and growing inequalities of wealth in the settled areas created a labor force willing to embrace cottage industry. A Pennsylvanian observed in 1773 that "many thousands, rather than go farther back into the country where lands are cheap or undertake the arduous task of clearing new lands, turn to manufacturing, and live upon a small farm, as in many parts of England." Manufacturing was important in some towns even before this period. Andrew Burnaby, who visited the colonies in 1760, reported that "above 60,000 pair" of stockings were made in a year at Germantown, near Philadelphia. During the 1760s Boston, New York, and Philadelphia all established large manufactories. Each of the institutions coordinated the work of several hundred spinners and of more than a dozen weavers. Advances also were recorded in the southern low country. Traditionally, southern planters had imported virtually all the cloth they needed, manufacturing only a small amount of coarse fabric for the slaves. After 1760, while still behind the North and local backcountry, spinning and weaving became more common on the plantations. Progress seems to have been most notable in Virginia and least marked in the rice lands of South Carolina and Georgia.

The production of footwear also expanded during the late colonial period, and a growing number of individuals were involved in this enterprise, particularly in the coastal towns of the northern colonies. Lynn, Massachusetts, for example, produced about 80,000 pairs of shoes in 1767. In New England, American-made shoes not only predominated in the rural areas, but also gradually replaced shoes of British manufacture in the trading towns where imported goods were plentiful.

The growth of colonial manufacturing had a significant impact on the standard of living in the different regions and on the subsequent course of economic development. Home and town industry helped raise per capita income in the northern colonies. Thus, while southern whites generally imported more British goods per capita than northern whites, this distinction cannot be taken as proof of northern backwardness (see Figures 1, 2, and 3). More plausibly it suggests the importance of textile and other manufacturing in the North. This local production provided an important base for industrial development in subsequent decades. There is a direct line from the manufactories of the 1760s, which organized the work of numerous spinners, to the spinning mills of the 1790s, which distributed machine-spun thread to local weavers, to the establishment of complete factories, based on the power loom, beginning in 1815.

Fourth, Britain's acquisition in 1763 of the land between the Appalachians and the Mississippi provided the colonists with a rich territory that seemed to be a guarantee of future economic growth. For some, this land also held the promise of immediate returns. Eventually western lands yielded rich profits to settlers, speculators, and the federal government, but during the late colonial period the territory proved a troublesome asset for those seeking immediate gains. Several companies, based for the most part in Virginia and Pennsylvania, projected schemes for the development of the West. These plans ran afoul of British desires to contain colonial expansion and reduce the costs of dealing with the Indians. The western lands perhaps were most important for the encouraging cast they gave to the nation's future.

The impetus for growth in per capita product provided by southern European demand, the home market, manufacturing, and western lands, although important, was not sufficient to make the late colonial period one of buoyant expansion. Movements in world prices and fluctuations in the flow of British capital were all-important for the American economy, and these were not favorable between 1760 and 1775. By 1800, economic historians have suggested, America's own productivity and resources, and not the stimulus of an international economy, had become the main source of economic growth. But in the late colonial period the home market and domestic resources were not yet sufficiently developed.

Nonetheless, a significant reweighting of the forces for growth had occurred in the years following 1760, and this change had serious ramifications. The domestic economy had become more important; the beneficial effects of the British Empire had been brought into question. This new economic balance helped shape the outlook of the Revolutionary generation. British restrictions on the local economy were questioned seriously, in many cases for the first time. Colonial pamphleteers and editorialists noted that royal proclamations and Parliamentary enactments prevented Americans from establishing private banks, disposing of western lands, imposing tariffs or navigation acts, or effectively regulating local currency. Some individuals observed that the lack of a unified colonial government hindered development. The sovereignty that Americans gained with Independence and the unity they secured with the Constitution would be of singular help in promoting economic growth.

The paradigm, or model, of colonial economic development set forth above is clearly a tentative one, and the reasons offered for the nature and timing of population increase and for changes in per capita income must bear the scrutiny of future empirical research. It is hoped, however, that the pattern of explanation presented here will help raise the debate over economic development to a higher level. With further studies we can draw still closer to an understanding of how the colonies grew and how that process affected the Revolutionary movement.

NOTES

1. Ralph L. Andreano, ed., *New Views on American Economic Development: A Selective Anthology of Recent Work* (Cambridge, Mass., 1965), 42.

2. See George Rogers Taylor, "American Economic Growth Before 1840: An Exploratory Essay," *Journal of Economic History,* XXIV (1964), 427–444; Stuart Bruchey, *The Roots of American Economic Growth, 1607–1861* (New York, 1965), 1–73; Douglass C. North, *Growth and Welfare in the American Past: A New Economic History* (Englewood Cliffs, N.J., 1966), 1–49; and Robert E. Gallman, "The Pace and Pattern of American Economic Growth," in Lance E. Davis *et al.,* eds., *American Economic Growth: An Economist's History of the United States* (New York, 1972), 15–25. One of the better accounts of colonial economic development is James A. Henretta, *The Evolution of American Society, 1700–1815: An Interdisciplinary Analysis* (Lexington, Mass., 1973), Chap. 2. See my review of Henretta's work in the *William and Mary Quarterly,* 3d ser., XXXI (1974), 510–511.

3. James F. Shepherd and Gary M. Walton, *Shipping, Maritime Trade, and the Economic Development of Colonial North America* (Cambridge, 1972), Chaps. 2–3, quotation on p. 25, n. I.

4. The contributions to this debate include Lawrence A. Harper, "The Effects of the Navigation Acts on the Thirteen Colonies," in Richard B. Morris, ed., *The Era of the American Revolution* (New York, 1939), 3–39; Oliver M. Dickerson, *The Navigation Acts and the American Revolution* (Philadelphia, 1951), 5–91; Robert Paul Thomas, "A Quantitative Approach to the Study of the Effects of British Imperial Policy upon Colonial Welfare: Some Preliminary Findings," *Jour. Econ. Hist.,* XXV (1965), 615–638; and Peter D. McClelland, "The Cost to America of British Imperial Policy," *American Economic Review,* LIX (1969), 370–381.

5. For a definition and discussion of the equivalent concepts of national income and national product see Simon Kuznets, *Economic Change: Selected Essays in Business Cycles, National Income, and Economic Growth* (New York, 1953), Chaps. 6–7. Kuznets's analysis is of particular value for colonial historians because it stresses the problems of dealing with a developing agricultural society. On the same question see also Robert E. Gallman, "The Statisitical Approach: Fundamental Concepts as Applied to History," in George Rogers Taylor and Lucius F. Ellsworth, eds., *Approaches to American Economic History* (Charlottesville, Va., 1971), 63–64. For a theoretical discussion of the

concept of "long swings" consult Simon Kuznets, *Secular Movements in Production and Prices: Their Nature and Their Bearing upon Cyclical Fluctuations* (Boston, 1930), 59–69, 324–325.

6. For a discussion of short-run fluctuations in the colonial period see Marc Egnal, "The Pennsylvania Economy, 1748–1762: An Analysis of Short-Run Fluctuations in the Context of Long-Run Changes in the Atlantic Trading Community" (Ph.D. diss., University of Wisconsin, 1974), esp. Chap. 3; John M. Hemphill II, "Virginia and the English Commercial System, 1689–1733: Studies in the Development and Fluctuation of a Colonial Economy under Imperial Control" (Ph.D. diss., Princeton University, 1964); and William S. Sachs, "The Business Outlook in the Northern Colonies, 1750–1775" (Ph.D. diss., Columbia University, 1957).

20. The Strolling Poor: Transiency in Eighteenth-Century Massachusetts

Douglas Lamar Jones

If prerevolutionary Massachusetts represented hundreds of bucolic, peaceful communities filled with freehold farmers, it also represented hundreds of communities whose citizens were wrestling more than ever before with the problems of transiency, the dependent poor, and poor relief. Douglas Lamar Jones (b. 1944), faculty member at Tufts University, points out that these problems were not easy to solve, even if Bay Colony peoples had a long history of antitransiency legislation. Dating back to the earliest settlements, the Puritans had earned a reputation for not welcoming the movement of strangers from town to town, unless purposes were known. In these earlier times antitransiency legislation reflected upon magistrates' concerns about uniform religious beliefs. They did not want dissenters to break down communal harmony in religious practices. But by the mid-eighteenth century, legal and spontaneous acts directed against transients arose primarily from other reasons, namely those of the economic costs involved in bearing responsibility for the poor.

Professor Jones places his discussion within the context of the "modernization" of human practices in providing for the poor. How did premodern communities in colonial America care for the indigent, the transient, and the poor? What made their practices premodern, as opposed to more modern? What were more modern forms of control? What was the changing role of the family in the modernization process, and why? Professor Jones's case-study approach, based on a full sampling of surviving records from Massachusetts, indicates that poorer persons faced increasingly difficult personal conditions. Was this a direct reflection of a growing maldistribution in wealth, or must other factors be taken into consideration? Based on all of the essays in this section, what seems the most flexible way to conceptualize the range of economic opportunity and the structure of provincial society on the eve of the American Revolution?

In 1790, William Bentley, the Salem diarist, observed two of the dominant changes occurring in Massachusetts society during the eighteenth century: the transiency of the poor and increased migration of economically diverse segments of the population.[1] Bentley noted that the Salem Selectmen debated "whether [or not] to warn Strangers out of Town in order to save the Town from the charges of

Source: Douglas Lamar Jones, "The Strolling Poor: Transiency in Eighteenth-Century Massachusetts," *Journal of Social History,* 8 (1975), pp. 28–54. Copyright 1975 by Peter N. Stearns. Reprinted by permission of Douglas Lamar Jones and Peter N. Stearns.

the Poor. It is found in fact that the greater part of the whole property is in the hands of persons not Town born, and in the best streets even a majority of freeholders [are newcomers]."[2] To Bentley, migration had become a way of life in eighteenth-century Salem, and one result was a realignment of the rules for defining the social order. One could no longer expect that one's neighbors were, in Bentley's felicitous phrase, "Town born," and had grown to adulthood within the same town and presumably with the same set of values.

Bentley's observations of a changing social order were not simply the particularistic sentiments of a local diarist; they were the articulation of the passing of traditional Massachusetts society and the emergence of a more modern one.[3] This process of modernization in Massachusetts was by no means abrupt or dramatic. Indeed, it is more useful to view the middle and late decades of the eighteenth century as a period of transition. During this transitional stage, structural change, social values, and personal behavior fluctuated amidst the demands of passage from the more simple, face-to-face society of the seventeenth century. This essay seeks to examine three aspects of transiency migration during this transitional stage: the magnitude of transiency during the eighteenth century; the social and economic characteristics of transients; and the legal response to increasing numbers of transient poor persons.

During the eighteenth century, an increase in the number of transients in eastern and western Massachusetts coincided with the secular trend in westward migration and declining levels of residential continuity. This transition to increased mobility during the eighteenth century became even more firmly established during the nineteenth century. Mostly poor and of lower-class origins, eighteenth-century transients were found in both the congested eastern Massachusetts counties and the frontier. Moving very short distances from town to town and job to job, this class of transients confronted traditional communities with mounting problems of social welfare and control. The process of increased migration caused the towns to live in uneasy tension with a growing class of poor persons for several decades during the eighteenth century.

In response to this class of transients, new legal mechanisms were developed to limit their impact on the traditional towns. The towns relinquished some but not all of their customary responsibilities for the transient poor while society at large gradually assumed a greater proportion of the duties of care and control. These new legal mechanisms did not completely alter the care provided by families and towns, but they did make clear that Massachusetts society required more routinized means for sustaining social order than face-to-face, local society offered.[4] Thus the appearance of a visible class of transients and the rationalization of legal means of welfare and control during the eighteenth century represent aspects of the transition from traditional to modern American society.

I

In premodern Massachusetts, there was a remarkably wide divergence in the rates of population persistence, ranging from 50 to 83 percent (see Table 1).[5] This broad pattern of residential continuity was accounted for, however, by the first generation of settlers. Their rates of persistence (from available local studies) ranged from 52 to 83 percent. As time passed and the population expanded, the range of persistence in eighteenth-century Massachusetts narrowed to 50 to 69 percent. While the minimum rate of population continuity in premodern Massachusetts never fell below 50 percent, the maximum range varied quite dra-

TABLE 1 Rates of Persistence in Selected Communities in Premodern New England*

Decade	Community**	Rate of Persistence	N	Range	Mean
				52–83%	67%
1643–1653	Rowley, Mass.	59%	(54)		
1648–1660	Dedham, Mass.	52%	(98)		
1660–1670	Dedham	78%	(91)		
	Hingham, Mass.	73%	(96)		
1676–1686	Windsor, Conn.	57%	(165)		
1680–1690	Dedham	73%	(113)		
1686–1696	Manchester, Mass.	61%	(34)		
1687–1695	Boston, Mass.	53%	(1224)		
1690–1700	Dedham	83%	(125)		
				50–69%	60%
1723–1733	Dedham	55%	(204)		
1731–1741	Wenham, Mass.	68%	(99)		
1741–1751	Beverly, Mass.	50%	(302)		
	Wenham	58%	(113)		
1751–1761	Beverley	58%	(304)		
	Wenham	53%	(105)		
1754–1765	Hingham	69%	(331)		
1761–1771	Beverly	64%	(368)		
	Wenham	59%	(99)		
1780–1790	Boston	56%	(2225)		
1790–1800	Hingham	68%	(347)		

Sources: In order of listing, calculated by the author from *The Early Records of the town of Roxley, Massachusetts, 1639–1672* (Rowley, Mass., 1894), pp. v–x; Kenneth A. Lockridge, "The Population of Dedham, Massachusetts, 1636–1736," *Economic History Review* XIX (1966): 322; Daniel Scott Smith, "Population, Family, and Society in Hingham, Massachusetts, 1635–1880," (Ph.D. diss., University of California, Berkeley, 1973); Linda Auwers Bissell, "From One Generation to Another: Mobility in Seventeenth-Century Windsor, Connecticut," *William and Mary Quarterly* XXXI (1974): 79–110, Table VIII; calculated by the author from *Manchester Town Records, 1636–1736* (Salem, 1889), pp. 30–31, 73; James A. Henretta, "Economic Development and Social Structure in Colonial Boston," *William and Mary Quarterly* XXII (1965): 74–92; tax list and reconstitution data of Wenham, Massachusetts; tax list and reconstitution data of Beverly, Massachusetts; Allan Kulikoff, "The Progress of Inequality in Revolutionary Boston," *William and Mary Quarterly* XXVIII (1971): 402.

* Computation of the persistence statistic displayed in this table was based on a determination of the number of persons listed in the first time period, and then a ratio of the persons who continued to the following time period was calculated. All persistence statistics in this table have been standardized to fit this method.

** All towns listed are located in Massachusetts unless otherwise noted.

matically over time. By the mid-eighteenth century, the overt residential stability found in some Massachusetts towns a century earlier had disappeared; taxpayers and their families began to move at a faster pace.

This mobility quickened even more during the early nineteenth century, as the secular patterns of persistence declined more sharply. From a longitudinal perspective, the decreased rates of the eighteenth century should be viewed as a transition to the more volatile rural and urban populations of nineteenth-century America.[6]

TABLE 2 New and Subdivided Settlement Formation in Massachusetts, 1621–1860, by Geographic Region*

Region and type of settlement	1621–1660		1661–1700		1701–1740	
	PERCENT	N	PERCENT	N	PERCENT	N
East**						
New settlements	75	(36)	52	(14)	14	(8)
Subdivisions	19	(9)	22	(6)	48	(28)
East—Total	94	(45)	74	(20)	62	(36)
West†						
New settlements	6	(3)	19	(5)	20	(12)
Subdivisions	—	(0)	7	(2)	19	(11)
West—Total	6	(3)	26	(7)	39	(23)
Massachusetts, all						
New settlements	81	(39)	70	(19)	34	(20)
Subdivisions	19	(9)	30	(8)	66	(39)
Grand Total		(48)		(27)		(59)

	1741–1780		1781–1820		1821–1860	
	PERCENT	N	PERCENT	N	PERCENT	N
East						
New settlements	—	(0)	—	(0)	—	(0)
Subdivisions	10	(10)	42	(22)	68	(21)
East—Total	10	(10)	42	(22)	68	(21)
West						
New settlements	40	(38)	11	(6)	3	(1)
Subdivisions	50	(48)	47	(25)	29	(9)
West—Total	90	(86)	58	(31)	32	(10)
Massachusetts, all						
New settlements	40	(38)	11	(6)	3	(1)
Subdivisions	60	(58)	89	(47)	96	(30)
Grand Total		(96)		(53)		(31)

Source: Compiled from Kevin H. White, *Historical Data Relating to Counties, Cities and Towns in Massachusetts* (The Commonwealth of Massachusetts, 1966).

* As used in this table, "date of settlement formation" is based on dates of founding of towns, districts, and plantations. In order to generate the most accurate time series of population dispersion using settlement formation as the index, I tried to use the earliest date of formation, particularly of districts and plantations. This definition of settlement formation—which focuses on the social organization of communities—offers the most useful way of portraying the dispersion of organized society by geographic area.

** Eastern Massachusetts includes all counties to the east of, but excluding, Worcester County: Barnstable, Bristol, Duke's, Essex, Middlesex, Nantucket, Norfolk, Plymouth, and Suffolk.

† Western Massachusetts includes all counties to the west of, and including, Worcester County: Berkshire, Franklin, Hampden, Hampshire, and Worcester. Several counties in Maine also received out-migrants, but they were omitted from this tabulation. Their inclusion would increase the proportion of new and subdivided settlements formed outside of eastern Massachusetts.

A useful index of eighteenth-century population redistribution through migration is the proportion of settlement dispersion occurring by geographic region. During the seventeenth century, almost all new settlements were formed in eastern Massachusetts. The western part of the colony remained relatively untouched except around Springfield and Northampton (see Table 2). By 1740, however, there was an absolute decline in settlement formation in the eastern counties as the

TABLE 3 Number of Transient Households Warned out of Essex and Hampshire Counties, 1739–1774, and the Rate of Increase or Decrease from the Previous Time Period

| | Households warned and the rate of increase or decrease from previous time period | | | | Average increase or decrease |
| | ESSEX COUNTY | | HAMPSHIRE COUNTY | | |
Dates	Percent	N	Percent	N	PERCENT
1739–1743	n.a.*	(257)	n.a.	(50)	n.a.
1750–1754	56	(400)	76	(88)	+58
1760–1764	+116	(862)	+248	(306)	+139
1770–1774	−93	(58)	−60	(122)	−85

Sources: Taken from the Court of General Sessions of the Peace, 1726–1796, Essex County, Massachusetts, Clerk of Courts Office, Salem, Massachusetts. Taken from the Court of General Sessions of the Peace, 1735–1781, Hampshire County, Massachusetts, Clerk of Courts Office, Northampton, Massachusetts.

* The designation n.a. means that the proportional increase for the given time period was not available.

white population began to shift to the west and the north. Almost 90 percent of the settlements founded between 1741 and 1780 were in the western counties.

Not all of the western settlements formed after 1741 were new, many were subdivisions which split off from older towns. While we normally think of the congested eastern towns as having to subdivide, the reverse was true between 1741 and 1780: almost no towns subdivided in the east. Out-migration was the primary response to population growth in many eastern towns during the transitional period. (There were, however, rural-urban differences in the extent of out-migration in the east.) Ultimately, western migration declined after 1781 as economic adjustments were made and higher population densities accepted. But the transition to increased mobility had been made during the eighteenth century.

Migration increased during the eighteenth century as a natural but unwanted response to demographic pressures on available economic resources.[7] This change to greater geographic mobility was neither abrupt nor dramatic. It was a slow process intimately related to population growth and the need for land in traditional, agricultural society. Migration became a stopgap attempt to limit the population sizes of many Massachusetts towns, particularly the older farming towns in the eastern counties. Not until family limitation emerged during the nineteenth century as a more effective control on population size was geographic mobility loosened from its mechanistic relationship to population growth.

Precisely during the peak periods of eighteenth-century migration and settlement formation, the number of unwanted persons—transients—in two representative Massachusetts counties, Essex and Hampshire, increased dramatically (see Table 3). In Essex, located to the north of Boston along the coast and established during the seventeenth century, the rate of increase in the number of transient households doubled in each of the two decades following 1739–43 (from 56 percent in 1750–54 to 112 percent in 1760–64). Despite the higher absolute number of transients in Essex County, a rapid increase in the proportion of transients was common in Hampshire as well.

Located in western Massachusetts, Hampshire County underwent a substantial population growth during the eighteenth century. But during the early 1760s, Hampshire witnessed a phenomenal increase in the proportion of persons warned out as transients. The rate of increase was so much greater than in any other time period in either Hampshire or Essex that it suggests that the impact of a growing class of transients occurred later in the demographic history of this frontier county.[8] Once this time-lag is accounted for, the ratio of transients in 1760–64 to the total population in 1765 in each county was almost identical (.106 in Essex and .104 in Hampshire). By the 1760s social exclusion of the poor was as common on the frontier of Massachusetts society as in the older, more established, eastern counties.[9]

The migration transition in eighteenth-century Massachusetts involved both an increase in general population redistribution and a rise in transiency mobility. The wandering poor person was not a completely new "type"; transients were found in smaller numbers in seventeenth-century towns. What was new, however, was the existence of a class of the transient poor who required economic assistance. This swelling population of dependent poor, many of whom were single persons, confronted the traditional towns with problems of poor relief. The visibility of eighteenth-century transients implicitly challenged the traditionalism of the communal society; unemployment, single-person households, and residential mobility were not accepted patterns of behavior.

II

During the eighteenth century, towns began to follow the practice of presenting the names and prior residential origins of transients to the courts of general sessions of the peace. Parents, their children, and servants (if any) were grouped together in the warnings which were prepared by local constables for the legal identification of all transients. Single persons were usually listed separately. The social unit warned out was the household, which consisted variously of a family, a single man or woman, or, more rarely, a family with a servant or slave.

The most distinctive feature of transient households in Essex and Hampshire Counties was the high proportion of single persons (see Table 4). The total proportions of single transients in Essex County ranged from 52 to 62 percent, while in Hampshire County there was a greater variation across time (from 26 to 54 percent). Although we do not know the ages of these single transients, their large proportion of the total suggests that many may have been young and unmarried— the most common characteristics of migrants.[10] Yet we cannot rule out the possibility that some were older persons, such as widows, who were unemployable and migrating for better living conditions as dependent poor.

Transiency among single persons was not restricted by sex; almost equal proportions of men and women were warned in Essex while in Hampshire, again, there was more variation over time. These regional variations in the numbers of single men and women may be explained by the different demographic histories of the two counties. Essex, a demographically "older" county than Hampshire, had the most unbalanced sex ratio of all Massachusetts counties. In many Essex County towns, native sons migrated during the eighteenth century because of economic and population pressures. This out-migration reduced the supply of males and created a demographic imbalance. Hampshire, however, expanded after 1730, when the number of towns increased sixfold and the number of adult men and women was almost equal.[11] Single transient women were perhaps more welcome in Hampshire because of the need for marriage mates in a developing area. In

TABLE 4 Household Status of Transients in Essex and Hampshire Counties, Massachusetts, During the Eighteenth Century

Household Status	1739–1743		1750–1754	
	ESSEX	HAMPSHIRE	ESSEX	HAMPSHIRE
Single persons				
Males	27%	28%	38%	33%
Females	27%	26%	30%	14%
Families*				
Two-parent	39%	38%	28%	42%
One-parent	7%	8%	4%	11%
Servants**	—	—	1%	—
Slaves	—	—	—	—
Total†	100%	100%	100%	100%
N	(257)	(50)	(400)	(88)

	1760–1764		1770–1774	
	ESSEX	HAMPSHIRE	ESSEX	HAMPSHIRE
Single persons				
Males	32%	30%	28%	11%
Females	31%	14%	24%	15%
Families				
Two-parent	29%	45%	40%	68%
One-parent	6%	10%	9%	6%
Servants	1%	—	—	1%
Slaves	1%	—	—	—
Total	100%	99%	101%	101%
N	(862)	(306)	(58)	(122)

Source: Taken from the Court of General Sessions of the Peace, 1726–1796, Essex County, Clerk of Courts Office, Salesm, Massachusetts; Court of General Sessions of the Peace, 1735–1781, Hampshire County, Clerk of Courts Office, Northampton, Massachusetts.

* Almost all one-parent families were headed by females. In Essex County, 46 of 51 one-parent families in 1760–1764 were headed by women. In Hampshire, 41 of the 52 one-parent families were headed by single mothers.

** Since occupations were not included in the warning out, this is only a minimal estimate of the number of servants.

† Percentages may not add to 100 percent due to rounding.

Essex, transient males were not the solution to a decline in available marriage mates because of their lower-class status. Caught between the pressures of increasing demands on economic resources and legal and moral strictures against the status of the single-person household, unmarried transients formed the major subclass of the dependent population.

The one-parent household was subject to very close scrutiny in eighteenth-century Massachusetts, particularly if headed by a woman. The overall proportion of one-parent families remained at a low level in both Essex and Hampshire, but the number of female-headed families almost tripled during the early 1760s. There may have been an incremental increase in widowhood following the French and Indian Wars which could account for this change.[12] But mothers with illegitimate children also fell victim to banishment by communities attempting to avoid poor

TABLE 5 Average Household and Family Size of Transients, 1760–1764, and of Persons Listed in the Census of 1765, in Essex and Hampshire Counties, Massachusetts

	Average household size*	Average family size**
Essex County		
1765 Census, whites only	5.34	n.a.
Transients, 1760–1764	2.10	4.10
Hampshire County		
1765 Census, whites only	5.95	n.a.
Transients, 1760–1764	2.65	4.03

Sources: For transients, see Table 3. 1765 calculations are taken from data in Joseph B. Felt, "Statistics of the Population in Massachusetts," *Collections of the American Statistical Association* I, part II (Boston, 1845), pp. 149–51.

* Definitions of the relationships among family members are not available in the 1765 Census. For this reason, I have adopted the term "household" to describe the average number of persons within each living unit. From the aggregated data available in the 1765 Census, "household" seems to be a more inclusive definition than the term "family," which was used by the census takers. Within the census category of "family," servants, apprentices, possibly slaves, and three-generational families seem to have co-resided together. Also, the term "household" permits us to categorize single individuals into separate households.

** The category of "average family size" omits single individuals and employs as the unit of analysis persons who were defined as biologically related members of the same family. While information of this type is not available from the census, it can be found in the warnings out. For a discussion of the definitions of family and household used here, see Peter Laslett, ed., *Household and Family in Past Time* (Cambridge, England, 1972), pp. 28–40.

relief and enforce moral censure.[13] The late eighteenth century was a period of increased sexual activity, as the rise in premarital pregnancy rates in Massachusetts suggests. Prosecution for illegitimacy also reflected increased sexual activity as well as the moral authority of the towns and county courts.[14] It seems likely that transient single mothers fell within this category of socially excluded persons.

Not all transients were unmarried; families comprised the second largest category of unwanted persons. These transient families generally included only biologically related members: husbands, wives, and their children. Rarely were three-generational households, apprentices, servants, or slaves found among transient families.

Smaller than the average, premodern American family, transient families averaged just about four persons (see Table 5). Since family size is an indication of the relative age of the parents, it seems clear that married transients were as youthful on the frontier as in older, eastern Massachusetts. But there were demographic differences between transient families in each county. Proportionally more transient families lived in Hampshire than in Essex, and the average household size was larger in the west as well. These differences suggest that more families migrated to Hampshire County, presumably for better economic opportunities. Essex County, on the other hand, became more congested during the last half of the eighteenth century.[15] Part of this congestion may have resulted from transients who were trapped geographically and economically by old age, ill health, and poverty.

These distinctions showed also in the type of community more likely to take action against the transients. Since warnings out were related to a town's efforts to avoid the costs of poor relief, we would expect that in Essex County, where the economy was under stress, both the wealthy and poor towns would have warned out transients in equal proportions. The wealthy towns would be motivated by the desire to preserve their wealth and economic order; the less wealthy towns by the need to preserve what wealth was available. This, in fact, was the case in Essex County during the 1760s. There was almost no relationship between per capita warnings and per capita wealth. Transiency migration in Essex County was common to all towns, regardless of their wealth or population size.[16]

But in Hampshire County there was a stronger relationship between per capita warnings and per capita wealth. In part, this relationship reflects greater economic opportunities in Hampshire than in Essex. Transients clearly were attracted to Hampshire County, as its population growth and proliferation of new settlements suggest. Some communities were more attractive than others, but exactly which ones is not clear at this time. For example, the sick, the aged, and widows may have been drawn to those towns with well-developed charitable and institutional support. More generally, younger transients showed some sense of economic advantage in seeking places in Hampshire County, though they were often rebuffed.

Overriding these differences, however, was the fact that transients in both counties came from the bottom of the social scale. Almost all of the Salem transients listed in 1791 (mostly males) were working-class artisans and lower-class mariners and laborers (see Table 6). Only a handful were in higher occupational groups. Compared to the complete occupational structure of Boston's males in 1790, the male transients from Salem were overwhelmingly lower class. Yet an important variation occurs when we control for country of origin. Nearly two-thirds of the foreign transients were mariners or fishermen while only about one-quarter of the domestic transients lived directly from the sea. Conversely, few foreign transients were artisans while a majority of domestic transients were dispersed among land- and sea-related crafts such as tailoring, ship's carpentry, and cabinet-making. Similar proportions of both domestic and foreign transients were unskilled workers.

Because Salem's foreign transients were primarily mariners, their transiency may have been a function of their occupations. On the other hand, the more balanced occupational profile of domestic transients suggests that they were attracted to Salem because of its diversified social structure. For example, the proportion of transient domestic artisans in Salem in 1791 was remarkably similar to the proportion of artisans in Boston. It is not surprising that skilled and semiskilled domestic artisans were drawn to a commercial town such as Salem; they sought economic opportunities where they were most available. More problematic was the future of unskilled laborers and husbandmen. These persons were least prepared to adjust to the economic life of a premodern, commercial town, and may have swelled the ranks of the transient poor.

Transient domestic artisans in Massachusetts should not be confused with English "tramping artisans" of the eighteenth and nineteenth centuries. Of course, their status as migrants was an important parallel, but English "tramping" was an organized form of unemployment relief and labor redistribution which operated with varying degrees of efficiency. In contrast, transiency in eighteenth-century Massachusetts was individualized and nonunionized. Some

TABLE 6 Occupational Status of Transients to Salem, Massachusetts, in 1791, by Residential Origins, Compared with the Occupational Structure of Boston, Massachusetts, 1790

Occupational status	Residential origins of Salem transients, 1791						Boston, 1790 ALL MALES	
	U.S.		FOREIGN		TOTAL			
	Percent	N	Percent	N	Percent	N	Percent	N
Government	—	(0)	—	(0)	—	(0)	3	(67)
Professional	—	(0)	1	(1)	1	(1)	9	(219)
Tradesmen	—	(0)	2	(2)	1	(2)	18	(474)
Clerical	—	(0)	1	(1)	1	(1)	3	(66)
Artisans	51	(59)	15	(12)	36	(71)	49	(1271)
Building crafts		(11)		(1)		(12)		(245)
Cloth trades		(17)		(2)		(19)		(289)
Food trades		(10)		(3)		(13)		(175)
Marine crafts		(6)		(4)		(10)		(219)
Metal crafts		(6)		(2)		(8)		(132)
Wood-workers		(3)		(0)		(3)		(106)
Miscellaneous		(6)		(0)		(6)		(205)
Service	—	(0)	—	(0)	—	(0)	7	(183)
Mariners	24	(27)	61	(50)	39	(77)	5	(117)
Unskilled	25	(29)	20	(16)	23	(45)	7	(188)
Total		(115)		(82)		(197)		(2585)

Sources: Calculated from "Salem Warnings, 1791," *Essex Institute Historical Collections* XLIII (1907): 345–52. Because of missing information as to occupations or residential origins, 26 males, 22 single women, and 14 widows were omitted. Calculated from Allan Kulikoff, "The Progress of Inequality in Revolutionary Boston," *William and Mary Quarterly* XXVIII (1971): 411–12, Appendix.

form of informal cooperation may have existed, particularly in the seaports of Salem and Boston, but nineteenth-century England had a more clearly defined subculture of migrant artisans.[17]

The low economic condition of Massachusetts transients raises the problem of whether they were capable of travelling long distances in search of employment or subsistence. An analysis of the residential origins of transients who entered three Massachusetts towns—Cambridge, Chelmsford and Salem—reveals two distinct types of migratory activity. First, foreign transients travelled long distances almost exclusively by water, immigrating from countries such as England or Ireland. Second, domestic transients relocated very short distances, usually not more than ten miles from the town of last residence. This pattern of domestic transients was likely to have been a repeating one, so that some transients circulated from town to town.

Long-distance movement of transients from other countries depended on the geographic contiguity of the destination to the point of origin. Both Salem and Boston received distinct migratory streams of European transients during the late eighteenth century. Only a trickle of transients entered the seaport towns from outside Massachusetts (see Table 7).

The major stream of transients in seaport and inland towns was from within Massachusetts. Primary economic and population centers such as Salem and Boston received a majority of their transients from within Massachusetts. Smaller

TABLE 7 Residential Origins of Transients in Three Massachusetts Towns
During the Eighteenth Century

Residential origins	Cambridge* 1761–1771	Chelmsford* 1761–1771	Salem** 1791
Massachusetts	96%	82%	52%
Foreign	2%	—	36%
U.S., other	2%	18%	10%
Unknown	1%	—	2%
Total†	101%	100%	100%
Within ten miles	76%	64%	30%
Essex County	5%	6%	30%
Middlesex County	49%	72%	7%
Suffolk County	32%	4%	7%
N	(189)	(103)	(260)

Sources: For Cambridge and Chelmsford—Court of General Sessions of the Peace, 1761–1771, Middlesex County, Clerk of Courts Office, Cambridge, Massachusetts. For Salem see Table 6.

* Transients from Cambridge and Chelmsford represent male and female housholds (single and married) who were warned by the Court of General Sessions of the Peace, 1761–1771, Middlesex County, Clerk of Courts Office, Cambridge, Massachusetts.

** Transients from Salem were warned by the local Selectmen. They represent male and female transients; marital status was not usually given.

† Percentages may not add up to 100 percent due to rounding.

inland towns, removed from initial contact with foreign immigrants, also received almost all of their transients from within Massachusetts. The main exceptions were towns which dotted the borders, thus coming into contact with transients from neighboring states such as New Hampshire or Connecticut. Chelmsford, for example, a small, agricultural town located near New Hampshire, received nearly one-fifth of its transients from outside Massachusetts. Cambridge, however, recorded only a bare 2 percent of its transient population as coming directly from outside Massachusetts.

Thus the general pattern of transient migration in eighteenth-century Massachusetts was one of localized mobility, as transients moved from town to town within discrete local areas. The long migratory move—except for foreign immigrants—was rare. More typically, transients circulated among towns within a ten-mile radius. It is important to distinguish between localized mobility among rural and urban (or seaport) towns. Major population sources such as Boston or Salem, with their large and diverse migratory streams, drew transients from distances greater than ten miles. Of the transients entering Boston and Salem, however, about one-half were from within ten miles.[19]

In contrast to the urban areas, two rural Middlesex County towns, Cambridge and Chelmsford, received most of their transients from within ten miles (see Table 7). With its close proximity to Boston, Cambridge was like a way station for transients. Three-fourths of Cambridge's transients came from within ten miles, and a third were from nearby Boston. Boston's transient migration stream seemed to feed directly into Cambridge, as a procession of migrants—many of foreign birth—paused briefly but moved on. Chelmsford, located outside of a large migration stream, experienced even fewer long-distance transients than Cambridge. Indeed, the county boundaries of Middlesex were as useful a guide to the extent of localized mobility into Chelmsford as the ten-mile radius (72 percent from within the County vs. 64 percent from within ten miles). Ultimately, the ten-mile radius provides the most useful measure of transiency migration. The nearer a town was to a major population stream, the more likely it was that the transient would cross a political boundary. Even during the transition from a traditional to a modern society, there was a pattern of rural to urban migration. Artisans, for example, were probably "pulled" across political boundaries to better opportunities; unskilled laborers may have been "pushed" from their jobs by poor working conditions or a declining economy.

Transiency thus reflected important but limited geographic mobility, which followed from frequently intense poverty and physical hardship. Constables and clerks conveyed a sense of poverty in some cases from which escape was almost impossible. William Pickett, for example, had been a prisoner in Canada during the French and Indian War. After suffering hardships of war and captivity, he returned to Springfield without even sufficient clothing. The London-born Pickett had been a servant before his capture during the war.[20]

Given the high proportions of single transients, it is plausible to suggest that many transients were ex-servants. Servitude of whites in Massachusetts usually was not permanent. At the end of their terms of service, men and women were often in their early twenties and ready to begin a new "stage" in their personal and economic growth. For example, over one-fifth of the privates from Essex County who served in the French and Indian War in 1758 were servants. For some, the experience of travelling to other parts of New England during military service may have opened up hitherto unknown opportunities for settlement. One such private, Daniel Buteman from Beverly, eventually appeared on the tax lists there, married a local woman and out-migrated.[21] The case of Buteman is but one example; the important point is that migration and military service were tied to improved economic opportunities for young ex-servants such as Buteman.

Others were less fortunate. Benjamin Baley, his wife, and their three children required poor relief from Topsfield in 1762. Baley bound himself to some Topsfield inhabitants who failed to fulfill their obligations, leaving him without a job, any form of income, and dependent upon the town.[22] Transients such as Baley, encumbered by economic responsibilities to the towns in which they settled, were taxed just as other inhabitants but lacked the ability to pay their shares. Appearance on an eighteenth-century tax list implied neither wealth nor residential stability. Peter Frost, for one, made an extreme choice when he was unable to solve his continuing problems of poverty and personal care. Frost, an Ipswich laborer, bound himself for life in 1700 to William Cogwell, Jr.[23]

Sickness plagued some transients. Reports of clerks commonly referred not only to their poverty but also ill health. The death of transients in unfamiliar towns was common; Samuel Graffam, for example, of Harpswell fell sick in Topsham and died there. In particular, young children were extremely vulnerable to the ardors of repeated migration. Jane Wing, a single mother, lost one of her three children in Bridgewater and the town reluctantly absorbed the cost of the burial.[24] The rigors of transiency—poverty, constant mobility, poor health, the inability to work, and few alternatives for improvement—confronted at least some of the transients of eighteenth-century Massachusetts with a circle of poverty which was difficult to break. Widows, the aged, children, and the mentally ill were most vulnerable to the conditions of transiency.

One ex-servant who fell into distress was Elizabeth Nicholson Stimson. Her history—brief as it is to us—reads like a microcosm of the transient's existence.[25] Elizabeth was born in Salem in 1775 but moved to Andover with her family in 1779. When she was fifteen or sixteen years old, Elizabeth left her family and worked as a "maid servant" for eight years, until 1798, primarily in Middleton but also in Reading. She lived on her wages, completed the term of service, and returned to Salem to live with her aunt. After a few months, she moved again, this time back to her father's home in Andover. There she lived until she married in 1799 at the age of twenty-four. With her husband, probably an itinerant mariner, she lived in Salem and bore three children until the entire family required poor relief in 1807. Elizabeth Stimson's mobility patterns seem typical of eighteenth-century Massachusetts: completely localized within a discrete geographical area. She married at an average age, but only after completing eight years as a servant. Precisely why she and her family required poor relief was not clear, but they, like hundreds of others, turned to the town for assistance in increasing numbers during the eighteenth century. Their ability to cope with poverty and illness depended in part on the institutional responses of the towns, the counties, and the General Court to the plight of the transients.

III

Both the rising numbers of transients and their economic dependency prompted institutions in eighteenth-century Massachusetts to develop new solutions to social welfare and control. During this transitional period, some continuity in traditional practices of welfare and control remained. But the thrust of the eighteenth-century response to the new class of transient poor was away from the seventeenth-century practices.

The seventeenth-century background of the institutional control of transients (as distinct from welfare) presents an incomplete record, but two themes emerge from the archives of the towns. First, the towns regulated very carefully the admission of new members. Viewed in this sense, close scrutiny of all types of migrants functioned to monitor the quality of potential townsmen and women in order to achieve a cohesive social order.[26] In addition to controlling the quality of new inhabitants, the regulation of transients was rooted in a suspicion of their possible criminal acts. Salem, for example, did not permit Indians in the town except during daylight hours, and constables were directed by the Selectmen to view as suspicious "night walkers" and others who were awake at unreasonable hours.[27] The most dangerous transients, often called vagabonds, required more specific public control. Persons who were unable to give "a good and satisfactory account of their wandering up and down" were included within this category.[28] They were subject to corporal punishment for their wanderings and returned to their legal residences. In this case, banishment was used because no police force existed which could maintain effective control over the more dangerous transients.

The second rationale for social control was economic; towns tried to minimize transiency in order to avoid responsibilities of poor relief. Theoretically, those persons most likely to require poor relief—foreign immigrants, ex-servants, the wandering poor, and the sick—could gain legal inhabitancy by residing for a specific length of time. Once a needy person was settled, his welfare was normally provided through families.[29] But the seventeenth-century towns took measures to prevent things from going this far. Ipswich, for example, regulated the flow of transients in a 1699 town law because such persons "may prove burdensome in several respects to the town." An earlier law in Wenham required a security bond from transients, while Salem sought to protect itself from economic burdens by permitting two joiners to enter the town in 1661 only because they had secure employment.[30] Employment defused the threat of poor relief, particularly if the transient was a servant and responsible to a master.

Local institutions monitored the activities of transients as well. Seventeenth-century churches and schools limited their participants to personally familiar inhabitants, as opposed to transients. In the 1640s, the elders of the church at Salem advised the newly formed Wenham Church to admit only those individuals "known [personally] to some of the congregation to be in Covenant elsewhere." In the small seventeenth-century communities, where relationships were conducted on a face-to-face basis, the distinction between personally familiar individuals and those without connections within the community was an important boundary between transients and residents. Ipswich went so far as to distinguish formally between the family and friends of town residents and unwelcome "strangers" who were outside of those networks. Even if transients lived side-by-side with local inhabitants, town institutions separated the transient. In Salem, transients could send their children to the local schoolmaster, but only at a fee of twice that of full inhabitants.[31]

While most of the evidence indicates that transients in seventeenth-century Massachusetts towns were treated with varying degrees of suspicion, it must be noted that the practice of geographic mobility was also an accepted one. Cambridge acknowledged the passage of travellers through that town by giving permission to Andrew Belcher in 1653 "to sell beer and bread for [the] entertainment of strangers and the good of the town." Such licensing was not uncommon. Similarly, the General Court recognized the status of the nonresident by creating special laws and courts to handle some of their financial and legal situations.[32] While geographic movement was a normal part of the life of some towns, particularly seaports such as Boston, transients held an ambiguous position—neither totally accepted nor completely rejected.

In most towns during the eighteenth century, resident dependents still received care in individual families. For dependents without families or close relatives, the usual practice was for Selectmen or overseers of the poor to pay residents for boarding disabled or indigent persons. Often dependents performed small household chores if physically able. Mary Cue, of Wenham, agreed "to keep" Aaron Jones for one year in 1745, a standard length of time for this contractual service. Her duties included providing Jones with food, "both in sickness and in health," as well as mending his clothes. For these services, the town paid her about four pounds and absorbed all medical expenses. By 1788 in Wenham, the care of local dependents remained with individual families but the town took steps to rationalize the economics of poor relief. Placement of dependents occurred through bidding, with the poor going to the family with the lowest bid. Wenham obtained care but at minimal public cost.[33]

Assistance of local dependents was an integral part of life in the Massachusetts towns, but these functions were performed with varying degrees of success and motives. On the one hand, care was extended to nonresidents such as widow Mercy Fiske, who entered Wenham without permission of the Selectmen in 1694. They nevertheless paid for a doctor and nurse to care for her.[34] Similarly, the smaller agricultural towns such as Manchester, Topsfield, and Wenham agreed to raise money to donate to the poor of Boston during the Revolution.[35]

On the other hand, disputes between towns and between individuals and towns over the responsibility for the care of the poor were common. The poor law of 1794 attempted to alleviate some of these questions of care by providing poor relief of up to three months for all persons. Indeed, one of the most striking features of the revised poor law was its meticulous provision for resolving disputes between towns. Usually the point of contention was the precise residential origin of the persons in need of care. Gloucester and Wenham, for example, disagreed over the legal residence of an "idiot boy" named Nathan Rolings, with Wenham claiming that he was brought into the town illegally.[36] The plight of Rolings, who required some form of permanent care, suggests that social welfare by families in colonial Massachusetts also had its problematic side. One can easily imagine a boy like Rolings having been buffeted from town to town and family to family.

Even families did not always care for their own relatives who were in need. Wenham and Beverly had to negotiate a contract in order to force a nonresident son to care for his widowed mother. Also, the overseers of the poor of Marblehead petitioned the court of general sessions of the peace in 1752 to force the relatives of two "aged" women to care for them.[37] Avoidance of familial responsibility, while not the usual practice, clearly was a part of the colonial experience.

With overseers of the poor empowered to bind out transients as well as children, social welfare and social control converged. In both rural and urban towns, overseers bound children of the poor and idle into service. Boston's and Wenham's overseers turned naturally to the servant and apprenticeship system. Children as well as adult transients received food, shelter, clothing, perhaps some form of training, and varying degrees of emotional relationships.[38] What must be understood here, though, was the conjunction of family life and its values and the community's resolution of economic dependency through the labor system. Not only did overseers minimize their relief expenses; they maximized social order by dispersing potential transients into the community.

Another alternative—formal institutionalization—was not used extensively in Massachusetts until the early nineteenth century. But the practice of grouping dependents under the same roof existed throughout the eighteenth century. Early forms of institutionalization were found not only in large population centers such as Boston or Salem; small agricultural towns such as Manchester, Wenham, and Ipswich also experimented with group housing.[39] Known as a workhouse or poorhouse, the typical eighteenth-century institution frequently housed the local poor and transients together. Also, towns combined the use of houses for transients and the poor with family welfare. As early as 1719, Ipswich built a poorhouse but in 1734 recommended that the poor be placed in private homes and employed outside. The use of workhouses for both the housing and employment of "idle and indigent" persons became widespread enough in Massachusetts by 1750 to require the General Court to regulate their operations. This law permitted the housing of poor, vagrant, and idle persons because all were deemed socially harmful.[40]

Transients who did not work had long been a source of intense concern to the General Court. The Court labelled transient vagrants as disruptive persons, accusing them of luring children and servants away from their "callings and employments." As early as 1682, the Court singled out Boston as a haven for "idle persons in families as well as single persons."[41] Transient vagrants who required specific controls were not only perceived as bad in themselves but as menaces to others and to the social order. This control was not confined to the large eastern towns. The General Court passed a special act at the end of the eighteenth century for the removal of vagrants and "strolling poor people" from the District of Marshpee on Cape Cod. Marshpee, according to the Court, had become a place of shelter for the transient poor, and was populated primarily by Indians and blacks.[42] And generally the more traditional forms of social welfare and control which relied on personal familiarity and residential continuity provided a stark contrast to the needs of a growing class of transient poor during the eighteenth century. Despite the continuities of care on a local level, the more complex and routine legal mechanisms of the eighteenth century represented a shift from traditional approaches to welfare and control.

As the eighteenth century progressed, the control of transiency depended less on each town as a unique social entity and more on the legal administration of a routine system of welfare and control. The customary statutory settlement laws before 1739 permitted a legal settlement if an individual resided in a town for a specified number of months. After 1739, residency requirements stiffened. Legal residency required the agreement of the town meeting or the Selectmen; even the payment of taxes did not create a de facto form of legal residence.[43] In practice, the control of the movement and settlement of eighteenth-century transients was an integral part of the social order. The granting of poor relief, the laws of settlement, and the practice of warning transients to leave town were interrelated aspects of the legal structure employed by towns in Massachusetts to preserve their social order.

Who held the responsibility for discovering the presence of transients and informing them that they had to leave a particular town? This important question of the legal responsibility for the detection of transients changed over the course of the eighteenth century. The purpose of the settlement and poor-relief laws—the social control of unwanted persons—remained substantially the same, but the methods for dealing with transients were transformed. While each town originally was accountable for discovery and notification, by the end of the eighteenth century the town no longer had the sole responsibility for transients in its midst. By focusing closely on the process of discovery and the burden of notification of the warnings-out system, we can ascertain the shifting legal relationships between the transients, the towns, and the county courts.

In 1692, the Province of Massachusetts enacted a settlement law which provided that persons not legally warned out of a town within three months became inhabitants, and entitled to poor relief.[44] This statute was a more formalized statement of seventeenth-century settlement laws passed by individual towns; however, it added several featured to the legal process of the control of transiency and of poor relief. First, the burden of discovering the presence of transients was placed on the towns themselves. Eager to avoid poor relief, warnings were returned by towns to their county courts as proof that the town had warned out all transients. These procedures meant that the costs of the discovery of transients and the legal notification of their presence became functions of the town governments and secondarily of the county courts. In most towns, populations were small and transients easily identifiable. But in more populous towns, or those with a greater turnover of new persons such as Boston and Salem, identification of transients required more than the customary reliance on the face-to-face encounters of the agricultural villages. As early as 1670, the Salem Selectmen hired Thomas Oliver to go to each house once a month to inquire about the presence of "strangers."[45]

During the late 1720s and 1730s, the General Court altered the settlement and poor-relief laws by shifting the burden of discovery of the transients from the towns themselves to the local inhabitants who provided them with food and shelter.[46] Called "entertainment" laws, these statutes provided that transients could not remain in a particular town longer than twenty days without special permission from that town. Inhabitants who housed transients were required to give the town clerk a written description of the transient's personal characteristics or be subject to a forty-shilling fine for noncompliance. As a device for the control of transiency and reduction of poor relief, warnings out were used contemporaneously with the "entertainment" laws. The former prevented the transient from becoming a legal resident; the latter provided a source of indemnity against the poor relief of transients. This dual form of control regulated not only the transients but also cautioned local inhabitants before they rented rooms to transients.

The operation of this law was straightforward and local inhabitants seem to have cooperated. For example, in 1738, Richard Dodge, a lifelong resident of Wenham, notified the Selectmen that he had "taken in" Thomas Colwell, his wife, and their three children. The Colwell family migrated to Wenham from New Hampshire, were given a dwelling house by Dodge, and probably hired as servants. Because this family was employed, they were exempted from the twenty-day restriction. It was not unusual for Dodge to hire a servant family. Married in 1724, Dodge's wife Mary gave birth to seven children by 1738—but only one was alive by the end of that year. Without maturing children in an agricultural economy, Richard Dodge was labor poor and in a position to need hired help for his farm.[47]

By 1767, the General Court removed the burden of discovery of transients from the towns and their inhabitants alike, placing it directly on the transients themselves. Instead of relying on local constables to warn transients through the county courts, the 1767 statute required all transients to inform the Selectment of their presence as they entered a town. Responsibility for being a transient came to rest with each migrant; status as a nonresident meant that persons were to submit themselves voluntarily to physical removal back to their towns of legal residence.[48]

Known transients were removed on authority of a warrant from a justice of the peace. Constables secured transients by warrants, and returned them from town to town until the transients reached their legal residences. If possible, the transient paid for the cost of this removal; otherwise, the town of legal residence bore the expense.[49] The General Court absorbed the costs of persons to destinations outside of Massachusetts. One important exception to this law exempted apprentices and servants from removal if attached to a master or family; the labor system remained intact while physical removal controlled potentially harmful transients. An important implication of this statute was the decline of the system of warnings out processed through the county court. Legal notification that transients were nonresidents was no longer necessary under the 1767 law.

Not until the 1790s did the General Court fully rewrite the settlement and poor-relief laws in operation during the middle years of the eighteenth century. Indeed, it seems as though the Revolution and its aftermath temporarily interrupted—rather than caused—revision of the policies regulating transients. Drawing on the principles of the 1767 statute, the revision of 1794 provided for an even more routinized procedure for the removal of transients.[50] The 1767 statute in effect had eliminated the warnings out as a device for controlling transiency, but some towns continued the practice both through the county court and local overseers of the poor. However, the 1794 statute specifically ended the warnings-out system, substituting a comprehensive procedure for the return of transients to their legal residences. With this added power of removal came expanded responsibilities; each town had to provide care and immediate relief for all persons regardless of resident status for a period of up to three months.

The shifting burdens of legal responsibility for the transients of eighteenth-century Massachusetts culminated in this statute of 1794. Poor transient persons became fully integrated into the legal structure but not the social order. Towns became legally responsible to the transients' need for care; yet these same towns also could employ removal procedures practiced earlier in the century. The difference was that the new procedures for removing transients and reducing the work of the county courts. Transients received some increased procedural rights, such as an appeal to the court for common pleas to contest removal, but the statute focused most extensively on the procedural aspects of removal, the control of dependent persons, and the arbitration of disputes among towns over questions of legal residences of transients. This revised law of 1794 clearly revealed continuities with past practices, but it also reflected divergences, particularly more precise, rational forms for the administration of poor relief. For while the 1794 poor law was a "legal institutionalization" of the transient poor, it also, paradoxically, maintained a resolution of dependency which relied heavily on the family.

By the end of the eighteenth century, local systems of welfare and control ultimately became integrated into the larger structure of Massachusetts society. The implications of this process of integration (by the General Court, the county courts, and the towns) suggest that the familiar communal assumptions of life in the premodern town experienced severe testing under the reality of increased transiency migration and economic stratification. Late eighteenth-century Massachusetts society was a dynamic one in transition; it was not a fixed, flat, "colonial" one. David Rothman, in his recent analysis of nineteenth-century penal and welfare practices uses a "noninstitutional" counterpoint based on a motionless view of colonial America as a contrast to the nineteenth-century society which "discovered" the asylum.[51] This leaves the impression that before 1800, social welfare was an unchanging, idyllic blend of assistance from one's family and neighbours. Rothman's point about the development of institutionalization during the nineteenth century is astute; the counterpoint, however, does not explain transitional change within the history of premodern systems of welfare and control. Rather than stressing a dichotomy between "colonial" and "Jacksonian" policies of social welfare and control, we must recognize a transitional period from the traditional forms to the more modern ones of the nineteenth century.

The eighteenth-century legal process of social control actively involved both the town and the county court. The role of the county court, however, did not supersede that of the town; the two interacted defensively in attempts to monitor transient migration, minimize poor relief, and preserve the social order. The decline in the use of warnings in 1767 and their disappearance from the revised poor law of 1794 as a technique of social and economic control represent part of the rationalization of the legal sanctions on transiency in Massachusetts. These more predictable, routine methods of limiting the economic and social impact of transients are characteristic of more modern societies.[52]

Social solidarity did not disappear as the towns shared their political authority with the county courts, but the boundaries of social interaction were redefined.[53] Localism, or the "Town born" in Bentley's words, was no longer a guarantee of homogeneity. The emerging social order in late eighteenth-century Massachusetts required support from general laws which defined transients as deviants from the cultural and economic norms of family life, residential stability, and secure employment. Banishment could no longer satisfy the needs of a transitional society. Increasing levels of transiency migration and reciprocal legal means of control indicate that premodern Massachusetts had passed from an explicitly communal society to a more complex, modern one. This transition was by no means complete by 1800. Yet the tensions of the structural change and legal adjustments pointed more in the direction of modern nineteenth-century America than toward communal continuity.

NOTES

1. The term "transient" appeared in eighteenth-century court records to describe unwanted persons. Other variations on the same term were "non-inhabitant," "vagrant," and "low and poor." In this essay, I have used "transient" to describe all unwanted persons. Most of these persons were of low economic status, including the "poor," the "near poor," and persons of working-class status. Examples of the terminology used to characterize unwanted transients may be found in the Court of General Sessions of the Peace, Hampshire County, Clerk of Courts Office, Northampton, Massachusetts, 1758–62: 247; 1762–64: 49–50, 88, 163.

2. William Bentley, *The Diary of William Bentley* (Gloucester, Mass., 1962), II: 188.

3. Several recent historical analyses of the trend towards modernization have appeared: Kenneth A. Lockridge, "Land, Population, and the Evolution of New England Society 1630–1800," *Past and Present* 39 (1968): 62–80; Richard D. Brown, "Modernization and the Modern Personality in Early America, 1600–1865: A Sketch of a Synthesis," *The Journal of Interdisciplinary History II* (1972): 201–28; and Lockridge, "Social Change and the Meaning of the American Revolution," *Journal of Social History* 6 (1973): 403–39. Many of the issues of modernization in early American history are discussed in Daniel Scott Smith, "Population, Family and Society in Hingham, Massachusetts, 1635–1880," (Ph.D. diss., University of California, Berkeley, 1973).

4. For a general discussion of the changes in legal structures in modernizing societies, see Marc Galanter, "The Modernization of Law," in Myron Weiner, ed., *Modernization: The Dynamics of Growth* (New York, 1966), pp. 153–65.

5. In determining trends of geographic mobility before 1800, in- and out-migration statistics are the most useful because they permit the direct control of mortality. But because source materials are sparse and normally underrecorded, complete measurement of migration for a substantial number of New England towns is not yet possible. In order to circumvent these problems, we must turn to the persistence statistic. As defined here, persistence rates include male taxpayers or landholders who appeared on consecutive lists of inhabitants at regularized time intervals. Not pure measures of migration, persistence rates permit us to understand the extent of residential continuity, and by implication, discontinuity.

6. Persistence rates in rural communities, 1800–1890, displayed a much lower range (21 to 59 percent) than in eighteenth-century New England; the range of persistence in nineteenth-century urban communities was also low (30 to 64 percent). The nineteenth-century data is most conveniently summarized in Stephan Thernstrom, *The Other Bostonians: Poverty and Progress in the American Metropolis, 1880–1970* (Cambridge, Mass. 1973), pp. 221–232, Tables 9.1 and 9.2.

7. Population growth in colonial New England came from within, due primarily to low age at marriage, generally uncontrolled fertility practices, and healthy conditions. For a discussion of the growth rate of New England's white population, see Daniel Scott Smith, "The Demographic History of Colonial New England," *Journal of Economic History* XXXII (1972): 174–83.

The limitations of migration as a means of controlling family and population sizes have been discussed by Nathan Keyfitz, "Migration as a Means of Population Control," *Population Studies* 25 (1971): 63–72. Some Massachusetts towns overtly attempted to rationalize the process of resettlement of younger sons or the generation of revenue from land ownership by petitioning the General Court to expand their boundaries or acquire new land. See petition of November 27, 1729, *Journal of the*

House of Representatives of Massachusetts 9 (1729-31), p. 134; *Wenham Town Records* (Wenham, Mass., 1940), III: 25; Thomas Franklin Waters, *Ipswich in the Massachusetts Bay Colony* (Ipswich, Mass., 1917), II: 398-401.

8. It is possible that a cyclical pattern of transiency migration occurred within the general secular trend of the eighteenth century. Definitive statements on this issue are difficult to make because of the type of records from which transient migration is drawn. Warnings out were legal actions taken by individual towns, and therefore reflected the values of each town as well as the needs and behavior of transients. Also, transients undoubtedly were warned more than once from nearby towns. This problem of recidivism in legal records further complicates any relationship between cyclical fertility patterns and levels of transiency migration. On cyclical issues in early American history, see P. M. G. Harris, "The Social Crisis of American Leaders: The Demographic Foundations," *Perspectives in American History* III (1969): 159-344.

9. About 1770, warnings out processed through the county courts declined because of a change in the statutory law. The 1767 settlement law no longer required notification of the presence of transients. Since this law was slow to take effect, some towns continued to warn transients according to the old practice; see *Massachusetts Acts and Resolves* IV (1757-68), ch. 17, pp. 911-12.

10. The youthfulness of migrants in industrial society is well documented; see Henry S. Shryock, Jr., *Population Mobility Within the United States* (Chicago, 1964), pp. 346-58; Sidney Goldstein, *Patterns of Mobility 1910-1950: The Norristown Study* (Philadelphia, 1958), pp. 203-06. But a dominant pattern of migratory young persons, especially males, was found in a preindustrial English village; see R. S. Schofield, "Age-Specific Mobility in an Eighteenth Century Rural English Parish," *Annales de Démographie Historique* (1970): 261-74.

11. The adult sex ratios in 1765 and 1800 in Essex County were 84 and 82 respectively; in Hampshire County, they were 99 and 98. For a delineation of the increasing pressure of population in one Essex County town, see Philip J. Greven, Jr., *Four Generations: Population, Land, and Family in Colonial Andover, Massachusetts* (Ithaca, 1970); for a suggestive formulation of the issues of population pressure and land supply, see Lockridge, "Land, Population, and the Evolution of New England Society 1630-1800." The critical issue, however, may not have been a persistent shortage of land, but the problems of transition to new types of agricultural methods as well as increasing commercialization.

12. For example, the proportion of widows taxed in Wenham increased from 3 percent to 8 percent from 1751 to 1761.

13. One witness in a divorce case in Boston testified against a single mother who was a servant, saying that he "got her warned out of Town because she was with child to prevent charge," Suffolk County Court Files, Divorce Cases, no. 129749, p. 112. I am indebted to Nancy F. Cott for bringing this case to my attention.

14. Daniel Scott Smith and Michael S. Hindus, "Pre-marital Pregnancy in America, 1640-1966: An Overview and Interpretation," (forthcoming, *The Journal of Interdisciplinary History* [winter, 1975]). Prosecutions for the crime of fornication in Middlesex County during the period 1760-74 accounted for 65 percent of all cases in the Superior and General Sessions Courts; see William E. Nelson, "Emerging Notions of Modern Criminal Law in the Revolutionary Era: An Historical Perspective," *New York University Law Review* 42 (1967): 452. Of course, premarital pregnancy rates and fornication prosecution rates are not identical; they only illustrate the increasing sexual activity of the eighteenth century. What is not clear, however, is if the incidence of prosecution compared favorably with the total pattern of premarital pregnancy.

15. The congestion in Essex County may be seen in its crowded housing patterns. Essex had an average of 7.6 persons per house in 1765, while Hampshire had only 6.7; this difference continued through the century. Yet the average household size was smaller in Essex than in Hampshire. It seems possible that some of this crowding was the result of transients sharing houses with local residents. For the analysis of persons per house and per family, see Philip J. Greven, Jr., "The Average Size of Families and Households in the Province of Massachusetts in 1764 and in the United States in 1790: An Overview," in Peter Laslett, ed., *Household and Family in Past Time* (Cambridge, England, 1972), pp. 545-60; also see Table 5.

16. In order to measure the relationship between transients, population size, and wealth of the towns in Essex and Hampshire Counties, I used a rank-order correlation test. To control for population size, I employed correlations based on per capita number of warnings per town and per capita wealth per town. The rank-order test was chosen because the quality of the data did not warrant a finer measure. This test measures the strength of the relationship between two variables on a scale of +1.0 (perfect agreement) to −1.0 (perfect disagreement). The conclusions in this paragraph and the following one are based on the following correlations of per capita warnings and per capita wealth dur-

ing the early 1760s:

Spearman's r_s
Essex County   +.070
Hampshire County   +.456

Population figures for 1765 were taken from Joseph B. Felt, "Statistics of the Population in Massachusetts," *Collections of the American Statistical Association* (Boston, 1845), I, part II: 149, 151, 211–12. Wealth rankings are from the proportion of county taxes assessed for each town within each county; see Court of General Sessions of the Peace, Essex County, 1764–77: 211; Court of General Sessions of the Peace, Hampshire County, 1758–62: 196. Transients for the period 1760–64 were used in order to provide a sufficient number of transients to rank per town; for sources, see notes to Table 3.

17. On English "tramping," see E. J. Hobsbawm, *Labouring Men: Studies in the History of Labour* (New York, 1967), pp. 41–72. For a discussion of vagabonds in Elizabethan England, see A. L. Beier, "Vagrants and the Social Order in Elizabethan England," *Past and Present* 64 (1974): 3–29. For a comparison of the changes in the laws affecting vagrants in England and America, see William J. Chambliss, "A Sociological Analysis of the Law of Vagrancy," *Social Problems* 12 (1964): 67–77. Chambliss argues, incorrectly in my view, that American vagrancy (i.e., transiency) laws were merely adaptations of their English counterparts. This interpretation of similarity fails to take into account the fact that Massachusetts laws were specific reactions to social change within the American experience. Clearly, increased regulation occurred in both England and America; but criminal sanctions against transients were more common in England than in Massachusetts.

18. In Boston, 28 percent of the transients warned in 1791 by the Overseers of the Poor were from foreign countries; 71 percent arrived from towns within Massachusetts. Boston figures are for the total population of transients, not households; see Kulikoff, "The Progress of Inequality in Revolutionary Boston," pp. 400–01, Table X.

19. Of the Salem transients who entered from within Massachusetts, 57 percent came from within ten miles. Forty-six percent of the Massachusetts transients who migrated to Boston were from within ten miles; see *Ibid.*, p. 401, Table X.

20. Court of General Sessions of the Peace, Hampshire County, Massachusetts, 1758–62: 247.

21. Computed from Beverly reconstitution data and Eben Putnam, "Soldiers in the French War from Essex County, 1755–1761," *Essex Institute Historical Collections* XXIX (1892): 169–76.

22. *Town Records of Topsfield, Massachusetts* (Topsfield, 1917), II: 217–18, 222, 229.

23. Waters, *Ipswich*, II: 391–92.

24. *Topsham v. Harpswell, 1 Mass. Reports* 517 (1805); *Bridgewater v. Dartmouth, 4 Mass. Reports* 273 (1808); *Quincy v. Braintree, 5 Mass. Reports* 86 (1809); *Town Records of Topsfield* II: 225.

25. *Salem v. Andover, 3 Mass. Reports* 436 (1807).

26. For examples, see Waters, *Ipswich*, II: 386, 392–93; *Wenham Town Records*, I: 5; *The Records of the Town of Cambridge, 1630–1703* (Cambridge, 1901), pp. 24, 108, 155, 193; *Town Records of Salem, Massachusetts* (Salem, 1913), II: 112; *Records of the Town of Braintree, 1640–1703* (Randolph, 1886): 2, 19–20; Josiah Henry Benton, *Warning Out in New England* (Boston, 1911), *passim*. Various types of controls of access to the community were used: Braintree limited land ownership and sale to approved persons, while Cambridge even fined one of its own inhabitants for "entertaining" his son.

27. *Town Records of Salem*, II: 303–04.

28. *The Charters and General Laws of the Colony and Province of Massachusetts Bay* (Boston, 1814), ch. XCIX (1662), 200. David J. Rothman, *The Discovery of the Asylum* (Boston, 1971), pp. 1–29, provides a discussion of some of these issues.

29. For discussions of the family as an institution of social welfare in seventeenth-century Massachusetts, see John Demos, *A Little Commonwealth: Family Life in Plymouth Colony* (New York, 1970) and Edmund S. Morgan, *The Puritan Family: Religion and Domestic Relations in Seventeenth-Century New England* (New York, 1966).

30. Waters, *Ipswich*, II: 392–393; *Wenham Town Records* (Wenham, Mass., 1930), I: 5; *Town Records of Salem*, II: 50.

31. Diary of John Fiske, 1637–75 (typescript copy), pp. 44–49, Essex Institute, Salem, Massachusetts; Waters, *Ipswich*, II: 393; *Town Records of Salem*, II: 50.

32. *Records of the Town of Cambridge*, 100; *Charters and General Laws*, ch. XCII (1641), pp. 191–92; ch. XXI (1665), 72–73; ch. XXXI (1639), 91.

33. *Wenham Town Records,* III: 81–82; IV: 81, 89. The Selectmen of Worcester also expressed concern that the poor of that town were placed "to the best advantage and Saving to the Town." *Worcester Town Records, 1784–1800* (Worcester, 1890), 146.

34. *Wenham Town Records,* I: 135–159.

35. *Ibid.,* IV: 11; *Town Records of Topsfield,* II: 344; *Manchester Town Records, 1718–1769* (Salem, 1889), II: 147.

36. *Wenham Town Records,* III: 99; also see *ibid.,* IV: 160, for another example of conflict over the legal residence of a transient.

37. *Ibid.,* IV: 80; Court of General Sessions of the Peace, Essex County, Massachusetts, petition dated December, 1752, 115.

38. A systematic study of the apprenticing of children in eighteenth-century Boston reveals that one-half of all children bound between 1734 and 1805 were between the ages of five and nine years, while the median age was nine. Potential transients or dependents, these children were apprenticed to families both within and outside Boston. A small rural town such as Wenham also apprenticed children, but with less of a geographic dispersion than Boston. See Lawrence W. Towner, "The Indentures of Boston's Poor Apprentices: 1734–1805," *Publications of the Colonial Society of Massachusetts* XLIII (Boston, 1966): 417–68; and *Wenham Town Records,* IV: 196–98, 206, 213.

39. See *Town Records of Manchester,* II: 105, 114; *Wenham Town Records,* III: 188: *Records of the Town of Braintree,* 236, 281–82.

40. Waters, *Ipswich,* II: 396–97; *Mass. Acts and Resolves,* III (1742–56): ch. 12, pp. 108–11.

41. *Charters and General Laws,* ch. XCIX (1662), 200; ch. LIII (1682), 128; also see *Mass. Acts and Resolves,* III (1742–56): ch. 43, p. 926; and *ibid.* (1792–93), ch. 59, pp. 479–93.

42. *Mass. Acts and Resolves* (1796–97), ch. 23, pp. 52–53.

43. *Ibid.,* II (1715–41): ch. 9, 995–95.

44. *Ibid.,* I (1692–1714): ch. 28, 64–68.

45. *Town Records of Salem,* II: 112.

46. *Mass. Acts and Resolves,* II (1715–41): ch. 6, 386; ch. 8, 616; ch. 9, 994–95; ch. 16, 835–36.

47. *Wenham Town Records,* III: 40, and reconstitution data. For other examples of compliance and enforcement of "entertainment" laws, see "Persons 'Warned Out' of the Town of Newbury, 1734–76," *Essex Institute Historical Collections* LXIX (1933): 36.

48. *Mass. Acts and Resolves,* IV (1757–68): ch. 17, 911–12.

49. Examples of physical removal may be found in *Worcester Town Records,* 66, 81, 91, 121, 174–75; and *Wenham Town Records,* IV: 57.

50. *Mass. Acts and Resolves* (1792–93): ch. 59, 479–93.

51. Rothman, *The Discovery of the Asylum,* especially pp. 3–56.

52. For example, the "instrumental conception" of early nineteenth-century American law fits this pattern of predictability; see Morton J. Horwitz, "The Emergence of an Instrumental Conception of American Law, 1780–1820," *Perspectives in American History* V (1971): 287–326.

53. Michael Zuckerman, *Peacable Kingdoms: New England Towns in the Eighteenth Century* (New York, 1970), has made the argument that the towns were the centers of a broad range of political, legal, moral, and social authority. His analysis has been faulted by legal historians in particular, who have argued implicitly and explicitly that there was more conflict and court participation in the affairs of eighteenth-century new England towns; see L. Kinvin Wroth, "Possible Kingdoms: The New England Town from the Perspective of Legal History," *The American Journal of Legal History* XV (1971): 318–30; and David Grayson Allen, "The Zuckerman Thesis and the Process of Legal nationalization in Provincial Massachusetts," *William and Mary Quarterly* XXXIX (1972): 443–60, and Zuckerman's reply in *ibid.,* pp. 461–68.

It seems to me, however, that we should not frame the question in terms of power located in either the town or the court system; to do so means any answer would have to overlook the complexity of shifting trends in authority and conflict. The more likely explanation is that which is suggested below: that power was becoming shared as demographic and economic changes posed shifts in the basic social order.

SECTION 5: SUGGESTIONS FOR FURTHER READING

An introductory work to colonial economic development of exceptional clarity is Stuart Bruchey's succinct *The Roots of American Economic Growth, 1607–1861* (1965). Two overview articles of value are C. P. Nettels, "British Mercantilism and the Economic Development of the Thirteen Colonies," *Journal of Economic History,* 12 (1952), pp. 105–115, and G. R. Taylor, "American Economic Growth before 1840: An Exploratory Essay," *Journal of Economic History,* 24 (1964), pp. 427–444. These investigations should be supplemented by J. F. Shepherd and G. M. Walton, *Shipping,*

Maritime Trade, and the Economic Development of Colonial North America (1972), and P. D. McClelland, "The Cost to America of British Imperial Policy," *American Economic Review,* 59 (1969), pp. 370–381, along with the essay presented here by Marc Egnal and the works dealing with the impact of the Navigation Acts on colonial economic development mentioned in the preceding bibliography.

A number of important regional studies have appeared over the years and should be consulted by those wanting a more detailed look at more localized economic patterns. Old but still useful is W. B. Weeden, *Economic and Social History of New England, 1620–1789* (2 vols., 1890). Also of importance for that region is Bernard and Lotte Bailyn, *Massachusetts Shipping, 1697–1714: A Statistical Study* (1959). For the middle colonies J. T. Lemon, *The Best Poor Man's Country: A Geographical Study of Early Southeastern Pennsylvania,* (1972), A. L. Jensen, *The Maritime Commerce of Colonial Philadelphia* (1963), and J. G. Lydon, "Philadelphia's Commercial Expansion, 1720–1739," *Pennsylvania Magazine of History and Biography,* 91 (1967), pp. 401–418, are important. For the South, key studies include J. M. Price, *France and the Chesapeake: A History of the French Tobacco Monopoly, 1674–1791, and of Its Relationship to the British and American Tobacco Trades* (2 vols., 1973), A. C. Land, "Economic Behavior in a Planting Society: The Eighteenth-Century Chesapeake," *Journal of Southern History,* 33 (1967), pp. 469–485, David Klingaman, "The Significance of Grain in the Development of the Tobacco Colonies," *Journal of Economic History,* 29 (1969), pp. 268–278, and S. M. Rosenblatt, "The Significance of Credit in the Tobacco Consignment Trade: A Study of John Norton & Sons," *William and Mary Quarterly,* 3rd ser., 19 (1962), pp. 383–399.

Carl Bridenbaugh has described provincial urbanization in his encyclopedic *Cities in the Wilderness: The First Century of Urban Life in America, 1625–1742* (1938), and *Cities in Revolt: Urban Life in America, 1743–1776* (1955). Urbanization related to job specialization is the important subject of J. M. Price, "Economic Function and the Growth of American Ports Towns in the Eighteenth Century," *Perspectives in American History,* 8 (1974), pp. 123–186, while J. H. Soltow, *The Economic Role of Williamsburg* (1965), explains how one southern town functioned as a local trade center. J. A. Ernst and H. R. Merrens, "'Camden's Turrets Pierce the Skies!': The Urban Process in the Southern Colonies during the Eighteenth Century," *William and Mary Quarterly,* 3rd ser., 30 (1973), pp. 549–574, explain why the concept of urbanization may be misplaced for the early South.

The merchant is introduced with documentary materials in Stuart Bruchey, ed., *The Colonial Merchant: Sources and Readings* (1966), while differing types of merchants may be studied in W. T. Baxter, *The House of Hancock: Business in Boston, 1724–1775* (1945), J. B. Hedges, *The Browns of Providence Plantation: Colonial Years* (1952), R. A. Davison, *Isaac Hicks: New York Merchant and Quaker, 1767–1820* (1964), and J. H. Soltow, "Scottish Traders in Virginia, 1750–1775," *Economic History Review,* 2nd ser., 12 (1959), pp. 83–98. Older but valuable contributions about agricultural activity and the economic role of farmers are P. W. Bidwell and J. I. Falconer, *History of Agriculture in the Northern United States, 1620–1860* (1925), and L. C. Gray, *History of Agriculture in the Southern United States to 1860* (1933). Students should also consult A. C. Land, "The Tobacco Staple and the Planter's Problems: Technology, Labor, and Crops," and D. A. Williams, "The Small Farmer in Eighteenth-Century Virginia," both in *Agricultural History,* 43 (1969), pp. 69–81, and pp. 91–101. A model community study investigating one farming town facing revolution is R. A. Gross, *The Minutemen and Their World* [Concord, Massachusetts] (1976). The impact of the commercial ethos on the Quaker religious community is treated in F. B. Tolles, *Meeting House and Counting House: The Quaker Merchants of Colonial Philadelphia, 1682–1763* (1948).

A pioneering, cyclical view of opportunity covering the sweep of American history is contained in P. M. G. Harris, "The Social Origins of American Leaders: The Demographic Foundations," *Perspectives in American History,* 3 (1969), pp. 157–344. Carl Bridenbaugh, *Myths and Realities: Societies of the Colonial South* (1963), is a perceptive analysis of the socioeconomic evolution of three distinct cultures in the prerevolutionary South. Those wanting to look at the subject of economic development beyond the period of the American Revolution should begin with J. A. Henretta, *The Evolution of American Society, 1700–1815: An Interdisciplinary Analysis* (1973), and D. C. North, *The Economic Growth of the United States, 1790–1860* (1961).

The modern debate about the range of opportunity for socioeconomic advancement stems from conclusions in R. E. Brown, *Middle-Class Democracy and the Revolution in Massachusetts, 1691–1780* (1955), the source of the first selection, and a companion volume by R. E. and B. K. Brown, *Virginia, 1705–1786: Democracy or Aristocracy?* (1964). The emphasis upon the emergence of an economically equalitarian society receives carefully qualified support from C. S. Grant, *Democracy in the Connecticut Frontier Town of Kent* (1961), G. B. Warden, *Boston, 1689–1776* (1970), and S. B. Kim, "A New Look at the Great Landlords of Eighteenth-Century New York," *William and Mary Quarterly,* 3rd ser., 27 (1970), pp. 581–614. Richard Hofstadter, *America at 1750: A Social Portrait* (1971), is an effective general summary of this interpretive point of view.

By comparison the bulk of recent studies demonstrate a widening gap between the wealthy and the poor in prerevolutionary America. The best place to begin is J. T. Main, *The Social Structure of Revolutionary America* (1965), along with J. T. Lemon and G. B. Nash, "The Distribution of Wealth in Eighteenth-Century America: A Century of Change in Chester County, Pennsylvania, 1693-1802," *Journal of Social History*, 2 (1968), pp. 1-24, as well as the essay by Aubrey C. Land appearing in this section. Also of importance are B. W. Labaree, *Patriots and Partisans: The Merchants of Newburyport, 1764-1815* (1962), J. A. Henretta, "Economic Base and Social Structure in Colonial Boston," *William and Mary Quarterly*, 3rd ser., 22 (1965), pp. 75-92, K. E. Lockridge, "Land, Population, and the Evolution of New England Society, 1630-1790," *Past & Present*, 39 (1968), pp. 62-80, E. M. Cook, Jr., "Social Behavior and Changing Values in Dedham, Massachusetts, 1700 to 1775," *William and Mary Quarterly*, 3rd ser., 27 (1970), pp. 546-580, and G. B. Nash, "Urban Wealth and Poverty in Pre-Revolutionary America," *Journal of Interdisciplinary History*, 6 (1976), pp. 545-584. G. B. Warden, "Inequality and Instability in Eighteenth-Century Boston: A Reappraisal," *Journal of Interdisciplinary History*, 6 (1976), pp. 585-620, should be read in conjunction with the Nash presentation, as Warden challenges those who have written about declining levels of economic opportunity.

K. E. Lockridge, "Social Change and the Meaning of the American Revolution," *Journal of Social History*, 6 (1973), pp. 403-439, relates the data in many of the foregoing studies to formative tensions in the Revolutionary period. J. T. Main, "The Distribution of Property in Colonial Connecticut," *The Human Dimensions of Nation Making: Essays in Colonial and Revolutionary America*, ed. J. K. Martin (1976), pp. 54-104, and G. L. Main, "Probate Records as a Source for Early American History," *William and Mary Quarterly*, 3rd ser., 32 (1975), pp. 89-99, explain the pitfalls of using quantifiable materials.

Historians of early America have only begun to investigate the problems of poverty and poor relief. Besides the important essay by Douglas Lamar Jones presented here, students should consult G. B. Nash, "Poverty and Poor Relief in Pre-Revolutionary Philadelphia," *William and Mary Quarterly*, 3rd ser., 33 (1976), pp. 3-30, Douglas Greenberg, *Crime and Law Enforcement in the Colony of New York, 1691-1776* (1977), Howard Mackey, "The Operation of the English Old Poor Law in Virginia," *Virginia Magazine of History and Biography*, 73 (1965), pp. 29-48, R. A. Mohl, "Poverty in Early America, A Reappraisal: The Case of Eighteenth-Century New York City," *New York History*, 50 (1969), pp. 5-27, and S. V. James, *A People among Peoples: Quaker Benevolence in Eighteenth-Century America* (1963).

The Nature of Provincial Politics

SECTION 6

The eighteenth century in Anglo-American history often has been described as the "era of salutary neglect." Imperial administrators paid relatively little attention to the American provinces. The empire seemed to run by the force of inertia. Few changes of lasting consequence occurred in the Navigation system. There were minor modifications in the trade acts intended to shut off the development of some nascent American manufactures threatening to compete directly with home products, and there was an act placing heavy duties on foreign molasses imported into the provinces. The idea was to eliminate outside competition for British West Indian suppliers, but customs officials did not enforce the Molasses Act with any regularity. The Board of Trade replaced the Lords of Trade in 1696 as the administrative agency of the empire, but the new Board had no legislative functions. It existed to collect information and to advise the King's Privy Council in what few policy decisions that body promulgated. On the whole, government officials in England were more interested in securing political patronage and profitable sinecures for themselves and their dependents. Most often the American world was a minor, irritating distraction for them, not really worthy of a gentleman's prolonged attention. Native American leaders, as a result, had a relatively free hand in charting the course of their own internal provincial political development.

There was one important policy decision that had a significant impact on colonial political life. English ministers, even though they often thought in military and autocratic terms, never again tried their Dominion experiment with regional centralization. Home officials did take over the administration of several proprietary ventures—New York, New Jersey, and the Carolinas—and each of these colonies received a royal governor. Hence, by the time Georgia became a royal province in the early 1750s, eight of the thirteen mainland colonies that later revolted were of the royalist type, and all thirteen had locally elected representative assemblies. A Crown-appointed governor headed the royalist structure as chief executive. Directly below the governor in the hierarchy was a council, consisting of men nominated by the governor and confirmed in their positions by ministers in England. Not only did councilors advise governors, but an equally important function was to sit in a legislative (and sometimes judicial) capacity as members of the upper houses of the colonial assemblies. The lower houses, consisting of popularly elected delegates, comprised the only branch of the three-tiered royalist structure in which local citizens had a direct voice in filling offices.

It was within this structural framework, guaranteeing English subjects in America at least modest participation in local political affairs, that patterned, almost standardized political debates took place. There were ongoing, at times bitter, disputes over the extent of royal prerogatives in decision making. In theory the governors enjoyed broad privileges. According to their "commissions" and "instructions," governors had the right to veto all provincial legislation appearing to be inconsistent with their instructions or imperial needs. They also had the authority to dispose of Crown lands and appoint men to petty offices as well as to establish the fees such officeholders received for their services. The governors held the power to determine new election districts and the meeting time and place for assembly sessions. They could adjourn, prorogue, or dissolve assemblies at will if local legislators went too far in challenging the Crown's prerogatives or causing problems for governors.

So much for what was on paper. In reality aggrandizing local leaders were not willing to accept such overpowering executive privileges. As Jack P. Greene explains, it was within the prerogative framework that steady resistence from assembly leaders resulted in the serious attrition of executive power. Lacking support from home government officials, royal governors were on the defensive until after the French and Indian War and the reinvigoration of imperial programs during the 1760s. But by that decade, which heralded the end of salutary neglect, the new question was whether the assemblies would compromise their growing autonomy.

Yet focusing exclusively upon the assemblies' quest for power does not convey a full picture of provincial politics. There is no doubt that the struggle over prerogatives helped in forming the backdrop for the coming of the American Revolution, but we also must consider what kind of a political culture was taking form in the provinces. What evidence is there of democratic tendencies? What relationships existed between common citizens and their legislators? May it be said that the provinces were passing through an incubator stage of democracy, emphasized by the rise of the elective assemblies? These questions have not resulted in easy answers.

We have already seen from Bernard Bailyn's essay about Virginia (selection 13) that dominant political theories in Old England assumed an indivisible relationship to exist between leadership in state and society. With full feudal overtones seventeenth-century Englishmen continued to think in hierarchical terms. They assumed that it was the natural function of the "better sort" of nobility and gentry to watch over and guide public policy formulation for the common people. The accepted tenet was that only men of family bloodline, landed status, and proven credentials could have the wisdom to provide disinterested and enlightened leadership.

A number of scholars have argued that these ideas did not take hold in the maturing provincial political milieu. Rather the colonies diverged sharply from English practices, largely because of widespread voting rights. The opportunity to own land, the requisite basis for a full stake in society and its decisions, and to vote, set the provincial world apart as more equalitarian. Property holding on such an extensive scale simply blurred class distinctions and undercut deferential assumptions about who should rule in local political matters.

To prove the point, a number of historians, following the lead of Robert E. and B. Katherine Brown (see selection 17) poured through surviving records on voting qualifications. They found that extraordinarily high numbers of free white adult males owned enough property to qualify for the franchise. Moreover, they voted with some regularity. Having developed an equation between voting rights for males—women, the unfree, and the poor were not offered a role in provincial politics—and representative democracy, these historians assumed that voting males insisted upon full and responsible representation of their interests in assembly decisions. When assembly leaders acted, they carried out the will of their voting constituents, or faced being turned out of office at the next election.

Yet even before the dust resettled on the local voting records, other historians were pointing out that notions about representative democracy before the Revolution were misleading, if not wholly erroneous. They brought forth evidence to demonstrate that the maturing provincial political culture was becoming more rather than less English in its political practices. They argued that common citizens, even those with enough property to fit into the middle class, deferred with increasing regularity to their socioeconomic "betters" in the formulation of public policy, that everyday citizens had no effective involvement in the nomination of candidates for office, that men of middling status rarely ran for elective positions, that few colony-wide offices were elective, and that adult males who went to polling places rarely determined more than which elite leader would attend assembly sessions, thereby hoping to win the favor of powerful elite families, rather than to gain power for themselves. The study of electoral practices and elected leaders indicated that the colonists were not reaching a stage of democratically representative government; if anything, the drift was in the other direction. What was occurring was the "Anglicization" or "Europeanization" of provincial politics. Consider the importance of hierarchical thinking among Virginians in selection 23 by Charles S. Sydnor on provincial electoral practices.

The degree of provincial democracy found by researchers depends somewhat upon their definition of that term. To those who combed through archives for evidence of widespread voting rights, the assumption was as follows: the more men who could vote, the greater the likelihood that democracy was developing. Yet this reflects modern assumptions. Many students of eighteenth-century America have shown recently that "democracy" had a somewhat different meaning in the prerevolutionary setting. Englishmen then believed that the best government mixed and balanced the three social orders of monarchy, aristocracy, and democracy (referring to the *demos* or the rank of common citizens) in its working branches. In England the House of Lords in Parliament was the branch representing the titled nobility while the House of Commons, although filled with men who were anything but common in socioeconomic terms, represented the interests of the democracy of "commoners." The term "democracy" was more often used in reference to a specific social order than to a process of political interaction. The most knowledgeable experts believed that pure democracies in which the people ruled themselves through open-field meetings or through unicameral assemblies could not work because commoners were not educated or enlightened enough to make anything but self-serving decisions. In fact, the term "democracy" often was interchangeable with such derisive epithets as the "lower sort," "the meaner sort," and "the rabble."

Allowing for the transmission of such thinking across the Atlantic, some historians have argued that colonial gentlemen elite leaders assumed that there were parallels between the structure of English government (the king in Parliament) and the three structural tiers (governor, council, and lower house) of royal and proprietary governments in America. Common citizens had their base in lower houses of assemblies, yet voters operating within a deferential framework most often elected men of wealth and local community standing to make appropriate political decisions for the whole community.

These men of standing in America, furthermore, became increasingly concerned in the 1760s that the king's ministers were attempting to destroy their assemblies and liberties, all because of the ministers' lust for personal gain and power. Even though accepting the structural basis of balanced governments in England and America, there was a mounting feeling that something was terribly wrong in the empire during the turbulent years just prior to the Revolution. As argued by Gordon S. Wood, it may not have been the reassertion of prerogatives by royal officials so much as provincial perceptions that a conspiracy was afoot to undermine English liberties in America. Rather than viewing the prerogative tradition as the key formative element, then, Professor Wood claims that a strain of ideological perceptions known as English radical Whiggism lay at the heart of concerns about impending doom for the American political order. As a result, Americans of all ranks were able to pull themselves together in trying to control the specter of tyranny from Britain, a form of tyranny in provincial perceptions reflecting back upon a serious imbalance among traditional social orders in governments.

In grappling with the nature of provincial politics, we must consider political ideology, perceptions, practices, institutional arrangements, and the people directly involved in decision making in conjunction with those having little or no political voice. And we must ask: What types of ideas or ideological perceptions helped to mold political reality? How constrained was the role of everyday citizens in political decision making? Who did the assemblies represent in their upsurge in authority? If assemblymen were responding with regularity to the will of their constituents, then how do we account for the frequent instances of mob violence in the provinces? Were crowds of dissatisfied citizens evidencing their disgust with insensitive provincial elite leaders, or were they in actual fact sustaining and broadening community political authority through extralegal acts?

Answering these questions will result in a broader understanding of the maturing American political culture. It will suggest how far Americans may have diverged from their English antecedents. The distance may not have been so great as once suspected, yet it is also possible that the formulation of decidedly equalitarian practices, compared to Old World models, may have been well under way in the decades prior to the American Revolution, making it possible for the latter half of the eighteenth century to become an era of profound political transformation.

21. The Role of the Lower Houses of Assembly in Eighteenth-Century Politics

Jack P. Greene

Professor Jack P. Greene (b. 1931) of John Hopkins University, a scholar who has written extensively about patterns of change in early American politics, offers here in a classic essay a general assessment of the rise of provincial assemblies in authority and stature. Greene stresses that in the latter seventeenth century English ministers conceived of the American assemblies in static terms. They considered these bodies as local units with circumscribed legislative functions, fit only to handle problems of the moment. The dynamic growth in assembly powers defied those assumptions, yet imperial administrators did not alter their static view to coincide with changing reality. Why? Professor Greene's working assumption is that the ministers were aware of the altered relationship but silent because they did not want to injure a generally harmonious rapport with colonial leaders also involved in making the thriving imperial economy work. Thus home government officials more often than not tacitly sanctioned the assemblies' aggressions upon royal prerogatives. Governors were often helpless, at least until a new departure in British policy helped precipitate revolutionary fervor.

Even though Professor Greene's presentation is well taken, it must be considered whether historical hindsight has been used to reconstruct a general trend in assembly behavior, that is whether colonial gentlemen caught up in the daily heat of political exchanges and debates would have recognized the pattern, let alone have allowed it to focus and affect their political actions. Considering the problem from another angle, did emerging local elites play a vital part in forming the contours of provincial political contests with royal and proprietary officials? What other factors besides prerogatives and elites need to be taken into consideration, and why? Professor Greene's findings must be compared with those of Gordon S. Wood in the next selection.

The rise of the representative assemblies was perhaps the most significant political and constitutional development in the history of Britain's overseas empire before the American Revolution. Crown and proprietary authorities had obviously intended the governor to be the focal point of colonial government with the lower houses merely subordinate bodies called together when necessary to levy taxes and ratify local ordinances proposed by the executive. Consequently, except in the

Source: Jack P. Greene, "The Role of the Lower Houses of Assembly in Eighteenth-Century Politics," *Journal of Southern History,* 27 (1961), pp. 451–474. Copyright 1961 by the Southern Historical Association. Reprinted with substantial additions from the author by permission of the *Journal of Southern History.*

New England charter colonies, where the representative bodies early assumed a leading role, they were dominated by the governors and councils for most of the period down to 1689. But beginning with the Restoration and intensifying their efforts during the years following the Glorious Revolution, the lower houses engaged in a successful quest for power as they set about to restrict the authority of the executive, undermine the system of colonial administration laid down by imperial and proprietary authorities, and make themselves paramount in the affairs of their respective colonies.

Historians have been fascinated by this phenomenon. For nearly a century after 1776 they interpreted it as a prelude to the American Revolution. In the 1780's the pro-British historian George Chalmers saw it as the early manifestation of a latent desire for independence, an undutiful reaction to the mild policies of the Mother Country.[1] In the middle of the nineteenth century the American nationalist George Bancroft, although more interested in other aspects of colonial history, looked upon it as the natural expression of American democratic principles, simply another chapter in the progress of mankind.[2] The reaction to these sweeping interpretations set in during the last decades of the nineteenth century, when Charles M. Andrews, Edward Channing, Herbert L. Osgood, and others began to investigate in detail and to study in context developments from the Restoration to the end of the Seven Years' War. Osgood put a whole squadron of Columbia students to work examining colonial political institutions, and they produced a series of institutional studies in which the evolution of the lower houses was a central feature. These studies clarified the story of legislative development in each colony, but this necessarily piecemeal approach, as well as the excessive fragmentation that characterized the more general narratives of Osgood and Channing, tended to emphasize the differences rather than the similarities in the rise of the lower houses and failed to produce a general analysis of the common features of their quest for power.[3] Among later scholars, Leonard W. Labaree in his excellent monograph *Royal Government in America* presented a comprehensive survey of the institutional development of the lower houses in the royal colonies and of the specific issues involved in their struggles with the royal governors, but he did not offer any systematic interpretation of the general process and pattern of legislative development.[4] Charles Andrews promised to tackle this problem and provide a synthesis in the later volumes of his magnum opus, *The Colonial Period of American History,* but he died before completing that part of the project.[5]

As a result, some fundamental questions have never been fully answered, and no one has produced a comprehensive synthesis. No one has satisfactorily worked out the basic pattern of the quest; analyzed the reasons for and the significance of its development; explored its underlying assumptions and theoretical foundations; or assessed the consequences of the success of the lower houses, particularly the relationship between their rise to power and the coming of the American Revolution. This essay is intended to suggest some tentative conclusions about these problems, not to present ultimate solutions. My basic research on the lower houses has been in the Southern royal colonies and in Nova Scotia. One of the present purposes is to test the generalizations I have arrived at about the Southern colonies by applying them to what scholars have learned of the legislatures in the other colonies. This procedure has the advantage of providing perspective on the story of Southern developments. At the same time, it may serve as one guidepost for a general synthesis in the future.

Any student of the eighteenth-century political process will sooner or later be struck by the fact that, although each of the lower houses developed independently and differently, their stories were similar. The elimination of individual variants, which tend to cancel out each other, discloses certain basic regularities, a clearly discernible pattern—or what the late Sir Lewis Namier called a morphology—common to all of them. They all moved along like paths in their drives for increased authority, and although their success on specific issues differed from colony to colony and the rate of their rise varied from time to time, they all ended up at approximately the same destination. They passed successively through certain vaguely defined phases of political development. Through most of the seventeenth century the lower houses were still in a position of subordination, slowly groping for the power to tax and the right to sit separately from the council and to initiate laws. Sometime during the early eighteenth century most of them advanced to a second stage at which they could battle on equal terms with the governors and councils and challenge even the powers in London if necessary. At that point the lower houses began their bid for political supremacy. The violent eruptions that followed usually ended in an accommodation with the governors and councils which paved the way for the ascendancy of the lower houses and saw the virtual eclipse of the colonial executive. By the end of the Seven Years' War, and in some instances considerably earlier, the lower houses had reached the third and final phase of political dominance and were in a position to speak for the colonies in the conflict with the imperial government which ensued after 1763.

By 1763, with the exception of the lower houses in the corporate colonies of Rhode Island and Connecticut, which had virtually complete authority, the Pennsylvania and Massachusetts houses of representatives were probably most powerful. Having succeeded in placing its election on a statutory basis and depriving the Council of direct legislative authority in the Charter of Privileges in 1701, the Pennsylvania House under the astute guidance of David Lloyd secured broad financial and appointive powers during the administrations of Daniel Gookin and Sir William Keith. Building on these foundations, it gained almost complete dominance in the 1730's and 1740's despite the opposition of the governors, whose power and prestige along with that of the Council declined rapidly.[6] The Massachusetts House, having been accorded the unique privilege of sharing in the selection of the Council by the royal charter in 1691, already had a strong tradition of legislative supremacy inherited from a half century of corporate experience. During the first thirty years under the new charter first the benevolent policies of Sir William Phips and William Stoughton and then wartime conditions during the tenures of Joseph Dudley and Samuel Shute enabled the House, led by Elisha Cooke, Jr., to extend its authority greatly. It emerged from the conflicts over the salary question during the 1720's with firm control over finance, and the Crown's abandonment of its demand for a permanent revenue in the early 1730's paved the way for an accommodation with subsequent governors and the eventual dominance of the House under Governor William Shirley after 1740.[7]

The South Carolina Commons and New York House of Assembly were only slightly less powerful. Beginning in the first decade of the eighteenth century, the South Carolina lower house gradually assumed an ironclad control over all aspects of South Carolina government, extending its supervision to the minutest details of local administration after 1730 as a succession of governors, including Francis Nicholson, Robert Johnson, Thomas Broughton, the elder William Bull, and James Glen offered little determined opposition. The Commons continued to grow in stature after 1750 while the Council's standing declined because of the Crown policy of filling it with placemen from England and the Common's successful attacks upon its authority.[8] The New York House of Assembly began to demand greater authority in reaction to the mismanagement of Edward Hyde, Viscount Cornbury, during the first decade of the eighteenth century. Governor Robert Hunter met the challenge squarely during his ten-year administration beginning in 1710, but he and his successors could not check the rising power of the House. During the seven-year tenure of George Clarke beginning in 1736, the House advanced into the final stage of development. Following Clarke, George Clinton made a vigorous effort to reassert the authority of the executive, but neither he nor any of his successors was able to challenge the power of the House.[9]

The lower houses of North Carolina, New Jersey, and Virginia developed more slowly. The North Carolina lower house was fully capable of protecting its powers and privileges and competing on equal terms with the executive during the last years of proprietary rule and under the early royal governors, George Burrington and Gabriel Johnston. But it was not until Arthur Dobbs' tenure in the 1750's and 1760's that, meeting more regularly, it assumed the upper hand in North Carolina politics under the astute guidance of Speaker Samuel Swann and Treasurers John Starkey and Thomas Barker.[10] In New Jersey the lower house was partially thwarted in its spirited bid for power during the 1740's under the leadership of John Kinsey and Samuel Nevill by the determined opposition of Governor Lewis Morris, and it did not gain superiority until the administrations of Jonathan Belcher, Thomas Pownall, Francis Bernard, and Thomas Boone during the Seven Years' War.[11] Similarly, the Virginia Burgesses vigorously sought to establish its control in the second decade of the century under Alexander Spotswood, but not until the administrations of Sir William Gooch and Robert Dinwiddie, when first the expansion of the colony and then the Seven Years' War required more regular sessions, did the Burgesses finally gain the upper hand under the effective leadership of Speaker John Robinson.[12]

Among the lower houses in the older colonies, only the Maryland House of Delegates and the New Hampshire House of Assembly failed to reach the final level of development in the period before 1763. The Maryland body made important advances early in the eighteenth century while under the control of the Crown and aggressively sought to extend its authority in the 1720's under the leadership of the older Daniel Dulany and again in the late 1730's and early 1740's under Dr. Charles Carroll. But the proprietors were usually able to thwart these attempts, and the Delegates failed to pull ahead of the executive despite a concerted effort during the last intercolonial war under the administration of Horatio Sharpe.[13] In New Hamsphire the House had exercised considerable power through the early decades of the eighteenth century, but Governor Benning Wentworth effectively challenged its authority after 1740 and prevented it from attaining the extensive power exercised by its counterparts in other colonies.[14] It should be emphasized, however, that neither the Maryland nor the New Hampshire lower house was in any sense impotent and along with their more youthful equivalent in Georgia gained dominance during the decade of debate with Britain after 1763. Of the lower houses in the continental colonies with pre-1763 political experience, only the Nova Scotia Assembly had not reached the final phase of political dominance by 1776.[15]

The similarities in the process and pattern of legislative development from colony to colony were not entirely accidental. The lower houses faced like problems and drew upon common traditions and imperial precedents for solutions: They all operated in the same broad imperial context and were affected by common historical forces. Moreover, family, cultural, and commercial ties often extended across colony lines, and newspapers and other printed materials, as well as individuals, often found their way from one colony to another. The result was at least a general awareness of issues and practices in neighboring colonies, and occasionally there was even a conscious borrowing of precedents and traditions. Younger bodies such as the Georgia Commons and Nova Scotia Assembly were particularly indebted to their more mature counterparts in South Carolina and Massachusetts Bay.[16] On the executive side, the similarity in attitudes, assumptions, and policies among the governors can be traced in large measure to the fact that they were all subordinate to the same central authority in London, which pursued a common policy in all the colonies.

Before the Seven Years' War the quest was characterized by a considerable degree of spontaneity, by a lack of awareness that activities of the moment were part of any broad struggle for power. Rather than consciously working out the details of some master plan designed to bring them liberty or self-government, the lower houses moved along from issue to issue and from situation to situation, primarily concerning themselves with the problems at hand and displaying a remarkable capacity for spontaneous action, for seizing any and every opportunity to enlarge their own influence at the executive's expense and for holding tenaciously to powers they had already secured. Conscious of the issues involved in each specific conflict, they were for the most part unaware of and uninterested in the long-range implications of their actions. Virginia Governor Francis Fauquier correctly judged the matter in 1760. "Whoever charges them with acting upon a premeditated concerted plan, don't know them," he wrote of the Virginia burgesses, "for they mean honestly, but are Expedient Mongers in the highest Degree."[17] Still, in retrospect it is obvious that throughout the eighteenth century the lower houses were engaged in a continuous movement to enlarge their sphere of influence. To ignore that continuity would be to miss the meaning of eighteenth-century colonial political development.

One is impressed with the rather prosaic manner in which the lower houses went about the task of extending their authority, with the infrequency of dramatic conflict. They gained much of their power in the course of routine business, quietly and simply extending and consolidating their authority of passing laws and establishing practices, the implications of which escaped both colonial executives and imperial authorities and were not always fully recognized even by the lower houses themselves. In this way they gradually extended their financial authority to include the powers to audit accounts of all public officers, to share in disbursing public funds, and eventually even to appoint officials concerned in collecting and handling local revenues. Precedents thus established soon hardened into fixed principles, "undoubted rights" or "inherent powers," changing the very fabric of their respective constitutions. The notable absence of conflict is perhaps best illustrated by the none too surprising fact that the lower houses made some of their greatest gains under those governors with whom they enjoyed the most harmony, in particular Keith in Pennsylvania, Shirley in Massachusetts, Hunter in New York, and the elder and younger Bull in South Carolina. In Virginia the House of Burgesses made rapid strides during the 1730's and 1740's under the benevolent government of Gooch, who discovered early in his administration that the secret of political success for a Virginia governor was to reach an accord with the plantation gentry.

One should not conclude that the colonies had no exciting legislative-executive conflicts, however. Attempts through the middle decades of the eighteenth century by Clinton to weaken the financial powers of the New York House, Massachusetts Governors Samuel Shute and William Burnet to gain a permanent civil list, Benning Wentworth to extend unilaterally the privilege of representation to new districts in New Hampshire, Johnston to break the extensive power of the Albemarle Counties in the North Carolina lower house, Dinwiddie to establish a fee for issuing land patents without the consent of the Virginia Burgesses, and Boone to reform South Carolina's election laws each provided a storm of controversy that brought local politics to a fever pitch.[18] But such conflicts were the exception and usually arose not out of the lower houses' seeking more authority but from the executives' attempts to restrict powers already won. Impatient of restraint and jealous of their rights and privileges, the lower houses responded forcefully and sometimes violently when executive action threatened to deprive them of those rights. Only a few governors, men of the caliber of Henry Ellis in Georgia and to a lesser extent William Henry Lyttelton in South Carolina and Bernard in New Jersey, had the skill to challenge established rights successfully without rasing the wrath of the lower houses. Clumsier tacticians—Pennsylvania's William Denny, New York's Clinton, Virginia's Dinwiddie, North Carolina's Dobbs, South Carolina's Boone, Georgia's John Reynolds—failed when pursuing similar goals.

Fundamentally, the quest for power in both the royal and the proprietary colonies was a struggle for political identity, the manifestation of the political ambitions of the leaders of emerging societies within each colony. There is a marked correlation between the appearance of economic and social elites produced by the growth in colonial wealth and population on the one hand and the lower houses' demand for increased authority, dignity, and prestige on the other. In the eighteenth century a group of planters, merchants, and professional men had attained or were rapidly acquiring within the colonies wealth and social position. The lower houses' aggressive drive for power reflects the determination of this new elite to attain through the representative assemblies political influence as well. In another but related sense, the lower houses' efforts represented a movement for autonomy in local affairs, although it is doubtful that many of the members recognized them as such. The lower houses wished to strengthen their authority within the colonies and to reduce to a minimum the amount of supervision, with the uncertainties it involved, that royal or proprietary authorities could exercise. Continuously nourished by the growing desire of American legislators to be masters of their own political fortunes and by the development of a vigorous tradition of legislative superiority in imitation of the imperial House of Commons, this basic principle of local control over local affairs in some cases got part of its impetus from an unsatisfactory experience early in the lower houses' development with a despotic, inefficient, or corrupt governor such as Thomas, Lord Culpeper, or Francis, Lord Howard or Effingham, in Virginia, Lionel Copley in Maryland, Sir Edmund Andros in Massachusetts, Seth Sothell in North Carolina, or the infamous Cornbury in New York and New Jersey.

With most of their contemporaries in Great Britain, colonial Americans were convinced that men were imperfect creatures, perpetually self-deluded, enslaved by their passions, vanities, and interests, confined in their vision and understanding, and incapable of exercising power over each other without abusing it. This cluster of assumptions with the associated ideals of a government of laws rather than of men and of a political structure that restrained the vicious tendencies of man by checking them against each other was at the heart of English constitutionalism. In Britain and in the colonies, wherever Englishmen encountered a seeming abuse of power, they could be expected to insist that it be placed under legal and constitutional restraints. Because the monarchy had been the chief offender in seventeenth-century England, it became conventional for the representative branch to keep an especially wary eye on the executive, and the Glorious Revolution tended to institutionalize this pattern of behavior. The necessity to justify the Revolution ensured both that the specter of Stuart despotism would continue to haunt English political arenas throughout the eighteenth century and that representative bodies and representatives would be expected—indeed obliged—to be constantly on the lookout for any signs of that excess of gubernatorial power that would perforce result in executive tyranny. When colonial lower houses demanded checks on the prerogative and sought to undermine executive authority, they were, then, to some extent, playing out roles created for them by their predecessors in the seventeenth-century English House of Commons and using a rhetoric and a set of ground rules that grew out of the revolutionary conditions of Stuart England. In every debate, and in every political contest, each American legislator was a potential Coke, Pym, or Hampden and each governor, at least in legislators' minds, a potential Charles I or James II.

But the lower houses' quest for power involved more than the extension of legislative authority within the colonies at the expense of the colonial executives. After their initial stage of evolution, the lower houses learned that their real antagonists were not the governors but the proprietors of Crown officials in London. Few governors proved to be a match for the respresentatives. A governor was almost helpless to prevent a lower house from exercising powers secured under his predecessors, and even the most discerning governor could fall into the trap of assenting to an apparently innocent law that would later prove damaging to the royal or proprietary prerogative. Some governors, for the sake of preserving amicable relations with the representatives or because they thought certain legislation to be in the best interest of a colony, actually conspired with legislative leaders to present the actions of the lower houses in a favorable light in London. Thus, Jonathan Belcher worked with Massachusetts leaders to parry the Crown's demand for a permanent revenue in the 1730's, and Fauquier joined with Speaker John Robinson in Virginia to prevent the separation of the offices of speaker and treasurer during the closing years of the Seven Years' War.

Nor could imperial authorities depend upon the colonial councils to furnish an effective check upon the representatives' advancing influence. Most councilors were drawn from the rising social and economic elites in the colonies. The duality of their role is obvious. Bound by oath to uphold the interests of the Crown or the proprietors, they were also driven by ambition and a variety of local pressures to maintain the status and power of the councils as well as to protect and advance their own individual interests and those of their group within the colonies. These two objectives were not always in harmony, and the councils frequently sided with the lower houses rather than with the governors. With a weakened governor and an unreliable council, the task of restraining the representative assemblies ultimately devolved upon the home government. Probably as much of the struggle for power was played out in Whitehall as in Williamsburg, Charleston, New York, Boston, or Philadelphia.

Behind the struggle between colonial lower houses and the imperial authorities were two divergent, though on the colonial side not wholly articulated, concepts of the constitutions of the colonies and in particular of the status of the lower houses. To the very end of the colonial period, imperial authorities persisted in the views that colonial constitutions were static and that the lower houses were subordinate governmental agencies with only temporary and limited lawmaking powers—in the words of one imperial official, merely "so many Corporations at a distance, invested with an Ability to make Temporary By Laws for themselves, agreeable to their respective Situations and Climates."[19] In working out a political system for the colonies in the later seventeenth century, imperial officials had institutionalized these views in the royal commissions and instructions. Despite the fact that the lower houses were yearly making important changes in their respective constitutions, the Crown never altered either the commissions or instructions to conform with realities of the colonial political situation and continued to maintain throughout the eighteenth century that they were the most vital part of the constitutional structure of the royal colonies. The Pennsylvania and to a lesser extent the Maryland proprietors were less rigid, although they also insisted upon their theoretical constitutional and political supremacy over the lower houses.

Colonial lower houses had little respect for and even less patience with such a doctrinaire position, and whether or not royal and proprietary instructions were absolutely binding upon the colonies was the leading constitutional issue in the period before 1763. As the political instruments of what was probably the most pragmatic society in the eighteenth-century Western World, colonial legislators would not likely be restrained by dogma divorced from reality. They had no fear of innovations and welcomed the chance to experiment with new forms and ideas. All they asked was that a thing work. When, the lower houses found that instructions from imperial authorities did not work in the best interests of the colonies, that they were, in fact, antithetic to the very measures they as legislatures were trying to effect, they openly refused to submit to them. Instructions, they argued, applied only to officials appointed by the Crown.

> Instructions from his majesty, to his governor, or the council, are binding to them, and esteemed as laws or rules; because if either should disregard them, they might immediately be displaced,

declared a South Carolina writer in 1756 while denying the validity of an instruction that stipulated colonial councils should have equal rights with the lower houses in framing money bills. "But, if instructions should be laws and rules to the people of this province, then there would be no need of assemblies, and all our laws and taxes might be made and levied by an instruction."[20] Clearly, then, instructions might bind governors, but never the elected branch of the legislature.

Even though the lower houses, filled with intensely practical politicians, were concerned largely with practical political considerations, they found it necessary to develop a body of theory with which to oppose unpopular instructions from Britain and to support their claims to greater political power. In those few colonies that had charters, the lower houses relied upon the guarantees in them as their first line of defense, taking the position that the stipulations of the charters were inviolate, despite the fact that some had been invalidated by English courts, and could not be altered by executive order. A more basic premise which was equally applicable to all colonies was that the constituents of the lower houses, as inhabitants of British colonies, were entitled to all the traditional rights of Englishmen. On this foundation the colonial legislatures built their ideological structure. In the early charters the Crown had guaranteed the colonists "all privileges, franchises and liberties of this our kingdom of England . . . any Statute, act, ordinance, or provision to the contrary thereof, notwithstanding."[21] Such guarantees, colonials assumed, merely constituted recognition that their privileges as Englishmen were inherent and unalterable and that it mattered not whether they stayed on the home islands or migrated to the colonies. "His Majesty's Subjects coming over to America," the South Carolina Commons argued in 1739 while asserting its exclusive right to formulate tax laws, "have no more forfeited this their most valuable Inheritance than they have withdrawn their Allegiance." No "Royal Order," the Commons declared, could "qualify or any wise alter a fundamental Right from the Shape in which it was handed down to us from our Ancestors."[22]

One of the most important of these rights was the privilege of representation, on which, of course, depended the very existence of the lower houses. Imperial authorities always maintained that the lower houses existed only through the consent of the Crown,[23] but the houses insisted that an elected assembly was a fundamental right of a colony arising out of an Englishman's privilege to be represented and that they did not owe their existence merely to the King's pleasure.

> Our representatives, aggreably to the general sense of their constituents [wrote New York lawyer William Smith in the 1750's] are tenacious in their opinion, that the inhabitants of this colony are entitled to all the privileges of Englishmen; that they have a right to participate in the legislative power, and that the session of assemblies here, is wisely substituted instead of a representation in parliament, which, all things considered, would, at this remote distance, be extremely inconvenient and dangerous.[24]

The logical corollary to this argument was that the lower houses were equivalents of the House of Commons and must perforce in their limited spheres be entitled to all the privileges possessed by that body in Great Britain. Hence, in cases where an invocation of fundamental rights was not appropriate, the lower houses frequently defended their actions on the grounds that they were agreeable to the practice of the House of Commons. Thus in 1755 the North Carolina Lower House denied the right of the Council to amend tax bills on the grounds that it was "contrary to Custom and Usage of Parliament."[25] Unintentionally, Crown officials encouraged the lower houses to make this analogy by forbidding them in the instructions to exercise "any power or privilege whatsoever which is not allowed by us to the House of Commons . . . in Great Britain."[26]

Because neither fundamental rights nor imperial precedents could be used to defend practices that were contrary to customs of the mother country or to the British constitution, the lower houses found it necessary to develop still another argument: that local precedents, habits, traditions, and statutes were important parts of their particular constitutions and could not be abridged by a royal or proprietary order. The assumptions were that the legislatures could alter colonial constitutions by their own actions without the active consent of imperial officials and that once the alterations were confirmed by usage they could not be counter-manded by the British government. They did not deny the power of the governor to veto or of the Privy Council to disallow their laws but argued that imperial acquiescence over a long period of time was tantamount to consent and that precedents thus established could not be undone without their approval. The implication was that the American colonists saw their constitutions as living, growing, and constantly changing organisms, a theory which was directly opposite to the imperial view. To be sure, precedent had always been an important element in shaping the British constitution, but Crown officials were unwilling to concede that it was equally so in determining the fundamental law of the colonies. They willingly granted that colonial statutes, once formally approved by the Privy Council, automatically became part of the constitutions of the colonies, but they officially took the position that both royal instructions and commissions, as well as constitutional traditions of the mother country, took precedence over local practice or unconfirmed statutes.[27] This conflict of views persisted throughout the period after 1689, becoming more and more of an issue in the decades immediately preceding the American Revolution.

In the last analysis it was the imperial denial of the validity of the constitu-tional defenses of the lower houses that drove colonial lawmakers to seek to extend the power of the lower houses at the very time they were insisting—and, in fact, deeply believed—that no one individual or institution should have a superiority of power in any government. No matter what kind of workable balance of power might be attained within the colonies, there was always the possibility that the home government might unleash the unlimited might of the parent state against the colonies. The chief fear of colonial legislators, then, was not the power of the governors, which they could control, but that of the imperial government, which in the circumstances they could never hope to control, and the whole movement for legislative authority in the colonies can be interpreted as a search for a viable constitutional arrangement in which the rights of the colonists would be secured against the preponderant power of the mother country. The failure of imperial authorities to provide such an arrangement or even to formalize what small con-cessions they did make, meant, of course, that the search could never be fulfilled, and the resulting anxiety, only partly conscious and finding expression through the classic arguments and ringing phrases of English political struggles of the seventeenth century, impelled the lower houses and the men who composed them relentlessly through the colonial period and was perhaps the most important single factor in the demand of patriot leaders for explicit, written constitutions after the Declaration of Independence.

It is nonetheless true that, if imperial authorities did not grant the validity of the theoretical arguments of the lower houses, neither did they make any systematic or concerted effort to force a rigid compliance with official policies for most of the period after 1689. Repressive measures, at least before 1763, rarely went beyond the occasional disallowance of an offending statute or the official reprimand of a rambunctious lower house. General lack of interest in the routine business of colonial affairs and failure to recognize the potential seriousness of the situation may in part account for this leniency, but it is also true that official policy under both Walpole and the Pelhams called for a light rein on the colonies on the assumption that contented colonies created fewer problems for the adminis-tration. "One would not Strain any point," Charles Delafaye, secretary to the lords justices, cautioned South Carolina's Governor Francis Nicholson in 1722, "where it can be of no Service to our King or Country." "In the Plantations," he added, "the Government should be as Easy and Mild as possible to invite people to Settle under it."[28] Three times between 1734 and 1749 the ministry failed to give enthusiastic support to measures introduced into Parliament to insure the supremacy of instructions over colonial laws.[29] Though the Calverts were somewhat more insistent upon preserving their proprietary prerogatives, in general the proprietors were equally lax as long as there was no encroachment upon their land rights or proprietary dues.

Imperial organs of administration were in fact inadquate to deal effectively with all the problems of the empire. Since no special governmental bodies were created in England to deal exclusively with colonial affairs, they were handled through the regular machinery of government—a maze of boards and officials whose main interests and responsibilities were not the supervision of overseas colonies. The only body sufficiently informed and interested to deal competently with colonial matters was the Board of Trade, and it had little authority, except for the brief period from 1748 to 1761 under the presidency of George Dunk, Earl of Halifax. The most useful device for restraining the lower houses was the Privy Council's right to review colonial laws, but even that was only partly effective, because the mass of colonial statutes annually coming before the Board of Trade made a thorough scrutiny impossible. Under such arrangements no vigorous colonial policy was likely. The combination of imperial lethargy and colonial aggression virtually guaranteed the success of the lower houses' quest for power. An indication of a growing awareness in imperial circles of the seriousness of the situation was Halifax's spirited, if piecemeal, effort to restrain the growth of the lower houses in the early 1750's. Symptomatic of these efforts was the attempt to make Georgia and Nova Scotia model royal colonies at the institution of royal government by writing into the instructions to their governors provisions designed to insure the continued supremacy of the executive and to prevent the lower houses from going the way of their counterparts in the older colonies. However, the outbreak of the Seven Years' War forced Halifax to suspend his activities and prevented any further reformation until the cessation of hostilities.

Indeed, the war saw a drastic acceleration in the lower houses' bid for authority, and its conclusion found them in possession of many of the powers held less than a century before by the executive. In the realm of finance they had imposed their authority over every phase of raising the distributing public revenue. They had acquired a large measure of independence by winning control over their compositions and proceedings and obtaining guarantees of basic English Parliamentary privileges. Finally, they had pushed their power even beyond that of the English House of Commons by gaining extensive authority in handling executive affairs, including the right to appoint executive officers and to share in formulating executive policy. These specific gains were symptoms of developments of much greater significance. To begin with, they were symbolic of a fundamental shift of the constitutional center of power in the colonies from the executive to the elected branch of the legislature. With the exception of the Georgia and Nova Scotia bodies, both of which had less than a decade of political experience behind them, the houses had by 1763 succeeded in attaining a new status, raising themselves from dependent lawmaking bodies to the center of political authority in their respective colonies.

But the lower houses had done more than simply acquire a new status in colonial politics. They had in a sense altered the structure of the constitution of the British Empire itself by asserting colonial authority against imperial authority and extending the constitutions of the colonies far beyond the limitations of the charters, instructions, or fixed notions of imperial authorities. The time was ripe for a re-examination and redefinition of the constitutional position of the lower houses. With the rapid economic and territorial expansion of the colonies in the years before 1763 had come a corresponding rise in the responsibilities and prestige of the lower houses and a growing awareness among colonial representatives of their own importance, which had served to strengthen their long-standing, if still imperfectly defined, impression that colonial lower houses were the American counterparts of the British House of Commons. Under the proper stimuli, they would carry this impression to its logical conclusion: that the lower houses enjoyed an equal status under the Crown with Parliament. Here, then, well beyond the embryonic stage, was the theory of colonial equality with the mother country, one of the basic constitutional principles of the American Revolution, waiting to be nourished by the series of crises that beset imperial-colonial relations between 1763 and 1776.

The psychological implications of this new political order were profound. By the 1750's the phenomenal success of the lower houses had generated a soaring self-confidence, a willingness to take on all comers. Called upon to operate on a larger stage during the Seven Years' War, they emerged from that conflict with an increased awareness of their own importance and a growing consciousness of the implications of their activities. Symptomatic of these developments was the spate of bitter controversies that characterized colonial politics during and immediately after the war. The Gadsden election controversy in South Carolina, the dispute over judicial tenure in New York, and the contests over the pistole fee and the two-penny act in Virginia gave abundant evidence of both the lower houses' stubborn determination to preserve their authority and the failure of Crown officials in London and the colonies to gauge accurately their temper or to accept the fact that they had made important changes in the constitutions of the colonies.

With the shift of power to the lower houses also came the development in each colony of an extraordinarily able group of politicians. The lower houses provided excellent training for the leaders of the rapidly maturing colonial societies, and the recurring controversies prepared them for the problems they would be called upon to meet in the dramatic conflicts after 1763. In the decades before Independence there appeared in the colonial statehouses John and Samuel Adams and James Otis in Massachusetts Bay; William Livingston in New York; Benjamin Franklin and John Dickinson in Pennsylvania; Daniel Dulany the younger in Maryland; Richard Bland, Richard Henry Lee, Thomas Jefferson, and Patrick Henry in Virginia; and Christopher Gadsden and John Rutledge in South Carolina. Along with dozens of others, these men guided their colonies through the debate with Britain, assumed direction of the new state governments after 1776, and played conspicuous roles on the national stage as members of the Continental Congress, the Confederation, and, after 1787, the new federal government. By the 1760's, then, almost every colony had an imposing group of native politicians thoroughly schooled in the political arts and primed to meet any challenge to the power and prestige of the lower houses.

Britain's "new colonial policy" after 1763 provided just such a challenge. It precipitated a constitutional crisis in the empire, creating new tensions and setting in motion forces different from those that had shaped earlier developments. The new policy was based upon concepts both unfamiliar and unwelcome to the colonists such as centralization, uniformity, and orderly development. Yet it was a logical culmination of earlier trends and, for the most part, an effort to realize old aspirations. From Edward Randolph in the last decades of the seventeenth century to the Earl of Halifax in the 1750's colonial officials had envisioned a highly centralized empire with a uniform political system in each of the colonies and with the imperial government closely supervising the subordinate governments.[30] But, because they had never made any sustained or systematic attempt to achieve these goals, there had developed during the first half of the eighteenth century a working arrangement permitting the lower houses considerable latitude in shaping colonial constitutions without requiring crown and proprietary officials to give up any of their ideals. That there had been a growing divergence between imperial theory and colonial practice mattered little so long as each refrained from challenging the other. But the new policy threatened to upset this arrangement by implementing the old ideals long after the conditions that produced them had ceased to exist. Aimed at bringing the colonies more closely under imperial control, this policy inevitably sought to curtail the influence of the lower houses, directly challenging many of the powers they had acquired over the previous century. To American legislators accustomed to the lenient policies of Walpole and the Pelhams and impressed with the rising power of their own lower houses, the new program seemed a radical departure from precedent, a frontal assault upon the several constitutions they had been forging over the previous century. To protect gains they had already made and to make good their pretensions to greater political significance, the lower houses thereafter no longer had merely to deal with weak governors or casual imperial administrators; they now faced an aggressive group of officials bent upon using every means at their disposal, including the legislative authority of Parliament, to gain their ends.

Beginning in 1763 one imperial action after another seemed to threaten the position of the lower houses. Between 1764 and 1766 Parliament's attempt to tax the colonists for revenue directly challenged the colonial legislatures' exclusive power to tax, the cornerstone of their authority in America. A variety of other measures, some aimed at particular colonial legislatures and others at general legislative powers and practices, posed serious threats to powers that the lower houses had either long enjoyed or were trying to attain. To meet these challenges, the lower houses had to spell out the implications of the changes they had been making, consciously or not, in the structures of their respective governments. That is, for the first time they had to make clear in their own minds and then to verbalize what they conceived their respective constitutions in fact were or should be. In the process, the spokesmen of the lower houses laid bare the wide gulf between imperial theory and colonial practice. During the Stamp Act crisis in 1764–1766 the lower houses claimed the same authority over taxation in the colonies as Parliament had over that matter in England, and a few of them even asserted an equal right in matters of internal policy.[31] Although justified by the realities of the colonial situation, such a definition of the lower houses' constitutional position within the empire was at marked variance with imperial ideals and only served to increase the determination of the home government to take a stricter tone. This determination was manifested after the repeal of the Stamp Act by Parliament's claim in the Declaratory Act of 1766 to "full power and authority" over the colonies "in all cases whatsoever."[32]

The pattern over the next decade was on the part of the home government one of increasing resolution to deal firmly with the colonies and on the part of

American lawmakers a heightened consciousness of the implications of the constitutional issue and a continuously rising level of expectation. In addition to their insistence upon the right of Parliament to raise revenue in the colonies, imperial officials also applied, in a way that was increasingly irksome to American legislators, traditional instruments of royal control like restrictive instructions, legislative review, the governors' power to dissolve the lower houses and the suspending clause requiring prior approval of the Crown before laws of an "extraordinary nature" could go into effect. Finally Parliament threatened the very existence of the lower houses by a measure suspending the New York Assembly for refusing to comply with the Quartering Act in 1767 and by another altering the substance of the Massachusetts constitution in the Massachusetts Government Act in 1774. In the process of articulating and defending their constitutional position, the lower houses acquired aspirations well beyond any they had had in the years before 1763. American representatives became convinced in the decade after 1766 not only that they knew best what to do for their constituents and the colonies and that anything interfering with their freedom to adopt whatever course seemed necessary was an intolerable and unconstitutional restraint but also that the only security for their political fortunes was in the abandonment of their attempts to restrict and define Parliamentary authority in America and instead to deny Parliament's jurisdiction over them entirely by asserting their equality with Parliament under the Crown. Suggested by Richard Bland as early as 1766, such a position was openly advocated by James Wilson and Thomas Jefferson in 1774 and was officially adopted by the First Continental Congress when it claimed for Americans in its declarations and resolves "a free and exclusive power of legislation in their several provincial legislatures, where their right of representation can alone be preserved, in all cases of taxation and internal polity."[33]

Parliament could not accept this claim without giving up the principles it had asserted in the Declaratory Act and, in effect, abandoning the traditional British theory of empire and accepting the colonial constitutional position instead. The First Continental Congress professed that a return to the *status quo* of 1763 would satisfy the colonies, but Parliament in 1774–1776 was unwilling even to go that far, much less to promise them exemption from Parliamentary taxation. Besides, American legislators now aspired to much more. James Chalmers, Maryland planter and later loyalist who was out of sympathy with the proceedings of American patriots between 1774 and 1776, correctly charged that American leaders had "been constantly enlarging their views, and stretching them beyond their first bounds, till at length they have wholly changed their ground."[34] Edward Rutledge, young delegate from South Carolina to the First Continental Congress, was one who recognized that the colonies would not "be satisfied with a restoration of such rights only, as have been violated since the year '63, when we have as many others, as clear and indisputable, that will even then be infringed."[35] The simple fact was that American political leaders, no matter what their professions, would not have been content to return to the old inarticulated and ambiguous pattern of accommodation between imperial theory and colonial practice that had existed through most of the period between 1689 and 1763. They now sought to become masters of their own political fortunes. Rigid guarantees of colonial rights and precise definitions of the constitutional relationship between the mother country and the colonies and between Parliament and the lower houses on American terms—that is, imperial recognition of the autonomy of the lower houses in local affairs and of the equality of the colonies with the mother country—would have been required to satisfy them.

No analysis of the charges in the Declaration of Independence can fail to suggest that the preservation and consolidation of the rights and powers of the lower houses were central in the struggle with Britain from 1763 to 1776, just as they had been the most important issue in the political relationship between Britain and the colonies over the previous century and a half. Between 1689 and 1763 the lower houses' contests with royal governors and imperial officials had brought them political maturity, a considerable measure of control over local affairs, capable leaders, and a rationale to support their pretensions to political power within the colonies and in the Empire. The British challenge after 1763 threatened to render their accomplishments meaningless and drove them to demand equal rights with Parliament and autonomy in local affairs and eventually to declare their independence. At issue was the whole political structure forged by the lower houses over the previous century. In this context the American Revolution becomes in form, if not in essence, a war for political survival, a conflict involving not only individual rights as traditionally emphasized by historians of the event but assembly rights as well.

NOTES

1. George Chalmers, *An Introduction to the History of the Revolt of the American Colonies* (2 vols., Boston, 1845), I, 223–26, and II, 226–28, particularly, for statements of Chalmers' position.

2. George Bancroft, *History of the United States* (14th ed., 10 vols., Boston, 1854–1875), III, I–108, 383–98, particularly.

3. Herbert L. Osgood, *The American Colonies in the Seventeenth Century* (3 vols., New York, 1904–1907) and *The American Colonies in the Eighteenth Century* (4 vols., New York, 1924–1925). For Edward Channing's treatment see *A History of the United States* (6 vols., New York, 1905–1925), II. Representative of the studies of Osgood's students are William R. Shepherd, *History of Proprietary Government in Pennsylvania* (New York, 1896); Newton D. Mereness, *Maryland As a Proprietary Province* (New York, 1901); W. Roy Smith, *South Carolina As a Royal Province, 1719–1776* (New York, 1903); Charles L. Raper, *North Carolina: A Study in English Colonial Government* (New York, 1904); William H. Fry, *New Hampshire As a Royal Province* (New York, 1908); Edwin P. Tanner, *The Province of New Jersey, 1664–1738* (New York, 1908); Edgar J. Fisher, *New Jersey As a Royal Province, 1738–1776* (New York, 1911); and Percy S. Flippin, *The Royal Government in Virginia, 1624–1775* (New York, 1919).

4. Leonard W. Labaree, *Royal Government in America* (New Haven, 1930), 172–311, particularly. Two other illuminating studies by Labaree's contemporaries are A. B. Keith, *Constitutional History of the First British Empire* (Oxford, 1930), which is legalistic in emphasis, and John F. Burns, *Controversies Between Royal Governors and Their Assemblies in the Northern American Colonies* (Boston, 1923), which fails to tie together in any satisfactory way developments in the four colonies it treats.

5. Charles M. Andrews, "On the Writing of Colonial History," *William and Mary Quarterly*, 3rd ser., I (January, 1944), 29–42. The line of interpretation that Andrews would probably have followed is briefly developed in his brilliant *The Colonial Background of the American Revolution* (New York, 1924), 3–65.

6. Developments in Pennsylvania may be traced in Shepherd, *Proprietary Government, op. cit.;* Benjamin Franklin, *A Historical Review of Pennsylvania* (London, 1759); Roy N. Lokken, *David Lloyd: Colonial Lawmaker* (Seattle, 1959); Sister Joan de Lourdes Leonard, *The Organization and Procedure of the Pennsylvania Assembly, 1682–1772* (Philadelphia, 1949); Winifred T. Root, *The Relation of Pennsylvania with the British Government, 1696–1765* (Philadelphia, 1912); and Theodore Thayer, *Pennsylvania Politics and the Growth of Democracy, 1740–1776* (Harrisburg, Pa., 1953). On Rhode Island and Connecticut see David S. Lovejoy, *Rhode Island Politics and the American Revolution, 1760–1776* (Providence, 1958), and Oscar Zeichner, *Connecticut's Years of Controversy, 1754–1775* (Chapel Hill, N.C., 1949).

7. Useful studies on Massachusetts are Robert E. Brown, *Middle-Class Democracy and the Revolution in Massachusetts, 1691–1780* (Ithaca, N.Y., 1955); Martin L. Cole, The Rise of the Legislative Assembly in Provincial Massachusetts (unpublished Ph.D. thesis, State University of Iowa, 1939); Thomas Hutchinson, *The History of the Colony and Province of Massachusetts-Bay*, Lawrence S. Mayo, ed. (3 vols., Cambridge, Mass., 1936); and Henry R. Spencer, *Constitutional Conflict in Provincial Massachusetts* (Columbus, O., 1905).

8. The best published study on South Carolina is Smith, *South Carolina As a Royal Province*. Also useful are David D. Wallace, *The Life of Henry Laurens* (New York, 1915); Jack P. Greene, The Quest for Power of the Lower Houses of Assembly in the Southern Royal Colonies, 1730–1763 (unpublished Ph.D. thesis, Duke University, 1956); and M. Eugene Sirmans, "The South Carolina Royal Council, 1720–1763," *William and Mary Quarterly,* 3rd ser., XVIII (July, 1961), 373–92.

9. Developments in New York can be followed in Carl L. Becker, *The History of Political Parties in the Province of New York, 1760–1776* (Madison, 1909); Milton M. Klein, "Democracy and Politics in Colonial New York," *New York History,* XL (July 1959), 221–46; Lawrence H. Leder, *Robert Livingston, 1654–1728, and the Politics of Colonial New York* (Chapel Hill, N.C., 1961); Beverly McAnear, Politics in Provincial New York, 1689–1761 (unpublished Ph.D. thesis, Stanford University, 1935); Irving Mark, *Agrarian Conflicts in Colonial New York, 1711–1775* (New York, 1940); William Smith, *The History of the Late Province of New York* (2 vols., New York, 1829); and Charles W. Spencer, *Phases of Royal Government in New York, 1691–1719* (Columbus, O., 1905).

10. Useful analyses of North Carolina are Raper, *North Carolina, op. cit.,* and Desmond Clarke, *Arthur Dobbs Esquire, 1689–1765* (Chapel Hill, N.C., 1957).

11. New Jersey developments can be traced in Donald L. Kemmerer's excellent study, *Path to Freedom: The Struggle for Self-Government in Colonial New Jersey, 1703–1776* (Princeton, 1940).

12. Among the more useful secondary works on Virginia are Flippin, *Royal Government, op. cit.;* Bernard Bailyn, "Politics and Social Structure in Virginia," in James M. Smith, ed., *Seventeenth-Century America: Essays on Colonial History* (Chapel Hill, N.C., 1959), 90–115; Lucille Blanche Griffith, The Virginia House of Burgesses, 1750–1774 (unpublished Ph.D. thesis, Brown University, 1957); Ray Orvin Hummel, Jr., The Virginia House of Burgesses, 1689–1750 (unpublished Ph.D. thesis, University of Nebraska, 1934); David J. Mays, *Edmund Pendleton, 1721–1803* (2 vols., Cambridge, Mass., 1952); Charles S. Sydnor, *Gentlemen Freeholders: Political Practices in Washington's Virginia* (Chapel Hill, N.C., 1952); Thomas J. Wertenbaker, *Give Me Liberty: The Struggle for Self-Government in Virginia* (Philadelphia, 1958); and David Alan Williams, Political Alignments in Colonial Virginia, 1698–1750 (unpublished Ph.D. thesis, Northwestern University, 1959).

13. On Maryland see two excellent studies, Charles A. Barker, *The Background of the Revolution in Maryland* (New Haven, 1940), and Aubrey Land, *The Dulanys of Maryland* (Baltimore, 1955).

14. New Hampshire developments can be followed in Fry, *New Hampshire, op. cit.,* and Jeremy Belknap, *History of New Hampshire* (3 vols., Boston, 1791–1792).

15. On Georgia see W. W. Abbott, *The Royal Governors of Georgia, 1754–1775* (Chapel Hill, N.C., 1959), and Albert B. Saye, *New Viewpoints in Georgia History* (Atlanta, 1943). John Bartlett Brebner, *The Neutral Yankees of Nova Scotia* (New York, 1937), is the best study of developments in that colony.

16. On this point see Abbot, *ibid.,* and Brebner, *ibid.*

17. "Fauquier to Board of Trade," June 2, 1760, in Colonial Office Papers (London, Public Record Office), Series 5/1330, folios 37–39.

18. The details of these disputes can be traced in Smith, *History of New York, op. cit.,* II, 68–151; Hutchinson, *History of Massachusetts Bay, op. cit.,* 163–280; Labaree, *Royal Government,* 180–185; Lawrence F. London, "The Representation Controversy in Colonial North Carolina," *North Carolina Historical Review,* XI (October, 1934), 255–270; Jack P. Greene, ed., "The Case of the Pistole Fee," *Virginia Magazine of History and Biography,* LXVI (October, 1958), 399–422, and "The Gadsden Election Controversy and the Revolutionary Movement in South Carolina," *Mississippi Valley Historical Review,* XLVI (December, 1959), 469–492.

19. Sir William Keith, "A Short Discourse on the Present State of the Colonies in America with Respect to the Interest of Great Britain," 1729, in Colonial Office Papers (London, Public Record Office), Series 5/4, folios 170–171.

20. *South Carolina Gazette,* May 13, 1756.

21. For instance, see the provision in the Maryland charter conveniently published in Merrill Jensen, ed., *English Historical Documents: American Colonial Documents to 1776* (New York, 1955), 88.

22. James H. Easterby and Ruth S. Green, eds., *The Colonial Records of South Carolina: The Journals of the Commons House of Assembly* (8 vols., Columbia, 1951–1961), *1736–1739* (June 5, 1739), 720.

23. This view was implicit in most thinking and writing about the colonies by imperial authorities. For the attitude of John Carteret, Lord Granville, an important figure in colonial affairs through the middle decades of the eighteenth century, see Benjamin Franklin to Isaac Norris, March 19, 1759, as quoted by William S. Mason, "Franklin and Galloway: Some Unpublished Letters," American Antiquarian Society, *Proceedings,* n.s., XXXIV (1925), 245–46. Other examples are Jack P. Greene, ed., "Martin Bladen's Blueprint for a Colonial Union," *William and Mary Quarterly,* 3rd ser., XVII

(October, 1960), 516–530, by a prominent member of the Board of Trade, and Archibald Kennedy, *An Essay on the Government of the Colonies* (New York, 1752), 17–18, by an official in the colonies.

24. Smith, *op. cit.*, I, 307.

25. Journals of the Lower House, January 4–6, 1755, William L. Saunders, ed., *The Colonial Records of North Carolina* (10 vols., Raleigh, 1886–1890), V, 287.

26. Leonard W. Labaree, ed., *Royal Instructions to British Colonial Governors, 1670–1776* (2 vols., New York, 1935), I, 112–113.

27. For a classic statement of the imperial argument by a modern scholar see Lawrence H. Gipson, *The British Empire Before the American Revolution* (10 vols., Caldwell, Idaho, and New York, 1936–1961), III (rev.), 275–281.

28. Delafaye to Nicholson, January 22, 1722, in Papers Concerning the Governorship of South Carolina (Houghton Library, Harvard University, Cambridge, Mass.), bMs Am 1455, Item 9.

29. For a discussion of these measures see Bernard Knollenberg, *Origin of the American Revolution, 1759–1766* (New York, 1960), 49.

30. On this point see Charles M. Andrews, *The Colonial Period of American History* (4 vols., New Haven, 1934–1938), IV, 368–425; Michael Garibaldi Hall, *Edward Randolph and the American Colonies, 1676–1703* (Chapel Hill, N.C., 1960); Arthur H. Basye, *Lords Commissioners of Trade and Plantations, 1748–1782* (New Haven, 1925); and Dora Mae Clark, *The Rise of the British Treasury: Colonial Administration in the Eighteenth Century* (New Haven, 1960).

31. See the sweeping claim of the Virginia House of Burgesses to the "Inestimable Right of being governed by such Laws respecting their internal Polity and Taxatior as are devised from their own Consent" in objecting to Grenville's proposed stamp duties. Henry R. McIlwaine and John P. Kennedy (eds.), *Journals of the House of Burgesses in Virginia* (13 vols., Richmond, 1905–1913), *1761–1765*, 302–304 (December 18, 1764). The protests of all the lower houses against the Stamp Act are conveniently collected in Edmund S. Morgan, ed., *Prologue to Revolution: Sources and Documents on the Stamp Act Crisis, 1764–1766* (Chapel Hill, N.C., 1959), 8–17, 46–69.

32. Danby Pickering, ed., *The Statutes at Large from Magna Carta to the End of the Eleventh Parliament of Great Britain, Anno 1761, Continued to 1806* (46 vols., Cambridge, Eng., 1762–1807), XXVII, 19–20.

33. Worthington C. Ford and others, eds., *Journals of the Continental Congress* (34 vols., Washington, 1904–1937), I, 68–69 (October 14, 1774).

34. Candidus [James Chalmers], *Plain Truth: Addressed to the Inhabitants of America* (London, 1776), 46.

35. Rutledge to Ralph Izard, Jr., October 29, 1774, in A. I. Deas, ed., *Correspondence of Mr. Ralph Izard of South Carolina* (New York, 1844), 22–23.

22. The Whig Science of Politics

Gordon S. Wood

Dynamic political development in the face of static home government images may have been a vital reason for the broadened powers of the lower houses of assemblies. According to Gordon S. Wood (b. 1933) of the Brown University history faculty, however, provincial Americans did not necessarily conceptualize politics in those terms. Rather other words and phrases, such as "balanced government," "liberty," "power," "corruption," and "tyranny" were much more important in energizing perceptions of political reality. English Whig opposition writing, or radical Whiggism, continually juxtaposed the individual lust for power with the need to preserve civil liberty; and opposition writers worried incessantly about whether the balanced structure of British government, the glory of the unwritten English constitution, could contain aggrandizing, power-hungry members of the king's party.

Professor Wood and others, such as Bernard Bailyn of Harvard University, have argued that provincial Americans not only imbibed radical Whiggism but also, as a result, came to perceive a conspiracy emanating from certain quarters in England to destroy American liberties, that is the right of the people to hold power and have their interests represented and protected through government. Not only that, Wood and others have pointed to evidence which suggests that prerevolutionary colonists viewed themselves as having a unique calling. In challenging the conspiracy they were performing a special mission for the Western world, similar in form (but not necessarily in content) to the early Puritans' belief in an urgent errand. What was that unique assignment? Is it not possible that the same sense of special duty and destiny could have arisen out of the prerogative tradition? Indeed, what are the possible relationships between these two strains of thought? Can the two be reconciled, allowing for a broader ideological explanation of political confrontation and change?

The author also notes that opposition writers of the era worried constantly about the peoples' general passiveness in politics. If such observations were at all accurate, then how can we be sure that the bulk of prerevolutionary Americans were uniformly reading opposition political literature, becoming active in

Source: From Gordon S. Wood, *The Creation of the American Republic, 1776-1787* (Chapel Hill: University of North Carolina Press, 1969), pp. 10–11, 13–43. Footnotes omitted. Reprinted by permission of the University of North Carolina Press and the Institute of Early American History and Culture.

politics, and reacting with stridency to a sense of ministerial conspiracy? Has Wood captured the popular mind, or only that of well-educated elite leaders?

THE ENGLISH CONSTITUTION

If any era of modern times found its political ideals incorporated in a particular national institution, it was the eighteenth century. For the Age of Enlightenment was also the classic age of the English constitution. Perhaps never before and surely never since has any single nation's constitution so dominated Western man's theorizing about politics. The Glorious Revolution of 1688, said John Toland, the late seventeenth-century editor of Harrington, had "settl'd the Monarchy for the future . . . under such wise Regulations as are most likely to continue it forever." By the beginning of the eighteenth century the English government was obviously "the most free and best constituted in all the world." By balancing within the confines of Parliament the ancient contending interests of English society and by mixing within a single government the several categories of politics that had been known to the Western world for centuries, the English, it seemed, had concretely achieved what political philosophers from antiquity on had only dreamed of. In the minds of the English colonists, indeed of the enlightened everywhere in the eighteenth century, the English constitution—"this beautiful system," as Montesquieu called it—seemed to possess no national or cultural limitations. It had "its foundation in nature," said Samuel Adams; its principles were from God and were universal, capable of application by all peoples who had the ability to sustain them. It was, declared one American in 1759, "the best model of Government that can be framed by Mortals." For the Americans the English constitution was always "the glorious fabrick of Britain's liberty," "the palladium of civil liberty . . . that firm foundation of the nation's peace," "the monument of accumulated wisdom, and the admiration of the world." Every day for fifty years, wrote John Adams in 1761, men had boasted that the English constitution was the finest under heaven. "No Government that ever existed, was so essentially free." Even members of the Stamp Act Congress gloried in "having been born under the most perfect form of government.". . .

The colonists were hardly aware that they were seeing the English constitution and their heritage differently from other Englishmen. To judge from their broad and varied references to English writers, they seemed to be reading the same literature, the same law books, the same histories as those being read by Englishmen in the mother country. They cited and borrowed promiscuously from almost every conceivable English writer—from Locke, Blackstone, Addison, Swift, Hale, Hume, and James Thompson, from everyone and anyone a good Englishman might read. Yet amidst their breadth of reading and references was a certain engagement of interest, a certain concentration on a particular strain of attitudes and ideas, that more than anything else ultimately implicated the Americans in a peculiar conception of English history and English life and in an extraordinarily radical perspective on the English constitution they were so fervently defending.

It is only now becoming clear how selective the colonists were in their use of British literature and how much they focused on those writings which expressed what may be termed an Opposition view of English politics. Since the full depth and extent of this Opposition thinking remains still unexplored, it is difficult to characterize precisely. Beneath the apparent complacency and stability of the age of Walpole were deep currents of dissatisfaction, both urban and rural, that eventually found political expression in the Wilkesite and county association movements in the 1760's and 1770's. Although the Opposition criticism inevitably tended to be Whiggish, many of the critics were not Whigs at all but old-fashioned Tories voicing in common terms with Whig radicals their alienation from a corrupted England. And while the tone of the dissatisfaction was generally and fervently nonconformist, some of its most articulate spokesmen were Anglicans. Indeed, so transcendent of traditional eighteenth-century political categories was this Opposition thought that it has been suggested that the eighteenth-century English political mind can be best understood in terms of a country-court division—an old seventeenth-century categorization which perhaps sums up as well as any other dichotomy the hostility of those who felt estranged from the established centers of power. At the heart of the country outlook was an independent view of politics, a widely shared conception about the way English public life should be organized—where the parts of the constitution were independent of one another, where the Commons were independent of the Crown, where members of Parliament were independent of any connection or party, in short, the kind of society where no man was beholden to another.

While this Opposition thinking can be broadly conceived, ranging from Bolingbroke to Burke, the expressions of it the Americans found most attractive, most relevant to their situation and needs, were precisely those with the least respectability and force in England—those expressions of radical intellectuals writing to the left of the official Whig line. The radicalism of the Real Whigs, as the most self-conscious of these early eighteenth-century writers called themselves, or Commonwealthmen, as they have recently been called, came not from the concrete proposals they offered for the reformation of English politics. For most of these proposals—prohibitions on placement in the House of Commons, attacks on the increasing debt and the representational system, and recommendations for shorter Parliaments and the right of constituents to instruct their representatives—were the stock reforms of Opposition politicians during the eighteenth century. The revolutionary character of these radical Whigs came more fundamentally from their fierce and total unwillingness to accept the developments of the eighteenth century. They were reacting against the maturation of the empire, with all that this meant in the use of money and bureaucracy in the running of government. They offered their fellow Englishmen a strident and impassioned critique of their society and politics, all set within a comprehensive understanding of centuries of English history and the ancient constitution, and grounded in the political and social ideals of the liberal writings of the previous century, especially those of the classical republicans—Harrington, Milton, and Sidney. For three generations—from John Trenchard and Thomas Gordon, through Thomas Hollis and Richard Baron, to Richard Price and James Burgh—the English radicals preserved and transmitted these ideals amidst a society which increasingly seemed to be paying only lip service to them. Yet whatever the intensity and stridency with which the radicals voiced their criticism, their thought was never developed systematically, and it easily blended into widely held opinions about the nature of English history and government. In fact, their thought never transcended the common political and social assumptions of the day.

However unrespected and unheeded this heritage of dissident thought was in England itself, it was eagerly received in the colonies across the Atlantic. The Americans too felt themselves alienated from the official world of cosmopolitan London; they too sensed beneath the apparent similarities the world of differences that separated them from established England. As American society had gradually and almost imperceptibly deviated in a century's time from the norms of English social and political life, pressures had been built up, intensified, and focused by the overlying imperial system. This remotely rooted and often arbitrary legal structure only further complicated the lines of authority in a society whose sanctions for political and social superiority were already inherently tenuous. With such a precariously maintained social hierarchy, sensitive to the slightest disturbance, politics necessarily had become an extraordinarily ticklish business; and almost all of the colonies had been continually racked by a bitter and kaleidoscopic factionalism. Since every political move, however small, was believed to have enormous repercussions, the most minor incidents had erupted into major constitutional questions involving the basic liberties of the people. Every accumulation of political power, however tiny and piecemeal, was seen as frighteningly tyrannical, viewed as some sinister plot to upset the delicately maintained relationships of power and esteem. Jealousy and suspicion, concluded Charles Carroll of Maryland in 1773, had become the very basis of American politics.

In such an atmosphere the ideas of radical Whiggism with their heightened language of intense liberalism and paranoiac mistrust of power were found to be a particularly meaningful way of expressing the anxieties Americans felt. Every point of strain, whether it was the clashing of religious groups, or a royal governor's indictment of a colonial printer, had called forth a new articulation of radical beliefs. Throughout the eighteenth century the Americans had published, republished, read, cited, and even plagiarized these radical writings in their search for arguments to counter royal authority, to explain American deviations, or to justify peculiar American freedoms. But, as in the case of Jonathan Mayhew's blatant borrowing from Bishop Hoadly, there could be no sense of shame or need for apology. What the Whig radicals were saying about English government and society had so long been a part of the American mind, had so often been reinforced by their own first-hand observations of London life, and had possessed such an affinity to their own provincial interests and experience that it always seemed to the colonists to be what they had been trying to say all along.

More than any other source this disaffected Whig thought fused and focused the elements that shaped the colonists' conception of the English constitution and English politics. In the years after 1763 when the need for explanation and understanding assumed a new and vital importance, the Americans could only marvel at the "many things much to the present purpose" offered by this Whig literature, which in those eventful years seemed to "look almost like prophecy." By drawing on the evidence of antiquity and their own English past as transmitted to them through the radical Whig tradition the colonists sought to formulate a science of politics and of history that would explain what was happening to England and to themselves—an explanation that when joined with a complicated medley of notions taken from Enlightenment rationalism and New England covenant theology possessed revolutionary implications.

POWER AGAINST LIBERTY

The theory of government that the Americans clarified in their reading and discussion possessed a compelling simplicity: politics was nothing more than a perpetual battle between the passions of the rulers, whether one or a few, and the united interest of the people—an opposition that was both inevitable and proportional. "Whatever is good for the People," Thomas Gordon had written, "is bad for their Governors; and what is good for the Governors, is pernicious to the People." This notion of political dualism between rulers and ruled, characteristic of all Western political theories except those during the heyday of nineteenth-century democratic idealism, was at the bottom of the Whigs' beliefs: their conception of a mutual contract, their understanding of allegiance and protection, their notion of a dichotomy between power and liberty, tyranny and licentiousness, their idea of governmental balance, and their theory of revolution.

Englishmen, like most men in the eighteenth century, continued to cling to a medieval conception of society, divided into estates or orders, with the people constituting a single unitary estate alongside the nobility and the Crown. There was as yet little clear understanding of classes or status groups in the modern sense. The aristocracy were of course rigidly separated from the people; their distinction, however, was not one so much of wealth or even of social outlook as it was one of legal and political privilege. The people were generally assumed to be a homogeneous entity, undeniably composed of an infinite number of gradations and ranks, but still an entity whose interests were considered to be connected and for the purposes of politics basically similar.

Each estate possessed certain rights and privileges recognized in law and by custom, the Crown with its prerogatives, however limited by the settlement of 1689, still having the major responsibility for governing the realm. Indeed, the eighteenth century's discussion of politics can only be understood in the context of this ancient notion of the Crown's prerogatives, the bundle of rights and powers adhering in the King's authority to rule, set against the rights and liberties of the people, or the ruled, represented in the House of Commons. As long as the idea of prerogative remained meaningful, the distinction between rulers and ruled was clear and vital and the rights of each were balanced in tension. "Liberty," said James Wilson in 1775 "is, by the constitution, of equal stability, of equal antiquity, and of equal authority with prerogative. The duties of the king and those of the subject are plainly reciprocal: they can be violated on neither side, unless they be [not] performed on the other." The magistracy, whatever the source of its authority, retained inherent legal rights and remained an independent entity in the society with which the people must bargain and contract in order to protect their own rights and privileges. The peers, "forming a balance of power between the king and the people," gave the state "the benefit of an aristocracy." It was their duty "to trim this boat of common wealth, and to skreen the people against the insults of the Prince, and the Prince against the popularity of the commons, since if either extreme prevails so far as to oppress the other, they are sure to be overwhelmed in their ruin."

Politics, in other words, was still commonly viewed along a classic power spectrum that ranged from absolute power in the hands of one person on one end, to absolute power or liberty in the hands of the people at the other end. The spectrum met in full circle when, it was believed, the disorder of absolute liberty would inevitably lead to the tyranny of the dictator. All the traditional forms of government could be located along this spectrum as they partook more or less of power and liberty measured by the nature and number of those allowed to share political authority. The ideal of politics since Aristotle had been of course to avoid either extreme, the degeneration "into tyranny on the one hand, or anarchy on the other: either of which is directly subversive of the ends of civil government." "The seeming theoretic excellence of the English constitution" consisted precisely in "that equipoise between the respective branches of the legislature," the "balance of power, being so judiciously placed, as to connect the force, and to preserve the rights of . . . each estate, armed with a power of self defense; against the encroachments of the other two."

Since the three social orders were thought to be fully embodied in the state, Parliament consisting "of all the estates, that composed the nation, in epitome, with the supreme sovereignty of the kingdom," eighteenth-century Englishmen generally had not yet made any clear distinction between state and society. Hence politics was still described in terms of these medieval social categories, as a kind of negotiating and maneuvering for political domination among the three estates of the realm; and not, as today, in terms of divisions among the people themselves, as a struggle among various groups for control of a semi-autonomous state in order to advance particular economic or class interests.

In this continuous contest among the estates of the society, a contest that since the seventeenth century had become more and more confined to one between Crown and Commons, the Whigs' loyalty was always with the people. Although the people were but a single estate in the realm it seemed self-evident to the Whigs that the promotion of the people's happiness was the sole purpose of government. The institution of government was of course "a wise, a necessary, and a sacred thing," an essential restraint on the lusts and passions that drove all men. Without it, "the strongest would be master, the weakest go to the wall. . . . Right, justice and property must give way to power." Hence certain men were "exalted, from among the people, to bear rule." Such magistrates explicitly or implicitly agreed to use their superior power to protect the rights of the people. In return the people pledged their obedience, but only, the Whigs continually emphasized, as long as the rulers promoted the public interest. But unhappily in the eyes of the Whigs the history of politics hardly appeared to be what it should have been; the people's welfare had too often been abused by their governors, and they had too often been compelled to surrender their power to the rulers' power.

The acquisition of power, of course, was what politics was all about. "The love of power is natural," said James Burgh quoting Bolingbroke; "it is insatiable; it is whetted, not cloyed, by possession." It was an obsession with the radical Whigs—this "intoxicating" desire by men for domination over others—and, as often with nagging aches, they could not leave it alone; but, however painful the process, they were driven "to enquire into the nature of power." Men struggled constantly, the Whigs believed, to secure power and if possible to aggrandize it at the expense of others, for power relationships were reciprocating: what was one man's increase of power was another's loss. The minimal amount of power a man deserved, because he was a man, the Whigs defined as liberty—"the Power," as Thomas Gordon put it, "which every Man has over his own Actions, and his Right to enjoy the Fruit of his Labour, Art, and Industry." This was personal liberty, "physical liberty," as Richard Price called it: it was individual; it was what gave a man control of his own destiny; it was the inherent right man had to his life and his property. Its instruments and remedies were all those natural rights that were "not the grants of princes or parliaments, but original rights, conditions of original contracts," protected in England by the common law and recognized by the bills and charters exacted from the rulers. Government itself was formed so "that every member of society may be protected and secured in the peaceable, quiet possession and enjoyment of all those liberties and privileges which the Deity has bestowed upon him." The end of government, in sum, was the preservation of liberty.

The greatest diffusion of this personal power or liberty was for the Whigs the ideal society. Hence most Whigs believed nothing as effectually prevented the abuse of power in a society "as an equality in the state." Some radicals were even inclined to limit liberty for its own sake, to restrict the amount of wealth or land a man could acquire in order to prevent its abuse. Most Commonwealthmen, however, were willing to grant the inevitability of differences of power among the people, differences that with the right kind of republican laws could not be perpetuated or made especially dangerous to the liberty of others. Economic and social inequalities among the people seemed slight and insignificant when compared to the differences of power that flowed from the institution of government. For in opposition to the magistracy the people were one. Although some writers were beginning to stress the overriding importance of class distinctions among the people, the only meaningful kind of power in most eighteenth-century thinking was still political. Therefore no men were further separated from the rest of the community, and hence more dangerous, than the rulers of a society.

"Such is the accursed nature of lawless ambition" that the great amount of power held by the political rulers—legitimized as no other power ever was—necessarily corrupted the "men of abilities, and influence" who commanded it. "Men in high stations . . . ," the Whigs knew, "increase their ambition, and study rather to be more powerful than wiser or better." "Voracious like the grave, they can never have enough, *i.e.* of power and wealth," and they thus drove on to pervert their governmental authority, an excessive abuse which the Whigs defined as tyranny or despotism: "Tyranny being nothing else but the government of one man, or a few, over many, against their inclination and interest." Therefore, as James Burgh had concluded, government by one or a few was "impossible without continual danger to liberty."

Liberty, defined as the power held by the people, was thus the victim and very antithesis of despotism. Yet the people, like the rulers, could abuse their power; such a perversion of liberty was called licentiousness or anarchy. It was not so much a collective as an individual perversion, each man doing what was right in his own eyes, running amuck and ultimately dissolving all social bonds. "Liberty," good Whigs continually emphasized, "does not consist in living without all restraint." For it seemed certain "that nothing next to *slavery* is more to be dreaded, than the anarchy and confusion that will ensue, if proper regard is not paid to the good and wholesome laws of government." Still slavery was the greater dread. As Josiah Quincy noted, "It is much easier to restrain liberty from running into licentiousness than power from swelling into tyranny and oppression." In the minds of the most extreme Commonwealthmen there could be only one peril confronting England: "the danger of the *people's* being enslaved by the servants of the crown." It was only the propaganda of the ministerial party, declared one irate Whig, "that power ought not to be given to the people." Faction, civil disturbance, and rebellion in history had resulted only from responses to acts of oppression by the rulers, not from any excess of liberty in the people. "It was therefore a want of power in the people which made the Revolution [of 1688] necessary, not a fulness of their power."

The ultimate sanction for the protection of the people's liberty, in the case of the ruler's breach of the mutual contract between them, was the people's right of resistance; but revolution was hardly a sanction that could be commonly used, for, as devout Whigs often said, the remedy must not be worse than the disease. "The Injury suffered ought to be so very notorious, that every eye may see it." Only the most "*extreme necessity*" justified the war and tumult revolution would bring. Another sanction, another means of protection for the people within the bounds of the constitution itself, was necessary. "Peace is seldom made, and never kept," Algernon Sidney had written, "unless the subject retain such a power in his hands as may oblige the prince to stand to what is agreed." Thus the people authorized their rulers to make and to execute laws to govern them, but "always provided they retain a right and power to choose a sufficient number from among themselves, to be a representative body of the whole people . . . to have a voice in the making of all such laws, . . . and in the management of all the most weighty concerns of the state." "For, deprive us of this barrier of our liberties and properties, our own consent; and there remains no security against tyranny and absolute despotism."

This participation by the people in the government was what the Whigs commonly meant by political or civil liberty, which Alexander Hamilton along with other Americans defined as the right of the people "to a *share* in the government." "CIVIL LIBERTY," said Richard Price, "is the power of a *Civil Society* or *State* to govern itself by its own discretion; or by laws of its own making." No Whig conception could have been more relevant for Americans. Liberty, Benjamin Church told his Boston audience in 1773, was "the happiness of living under laws of our own making." "Therefore," for Church and all American Whigs, "the liberty of the people is exactly proportioned to the share the body of the people have in the legislature; and the check placed in the constitution on executive power."

Public liberty was thus the combining of each man's individual liberty into a collective governmental authority, the institutionalization of the people's personal liberty, making public or political liberty equivalent to democracy or government by the people themselves. "According to the celebrated Dr. Price," declared a Boston writer, "liberty in a State is self-government." No government could possibly be free, could possibly protect each man's individual liberty, unless it partook of democracy, unless, in other words, the people participated in it. Without the pooling of each man's liberty into a common body, no property would be secure. "For power is entire and indivisible; and property is single and pointed as an atom." Liberty was therefore more than a helpless victim of the rulers' hunger; collectively the people's liberty became the essential barrier against arbitrary power. Free people, declared an American orator in 1771, were not those who were merely spared actual oppression, "but those who have a *constitutional check upon the power* to oppress."

Of course there were problems, the Whigs realized, in translating the people into the government. Naturally public liberty was most fully realized when the people themselves exercised their role in government. Hence, it was "obvious that *Civil Liberty*, in its most perfect degree, can be enjoyed only in small states"— where the people could meet and conduct public affairs personally. When the state became so large as to make this impossible, the people were compelled to appoint substitutes or representatives, resulting in a necessary "diminution of Liberty." Here arose "the great Point of Nicety and Care in forming the Constitution," said John Trenchard: "that the Persons entrusted and representing, shall either never have any Interest detached from the Persons entrusting and represented, or never the Means to pursue it."

Representation was indeed a delicate point, surely the most confusing and important in the Whig conception of politics, which rested on a rigid distinction between rulers and ruled, magistracy and people. The people's role in the government was confined to the House of Commons; there the representatives should meet frequently and for a short time to correct the laws, returning immediately to private life to experience the consequence of their actions along with other members of the society. Such frequent and short Parliaments could presumably never enact legislation contrary to the interests of the whole people. This anachronistic conception of Parliament assumed that the Commons, although the conservators of liberty, had nothing whatever to do with the actual process of governing the realm. Continuous, day-to-day government, including even what we would call the necessary prerogatives of the legislature, was still the responsibility of the Crown or the rulers. To those who thought in such antiquated terms the King was the people's "sovereign and ruler," while the representatives in Parliament were only "fellow subjects." Many independent-minded Englishmen continued to believe that Parliament "had no right to interfere with the executive power," some going so far as to state that "it was the business of Parliament to raise supplies, not to debate on the measures of Government."

Yet eighteenth-century practice was rapidly undermining this old-fashioned theory of the role of Parliament, creating disturbing implications for the way men thought about politics. The people's increased participation in the actual affairs of state, through their participation in the ever-stronger House of Commons, was tending to blur the rigid distinction between rulers and ruled that lay at the heart of the Whig theory of politics. By their added responsibilities, their long tenure in office, and their consequent separation from the body of the people, the members of the Commons were coming to resemble more the character of rulers than representatives of the ruled. Under the pressure of these changes many Englishmen were beginning to describe this quasi-magisterial quality of the representatives as an advantageous way of enabling the wisest and most virtuous men to speak for the populace, making the House of Commons a kind of independent body distinct from the people and "intended as a balance between them and the sovereign." Some such notion was involved in the prevailing belief in the detached and virtual representation of the people and the correlative conception of the sovereignty of Parliament, that is, that Parliament was the final and supreme authority for all law even against the wishes of the people whom it supposedly represented. For the members of Parliament were "the Judges, and the only Judges of the Public Good," and unless "we are to submit to their determinations, . . . we will make all our Laws useless, our Constitution and Government precarious."

Although such changes as the Septennial Act, lengthening and regularizing the life of Parliaments, were actually responsible for the Commons' enhanced importance in the eighteenth-century English constitution, most radical Whigs saw little advantage in them, and repeatedly decried the abandonment of the short Parliaments and frequent elections of earlier days. As one critic pointed out, the reformers were, without fully realizing the significance of what they were saying, calling for a revival of those "ages when the House of Commons was an insignificant part of the Constitution," and when legislation was largely an exceptional and remedial matter. Yet to the radical Whigs the emergent independence of long-tenured Parliaments seemed dangerous to the people's liberty. While it might be necessary for the people "to appoint a power in the State, to which they individually transfer their wills, dress it up in the insignia of sovereignty, and arm it with legislative authority," the radicals had no doubt that this "sovereign power" was "no more than the representative of the people declaratory of their will, and bound to act in subservience to their interest." The idea that the representatives could do what they liked was "almost too monstrous to conceive." "Can there be imagined a more striking absurdity than that the trustee should become independent of the person reposing the trust . . . the creature stronger than the creator?" Parliamentary actions, like the expulsion of John Wilkes from the House of Commons despite his repeated election, only aggravated this fear of the arbitrary independence of the House of Commons, a fear that had run through the radical English mind since the seventeenth century, "when," as Catharine Macaulay recalled, "the representatives had affected an intire independency on, or rather an absolute sovereignty over their constitutents."

Despite this fear, however, most Commonwealthmen were not yet ready to give up on the representational process. They realized that government by representation "deviates more or less from Liberty, in proportion as the representation is more or less imperfect." And representation in the House of Commons seemed so imperfect, so antiquated, and cried out so for reform that its evils would have to be remedied before men could clearly explore the implications of representation for their traditional understanding of politics. They thus concentrated not on denying the efficacy of representation itself, but on anchoring the drifting representatives to the people, so that through the institution of certain safeguards and reforms, like more proportional representation, freer elections, and more frequent Parliaments, the interests of the people and their representatives could "be engaged upon the same Bottom, that Principals and Deputies must stand and fall together." Still the deeply rooted mistrust of any body set above the people, the frightening discrepancy between the people and their spokesmen, however equally or frequently elected, always remained (as the Americans exposed fully in the coming years) a point of nagging confusion in the English understanding of politics. Indeed, lack of confidence in the representational system become the most important means of measuring degrees of radicalism among a Whiggish people.

ENGLISH CORRUPTION

This Whig theory of politics, assumed by the Americans with varying degrees of precision during their decade-long debate with England, was not simply a series of political maxims or abstractions isolated from any social or historical context, unrelated to time and place. "As the interests of People vary with their circumstances," declared one early eighteenth-century English pamphlet republished in America in 1775, "so the Form of Government may be various, and yet each be best in its Proper Place, and by consequence one Form of Government may be best for this People, another for that." The common belief of the age that human nature was forever the same referred essentially to the raw biological nature upon which the environment operated. Most thinkers had little doubt that the cultural natures of men varied with the circumstances in which they lived. The Augustan age was scarcely unhistorical, although it was decidedly contemptuous of mere antiquarianism or storytelling. It was not history for its own sake, not even the evolution through time of a particular people or culture, that attracted men of the age, but rather the abstract process of development, the laws or uniformities which applied equally to all peoples. As in politics it was generalizations, scientific principles about the historical process that the age was after, and men were engrossed in discovering the connectedness of things, particularly the relations between governmental institutions and society, and the principles that governed their changes through time. In this sense eighteenth-century English political thought perhaps owed more to Machiavelli and Montesquieu than it did to Locke. Most English colonists did not conceive of society in rational, mechanistic terms; rather society was organic and developmental. The macrocosm was still like the microcosm. "It is with states as it is with men," was a commonplace of the day; "they have their infancy, their manhood, and their decline." The history of particular nations and peoples, whatever may have been the history of mankind in general, was not a linear progression, but a variable organic cycle of birth, maturity, and death, in which states, like the human body, carried within themselves the seeds of their own dissolution, "which ripen faster or slower," depending on the changing spirit of the society.

However much American Whigs were convinced that men were "just beginning to emerge from Egyptian darkness, with respect to the rights of human nature," they well knew that in comparison with the past "the present age shews equal absurdities and vices upon the theatre of politicks . . . everything for which we condemn our ancestors." In those troublesome years approaching the Revolution countless American writings, steeped in radical Whig pessimism, sought to expose the regressive tendencies in politics that lay beneath the promising progress in theoretical science. Politics in the jaundiced eyes of the radical Whigs had always been a tale of "bloodshed and slaughter, violence and oppression," where the "Monarchs of every age . . . surrounded by a banditti which they call a standing army" had committed havoc on the liberty, property, and lives of hapless peoples. "Fountains of tears have been shed, and rivers of blood have been spilt at the shrine of arbitrary power. History both antient and modern is but a detail of calamities which have been brought upon mankind from this quarter." Indeed, the present "degenerate age" seemed even worse than the past, since by the middle of the eighteenth century the world had witnessed "a greater annihilation of public freedom than seen a century before." The very idea of liberty was unknown in Africa and Asia; and it seemed to the alienated Whigs that it might soon be only a memory in Europe, for everywhere "liberty is absorbed by monarchy; and the many must be subject to one." In the course of a single year both Sweden and Poland had been enslaved, leaving on the continent only the Swiss cantons and the Dutch provinces free; and their liberty appeared shortlived. "Where is the kingdom," devout Whigs asked, "that does not groan under the calamities of military tyranny?"

But then in every Englishman's eyes it had always been so. Amidst a tyrannical world England had always stood as a solitary bastion in defense of freedom. No people in history, said John Dickinson, had ever been "so constantly watchful of their liberty, and so successful in their struggles for it, as the *English*." It had not been easy, since for seven hundred years the English had struggled with the forces of tyranny. Although some Whigs, like Joseph Hawley, saw "the origin of the British state . . . too far sunk in the dark ages of antiquity to investigate the manner, or trace the means by which it was formed," most presumed the existence of a Saxon golden age of liberty and equality with a pristine gothic constitution which had been ruthlessly invaded by "that barbarous system of despotism imposed by the Norman tyrant." From that time on the English people, as Jefferson described it, had fought vigorously to regain their liberties from the Crown and to restore "that antient constitution, of which our ancestors had been defrauded," each clash resulting in landmarks in the development of English freedom and representative institutions. In this bitter "continued struggle between the prince and the people" the seventeenth century seemed to be of crucial importance; for the Crown under the Stuarts had made a grand and desperate effort to snuff out the liberty of the people once and for all, causing a fierce and bloody civil war and a disruption of the constitution that had eventually been settled by "that happy establishment" of 1688.

For most radical Whigs the Glorious Revolution had not marked the end of the struggle. In their aversion to the developments of eighteenth-century England they refused to turn their backs on the disordered but exhilarating and promising experience of the seventeenth century and to accept the Revolution of 1688 as a final solution to the problems of English public life. While few Americans were willing to go so far as to declare that "England was never more happy before, nor much more since, than after the head of the first Stuart was severed from his body," all true Whigs were forced to conclude that the Revolution of 1688 had not after all been able to preserve the liberty that the great men of the seventeenth century—the Hampdens, the Sidneys—had sought. Especially in the decade after the accession of George III there could be no place for confidence in their writings, only pessimism and an agonizing despair for the future of liberty, not only in Europe but in England itself.

The colonists in these prerevolutionary years watched England in bewilderment as what had long been predicted by "her senators and historians" seemed actually to be happening—the English constitution, formerly "the noblest improvement of human reason," was at last succumbing to the forces of tyranny, "shaken to its very basis." England, the Americans said over and over again, "once the land of liberty—the school of patriots—the nurse of heroes, has become the land of slavery—the school of parricides and the nurse of tyrants." By the 1770's the metaphors describing England's course were all despairing: the nation was fast streaming toward a cataract, hanging on the edge of a precipice; the brightest lamp of liberty in all the world was dimming. Internal decay was the most common image. A poison had entered the nation and was turning the people and the government into "one mass of corruption." On the eve of the Revolution the belief that England was "sunk in corruption" and "tottering on the brink of destruction" had become entrenched in the minds of disaffected Englishmen on both sides of the Atlantic.

These widely voiced fears for the fate of the English constitution, "the mighty ruin of a once noble fabrick," were not simply the bombastic expressions of revolutionary-minded men. They represented the rational and scientific conclusions of considered social analysis. For all of its rhetorical exaggeration, the ideology of Whig radicalism, embraced by Americans of varying political persuasions and at every social level, was grounded in the best, most enlightened knowledge of the eighteenth century; it was this grounding that gave the Whig ideology much of its persuasive force. When the American Whigs described the English nation and government as eaten away by "corruption," they were in fact using a technical term of political science, rooted in the writings of classical antiquity, made famous by Machiavelli, developed by the classical republicans of seventeenth-century England, and carried into the eighteenth century by nearly everyone who laid claim to knowing anything about politics. And for England it was a pervasive corruption, not only dissolving the original political principles by which the constitution was balanced, but, more alarming, sapping the very spirit of the people by which the constitution was ultimately sustained.

The corruption of the constitution's internal principles was the more obvious and the more superficial danger. The marvelous mixture of the English constitution was dependent, the Whigs believed, on "the three distinct powers, or bodies" of the legislature being "entirely independent of each other." But as the Whigs interpreted the events of the eighteenth century, the Crown had been able to evade the restrictions of the revolutionary settlement of 1688 and had "found means to corrupt the other branches of the legislature," upsetting the delicately maintained balance of the constitution from within. Throughout the eighteenth century the Crown had slyly avoided the blunt and clumsy instrument of prerogative, and instead had resorted to influencing the electoral process and the representatives in Parliament in order to gain its treacherous ends. This seemed in the minds of devout Whigs a far more subtle tyranny than the Stuarts' usurpations of the previous century, because "the very means which were devised to secure and protect" the people had become "the engines of destruction." George III was "now tearing up the constitution by the roots, under the form of law." Nothing angered radicals and independent-minded Englishmen in the eighteenth century more than the attempts by a frustrated ministry to carry out the Crown's supposed responsibility for governing the realm with the necessary but often little understood cooperation of a balky Parliament—a cooperation that was possible only through ministerial management and influencing of the House of Commons. It appeared to those who clung to the original principles of the constitution and the growing tradition of separation of powers that the Crown, in its painful efforts to build majorities through borough-mongering and the distribution of patronage, was in fact bribing its way into tyranny. "It is upon this principle," Americans concluded, "that the King of Great-Britain is absolute; for though he doth not act without the parliament, by places, pensions, honours and promises, he obtains the sanction of the parliament for doing as he pleases. The ancient form is preserved, but the spirit of the constitution is evaporated."

Nonetheless, this disruption of the internal workings of the constitution was not profoundly frightening to good Whigs; indeed it was to be expected, for time did not stand still, and men knew they lived in "a changeable world." Had not Machiavelli and Sidney both written that "all human Constitutions are subject to Corruption and must perish, unless they are *timely renewed* by reducing them to their first Principles"? The constitution's disorder should have been an inevitable but temporary aberration, eventually correctable by the people. Yet everyone knew that reducing the constitution to its first principles—"restoring it to its pristine Perfection"—was impossible if the people themselves had become corrupted and sunk in vice. Until the society itself had been infected, until there was "a general depravity of morals, a total alienation from virtue, a people cannot be compleatly enslaved." It was not any inherent weakness in the principles of the British constitution that had made it defective, since "the strongest constitutions are most liable to certain diseases." But if the diseases remained unremedied, if the constitution could not be restored to its first principles, then the fault could only be the people's. For it was the "distinguished happiness" of the British constitution that "when by any means" it became corrupted, "nothing is wanting to a restoration, but the virtue of the people." Indeed, "all men might be free, if they had but virtue enough to be so."

Borrowing pointedly from the relevant writings of history, especially from classical antiquity, eighteenth-century intellectuals—Montesquieu being but the best among many—had worked out the ambiguous but necessary and mutual relation they believed existed between the moral spirit of a society and its political constitution. It was a fascinating subject, the kind that commencement speakers at American colleges in the 1770's could not resist. "Empires," declared one orator lecturing "On the Fall of Empires," "carry in them their own bane, and proceed, in fatal round, from virtuous industry and valour, to wealth and conquest; next to luxury, then to foul corruption and bloated morals; and, last of all, to sloth, anarchy, slavery and political death." History, as written by Sallust and Plutarch, only too grimly showed the fate of empires grown too fat with riches. While the Romans, for example, maintained their love of virtue, their simplicity of manners, their recognition of true merit, they raised their state to the heights of glory. But they stretched their conquests too far and their Asiatic wars brought them luxuries they had never before known. "From that moment virtue and public spirit sunk apace: dissipation vanished temperance and independence." "From a People accustomed to the Toils of War, and Agriculture, they became a People who no longer piqued themselves on any other Merit than a pretended fine Taste for all the Refinements of a voluptuous Life." They became obsessed with the "Grandeur and Magnificence in Buildings, of Sumptuousness and Delicacy in their Tables, of Richness and Pomp in their Dress, of Variety and Singularity in their Furniture." That corruption "which always begins amongst the Rich and the Great" soon descended to the common people, leaving them "enfeebled and their souls depraved." The gap between rich and poor widened and the society was torn by extortion and violence. "It was no longer virtue that raised men up to the first employments of the state, but the chance of birth, and the caprice of fortune." With the character of the Roman people so corrupted, dissolution had to follow. "The empire tottered on its foundation, and the mighty fabric sunk beneath its own weight."

The analogy with the present was truly frightening. "Those very symptoms which preceded the fall of Rome, appear but too evidently in the British constitution." And as everyone in the eighteenth century knew, "Similar causes must ever produce similar effects." Both John Adams and William Hooper saw venality in England at the pitch it was when Jugurtha left Rome. All the signs of England's economic and social development in the eighteenth century—the increasing capitalization of land and industry, the growing debt, the rising prices and taxes, the intensifying search for distinctions by more and more people—were counted as evidence of "its present degeneracy, and its impending destruction." A "long succession of abused prosperity" drawn into "ruinous operation by the Riches and Luxuries of the East"—England's very greatness as an empire—had created a poison which was softening the once hardy character of the English people, sapping their time-honored will to fight for their liberties, leaving them, as never before in their history, weakened prey to the designs of the Crown. It seemed to radical Whigs and Americans alike that "Gangrene has taken too deep Hold to be eradicated in these Days of Venality." The English people had at last become too corrupted, too enfeebled, to restore their constitution to its first principles and rejuvenate their country. "The whole fabric," warned James Burgh, was "ready to come down in ruins upon our heads."

THE PATTERN OF TYRANNY

It was in the context of this frightening diagnosis of the state of the British constitution and society that the Americans viewed the attempts of the British government in the years after 1763 to put its empire on a surer footing. Some, like James Iredell, continued to the very end of the debate to be "far from thinking" that the English people were "universally corrupt, though too many, God knows, are." But whatever the degree of corruption in England may have been, it seemed even to someone as skeptical as Iredell that "this has been the cause of all our present calamity." True Whigs were well aware that in the last stages of a nation's life "luxury and its never failing attendant corruption, will render easy the attempts of an arbitrary prince, who means to subvert the liberty of his country." Only in such a venal and degenerate climate did tyrants flourish. If indeed England were "on the verge of ruin," as "by the best accounts, we are assured," then events would confirm that the long anticipated crisis of liberty was at hand. It therefore became the responsibility of the colonial leaders to make clear to their fellow subjects what was happening, to disperse "the clouds of obscuring ignorance" and "trace with enquiring minds the principles of government . . . closely investigate the origin of power, and deduce from unvarying laws" the insidious designs of the British King and ministers that lay behind the events of the 1760's and seventies. The result of their efforts in the years leading up to the Revolution was an extraordinary display of the writing of contemporary history— a scientific analysis of the workings of men and events through time that was at once highly refined and yet extremely crude—designed to enable the colonists, as no people before them ever had, to expose and thus resist the forces of tyranny before they were actually enslaved.

Those Whig spokesmen who bothered to go beyond a simple articulation of Whig maxims offered an especially impressive conception of the patterns of culture and history. They knew it would be no simple task to awaken the people to the dangers confronting their liberties. "The experience of all ages" showed that the people were "inattentive to the calamities of others, careless of admonition, and with difficulty roused to repel the most injurious invasions." The Whigs were struck with "the easiness with which the many are governed by the few, . . . the implicit submission with which men resign their own sentiments and passions to those of their rulers." Many could therefore conclude with David Hume that it was on custom or "opinion only that government is founded, and this maxim extends to the most despotic and most military governments, as well as to the most free and most popular." The people through history, Americans noted over and over again, were generally docile and obedient, disposed "to be as submissive and passive and tame under government as they ought to be." In fact the people were naturally "so gentle that there never was a government yet in which thousands of mistakes were not overlooked." Men were born to be deluded, "to believe whatever is taught, and bear all that is imposed."

This customary deference of the people was really what explained the over-weening dominance of the ruling few through so many centuries of history, for it "gradually reconciles us to objects even of dread and detestation." Because of the Whigs' particular conception of politics, their otherwise sophisticated understanding of the historical process took on a primitive cast, and history became the product of self-conscious acts by rulers seeking to extend their power over an unsuspecting populace. Insignificant, piecemeal changes, none of which seemed decisive or unbearable at the time, "spread over the multitude in such a manner, as to touch individuals but slightly." In a variety of metaphors the colonists sought to express their understanding of how the rulers, possessing their own "particular purposes," slyly used the historical process. Every one of their acts of usurpation was "like a small spark [which] if not extinguished in the beginning will soon gain ground and at last blaze out into an irresistible Flame"; or it was "like the rollings of mighty waters over the breach of ancient mounds,—slow and unalarming at the beginning; rapid and terrible in the current; a deluge and devastation at the end"; or it was like "a spot, a speck of decay, however small the limb on which it appears, and however remote it may seem from the vitals," that would grow and corrupt "till at length the inattentive people are compelled to perceive the heaviness of their burthens," usually, however, too late for the people to resist. "They find their oppressors so strengthened by success, and themselves so entangled in examples of express authority on the part of the rulers, and tacit recognition on their own part, that they are quite confounded." All history was therefore an object lesson in the power of the seemingly insignificant. "Innumerable instances might be produced to shew," said John Dickinson in the most acute analysis of the way history and politics worked that was written in these years, "from what slight beginnings the most extensive consequences have flowed."

Yet the power of custom and the habitual deference of the people to established authority also worked to protect the people against wanton civil disturbance and to prevent rebellion for light and transient causes. Most American Whigs were sure that no people could be falsely incited into revolution by sheer demagoguery, as the Tories were charging. No popular leaders, wrote John Adams, had ever been able "to persuade a large people, for any length of time together, to think themselves wronged, injured, and oppressed, unless they really were, and saw and felt it to be so." Only irrefutable proof, only evidence which was "as clear as the sun in its meridian brightness," could convince the people that they were really threatened with enslavement at the hands of their rulers. By the eve of the Revolution most Whigs believed that they possessed that kind of proof.

It was obvious to the Americans that the events of the years after 1763, "these unheard of intolerable calamities, spring not of the dust, come not causeless." "Ought not the PEOPLE therefore," asked John Dickinson in 1768, "to watch? to observe facts? to search into causes? to investigate designs?" And as their search into the causes for what was happening proceeded, the otherwise inexplicable series of events increasingly seemed to be but pieces of a grand design, nothing less than, in Jefferson's words, "a deliberate, systematical plan of reducing us to slavery." By the 1770's there was hardly a piece of Whig writing, whether pamphlet, newspaper essay, letter, or even diary, that did not dwell on this obsessive fear of a "Conspiracy . . . [against the public liberty] first regularly formed, and begun to be executed, in 1763 or 4." It was scarcely believable, said William Henry Drayton in 1776, "but, nothing less *than absolute proof* has convinced us" that the British government had for the past dozen years carried on a "conspiracy against the rights of humanity." Some out of a deep reverence for England had struggled "long against the evidence of facts" that had by 1775 "become irresistible." The colonists had simply "too many Proofs that a regular System has been formed to bow down the Neck of America to the *Feet* of the *Ministry*." The cumulative momentum of this belief in a British ministerial conspiracy against the colonists' liberties not only was symptomatic of the rising intensity of the Americans' revolutionary fever, but it also formed for the Americans, as has recently and amply been demonstrated, the only frame of mind with which they could justify and explain their revolution. For in the Whig creed no specific acts of the government against the people could sanction revolution. Only "repeated, multiplied oppressions," placing it beyond all doubt "that their rulers had formed settled plans to deprive them of their liberties," could warrant the concerted resistance of the people against their government.

The notion of conspiracy was not new in Western history. From Sallust's description of Catiline through Machiavelli's lengthy discussion men were familiar with the use of conspiracy in politics. Yet the tendency to see events as the result of a calculated plot, especially events in times of public tumult, appears particularly strong in the eighteenth century, a product, it seems, not only of the political realities and assumptions of the age, but of its very enlightenment, a consequence of the popularization of politics and the secularization of knowledge. Those Americans who continued to see themselves as a specially covenanted people could and did look beyond the earth to Providence for an explanation of the events in the years after 1763: a divinely favored people were being justly punished for their sins. But to those captivated by the Enlightenment of the eighteenth century the wonder-working ways of Providence were not satisfying enough. The explanation of human phenomena lay in the ways of man alone, in human purposes, in political and social science. Whatever happened in history was intended by men to have happened. Enlightened rationalists as well as Calvinist clergy were obsessed with the motives that lay hidden behind deceiving, even self-deceiving, statements, and they continually sought to penetrate beneath the surface of events in order to find their real significance in the inner hearts of men. Yet in replacing Providence with human motivation as a source of historical explanation, men still felt the need to discover the design, "the *grand plan*," that lay beneath the otherwise incomprehensible jumble of events. Now it seemed possible to the men of this enlightened age that they would be able, as the scrutinizers of Providence had been unable, "to trace things into their various connections, or to look forward into all their remote and distant consequences," to disclose at last what had always been in darker days "the hidden and . . . uncertain connection of events." It was precisely this task of tracing, predicting, disclosing, and connecting motives and events that American Whig leaders had set for themselves in the debate with Great Britain. And thus their attributing what was happening to the relations between Britain and her colonies to the conspiratorial designs of a few men in high places became another example of their application of science to human affairs, a noble effort to make natural sense of the complexity of phenomena, a humanization of Providence, an impassioned attempt to explain the ways of man to man, the crude beginnings of what has come to be called the Whig interpretation of history.

The pieces all fell into place, as Whig intellectuals on both sides of the Atlantic worked to make clear the nature of English society and the pattern of the Crown's policy for all to see. This clarification, this growing belief that the English government was conspiratorially making "a bold push for our entire subjection," was, it has been argued, more than anything else responsible for the Americans' decision to revolt. Certainly there can be little doubt of the pervasiveness of these revolutionary beliefs in the minds of the American Whigs. It seemed increasingly evident to the colonists that the forces of tyranny, rapacious as they were, were not content with the conquest of Europe, but now had cast their "jealous eye on this new world" and threatened "to involve it in the miseries of the old." Every successive step by the Crown, under the guise of a corrupted and pliant Parliament, only confirmed American fears of a despotic conspiracy against freedom. The multiplication of new government officials was obviously the beginning of the Court's plan "that millions of leading men's dependents shall be provided for in America, for whom places can by no means be found at home." The sending of new troops to America was merely the introduction of despotism's traditional instrument—a standing army. The new admiralty courts were only the first stage in the eventual elimination of trial by jury. The invigoration of the Anglican establishment could only be directed toward the ultimate destruction of America's religious freedom. The Quebec Act was actually an insidious attempt by the ministry to introduce through the colonies' back door the evils of popery, civil law, and eventual absolutism. And in such a mental atmosphere the Coercive Acts could be but flagrant confirmation of the Crown's grand strategy.

Under the pressures of this intensifying controversy the Americans' conception of their place in history—suggested intermittently in their writings since the seventeenth century and deduced from their understanding of the nature of social development—was raised to a new and powerful height of comprehensiveness. While the mother country grew old and haggard, the colonies seemed "as yet a new and uncorrupted people." In the seventeenth century they had carried "the spirit of liberty" from England to the wilderness "at the time when it was in its greatest purity and perfection"; and in the New World it had flourished. No wonder, then, that "there seldom ever was a nation . . . more violently assaulted, than we have been." America had become a disconcerting obstacle in the Crown's march to absolutism, a shining symbol to oppressed peoples everywhere that freedom still lived. The crisis with England, so "strange," so "unnatural," seemed by 1774 "to foretell some great event," leading Americans "to imagine there is something at hand that shall greatly augment the history of the world." Out of the frenzied thinking of disaffected Englishmen and the scattered writings of European intellectuals—all grounded in the best scientific knowledge of the day— and out of their own ethnocentric traditions, the Americans began piecing together the immense significance of what they were involved in, ultimately creating one of the most coherent and powerful revolutionary ideologies the Western world had yet seen. They could not help believing—all the evidence, all the enlightened everywhere confirmed it—that liberty was fleeing the Old World entirely and "seeking an asylum westward." Out of the tumult that was sure to come they could only hope that "a great and mighty empire may rise up in this western world," an empire peculiarly dedicated to the principles of liberty.

23. Swilling the Planters with Bumbo

Charles S. Sydnor

Many political scientists would argue that contemporary American voters are only nominally issue oriented. They would say that in today's political culture individuals vote for a candidate because of deeply ingrained party affiliations or because of psychological attachments to the personalities (and physical characteristics and mannerisms) of particular candidates. Rarely are there elections when the issues are clear and citizens go to the polls specifically to drive an incumbent from office for having initiated or supported unpopular or unwise legislation.

But what was electioneering like in the eighteenth century when pervasive party labels rarely existed? What distinguished particular candidates? Why did men vote? The late Charles S. Sydnor (1899–1954), who served on the faculty of Duke University, provided lively answers to these questions as they relate to the political practices of prerevolutionary Virginia. Sydnor argued that electioneering in the Old Dominion had many democratic overtones. Yet, notice the names of the Virginians being elected to office. What stratum of society did candidates generally come from? Was it the practice of "treating," furthermore, that drew so many men to polling places? Was it the conviviality of election time, indicating a holiday-like mood breaking the tedium of farm life, that filled Virginians with the "democratic spirit," or was there something more meaningful that brought voters to the polls, such as making sure that representatives fully understood constituency political demands? Are the characteristics of election activities fundamentally deferential and elitist, or more democratic in content?

It would be pleasant to think that voters were good and wise in the bright, beginning days of the American nation; that in Jefferson's Arcadia, to use a popular euphemism, the sturdy, incorruptible freeholders assembled when occasion demanded and, with an eye only to the public good and their own safety, chose the best and ablest of their number to represent them in the Assembly. It is true that the voters of early Virginia chose their representatives and that often they chose remarkably well; but it is an error to think that the voters were the only positive active force at work in elections. For good or ill, the candidates and their friends also played an important part by using many forms of persuasion and pressure upon the voters.

Source: From Charles S. Sydnor, *Gentlemen Freeholders: Political Practices in Washington's Virginia* (Chapel Hill: University of North Carolina Press, 1952), pp. 39–59. Footnotes omitted. Reprinted by permission of the University of North Carolina Press and the Institute of Early American History and Culture.

A play called *The Candidates; or, the Humours of a Virginia Election,* written about 1770 by Colonel Robert Munford of Mecklenburg County, Virginia, provides valuable insight into the part played by candidates in the elections of eighteenth-century Virginia. In this play one of the former delegates to the Assembly, Worthy by name, has decided not to stand for reelection. The other, Wou'dbe, offers himself once more "to the humours of a fickle croud," though with reluctance, asking himself: "Must I again resign my reason, and be nought but what each voter pleases? Must I cajole, fawn, and wheedle, for a place that brings so little profit?" The second candidate, Sir John Toddy, "an honest blockhead," with no ability except in consuming liquor and no political strength except his readiness to drink with the poor man as freely as with the rich, looks for support among the plain people who like him because he "wont turn his back upon a poor man, but will take a chearful cup with one as well as another." Scorned by the leading men of the county, the other two candidates, Smallhopes and Strutabout, a vain, showy fellow, are adept in the low arts of winning the support of ignorant men.

Each of these candidates had some influence, following, or support which, in the language of that day, was known as his interest. It was common practice at this time for two candidates to join interests, as the phrase went, in hopes that each could get the support of the friends of the other. When Sir John suggests to Wou'dbe a joining of interests by asking him "to speak a good word for me among the people," Wou'dbe refuses and tells him plainly "I'll speak a good word to you, and advise you to decline" to run. Because Wou'dbe could not, from principle, join interests with any one of the three other candidates, he loses votes by affronting first one and then another of them. Just in the nick of time, Wou'dbe's colleague Worthy descends from the upper reaches of respectability and greatness to save Wou'dbe from defeat and political virtue from ruin. With stilted phrase Worthy denounces "the scoundrels who opposed us last election" and directs Wou'dbe to "speak this to the people, and let them know I intend to stand a poll." The good men of the county rally to the side of righteousness; Sir John (between alcoholic hiccoughs) announces "I'm not so fitten" as "Mr. Worthy and Mr. Wou'dbe"; Strutabout and Smallhopes, looking as doleful as thieves upon the gallows, are ignominiously defeated; and Worthy and Wou'dbe are triumphantly reelected.

Among the more important of the unwritten rules of eighteenth-century Virginia politics, a rule which the candidates and their advisers often mentioned was the necessity for candidates to be present at elections. Judge Joseph Jones, out of his ripe experience, wrote in 1785 to his young nephew James Monroe, "respecting your offering your service for the County the coming year, ... it would be indispensably necessary you should be in the County before the election and attend it when made." In 1758 several of Washington's friends wrote him to "come down" from Fort Cumberland, where he was on duty with his troops, "and show your face" in Frederick County where he was a candidate for burgess. One of his supporters warned him that "you being elected absolutely depends on your presence." Thanks to the hard work of his friends and the patriotic circumstances of his absence, Washington was elected; but it is evident that the absence of a candidate from the county before and during the taking of the poll was regarded as a distinct handicap.

Fifty years later Henry St. George Tucker, who planned to stand for election at Winchester, was delayed by bad weather and other circumstances at Staunton.

He wrote to his father: "I shall not be able to reach Winchester time enough for the election and I presume I shall be withdrawn in consequence of what I have written to my friends in Winchester." But by hard driving he made it, arriving "a few moments before the polls were opened"; and he was elected. As late as 1815 Tucker continued to place himself personally before the people while the voting was in process. Even though he was "still very weak" from illness, he played his part in an election of that year while the enormous number of 737 votes was polled until, as he wrote his father, "fatigue well nigh overcame me."

A sharp distinction must be made between election-day and pre-election behavior of the candidate toward the voter. The code of the times required that in the days before the election the candidate maintain a dignified aloofness from the voters; however, this rule was broken perhaps as often as it was observed. The tipsy Sir John Toddy, in *The Candidates,* assisted by his henchman Guzzle, tries unabashedly to work himself into the good graces of three freeholders named Prize, Twist, and Stern. As they and their wives are sitting on a rail fence, with other freeholders standing about, Sir John comes up to a group. At his shoulder stands Guzzle to whisper the names of the prospective voters to him.

> SIR JOHN. Gentlemen and ladies, your servant, hah! my old friend Prize, how goes it? how does your wife and children do?
> SARAH. At your service, sir. (*making a low courtsey.*)
> PRIZE. How the devil come he to know me so well, and never spoke to me before in his life? (*aside.*)
> GUZZLE. (*whispering to Sir John*) Dick Stern.
> SIR JOHN. Hah! Mr. Stern, I'm proud to see you; I hope your family are well; how many children? does the good woman keep to the old stroke?
> CATHARINE. Yes, an't please your honour, I hope my lady's well, with your honour.
> SIR JOHN. At your service, madam.
> GUZZLE. (*whispering* [to] *Sir John*) Roger Twist.
> SIR JOHN. Hah! Mr. Roger Twist! your servant, sir. I hope your wife and children are well.
> TWIST. There's my wife. I have no children, at your service.

James Littlepage, a candidate for burgess in Hanover County in 1763, practiced nearly every art known to his generation for getting his candidacy before the people and winning their support. The gathering of worshippers at church services afforded him an opportunity to meet people; but unfortunately, he could not be at two churches at the same time. Deciding that it was more important to go to a dissenting congregation, he prepared the way by letters to two freeholders in which he announced that he would "be at your Church To-morrow Se'nnight," and asked their support, setting forth the platform on which he was campaigning and circulating the false rumor that his opponent had "declined serving this County."

To take care of matters at the other church which he was unable to attend personally, he sent a letter to three freeholders for them to read and pass about among those in attendance. As one of those who saw the letter recalled its substance, Littlepage wrote that he "was the Day gone to the lower Meeting House of the Dissenters, to know their Sentiments whether they would submit to the damned Tobacco Law, and desired to know whether they also would submit to it; that if they would send him Burgess he would be hanged, or burnt (or Words to that Effect) if he did not get that Part of it, directing a Review of Tobacco, repealed, as being an Infringement on the Liberty of the Subjects, the Inspectors being so intimidated by it that they refused the greater Part of their Tobacco; and that he would endeavor to have the Inspectors chosen by the People."

To meet the voters who could not be found in assemblies, Littlepage went on a house-to-house canvass. After discussing his chances in one part of the county with his friend John Boswell, and being assured that "he might have a good Chance, if he would go up amongst them," Littlepage "accordingly went up, and the said *Boswell* rode about with him among the People." He was the soul of hospitality, inviting those who lived at some distance from the courthouse to spend the night with him on their way to the poll. Littlepage was elected.

James Madison in his old age recalled that when he entered politics it was "the usage for the candidates to recommend themselves to the voters . . . by personal solicitation." Madison thoroughly disliked this practice. Shortly before the election of representatives to the first Congress of the United States he wrote from Philadelphia to George Washington: "I am pressed much in several quarters to try the effect of presence on the district into which I fall, for electing a Representative; and am apprehensive that an omission of that expedient, may eventually expose me to blame. At the same time I have an extreme distaste to steps having an electioneering appearance, altho' they should lead to an appointment in which I am disposed to serve the public; and am very dubious moreover whether any step which might seem to denote a solicitude on my part would not be as likely to operate against as in favor of my pretensions."

Colonel Landon Carter, writing in 1776, said that he had once been "turned out of the H. of B." because "I did not familiarize myself among the People," whereas he well remembered his "son's going amongst them and carrying his Election." The contrasting experiences of father and son suggest that going among the people was important to get a man elected. However, the son, Robert Wormeley Carter, lost his seat in an election in Richmond County in 1776 even though, according to his father, he had "kissed the ——— of the people, and very seriously accommodated himself to others." With mounting anger the Colonel wrote: "I do suppose such a Circumstance cannot be parallelled, but it is the nature of Popularity. She, I long discovered to be an adultress of the first order." The son was likewise displeased with the decision of the voters, but he naturally thought that his campaign methods were above reproach. He wrote in his diary "as for myself I never ask'd but one man to vote for me since the last Election; by which means I polled but 45. votes an honorable number."

Father and son were miles apart in describing what the son had done; but they were in complete agreement as to what he ought to have done. Both thought that candidates should not solicit votes, and there were other men who thought exactly as they did. Henry St. George Tucker wrote to his father before an election to be held on April 6, 1807, "Please to take notice also, that I am no *electionerer*." "I have studiously avoided anything like canvassing. . . . My opponents are sufficiently active I learn." Of his victory he wrote: "it has been entirely without solicitation on my part." Eight years later he was again elected though he declared that he had "never attended a public meeting or been at the home of a single individual, and though my adversary and his friends had ransacked the county in the old Electioneering Style."

The contrast between ideal and reality was well illustrated by statements made during an election quarrel in Accomac County. The following advice was given to the freeholders: "If a man sollicits you earnestly for your vote, avoid him; self-interest and sordid avarice lurk under his forced smiles, hearty shakes by the hand, and deceitfully enquires after your wife and family." However, it was said, referring to the candidates, that "every person who observes the two gentlemen, allows that the smiles of Mr. S——h are more forced than Mr. H——ry's, and of this Mr. S——h himself is so conscious that he has declared, he would give an Hundred Pounds could he shake hands with the freeholders, and smile in their faces with as good a grace as Col. Pa——e, that he might be more equally match'd."

Some candidates sought to injure a rival by starting the rumor that he was withdrawing from the race, that he had joined interests with an unpopular man, that he was a common drunkard, that he despised poor folks, or that "It's his doings our levies are so high." If the rumor was false, it was better for the candidate to keep silent and let one of his supporters circulate it. More often, the candidate, with the help of his friends, undertook to set himself and his views on current issues in a favorable light.

Sir John Toddy, whose supporters were great lovers of rum, promised to get the price of that article reduced, and it is said of Strutabout that "he'll promise to move mountains. He'll make the rivers navigable, and bring the tide over the tops of the hills, for a vote." The noble Worthy promised no more than to "endeavour faithfully to discharge the trust you have reposed in me." And Wou'dbe answered the questions of the voters with carefully measured words. When asked if he would reduce the price of rum and remove an unpopular tax, he answered, "I could not," explaining that it would be beyond his power to accomplish these things. His position on other matters is set forth in the following dialogue.

STERN. Suppose, Mr. Wou'dbe, we that live over the river, should want to come to church on this side, is it not very hard we should pay ferryage; when we pay as much to the church as you do?

WOU'DBE. Very hard.

STERN. Suppose we were to petition the assembly could you get us clear of that expense?

WOU'DBE. I believe it to be just; and make no doubt but it would pass into a law.

STERN. Will you do it?

WOU'DBE. I will endeavour to do it.

STERN. Huzza for Mr. Wou'dbe! Wou'dbe forever!

PRIZE. Why don't you burgesses, do something with the damn'd pickers? If we have a hogshead of tobacco refused, away it goes to them; and after they have twisted up the best of it for their own use, and taken as much as will pay them for their trouble, the poor planter has little for his share.

WOU'DBE. There are great complaints against them; and I believe the assembly will take them under consideration.

PRIZE. Will you vote against them?

WOU'DBE. I will, if they deserve it.

Littlepage, it will be recalled, promised to fight the existing system of tobacco inspection, and thereby was said to have gained much favor with the people. He also proposed to have the inspectors chosen yearly by the freeholders of the county, an extension of democracy which must have seemed radical to some men of the time. Friends of George Wythe, appealing to those who felt burdened by taxes, declared that "he would serve as Burgess for the said County for nothing," and they offered to "give Bond to repay any Thing that should be levied on the County for him." A rival candidate, William Wager, realizing that he must follow suit, immediately upon "hearing this Declaration, came up and said, he would serve on the same terms."

There is some evidence that the House of Burgesses frowned upon campaign commitments by candidates, especially upon those which reflected upon the prerogative of the House by promising that it would act according to the will of a single member. The powerful Committee of Privileges and Elections investigated the making of campaign promises by some of the candidates, and the committee gave detailed reports to the House of its findings. Perhaps it was to protect himself against the disapproval of the House that Littlepage, who had promised much during his campaign, "Just before the Poll was opened . . . publickly and openly declared, in the Court House, before a great Number of People, that he did not look upon any of the Promises he had made to the People as binding on him, but that they were all void."

There is no way of knowing how many of the candidates followed the rule approved by the Carters, Tucker, and Munford's character Wou'dbe: "never to ask a vote for myself," and how many of them followed the example of Littlepage in unashamedly and energetically courting the voters wherever they could find them, even going on house-to-house canvasses. Most of the candidates seem to have operated between these extremes. While they did not insulate themselves from the voters before elections, they avoided unseemly and ostentatious activity in their mingling with the people. The distinction between approved and disapproved conduct was close, and it is easier to be sure that a line was drawn than to be sure just where it was drawn. A man was likely to shift it a bit, depending on whether he was judging his own actions or those of his rival. John Clopton once gave his candidate son shrewd advice about cultivating the people and tricking a rival at the very time that he was fulminating against the tricks, deceptions, and intimidations practiced by the son's opponents!

Whether the candidates actively campaigned or not, a good many votes were committed before the election. The Quakers or the Presbyterians, the men along the south side of a river or in the northern corner of a county—these and other groups might discuss the candidates and decide which of them to support. Similarly, powerful men would let their friends, relatives, and dependents know how they stood toward the candidates. Thus, elections were often settled before they were held. A curious attempt to hold back this natural operation of democracy was made in a brief notice published in the *Virginia Gazette*. It was addressed "To the free and independent ELECTORS of the borough of NORFOLK," and it desired them "not to engage your votes or interest until the day of election, as a Gentleman of undoubted ability intends to declare himself as a candidate on that day, and hopes to succeed."

From these cases it is evident that although many candidates entered the race several weeks before election day, a few of them, like the unnamed gentleman of Norfolk or like Worthy in Munford's play, waited until the last minute before announcing their decision to stand a poll. John Marshall recalled in his old age that he had the unusual experience of being made a candidate contrary to his wishes. He described the event, which occurred at Richmond during an election to the Virginia legislature in the spring of 1795, in the following words.

> I attended at the polls to give my vote early & return to the court which was then in session at the other end of the town. As soon as the election commenced a gentleman came forward and demanded that a poll should be taken for me. I was a good deal surprized at this entirely unexpected proposition & declared my decided dissent. I said that if my fellow citizens wished it I would become a candidate at the next succeeding election, but that I could not consent to serve this year because my wishes & my honour were engaged for one of the candidates. I then voted for my friend & left the polls for the court which was open and waiting for me. The gentleman said that he had a right to demand a poll for whom he pleased, & persisted in his demand that one should be opened for me—I might if elected refuse to obey the voice of my constituents if I chose to do so. He then gave his vote for me.
>
> As this was entirely unexpected—not even known to my brother who though of the same political opinions with myself was the active & leading partisan of the candidate against whom I voted, the election was almost suspended for ten or twelve minutes, and a consultation took place among the principal freeholders. They then came in and in the evening information was brought me that I was elected. I regretted this for the sake of my friend. In other respects I was well satisfied at being again in the assembly.

Many of the candidates may have been perfectly circumspect in their preelection behavior, but all of them, with hardly an exception, relied on the persuasive powers of food and drink dispensed to the voters with openhanded liberality. Theoderick Bland, Jr., once wrote with apparent scorn that "Our friend, Mr. Banister, has been very much ingaged ever since the dissolution of the assembly, in swilling the planters with bumbo." When he supplied the voters with liquor Banister was in good company; it included Washington, Jefferson, and John Marshall.

The favorite beverage was rum punch. Cookies and ginger cakes were often provided, and occasionally there was a barbecued bullock and several hogs. The most munificent as well as democratic kind of treat was a public occasion, a sort of picnic, to which the freeholders in general were invited. George Washington paid the bills for another kind of treat in connection with his Fairfax County campaigns for a seat in the House of Burgesses. It consisted of a supper and ball on the night of the election, replete with fiddler, "Sundries &ca." On at least one occasion he shared the cost of the ball with one or more persons, perhaps with the other successful candidate, for his memorandum of expenses closes with the words: "By Cash paid Captn. Dalton for my part of ye Expense at the Election Ball. £8.5.6."

A supper and ball of this kind was probably more exclusive than a picnic-type of treat. Hospitality was often shown also to small groups, usually composed of important and influential men. Munford describes a breakfast given the morning of the election by Wou'dbe for the principal freeholders. Worthy was the guest of honor; fine salt shad, warm toast and butter, coffee, tea, or chocolate, with spirits for lacing the chocolate, were set before the guests; and although it was said that "we shall have no polling now," it was understood that all were for Worthy and Wou'dbe.

It was a common practice for candidates to keep open house for the freeholders on their way to the election, and it is a marvel where space was found for all to sleep. When Littlepage heard that some of the voters who lived more than twenty-five miles from the courthouse were unwilling to ride so far in cold weather, he invited them to call at his house which was about five miles from the courthouse. Some ten of them came and were hospitably entertained, "though their Entertainment was not more than was usual with him." Some of the company "were pretty merry with Liquor when they came" to his home. That evening "they chiefly drank Cider." "Some of them drank Drams in the Morning, and went merry to the Court House."

Candidates frequently arranged for treats to be given in their names by someone else. Lieutenant Charles Smith managed this business for George Washington during a campaign in Frederick County in 1758. Two days after the election, which Washington had not been able to attend, Smith sent him receipts for itemized accounts that he had paid to five persons who had supplied refreshments for the voters. A year or two earlier in Elizabeth City County Thomas Craghead sought to repay William Wager, a candidate for burgess, for help he had once received in time of distress. He invited several people to Wager's house and out of his own purse entertained them with "Victuals and Drink." He also had a share in treating all who were present at a muster of Captain Wager's militia company, after which they drank Wager's health.

Samuel Overton, a candidate in Hanover County, directed Jacob Hundley "to prepare a Treat for some of the Freeholders of the said County at his House." Later, Overton withdrew from the race, but a group of freeholders, perhaps ignorant of Overton's withdrawal, came to Hundley's house. He thereupon sent a messenger, desiring Overton's "Directions whether they were to be treated at his Expense," and Overton ordered him "to let them have four Gallons of Rum made into punch, and he would pay for it."

At this juncture some of the finer points of campaigning begin to appear. Littlepage, an active candidate, was among those present at Hundley's house; and Littlepage had agreed in return for Overton's withdrawal to reimburse Overton the sum of £75, which was the expense he had incurred in this and a previous election. As a codicil it was agreed that Littlepage would pay only £50 in case "Mr. Henry," presumably Patrick Henry, should enter the race and be elected. While the treat was in progress Hundley told Littlepage "that the Liquor was all drank." He immediately ordered two gallons more, telling Hundley that he supposed Overton would pay for it. Whether any of the company heard this conversation is in doubt; but this much is clear, that Littlepage paid Overton to withdraw, that Littlepage attended a treat for Overton's friends, and that Littlepage succeeded, according to the testimony of one of the guests, in winning "the Interest" of most of them.

On election day the flow of liquor reached high tide. Douglas S. Freeman calculated that during a July election day in Frederick County in the year 1758, George Washington's agent supplied 160 gallons to 391 voters and "unnumbered hangers-on." This amounted to more than a quart and a half a voter. An itemized list of the refreshments included 28 gallons of rum, 50 gallons of rum punch, 34 gallons of wine, 46 gallons of beer, and 2 gallons of cider royal. During the close and bitter struggle between John Marshall and John Clopton for a seat in Congress in 1799, a "barrel of whiskey . . . with the head knocked in" was on the courthouse green.

Defeated candidates often complained of the wrongdoing of their successful opponents. George Douglas of Accomac County alleged before the Committee of Privileges and Elections that Edmund Scarburgh, shortly before the issuance of the writ of election, had twice given "strong Liquors to the People of the said County; once at a Race, and the other Time as a Muster; and did, on the Day of Election, cause strong Liquor to be brought in a Cart, near the Court-house Door, where many People drank thereof, whilst the Polls of the Election were taking; and one Man in particular, said, *Give me a Drink, and I will go and vote for Col. Scarburgh,* . . . and drink was accordingly given him out of the said Cart, where several People were merry with Drink: But it doth not appear, whether that Person voted for the said *Scarburgh,* or not; or was a Freeholder." Contrary to the recommendation of the Committee, Scarburgh was seated.

Captain Robert Bernard was charged with intimidation as well as improper treating in his efforts to help Beverley Whiting win an election in Gloucester County. He attended a private muster of Captain Hayes' men and solicited the freeholders among them to vote for Whiting. "And the next Day, at a Muster of his own Company, the said *Bernard* brought 40 Gallons of Cyder, and 20 Gallons of Punch into the Field, and treated his Men, solliciting them to vote for Mr. *Whiting,* as they came into the Field; and promised one *James Conquest,* to give him Liquor, if he would vote for Mr. *Whiting,* which *Conquest* refused; and then *Bernard* said he should be welcome to drink, tho' he would not vote for him: That the said *Bernard* promised one *Gale,* a Freeholder to pay his Fine, if he would stay from the Election; which *Gale* accordingly did: That the Day of Election, the said *Bernard* treated several Freeholders, who said they would vote for Mr. *Whiting,* at one *Sewell's* Ordinary: And that, at the Election, one of the Freeholders said, he was going to vote for Mr. *Whiting,* because he had promised Capt. *Bernard* so to do; but that he had rather give Half a Pistole than do it: And other Freeholders, who were indebted to Col. *Whiting,* said, that Capt. *Bernard* told them, that Col. *Whiting* would be angry with them if they voted against Mr. *Whiting;* which the said *Bernard* denied, upon his Oath, before the Committee."

The House of Burgesses compelled Bernard to acknowledge his offense, to ask the pardon of the House, and to pay certain fees; and it requested the Governor to issue a writ for a new election in Gloucester County.

The law strictly prohibited any person "directly or indirectly" from giving "money, meat, drink, present, gift, reward, or entertainment . . . in order to be elected, or for being elected to serve in the General Assembly"; but in one way or another nearly all the candidates gave treats, and seldom was a voice raised in protest. One of the rare protests was adopted at a general meeting of the citizens of Williamsburg two years before the Declaration of Independence. In an address to Peyton Randolph, who was a candidate for re-election to the House of Burgesses, the townsmen declared themselves to be "greatly scandalized at the Practice which has too much prevailed throughout the Country of entertaining the Electors, a Practice which even its Antiquity cannot sanctify; and being desirous of setting a worthy Example to our Fellow Subjects, in general, for abolishing every Appearance of Venality (that only Poison which can infect our happy Constitution) and to give the fullest Proof that it is to your singular Merit alone you are indebted for the unbought Suffrages of a free People; moved, Sir, by these important Considerations, we earnestly request that you will not think of incurring any Expense or Trouble at the approaching Election of a Citizen, but that you will do us the Honour to partake of an Entertainment which we shall direct to be provided for the Occasion."

Three years later young James Madison, feeling that "the corrupting influence of spiritous liquors, and other treats," was "inconsistent with the purity of moral and republican principles," and wishing to see the adoption of "a more chaste mode of conducting elections in Virginia," determined "by an example, to introduce it." He found, however, that voters preferred free rum to the high ideals of a young reformer; "that the old habits were too deeply rooted to be suddenly reformed." He was defeated by rivals who did not scruple to use "all the means of influence familiar to the people." For many years to come liquor had a large part in Virginia elections. In 1795 Jefferson wrote that he was in despair because "the low practices" of a candidate in Albemarle County were "but too successful with the unthinking who merchandize their votes for grog." In 1807 Nathaniel Beverley Tucker, writing from Charlotte Court House, informed his father, St. George Tucker, that "In this part of the state . . . every decent man is striving to get a seat in the legislature. There are violent contests every where that I have been, to the great annoyance of old John Barleycorn, who suffers greatly in the fray."

Although the custom of treating was deeply ingrained, the law was not entirely disregarded. It did not prohibit a man's offering refreshment to a friend; it only prohibited treating "in order to be elected." Through various interpretations of these words most of the candidates found ways of dispensing largess to the freeholders without incurring the censure of the House of Burgesses and perhaps without suffering from an uneasy conscience. Everyone would agree that it was wrong to give liquor to "one *Grubbs,* a Freeholder," who announced at an election that "he was ready to vote for any one who would give him a Dram." Neither should a candidate ask votes of those whom he was entertaining though it was perhaps all right for him to make the general remark "that if his Friends would stand by him he should carry his Election." Some men thought that there should be no treating after the election writ was issued until the poll had been taken. James Littlepage "expressly ordered" Paul Tilman, whom he had employed "to prepare his Entertainment at the Election . . . not to give the Freeholders any Liquor until after the closing of the Poll," and Littlepage produced evidence to show that "none of them had any Liquor, except some few who insisted on it, and paid for it themselves."

To avoid the appearance of corruption, it was well for the candidate to have the reputation of being hospitable at all times. When William Wager's campaign was under investigation, especially in the matter of the treat given in his home by one of his friends and another treat given in his honor to his militia company, Wager introduced evidence to show that he customarily entertained all who came to his house, strangers as well as freeholders, and that he usually treated the members of his militia company with punch after the exercises were over. "They would after that come before his Door and fire Guns in Token of their Gratitude, and then he would give them Punch 'til they dispersed, and that this had been a frequent Practice for several Years."

To avoid the reality as well as the appearance of corruption, the candidates usually made a point of having it understood that the refreshments were equally free to men of every political opinion. If a candidate's campaign was under investigation, it was much in his favor if he could show that among his guests were some who had clearly said that they did not intend to vote for him. Washington reflected an acceptable attitude when he wrote while arranging for the payment of large bills for liquor consumed during a Frederick County election: "I hope no Exception were taken to any that voted against me but that all were alike treated and all had enough; it is what I much desir'd." Washington seems to have followed this policy in subsequent elections. A young Englishman, who witnessed an election at Alexandria in 1774 when Washington was one of the two successful candidates, wrote: "The Candidates gave the populace a Hogshead of Toddy (what we call Punch in England). In the evening the returned Member gave a Ball to the Freeholders and Gentlemen of the town. This was conducted with great harmony. Coffee and Chocolate, but no Tea. This Herb is in disgrace among them at present."

Bountiful supplies of free liquor were responsible for much rowdiness, fighting, and drunkenness, but the fun and excitement of an election and the prospect of plentiful refreshments of the kind customarily consumed in that day helped to bring the voters to the polls. Thus in a perverse kind of way treating made something of a contribution to eighteenth-century democracy. Although one sometimes found a man who lived by the rule, "never to taste of a man's liquor unless I'm his friend," most of the voters accepted such refreshments as were offered. As they drank, they were less likely to feel that they were incurring obligations than that the candidate was fulfilling his obligation. According to the thinking of that day, the candidate ought to provide refreshments for the freeholders. His failure to fulfill this obligation would be interpreted as a sign of "pride or parsimony," as a "want of respect" for the voters, as James Madison found to his sorrow.

The Virginia voter expected the candidate to be manly and forthright, but he wanted the candidate to treat him with due respect. He had the power to approve and reject, and the sum total of this consciousness of power among the voters was a strong and significant aspect of the democratic spirit in eighteenth-century Virginia.

24. Popular Uprisings and Civil Authority in Eighteenth-Century America

Pauline Maier

The preceding selections suggest the contours of provincial political ideas, practices, and concerns within the context of legally sanctioned institutions of government. But how do we interpret the extralegal activity of provincial political crowds? Why did citizens so often turn to mob violence instead of to the normal channels of government? Marxist historians would assert that crowds came together to fight against oppression from those in power. If poorer people lacked political rights, then mob violence could have been their only alternative in the expression of their needs and wants. But Professor Pauline Maier (b. 1938) of the University of Massachusetts at Boston in the following essay directly challenges such reasoning as it relates to mob action in provincial and revolutionary America. Maintaining that colonial crowds did not as a rule consist only of the poor, she argues that such mobs formed in communities when local magistrates could not obtain what the citizens considered essential through normal political channels.

Mob violence, then, was not necessarily directed against the institutions of government, nor were crowds irrational in their activities. Rather they struck out selectively against the sources of their grievances and then they disbanded, very much like the European mobs of the time. Is it possible, however, that Professor Maier has misled us in asserting the middle-class character and general representativeness of early American mobs? What are possible alternative explanations for the high incidence of crowd action, if the late colonial political culture is defined in elitist, deferential, and increasingly Anglicized terms? How might the growing concentration of wealth in prerevolutionary America relate to incidents of crowd violence? Does it seem plausible that attitudes about the function and legitimacy of mob behavior changed radically because of the new ideals in government inherent in the American Revolution?

It is only natural that the riots and civil turbulence of the past decade and a half have awakened a new interest in the history of American mobs. It should be emphasized, however, that scholarly attention to the subject has roots independent of contemporary events and founded in long-developing historiographical trends. George Rudé's studies of pre-industrial crowds in France and England, E. J. Hobsbawm's discussion of "archaic" social movements, and recent works linking eighteenth-century American thought with English revolutionary tradition have

Source: Pauline Maier, "Popular Uprisings and Civil Authority in Eighteenth-Century America," *William and Mary Quarterly*, 3rd ser., 27 (1970), pp. 3–35. Reprinted by permission of Pauline Maier and the *William and Mary Quarterly*.

all, in different ways, inspired a new concern among historians with colonial uprisings.[1] This discovery of the early American mob promises to have a significant effect upon historical interpretation. Particularly affected are the Revolutionary struggle and the early decades of the new nation, when events often turned upon well-known popular insurrections.

Eighteenth-century uprisings were in some important ways different than those of today—different in themselves, but even more in the political context within which they occurred. As a result they carried different connotations for the American Revolutionaries than they do today. Not all eighteenth-century mobs simply defied the law: some used extralegal means to implement official demands or to enforce laws not otherwise enforceable, others in effect extended the law in urgent situations beyond its technical limits. Since leading eighteenth-century Americans had known many occasions on which mobs took on the defense of the public welfare, which was, after all, the stated purpose of government, they were less likely to deny popular upheavals all legitimacy than are modern leaders. While not advocating popular uprisings, they could still grant such incidents an established and necessary role in free societies, one that made them an integral and even respected element of the political order. These attitudes, and the tradition of colonial insurrections on which they drew, not only shaped political events of the Revolutionary era, but also lay behind many laws and civil procedures that were framed during the 1780's and 1790's, some of which still have a place in the American legal system.

I

Not all colonial uprisings were identical in character or significance. Some involved no more than disorderly vandalism or traditional brawls such as those that annually marked Pope's Day on November 5, particularly in New England. Occasional insurrections defied established laws and authorities in the name of isolated private interests alone—a set of Hartford County, Connecticut, landowners arose in 1722, for example, after a court decision imperiled their particular land titles. Still others—which are of interest here—took on a broader purpose, and defended the interests of their community in general where established authorities failed to act.[2] This common characteristic linked otherwise diverse rural uprisings in New Jersey and the Carolinas. The insurrectionists' punishment of outlaws, their interposition to secure land titles or prevent abuses at the hands of legal officials followed a frustration with established institutions and a belief that justice and even security had to be imposed by the people directly.[3] The earlier Virginia tobacco insurrection also illustrates this common pattern well: Virginians began tearing up young tobacco plants in 1682 only after Governor Thomas Culpeper forced the quick adjournment of their assembly, which had been called to curtail tobacco planting during an economic crisis. The insurrections in Massachusetts a little over a century later represent a variation on this theme. The insurgents in Worcester, Berkshire, Hampshire, Middlesex, and Bristol counties—often linked together as members of "Shays's Rebellion"—forced the closing of civil courts, which threatened to send a major portion of the local population to debtors' prison, only until a new legislature could remedy their pressing needs.[4]

This role of the mob as extralegal arm of the community's interest emerged, too, in repeated uprisings that occurred within the more densely settled coastal areas. The history of Boston, where by the mid-eighteenth century "public order

. . . prevailed to a greater degree than anywhere else in England or America," is full of such incidents. During the food shortage of 1710, after the governor rejected a petition from the Boston selectmen calling for a temporary embargo on the exportation of foodstuffs one heavily laden ship found its rudder cut away, and fifty men sought to haul another outward bound vessel back to shore. Under similar circumstances Boston mobs again intervened to keep foodstuffs in the colony in 1713 and 1729. When there was some doubt a few years later whether or not the selectmen had the authority to seize a barn lying in the path of a proposed street, a group of townsmen, their faces blackened, levelled the structure and the road went through. Houses of ill fame were attacked by Boston mobs in 1734, 1737, and 1771; and in the late 1760's the *New York Gazette* claimed that mobs in Providence and Newport had taken on responsibility for "disciplining" unfaithful husbands. Meanwhile in New London, Connecticut, another mob prevented a radical religious sect, the Rogerenes, from disturbing normal Sunday services, "a practice they . . . [had] followed more or less for many years past; and which all the laws made in that government, and executed in the most judicious manner could not put a stop to."[5]

Threats of epidemic inspired particularly dramatic instances of this community oriented role of the mob. One revealing episode occurred in Massachusetts in 1773–1774. A smallpox hospital had been built on Essex Island near Marblehead "much against the will of the multitude" according to John Adams. "The patients were careless, some of them wantonly so; and others were suspected of designing to spread the smallpox in the town, which was full of people who had not passed through the distemper." In January 1774 patients from the hospital who tried to enter the town from unauthorized landing places were forcefully prevented from doing so; a hospital boat was burned; and four men suspected of stealing infected clothes from the hospital were tarred and feathered, then carted from Marblehead to Salem in a long cortege. The Marblehead town meeting finally won the proprietors' agreement to shut down the hospital; but after some twenty-two new cases of smallpox broke out in the town within a few days "apprehension became general," and some "Ruffians" in disguise hastened the hospital's demise by burning the nearly evacuated building. A military watch of forty men were needed for several nights to keep the peace in Marblehead.[6]

A similar episode occurred in Norfolk, Virginia, when a group of wealthy residents decided to have their families inoculated for smallpox. Fears arose that the lesser disease brought on by the inoculations would spread and necessitate a general inoculation, which would cost "more money than is circulating in Norfolk" and ruin trade and commerce such that "the whole colony would feel the effects." Local magistrates said they could not interfere because "the law was silent in the matter." Public and private meetings then sought to negotiate the issue. Despite a hard-won agreement, however, the pro-inoculation faction persisted in its original plan. Then finally a mob drove the newly inoculated women and children on a five-mile forced march in darkness and rain to the common Pest House, a three-year old institution designed to isolate seamen and others, particularly Negroes, infected with smallpox.[7]

These local incidents indicate a willingness among many Americans to act outside the bounds of law, but they cannot be described as antiauthoritarian in any general sense. Sometimes in fact—as in the Boston bawdy house riot of 1734, or the Norfolk smallpox incident—local magistrates openly countenanced or participated in the mob's activities. Far from opposing established institutions, many supporters of Shays's Rebellion honored their leaders "by no less decisive marks of popular favor than elections to local offices of trust and authority."[8] It was above all the existence of such elections that forced local magistrates to reflect community feelings and so prevented their becoming the targets of insurrections. Certainly in New England, where the town meeting ruled, and to some extent in New York, where aldermen and councilmen were annually elected, this was true; yet even in Philadelphia, with its lethargic closed corporation, or Charleston, which lacked municipal institutions, authority was normally exerted by residents who had an immediate sense of local sentiment. Provincial governments were also for the most part kept alert to local feelings by their elected assemblies. Sometimes, of course, uprisings turned against domestic American institutions—as in Pennsylvania in 1764, when the "Paxton Boys" complained that the colony's Quaker assembly had failed to provide adequately for their defense against the Indians. But uprisings over local issues proved *extra-institutional* in character more often than they were anti-institutional; they served the community where no law existed, or intervened beyond what magistrates thought they could do officially to cope with a local problem.

The case was different when imperial authority was involved. There legal authority emanated from a capital an ocean away, where the colonists had no integral voice in the formation of policy, where governmental decisions were based largely upon the reports of "king's men" and sought above all to promote the king's interests. When London's legal authority and local interest conflicted, efforts to implement the edicts of royal officials were often answered by uprisings, and it was not unusual in these cases for local magistrates to participate or openly sympathize with the insurgents. The colonial response to the White Pines Acts of 1722 and 1729 is one example. Enforcement of the acts was difficult in general because "the various elements of colonial society . . . seemed inclined to violate the pine laws—legislatures, lumbermen, and merchants were against them, and even the royal governors were divided." At Exeter, New Hampshire, in 1734 about thirty men prevented royal officials from putting the king's broad arrow on some seized boards; efforts to enforce the acts in Connecticut during the 1750's ended after a deputy of the surveyor-general was thrown in a pond and nearly drowned; five years later logs seized in Massachusetts and New Hampshire were either "rescued" or destroyed.[9] Two other imperial issues that provoked local American uprisings long before 1765 and continued to do so during the Revolutionary period were impressment and customs enforcement.

As early as 1743 the colonists' violent opposition to impressment was said to indicate a "Contempt of Government." Some captains had been mobbed, the Admiralty complained, "others emprisoned, and afterwards held to exorbitant Bail, and are now under Prosecutions carried on by Combination, and by joint Subscription towards the expense." Colonial governors, despite their offers, furnished captains with little real aid either to procure seamen or "even to protect them from the Rage and Insults of the People." Two days of severe rioting answered Commodore Charles Knowles's efforts to sweep Boston harbor for able-bodied men in November 1747. Again in 1764 when Rear Admiral Lord Alexander Colville sent out orders to "procure" men in principal harbors between Casco Bay and Cape Henlopen, mobs met the ships at every turn. When the *St. John* sent out a boat to seize a recently impressed deserter from a Newport wharf, a mob protected him, captured the boat's officer, and hurled stones at the crew; later fifty Newporters joined the colony's gunner at Fort George in opening fire on the king's ship itself. Under threat to her master the *Chaleur* was forced to release four fishermen seized off Long Island, and when that ship's captain went ashore at New York a mob seized his boat and burned it in the Fields. In the spring of 1765 after the *Maidstone* capped a six-month siege of Newport harbor by seizing "all the Men" out of a brigantine from Africa, a mob of about five hundred men similarly seized a ship's officer and burned one of her boats on the Common. Impressment also met mass resistance at Norfolk in 1767 and was a major cause of the famous *Liberty* riot at Boston in 1768.[10]

Like the impressment uprisings, which in most instances sought to protect or rescue men from the "press," customs incidents were aimed at impeding the customs service in enforcing British laws. Tactics varied, and although incidents occurred long before 1764—in 1719, for example, Caleb Heathcote reported a "riotous and tumultuous" rescue of seized claret by Newporters—their frequency, like those of the impressment "riots," apparently increased after the Sugar Act was passed and customs enforcement efforts were tightened. The 1764 rescue of the *Rhoda* in Rhode Island preceded a theft in Dighton, Massachusetts, of the cargo from a newly seized vessel, the *Polly,* by a mob of some forty men with blackened faces. In 1766 again a mob stoned a customs official's home in Falmouth (Portland), Maine, while "Persons unknown and disguised" stole sugar and rum that had been impounded that morning. The intimidation of customs officials and of the particularly despised customs informers also enjoyed a long history. In 1701 the South Carolina attorney general publicly attacked an informer "and struck him several times, crying out, this is the Informer, this is he that will ruin the country." Similar assaults occurred decades later, in New Haven in 1766 and 1769, and New London in 1769, and were then often distinguished by their brutality. In 1771 a Providence tidesman, Jesse Saville, was seized, stripped, bound hand and foot, tarred and feathered, had dirt thrown in his face, then was beaten and "almost strangled." Even more thorough assaults upon two other Rhode Island tidesmen followed in July 1770 and upon Collector Charles Dudley in April 1771. Finally, customs vessels came under attack: the *St. John* was shelled at Newport in 1764 where the customs ship *Liberty* was sunk in 1769—both episodes that served as prelude to the destruction of the *Gaspée* outside Providence in 1772.[11]

Such incidents were not confined to New England. Philadelphia witnessed some of the most savage attacks, and even the surveyor of Sassafras and Bohemia in Maryland—an office long a sinecure, since no ships entered or cleared in Sassafras or Bohemia—met with violence when he tried to execute his office in March 1775. After seizing two wagons of goods being carried overland from Maryland toward Duck Creek, Delaware, the officer was overpowered by a "licentious mob" that kept shouting "Liberty and Duck Creek forever" as it went through the hours-long rituals of tarring and feathering him and threatening his life. And at Norfolk, Virginia, in the spring 1766 an accused customs informer was tarred and feathered, pelted with stones and rotten eggs, and finally thrown in the sea where he nearly drowned. Even Georgia saw customs violence before independence, and one of the rare deaths resulting from a colonial riot occurred there in 1775.[12]

White Pines, impressment, and customs uprisings have attracted historians' attention because they opposed British authority and so seemed to presage the Revolution. In fact, however, they had much in common with many exclusively local uprisings. In each of the incidents violence was directed not so much against the "rich and powerful"[13] as against men who—as it was said after the Norfolk smallpox incident—"in every part of their conduct . . . acted very inconsistently as good neighbors or citizens." The effort remained one of safeguarding not the interests of isolated groups alone, but the community's safety and welfare. The White Pines Acts need not have provoked this opposition had they applied only to trees of potential use to the Navy, and had they been framed and executed with concern for colonial rights. But instead the acts reserved to the Crown all white pine trees including those "utterly unfit for masts, yards, or bowsprits," and prevented colonists from using them for building materials or lumber exportation even in regions where white pine constituted the principal forest growth. As a result the acts "operated so much against the convenience and even necessities of the inhabitants," Surveyor John Wentworth explained, that "it became almost a general interest of the country" to frustrate the acts' execution. Impressment offered a more immediate effect, since the "press" could quickly cripple whole towns. Merchants and masters were affected as immediately as seamen: the targeted port, as Massachusetts' Governor William Shirley explained in 1747, was drained of mariners by both impressment itself and the flight of navigation to safer provinces, driving the wages for any remaining seamen upward. When the press was of long duration, moreover, or when it took place during a normally busy season, it could mean serious shortages of food or firewood for winter, and a general attrition of the commercial life that sustained all strata of society in trading towns. Commerce seemed even more directly attacked by British trade regulations, particularly by the proliferation of customs procedures in the mid-1760's that seemed to be in no American's interest, and by the Sugar Act with its virtual prohibition of the trade with the foreign West Indies that sustained the economies of colonies like Rhode Island. As a result even when only a limited contingent of sailors participated in a customs incident officials could suspect—as did the deputy collector at Philadelphia in 1770—that the mass of citizens "in their Hearts" approved of it.[14]

Because the various uprisings discussed here grew out of concerns essential to wide sections of the community, the "rioters" were not necessarily confined to the seamen, servants, Negroes, and boys generally described as the staple components of the colonial mob. The uprising of Exeter, New Hampshire, townsmen against the king's surveyor of the woods in 1754 was organized by a member of the prominent Gillman family who was a mill owner and a militia officer. Members of the upper classes participated in Norfolk's smallpox uprising, and Cornelius Calvert, who was later attacked in a related incident, protested that leading members of the community, doctors and magistrates, had posted securities for the good behavior of the "Villains" convicted of mobbing him. Captain Jeremiah Morgan complained about the virtually universal participation of Norfolkers in an impressment incident of 1767, and "all the principal Gentlemen in Town" were supposedly present when a customs informer was tarred and feathered there in 1766. Merchant Benedict Arnold admitted leading a New Haven mob against an informer in 1766; New London merchants Joseph Packwood and Nathaniel Shaw commanded the mob that first accosted Captain William Reid the night the *Liberty* was destroyed at Newport in 1769, just as John Brown, a leading Providence merchant, led that against the *Gaspée*. Charles Dudley reported in April 1771 that the men who beat him in Newport "did not come from the . . . lowest class of Men," but were "stiled Merchants and the Masters of their Vessels"; and again in 1775 Robert Stratford Byrne said many of his Maryland and Pennsylvania attackers were "from Appearance . . . Men of Property." It is interesting, too, that during Shays's Rebellion—so often considered a class uprising—"men who were of good property and owed not a shilling" were said to be "involved in the train of desperado's to suppress the courts."[15]

Opposition to impressment and customs enforcement in itself was not, moreover, the only cause of the so-called impressment or customs "riots." The complete narratives of these incidents indicate again not only that the crowd acted to support local interests, but that it sometimes enforced the will of local magistrates by extralegal means. Although British officials blamed the *St. John* incident upon that ship's customs and impressment activities, colonists insisted that the confrontation began when some sailors stole a few pigs and chickens from a local miller and the ship's crew refused to surrender the thieves to Newport officials. Two members of the Rhode Island council then ordered the gunner of Fort George to detain the schooner until the accused seamen were delivered to the sheriff, and "many People went over the Fort to assist the Gunner in the Discharge of his Duty." Only after this uprising did the ship's officers surrender the accused men.[16] Similarly, the 1747 Knowles impressment riot in Boston and the 1765 *Maidstone* impressment riot in Newport broke out after governors' request for the release of impressed seamen had gone unanswered, and only after the outbreaks of violence were the governors' requests honored. The crowd that first assembled on the night the *Liberty* was destroyed in Newport also began by demanding the allegedly drunken sailors who that afternoon had abused and shot at a colonial captain, Joseph Packwood, so they could be bound over to local magistrates for prosecution.[17]

In circumstances such as these, the "mob" often appeared only after the legal channels of redress had proven inadequate. The main thrust of the colonists' resistance to the White Pines Acts had always been made in their courts and legislatures. Violence broke out only in local situations where no alternative was available. Even the burning of the *Gaspée* in June 1772 was a last resort. Three months before the incident a group of prominent Providence citizens complained about the ship's wanton severity with all vessels along the coast and the colony's governor pressed their case with the fleet's admiral. The admiral, however, supported the *Gaspée*'s commander, Lieutenant William Dudingston; and thereafter, the *Providence Gazette* reported, Dudingston became "more haughty, insolent, and intolerable, . . . personally ill treating every master and merchant of the vessels he boarded, stealing sheep, hogs, poultry, etc. from farmers round the bay, and cutting down their fruit and other trees for firewood." Redress from London was possible but time-consuming, and in the meantime Rhode Island was approaching what its governor called "the deepest calamity" as supplies of food and fuel were curtailed and prices, especially in Newport, rose steeply. It was significant that merchant John Brown finally led the Providence "mob" that seized the moment in June when the *Gaspée* ran aground near Warwick, for it was he who had spearheaded the effort in March 1772 to win redress through the normal channels of government.[18]

II

There was little that was distinctively American about the colonial insurrections. The uprisings over grain exportations during times of dearth, the attacks on brothels, press gangs, royal forest officials, and customsmen, all had their counterparts in seventeenth- and eighteenth-century England. Even the Americans' hatred of the customs establishment mirrored the Englishman's traditional loathing of excise men. Like the customsmen in the colonies, they seemed to descend into localities armed with extraordinary prerogative powers. Often, too, English excisemen were "thugs and brutes who beat up their victims without compunction or stole or wrecked their property" and against whose extravagances little redress was possible through the law.[19] Charges of an identical character were made in the colonies against customsmen and naval officials as well, particularly after 1763 when officers of the Royal Navy were commissioned as deputy members of the customs service,[20] and a history of such accusations lay behind many of the best-known waterfront insurrections. The Americans' complaints took on particular significance only because in the colonies those officials embodied the authority of a "foreign" power. Their arrogance and arbitrariness helped effect "an estrangement of the Affections of the People from the Authority under which they act," and eventually added an emotional element of anger against the Crown to a revolutionary conflict otherwise carried on in the language of law and right.[21]

The focused character of colonial uprisings also resembled those in England and even France where, Rudé has pointed out, crowds were remarkably single-minded and discriminating.[22] Targets were characteristically related to grievances: the Knowles rioters sought only the release of the impressed men; they set free a captured officer when assured he had nothing to do with the press, and refrained from burning a boat near Province House for fear the fire would spread. The Norfolk rioters, driven by fear of smallpox, forcefully isolated the inoculated persons where they would be least dangerous. Even the customs rioters vented their brutality on customs officers and informers alone, and the Shaysite "mobs" dispersed after closing the courts which promised most immediately to effect their ruin. So domesticated and controlled was the Boston mob that it refused to riot on Saturday and Sunday nights, which were considered holy by New Englanders.[23]

When colonists compared their mobs with those in the Mother Country they were struck only with the greater degree of restraint among Americans. "These People bear no Resemblance to an English Mob," John Jay wrote of the Shaysites in December 1786, "they are more temperate, cool and regular in their Conduct—they have hitherto abstained from Plunder, nor have they that I know of committed any outrages but such as the accomplishment of their Purpose made necessary." Similar comparisons were often repeated during the Revolutionary conflict, and were at least partially grounded in fact. When Londoners set out to "pull down" houses of ill fame in 1688, for example, the affair spread, prisons were opened, and disorder ended only when troops were called out. But when eighteenth-century Bostonians set out on the same task, there is no record that their destruction extended beyond the bordellos themselves. Even the violence of the customs riots—which contrast in that regard from other American incidents—can sometimes be explained by the presence of volatile foreign seamen. The attack on the son of customsman John Hatton, who was nearly killed in a Philadelphia riot, occurred, for example, when the city was crowded by over a thousand seamen. His attackers were apparently Irish crew members of a vessel he and his father had tried to seize off Cape May, and they were "set on," the Philadelphia collector speculated, by an Irish merchant in Philadelphia to whom the vessel was consigned. One of the most lethal riots in the history of colonial America, in which rioters killed five people, occurred in a small town near Norfolk, Virginia, and was significantly perpetrated entirely by British seamen who resisted the local inhabitants' efforts to reinstitute peace.[24] During and immediately after the Revolutionary War some incidents occurred in which deaths are recorded; but contemporaries felt these were historical aberrations, caused by the "brutalizing" effect of the war itself. "Our citizens, from a habit of putting . . . [the British] to death, have reconciled their minds to the killing of each other," South Carolina Judge Aedanus Burke explained.[25]

To a large extent the pervasive restraint and virtual absence of bloodshed in American incidents can best be understood in terms of social and military circumstance. There was no large amorphous city in America comparable to London, where England's worst incidents occurred. More important, the casualties even in eighteenth-century British riots were rarely the work of rioters. No deaths were inflicted by the Wilkes, Anti-Irish, or "No Popery" mobs, and only single fatalities resulted from other upheavals such as the Porteous riots of 1736. "It was authority rather than the crowd that was conspicuous for its violence to life and limb": all 285 casualties of the Gordon riots, for example, were rioters.[26] Since a regular army was less at the ready for use against colonial mobs, casualty figures for American uprisings were naturally much reduced.

To some extent the general tendency toward a discriminating purposefulness was shared by mobs throughout western Europe, but within the British Empire the focused character of popular uprisings and also their persistence can be explained in part by the character of law enforcement procedures. There were no professional police forces in the eighteenth century. Instead the power of government depended traditionally upon institutions like the "hue and cry," by which the community in general rose to apprehend felons. In its original medieval form the "hue and cry" was a form of summary justice that resembled modern lynch law. More commonly by the eighteenth century magistrates turned to the *posse commitatus,* literally the "power of the country," and in practice all able-bodied men a sheriff might call upon to assist him. Where greater and more organized support was needed, magistrates could call out the militia.[27] Both the *posse* and the militia drew upon local men, including many of the same persons who made up the mob. This was particularly clear where these traditional mechanisms failed to function effectively. At Boston in September 1766 when customsmen contemplated breaking into the house of merchant Daniel Malcom to search for contraband goods, Sheriff Stephen Greenleaf threatened to call for support from members of the very crowd suspected of an intent to riot; and when someone suggested during the Stamp Act riots that the militia be raised Greenleaf was told it had already risen. This situation meant that mobs could naturally assume the manner of a lawful institution, acting by habit with relative restraint and responsibility. On the other hand, the militia institutionalized the practice of forcible popular coercion and so made the formation of extralegal mobs more natural that J. R. Western has called the militia "a relic of the bad old days," and hailed its passing as "a step towards . . . bringing civilization and humanity into our [English] political life."[28]

These law enforcement mechanisms left magistrates virtually helpless whenever a large segment of the population was immediately involved in the disorder, or when the community had a strong sympathy for the rioters. The Boston militia's failure to act in the Stamp Act riots, which was repeated in nearly all the North American colonies, recapitulated a similar refusal during the Knowles riot of 1747.[29] If the mob's sympathizers were confined to a single locality, the governor could try to call out the militias of surrounding areas, as

Massachusetts Governor William Shirley began to do in 1747, and as, to some extent, Governor Francis Bernard attempted after the rescue of the *Polly* in 1765.[30] In the case of sudden uprisings, however, these peace-keeping mechanisms were at best partially effective since they required time to assemble strength, which often made the effort wholly pointless.

When the disorder continued and the militia either failed to appear or proved insufficient, there was, of course, the army, which was used periodically in the eighteenth century against rioters in England and Scotland. Even in America peacetime garrisons tended to be placed where they might serve to maintain law and order. But since all Englishmen shared a fear of standing armies the deployment of troops had always to be a sensitive and carefully limited recourse. Military and civil spheres of authority were rigidly separated, as was clear to Lord Jeffery Amherst, who refused to use soldiers against antimilitary rioters during the Seven Years' War because that function was "entirely foreign to their command and belongs of right to none but the civil power." In fact troops could be used against British subjects, as in the suppression of civil disorder, only upon the request of local magistrates. This institutional inhibition carried, if anything, more weight in the colonies. There royal governors had quickly lost their right to declare martial law without the consent of the provincial councils that were, again, usually filled with local men.[31]

For all practical purposes, then, when a large political unit such as an entire town or colony condoned an act of mass force, problems were raised "almost insoluble without rending the whole fabric of English law." Nor was the situation confined to the colonies. After describing England's institutions for keeping the peace under the later Stuarts, Max Beloff suggested that no technique for maintaining order was found until nineteenth-century reformers took on the task of reshaping urban government. Certainly by the 1770's no acceptable solution had been found—neither by any colonists, nor "anyone in London, Paris, or Rome, either," as Carl Bridenbaugh has put it. To even farsighted contemporaries like John Adams the weakness of authority was a fact of the social order that necessarily conditioned the way rulers could act. "It is vain to expect or hope to carry on government against the universal bent and genius of the people," he wrote, "we may whimper and whine as much as we will, but nature made it impossible when she made man."[32]

The mechanisms of enforcing public order were rendered even more fragile since the difference between legal and illegal applications of mass force was distinct in theory, but sometimes indistinguishable in practice. The English common law prohibited riot, defined as an uprising of three or more persons who performed what Blackstone called an "unlawful act of violence" for a private purpose. If the act was never carried out or attempted the offense became unlawful assembly; if some effort was made toward its execution, rout; and if the purpose of the uprising was public rather than private—tearing down whore houses, for example, or destroying all enclosures rather than just those personally affecting the insurgents—the offense became treason since it constituted a usurpation of the king's function, a "levying war against the King." The precise legal offence lay not so much in the purpose of the uprising as in its use of force and violence "wherein the Law does not allow the Use of such Force." Such unlawful assumptions of force were carefully distinguished by commentators upon the common law from other occasions on which the law authorized a use of force. It was, for example, legal for force to be used by a sheriff, constable, "or perhaps even . . . a private Person" who assembled "a competent Number of People, in Order with Force to suppress Rebels, or Enemies, or Rioters"; for a justice of the peace to raise the *posse* when opposed in detaining lands, or for Crown officers to raise "a Power as may effectually enable them to over-power any . . . Resistance" in the execution of the King's writs.[33]

In certain situations these distinctions offered at best a very uncertain guide as to who did or did not exert force lawfully. Should a *posse* employ more force than was necessary to overcome overt resistance, for example, its members acted illegally and were indictable for riot. And where established officials supported both sides in a confrontation, or where the legality of an act that officials were attempting to enforce was itself disputed, the decision as to who were or were not rioters seemed to depend upon the observer's point of view. Impressment is a good example. The colonists claimed that impressment was unlawful in North America under an act of 1708, while British authorities and some—but not all—spokesmen for the government held that the law had lapsed in 1713. The question was settled only in 1775, when Parliament finally repealed the "Sixth of Anne." Moreover, supposing impressment could indeed be carried on, were press warrants from provincial authorities still necessary? Royal instructions of 1697 had given royal governors the "sole power of impressing seamen in any of our plantations in America or in sight of them." Admittedly that clause was dropped in 1708, and a subsequent parliamentary act of 1746, which required the full consent of the governor and council before impressment could be carried on within their province, applied only to the West Indies. Nonetheless it seems that in 1764 the Lords of the Admiralty thought the requirement held throughout North America.[34] With the legality of impressment efforts so uncertain, especially when opposed by local authorities, it was possible to see the press gangs as "rioters" for trying *en masse* to perpetrate an unlawful act of violence. In that case the local townsmen who opposed them might be considered lawful defenders of the public welfare, acting much as they would in a *posse*. In 1770 John Adams cited opposition to press gangs who acted without warrants as an example of the lawful use of force; and when the sloop of war *Hornet* swept into Norfolk, Virginia, in September 1767 with a "bloody riotous plan . . . to impress seamen, without consulting the Mayor, or any other magistrate," the offense was charged to the pressmen. Roused by the watchman, who called out *"a riot by man of war's men,"* the inhabitants rose to back the magistrates, and not only secured the release of the impressed men but also imprisoned ten members of the press gang. The ship's captain, on the other hand, condemned the townsmen as "Rioters." Ambiguity was present, too, in Newport's *St. John* clash, which involved both impressment and criminal action on the part of royal seamen and culminated with Newporters firing on the king's ship. The Privy Council in England promptly classified the incident as a riot, but the Rhode Island governor's report boldly maintained that "the people meant nothing but to assist [the magistrates] in apprehending the Offenders" on the vessel, and even suggested that "their Conduct be honored with his Majesty's royal Approbation."[35]

The enforcement of the White Pines Acts was similarly open to legal dispute. The acts seemed to violate both the Massachusetts and Connecticut charters; the meaning of provisions exempting trees growing within townships (act of 1722) and those which were "the property of private persons" (act of 1729) was contested, and royal officials tended to work on the basis of interpretations of the laws that Bernhard Knollenberg has called farfetched and, in one case, "utterly untenable." The Exeter, New Hampshire, "riot" of 1734, for example, answered an attempt of the surveyor to seize boards on the argument that the authorization to seize logs from allegedly illegally felled white pine trees in the act of 1722 included an authorization to seize processed lumber. As a result, Knollenberg concluded, although the surveyors' reports "give the impression that the New Englanders were an utterly lawless lot, . . . in many if not most cases they were standing for what they believed, with reason, were their legal and equitable rights in trees growing on their own lands."[36]

Occasions open to such conflicting interpretations were rare. Most often even those who sympathized with the mobs' motives condemned its use of force as illegal and unjustifiable. That ambiguous cases did arise, however, indicates that legitimacy and illegitimacy, *posses* and rioters, represented but poles of the same spectrum. And where a mob took upon itself the defense of the community, it benefited from a certain popular legitimacy even when the strict legality of its action was in doubt, particularly among a people taught that the legitimacy of law itself depended upon its defense of the public welfare.

Whatever quasi-legal status mobs were accorded by local communities was reinforced, moreover, by formal political thought. "Riots and rebellions" were often calmly accepted as a constant and even necessary element of free government. This acceptance depended, however, upon certain essential assumptions about popular uprisings. With words that could be drawn almost verbatim from John Locke or any other English author of similar convictions, colonial writers posited a continuing moderation and purposefulness on the part of the mob. "Tho' innocent persons may sometimes suffer in popular Tumults," observed a 1768 writer in the *New York Journal,* "yet the general Resentment of the People is principally directed according to Justice, and the greatest Delinquent feels it most." Moreover, upheavals constituted only occasional interruptions in well-governed societies. "Good Laws and good Rulers will always be obey'd and respected"; "the Experience of all Ages proves, that Mankind are much more likely to submit to bad laws and wicked Rulers, than to resist good ones." "Mobs and Tumults," if was often said, "never happen but thro' Oppression and a scandalous Abuse of Power."[37]

In the hands of Locke such remarks constituted relatively inert statements of fact. Colonial writers, however, often turned these pronouncements on their heads such that observed instances of popular disorder became *prima facie* indictments of authority. In 1747, for example, New Jersey land rioters argued that "from their Numbers, Violences, and unlawful Actions" it was to be "inferred that . . . they are wronged and oppressed, or else they would never *rebell agt. the Laws.*" Always, a New York writer said in 1770, when "the People of any Government" become "turbulent and uneasy," it was above all "a certain Sign of Maladministration." Even when disorders were not directly levelled against government they provided "strong proofs that something is much amiss in the state" as William Samuel Johnson put it; that—in Samuel Adams's words—the "wheels of good government" were "somewhat clogged." Americans who used this argument against Britain in the 1760's continued to depend upon it two decades later when they reacted to Shays's Rebellion by seeking out the public "Disease" in their own independent governments that was indicated by the "Spirit of Licentiousness" in Massachusetts.[38]

Popular turbulence seemed to follow so naturally from inadequacies of government that uprisings were often described with similes from the physical world. In

1770 John Adams said that there were "Church-quakes and state-quakes in the moral and political world, as well as earthquakes, storms and tempests in the physical." Two years earlier a writer in the *New York Journal* likened popular tumults to "Thunder Gusts" which "commonly do more Good than Harm." Thomas Jefferson continued the imagery in the 1780's, particularly with his famous statement that he liked "a little rebellion now and then" for it was "like a storm in the atmosphere." It was, moreover, because of the "imperfection of all things in this world," including government, that Adams found it "vain to seek a government in all points free from a possibility of civil wars, tumults and seditions." That was "a blessing denied to this life and preserved to complete the felicity of the next."[39]

If popular uprisings occurred "in all governments at all times," they were nonetheless most able to break out in free governments. Tyrants imposed order and submission upon their subjects by force, thus dividing society, as Jefferson said, into wolves and sheep. Only under free governments were the people "nervous," spirited, jealous of their rights, ready to react against unjust provocations; and this being the case, popular disorders could be interpreted as "Symptoms of a strong and healthy Constitution" even while they indicated some lesser shortcoming in administration. It would be futile, Josiah Quincy, Jr., said in 1770, to expect "that pacific, timid, obsequious, and servile temper, so predominant in more despotic governments" from those who lived under free British institutions. From "our happy constitution," he claimed, there resulted as "very natural Effects" an "impatience of injuries, and a strong resentment of insults."[40]

This popular impatience constituted an essential force in the maintenance of free institutions. "What country can preserve it's [*sic*] liberties if their rulers are not warned from time to time that their people preserve the spirit of resistance?" Jefferson asked in 1787. Occasional insurrections were thus "an evil . . . productive of good": even those founded on popular error tended to hold rulers "to the true principles of their institution" and generally provided "a medecine necessary for the sound health of government." This meant that an aroused people had a role not only in extreme situations, where revolution was requisite, but in the normal course of free government. For that reason members of the House of Lords could seriously argue—as A. J. P. Taylor has pointed out—that "rioting is an essential part of our constitution"; and for that reason, too, even Massachusetts's conservative Lieutenant Governor Thomas Hutchinson could remark in 1768 that "mobs a sort of them at least are constitutional."[41]

III

It was, finally, the interaction of this constitutional role of the mob with the written law that makes the story of eighteenth-century popular uprisings complexity itself.[42] If mobs were appreciated because they provided a check on power, it was always understood that, insofar as upheavals threatened "running to such excesses, as will overturn the whole system of government," "strong discouragements" had to be provided against them. For eighteenth-century Americans, like the English writers they admired, liberty demanded the rule of law. In extreme situations where the rulers had clearly chosen arbitrary power over the limits of law, men like John Adams could prefer the risk of anarchy to continued submission because "anarchy can never last long, and tyranny may be perpetual," but only when "there was any hope that the fair order of liberty and a free constitution would arise out of it." This desire to maintain the orderly rule of law led legislatures in England and the colonies to pass antiriot statutes and to make strong efforts—in the words of a 1753 Massachusetts law—to discountenance "a mobbish temper and spirit in . . . the inhabitants" that would oppose "all government and order."[43]

The problem of limiting mass violence was dealt with most intensely over a sustained period by the American Revolutionary leadership, which has perhaps suffered most from historians' earlier inattention to the history of colonial uprisings. So long as it could be maintained—as it was only fifteen years ago—that political mobs were "rare or unknown in America" before the 1760's, the Revolutionaries were implicitly credited with their creation. American patriots, Charles McLean Andrews wrote, were often "lawless men who were nothing more than agitators and demagogues" and who attracted a following from the riffraff of colonial society. It now seems clear that the mob drew on all elements of the population. More important, the Revolutionary leaders had no need to create mob support. Instead they were forced to work with a "permanent entity," a traditional crowd that exerted itself before, after, and even during the Revolutionary struggle over issues unrelated to the conflict with Britain, and that, as Hobsbawm has noted, characteristically aided the Revolutionary cause in the opening phases of conflict but was hard to discipline thereafter.[44]

In focusing popular exuberance the American leaders could work with long-established tendencies in the mob toward purposefulness and responsibility. In doing so they could, moreover, draw heavily upon the guidelines for direct action that had been defined by English radical writers since the seventeenth century. Extralegal action was justified only when all established avenues to redress had failed. It could not answer casual errors or private failings on the part of the magistrates, but had to await fundamental public abuses so egregious that the "whole people" turned against their rulers. Even then, it was held, opposition had to be measured so that no more force was exerted than was necessary for the public good. Following these principles colonial leaders sought by careful organization to avoid the excesses that first greeted the Stamp Act. Hutchinson's query after a crowd in Connecticut had forced the resignation of stampman Jared Ingersoll—whether "such a public regular assembly can be called a mob"—could with equal appropriateness have been repeated during the tea resistance, or in 1774 when Massachusetts *mandamus* councillors were forced to resign.[45]

From the first appearance of an organized resistance movement in 1765, moreover, efforts were made to support the legal magistrates such that, as John Adams said in 1774, government would have "as much vigor then as ever" except where its authority was specifically under dispute. This concern for the maintenance of order and the general framework of law explains why the American Revolution was largely free from the "universal tumults and all the irregularities and violence of mobbish factions [that] naturally arise when legal authority ceases." It explains, too, why old revolutionaries like Samuel Adams or Christopher Gadsden disapproved of those popular conventions and committees that persisted after regular independent state governments were established in the 1770's. "Decency and Respect [are] due to Constitutional Authority," Samuel Adams said in 1784, "and those Men, who under any Pretence or by any Means whatever, would lessen the Weight of Government lawfully exercised must be Enemies to our happy Revolution and the Common Liberty."[46]

In normal circumstances the "strong discouragements" to dangerous disorder were provided by established legislatures. The measures enacted by them to deal with insurrections were shaped by the eighteenth-century understanding of civil uprisings. Since turbulence indicated above all some shortcoming in government, it was never to be met by increasing the authorities' power of suppression. The "weakness of authority" that was a function of its dependence upon popular support appeared to contemporary Americans as a continuing virtue of British institutions, as one reason why rulers could not simply dictate to their subjects and why Britain had for so long been hailed as one of the freest nations in Europe. It was "far less dangerous to the Freedom of a State" to allow "the laws to be trampled upon, by the licence among the rabble . . . than to dispence with their force by an act of power." Insurrections were to be answered by reform, by attacking the "Disease"—to use John Jay's term of 1786—that lay behind them rather than by suppressing its "Symptoms." And ultimately, as William Samuel Johnson observed in 1768, "the only effectual way to prevent them is to govern with wisdom, justice, and moderation."[47]

In immediate crises, however, legislatures in both England and America resorted to special legislation that supplemented the common law prohibition of riot. The English Riot Act of 1714 was passed when disorder threatened to disrupt the accession of George I; a Connecticut act of 1722 followed a rash of incidents over land title in Hartford County; the Massachusetts act of 1751 answered "several tumultuous assemblies" over the currency issue and another of 1786 was enacted at the time of Shays's Rebellion. The New Jersey legislature passed an act in 1747 during that colony's protracted land riots; Pennsylvania's Riot Act of 1764 was inspired by the Paxton Boys; North Carolina's of 1771 by the Regulators; New York's of 1774 by the "land wars" in Charlotte and Albany Counties.[48] Always the acts specified that the magistrates were to depend upon the *posse* in enforcing their provisions, and in North Carolina on the militia as well. They differed over the number of people who had to remain "unlawfully, riotously, and tumultuously assembled together, to the Disturbance of the Publick Peace" for one hour after the reading of a prescribed riot proclamation before becoming judicable under the act. Some colonies specified less punishments than the death penalty provided for in the English act, but the American statutes were not in general more "liberal" than the British. Two of them so violated elementary judicial rights that they were subsequently condemned—North Carolina's by Britain, and New York's act of 1774 by a later, Revolutionary state legislature.[49]

In one important respect, however, the English Riot Act was reformed. Each colonial riot law, except that of Connecticut, was enacted for only one to three years, whereas the British law was perpetual. By the provision colonial legislators avoided the shortcoming which, it was said, was "more likely to introduce *arbitrary Power* than even an *Army* itself," because a perpetual riot act meant that "in all future time" by "reading a Proclamation" the Crown had the power "of hanging up their Subjects wholesale, or of picking out Those, to whom they have the greatest Dislike." If the death penalty was removed, the danger was less. When, therefore, riot acts without limit of time were finally enacted—as Connecticut had done in 1722, Massachusetts in 1786, New Jersey in 1797—the punishments were considerably milder, providing, for example, for imprisonment not exceeding six months in Connecticut, one year in Massachusetts, and three years in New Jersey.[50]

Riot legislation, it is true, was not the only recourse against insurgents, who throughout the eighteenth century could also be prosecuted for treason. The colonial and state riot acts suggest, nonetheless, that American legislators recognized the participants in civil insurrections as guilty of a crime peculiarly complicated because it had social benefits as well as damages. To some degree, it appears, they shared the idea expressed well by Jefferson in 1787: that "honest republican governors" should be "so mild in their punishments of rebellions, as not to discourage them too much."[51] Even in countering riots the legislators seemed as intent upon preventing any perversion of the forces of law and order by established authorities as with chastising the insurgents. Reform of the English Riot Act thus paralleled the abolition of constituent treasons—a traditional recourse against enemies of the Crown—in American state treason acts of the Revolutionary period and finally in Article III of the Federal Constitution.[52] From the same preoccupation, too, sprang the limitations placed upon the regular army provided for in the Constitution in part to assure the continuation of republican government guaranteed to the states by Article IV, Section IV. Just as the riot acts were for so long limited in duration, appropriations for the army were never to extend beyond two years (Article I, Section viii, 12); and the army could be used within a state against domestic violence only after application by the legislature or governor, if the legislature could not be convened (Article IV, Section iv).

A continuing desire to control authority through popular action also underlay the declaration in the Second Amendment that "a well regulated Militia being necessary to the security of a free State," citizens were assured the "right . . . to keep and bear Arms." The militia was meant above all "to prevent the establishment of a standing army, the bane of liberty"; and the right to bear arms—taken in part from the English Bill of Rights of 1689—was considered a standing threat to would-be tyrants. It embodied "a public allowance, under due restrictions, of the *natural right of resistance and self preservation,* when the sanctions of society and laws are found *insufficient* to restrain the *violence of oppression.*" And on the basis of their eighteenth-century experience, Americans could consider that right to be "perfectly harmless. . . . If the government be equitable; if it be reasonable in its exactions; if proper attention be paid to the education of children in knowledge, and religion," Timothy Dwight declared, "few men will be disposed to use arms, unless for their amusement, and for the defence of themselves and their country."[53]

The need felt to continue the eighteenth-century militia as a counter-weight to government along with the efforts to outlaw rioting and to provide for the use of a standing army against domestic insurrections under carefully defined circumstances together illustrate the complex attitude toward peace-keeping that prevailed among the nation's founders. The rule of law had to be maintained, yet complete order was neither expected nor even desired when it could be purchased, it seemed, only at the cost of forcefully suppressing the spirit of a free people. The constant possibility of insurrection—as institutionalized in the militia—was to remain an element of the United States Constitution, just as it had played an essential role in Great Britain's.

This readiness to accept some degree of tumultuousness depended to a large degree upon the lawmakers' own experience with insurrections in the eighteenth century, when "disorder" was seldom anarchic and "rioters" often acted to defend law and justice rather than to oppose them. In the years after independence this toleration declined, in part because mass action took on new dimensions. Nineteenth-century mobs often resembled in outward form those of the previous century, but a new violence was added. Moreover, the literal assumption of popular rule in the years after Lexington taught many thoughtful Revolutionary partisans what was for them an unexpected lesson—that the people were "as capable of despotism as any prince," that "public liberty was no guarantee after all of private liberty."[54] With home rule secured, attention focused more exclusively upon minority rights, which mob action had always to some extent imperiled. And the danger that uprisings carried for individual freedom became ever more egregious as mobs shed their former restraint and burned Catholic convents, attacked nativist speakers, lynched Mormons, or destroyed the presses and threatened the lives of abolitionists.

Ultimately, however, changing attitudes toward popular uprisings turned upon fundamental transformations in the political perspective of Americans after 1776. Throughout the eighteenth century political institutions had been viewed as in a constant evolution: the colonies' relationship with Britain and with each other, even the balance of power within the governments of various colonies, remained unsettled. Under such circumstances the imputations of governmental shortcoming that uprisings carried could easily be accepted and absorbed. But after Independence, when the form and conduct of the Americans' governments were under their exclusive control, and when those governments represented, moreover, an experiment in republicanism on which depended their own happiness and "that of generations unborn," Americans became less ready to endure domestic turbulence or accept its disturbing implications. Some continued to argue that "distrust and dissatisfaction" on the part of the multitude were "always the consequence of tyranny or corruption." Others, however, began to see domestic turbulence not as indictments but as insults to government that were likely to discredit American republicanism in the eyes of European observers. "Mobs are a reproach to Free Governments," where all grievances could be legally redressed through the courts or the ballot box, it was argued in 1783. They originated there "not in Oppression, but in Licentiousness," an "ungovernable spirit" among the people. Under republican governments even that distrust of power colonists had found so necessary for liberty, and which uprisings seemed to manifest, could appear outmoded. "There is some consistency in being jealous of power in the hands of those who assume it by birth . . . and over whom we have no controul . . . as was the case with the Crown of England over America," another writer suggested. "But to be jealous of those whom we chuse, the instant we have chosen them" was absurd: perhaps in the transition from monarchy to republic Americans had "bastardized" their ideas by placing jealousy where confidence was more appropriate.[55] In short, the assumptions behind the Americans' earlier toleration of the mob were corroded in republican America. Old and new attitudes coexisted in the 1780's and even later. But the appropriateness of popular uprisings in the United States became increasingly in doubt after the Federal Constitution came to be seen as the final product of long-term institutional experimentation, "a momentous contribution to the history of politics" that rendered even that most glorious exertion of popular force, revolution itself, an obsolete resort for Americans.[56]

Yet this change must not be viewed exclusively as a product of America's distinctive Revolutionary achievement. J. H. Plumb has pointed out, that a century earlier, when England passed beyond her revolutionary era and progressed toward political "stability," radical ideology with its talk of resistance and revolution was gradually left behind. A commitment to peace and permanence emerged from decades of fundamental change. In America as in England this stability demanded that operative sovereignty, including the right finally to decide what was and was not in the community's interest, and which laws were and were not constitutional, be entrusted to established governmental institutions. The result was to minimize the role of the people at large, who had been the ultimate arbiters of those questions in English and American Revolutionary thought. Even law enforcement was to become the task primarily of professional agencies. As a result in time all popular upheavals alike became menacing efforts to "pluck up law and justice by the roots," and riot itself gradually became defined as a purposeless act of anarchy, "a blind and misguided outburst of popular fury," of "undirected violence with no articulated goals."[57]

NOTES

1. See the following by George Rudé: *The Crowd in the French Revolution* (Oxford, 1959); "The London 'Mob' of the Eighteenth Century," *The Historical Journal*, II (1959), 1–18; *Wilkes and Liberty: A Social Study of 1763 to 1774* (Oxford, 1962); *The Crowd in History: A Study of Popular Disturbances in France and England, 1730–1848* (New York, 1964). See also E. J. Hobsbawm, *Primitive Rebels: Studies in Archaic Forms of Social Movement in the 19th and 20th Centuries* (New York, 1959), esp. "The City Mob," 108–125. For recent discussions of the colonial mob see: Bernard Bailyn, *Pamphlets of the American Revolution* (Cambridge, Mass., 1965), I, 581–584; Jesse Lemisch, "Jack Tar in the Street: Merchant Seamen in the Politics of Revolutionary America," *William and Mary Quarterly*, 3d ser., XXV (1968), 371–407; Gordon S. Wood, "A Note on Mobs in the American Revolution," *Wm. and Mary Qtly.*, 3rd Ser., XXIII (1966), 635–642, and more recently Wood's *Creation of the American Republic, 1776–1787* (Chapel Hill, 1969), *passim*, but esp. 319–328. Wood offers an excellent analysis of the place of mobs and extralegal assemblies in the development of American constitutionalism. Hugh D. Graham and Ted R. Gurr, *Violence in America: Historical and Comparative Perspectives* (New York, 1969) primarily discusses uprisings of the 19th and 20th centuries, but see the chapters by Richard M. Brown, "Historical Patterns of Violence in America," 45–84, and "The American Vigilante Tradition," 154–226.

2. Carl Bridenbaugh, *Cities in the Wilderness: The First Century of Urban Life in America, 1625–1742* (New York, 1964), 70–71, 223–224, 382–384; and Carl Bridenbaugh, *Cities in Revolt: Urban Life in America, 1743–1776* (New York, 1964), 113–118; Charles J. Hoadly, ed., *The Public Records of the Colony of Connecticut . . .* (Hartford, 1872), VI, 332–333, 341–348.

3. See particularly Richard M. Brown, *The South Carolina Regulators* (Cambridge, Mass., 1963). There is no published study of the New Jersey land riots, which lasted over a decade and were due above all to the protracted inability of the royal government to settle land disputes stemming from conflicting proprietary grants made in the late 17th century. See, however, "A State of Facts concerning the Riots and Insurrections in New Jersey, and the Remedies Attempted to Restore the Peace of the Province," William A. Whitehead, *et al.*, eds., *Archives of the State of New Jersey* (Newark, 1883), VII, 207–226. On other rural insurrections see Irving Mark, *Agrarian Conflicts in Colonial New York, 1711–1775* (New York, 1940), Chap. IV, V; Staughton Lynd, "The Tenant Rising at Livingston Manor," *New-York Historical Society Quarterly*, XLVIII (1964), 163–177; Matt Bushnell Jones, *Vermont in the Making, 1750–1777* (Cambridge, Mass., 1939), Chap. XII, XIII; John R. Dunbar, ed., *The Paxton Papers* (The Hague, 1957), esp. 3–51.

4. Richard L. Morton, *Colonial Virginia* (Chapel Hill, 1960), I, 303–304; Jonathan Smith, "The Depression of 1785 and Daniel Shays' Rebellion," *Wm. and Mary Qtly.*, 3d ser., V (1948), 86–87, 91.

5. Bridenbaugh, *Cities in Revolt*, 114; Bridenbaugh, *Cities in the Wilderness*, 196, 383, 388–389; Edmund S. and Helen M. Morgan, *The Stamp Act Crisis*, rev. ed. (New York, 1963), 159; Anne Rowe Cunningham, ed., *Letters and Diary of John Rowe, Boston Merchant, 1759–1762, 1764–1779* (Boston, 1903), 218. On the marriage riots, see *New-York Gazette* (New York City), July 11, 1765—and note, that when the reporter speaks of persons "concern'd in such unlawful Enterprises" he clearly is referring to the husbands, not their "Disciplinarians." On the Rogerenes, see item in *Connecticut Gazette* (New Haven), Apr. 5, 1766, reprinted in Lawrence H. Gipson, *Jared Ingersoll* (New Haven, 1920), 195, n. 1.

6. John Adams, "Novanglus," in Charles F. Adams, ed., *The Works of John Adams* (Boston, 1850–1856), IV, 76–77; Salem news of Jan. 25 and Feb. 1, 1774, in *Providence Gazette* (Rhode Island), Feb. 5, and Feb. 12, 1774.

7. Letter from "Friend to the Borough and county of Norfolk," in Purdie and Dixon's *Virginia Gazette Postscript* (Williamsburg), Sept. 8, 1768, which gives the fullest account. This letter answered an earlier letter from Norfolk, Aug. 6, 1768, available in Rind's *Va. Gaz. Supplement* (Wmsbg.), Aug. 25, 1768. See also letter of Cornelius Calvert in Purdie and Dixon's *Va. Gaz.* (Wmsbg.), Jan. 9, 1772. Divisions over the inoculation seemed to follow more general political lines. See Patrick Henderson, "Smallpox and Patriotism, The Norfolk Riots, 1768–1769," *Virginia Magazine of History and Biography,* LXXIII (1965), 413–424.

8. James Madison to Thomas Jefferson, Mar. 19, 1787, in Julian P. Boyd, ed., *The Papers of Thomas Jefferson* (Princeton, 1950–), XI, 223.

9. Bernard Knollenberg, *Origin of the American Revolution: 1759–1766* (New York, 1965), 126, 129. See also, Robert G. Albion, *Forests and Sea Power* (Cambridge, Mass., 1926), 262–263, 265. Joseph J. Malone, *Pine Trees and Politics* (Seattle, 1964), includes less detail on the forceful resistance to the acts.

10. Admiralty to Gov. George Thomas, Sept. 26, 1743, in Samuel Hazard *et al.*, eds., *Pennsylvania Archives* (Philadelphia, 1852–1949), I, 639. For accounts of the Knowles riot, see Gov. William Shirley to Josiah Willard, Nov. 19, 1747, Shirley's Proclamation of Nov. 21, 1747, and his letter to the Board of Trade, Dec. 1, 1747, in Charles H. Lincoln, ed., *The Correspondence of William Shirley . . . 1731–1760* (New York, 1912), I, 406–419; see also Thomas Hutchinson, *History of the Province of Massachusetts Bay,* ed. Lawrence S. Mayo (Cambridge, Mass., 1936), II, 330–333; and *Reports of the Record Commissioners of Boston* (Boston, 1885), XIV, 127–130. David Lovejoy, *Rhode Island Politics and the American Revolution, 1760–1776* (Providence, 1958), 36–39, and on the *Maidstone* in particular see "O. G." in *Newport Mercury* (Rhode Island), June 10, 1765. Bridenbaugh, *Cities in Revolt,* 309–311; documents on the *St. John* episode in *Records of the Colony of Rhode Island and Providence Plantations* (Providence, 1856–1865), VI, 427–430. George G. Wolkins, "The Seizure of John Hancock's Sloop 'Liberty,'" Massachusetts Historical Society, *Proceedings* (1921–1923), LV, 239–284. See also Lemisch, "Jack Tar," *Wm. and Mary Qtly.,* 3d ser., XXV (1968), 391–393; and Neil R. Stout, "Manning the Royal Navy in North America, 1763–1775," *American Neptune,* XXIII (1963), 179–181.

11. Heathcote letter from Newport, Sept. 7, 1719, *Records of the Colony of Rhode Island,* IV, 259–260; Lovejoy, *Rhode Island Politics,* 35–39. There is an excellent summary of the *Polly* incident in Morgan, *Stamp Act Crisis,* 59, 64–67; and see also *Providence Gaz.* (R.I.), Apr. 27, 1765. On the Falmouth incident see the letter from the collector and comptroller of Falmouth, Aug. 19, 1766, Treasury Group 1, Class 453, Piece 182, Public Records Office. Hereafter cited as T. 1/453, 182. See also the account in Appendix I of Josiah Quincy, Jr., *Reports of the Case Argued and Adjudged in the Superior Court of Judicature of the Province of Massachusetts Bay, between 1761 and 1772* (Boston, 1865), 446–447. W. Noel Sainsbury *et al.*, eds., *Calendar of State papers, Colonial Series, America and the West Indies* (London, 1910), *1701,* no. 1042, xi, a. A summary of one of the New Haven informer attacks is in Willard M. Wallace, *Traitorous Hero: The Life and Fortunes of Benedict Arnold* (New York, 1954), 20–23. Arnold's statement on the affair which he led is in Malcolm Decker, *Benedict Arnold, Son of the Havens* (Tarrytown, N.Y., 1932), 27–29. Gipson, in *Jared Ingersoll, 277–278,* relates the later incidents. For the New London informer attacks, see documents of July 1769 in T. 1/471. On the Saville affair see Saville to collector and comptroller of customs in Newport, May 18, 1769, T. 1/471, and *New York Journal* (New York City), July 6, 1769. On later Rhode Island incidents see Dudley and John Nicoll to governor of Rhode Island, Aug. 1, 1770, T. 1/471. Dudley to commissioners of customs at Boston, Newport, Apr. 11, 1771, T. 1/482. On the destruction of the *Liberty* see documents in T. 1/471, esp. comptroller and collector to the governor, July 21, 1769.

12. On Philadelphia violence see William Sheppard to commissioners of customs, Apr. 21, 1769, T. 1/471; Deputy Collector at Philadelphia John Swift to commissioners of customs at Boston, Oct. 13, 1769, *ibid.;* and on a particularly brutal attack on the son of customsman John Hatton, see Deputy Collector John Swift to Boston customs commissioners, Nov. 15, 1770, and related documents in T. 1/476. See also Alfred S. Martin, "The King's Customs: Philadelphia, 1763–1774," *Wm. and Mary Qtly.,* 3d ser., V (1948), 201–216. Documents on the Maryland episode are in T. 1/513, including the following: Richard Reeve to Grey Cooper, Apr. 19, 1775; extracts from a Council meeting, Mar. 16, 1775; deposition to Robert Stratford Byrne, surveyor of His Majesty's Customs at Sassafras and Bohemia, and Byrne to customs commissioners, Mar. 17, 1775. On the Virginia incident see William Smith to Jeremiah Morgan, Apr. 3, 1766, Colonial Office Group, Class 5, Piece 1331, 80, Public Record Office. Hereafter cited as C. O. 5/1331, 80. W. W. Abbot, *The Royal Governors of Georgia, 1754–1775* (Chapel Hill, 1959), 174–175. These customs riots remained generally separate from the more central intercolonial opposition to Britain that emerged in 1765. Isolated individuals like John Brown of providence and Maximilian Calvert of Norfolk were involved in both the organized intercolonial Sons of Liberty and in leading mobs against customs functionaries or informers. These roles,

however, for the most part were unconnected, that is, there was no radical program of customs obstruction *per se*. Outbreaks were above all local responses to random provocations and, at least before the Townshend duties, usually devoid of explicit ideological justifications.

13. Hobsbawm, *Primitive Rebels,* 111. For a different effort to see class division as relevant in 18th century uprising, see Lemisch, "Jack Tar," *Wm. and Mary Qtly.,* 3d ser., XXV (1968), 387.

14. "Friends to the borough and county of Norfolk," Purdie and Dixon's *Va. Gaz. Postscrpt.* (Wmsbg.), Sept. 8, 1768. Wentworth quoted in Knollenberg, *Origin of American Revolution,* 124–125. Lemisch, "Jack Tar," *Wm. and Mary Qtly.,* 3d ser., XXV (1968), 383–385. Shirley to Duke of Newcastle, Dec. 31, 1747, in Lincoln, ed., *Shirley Correspondence,* I, 420–423. Dora Mae Clark, "The Impressment of Seamen in the American Colonies," *Essays in Colonial History Presented to Charles McLean Andrews* (New Haven, 1931), 199–200; John Swift to Boston customs commissioners, Nov. 15, 1770, T. 1/476.

15. Malone, *White Pines,* 112. "Friends to the borough and county of Norfolk," Purdie and Dixon's *Va. Gaz. Postscrpt.* (Wmsbg.), Sept. 8, 1768; Calvert letter, *ibid.,* Jan. 9, 1772, Capt. Jeremiah Morgan, quoted in Lemisch, "Jack Tar," *Wm. and Mary Qtly.,* 3d ser., XXV (1968), 391; and William Smith to Morgan, Apr. 3, 1766, C. O. 5/1331, 80. Decker, *Benedict Arnold,* 27–29; deposition of Capt. William Reid on the *Liberty* affair, July 21, 1769, T. 1/471; Ephraim Bowen's narrative on the *Gaspée* affair, *Records of the Colony of Rhode Island,* VII, 68–73; Charles Dudley to Boston customs commissioners, Apr. 11, 1771, T. 1/482, and deposition by Byrne, T. 1/513. Edward Carrington to Jefferson, June 9, 1787, Boyd, ed., *Jefferson Papers,* XI, 408; and see also Smith, "Depression of 1785," *Wm. and Mary Qtly.,* 3d ser., V (1948), 88—of the 21 men indicated for treason in Worcester during the court's April term 1787, 15 were "gentlemen" and only 6 "yeomen."

16. Gov. Samuel Ward's report to the Treasury lords, Oct. 23, 1765, Ward Manuscripts, Box 1, fol. 58, Rhode Island Historical Society, Providence. See also deposition of Daniel Vaughn of Newport—Vaughn was the gunner at Fort George—July 8, 1764, Chalmers Papers, Rhode Island, fol. 41, New York Public Library, New York City. For British official accounts of the affair, see Lieut. Hill's version in James Munro, ed., *Acts of the Privy Council of England, Colonial Series* (London, 1912), VI, 374–376, and the report of John Robinson and John Nicoll to the customs commissioners, Aug. 30, 1765, Privy Council Group, Class I, Piece 51, Bundle 1 (53a), Public Record Office. Hill, whose report was drawn up soon after the incident, does not contradict Ward's narrative, but seems oblivious of any warrant-granting process on shore; Robinson and Nicoll—whose report was drawn up over a year later, and in the midst of the Stamp Act turmoil—claimed that a recent customs seizure had precipitated the attack upon the *St. John.*

17. On the Knowles and *Maidstone* incidents see above, n. 10. On the *Liberty* affair see documents in T. 1/471, esp. the deposition of Capt. William Reid, July 21, 1769, and that of John Carr, the second mate, who indicates that the mob soon forgot its scheme of delivering the crew members to the magistrates.

18. Malone, *White pines,* 8–9, and *passim. Records of the Colony of Rhode Island,* VII, 60, 62–63, 174–175, including the deposition of Dep. Gov. Darius Sessions, June 12, 1772, and Adm. Montagu to Gov. Wanton, Apr. 8, 1772. Also, Wanton to Hillsborough, June 16, 1772, and Ephraim Bowen's narrative, *ibid.,* 63–73, 90–92. *Providence Gaz.* (R.I.), Jan. 9, 1773).

19. Max Beloff, *Public Order and Popular Disturbances, 1660–1714* (London, 1938), *passim;* Albion, *Forests and Sea Power,* 263; J. H. Plumb, *England in the Eighteenth Century* (Baltimore, 1961 [orig. publ., Oxford, 1950]), 66.

20. See, for example, "A Pumkin" in the *New London Gazette* (Connecticut), May 14, 18, 1773; "O. G." in *Newport Merc.* (R.I.), June 10, 1765; *New London Gaz.* (Conn.), Sept. 22, 1769; complaints of Marylander David Bevan, reprinted in Rind's *Va. Gaz.* (Wmsbg.), July 27, 1769, and *New London Gaz.* (Conn.), July 21, 1769. Stout, "Manning the Royal Navy," *American Neptune,* XXIII (1963), 174. For a similar accusation against a surveyor-general of the king's woods, see Albion, *Forests and Sea Power,* 262.

21. Joseph Reed to the president of Congress, Oct. 21, 1779, in Hazard *et al.,* eds., *Pennsylvania Archives,* VII, 762. Five years earlier Reed had tied to impress upon Lord Dartmouth the importance of constraining Crown agents in the colonies if any reconciliation were to be made between Britain and the colonies. See his letter to Earl of Dartmouth, Apr. 4, 1774, in William B. Reed, *Life and Correspondence of Joseph Reed* (Philadelphia, 1847), I, 56–57. For a similar plea, again from a man close to the American Revolutionary leadership, see Stephen Sayre to Lord Dartmouth, Dec. 13, 1766, Dartmouth papers, D 1778/2/258, William Salt Library, Stafford, England.

22. Rudé, *Crowd in History,* 60, 253–254. The restraint exercised by 18th century mobs has often been commented upon. See, for example, Wood, "A Note on Mobs," *Wm. and Mary Qtly.,* 3d ser., XXIII (1966), 636–637.

23. Joseph Harrison's testimony in Wolkins, "Seizure of Hancock's Sloop 'Liberty,'" Mass. Hist. Soc., *Proceedings,* LV, 254.

24. Jay to Jefferson, Dec. 14, 1786, Boyd, ed., *Jefferson papers,* X, 597. Beloff, *Public Order,* 30. John Swift to Boston customs commissioners, Nov. 15, 1770, Gov. William Franklin's Proclamation, Nov. 17, 1770, and John Hatton to Boston custom commissioners, Nov. 20, 1770, T. 1/476. The last mentioned riot occurred in November 1762. A cartel ship from Havana had stopped for repairs in October. On Nov. 21 a rumor spread that the Spaniards were murdering the inhabitants, which drew seamen from His Majesty's ship, *Arundel,* also in the harbor, into town, where the seamen drove the Spaniards into a house, set fire to it, and apparently intended to blow it up. A dignitary of the Spanish colonial service, who had been a passenger on the cartel ship, was beaten and some money and valuables were stolen from him. Local men tried to quell the riot without success. It was eventually put down by militiamen from Norfolk. See "A Narrative of a Riot in Virginia in November 1762," T. 1/476.

25. Burke and others to the same effect, quoted in Jerome J. Nadelhaft, The Revolutionary Era in South Carolina, 1775–1788 (unpubl. Ph.D. diss., University of Wisconsin, 1965), 151–152. See also account of the "Fort Wilson" riot of October 1779 in J. Thomas Scharf and Thompson Westcott, *History of Philadelphia, 1609–1884* (Philadelphia, 1884), I, 401–403.

26. Rudé, *Crowd in History,* 255–257.

27. On the "hue and cry" see Frederick Pollock and Frederic W. Maitland, *The History of English Law before the Time of Edward I* (Cambridge, Eng., 1968 [orig. publ., Cambridge, Eng., 1895]), II, 578–580, and William Blackstone, *Commentaries on the Laws of England* (Philadelphia, 1771), IV, 290–291. John Shy, *Toward Lexington: The Role of the British Army in the Coming of the American Revolution* (Princeton, 1965), 40. The English militia underwent a period of decay after 1670 but was revived in 1757. See J. R. Western, *The English Militia in the Eighteenth Century* (London, 1965).

28. Greenleaf's deposition, T. 1/446; *Providence Gaz.* (R.I.), Aug. 24, 1765. Western, *English Militia,* 74.

29. Gov. William Shirley explained the militia's failure to appear during the opening stages of the Knowles riot by citing the militiamen's opposition to impressment and consequent sympathy for the rioters. See his letter to the Lords of Trade, Dec. 1, 1747, in Lincoln, ed., *Shirley Correspondence,* I, 417–418. The English militia was also unreliable. It worked well against invasions and unpopular rebellions, but was less likely to support the government when official orders "clashed with the desires of the citizens" or when ordered to protect unpopular minorities. Sir Robert Walpole believed "that if called on to suppress smuggling, protect the turnpikes, or enforce the gin act, the militia would take the wrong side." Western, *English Militia,* 72–73.

30. Shirley to Josiah Willard, Nov. 19, 1747, Lincoln, ed., *Shirley Correspondence,* I, 407; Bernard's orders in *Providence Gaz.* (R.I.), Apr. 27, 1765.

31. Shy, *Toward Lexington,* 39–40, 44, 47, 74. Amherst, quoted in J. C. Long, *Lord Jeffrey Amherst* (New York, 1933), 124.

32. Shy, *Toward Lexington,* 44, Beloff, *Public Order,* 157–158; Bridenbaugh, *Cities in Revolt,* 297; C. F. Adams, ed., *Works of Adams,* IV, 74–75, V, 209.

33. The definition of the common law of riot most commonly cited—for example, by John Adams in the Massacre trials—was from William Hawkins, *A Treatise of the Pleas of the Crown* (London, 1716), I, 155–159. See also, Blackstone, *Commentaries,* IV, 146–147, and Edward Coke, *The Third Part of the Institutes of the Laws of England* (London, 1797), 176.

34. Clark, "Impressment of Seamen," *Essays in Honor of Andrew,* 198–224; Stout, "Manning the Royal Navy," *American Neptune,* XXIII (1963), 178–179; and Leonard W. Labaree, ed., *Royal Instructions to British Colonial Governors, 1670–1776* (New York, 1935), I, 442–443.

35. L. Kinvin Wroth and Hiller B. Zobel, eds., *Legal Papers of John Adams* (Cambridge, Mass., 1965), III, 253. Account of the Norfolk incident by George Abyvon, Sept. 5, 1767, in Purdie and Dixon's *Va. Gaz.* (Wmsbg.), Oct. 1, 1767. Capt. Morgan quoted in Lemisch, "Jack Tar," *Wm. and Mary Qtly.,* 3d ser., XXV (1968), 391. Munro, ed., *Acts of the privy Council, Colonial Series,* VI, 374; Gov. Samuel Ward to Treasury lords, Oct. 23, 1765, Ward MSS, Box 1, fol. 58.

36. Knollenberg, *Origin of the Revolution,* 122–130; Albion, *Forests and Sea Power,* 255–258.

37. *N.Y. Jour.* (N.Y.C.), Aug. 18, 1768 (the writer was allegedly drawing together arguments that had recently appeared in the British press); and *N.Y. Jour. Supplement* (N.Y.C.), Jan. 4, 1770. Note also that Jefferson accepted Shays's Rebellion as a sign of health in American institutions only after he had been assured by men like Jay that the insurgents had acted purposefully and moderately, and after he had concluded that the uprising represented no continuous threat to established government. "An insurrection in one of the 13. states in the course of 11. years that they have subsisted amounts to one

in any particular state in 143 years, say a century and a half," he calculated. "This would not be near as many as has happened in every other government that has ever existed," and clearly posed no threat to the constitutional order as a whole. To David Hartley, July 2, 1787, Boyd, ed., *Jefferson Papers,* XI, 526.

38. John Locke, *The Second Treatise of Government,* paragraphs 223–225. "A State of Facts Concerning the Riots ... in New Jersey," *New Jersey Archives,* VII, 217, *N.Y. Jour., Supp.* (N.Y.C.), Jan. 4, 1770. Johnson to Wm. Pitkin, Apr. 29, 1768, Massachusetts Historical Society, *Collections,* 5th ser., IX (1885), 275. Adams as "Determinus" in *Boston Gazette,* Aug. 8, 1768; and Harry A. Cushing, ed., *The Writings of Samuel Adams* (New York, 1904–1908), I, 237. Jay to Jefferson, Oct. 27, 1786, Boyd, ed., *Jefferson Papers,* X, 488.

39. Wroth and Zobel, eds., *Adams Legal Papers,* III, 249–250; *N.Y. Jour. Supp.* (N.Y.C.), Aug. 18, 1768; Jefferson to Abigail Adams, Feb. 22, 1787, Boyd, ed., *Jefferson Papers,* XI, 174. C. F. Adams, ed., *Works of Adams,* IV, 77, 80 (quoting Algernon Sydney).

40. Jefferson to Edward Carrington, Jan. 16, 1787, Boyd, ed., *Jefferson Papers,* XI, 49, and Rev. James Madison to Jefferson, Mar. 28, 1787, *ibid.,* 252. Wroth and Zobel, eds., *Adams Legal Papers,* III, 250. Quincy's address to the jury in the soldiers' trial after the Boston Massacre in Josiah Quincy, *Memoir of the life of Josiah Quincy, Junior, of Massachusetts Bay, 1744–1775,* ed. Eliza Susan Quincy, 3d ed. (Boston, 1875), 46. See also Massachusetts Assembly's similar statement in its address to Gov. Hutchinson, Apr. 24, 1770, Hutchinson, *History of Massachusetts Bay,* ed. Mayo, III, 365–366. This 18th century devotion to political "jealousy" resembles the doctrine of "vigilance" that was defended by 19th century vigilante groups. See Graham and Gurr, *Violence in America,* 179–183.

41. Jefferson to William Stephen Smith, Nov. 13, 1787, Boyd, ed., *Jefferson Papers,* XII, 356, Jefferson to Carrington, Jan. 16, 1787, *ibid.,* XI, 49, Jefferson to James Madison, Jan. 30, 1787, *ibid.,* 92–93. Taylor's remarks in "History of Violence," *The Listener,* CXXIX (1968), 701. ("Members of the House of Lords ... said ... if the people really don't like something, then they wreck our carriages and tear off our wigs and throw stones through the windows of our town-houses. And this is an essential thing to have if you are going to have a free country.") Hutchinson to [John or Robert] Grant, July 27, 1768, Massachusetts Archives, XXVI, 317, State House, Boston. See also the related story about John Selden, the famous 17th century lawyer, told to the House of Commons in Jan. 1775 by Lord Camden and recorded by Josiah Quincy, Jr., in the "Journal of Josiah Quincy, Jun., During his Voyage and Residence in England from September 28th, 1774, to March 3d, 1775," Massachusetts Historical Society, *Proceedings,* L (1916–1917), 462–463. Seldom was asked what lawbook contained the laws for resisting tyranny. He replied he did not know, "but I'll tell [you] what is most certain, that it has always been the custom of England—and the Custom of England is the *Law* of the *Land.*"

42. On the developing distinction Americans drew between what was legal and constitutional, see Wood, *Creation of the American Republic,* 261–268.

43. *N.Y. Jour. Supp.* (N.Y.C.), Jan. 4, 1770; Wroth and Zobel, eds., *Adams Legal papers,* III, 250, and C. F. Adams, ed., *Works of Adams,* VI, 151. Adams's views were altered in 1815, *ibid.,* X, 181. It is noteworthy that the Boston town meeting condemned the Knowles rioters not simply for their method of opposing impressment but because they insulted the governor and the legislature, and the Massachusetts Assembly acted against the uprising only after Gov. Shirley had left Boston and events seemed to be "tending to the destruction of all government and order." Hutchinson, *History of Massachusetts Bay,* ed. Mayo, II, 332–333. *Acts and Resolves of the Province of Massachusetts Bay,* III, 647. (Chap. 18 of the Province laws, 1752–1753, "An Act for Further Preventing all Riotous, Tumultuous and Disorderly Assemblies or Companies of Persons. . . .") This act, which was inspired particularly by Pope's Day violence, was renewed after the Boston Massacre in 1770 even though the legislature refused to renew its main Riot Act of 1751. *Ibid.,* IV, 87.

44. Arthur M. Schlesinger, "Political Mobs and the American Revolution, 1765–1776," *Proceedings of the American Philosophical Society,* XCIX (1955), 246; Charles M. Andrews, *The Colonial Background of the American Revolution,* rev. ed. (New Haven, 1939), 176; Charles M. Andrews, "The Boston Merchants and the Non-Importation Movement," Colonial Society of Massachusetts, *Transactions,* XIX (1916–1917), 241, Hobsbawm, *Primitive Rebels,* 111, 123–124.

45. Hutchinson to Thomas Pownall, [Sept. or Oct. 1765], Mass. Archives, XXVI, 157. Pauline Maier, From Resistance to Revolution: American Radicals and the Development of Intercolonial Opposition to Britain, 1765–1776 (unpubl. Ph.D. diss., Harvard University, 1968), I, 37–45, 72–215.

46. C. F. Adams, ed., *Works of Adams,* IV, 51; Rev. Samuel Langdon's election sermon to third Massachusetts provincial Congress, May 31, 1775, quoted in Richard Frothingham, *Life and Times of Joseph Warren* (Boston, 1865), 499: Samuel Adams to Noah Webster, Apr. 30, 1784, Cushing, ed., *Writings of Samuel Adams,* IV, 305–306. On Gadsden see Richard Walsh, *Charleston's Sons of Liberty* (Columbia, 1959), 87.

47. *N.Y. Jour. Supp.* (N.Y.C.), Jan. 4, 1770; Jay to Jefferson, Oct. 27, 1786, Boyd, ed., *Jefferson Papers*, X, 488; Johnson to William Pitkin, July 23, 1768, Massachusetts Historical Society, *Collections*, 5th Ser., IX, 294–295.

48. *The Statutes at Large* [of Great Britain] (London, 1786), V, 4–6; Hoadly, ed., *Public Records of Connecticut*, VI, 346–348 for the law, and see also 332–333, 341–348; *Acts and Resolves of Massachusetts Bay*, III, 544–546, for the Riot Act of 1751, and see also Hutchinson, *History of Massachusetts Bay*, ed. Mayo, III, 6–7; and *Acts and Laws of the Commonwealth of Massachusetts* (Boston, 1893), 87–88, for Act of 1786; "A State of Facts Concerning the Riots . . . in New Jersey," *N.J. Archives*, VII, 211–212, 221–222; *The Statutes at large of Pennsylvania* . . . (n.p., 1899), VI, 325–328; William A. Saunders, ed., *The Colonial Records of North Carolina* (Raleigh, 1890), VIII, 481–486; *Laws of the Colony of New York in the years 1774 and 1775* (Albany, 1888), 38–43.

49. See additional instruction to Gov. Josiah Martin, Saunders, ed., *Colonial Records of North Carolina*, VIII, 515–516; and *Laws of the State of New York* (Albany, 1886), I, 20.

50. *The Craftsman*, VI (London, 1731), 263–264. Connecticut and Massachusetts laws cited in n. 45; and *Laws of the State of New Jersey* (Trenton, 1821), 279–281.

51. Jefferson to Madison, Jan. 30, 1787, Boyd, ed., *Jefferson Papers*, XI, 93.

52. See Bradley Chapin, "Colonial and Revolutionary Origins of the American Law of Treason," *Wm. and Mary Qtly.*, 3d ser., XVII (1960), 3–21.

53. Elbridge Gerry in Congressional debates, quoted in Irving Brant, *The Bill of Rights, Its Origin and Meaning* (Indianapolis, 1965), 486; Samuel Adams, quoting Blackstone, as "E. A." in *Boston Gaz.*, Feb. 27, 1769, and Cushing ed., *Writings of Samuel Adams*, I, 317. Timothy Dwight, quoted in Daniel J. Boorstin, *The Americans: The Colonial Experience* (New York, 1958), 353.

54. Wood, *Creation of the American Republic*, 410.

55. Judge Aedanus Burke's Charge to the Grand Jury at Charleston, June 9, 1783, in *South-Carolina Gazette and General Advertiser* (Charleston), June 10, 1783; "A Patriot," *ibid.*, July 15, 1783; and "Another Patriot," *ibid.*, July 29, 1783; and on the relevance of jealousy of power, see a letter to Virginia in *ibid.*, Aug. 9, 1783. "Democratic Gentle-Touch," *Gazette of the State of South Carolina* (Charleston), May 13, 1784.

56. Wood, *Creation of the American Republic*, 612–614.

57. J. H. Plumb, *The Origins of Political Stability, England 1675–1725* (Boston, 1967), xv, 187; John Adams on the leaders of Shays's Rebellion in a letter to Benjamin Hitchborn, Jan. 27, 1787, in C. F. Adams, ed., *Works of Adams*, IX, 551; modern definitions of riot in "Riot Control and the use of Federal Troops," *Harvard Law Review*, LXXXI (1968), 643.

SECTION 6: SUGGESTIONS FOR FURTHER READING

Those wanting to broaden their understanding of the institutional growth of American assemblies should consult L. W. Labaree, *Royal Government in America: A Study of the British Colonial System before 1783* (1930), and J. P. Greene, *The Quest for Power: The Lower Houses of Assembly in the Southern Royal Colonies, 1689–1776* (1963), as well as various other books and articles cited in the footnotes of Professor Greene's essay. Essential for comprehending the English background in the era of salutary neglect are J. H. Plumb, *Sir Robert Walpole* (2 vols., 1956), Isaac Kramnick, *Bolingbroke and His Circle: The Politics of Nostalgia in the Age of Walpole* (1968), L. B. Namier's *England in the Age of the American Revolution* (2nd ed., 1961), and *The Structure of Politics at the Accession of George III* (2nd ed., 1965), and J. A. Henretta, *"Salutary Neglect": Colonial Administration under the Duke of Newcastle* (1972).

Many historians have been moving away from the position that the provincial contest over royal prerogatives had an essential formative influence in colonial political development. Rather they have been stressing the significance of radical Whiggism, as described in Caroline Robbins, *The Eighteenth-Century Commonwealthman: Studies in the Transition, Development, and Circumstance of English Liberal Thought from the Restoration of Charles II until the War with the Thirteen Colonies* (1959). Robbins should be supplemented with J. G. A. Pocock's "Machiavelli, Harrington, and English Political Ideologies in the Eighteenth Century," *William and Mary Quarterly*, 3rd ser., 22 (1965), pp. 549–583, "Virtue and Commerce in the Eighteenth Century," *Journal of Interdisciplinary History*, 3 (1972), pp. 119–134, and *The Machiavellian Moment: Florentine Political Thought and the Atlantic Republican Tradition* (1975). Bernard Bailyn, *The Ideological Origins of the American Revolution* (1967), and *The Origins of American Politics* (1968), along with Gordon S. Wood, *The Creation of the American Republic, 1776–1787* (1969), the source of the second selection, have been most influential in relating radical Whiggism to the Revolution and the concept of republicanism. A healthy sampling of radical Whig writings has been edited by D. L. Jacobson, *The English Libertarian Heri-*

tage: From the Writings of John Trenchard and Thomas Gordon in The Independent Whig and Cato's Letters (1965). Similarly, William Livingston et al., *The Independent Reflector*, ed. M. M. Klein (1963), represents a major provincial expression of opposition Whiggism. Students should also look at the important studies of H. T. Colbourn, *The Lamp of Experience: Whig History and the Intellectual Origins of the American Revolution* (1965), R. M. Weir, "'The Harmony We Were Famous For': An Interpretation of Pre-Revolutionary South Carolina Politics," *William and Mary Quarterly*, 3rd ser., 26 (1969), pp. 473–501, and Alan Rogers, *Empire and Liberty: American Resistance to British Authority, 1755–1763* (1974).

Professor Greene has challenged those stressing radical Whiggism in "Political Mimesis: A Consideration of the Historical and Cultural Roots of Legislative Behavior in the British Colonies in the Eighteenth Century," *American Historical Review*, 75 (1969) pp. 337–367, which also contains a rejoinder by Bernard Bailyn. A valuable critique of both approaches is Paul Lucas, "A Note on the Comparative Study of the Structure of Politics in Mid-Eighteenth-Century Britain and Its American Colonies," *William and Mary Quarterly*, 3rd ser., 28 (1971), pp. 301–309. For an approach emphasizing the utilitarian selection of political ideas, consult C. L. Rossiter, *Seedtime of the Republic: The Origin of the American Tradition of Political Liberty* (1953), and L. H. Leder, *Liberty and Authority: Early American Political Ideology, 1689–1763* (1968).

The actual operation of provincial politics, regardless of ideological assumptions, has produced a number of important investigations. C. S. Sydnor, *Gentlemen Freeholders: Political Practices in Washington's Virginia* (1952), from which the third selection is taken, Patricia Bonomi, *A Factious People: Politics and Society in Colonial New York* (1971), and S. E. Patterson, *Political Parties in Revolutionary Massachusetts* (1973), are quite suggestive in terms of relating political operations to ideology. Also of importance are Chilton Williamson, *American Suffrage from Property to Democracy, 1760–1860* (1960), J. R. Pole, *Political Representation in England and the Origins of the American Republic* (1966), E. E. Brennan, *Plural Office-Holding in Massachusetts, 1760–1780: Its Relation to the "Separation of Departments of Government"* (1945), S. N. Katz, *Newcastle's New York: Anglo-American Politics, 1732–1753* (1968), J. A. Schutz, *William Shirley: King's Governor of Massachusetts* (1961), and J. R. Daniell, "Politics in New Hampshire under Governor Benning Wentworth, 1741–1767, *William and Mary Quarterly*, 3rd ser., 23 (1966), pp. 76–105.

There has been open disputing about what kinds of men filled political offices in the colonies. Those who argue that leadership in provincial America had taken on an upper-class, deferential character include Carl Bridenbaugh, *Seat of Empire: The Political Role of Eighteenth-Century Williamsburg* (1950), J. P. Greene, "Foundations of Political Power in the Virginia House of Burgesses, 1720–1776," *William and Mary Quarterly*, 3rd ser., 16 (1959), pp. 485–506, J. B. Kirby, "Early American Politics—The Search for Ideology: An Historiographical Analysis and Critique of the Concept of 'Deference'," *Journal of Politics*, 32 (1970), pp. 808–838, Lucille Griffith, *The Virginia House of Burgesses, 1750–1776* (rev. ed., 1970), J. T. Main, "The One Hundred," and "Government by the People: The American Revolution and the Democratization of the Legislatures," both in the *William and Mary Quarterly*, 3rd ser., 11 (1954), pp. 354–384, and 23 (1966), pp. 391–407, J. K. Martin's "A Model for the Coming American Revolution: The Birth and Death of the Wentworth Oligarchy in New Hampshire, 1741–1776," *Journal of Social History*, 4 (1970), pp. 41–60, and "Men of Family Wealth and Personal Merit: The Changing Social Basis of Executive Leadership Selection in the American Revolution," *Societas—A Review of Social History*, 2 (1972), pp. 43–70, and J. R. Pole, "Historians and the Problem of Early American Democracy," *American Historical Review*, 67 (1962), pp. 626–646.

R. E. and B. K. Brown, cited in the previous bibliography, disagree and argue that everyday citizens dominated the political arena. With modifications their position has received support from M. M. Klein, "Democracy and Politics in Colonial New York," *New York History*, 40 (1959), pp. 221–246, and J. C. Rainbolt, "The Alteration in the Relationship between Leadership and Constituents in Virginia, 1660 to 1720," *William and Mary Quarterly*, 3rd ser., 27 (1970), pp. 411–434. Carefully stating possible democratic limits are G. B. Nash, *Quakers and Politics: Pennsylvania, 1681–1726* (1968), Michael Zuckerman, *Peaceable Kingdoms: New England Towns in the Eighteenth Century* (1970), and R. M. Zemsky, *Merchants, Farmers, and River Gods: An Essay on Eighteenth-Century American Politics* (1971). The findings in the latter two volumes must be considered in conjunction with E. M. Cook, Jr.'s "Local Leadership and the Typology of New England Towns, 1700–1785," *Political Science Quarterly*, 86 (1971), pp. 586–608, and *The Fathers of the Towns: Leadership and Community Structure in Eighteenth-Century New England* (1976). An important critique of the Browns' position with their reply is John Cary, "Statistical Method and the Brown Thesis on Colonial Democracy," *William and Mary Quarterly*, 3rd ser., 20 (1963), pp. 251–276, while R. N. Lokken, "The Concept of Democracy in Colonial Political Thought," *William and Mary Quarterly*,

3rd ser., 16 (1959), pp. 568–580, and Richard Buel, Jr., "Democracy and the American Revolution: A Frame of Reference," *William and Mary Quarterly*, 3rd ser., 21 (1964), pp. 165–190, are fundamental to understanding that term in its context.

Scholars have also been discussing the phenomenon of heightened European social and political norms in prerevolutionary America. Important contributions include J. P. Greene's "Search for Identity: An Interpretation of the Meaning of Selected Patterns of Social Response in Eighteenth-Century America," *Journal of Social History*, 3 (1970), pp. 189–220, and "An Uneasy Connection: An Analysis of the Preconditions of the American Revolution," appearing in the same volume as Rowland Berthoff and J. M. Murrin, "Feudalism, Communalism, and the Yeoman Freeholder: The American Revolution Considered as a Social Accident," *Essays on the American Revolution*, ed. S. G. Kurtz and J. H. Hutson (1973), pp. 32–80, and pp. 256–288 respectively, and R. M. Weir, "Who Shall Rule at Home: The American Revolution as a Crisis of Legitimacy for the Colonial Elite," *Journal of Interdisciplinary History*, 6 (1976), pp. 679–700.

Pauline Maier's conclusions about the composition and nature of crowd activities need to be compared with Jesse Lemisch, "Jack Tar in the Streets: Merchant Seamen in the Politics of Revolutionary America," *William and Mary Quarterly*, 3rd ser., 25 (1968), pp. 371–407, J. H. Hutson, "An Investigation of the Inarticulate: Philadelphia's White Oaks," *William and Mary Quarterly*, 3rd ser., 28 (1971), pp. 3–35, Edward Countryman, "The Problem of the Early American Crowd," *Journal of American Studies*, 7 (1973), pp. 77–90, and G. B. Nash, "Social Change and the Growth of Prerevolutionary Urban Radicalism," *The American Revolution: Explorations in the History of American Radicalism*, ed. A. F. Young, (1976), pp. 5–36, none of which describe crowds as essentially middle class. A good general introduction is R. M. Brown, *Strain of Violence: Historical Studies of American Violence and Vigilantism* (1975).

Religion, Piety, and the Great Awakening

SECTION 7

The seventeenth century was a transitional era in the approach to modernity of Western civilization. Many listened to the powerful voices of the Protestant reformers and searched for the true way to worship God. Others began to forsake religious experience in favor of worldly quests. It was a century when men of commerce rose to new stature, but it was also an age when individuals like the Puritans sought to create a harmonious, utopian biblical order both in Old and New England. The first generation of Bay Colony Puritans adhered to their original mission, but each successive generation grew more fascinated with material acquisitions than with spiritual fulfillment. Thus by the eighteenth century almost all that was left of the original "errand" to New England was the state-supported Congregational Church. Commitment to a biblical order was giving way to perfunctory religious formalism. More and more individuals observed religious customs out of habit, and only so long as worship did not shackle their secular aspirations.

Sometimes, parishioners found that they had ministers who were becoming more strikingly "Arminian" in their doctrines. The term refers to the principles of Jacobus Arminius (1560–1609), the Dutch theologian who softened the harsh doctrines of Calvinism by asserting that predestination was not absolute, that free will was paramount, and that individuals who performed good works and lived godly lives would be able to enter the heavenly kingdom. The conversion experience, depending upon preparation and the grace of God through His son Jesus Christ, was no longer considered so central an aspect of Puritan theology. People who acted godly were godly, according to the new clergy, and God would not reject them in death. Arminianism was a comforting theology for individuals of a worldly persuasion. It was not as time consuming as the more orthodox Calvinist-Puritan doctrine, and it reduced the sense of personal guilt in the acquisition of riches.

Yet it was not only the growing commercial ethos and the waning of traditional Puritan theology that made the act of preparing for conversion and saving grace seem ever more superfluous to many people. There were new intellectual currents in the air. A number of individuals were arguing that modern people could use their rational powers in discovering the immutable laws of nature; such an approach to learning implied that man could use his own mind in establishing more perfect human relationships and institutions. Rationalism meant that God could be relegated to the status of a "prime mover" (Deism) in creating the world and nature's laws. If that was the case, then there was no reason to believe that God continued to intervene directly in the affairs of man, as the original Puritans believed. For example, Calvinists took as doctrine that God would afflict people with forms of divine wrath, such as earthquakes or plagues, when commandments or covenants were broken. But if God was not the activating source, then it became necessary to explain why earthquakes or plagues occurred. Scientific inquiry, rationalism, and the Enlightenment, on the one hand, and the increasingly dry formalism of institutionalized religion, on the other hand, were factors working together. Their effect was to turn growing numbers of people away from religious believing and toward the exploration, classification, and deification of secular knowledge.

Yet there remained pockets of resistance to the new intellectualism. Certain German pietist groups, migrating to the middle colonies in the early eighteenth century, kept the angry God of the Old Testament as the focal point of their believing. They insisted that individuals must repent and accept saving grace, or else face eternal damnation. Also, there were sporadic outbursts of revivalism in Europe and in the provinces before the full fury of the Great Awakening struck the American colonies during the late 1730s and the 1740s. A Dutch Reformed pastor, Theodorus Frelinghuysen, led a revival among his parishioners during the 1720s in the Raritan River Valley of central New Jersey. Later in the decade Gilbert Tennent, a man who breathed theological fire on his Presbyterian congregation, joined Frelinghuysen. Then in the early 1730s youthful Jonathan Edwards, perhaps the most brilliant theologian of America's early years, began his "harvests" in the town of Northampton, Massachusetts. At first he appealed primarily to the young, preaching about the wrath awaiting the unregenerate; he exorted his flock to prepare themselves and to seek grace and salvation. Within a short time Edwards had started a full-scale revival movement in the Connecticut River Valley, though the local enthusiasm over traditional doctrine died down as quickly as it flared up.

The "first murmurings" of massive religious repentance, which set the stage for the general Awakening, occurred when another youthful divine, George Whitefield, started on the first of several preaching tours through the colonies in 1739. Whitefield was a native Englishman who had imbibed Methodist piety and had rejected the Arminianism of the state Anglican Church. A man of unusual vigor, melodious voice, and charismatic personality, Whitefield journeyed from province to province preaching the necessity for conversion and saving grace. The height of his oratorical influence came in the autumn of 1740 when he preached to an estimated 19,000 people while in Boston during a three-day period. Whitefield had no compunctions about invading the territories of established ministers and challenging parishioners to search for grace. And at first local clerics appreciated the resurgence of religious feeling (it was good for church attendance), but that brief infatuation soon passed.

The problem was that where Whitefield walked other itinerant ministers of lesser caution followed. In the early 1740s several of them traveled through New England preaching the "New Light" message, and some openly attacked the spiritual qualifications of local pastors. Before Gilbert Tennent ventured into New England he published a sermon entitled "The Danger of an Unconverted Ministry," in which he denounced Arminian ministers as little more than agents of the Devil because they did not teach the truth of the Bible and led their flocks astray with comforting assurances that "good works" were enough for salvation.

The most extreme revivalist preacher was James Davenport, who was convinced that he could identify those who had experienced conversion as opposed to those who were not converted. Unfortunately for Davenport's reputation, too many "Old Light" ministers were on the wrong side in his determination. He was deported from both Connecticut and Massachusetts.

Itinerant evangelists, the most important of whom were Whitefield and Tennent, not only revived vital religion but also soon called established ministers to account. The Old Light ministers, threatened as never before, reacted with impunity. In New England they saw to it that laws were passed against traveling, itinerant preachers. Yet the theological split did not evaporate that easily. New Light members of congregations, if they were in a minority, broke away and tried to form their own parishes. When a majority, they made the lives of the more staid clergy extremely unpleasant. The old guard fought back with scare words. They charged the New Lights with fanaticism, anti-intellectualism, anti-institutionalism. But in the minds of Whitefield, Edwards, Tennent, and other New Light preachers, their harvests of regenerated peoples were worth every type of resistance emanating from the Old Light group.

Thus it was that the 1740s became one of the most divisive decades in early American history. Many thousands returned to vital religion and piety, in striking juxtaposition to the long-term historical trend toward secularization of life and society. Since those disquieting years historians have been perplexed by the drama, the excitement, the furor, and the contention of the Great Awakening. For the most part historians have concentrated scholarly concerns on New England where the Awakening spread so rapidly for a few years before it became a source of continuing theological and community disagreements in the decades to come. Naturally many questions arise from such a turbulent sequence of events. Why did the Awakening occur when it did? Was it the result of youthful ministers rising up against the wisdom of their church elders? Or were people reacting against undesirable social conditions? What socioeconomic groups were most affected? Was it only the poor and ignorant on the frontier, or did the Awakening encompass all age and social groups, the high as well as the low, the dignified as well as the rude, the well educated as well as the uneducated? Why did itinerant preachers cause so much excitement? Was it the "New Birth" message, or did people flock to hear and be moved in order only to relieve the starkness in their lives? And finally, what were the consequences of the Awakening? Did it build a sense of a spiritual community among the individuals affected by the new preaching, or was the Awakening at most divisive in its impact? What relationship might there be between the reasons for the Awakening and the causes of the American Revolution? The readings that follow attempt to answer such questions. There is no doubt that the Great Awakening had a complex impact on provincial patterns of existence, and it is from this vantage point that we should seek to understand its significance.

25. Jonathan Edwards and the Great Awakening

Perry Miller

Perry Miller never failed to demonstrate his personal power of historical conceptualization when he wrote about the New England mind. In the essay below Miller explores more than a hundred years of the New England experience in order to establish what he felt was the proper context for the Great Awakening. Miller's focus rests upon Jonathan Edwards (1703–1758) and what Edwards's theology reveals about the impact of frontier thought on the political and intellectual milieu of the provincial experience. Even though Miller realized that there were European precedents for the Awakening, he concluded that they were not germaine in gaining an understanding of the significance of the movement in America. The critical factor was that the Awakening through Edwards, according to Miller, unleashed a new, more equalitarian influence in political thought (a product of frontier influences working upon the New England mind). Furthermore, the Awakening represented a rejection of the European aristocratic model of socioeconomic and political leadership.

Thus it seems that the "excesses" of the Awakening and its clergy, more so than anything else, stirred the anger of elite leaders in eastern Massachusetts and elsewhere. Is Miller suggesting, then, that the Awakening as a "crisis" in American history sped up the process of democratization in provincial life? Does he indicate that class and sectional lines separated proponents and opponents of the Awakening? Is there any way that we can be confident that Edwards, no doubt a brilliant man and Awakening leader, was fully representative of other individuals and other influences in the movement? Is it possible to make meaningful generalizations about a widespread social movement when intellectual currents are seen through the eyes of only one participant?

I

Although in the year 1740 some fairly flagrant scenes of emotional religion were being enacted in Boston, it was mainly in the Connecticut Valley that the frenzy raged and whence it spread like a pestilence to the civilized East. The Harvard faculty of that time would indeed have considered the Great Awakening a "crisis," because to them it threatened everything they meant by culture or reli-

Source: From Perry Miller, *Errand into the Wilderness* (Cambridge, Mass.: Harvard University Press (Belknap Press), 1956), pp. 154–166. Copyright 1956 by the President and Fellows of Harvard College and reprinted by permission of the Harvard University Press.

gion or just common decency. It has a horrible business that should be suppressed and altogether forgotten. Certainly they would not have approved its being dignified as a starting point in a series of great American crises.

As far as they could see, it was nothing but an orgy of the emotions. They called it—in the lexicon of the Harvard faculty this word conveyed the utmost contempt—"enthusiasm." It was not a religious persuasion: it was an excitement of overstimulated passions that understandably slopped over into activities other than the ecclesiastical and increased the number of bastards in the Valley, where already there were too many. And above all, in the Valley lived their archenemy, the deliberate instigator of this crime, who not only fomented the frenzy but was so lost to shame that he brazenly defended it as a positive advance in American culture. To add insult to injury, he justified the Awakening by employing a science and a psychological conception with which nothing they had learned at Harvard had prepared them to cope.

It was certainly a weird performance. Edwards delivered his revival sermons—for example the goriest, the one at Enfield that goes by the title "Sinners in the Hands of an Angry God" and is all that most people nowadays associate with his name—to small audiences in country churches. In these rude structures (few towns had yet prospered enough to afford the Georgian churches of the later eighteenth century which are now the charm of the landscape) the people yelled and shrieked, they rolled in the aisles, they crowded up to the pulpit and begged him to stop, they cried for mercy. One who heard him described his method of preaching: he looked all the time at the bell rope (hanging down from the roof at the other end of the church) as though he would look it in two; he did not stoop to regard the screaming mass, much less to console them.

Of course, in a short time the opinion of the Harvard faculty appeared to be vindicated. In 1740 Edwards had writhing in the churches not only his own people but every congregation he spoke to, and he dominated the entire region. Ten years later he was exiled, thrown out of his church and town after a vicious squabble (the fight against him being instigated by certain of the first citizens, some of them his cousins, who by adroit propaganda mobilized "the people" against him), and no pulpit in New England would invite this terrifying figure. He had no choice but to escape to the frontier, as did so many misfits in American history. He went to Stockbridge, where he eked out his last years as a missionary to a lot of moth-eaten Indians. Because of the works he produced under these—shall we call them untoward?—circumstances, and because he was still the acknowledged leader of the revival movement, he was invited in 1758 to become president of the College of New Jersey (the present-day Princeton), but he died a few weeks after his inauguration, so that his life really belongs to the Connecticut Valley.

One may well ask what makes such a chronicle of frenzy and defeat a "crisis" in American history. From the point of view of the social historian and still more from that of the sociologist it was a phenomenon of mass behavior, of which poor Mr. Edwards was the deluded victim. No sociologically trained historian will for a moment accept it on Edwards' terms—which were, simply, that it was an outpouring of the Spirit of God upon the land. And so why should we, today, mark it as a turning point in our history, especially since thereafter religious revivals became a part of the American social pattern, while our intellectual life developed, on the whole, apart from these vulgar eruptions? The answer is that this first occurrence did actually involve all the interests of the community, and the definitions that arose out of it were profoundly decisive and meaningful. In that perspective Jonathan Edwards, being the most acute definer of the terms on which the revival was conducted and the issues on which it went astray, should be regarded—even by the social historian—as a formulator of propositions that the American society, having been shaken by this experience, was henceforth consciously to observe.

There is not space enough here to survey the Awakening through the vast reaches of the South and the Middle Colonies, nor even to list the intricate consequences for the social ordering of New England. The splintering of the churches and the increase of sectarianism suggest one way in which Americans "responded" to this crisis, and the impulse it gave to education, most notably in the founding of Princeton, is another. Such discussions, however valuable, are external and statistical. We come to a deeper understanding of what this crisis meant by examining more closely a revelation or two from the most self-conscious—not to say the most literate—theorist of the Awakening.

The theme I would here isolate is one with which Edwards dealt only by indirection. He was skilled in the art of presenting ideas not so much by expounding as by vivifying them, and he achieved his ends not only by explicit statement but more often by a subtle shift in emphasis. In this case, it is entirely a matter of divining nuances. Nevertheless, the issue was present throughout the Awakening and, after the temporary manifestations had abated, on this proposition a revolution was found to have been wrought that is one of the enduring responses of the American mind to crisis.

I mean specifically what it did to the conception of the relation of the ruler—political or ecclesiastical—to the body politic. However, before we can pin down this somewhat illusive development, we are confronted with the problem of whether the Great Awakening is properly to be viewed as a peculiarly American phenomenon at all. It would be possible to write about it—as has been done—as merely one variant of a universal occurrence in Western culture. Between about 1730 and 1760 practically all of Western Europe was swept by some kind of religious emotionalism. It was present in Germany, Holland, Switzerland, and France, and in Catholic circles there was an analogous movement that can be interpreted as an outcropping of the same thing: this the textbooks call "Quietism." And most dramatically, it was present in England with the Wesleys, Whitefield, and Methodism.

Once this international viewpoint is assumed, the American outburst becomes merely one among many—a colonial one at that—and we hesitate to speak about it as a crisis in a history specifically American. What was at work throughout the Western world is fairly obvious: the upper or the educated classes were tired of the religious squabbling of the seventeenth century, and turned to the more pleasing and not at all contentious generalities of eighteenth-century rationalism; the spiritual hungers of the lower classes or of what, for shorthand purposes, we may call "ordinary" folk were not satisfied by Newtonian demonstrations that design in the universe proved the existence of God. Their aspirations finally found vent in the revivals, and in each country we may date the end of a Calvinist or scholastic or, in short, a theological era by the appearance of these movements, and thereupon mark what is by now called the era of Pietism or Evangelicalism.

In this frame of reference, the Great Awakening was only incidentally American. It is merely necessary to translate the European language into the local terminology to have an adequate account. In this phraseology, the Great Awakening in New England was an uprising of the common people who declared that what Harvard and Yale graduates were teaching was too academic. This sort of rebellion has subsequently proved so continuous that one can hardly speak of it as a crisis. It is rather a chronic state of affairs. And in this view of it, the uprising of 1740 belongs to the international history of the eighteenth century rather than to any account of forces at work only on this continent.

Told in this way, the story will be perfectly true. Because we talk so much today of the unity of Western European culture, maybe we ought to tell it in these terms, and then stop. But on the other hand there is a curiously double aspect to the business. If we forget about Germany and Holland and even England—if we examine in detail the local history of Virginia, Pennsylvania, and New England— we will find that a coherent narrative can be constructed out of the cultural developments in each particular area. This Awakening can be seen as the culmination of factors long at work in each society, and as constituting, in that sense, a veritable crisis in the indigenous civilization.

II

The church polity established in New England was what today we call congregational. This meant, to put it crudely, that a church was conceived as being composed of people who could certify before other people that they had a religious experience, that they were qualified to become what the founders called "visible saints." The founders were never so foolish as to suppose that everybody who pretended to be a saint *was* a saint, but they believed that a rough approximation of the membership to the covenant of grace could be worked out. A church was composed of the congregation, but these were only the professing Christians. The rest of the community were to be rigorously excluded; the civil magistrate would, of course, compel them to come to the church and listen to the sermon, collect from them a tax to support the preacher, but they could not be actual members. Those who qualified were supposed to have had something happen to them that made them capable—as the reprobate was not—of swearing to the covenant of the church. They were able, as the others were not, *physically* to perform the act.

The basic contention of the founders was that a church is based upon the covenant. Isolated individuals might be Christians in their heart of hearts, but a corporate body could not come into being unless there was this preliminary clasping of hands, this taking of the official oath in the open and before all the community, saying in effect: "We abide by this faith, by this covenant." In scholastic language, the congregation were the "matter" but the covenant was the "form" of the church. They objected above all things to the practice in England whereby churches were made by geography; that a lot of people, merely because they resided in Little Willingdon, should make the church of Little Willingdon, seemed to them blasphemy. That principle was mechanical and unreal; there was no spiritual participation in it—no covenant.

That was why they (or at any rate the leaders and the theorists) came to New England. On the voyage over, in 1630, John Winthrop said to them: "For wee must Consider that wee shall be as a Citty vppon a Hill, the eies of all people are vppon us." They had been attempting in England to lead a revolution; after the King's dismissal of Parliament in 1629 it looked as though there was no longer any hope of revolution there, and so they migrated to New England, to build the revolutionary city, where they could exhibit to Englishmen an England that would be as all England should be.

The essence of this conception was the covenant. As soon as they were disembarked, as soon as they could collect in one spot enough people to examine each other and acknowledge that each seemed visibly capable of taking the oath, they incorporated churches—in Boston, Charlestown, and Watertown, and, even in the frst decade, in the Connecticut Valley. But we must always remember that even in those first days, when conviction was at its height, and among so highly selected and dedicated numbers as made up the Great Migration, only about one fifth of the population were found able, or could find themselves able, to take the covenant. The rest of them—with astonishingly few exceptions—accepted their exclusion from the churches, knowing that they were not "enabled" and praying for the grace that might yet empower them.

From that point on, the story may seem somewhat peculiar, but after a little scrutiny it becomes an old and a familiar one: it is what happens to a successful revolution. The New Englanders did not have to fight on the barricades or at Marston Moor; by the act of migrating, they *had* their revolution. Obeying the Biblical command to increase and multiply, they had children—hordes of them. Despite the high rate of infant mortality, numbers of these children grew up in New England knowing nothing, except by hearsay and rumor, of the struggles in Europe, never having lived amid the tensions of England. This second generation were, for the most part, good people; but they simply did not have—they could not have—the kind of emotional experience that made them ready to stand up before the whole community and say: "On Friday the 19th, I was smitten while plowing Deacon Jones's meadow; I fell to the earth, and I knew that the grace of God was upon me." They were honest people, and they found it difficult to romanticize about themselves—even when they desperately wanted to.

In 1662 the churches of New England convoked a synod and announced that the children of the primitive church members were included in the covenant by the promise of God to Abraham. This solution was called at the time the halfway covenant, and the very phrase itself is an instructive demonstration of the New Englanders' awareness that their revolution was no longer revolutionary. These children, they decided, must be treated as members of the church, although they had not had the kind of experience that qualified their fathers. They must be subject to discipline and censures, because the body of the saints must be preserved. But just in case the authorities might be mistaken, they compromised by giving to these children only a "halfway" status, which made them members but did not admit them to the Lord's Supper.

This provision can easily be described as a pathetic, where it is not a ridiculous, device. It becomes more comprehensible when we realize that it was an accommodation to the successful revolution. Second and third generations grow up inheritors of a revolution, but are not themselves revolutionaries.

For the moment, in the 1660's and 1670's, the compromise worked, but the situation got worse. For one thing, New England suffered in King Philip's War, when the male population was decimated. Then, in 1684, the charter of Massachusetts was revoked, and after 1691 the colony had to adjust itself to the notion that its governor was imposed by the royal whim, not by the election of the saints. Furthermore, after 1715 all the colonies were prospering economically; inevitably they became more and more concerned with earthly things—rum, land, furs. On the whole they remained a pious people. Could one go back to Boston of 1710 or 1720—when the ministers were asserting that it was as profligate as Babylon—I am sure that one would find it, compared with modern Hollywood, a strict and moral community. Nevertheless, everybody was convinced that the cause of religion had declined. Something had to be done.

As early as the 1670's, the ministers had found something they could do: they could work upon the halfway members. They could say to these hesitants: "You were baptized in this church, and if you will now come before the body and 'own' the covenant, then your children can in turn be baptized." Gradually a whole segment of doctrine was formulated that was not in the original theory—which made it possible to address these citizens who were neither outside the pale nor yet snugly inside, which told them that however dubious they might be as saints, visible or invisible, they yet had sufficient will power to perform the public act of "owning the covenant."

With the increasing pressures of the late seventeenth and early eighteenth centuries, the practice of owning the covenant gradually became a communal rite. It was not enough that the minister labored separately with John or Elizabeth to make an acknowledgment the next Sunday: a day was appointed when all the Johns and Elizabeths would come to church and do it in unison, the whole town looking on. It is not difficult to trace through the increasing reenactments of this ceremony a mounting crescendo of communal action that was, to say the least, wholly foreign to the original Puritanism. The theology of the founders conceived of man as single and alone, apart in a corner or in an empty field, wrestling with his sins; only after he had survived this experience in solitude could he walk into the church and by telling about it prove his right to the covenant. But this communal confession—with everybody doing it together, under the urgencies of an organized moment—this was something new, emerging so imperceptibly that nobody recognized it as an innovation (or rather I should say that some did, but they were shouted down) that by the turn of the century was rapidly becoming the focus for the ordering of the spiritual life of the town.

The grandfather of Jonathan Edwards, Solomon Stoddard of Northampton, was the first man who openly extended the practice or renewal of covenant to those who had never been in it at all. In short, when these occasions arose, or when he could precipitate them, he simply took into the church and up to the Lord's Supper everyone who would or could come. He called the periods when the community responded en masse his "harvests," of which he had five: 1679, 1683, 1696, 1712, 1718. The Mathers attacked him for so completely letting down the bars, but in the Connecticut Valley his success was envied and imitated.

The Great Awakening of 1740, seen in the light of this development, was nothing more than an inevitable culmination. It was the point at which the method of owning the covenant became most widely and exultingly extended, in which the momentum of the appeal got out of hand, and the ministers, led by Jonathan Edwards, were forced by the logic of evolution not only to admit all those who would come, but to excite and to drive as many as possible, by such rhetorical stimulations as "Sinners in the Hands of an Angry God," into demanding entrance.

All of this, traced historically, seems natural enough. What 1740 did was present a number of leading citizens, like the Harvard faculty, with the results of a process that had been going on for decades but of which they were utterly unaware until the explosion. Then they found themselves trying to control it or censure it by standards that had in fact been out of date for a century, although they had all that while professed them. In this sense—which I regret to state has generally eluded the social historian—the Great Awakening was a crisis in the New England society.

Professional patriots, especially those of New England descent, are fond of celebrating the Puritans as the founders of the American tradition of rugged individualism, freedom of conscience, popular education, and democracy. The Puritans were not rugged individualists; they did indeed believe in education of a sort, but not in the "progressive" sense; they abhorred freedom of conscience; and they did not believe at all in democracy. They advertised again and again that their church polity was not democratic. The fact that a church was founded on a covenant and that the minister happened to be elected by the mass of the church—this emphatically did not constitute a democracy. John Cotton made the position of the founders crystal clear when he told Lord Say and Seal that God never ordained democracy as a fit government for either church or commonwealth; although at first sight one might suppose that a congregational church was one, in that the people chose their governors, the truth was that "the government is not a democracy, if it be administered, not by the people, but by the governors." He meant, in short, that even though the people did select the person, the office was prescribed; they did not define its functions, nor was it responsible to the will or the whim of the electors. "In which respect it is, that church government is justly denied . . . to be democratical, though the people choose their owne officers and rulers."

The conception ran through every deparment of the social thinking of New England in the seventeenth century, and persisted in the eighteenth up to the very outbreak of the Awakening. The essence of it always was that though officers may come into their office by the choice of the people, nevertheless the definition of the function, dignity, and prerogatives of the position does not depend upon the intentions or wishes of the electorate, but upon an abstract, divinely given, absolute prescription, which has nothing—in theory—to do with such practical or utilitarian considerations as may, at the moment of the election, be at work among the people.

The divine and immutable pattern of church government was set, once and for all, in the New Testament; likewise, the principles of political justice were given in an eternal and definitive form. The machinery by which a particular man was chosen to fulfill these directives (as the minister was elected by the vote of a congregation, or as John Winthrop was made governor of the Massachusetts Bay Company by a vote of the stockholders) was irrelevant. The existence of such machinery did not mean that the elected officer was in any sense responsible to the electorate. He knew what was expected of him from an entirely other source than their temporary passions; he knew what he, upon becoming such a being, should do—as such!

The classic statement, as is widely known, was the speech that John Winthrop delivered before the General Court on July 3, 1645. He informed the people that the liberty of the subject may sometimes include, as happily it did in Massachusetts, the privilege of selecting this or that person for office, but that it did not therefore mean the right to tell the officer what he should do once he was installed. The liberty that men enjoy in civil society, he said, "is the proper end and object of authority, and cannot subsist without it." It is not a liberty to do what you will, or to require the authority to do what you want: "It is a liberty to do that only which is good, just, and honest." Who defines the good, the just, and the honest? Obviously, the authority does.

In other words, the theory of early New England was basically medieval. Behind it lay the conception of an authoritative scheme of things, in which basic principles are set down once and for all, entirely antecedent to, and utterly without regard for, political experience. The formulation of social wisdom had nothing to do with the specific problems of any one society. It was not devised by a committee on ways and means. Policy was not to be arrived at by a discussion of strategy—for example (in modern terms), shouldn't we use the atomic bomb now? This sort of argument was unavailing, because the function of government was to maintain by authority that which was inherently—and definably—the true, just, and honest.

In Hartford, Connecticut, Samuel Stone, colleague of the great Thomas Hooker, summarized the argument by declaring that congregationalism meant a silent democracy in the face of a speaking aristocracy. There might be something which we call democracy in the form of the church, but the congregation had to keep silent when the minister spoke. And yet, for a hundred years after the death of Hooker, this strange alteration went on inside the institution. The official theory remained, down to the time of Edwards, that the spokesman for the society—be he governor or minister—told the society, by right divine, what it should or should not do, without any regard to its immediate interests, whether emotional or economic. He had laid upon him, in fact, the duty of forgetting such wisdom as he might have accumulated by living as a particular person in that very community or having shared the hopes and qualities of precisely these people.

What actually came about, through the device of renewing the covenant, was something that in fact completely contradicted the theory. (We must remember that the church was, during this century, not merely something "spiritual," but the institutional center of the organized life.) Instead of the minister standing in his pulpit, saying: "I speak; you keep quiet," he found himself, bit by bit, assuming the posture of pleading with the people: "Come, and speak up." He did not know what was happening. He began to find out only in the Great Awakening, when the people at last and multitudinously spoke up.

III

The greatness of Jonathan Edwards is that he understood what had happened. But note this carefully. He was not Thomas Jefferson: he did not preach democracy, and he had no interest whatsoever in any social revolution. He was the child of this aristocratic, medieval system; he was born to the purple, to ecclesiastical authority. Yet he was the man who hammered it home to the people that they *had* to speak up, or else they were lost.

Edwards was a Puritan and a Calvinist. He believed in predestination and original sin and all those dogmas which modern students hold to be outworn stuff until they get excited about them as slightly disguised by Franz Kafka. Edwards did not submit these doctrines to majority vote, and he did not put his theology to the test of utility. But none of this was, in his existing situation, an issue. Granting all that, the question he had to decide was: What does a man do who leads the people? Does he, in 1740, say with the Winthrop of 1645 that they submit to what he as an ontologist tells them is good, just, and honest?

What he realized (lesser leaders of the Awakening, like Gilbert Tennent, also grasped the point, but none with the fine precision of Edwards) was that a leader could no longer stand before the people giving them mathematically or logically impregnable postulates of the eternally good, just, and honest. That might work in 1640, or in Europe (where to an astonishing extent it still works), but it would not work in the American wilderness. By 1740 the leader had to get down amongst them, and bring them by actual participation into an experience that was no longer private and privileged, but social and communal.

In other words, Edwards carried to its ultimate implication—this constitutes his "relation to his times," which no purely social historian can begin to diagnose—that slowly forming tendency which had been steadily pressing through enlargements of the ceremonial owning of the covenant. He carried it so far that at last everybody could see what it really did mean. Then the Harvard faculty lifted their hands in horror—because this ritual, which they had thought was a segment of the cosmology of John Winthrop, was proved by Edwards' use to flow from entirely alien principles. For this reason, his own Yale disowned him.

IV

In the year 1748 Edwards' revolutionary effort—his leadership of the Awakening must be seen as a resumption of the revolutionary thrust that had been allowed to dwindle in the halfway covenant—was almost at an end. The opposition was mobilizing, and he knew, even before they did, that they would force him out. When the fight had only begun, his patron and friend, his one bulwark in the civil society, Colonel John Stoddard, chief of the militia and warden of the marches, died. There was now no civil power that could protect him against the hatred of the "river gods." Out of all New England, Stoddard had been really *the* outstanding magistrate in that tradition of aristocratic leadership which had begun with Winthrop and had been sustained through a massive succession. As was the custom in New England, the minister gave a funeral sermon; Edwards preached over the corpse of the town's greatest citizen—who happened, in this case, to be also his uncle and his protector. Those who were now certain, with Colonel Stoddard in the ground, that they could get Edwards' scalp were in the audience:

Edwards delivered a discourse that at first sight seems merely one more Puritan eulogy. He told the people that when great and good men like Stoddard are taken away, this is a frown of God's displeasure, which indicates that they ought to reform their vices. This much was sheer convention. But before he came, at the end, to the traditional berating of the populace, Edwards devoted the major part of his oration to an analysis of the function and meaning of authority.

It should be remembered that Winthrop had commenced the New England tradition by telling the people that they had the liberty to do only that which is in itself good, just, and honest; that their liberty was the proper end and object of authority thus defined; that the approbation of the people is no more than the machinery by which God calls certain people to the exercise of the designated powers. And it should also be borne in mind that these powers are given apart from any consideration of the social welfare, that they derive from ethical, theological—a priori—considerations.

Jonathan Edwards says that the supreme qualification of a ruler is that he be a man of "great ability for the management of public affairs." This is his first and basic definition! Let us follow his very words, underlining those which carry revolutionary significance. Rulers are men "of great *natural* abilities" who are versed in discerning "those things wherein the *public welfare or calamity consists,* and the proper *means* to avoid the one and promote the other." They must have lived among men long enough to discover how the mass of them disguise their motives, must have learned how to "unravel the false, subtle arguments and cunning sophistry that is often made use of to defend *iniquity.*" They must be men who have improved their talents by—here are his great criteria—*study, learning, observation,* and *experience.* By these means they must have acquired "skill" in public affairs, "a great understanding of *men and things,* a great *knowledge of human nature,* and of the way of *accommodating* themselves to it." Men are qualified to be rulers if and when they have this "very extensive knowledge of men with whom they are concerned," and when also they have a full and particular understanding "of the *state and circumstances* of the country or people that they have the care of." These are the things—not scholastical articles—that make those in authority "fit" to be rulers!

Look closely at those words and phrases: skill, observation, men and things, state and circumstances—above all, experience! Is this the great Puritan revivalist? It is. And what is he saying, out of the revival? He is telling what in political terms the revival really meant: that the leader has the job of accommodating himself to the realities of human and, in any particular situation, of social, experience. No matter what he may have as an assured creed, as a dogma—no matter what he may be able to pronounce, in the terms of abstract theology concerning predestination and original sin—as a public leader he must adapt himself to public welfare and calamity. He cannot trust himself to a priori rules of an eternal and uncircumstanced good, just, and honest. There are requirements imposed by the office; authority does indeed consist of propositions that pertain to it, but what are they? They are the need for knowing the people, the knack of properly manipulating and operating them, the wit to estimate their welfare, and the cunning to foresee what may become their calamity.

When we are dealing with so highly conscious an artist as Edwards, we not only are justified in submitting this crucial paragraph to close analysis, we are criminally obtuse if we do not. So it becomes significant to note what Edwards says immediately after his radically new definition of the ruler. Following his own logic, he is prepared at once to attack what, in the state and circumstances of the Connecticut Valley, constituted the primary iniquity, from which the greatest social calamity might be expected.

He says it without, as we might say, pulling punches: a ruler must, on these considerations of welfare, be unalterably opposed to all persons of "a mean spirit," to those "of a narrow, private spirit that may be found in little tricks and intrigues to promote their private interest, [who] will shamefully defile their hands to gain a few pounds, are not ashamed to hip and bite others, grind the faces of the poor, and screw upon their neighbors; and will take advantage of their authority or commission to line their own pockets with what is fraudulently taken or withheld from others." At the time he spoke, there sat before him the merchants, the sharp traders, the land speculators of Northampton; with the prompt publication of the sermon, his words reached similar gentlemen in the neighboring towns. Within two years, they hounded him out of his pulpit.

The more one studies Edwards, the more one finds that much of his preaching is his condemnation, in this language of welfare and calamity rather than of "morality," of the rising and now rampant businessmen of the Valley. It was Edwards' great perception—and possibly his greatest value for us today is precisely here—that the get-rich-quick schemes of his contemporaries were wrong not from the point of view of the eternal values but from that of the public welfare. The ruler, he said, must know the "theory" of government in such a way that it becomes "natural" to him, and he must apply the knowledge he has obtained by study and observation "to that business, so as to perform it most advantageously and effectually." Here he was, at the moment his protector was gone, when he knew that he was lost, telling those about to destroy him that the great man is he who leads the people by skill and experiential wisdom, and not by making money.

It is further revealing that, after Edwards had portrayed the ruler in this frame of utility and calculation, as he came to his fourth point, he then for the first time said that the authority ought to be a pious man, and only in his fifth and last did he suggest the desirability of a good family. For Winthrop these qualifications had been essentials of the office; for Edwards they were radically submitted to a criterion of utility. "It also contributes to the strength of a man in authority . . . when he is in such circumstances as give him advantage for the exercise of his strength, for the public good; as his being a person of honorable descent, of a distinguished education, his being a man of estate." But note—these are all "useful" because they "add to his strength, and increase his ability and advantage to serve his generation." They serve "in some respect" to make him more effective. It had never occurred to John Winthrop that the silent democracy should imagine for a moment that the elected ruler, in church or state, would be anyone but a pious, educated, honorably descended person, of adequate economic substance. Edwards (who was pious, educated, and very well descended, but not wealthy) says that in some respects these advantages are helps to efficiency.

From one point of view, then, this was what actually was at work inside the hysterical agonies of the Great Awakening. This is one thing they meant: the end of the reign over the New England and American mind of a European and scholastical conception of an authority put over men because men were incapable of recognizing their own welfare. This insight may assist us somewhat in comprehending why the pundits of Boston and Cambridge, all of whom were rational and tolerant and decent, shuddered with a horror that was deeper than mere dislike of the antics of the yokels. To some extent, they sensed that the religious screaming had implications in the realm of society, and those implications they—being businessmen and speculators, as were the plutocracy of Northampton—did not like.

Again, I would not claim too much for Edwards, and I have no design of inscribing him among the prophets of democracy or the New Deal. What he marks—and what he alone could make clear—is the crisis of the wilderness' Awakening, in which the social problem was taken out of the arcana of abstract morality and put into the arena of skill, observation, and accommodation. In this episode, the Americans were indeed participating in an international movement; even so, they came—or Edwards brought them—to sharper formulations of American experience. What the Awakening really meant for Americans was not that they too were behaving like Dutchmen or Germans or Lancashire workmen, but that in the ecstasy of the revival they were discovering, especially on the frontier, where life was the toughest, that they rejected imported European philosophies of society. They were now of themselves prepared to contend that the guiding rule of this society will be its welfare, and the most valuable knowledge will be that which can say what threatens calamity for the state.

26. Religion, Finance, and Democracy in Massachusetts: The Town of Norton as a Case Study

J. M. Bumsted

Professor J. M. Bumsted (b. 1938) of Simon Fraser University is another in a group of social historians who have pioneered in applying the techniques of demographic and quantitative analysis to the study of major historical problems. Bumsted demonstrates below how a meaningful hypothesis may emerge from microanalysis, in this case the detailed investigation of extant local records. Probing the spiritual outpouring of the Awakening as it touched citizens in Norton, Massachusetts, Professor Bumsted observes that young adults were finding it harder to obtain enough land in sustaining themselves economically as population grew in Norton during the eighteenth century. Young men and women of the third generation, many of whom were coming of age around 1740, also had to contend with a serious monetary crisis—the Land Bank controversy. For a time it looked as though paper money might disappear altogether, making it virtually impossible to get a mortgage, purchase a farm, achieve freehold status, and become a respected member of the community. Frustrations in one area somehow released themselves through the local Awakening in Norton. Key questions are how and why, which form the core of Bumsted's explanation.

Professor Bumsted has integrated measurable demographic variables— population growth and age—with land distribution to produce a thesis that the Awakening had certain "generation gap" overtones. In the process the author clarifies the ways in which pressures upon one demographic group (young adults) might explain differing responses to the evangelical fervor of the Awakening. But has Bumsted, in relying upon demographic data, captured the essence of what he admits was primarily a religious phenomenon? How do we account for the Awakening in communities not plagued by "overcrowding?" Where should we strike the balance between quantitative and literary sources in developing historical explanations?

In October 1740, the English evangelist George Whitefield stepped ashore in Newport, Rhode Island, and ignited in New England the religious revival known ever since as the "Great Awakening." Most discussions of the coming of the Awakening to New England emphasize the place of the revival in the historical development of religion and particularly of New England Puritanism.[1] John C.

Source: J. M. Bumsted, "Religion, Finance, and Democracy in Massachusetts: The Town of Norton as a Case Study," *Journal of American History,* 57 (1971), pp. 817–831. Reprinted by permission of J. M. Bumsted and the *Journal of American History.*

Miller, one of the few scholars who offered a socio-economic explanation for the coming of the Great Awakening, argued a relationship in the Bay Colony between the Land Bank controversy and the revival.[2] The Miller thesis has been often attacked and refuted on a variety of grounds.[3] Indeed, in his most recent consideration of the Awakening, Miller views the revival as a popular reaction to an "over-intellectualization" or formalization of religion and makes no reference to it as a socio-economic movement.[4]

While it may be impossible—as Miller himself may have realized—to take seriously his particular thesis, the demolition of his argument has left historians almost bereft of meaningful socio-economic explanations for the Great Awakening in New England.[5] Part of the difficulty has been that most studies of the revival— including Miller's—have been based on literary sources, which simply cannot be employed for socio-economic analysis. Contemporaries did not think in these terms except in a polemical sense, and polemics are not satisfactory evidence.[6] To deal with socio-economic questions, historians must know something about the structure of society, and this requires detailed research in local records. Such detailed analysis can reveal much more complex socio-economic dimensions than scholars have previously entertained. The following detailed analysis of one rural community in Massachusetts—the town of Norton—offers a partial substantiation of these assertions.

Norton, located in Bristol County, approximately fifteen miles east of Providence, twenty-five miles west of Plymouth, and forty miles south of Boston,[7] was part of a large tract of land known as Taunton North Purchase, obtained from the Indians by the Plymouth Colony and sold in 1668 to fifty-three proprietors from Taunton for £100. Most of the original proprietors did not gain advantage from their purchase, for the tract was not actually subdivided until 1696. The original town of Norton, as incorporated in 1711, included most of the original Taunton North Purchase, but about half of the tract was set off in 1725 as the town of Easton. In 1731, Norton was ecclesiastically subdivided into two parishes.[8] This analysis is concerned with the post-1725 town of Norton, particularly that part served by Norton's First Church. Although in one of the oldest settled regions of New England, Norton in 1740 was neither an ancient town nor a recently settled one. It was a growing and expanding community with two generations of settlement behind it, largely agricultural but with an increasing amount of domestic industry, particularly that connected with the iron trade. Clearly beyond and outside a "frontier" stage of development, Norton was not yet in a stage of stabilization—or even stagnation—which seemed to characterize many of New England's older rural communities. In 1740, Norton had not yet reached the point of throwing off large numbers of settlers to found new communities on the fringes of settlement in New England.

Norton is significant in two ways. Norton's First Church experienced a rather sizeable increase in full membership during the years of the Great Awakening. From the founding of the church in 1714 to 1739, a total of 179 persons joined it in full communion, an average of 6.8 per year. From 1740 to 1743, seventy joined in full communion, an average of 18.2 annually.[9] Norton's figures are not of the same magnitude as those of some of its neighbors: Attleborough's First Church had 189 admissions in the same four-year period; and Middleborough's First Church had 174.[10] While admissions to full communion are obviously not a perfect measure of the impact of the revival in any area, they are the only quantitative means available for measurement and were frequently used by contemporaries as yardsticks. Although Attleborough and Middleborough were similar to Norton in terms of being rapidly growing inland towns settled by proprietors upon Indian purchases at the close of the seventeenth century, they were different from Norton in one crucial respect: they both had enthusiastic New-Light ministers who consciously attempted to foster revival in their parishes.[11] Joseph Avery of Norton, however, never supported the Awakening and was a firm opponent of what he considered to be its excesses.[12] Norton was therefore a town which experienced a considerable revival without benefit of assiduous cultivation by the religious leader of the community. This is not to say that inhabitants of Norton did not have access to evangelical preaching in neighboring communities, but they had to travel to revival meetings rather than having them readily available at home.

Like most towns in Massachusetts, Norton lacks annual rate lists and militia lists, and no regular census of the town was taken until 1765, when it had 295 houses, 343 families, and 1,942 total inhabitants. All available evidence points to a rapid growth of population from sixty inhabitants in 1696 to 300 in 1711–1712, to 750 in 1725 (when 300 were set off to Easton), to 600 in 1731, and to 1,000 in 1740.[13] The vital records of the town indicate that the significant increase in births came after 1710 and increase in marriages after 1720. Births increased almost fourfold from 1700–1710 to 1711–1720, and marriages increased over fourfold from 1711–1720 to 1721–1730.

Years	Births	Marriages
1700–1710	66	1
1711–1720	213	27
1721–1730	230	89
1731–1740	358	108

Such crude indicators do not provide the basis for any sophisticated demographic conclusions. But it can be safely asserted that Norton experienced a sharp natural increase in population beginning around 1711, an increase which meant that around 1740 a disproportionately large number of young people were coming of age, seeking to acquire land, marrying and rearing families, and trying to establish themselves in the world.

While the number of individuals seeking access to land was constantly increasing, with the sharpest jump in the 1730s, the amount of land available was not keeping pace. In the early years of settlement sufficient land rationally located and of reasonable quality for all was available. The Taunton North Purchase was the property of proprietors, but most of those who settled in the tract had some access to the sizeable amount of undivided land in existence. The original proprietors—or their heirs or assignees—received 100 acres each of upland in the division of 1696. In 1699 the proprietors divided the "Great Cedar Swamp" into nine shares of six lots each, every lot included about eight acres to be used for meadow and woodlot. Another 100 acres of upland per share was allotted in 1700, but beginning with this division, the holder of the land right was required to "pitch" for it—that is, to state to the company how much land he desired and where it was to be located. All subsequent divisions—before 1740 there was a fifty-acre division in 1705, a sixty-acre division in 1714, a forty-acre division in 1724, a thirty-acre division in 1729, and a forty-five-acre division in 1731—were similarly pitched. With the 1731 division, about 70 percent of the total tract had been allocated, and most of the arable land apparently spoken for; after 1735, the number of pitches in the proprietor's records were negligible and the average acreage in each pitch small.

Years	Total Pitches	Average Acreage Size	Total Acreage Pitched
1700–1705	20	58.5	1170
1706–1710	34	29.1	994
1711–1715	131	19.0	2488
1716–1720	42	12.8	538
1721–1725	30	11.3	334
1726–1730	144	14.1	2029
1731–1735	106	15.8	1674
1736–1740	24	10.5	252
1741–1745	47	8.1	380
1746–1750	28	9.6	269

Apparently, in an effort to make more of the limited additional land available to those who were using it, beginning with a division in 1744, pitches were restricted only to those who had fully utilized their previous rights.[14] The effect of this restriction, of course, was to make it almost impossible for a newcomer to gain land from the proprietors. After 1739, the price of a share of the Taunton North Purchase, which had risen as high as £200 in 1717, levelled at about £10 lawful money, and the shares had become so divided through inheritance and sale that only fractional rights could be obtained. By 1740, therefore, the opportunity to obtain large quantities of undivided (and inexpensive since unimproved) land in Norton had virtually vanished.

With access to undivided land in Norton steadily decreasing and ultimately closing, anyone desirous of accumulating land had to look to other sources. One possibility was to purchase divided and perhaps improved or semi-improved land from others. But in a town with a steadily growing population, the amount of land changing hands through sale remained remarkably constant. A marked increase in the number of transactions and the total amount of acreage involved occurred in the years immediately following 1710, but from 1710 to 1740—calculating five year averages—the average annual number of transactions, the average annual acreage per transaction, and the average annual total acreage changed very little. (See below for tabulation of transactions.)

The one feature of land transactions which did alter was price, increasing from an average of 15.5 paper shillings per acre in the years 1711–1715 to 84.8 paper shillings per acre in the years 1736–1740. Because of steady inflation, this more than fivefold increase is a bit deceptive; the increase in terms of 1700 paper shillings was only from 13.3 shillings per acre to 21.7 shillings per acre.[15] But over the same period, the average wholesale price of a bushel of wheat only doubled from 6.78 to 13.45 paper shillings, and in terms of 1700 paper shillings actually decreased from 5.49 shillings to 3.45.[16] Land prices in Norton, therefore, were increasing far more rapidly than was the cost of living.

Years	Annual Average Number Trans.	Annual Average Acreage Trans.	Annual Average Total Acre
1701–1705	2.0	33.2	66.4
1706–1710	4.6	39.2	180.0
1711–1715	18.2	33.7	614.1
1716–1720	17.2	33.5	575.9
1721–1725	18.8	34.7	652.9
1726–1730	24.0	27.3	658.4
1731–1735	21.4	23.7	508.4
1736–1740	21.2	29.8	632.3

The young Nortonian did not necessarily have to purchase land in order to acquire it. It could be obtained from his parents, either as an inheritance or a gift. These sources were fairly limited in the years before 1740, however. The first generation of settlers—those who had participated in the early divisions of the North Purchase and were rated for support of the minister of 1711–1712—remained dominant in the town only until the early 1720s, when they were replaced by a second generation born in the last decades of the seventeenth century. This second generation was the one active in acquiring land, wealth, and power between 1720 and 1740. Its children, born primarily in Norton in the years after 1711, represented a third generation, coming of age in about 1740. But the second generation was neither an ancient nor a decrepit one, and only about a dozen had died in the years before the Awakening. Inheritance of land and wealth by the third generation was clearly an expectation, but not yet a reality by the time of the revival. A young Nortonian could always hope to be given land by parents still living, and the Land Registry records disclose over twenty such gifts in the 1730s. But, since the average age of the recipients of such parental largesse was thirty-three years, it is unlikely that those born in Norton after 1710 counted on acquiring land from their parents much before the 1740s. Many of the younger generation could—and perhaps did—seek their fortunes outside Norton.

Occupations, as recorded in the land transactions in Norton, indicate that the percentage of husbandmen in the town was constantly decreasing (from 56.2 percent in 1711–1720 to 37.1 percent in 1731–1740) while the percentage of artisans and laborers was increasing (artisans from 31.2 percent in 1711–1720 to 40.8 percent in 1731–1740 and laborers from 6.2 percent to 17.1 percent in the same years). Most inhabitants could aspire to the status of "husbandman." They would ultimately receive property from parents (or inlaws) and might in a thriving economy acquire sufficient funds through their own efforts to purchase land. But the sort of land and property the younger Nortonian could hope to gain from his parents—a fully improved and stocked farm—was probably better than he could expect to achieve on his own. In the years 1737–1739, three farms of approximately forty acres each changed hands for between £340 and £400 lawful money. Part of this high price (around 200 paper shillings per acre) was because a farm included improved upland, meadowland, woodland, and perhaps even an orchard. Then too, buildings, stock, and equipment were usually included. In 1740, a house, two cows, nine sheep, two swine, two featherbeds, furniture, brass, iron ware, wooden ware, farming tools, all the corn and grain on the ground, six bushels of rye, fencing stuff, cordwood, and boards—the equipage of an operating farm—sold in Norton for £50.[17]

If in economic terms, a large number of Norton's younger generation had not yet "arrived" in 1740, the same was true in political and religious terms as well. Before 1740, the average age in Norton for first election to town office was thirty-seven. The average age of officeholders chosen in the elections of 1739–1740 was 45.9 years; only 11.1 percent of the officeholders were under thirty years of age, and all were elected to minor onerous offices. If we examine the major officeholders (moderator, town clerk, selectmen, assessors, and treasurer), the average age was forty-seven—seven of the nine individuals involved were militia officers, and seven owned over 100 acres of land. It was occasionally possible for a young man to enter local politics at decision-making levels, but those who did so— like George Leonard, who was chosen town clerk at the age of twenty-three— came from the leading families of the town. The average young Nortonian had to wait considerably longer than a Leonard to gain political recognition, let alone an office of importance. Without land, he could expect very little, for only a small number of those elected to any office were landless.

Before 1740 that other mark of local status beside election to office—admission to the ranks of the visible saints—did not come typically to the young, although it was available to all who could make a relation (usually written) of a conversion experience. In the years before the Great Awakening the average age of males first admitted to communion in Norton's First Church was 39.7 years, and only 21.6 percent of admissions involved those under thirty years of age. Furthermore, those admitted to the church before 1740 included a fairly high percentage of those who could be said to have arrived at the time of their conversion. Town office had already been held by 36.4 percent; 46.7 percent were proprietors in the Taunton North Purchase; 79.1 percent owned more than thirty acres of land; 41.9 percent were husbandmen; and only 9.4 percent were laborers.

Norton was not a community which placed any particular premium on or granted much recognition to youth. Recent research has indicated that Norton was probably not atypical in this, and the commonly accepted notions of the endless opportunities afforded young men in colonial America may generally have to be revised.[18] The problem was not that upward progress and the achievement of full recognition as an adult member of the community did not come, but rather that a number of interrelated steps were involved in the process. A man was usually in his thirties before everything had fallen into place.

A brief outline of the major events of the life of Nathaniel Brintnal offers an excellent illustration of the process. Nathaniel Brintnal was born in 1704, son of Lieutenant Samuel and Esther Brintnal. In 1734 he was given 54¼ acres of land by his father, and the town elected him hog-reeve (his first political office) that same year. He married Sarah Hardin in 1736–1737, and their first child was born in 1738, when Nathaniel Brintnal was thirty-four years old. Elected to minor office irregularly from 1734 to 1748, Nathaniel Brintnal failed to acquire much additional land beyond that received from his parents; and he reached his high point of recognition in 1748, when he was elected sergeant of the Second Militia Company of Norton.

Most of Norton's younger generation probably chafed at the bit, but those who did not leave for greener pastures apparently accepted their situation. However, anything which might threaten to disturb the process of upward mobility for the rising generation—disturbing, arresting, decreasing, or even eradicating the expectations of the rising generation—was a great calamity. Such a disaster was clearly inherent in the decision of the Massachusetts government in 1739 to retire the colony's outstanding bills of public credit on the dates specified in their issue and, thereafter, to issue only a small amount of bills for current charges. By 1741, £250,000 of bills would be withdrawn from circulation, and the province would have virtually no medium of exchange. Seizing on the absence of regulation of bills of credit issued privately rather than by the government, several groups of promoters proposed to emit private bills of exchange to fill the currency void.[19] One of these schemes, backed by a large number of entrepreneurs important in their local communities (including Leonard of Norton), would loan bills of credit to individuals secured by mortgages on their lands, the mortgage to be repaid over a number of years in bills or in certain manufactured products. This was called the "Land Bank" or "Manufactory" scheme. A rival plan, organized chiefly by Boston merchants and backed by the government, was to issue bills secured by or exchangeable for silver upon demand.

In the controversies in Massachusetts over currency which had been endemic since the end of the seventeenth century, emphasis was always on the commercial aspects of the money problem. This was hardly surprising, since most of the controversial literature originated in Boston among commercial classes and their spokesmen. Particularly evident were concerns about the overseas balance of trade and the inflationary effects of paper currency. The persistent charge by hard money men that advocates of paper currency were idle, extravagant debtors hoping to employ inflation to their own nefarious advantage retained a long vitality. It is difficult to analyze with any certainty the motives of those who subscribed to the Land Bank in Massachusetts, particularly those outside the urban areas. But for those in rural Massachusetts in 1740, as for a very long period thereafter in American history, an easy money policy made very good sense.[20]

Even Thomas Hutchinson—and he was no friend of the Land Bank—allowed that its proponents had good reasons for their support.[21] The province needed a circulating medium of exchange to survive, grow, and expand. The alternative seemed to many a return to a barter economy.[22] Beyond this and the argument of paper-currency advocates of the need to encourage manufactures to decrease the province's unfavorable trade balance lurked an insistence that currency shortages and high interest rates made it difficult for farmers to obtain and improve land. As early as 1716, one author had argued:

> Some that are good Farmers, who observing that the Lands are so generally Ingrost, fear they shall not procure sufficient to settle their Children upon, have straitned themselves, and perhaps run in debt to buy Land, to the disabling them to improve the Lands they before had. For inabling such to improve their Lands, if the Country should lend 100 l. [£] without Interest, upon Condition that in ten Years time they break up and keep subdued 50 Acres of Land; this would be a great Encouragement to them, and would much Increase the Produce of the Country.[23]

Another pamphleteer in 1737 wrote: "No Man can afford to give *10 Per Cent* for Money to Trade with; neither can the Farmer afford to give such an Interest for Money to stock and improve his Land with: such an Interest would soon eat out his Farm: but at a moderate Interest Men would be encouraged to stock and improve much more Land than now they do, which would advance their Families, and serve the Publick also."[24] Even more to the point, in 1740 a newspaper correspondent argued that the Land Bank "will inrich the Province so many Hundred Thousand Pounds, and enable the Farmers to improve their Waste Lands and settle their Children on them."[25] Land meant status, and the acquisition of land became closely equated with a paper currency scheme which was ruthlessly suppressed by the provincial government.

On November 5, 1740, Governor Jonathan Belcher issued a proclamation warning sheriffs, undersheriffs, and constables to post notice to all persons holding commissions from his government (mostly county judges and officials, and militia officers) of the dangers of supporting the Land Bank currency "directly or indirectly." Removal from office was threatened for those who remained obdurate.[26] A month later, Belcher demonstrated that he was not making idle threats by dismissing a number of officeholders for having continued to encourage the bills; one of those dismissed was Norton's Leonard, who lost his posts as justice of the peace and justice of the Inferior Court of Common Pleas in Bristol County.[27] The governor followed these moves with orders that all county registrars of deeds furnish him with the names of Land Bank mortgagees.[28] In addition, the provincial secretary advised justices of the peace to use their "Power and Authority in every legal Method" to prevent passage of the bills, and singled out the use of the licensing authority over taverners, retailers, and common victualers.[29] Even before Massachusetts received word in the spring of 1741 that the Land Bank had been abolished in Britain by parliamentary act, Belcher had arrested its growth.

By the end of 1740, certainly by May 1741, the Land Bank had been successfully repressed, foreboding economic troubles for rural Massachusetts. The same period saw other developments which pointed in the same direction. The winter of 1740–1741, for example, had been a particularly difficult one; Josiah Cotton of Plymouth described it as "the most terrible that I (who am . . . 62 years old) remember; near 40 distinct Snows some very deep & of long continuance, which occasioned a vast consumption of Hay Corn &c. whereby Grain became very scarce & dear."[30] The war with Spain, which had begun in 1739, and the threat of war with France tended to keep many close to home, and high grain prices combined with a poor summer in 1741 produced a poor harvest in that year. In 1741 Cotton's son decided to remain at home "by reason of Presses War &c" and agreed to take over his father's farm for two years. But, his father reported, "being at a considerable charge in hiring Labourers, buying a Stock &c" young Cotton gave up his attempt in the autumn of 1741.[31]

No diarists in Norton give us a picture of conditions in the town, but the uncertainty of the economic situation was reflected in land transactions, which after averaging 21.3 per year in number over the decade 1730–1740, dropped to only ten in 1741, most of them in the early days of the year. It was in 1741, especially after the harvest, that religious excitement built to fever pitch in the area. Eleazer Wheelock's tour in late October and early November on his way to Boston saw real beginnings of revival.[32] By the end of the year, much of the area around Norton was in a state of emotional turmoil, and the churches harvested the results into the year 1742. In the years 1731–1740 in southeastern Massachusetts, an average of 2.39 males and 4.18 females per church had been admitted to full communion. Admissions crept up to 3.35 males and 4.69 females in 1741, but in 1742 soared to an average per church of 16.90 males and 20.50 females.[33] In

Norton's First Church, eighteen males and thirty-three females became full members the same year.

By itself, the chronology of events does not demonstrate a relationship between economic uncertainty spearheaded by the Land Bank suppression and the Awakening, although the sequence of events does not negate such a connection. But after a detailed examination of the sorts of people who joined the church in Norton, the likelihood of such a relationship becomes much stronger. In Norton, the males who joined the church during the Great Awakening were significantly younger, less established, and less successful in the world than were those males who had joined before 1740. The average age of admission to communion before 1740 had been 39.7 years, with only 21.6 percent of those admitted under age thirty. During the revival, the average age of male admissions was 29.9, and 71.3 percent were under the age of thirty, over half (57 percent) between the ages of twenty and thirty. Before 1740, 36.4 percent of those admitted had previously held town office; during the Awakening, the figure was 13.2 percent. Before 1740, 46.7 percent were proprietors of the North Purchase; during the revival, only one additional (3 percent of the total) held proprietorial rights. Before 1740, 79.1 percent had owned more than thirty acres of land; during the Awakening, only 36.3 percent held more than thirty acres, and another 36.3 percent (compared with 14.5 percent before 1740) owned no land at all. Before 1740, only 9.4 percent of the members admitted to the church had been laborers; during the Awakening, 25 percent held such an occupational listing.

Most of those who joined Norton's First Church during the Awakening would get elected to town office, acquire land, and become established. Responding to the Awakening was not an action of the permanently disinherited, but of the temporarily frustrated. It was all a matter of timing. The Awakening arrived in Norton and its vicinity, at least, at a particularly propitious moment: when a combination of developments, especially the suppression of the Land Bank, seemed to be arresting the ambitions and expectations of the younger generation. Significantly, none of the seventeen subscribers to the Land Bank in Norton joined the church at this time. It was not the Land Bankers themselves who felt thwarted. They were more intimidated by government action and eager to preserve an achieved status than they were frustrated about the crushed opportunities to obtain one. But for the younger generation, the appeal of a religious message which was, in a sense, levelling—since it exalted the achievement of conversion over all other attainments and rejected worldly success as superfluous—was very strong. Given a sense of frustration, it was hardly surprising that many younger people would turn to the one factor in their experience which did not depend upon success in the world— religion. And having turned to religion, they discovered that the message currently being emphasized over all others was that of the necessity for the crisis conversion experience, an experience which came only to some, and which seemed curiously to avoid those in the town who had arrived.

Economic prospects took a distinct turn for the better in 1742, as it became evident that the destruction of the Land Bank would not mean an end to large currency emissions by the province so long as it was at war. Land purchases in Norton increased from ten in 1741 to thirty in 1742, and a number of parents transferred property to their sons. Throughout southeastern Massachusetts, 1743 saw admissions to church membership fall off to 5.37 males and 6.95 females per church; and in Norton's First Church, only 2 males and 2 females were admitted. By 1744 both the economic situation and church admissions returned to normal, and all that remained of the Awakening was the clerical controversy over what opponents called its excesses.

The revival in Norton did not produce class conflict. It was probably a result of an implicit struggle between generations, but there is no evidence that the younger generation which joined the church saw the older generation as an enemy to be overthrown. There were no revolutions, overt or silent, within either town, church, or parish, in which the younger generation overturned the elder or attempted to assert its numerical power. The two outstanding occurrences in the town—the founding of a separate church in 1747 and a subsequent church-parish struggle which resulted in the dismissal of Avery as minister in 1749—both produced factions which cut across generations, socio—economic status, and the Awakening itself.[34] But Norton does suggest that the observed impact of the Awakening on the youth of New England, particularly on younger males, and the high incidence of revivalism in areas of economic unrest and land hunger—those regions which began throwing off large numbers to seek new land on the unsettled frontiers of colonial America—may have been related.

While one case study cannot substantiate a thesis, there are several pieces of corroborating evidence from outside Norton which are suggestive. One emerges from figures on the incidence of revival impact in southeastern Massachusetts, measured in terms of admission to full communion. The churches which experienced the largest upsurge in membership were located in areas settled at approximately the same time as Norton.[35]

Date of Settlement	Average Number of Admissions, 1741–1744
1620–1690	47.3
1691–1715	83.2
1716–1740	54.8

While it might be argued that these figures could be explicable in terms of religious dynamic rather than socio-economic factors, any positive correlation between high admissions and church practices, doctrine, or ministerial attitudes toward the Awakening cannot be established.[36] Nor does there appear to be any correlation between the population size of a community and the amplitude of its revival.[37]

Years of Age	Percentages of Admission to Full Communion in Middleborough First Church	Percentages of Admission to Full Communion in Norton
0–20	27.4	14.3
21–30	45.2	57.0
31–40	19.2	14.3
41–50	5.5	4.7
51–60	2.7	0.0
60–	0.0	9.5

High admissions tended to occur in communities which, like Norton, had a large number of young men coming of age and offered only limited opportunities for their full acceptance into adult society. This assertion receives some substantiation in figures from Middleborough, a community settled approximately the same time as Norton, where the average age of admission to full communion dropped as markedly as in Norton in the years of revival, and where age distributions were markedly similar.

The older communities of southeastern Massachusetts had already made their adjustments to population pressures; as coastal settlements they offered more alternatives for younger men.[38] As Cotton of Plymouth put it: "The Sea Swallows up the land."[39] Certainly those regions most responsive to the Great Awakening —eastern Connecticut and southeastern Massachusetts—were those which a generation after the revival were most active in providing settlers for newly opened backcountry areas such as New Hampshire and Nova Scotia.[40]

The Great Awakening was in one sense a regional, indeed national, phenomenon, particularly in terms of the public controversy which in engendered. But the Awakening was also the sum total of all the local revivals—like that in Norton—which occurred in the 1740s. Since the revival was essentially a religious movement, it would be chimeric to deny the prominence which religious factors played in its creation and propagation. But socio-economic factors were important as well in explaining why such a large proportion of the population responded so eagerly to the question: "What must I do to be saved?"

NOTES

1. See, for example, Edwin Scott Gaustad, *The Great Awakening in New England* (New York, 1957), 1–15; C. C. Goen, *Revivalism and Separatism in New England, 1740–1800* (New Haven, 1962), 1–8; Perry Miller, *The New England Mind: From Colony to province* (Cambridge, Mass., 1953); Perry Miller, *Jonathan Edwards* (New York, 1949).

2. John C. Miller, "Religion, Finance, and Democracy in Massachusetts," *New England Quarterly*, VI (March 1933), 29–58.

3. Robert E. Brown, *Middle-Class Democracy and the Revolution in Massachusetts, 1691–1780* (Ithaca, 1955), 128–29 n; George Athan Billias, *The Massachusetts Land Bankers of 1740* (Orono, Maine, 1959), 17–31; Gaustad, *The Great Awakening,* 43.

4. John C. Miller, *The First Frontier: Life in Colonial America* (New York, 1966), 266–79.

5. One exception is Richard L. Bushman, *From Puritan to Yankee: Character and the Social Order in Connecticut, 1690–1765* (Cambridge, Mass., 1967).

6. The danger of using the socio-economic cant of such propagandists as Old-Light Charles Chauncy or hard-money advocate William Douglass should be somewhat more obvious than it has been.

7. Most of the data on which this paper is based comes from the following sources: Norton First Church Records, I, 1714–1846 (Norton Public Library, Norton, Mass.); Norton First Precinct Records, I, 1734–1834 (Norton Public Library, Norton, Mass.); Norton North (2nd) Precinct Records, 1734–1765 (Norton Unitarian Church, Norton, Mass.); Norton Town Records, I, 1712–1769 (Norton Town Hall, Norton, Mass.); Bristol County Probate Records, I–XII, 1685–1750 (Bristol County Courthouse, Taunton, Mass.); Bristol County Land Records (Bristol County Courthouse, Taunton, Mass.); Taunton North Purchase Old Proprietary records, I–VII (Bristol County Courthouse, Taunton, Mass.); and *Vital Records of Norton, Massachusetts, to the year 1850* (Boston, 1906).

8. George F. Clark, *A History of the Town of Norton, from 1669–1859* (Boston, 1859); William L. Chaffin, *History of the Town of Easton Massachusetts* (Cambridge, Mass., 1886).

9. Norton First Church Records, I.

10. Figures are based on Attleborough First Church Records, I, 1741–1840 (Oldtown Congregational Church, North Attleborough, Mass.), and the catalogue of members contained in I. W. Putnam, *First Church in Middleborough, Mass: Mr. Putnam's Century and Half Discourses: An Historical Account; and a Catalogue of Members* (Boston, 1854), 89–94.

11. Clifford K. Shipton, *Biographical Sketches of Those Who Attended Harvard College* (15 vols., Boston, 1873–1970), V, 317–22, VII, 268–72.

12. *Ibid.,* V, 305–07.

13. Evarts B. Greene and Virginia D. Harrington, *American Population before the Federal Census of 1790* (New York, 1932), 29; Chaffin, *History of Easton,* 39; Clark, *History of Norton,* 63–65.

14. Taunton North Purchase Old Proprietary Records, IV, 53.

15. Based on a conversion table in Arthur Harrison Cole, *Wholesale Commodity Prices in the United States 1700–1861* (Cambridge, Mass., 1938), 119.

16. *Ibid.,* 117.

17. Bristol County land Records, XXX, 364.

18. For example, John Demos, *A Little Commonwealth: Family Life in Plymouth Colony* (New York, 1970); Philip J. Greven, Jr., *Four Generations: Population, Land, and Family in Colonial Andover, Massachusetts* (Ithaca, 1970); Kenneth A. Lockridge, *A New England Town The First Hundred Years: Dedham, Massachusetts, 1636–1736* (New York, 1970).

19. Andrew McFarland Davis, *Currency and Banking in the Province of Massachusetts Bay* (New York, 1901); Joseph B. Felt, *An Historical Account of Massachusetts Currency* (Boston, 1839); Billias, *The Massachusetts Land Bankers of 1740.*

20. Herman Belz, "Paper Money in Colonial Massachusetts," *Essex Institute Historical Collections,* CI (April 1965), 149–63.

21. Thomas Hutchinson, *The History of the Colony and Province of Massachusetts-Bay,* Lawrence Shaw Mayo, ed. (3 vols., Cambridge, Mass., 1936), II, 301.

22. Boston *Gazette,* Aug. 27, 1739.

23. *SOME CONSIDERATIONS Upon the several sorts of BANKS Propos'd as a Medium of Trade: AND Some Improvements that might be made in this Province, hinted at* (Boston, 1716), 14.

24. *A PROPOSAL to supply the Trade with a Medium of Exchange, and to sink the Bills of the other Governments* (Boston, 1737), vi.

25. *New England Weekly Journal,* Sept. 23, 1740.

26. Boston *Weekly News-Letter,* Nov. 6, 1740.

27. *Ibid.,* Dec. 4, 1740.

28. *Ibid.,* Dec. 18, 1740.

29. *Ibid.,* Dec. 18, 1740.

30. Josiah Cotton, "Memoirs containing Some Account of the Predecessors, Relations, Posterity & Alliances (with some remarkable Occurencies in The Life and Circumstances) of JOSIAH COTTON of Plymouth in New-England . . . ," 303–04 (Massachusetts Historical Society).

31. *Ibid.,* 303.

32. "Diary of Rev. Eleazer Wheelock, D.D., During His Visit to Boston, October 19, Until November 16, 1741," *Historical Magazine, and Notes and Queries Concerning the Antiquities, History and Biography of America,* V (1869), 237–40.

33. John M. Bumsted, "The Pilgrims' Progress: the Ecclesiastical History of Southeastern Massachusetts, 1620–1776" (doctoral dissertation, Brown University, 1965), Appendix I, Table 1.

34. *Ibid.,* 220–28, 262–64.

35. *Ibid.* 436–37.

36. *Ibid.*

37. Since no general population figures exist for 1740, these figures are from the 1765 census in Greene and Harrington, *American Population before the Federal Census of 1790,* 21–30.

38. For an expansion of this point, see J. M. Bumsted and J. T. Lemon, "New Approaches in Early American Studies: The Local Community in New England," *Histoire Sociale/Social History* (Nov. 1968), 98–112.

39. Cotton, "Memoirs . . . of JOSIAH COTTON . . . ," 291.

40. H. J. Mays, "Early New England Settlement of Nova Scotia" (seminar paper, McMaster University, 1968). See, for example, Alan Heimert, *Religion and the American Mind from the Great Awakening to the Revolution* (Cambridge, Mass., 1966), 49–50.

27. The Crisis of the Churches in the Middle Colonies, 1720-1750

Martin E. Lodge

The Congregational Church held a firm institutional grip upon religious expression in New England before the Awakening, though its grasp was weakened by the exhortations of Jonathan Edwards and other New Light ministers. In the middle colonies no one church group or sect was established by law, nor was there a preferred denomination. In this setting there was a lack of religious stability which, according to Professor Martin E. Lodge (b. 1937), who teaches at the State University College of New York at New Paltz, lay at the heart of theological tensions resulting in manifestations of the Awakening south of New England. Church organizations attempting to establish authority over their parishioners were not equipped to handle the new circumstances of America or the rapid growth in population in the middle colonies during the early decades of the eighteenth century. At first church members responded to religious instability in diverse ways. In the end, though, they turned to the "New Birth" preachings of such Awakening figures as George Whitefield and Gilbert Tennent as well as to those who denounced them.

Professor Lodge hypothesizes that the Awakening convulsed the middle colonies because it served as an outlet for people who were frustrated by so many competing church groups. Yet the revival experience itself was quite similar in content to that of New England where the Congregational Church was anything but unstable before the Awakening. Is it possible that dissimilar circumstances could cause uniform religious responses? Or must we contend also with the New Birth message itself and the personal charisma of itinerant preachers like George Whitefield if we are to fully understand the Great Awakening as it spread throughout the American provinces?

Fifty years ago Herbert L. Osgood described the Great Awakening in America as "the first great and spontaneous movement in the history of the American people."[1] The profound significance that Osgood attached to the Great Awakening has spurred two generations of historians to explore in depth its impact upon the development of American life, institutions, and thought. In this preoccupation with the influence of the Awakening upon the later phases of American history, however, scholars have tended to overlook the origins of the upheaval. Nowhere is

Source: Martin E. Lodge, "The Crisis of the Churches in the Middle Colonies, 1720–1750," *Pennsylvania Magazine of History and Biography,* 95 (1971), pp. 195–220. Reprinted by permission of Martin E. Lodge and the *Pennsylvania Magazine of History and Biography.*

this hiatus more evident than in the historiography of the Middle Colonies. No one has ever attempted to explain why the Great Awakening happened there, or why it was a "great and spontaneous" popular movement.[2]

The reason for this oversight, perhaps, has been the spell that the sectarians inhabiting the Middle Colonies have cast over modern historians. Their fascination with the Quakers and such German sects as the Mennonites seems to have blinded most students of the Middle Colonies to the significance of the denominations most affected by the revivals of the 1740's: the Presbyterian, Reformed, and Lutheran Churches.[3]

The Great Awakening in the Middle Colonies was almost exclusively a movement among the church people—those settlers whose religious heritage can be traced to the established churches of Europe. The anglican George Whitefield and the New Brunswick party of the Presbyterian Church dominated the awakening of the English-speaking colonists. These evangelists drew their following either from settlers raised in the Calvinistic traditions of the churches of Scotland, Ireland, and New England or from previously "indifferent" people whose religious background was unknown[4] but who usually became Presbyterians as the result of their conversions. The Quakers, the principal English-speaking sect, were affected only superficially.[5]

The German Awakening was staged by the Dunkers and the Moravians, two pietistic sects recently organized in Germany out of separatists from the established churches.[6] Neither group had much impact upon the older Mennonite and Schwenkfelder sects; they soon found their appeal was infinitely greater among the Lutheran and Reformed laymen. Conrad Beissel, for instance, an erstwhile Dunker, who was the most successful German evangelist of the 1730's, was only an annoyance to the Mennonites, but he infuriated Reformed circles by his inroads on their congregations.[7] Similarly, the Moravian revivals of the following decade were confined to the church people after the Pennsylvania sects, led by the Schwenkfelders, thwarted Count Zinzendorf's design to create a "church of the spirit" embracing all denominations.[8]

In this essay we will attempt to show how the breakdown of church religion in the Middle Colonies created a situation which made the church people unusually susceptible to evangelism.[9] Our thesis, simply stated, is that the churches of the Middle Colonies failed to establish institutions capable of fulfilling the religious needs of a rapidly expanding population. Before the late 1740's, neither the Church of England nor the several national branches of the Lutheran and Reformed Churches founded any American institution above the level of the congregation. The Presbyterians managed, early in the century, to reproduce the ecclesiastical system of Scotland, but when this organization could not cope with the demands of its congregations, it fell apart in 1741. While the young churches were faltering in their struggle to gain an institutional foothold in the New World, they were swamped by the vast immigration of church people from the British Isles and Germany which flooded the Middle Colonies after 1718. Unprepared to offer the stability the new arrivals so desperately needed amidst the moral and social confusion attending their settlement, the churches stood helplessly by as hundreds of laymen turned away from their inherited faith, went over to the sects or lapsed into religious indifference. Organized religion seemed on the verge of collapse when the Great Awakening, though at first adding to the disorder, rescued the floundering churches. By 1750, the strength and effectiveness of every church was increasing rapidly.[10]

The first prerequisite of a thriving church is an effective ministry. A minister is essential to the functioning of every congregation because only he can lawfully administer the sacraments and preach the Word of God. Furthermore, because of his specialized training in matters of the Spirit, the minister is the person best qualified to guide individual laymen in their private quest for righteousness and salvation. At the root of the institutional failure of the churches in the Middle Colonies, therefore, lay the churches' inability to establish a clergy numerous enough, or effective enough, to supply these elemental needs.

The most obvious symptom of the unhealthy condition of the churches in the Middle Colonies was the great disparity between the numbers of ministers and the number of congregations. The situation was particularly desperate in the German churches of Pennsylvania, where by 1740 there were but three German Reformed pastors for twenty-six congregations,[11] and only one clergyman for the twenty-seven German Lutheran congregations.[12] The Anglicans, the Dutch Reformed, and the Dutch and Swedish Lutherans were all better served than the Germans, although on any given Sabbath no more than half the pulpits of these denominations were ever occupied by ordained ministers.[13] The Presbyterian Church kept pace with the demands of its multiplying congregations throughout the 1720's.[14] During the following decade, however, the Church was overwhelmed by the influx of Scotch-Irish immigrants. By sending their younger members on strenuous itinerations the presbyteries managed to bridge the widening gap between the supply of ministers and the number of congregations until the end of the 1730's, when it became impossible, even with some fifty clergymen enrolled in the American church, to honor every request for a preacher.[15]

The scarcity of ministers in the Middle Colonies stemmed ultimately from the churches' dependence upon Europe for their clergy. A church congregation could not simply appoint its minister from the ranks of the lay membership, as could a sectarian congregation. He had to be educated and ordained by institutions which were usually found only in the Old World. This reliance upon Europe (and upon New England, too, for the Presbyterians) was fatal because Europe could not begin to satisfy the colonial churches' demands for clergymen. Ministers were reluctant to emigrate to the New World. Unlike the Puritan hegira to New England or the immigration of the sects, the migration of church peoples to the Middle Colonies was not a movement of religious communities conducted by their religious leaders in pursuit of a religious ideal. Only the Scotch-Irish were driven at all by religious motives, and, partly for that reason, only Presbyterian ministers came to America in significant numbers.[16] Other denominations were reduced to cajoling clergymen into undertaking an American mission by offering them such worldly advantages as a handsome salary or preferment at home after a period of service abroad.[17]

Because the immigration of clergymen did not allow the American churches to prosper, their only alternative was to become self-sufficient. Self-sufficiency, unfortunately, required institutions that were beyond the capacity of most churches to create at so primitive a stage of their development. Each denomination had to set up an ecclesiastical organization, independent of Europe and invested with the power of ordination, and then found a college to train a native ministry.

Only the Presbyterian church attained self-sufficiency during the first half of the eighteenth century, reaching it at the very end of the period. With the founding of the Presbytery of Philadelphia in 1706, the authority to ordain and regulate the American clergy was permanently located in the New World. The development of educational institutions, however, was much slower. William Tennent's "Log College," established at Neshaminy, Pennsylvania, in 1727, did little before the Great Awakening to relieve the Presbyterians of their dependence upon New England and the British Isles for training their ministers. By 1738 Tennent had supplied just five men to the ministry, four of them his sons, and his seminary had become so entangled in the controversy over revivalism that its very existence was threatened.[18] Not until the Great Awakening saved Tennent's College and goaded the evangelical party to found the College of New Jersey in 1746 did the Presbyterian Church acquire an institution capable of preserving its independence.

The other churches lagged far behind the Presbyterians. None of them so much as attempted to found a college, and, until the late 1740's, their organization above the level of the congregations was rudimentary and dependent upon foreign authority. The episcopacy of the Church of England was represented in the Middle Colonies by two commissaries appointed by the Bishop of London, one at Philadelphia and the other in the city of New York. Their authority was small: they could hold visitations, call the clergy to informal meetings, report to the bishop on clerical conduct, and, in an emergency, temporarily suspend a wayward minister. Ordination and discipline, the two powers essential to ecclesiastical independence, remained the prerogative of the English hierarchy.[19]

At the beginning of the eighteenth century the Lutherans in the Middle Colonies—Dutch, Swedish, and German—were supervised by a provost, a deputy of the Archbishop of Sweden. With the exception of three occasions when the Archbishop permitted his agent to ordain a candidate for the ministry, the powers of this official were identical to those of an Anglican commissary. Sweden, however, thoughtlessly neglected to designate a provost between 1730 and 1748, leaving the American Lutherans with no government at all during the most crucial years of their growth.[20]

The Dutch and German Reformed ministers never had an overseeing official, such as a provost or a commissary. They were completely unorganized until after the Great Awakening, although the Dutch ministers in New York sometimes met informally to discuss matters of policy, as during the controversy over Frelinghuysen's revival in the 1720's. Twice the Classis of Amsterdam grudgingly granted the New York clergy the power to ordain a minister, but it was only in 1747, following a decade of petitioning, that the Classis permitted the Dutch and the German churches each to erect an independent Coetus.[21]

When the Lutherans established a synod the following year, all the churches in the Middle Colonies, except the Anglican, which did not receive a bishop until after the Revolution, were ecclesiastically independent of Europe. Only then, by ordaining and regulating their own clergy, did these churches begin to grapple effectively with the shortage of ministers.

Supplying their congregations with pastors was only the most immediate problem the churches faced in the Middle Colonies. An even greater obstacle was the difficulty every church experienced in preserving the authority of the clerical office. The social status of the American ministers, and especially their control over the congregations, had to be enforced if they were to perform effectively. But for reasons which were only partly understood at the time, respect for the cloth seemed to vanish in the free air of the New World.

This disregard for the status of the ministry was due in part, as many contemporaries perceived, to the fact that the young churches enjoyed none of the wealth and power of their established parents. In Europe the spiritual authority of the clerical office, imparted to it by the rite of ordination, was enforced by powerful ecclesiastical bodies which were financially secure and backed by the state. But in the Middle Colonies the Presbyterians alone had any ecclesiastical organization; only the Anglicans in the vicinity of New York City received encouragement from the civil authorities;[22] and, except for some individual congregations, all the churches were destitute. Stripped of the secular props that would have assured his authority, an American minister could count only on the sanctity of his office to command the respect and submission of the laity. In the words of Henry Melchior Muhlenberg: "A preacher must fight his way through with the sword of the Spirit alone . . . if he wants to be a preacher and proclaim the truth."[23]

The prestige of the clergy was eclipsed also by the influence the sectarians had attained in many parts of the Middle Colonies. The churches in Europe had cruelly persecuted the sects, but in America the shoe was often on the other foot, and the sects tormented their erstwhile oppressors by blackening the character of individual ministers and publicly denouncing them as "hireling preachers" who earned their bread by gulling the people. So low did the reputation of some clergymen sink under the brunt of this anticlericalism that parents disciplined their children with stories of what the wicked parson would do if he caught them.[24]

The most ominous challenge to the ministers' authority, however, came not from the anticlericalism of the sects, nor even from the want of governmental support, but from the unruliness of their own congregations. Clergymen in the Middle Colonies found themselves at the mercy of the people they served. This perversion of the "normal" relationship between a pastor and his flock was intolerable to ministers who were accustomed to the freedom European clergymen enjoyed from the popular will of their parishioners. The withering of the clergy's control over the congregations seemed to poison the very roots of organized religion.

This displacement of pastoral power arose initially out of the circumstances surrounding the founding of congregations. Clergymen being so scarce in the Middle Colonies, particularly in the newer settlements, ministers were seldom present at the gathering of a congregation. Neighbors simply banded together, chose their officers, and, later on, at great sacrifice to themselves, bought a lot and erected a meetinghouse. All this was done without the authorization of the clergy; at most a minister would be called in to sanction the work of the laymen by installing church officers and celebrating communion.[25] By the time the laymen could afford to settle a minister permanently, they had secured an unbreakable hold over the affairs of the congregation. They owned the church property, they were liable for the debts incurred in purchasing a lot and building the meetinghouse, and, because of these responsibilities, they were unwilling to relinquish any of their control to the pastor.[26]

The minister's position in his congregation was further hampered by the control the laymen usually gained over his salary. No church in the Middle Colonies was independently wealthy: only in New York were tithes fixed by civil law;[27] the few congregations endowed with land often seem to have derived little income from it;[28] and only the Anglican missionaries employed by the Society for the Propagation of the Gospel consistently received allowances from the mother country.[29] Nearly every congregation, therefore, supported its minister by a voluntary subscription to his salary, an arrangement irksome to layman and clergyman alike. Because most church people were poor, these salaries were small, difficult to collect, and the frequent cause of ill feeling between pastors and their flocks.[30]

Worst of all, the ministers' financial dependence crippled their authority over the congregations. Disciplining unruly parishioners could be costly because the chastened sometimes refused to pay their share of the pastor's salary. For the same reason, an entire congregation might be disrupted if some members took a dislike to the minister. His salary would diminish as his unpopularity spread until even the contented parishioners would turn against him for fear the burden of support would fall upon them alone. Under these conditions, only a foolish minister, or an uncommonly courageous one, opposed the will of his people for long. Even preaching upon some unpleasant subject was risky: "I pay [the parson] by the year," explained one of Muhlenberg's parishioners, "but if his preaching does not please my taste, I'll go to another church where I can get it for nothing." The prevalence of such attitudes brought Muhlenberg to conclude, "it is easier to be a cowherd or a shepherd in many places in Germany than to be a preacher here, where every peasant wants to act the part of a patron of the parish, for which he has neither the intelligence nor the skill."[31]

The growth of popular control over the congregations was most noticeable in the German churches of Pennsylvania, where the clergy was too undermanned and too disorganized to offer much resistance. When Muhlenberg arrived in 1742, he immediately perceived how widely the American churches had deviated from the European norm: "In religious and church matters, each has the right to do what he pleases. . . . Everything depends on the vote of the majority."[32] The clergy was abashed by this drift toward lay rule. The one minister who dared to justify it, the Reformed pastor John Peter Miller, was scorned by his colleagues and took refuge in Conrad Beissel's cloister at Ephrata.[33] Other ministers fought stubbornly against the unruliness of their people, but they got nowhere until they organized themselves toward the end of the 1740's.

Meanwhile the Presbyterian Church managed to keep its congregations under restraint by wielding the authority of the presbyteries. In 1737, for instance, when the vacant congregation at Paxton refused to receive Thomas Craighead, the supply sent by the Presbytery of Donegal, the Presbytery declared that the Paxton church had shown disrespect for the ministry and decreed that the congregation would receive no more supplies until it acknowledged its fault and promised "more kindly entertainment" to the ministers sent its way. The people yielded at once, and ministerial supplies were renewed.[35]

The restraining hand of the presbyteries, however, was lifted after Gilbert Tennent preached his famous Nottingham sermon in March, 1740. This utterance, the most significant of the Great Awakening in the Middle Colonies, justified, as never before, the popular tendencies within the congregations by defending the right of the layman to hear any minister he chose.[36] By accepting, rather than resisting, the increased independence of laymen in church affairs, Tennent unleashed a great popular upheaval. Responding to this passionate appeal, the laity revolted against their pastors and split their congregations, eventually rending the entire Presbyterian Church into Old and New Side.

The development of lay control in the Anglican congregations differed from the other churches in one significant respect. Because most Anglican clergymen in the Middle Colonies were missionaries employed by the Society for the Propagation of the Gospel, they received a handsome annuity from England, and consequently they were economically independent of their people. There were several instances of unpopular missionaries being hounded out of their pulpits by their congregations,[37] but, in general, clerical authority in the Church of England was somewhat better preserved than was the case elsewhere. Anglican ministers, for example, were able to preach against the Great Awakening, even while their people were swept up in it, without the dire consequences that overtook many Presbyterian opponents of the revival.[38]

Nevertheless, a minister who was not subsidized by the Society, such as the rector of Christ Church in Philadelphia, was vulnerable to the same popular pressures as the pastors of other denominations. In 1737, for example, a quarrel broke out in Christ Church which epitomizes the tensions existing in all the churches of the Middle Colonies. The vestry, representing the desires of a large part of the parish, tried to install Richard Peters as assistant to the pastor, Archibald Cummings. Cummings sternly opposed the vestry's wishes, but, seeking to avoid a bitter confrontation, he deferred the matter to the Bishop of London, arguing that the Bishop alone possessed the authority to nominate and appoint an American clergyman. The vestry then claimed the right to present candidates for the Bishop's licensing because the members of the parish had built the church themselves and supported its minister solely by their voluntary contributions. Some parishioners were even inclined to doubt whether the Bishop had any jurisdiction at all in the affair. Although the controversy ended with the vestry's complete submission to the authority of the hierarchy, Cummings' reflection on the Peters case echoed the misgivings of many ministers who had opposed the will of their people with less success:

> This and the like Disturbances might be prevented or easily cured had we a B[isho]p in these parts: Indeed in this Church 'tis no wonder Differences happen so often seeing there's no fixed Salary, but everything precarious, entirely at the will of the people; were it so in Old England I doubt not but in many parishes the like would frequently happen.[39]

There was a saying current in the middle of the eighteenth century which depicted Pennsylvania as a "hell for . . . preachers."[40] This description might well have included the Middle Colonies as a whole because everywhere the ministers worked under the severest handicaps. Their authority and social status had been drastically undermined by the lack of government support, by inadequate ecclesiastical organization, and, above all, by the unruliness of their own people, to say nothing of the open contempt in which they were held by the sectarian population. At the same time, the scarcity of ministers, combined with the vastness of the country, greatly increased the physical burdens of their office. Most ministers traveled hundreds of miles through the wilderness every year preaching in vacant pulpits and administering to their own widely scattered flocks.[41]

When all these hardships are considered together, it is not surprising that the effectiveness of the ministry in the Middle Colonies was considerably reduced, and that a decline in religion among the churches inevitably resulted. Standards of religious observance suffered everywhere, in spite of the clergy's best efforts, and the religious needs of many church people went unfulfilled.

The journals of Henry Melchior Muhlenberg, written during his early ministry in Pennsylvania, illustrate how impossible it was to maintain European standards of worship. Because Muhlenberg's parishioners were so widely scattered over the countryside, his performance of routine duties, such as pastoral visits, inevitably fell short of standards set in Germany where congregations were huddled together in villages and the members could easily be visited several times a year. For similar reasons, Muhlenberg was forced to lower the requirements for confirmation. Children in Germany had to know their catechism by heart, but Muhlenberg could not supervise the instruction of the young so carefully, and he accepted them if they merely understood the most elementary doctrines. When ministering away from his own pulpit, Muhlenberg tailored his services to the ignorance of the people by shortening his sermons and spending the rest of the time catechizing his listeners. The celebration of communion in congregations where he did not personally know the qualifications of the members posed a particularly delicate problem of weeding out the ineligible. Muhlenberg's method was to cross-examine the deacons and elders about each applicant, hoping this would suffice, but he also soothed his ruffled conscience with the thought, "the Lord knoweth the heart."[42]

By these compromises with accepted standards, Muhlenberg actually made himself as effective as a clergyman could be in the Middle Colonies. Few ministers, however, possessed Muhlenberg's genius. They were generally men of only ordinary capacities, no better and no worse qualified than their European brethren.[43] But in America they faced extraordinary conditions which required unusual character, insight, and flexibility. Inevitably, many of them stumbled, and their blunders further impaired their effectiveness.

The most common kind of blunder, as one might expect, was the failure to adjust European usages to American conditions. Pastors who were unwilling to compromise with necessity risked destroying their usefulness altogether by alienating their congregations. Muhlenberg summarized their plight thus:

> Young beginners in this important office of the ministry do not have sufficient experience and possess more efficiency than insight. They start out vigorously and use European standards which do not always fit the complicated conditions in America. They usually stand alone without anyone with whom they might confer concerning the trials that occur. They are beset on every side by *spectateurs* and hostile lurkers who watch not only their whole work, but every little move they make, and treat even the smallest mistake as a criminal act.[44]

John Pugh, an Anglican missionary in Delaware, was such a stickler for European practices. In 1738 he wrote desperately to the Society for the Propagation of the Gospel asking whether he should adapt baptismal requirements to the demands of the settlers. He feared that his people, objecting to his rigid insistence upon qualified sponsors, would be driven over to the Presbyterians.[45] If a minister was to retain any effectiveness at all, therefore, he had to accept changes in religious observance.

It is not surprising that some ministers broke under the strain of such adjustments, while others became entangled in useless disputes with their parishioners, or, possessed by a sense of their inadequacy, fell into the dull, lifeless legalism which the revivalists were to exploit so pitilessly. Whatever the particular causes of individual failures, however, enough has been said to suggest that ministers in the Middle Colonies were considerably less effective than they probably would have been in Europe.

During the 1730's the impotence of the clergy brought organized religion to the brink of disintegration. When the ministry was unable to administer its office effectively, church institutions could no longer fulfill the religious needs of the laymen. This institutional breakdown became ever more serious as immigration swelled the numbers of church people, thus multiplying the burdens of the undermanned ministry and resulting ultimately in widespread discontent. A spiritual crisis developed among the church people which enabled the revivalists to touch off the popular outbursts of the 1740's.

The breakdown of organized religion, by seeming to close off the normal approaches to heaven, was intolerable to most church people because they were still deeply concerned with the hereafter. Despite all that has been written about the secularization of thought during the early eighteenth century, salvation remained the ultimate goal in the lives of ordinary laymen.[46] Consequently, when church institutions failed, this fundamental religiosity was often deflected into unexpected channels, none of which were fully satisfying. Three such deflections were of especial importance in preparing the church people for the evangelical movements of the 1740's: a peculiar kind of religious indifference, legalism, and anticlericalism.

The most obvious symptom of religious malaise, to contemporaries of the Great Awakening, was the shocking growth of religious indifference. Although religious indifference assumed a variety of forms, ranging from hardened un- belief[47] to mere religious slothfulness,[48] there was one type of indifference which is considerably more important than the rest for understanding the mood of the church people before the Great Awakening. Many laymen no longer knew what religion to believe; they had come to doubt the validity of their own creed without having found a satisfying substitute. Such people were not indifferent in the stric- test sense of the term because they were still spiritually concerned, and often deeply troubled, but in their uncertainty they frequently abandoned organized religion altogether and adopted a position indistinguishable, on the surface, from the slothfulness and hardened unbelief around them.

Among Muhlenberg's converts were several persons whose case histories illustrate this type of indifference in its purest form. The father of a young man in Muhlenberg's care, for example, told Muhlenberg that he had become skeptical of his Reformed beliefs and had allowed his children to grow up unbaptized because he was thoroughly confused by the multitude of denominations in Pennsylvania, each crying, "Here is Christ; we have the best medicine and the nearest road to heaven!" In spite of his own uncertainty, however, the father taught his children to read the Bible, hoping they would eventually be able to choose for themselves the religion most in agreement with God's Word.[49]

This unwillingness to commit oneself to a denomination was frequently pre- ceded by several changes in religion. Another of Muhlenberg's future parishioners, though raised in the Reformed Church, attended services with his Lutheran wife until he became disillusioned with the churches in general. He then tried some of the sects, but finding them equally unsatisfying, he resolved thereafter to hold aloof from all communions and seek peace only in Christ. The spiritual odyssey of Conrad Weiser, the famous Indian agent, followed a similar course. During the 1730's, Weiser progressed from Lutheranism, his ancestoral religion, through the Reformed faith to Conrad Beissel's monastery at Ephrata, which he later quit after a brief flirtation with the Moravians. Weiser no longer knew where to go when Muhlenberg met him in 1742, and for five years he lived in a religious limbo until Muhlenberg finally persuaded him again to receive communion in the Lutheran Church.[50]

In each case, the uncertainty which drove these men to adopt an attitude of outward indifference is closely related to the denominational heterogeneity of the Middle Colonies. The multiplicity of religions, more than any other single factor, appears to have provided the layman with the incentive to question his inherited faith. Opportunities for doubting one's beliefs were more limited in Europe and in New England where a dominant church either suppressed its rivals or relegated them to a distinctly inferior position. But in the Middle Colonies dozens of denominations competed on a more or less equal footing and the babble of creeds inevitably obscured the old certainties. Consequently, an unusually large number of settlers abandoned their beliefs and either joined another denomination or fell into a skeptical indifference.

Religious belief might have been better preserved had the Middle Colonies not been a veritable battleground of warring religions. All denominations were inflamed with a lust for proselytes. The Anglican missionaries, as instruments of their employers' grand design to bring the plantations under the sway of the Church of England,[51] were probably the most ambitious soul gatherers of any group of clergymen. Though their accomplishments fell far short of their objectives, they sustained their zeal and justified their salaries with glowing accounts of every little triumph over the "dissenters."[52] Nor were the Presbyterians remiss in propagating their version of the Gospel. During the 1730's, for example, the Anglicans in the Pequea Valley of Pennsylvania pleaded desperately for a missionary to do battle with the Presbyterians who were leaving no stone unturned to draw them into their communion.[53]

The sects, rather than the churches, were the most successful proselytizers. Not only did the sectarians dominate many parts of the Middle Colonies in wealth and prestige, but the confused and disillusioned church people were unusually easy prey. Numerous immigrants from the British Isles quickly forsook their churches and joined the Quakers, while many Germans, impressed with the prestige of the Friends, became indolent in the practice of their own religion.[54] The greatest inroads among the German church people, however, were made by the pietistic sects, whose missionary efforts led directly to the German Awakening of the 1740's. The Mennonites too, though less zealous for converts than either the Quakers or the pietists, seldom shunned the opportunity to entangle an occasional stray in their nets.[55] Even unbelievers and "deists" joined the competition for proselytes, causing more than one Anglican priest to complain of "bad men" who promoted infidelity and profaneness throughout the country by sowing "loose and Atheistical" principles.[56]

It was difficult to avoid having one's religious beliefs challenged, because so many laymen, particularly from the sects, dabbled in missionary work among their neighbors. These zealots employed the crudest techniques, ridicule and insult, to destroy the faith of their victims. Typical of the heckling the church people endured was the scrape of an elderly Englishman with a local Quaker magnate: upon hearing his neighbor had just been baptized, the Friend jeered, "Why didn't thee desire the Minister rather to piss upon thy Head . . . ; that would have been of more effect." Such an incident, though trivial in itself, could discourage even a devout person if it became an everyday experience. Muhlenberg tells of an old couple, staunch Lutherans in Germany, who were so ridiculed by their sectarian neighbors in Pennsylvania that by the time he found them "their candlewick scarcely glimmer[ed]." Not all laymen, of course, submitted to these attacks quietly. Whenever the sectarians challenged Frederick Stengle, one of Muhlenberg's most ardent parishioners, and provoked him to argument, he was so heated in the defense of his religion that they eventually learned to leave him alone. Disputatious fellows like Stengel lived dangerously, however, for, as Muhlenberg observed, if the sectarians found someone who was not solidly grounded in doctrine, they would relentlessly entangle him in his own arguments and lead him away from the church.[57]

Indentured servitude and religious intermarriage also encouraged lay prose-lytizing. An indentured servant, cut off from the fellowship of his co-religionists, was all but helpless before the indoctrination of his master. Such was the experience of the Lutheran, Michael Walker, for many years the servant of a prominent Friend. Walker was often tempted to join the Quakers and attended their meetings regularly, but eventually his earlier religious training prevailed, and, when freed, he became a Lutheran schoolmaster. Muhlenberg relates several other cases of Anglicans or Lutherans, indented to sectarians, who also survived to join his congregations.[58] One can presume, however, without stretching the imagination, that numerous church people succumbed to the propaganda of their employers and abandoned their original faith. Matrimonial converts were common, too, despite the strictures of every denomination against religious intermar-riage. In 1741, for example, an Anglican missionary lamented the inroads the Presbyterians were making on his parish by marrying his young people, and Muhlenberg mentions several persons who married into the Lutheran Church.[59]

Religious intermarriage, indentured servitude, and the daily clashes with sectarians, therefore, all combined to undermine the religious beliefs of the church people. At the same time, the inefficacy of church institutions, and the economic burden of their support,[60] severely strained the layman's loyalty to his denomina-tion. Unable to cope with such pressures, hundreds of people abandoned the churches. Many changed their beliefs and joined another communion, while countless others, hopelessly bewildered but still spiritually concerned, quit organized religion altogether.

Meanwhile, the laymen who remained steadfast in the practice of their reli-gion were subjected to a legalism which was virtually a compromise with indif-ference. Many ministers, aware of the pressures driving the laymen away from the churches, sought to preserve the allegiance of their parishioners by easing the requirements for Christian fellowship. They made few demands upon the inward spirituality of their people, being content merely if their congregations attended worship regularly and were correct in doctrine and outward behavior.

This was the policy, for example, of Jedediah Andrews, pastor of the Presby-terian church in Philadelphia, whose legalistic preaching Benjamin Franklin immortalized in the pages of his *Autobiography*. Franklin, who at the time was nominally a Presbyterian, occasionally went to hear Andrews, though with grow-ing reluctance because: "His discourses were chiefly either polemic arguments, or explications of the peculiar doctrines of our sect, and were all to me very dry, uninteresting, and unedifying, since not a single moral principle was inculcated or enforc'd, their aim seeming to be rather to make us good Presbyterians rather than good citizens." Eventually Andrews hit upon a text, which Franklin thought "could not miss of having some morality," but to his disgust Andrews confined the sermon to five points only: "1. Keeping holy the Sabbath day. 2. Being diligent in reading the holy Scriptures. 3. Attending duly the public worship. 4. Partaking of the Sacrament. 5. Paying due respect to God's ministry." This was not the useful, social morality Franklin had in mind, and he "attended his preaching no more."[61]

Though we may sympathize with Franklin's disillusionment, Andrews' legalistic preaching was, nevertheless, a necessary response to the plight of his people. His congregation, like many in the Middle Colonies, was a mixture of "divers Nations of different sentiments,"[62] and it was forever threatened from within by the disintegration of religious belief and from without by sectarian criticism. Under these conditions, Andrews had little choice but to inculcate and defend the "peculiar doctrines" of Presbyterianism if he expected to hold such a group together and bolster its wavering faith. He had to insist, furthermore, that his people perform at least the minimum religious duties—read the Bible, attend church, etc.—if he was to prevent many of them from becoming outwardly indifferent.

Legalistic preaching, therefore, may not have been very inspired, but, because it dealt directly with many of the problems undermining church religion, it probably helped stave off a complete disintegration of religious belief. By preaching doctrine and good behavior, ministers, such as Andrews, instilled their congregations with a sense of denominational identity and pride. No doubt, too, the spiritual needs of some colonists were completely satisfied by this easy-going formalism, while others, inwardly shaken by the religious anarchy around them, suppressed their doubts and accepted legalism for want of anything better. Consequently, until the revivalists offered a more fulfilling alternative, legalism prevailed in congregations throughout the Middle Colonies.[63]

Though some people found solace in legalism, other laymen were unhappy with its cold formalism, which could not satisfy the inward needs created by the spiritual crisis they were undergoing. Persons who were baffled by the variety of religions in the Middle Colonies, and had come to doubt their beliefs, could not be consoled by doctrines and rules. When their religion was reduced to a set of dogmas, it appeared to these troubled souls as just another creed, with only its familiarity to recommend it over the teachings of other denominations. Few settlers were qualified to undertake the comparative examination of theologies needed to decide whether their creed was the one most in accord with God's Word. Nor were they capable of making so weighty an intellectual decision without a deeper emotional affirmation. By failing to supply that emotional affirmation, legalism probably intensified the uncertainty of numerous laymen.

Because legalism was unable to mollify the spiritual confusion of the laity, there was nothing to prevent the discontent of the church people from spreading during the decade before the Great Awakening. John Peter Miller observed that by 1730 many church people in Pennsylvania were "so confused they no longer knew what to believe."[64] In a sermon in 1733, T. J. Frelinghuysen described the religious uncertainty he had detected among the settlers of New Jersey: "I would be religious, did I only know which religion is the true one; but how shall I who am young, arrive at a correct conclusion? One pursues this course, and another that—one professes this belief, and another that, and a third rejects both!"[65] The Anglican missionaries commented frequently, throughout these years, on the spiritual restlessness of the population. Robert Weyman, for example, noted with some surprise a "general disposition" of Pennsylvanians to hear him out, "notwithstanding the Prejudices they had been brought up in against the Church of England." Other missionaries in Pennsylvania and Delaware also reported "dissenters of all persuasions" flocking to their services.[66] More and more laymen, it seems, were ignoring denominational lines and looking for solace in any religion that was close at hand.

The ugliest symptom of the church people's uneasiness, however, was the growth of anticlericalism within the congregations. Reading through the church records of the 1730's, one becomes increasingly aware of a deep hostility on the part of many congregations toward their pastors, a hostility manifested in the readiness of laymen to exaggerate and denounce the pettiest professional and moral failures of the ministry.[67] The existence of this undercurrent of contempt for the clergy is confirmed by the Great Awakening itself, when one congregation after another, openly aired its hatred, blackened its pastor's character, and tried to turn him out of his pulpit.[68] Historians have missed the full significance of this bitter censoriousness by attributing it simply to the barbarizing effect of the frontier or, in the case of the Scotch-Irish, to "racial" characteristics. But if we accept these denunciations of the clergy at face value, they are obviously an unequivocal expression of the laymen's profound discontent with their ministers.

That discontent can be traced ultimately to the inability of the clergy to deal with the needs of their people. In the eyes of ordinary laymen, the clergy had failed to provide the institutional stability they so desperately desired. Church members were disturbed by the puzzling weakness of clerical authority and distressed by the ineffectual performance of their pastors. Preaching seemed to have declined too, because doctrines which had been accepted as self-evident in the Old World, now often appeared to be no more worthy of belief than the creeds of the most fantastic sects. The clergy's insistence that their parishioners give them a comfortable maintenance, after the laymen had already sacrificed so much to establish the congregations, deepened popular resentment. Encouraged, perhaps, by the anticlericalism of the sects, the laity's frustration came to focus, half-consciously, upon the simplest possible explanation of these vexing conditions: their pastors were incompetent, avaricious, and morally degenerate.

Although the failures attributed to the clergy were exaggerated and often unavoidable, the latent hostility they engendered in the congregations provided much of the raw emotion necessary to the success of the Great Awakening as a popular movement. When revivalists, such as Gilbert Tennent and George Whitefield, publicly condemned their ministerial opponents as "unregenerate," blamed them for the languishing condition of the congregations, and urged the laity to abandon them,[69] hundreds of laymen thought they had found the answer to their religious predicament. "Unregenerate" ministers suddenly became the scapegoats for all the bitterness arising from the breakdown of religious institutions and beliefs. By striking down the "pharisee preachers," many people felt they could free themselves from the unbearable psychological burden of their years in the Middle Colonies.[70]

The Great Awakening, however, was only incidentally a crusade against an unregenerate ministry. The central teaching of the revivalists, their doctrine of the New Birth, led them to a more enduring solution to the problems we have been discussing as constituting the "crisis of the churches" in the Middle Colonies. Their reinterpretation of conversion as an emotional experience provided the laity with an experimental basis for religious belief. A person experiencing the New Birth could know with some certainty that he was on the path to salvation, no matter what his denominational creed.[71] And when the New Birth was wedded to a specific set of doctrines, such as Calvinism, these doctrines, too, were empirically reaffirmed.[72] By resolving the layman's crisis of faith, the evangelists not only brought hundreds of people back into organized religion, but they also restored some of the prestige and moral authority the clergy had lacked before 1740. Pastors could once again minister to the innermost religious needs of their flocks, thus removing the most dangerous source of the tensions that had existed between ministers and their people. Once these tensions subsided, and the methods of the Great Awakening became common practice, the churches in the Middle Colonies could be rebuilt independent of the Old World and rooted in the peculiar conditions of America.

The Great Awakening in the Middle Colonies, therefore, was intimately bound up with the process of immigration and settlement. It arose out of the difficulties the churches experienced in establishing their religious institutions and maintaining their religious beliefs in a perplexing and often hostile environment. Before the 1740's the church people were confused Europeans, dependent upon the institutions and outlook they had left in the Old World. By 1750 this was, in general, no longer true. The Great Awakening had provided them with a set of principles that could reconcile their Old World heritage with their New World experience.

NOTES

1. Herbert L. Osgood, *The American Colonies in the Eighteenth Century* (New York, 1924; reprinted by Peter Smith, Gloucester, Mass., 1958), III, 409. I would like to thank Carl Bridenbaugh, Robert L. Middlekauff, and Russell F. Weigley for their criticism and their encouragement.

2. New England has been better served in this respect than have the rest of the colonies, particularly by Richard L. Bushman, *From Puritan to Yankee: Character and the Social Order in Connecticut, 1690–1765* (Cambridge, Mass., 1967), Chapters 9–12. Though Professor Bushman's book deals only with Connecticut, no other work discusses the background of the Awakening so comprehensively or with such insight. It should serve as a model for all future studies of the Great Awakening. The works of Perry Miller are invaluable for the intellectual origins of the revivals, especially his *The New England Mind; From Colony to Province* (Cambridge, Mass., 1953), and *Jonathan Edwards* (New York, 1949).

The only comprehensive study for the Middle Colonies is Charles Hartshorn Maxson, *The Great Awakening in the Middle Colonies* (Chicago, 1920; reprinted by Peter Smith, Gloucester, Mass., 1958), which is still a useful survey, particularly because it includes the German revivals. The most valuable study of the background of the Awakening, at least among the English speaking settlers, is Leonard J. Trinterud, *The Forming of an American Tradition: A Re-examination of Colonial Presbyterianism* (Philadelphia, 1949). Professor Trinterud examines Presbyterian evangelism in the light of the constitutional crises in the presbyterian Church and he includes some useful information on the religious conditions among the clergy and the laity, information which should be supplemented by Guy Soullrard Klett, *Presbyterians in Colonial Pennsylvania* (Philadelphia, 1937), and Nelson R. Burr, *The Anglican Church in New Jersey* (Philadelphia, 1954). None of these books, however, though they contain much of the material used in this article, attempt to explain why the revivalists got such a tremendous response from the laymen.

The intellectual origins of the Great Awakening in the Middle Colonies will not be explored in this article. For German evangelism, the student should begin with the several studies of the Dunkers and especially the Moravians. Professor Trinterud's work is excellent for the intellectual background of the Tennent party, although his observations on the significance of pietism have been corrected by James Tanis, *Dutch Calvinistic Pietism in the Middle Colonies: A Study in the Life and Theology of Theodorus Jacobus Frelinghuysen* (The Hague, 1967).

3. Throughout this article we will refer to "sect" and "sectarians," "church" and "church people." The term "sect" includes the Quakers, Mennonites, Schwenkfelders, Moravians, Dunkers, and such smaller groups as Conrad Beissel's Seventh Day Baptists encloistered at Ephrata, Pa. By the term "church" we mean the Church of England, the Presbyterians, the Congregationalists, and the various national branches of the Lutheran and Reformed Churches. For the difference between these two types of denominations, see footnote 9.

4. *The Querists, or Extract of sundry Passages taken out of Mr. Whitefield's printed Sermons, Journals and Letters* (Philadelphia, 1740), 32; Samuel Blair, *A Particular Consideration of a Piece, Entitled, The Querists* (Philadelphia, 1741), 61–62; Thomas Prince, *The Christian History . . . For the Years 1744-5* (Boston, 1745), 295. There is good reason to believe that most of these "indifferent" people had once been affiliated with some church.

5. Frederick B. Tolles, "Quietism versus Enthusiasm: The Philadelphia Quakers and the Great Awakening," *Pennsylvania Magazine of History and Biography,* LXIX (1945), 26–49.

6. On Dunker origins see Donald F. Durnbaugh, *European Origins of the Brethren* (Elgin, Ill., 1958), Chapter 1. On the Moravians see John Jacob Sessler, *Communal Pietism among the Early American Moravians* (New York, 1933), 8–12.

7. C. Henry Smith, *The Story of the Mennonites* (Newton, Kans., 1950), 547; John C. Wenger, *History of the Mennonites of the Franconia Conference* (Telford, Pa., 1937), 81; [John Peter Miller], *Chronicon Ephratense: A History of the Community of Seventh Day Baptists at Ephrata,* Translated by J. Max Hark (Lancaster, Pa., 1889), 70–73; William J. Hinke, ed., *Life and Letters of the Rev. John Philip Boehm, Founder of the Reformed Church in Pennsylvania: 1638-1749* (Philadelphia, 1916), 200–203, 274–275, 353–355, hereinafter cited as Boehm.

8. Sessler, 34–37; Smith, 547.

9. To keep this article down to a reasonable length, we will not deal in detail with the accompanying question of why the older sects—especially the Quakers, Mennonites, and Schwenkfelders—failed to participate in the Great Awakening. It seems proper, however, to outline the answer to that question, particularly since it is implicit in the paragraphs that follow.

In general, the sects were more successful than the churches in establishing their religious institutions, thus avoiding the crisis that came to confront the struggling churches. There were two basic reasons for the greater ease the sects enjoyed in settling the Middle Colonies: (1) Almost without exception, the immigration of the sectarians was better planned, organized, and financed than was the migration of the church people; but more importantly, (2) sectarian institutions were better adapted to the primitive conditions of the New World than were church institutions. The essential difference between a church and a sect, in this context, lay in their different conceptions of the ministry. A church minister was distinctly set apart from the layman by education, by calling, and by a special ordination. Furthermore, his profession was considered so sacred that he was not supposed to labor in a secular occupation. The sectarians, on the other hand, held a less exalted view of the ministerial office. No special qualifications or training were required of a sectarian minister. He was chosen directly from the ranks of the lay membership, and he was expected to earn his livelihood in a secular calling. Because of this simplicity, sectarian institutions became fully effective as soon as a congregation banded together and elected its officers, but a church congregation was crippled until it could secure the services of a specially trained and lawfully ordained clergyman and find the means to support him.

10. It should be pointed out that the generalizations we will develop in this article must be applied with some caution to the province of New York. First of all, the revivals on Long Island, and to some extent those among the New Englanders in northern New Jersey, follow the pattern of the New England Awakening rather than that of the Middle Colonies. New England revivalism grew out of the tensions that had arisen in an older, more homogeneous society, whose religious institutions were firmly established, while the Great Awakening in the Middle Colonies was largely a response to problems created by the process of settlement. Secondly, conditions in New York City and its immediate environs also varied in several respects from the rest of the Middle Colonies. The Church of England and the Dutch Reformed Church were more securely entrenched there, the sectarians were weaker, and the influx of immigrants much smaller.

11. Boehm, 83, 88–89.

12. *Ibid.,* 83; Henry Eyster Jacobs, *A History of the Evangelical Lutheran Church in the United States* (New York, 1893), 191.

13. The Anglicans in New York were always well supplied, but in the other provinces the Church of England only managed to keep about half its parishes in ministers. In 1724, for example, all six parishes in New York had ministers. In Pennsylvania, New Jersey, and Delaware, however, there were eight ministers for sixteen parishes, two of which were considered too weak to support a minister. Fulham Papers, XXXVI, 54–57, Lambeth Palace Library. New Jersey had five ministers for ten parishes in 1740. Burr, 86, 113. For further data on Pennsylvania and Delaware see William Stevens Perry (ed.), *Historical Collections Relating to the American Colonial Church,* Volume 2: *Pennsylvania* (Hartford, 1871), 131–133, 145–146.

In 1737 the Dutch Reformed church, though it had had over a century to establish itself, could muster only nineteen ministers for sixty-five congregations. E. T. Corwin, J. H. Dubbs, and J. T. Hamilton, *A History of the Reformed Church, Dutch, the Reformed Church, German, and the*

Moravian Church in the United States (New York, 1895), 136. There were usually one or two German clergymen in New York and another in New Jersey ministering to the scattered Dutch and German Lutherans in those provinces. Jacobs, 117–126.

The four congregations that made up the Swedish Lutheran Church were better off than any of the above denominations. During the first half of the eighteenth century the Wicacoa congregation near Philadelphia was vacant ten years, Racoon and Pennsneck in New Jersey twenty-one years each, and Christina, in what is now Wilmington, Del., just two years. Israel Acrelius, *A History of New Sweden* (Ann Arbor, 1966), 363. Besides their regular congregations, however, all the churches in the Middle Colonies had numerous outparishes, or preaching stations, which were supplied haphazardly.

14. Jedediah Andrews to Thomas Prince, Oct. 14, 1730, Samuel Hazard, *Register of Pennsylvania*, XV (March, 1835), 200–201.

15. Presbytery of Philadelphia Minutes, 12–13, 48, 54, 56, 66 in Presbyterian Historical Society, hereinafter PHS; Presbytery of New Brunswick "Minutes," *Journal of the Presbyterian Historical Society*, VI, 230–232. Fifty-four ministers were members of the Synod of Philadelphia in 1739. *Records of the Presbyterian Church in the United States of America* (Philadelphia, 1841), 141.

16. According to the most recent authority, religious persecution was only a secondary factor in prompting Presbyterian ministers to leave Ireland; they seem to have been driven chiefly by economic want. R. J. Dickson, *Ulster Emigration to Colonial America 1718–1775* (London, 1966), 27–28.

17. Anglican ministers employed as missionaries by the Society for the Propagation of the Gospel were very well paid. See footnote 29. Swedish ministers were "provided with honorable situations" when they returned from an American mission. Acrelius, 369.

18. Trinterud, 30, 71 ff.

19. Osgood, II, 23.

20. Jacobs, 105–106; Acrelius, 364.

21. Boehm, 173; Corwin, 134, 136, 139.

22. Osgood, II, 14–22; III, 117.

23. Henry Melchior Muhlenberg, *The Journals of . . .* , Translated by Theodore G. Tappett and John W. Doberstein (Philadelphia, 1942), I, 67.

24. *Ibid.,* I, 143, 221–222. For other examples of sectarian anticlericalism see *ibid.,* 96, 97, 122, 154, 204; John Holbrooke to Secretary S.P.G., Salem, N.J. Aug. 19, 1730, copy in H. E. Wallace Collection—New Jersey, Historical Society of Pennsylvania (HSP).

25. For a particularly good description of the gathering of a congregation see Boehm, 157–158; also *Journal of the Presbyterian Historical Society,* III, 36, 86. For examples of the congregations' financial difficulties see Boehm, 241–242, 265–266, 281, 286, 413, 415–416, 457–458; Muhlenberg, *Journals,* I, 87, 94–95; William Becket Manuscript, 125, HSP.

26. Boehm, 332.

27. Osgood, II, 14–17.

28. Perry, II, 223; Acrelius, 239–240, 253, 284, 289, 291–293, 297–298, 318, 328.

29. Consequently, the Anglican clergy was the best paid ministry in the Middle Colonies. In 1724, for instance, the New York missionaries were given £50 sterling annually by the Society supplemented by a grant from the Assembly and voluntary contributions. The missionaries in New Jersey, Pennsylvania, and Delaware received between £60 and £70 sterling plus a small voluntary contribution from their congregations. Fulham Papers, XXXVI, 54–57. The Presbyterian ministers in Pennsylvania, by contrast, seem rarely to have received more than £60 local money from their congregations, often half of it in farm produce. Presbytery of Donegal Minutes, 128–129, 145, 181, PHS; Klett, 109.

30. Salary squabbles are rife in the church records. For some examples see Presbytery of Donegal Minutes, 110–111, 141, 158–162, 164–165, 184, and Presbytery of Philadelphia Minutes, 59, 66, PHS; Perry, II, 152–153, 196, 217, 221–222; Acrelius, 257, 278.

31. Muhlenberg, *Journals,* I, 100, 122, 251.

32. *Ibid.,* I, 67.

33. Boehm, 199–200, 254–256.

34. For an example of one such struggle see *ibid.,* 198, 223–225, 281, 300–305, 324, 409–411, 430.

35. Presbytery of Donegal Minutes, 137–138, 144, PHS.

36. Gilbert Tennent, *The Danger of an Unconverted Ministry* (Philadelphia, 1740), 21.

37. Perry, II, 217; Fulham Papers, VII, 174, 176.

38. When the Presbyterian congregations split over the Great Awakening, some Old Side ministers asked to be dismissed chiefly because they could not subsist on their reduced salaries. This is clearly what happened in the case of John Elder and seems to have been the determining factor in the dismissals of Adam Boyd and John Thomson. Richard Webster, *A History of the Presbyterian Church in*

America (Philadelphia, 1857), 454–455; Presbytery of Donegal Minutes, 230, 264, 286–289, PHS. This did not happen to the Anglican missionaries when many of their people abandoned them. Perry, II, 203–235 *passim*; Becket Manuscript, 101–112, 116–134, HSP.

39. Fulham Papers, VII, 170, 175, 179, 189, 200, 201, 242; Hubertis Cummings, *Richard Peters: Provincial Secretary and Cleric 1704–1776* (Philadelphia, 1944), 13–23. An identical controversy arose in 1741 over establishing Peters as Cummings' successor. Fulham Papers, VII, 254, 291, 292, 300; Cummings, 42–70.

40. "Pennsylvania is heaven for farmers, paradise for artisans, and hell for officials and preachers." Gottlieb Mittelberger, *Journey to Pennsylvania,* edited and translated by Oscar Handlin and John Clive (Cambridge, Mass., 1960), 48.

41. For examples of the strenuousness and dangers of the clergy's peregrinations see William Becket Manuscript, 145, HSP; Perry, II, 126, 167, 179, 182; Muhlenberg, *Journals,* I, 183, 187–188, 210.

42. *Ibid.,* I, 98, 118–120, 194–195, 235.

43. The German churches were repeatedly scandalized by ministers fleeing an evil reputation in Europe, but the other churches seem to have done quite well in keeping unqualified men out of their pulpits. The Swedish Lutherans, Anglican, and Dutch Reformed ministries were selected with care by the European authorities, while the American presbyteries, though sometimes lax in disciplining their members, performed the same services for the Presbyterian church.

44. Muhlenberg, *Journals,* I, 249.

45. Perry, II, 201. The Anglican rite of baptism was a frequent source of difficulty for the missionaries. Burr, 173–174.

46. For a description of the religious conscience of the layman, see Ebenezer Pemberton, *Sermons on Several Subjects* (Boston, 1738), 17–19.

47. For examples see Muhlenberg, *Journals,* I, 138; Perry, II, 161, 178.

48. For example see John Pierson to Dr. Bearcroft, Salem, N.J., Oct. 30, 1744, copy in H. E. Wallace Collection—New Jersey, HSP.

49. Muhlenberg, *Journals,* I, 236.

50. *Ibid.,* I, 143–144, 102–103, 170, 172, 188–190.

51. Carl Bridenbaugh, *Mitre and Sceptre; Transatlantic Faiths, Ideals, Personalities, and Politics 1689–1775* (New York, 1962), 26.

52. For examples see Perry, II, 161–162, 170–171, 189–190, 194.

53. *Ibid.,* II, 183.

54. John Holbrook to Secretary S.P.G., Salem, N.J., Dec. 5, 1729, copy in H. E. Wallace Collection—New Jersey, HSP; Muhlenberg, *Journals,* I, 197.

55. Smith, 547; Muhlenberg, *Journals,* I, 127–128, 144.

56. Perry, II, 195–196, 177; William Becket Manuscript, 53, HSP.

57. Muhlenberg, *Journals,* I, 198, 151, 232.

58. *Ibid.,* I, 202, 205, 213, 234.

59. Perry, II, 215; Muhlenberg, *Journals,* I, 202, 241.

60. Perry, II, 201. Presbytery of Donegal Minutes, 4, PHS.

61. Benjamin Franklin, *The Autobiography of . . .* (New York, 1950), 92.

62. Jedediah Andrews to Benjamin Colman, Apr. 7, 1729, Ebenezer Hazard Manuscript Notes, I, PHS.

63. For the prevalence of legalism in the Presbyterian Church see the testimonies of the antirevivalists against it: John Thomson, *The Government of the Church of Christ* (Philadelphia, 1741), 120–124; George Gillespie, *A Sermon against Divisions in Christ's Churches* (Philadelphia, 1740), Appendix, i–ii. In 1738 J. B. Boehm was accused of insufferable dullness by some of his people. Boehm, 261, 314.

64. *Chronicon Ephratense,* 70.

65. Theodorus Jacobus Frelinghuysen, *Sermons by . . . ,* Translated by William Demarest (New York, 1856), 168–169.

66. Perry, II, 162, 196, 197.

67. The Minutes of the Presbytery of Donegal are the best source for studying this phenomenon because they are the most thorough. See especially the disputes between William Orr and the Nottingham congregation, 13–22, 67–81, 85–96, 99–109, 112–115, 119–121. A similar hostility toward J. P. Boehm can be detected throughout his collected letters, but it is not very evident in Muhlenberg's *Journals.*

68. See Presbytery of Donegal Minutes, 192 ff, and Presbytery of Philadelphia Minutes, 78–80, 82–87, 97–99, PHS.

69. Tennent, *Danger of an Unconverted Ministry*; George Whitefield, *Journals* (London, 1960), 345–346, 350–351.

70. Anticlericalism does not seem to have been a significant factor in the German Awakening, probably because there were so few ministers for the Moravian evangelists to oppose. Its importance for the Awakening among the Presbyterians, however, has been drastically underestimated. Condemning and overthrowing "unregenerate" ministers may have been more important than conversion to many laymen. Both conversion and anticlerical revolt served to remove the sense of guilt which had arisen among the church people as a result of the tensions we have been describing. Conversion purified the acknowledged sinner by giving him an experience of the grace of God. Anticlericalism operated more crudely, but it too relieved the individual of his burden of guilt by transferring it to the minister who was then denounced and, if possible, driven away. If this is an accurate interpretation of the significance of anticlericalism, the immediate emotional and psychological impact of the Great Awakening was broader and deeper than the rather small number of conversions would indicate.

71. This was essentially the approach of Whitefield and Zinzendorf.

72. Gilbert Tennent and the New Brunswick evangelists generally took this tack.

28. Religion and the American Mind

Alan Heimert

Professor Alan Heimert (b. 1928) of the Harvard University English department is a leading disciple of Perry Miller. He has raised many an eyebrow with his interpretation of the Great Awakening's impact on the American Revolution. Like Perry Miller, Heimert has focused his scholarly interests upon exploring the American mind. What the Awakening did, according to Heimert, was to split that mind into two identifiable parts—the Calvinist and the rationalist. What any individual felt about revolution was often a function of whichever of these parts was dominant. The Calvinists, in a striking reversal of their usual historical role, became the ones who gave driving energy to Revolutionary activity. Intensely conscious of sin and always trying to eradicate evil in society, the Calvinists objected to the corrupting influence of British ministers and their provincial appointees who, they said, were trying to plunder the American civil and ecclesiastical environment. The rationalists, on the other hand, were more compromising, conservative, and protective of upper-class interests. At best they were reluctant revolutionaries.

Heimert has been criticized for setting up such a sharp dichotomy between post-Awakening Calvinists and rationalists on the issue of revolution. Obviously it is difficult to explain the behavior of a Jefferson or a Franklin within his conceptual framework. But Heimert also has demonstrated the absurdity of an earlier mold which attributed all positive, driving energy in eighteenth-century history to Enlightenment rationalists. Is the problem, then, that writing about so amorphous a subject as the American mind has the tendency to oversimplify the rich variety in human thoughts and deeds?

In 1790 New Jersey's Governor William Livingston, looking back on the years of the Revolution, recalled that the clergy of America had been "almost all universally good Whigs."[1] His estimate has been sustained by later historians, most of whom have likewise tended to see the "black regiment" as something of a monolithic phalanx. The exception of the northern Episcopalians is duly noted, but it is otherwise assumed that the Protestant preachers of America were indistinguishably united in resistance to tyranny and obedience to God. Actually, the clergy's involvement in the Revolution was such that not even the most exhaustive denominational roll call would do justice to the differences among them. The

Source: From Alan Heimert, *Religion and the American Mind: From the Great Awakening to the Revolution* (Cambridge, Mass.: Harvard University Press, 1966), pp. 1–15. Copyright 1966 by the President and Fellows of Harvard College. Reprinted by permission of the Harvard University Press.

diversity was reflected as well in the response of the laity to the various episodes and issues of the imperial crisis. In Massachusetts, for instance, the great majority of citizens were nominally Congregationalists. Yet wide variations in political outlook were observable during the Stamp Act difficulties of 1765–1766. "The general discontent" of those years, observed one participant, was expressed quite differently within various elements of the populace, depending on what "religious principles" each espoused.[2] Similar differences were evident elsewhere in the colonies, not merely in 1765, but in the variety of reactions to most of the events and issues of the next ten years.

To comprehend the nature of Americans' intellectual differences in the years of the Revolution it is necessary to explore the progress of the American mind in the preceding generation. The divisions as to religious principles were an inheritance from one of the most critical episodes in the history of the American mind: the Great Awakening of the 1740's. Indeed the great revival with its intellectual aftermath is itself probably a more fascinating subject of inquiry than any of the ramifications of religious thought in the years of the Revolution. The intellectual division revealed in the Awakening, and codified in subsequent years by American theologians, persisted long after the Revolution, and in that perspective, the struggle for Independence may well have been only an incidental episode. The subject of this volume, however, is limited to the Awakening and the Revolution, and the continuities in American thought in the decades between them. This Introduction is designed to indicate, by way of anticipatory synopsis and not as demonstration or argument, the broader intellectual contours of that period, and to indicate something of the manner of defining and interpreting the religious principles and divisions of eighteenth-century America.

The Great Awakening was the series of religious revivals which, foreshadowed in the "refreshings" in New Jersey and New England in 1734–1735, rose to intercolonial crescendo in 1740. In the estimation of the Awakening's most outspoken critic, the revivals of the 1740's caused American Protestantism to be "divided into Parties" for the first time since the Antinomian Crisis of the 1630's.[3] Actually, divisions existed within the American churches even before the Great Awakening. The Presbyterian Church, for instance, was torn by various issues throughout the 1730's. Likewise the Congregational ministers of New England differed on such questions as the standards of church membership and, though no open breach had as yet appeared, were aligning themselves into clearly identifiable groups. What the Awakening did was crystallize these differences, giving them objective form, and more importantly, expand them beyond the clergy, making partisans of the laity as well. The "two armies, separated, and drawn up in battle array" which Jonathan Edwards espied in 1742 were not clerical factions merely but hosts whose confrontation embodied a fundamental cleavage within the colonial populace itself.[4]

One way of assessing the divisive consequences of the Awakening is that which has often been followed by historians of American Christianity—by considering the manner in which the Awakening altered the denominational structure of the colonies. The two churches most directly involved in the revival were fragmented. Presbyterianism was split into the Synod of Philadelphia, dominated by the "Old Side" opposers of the Awakening, and that of New York, whose members were the "New Side" partisans of the revival. In Connecticut the Congregational Church was similarly, though not so dramatically, sundered into "Old Lights" and "New Lights." There, also, "Separate" conventicles were established in defiance of the parish system and the semi-Presbyterial Saybrook Platform. Indeed, throughout New England evangelical congregations declared their independence from the associations and consociations that had developed over the course of a century. Some defined themselves as Baptists, and a few even as Presbyterians, but most simply stood as autonomous, and disaffected, seceders from the New England Way. Moreover, the revival impulse encouraged the growth of Presbyterianism in the South, where previously the Anglican Church had enjoyed a near monopoly. In Pennsylvania and New Jersey, and eventually in New England, the Baptists rose into new prominence as the beneficiaries of the revival. Throughout the North the Church of England, whose spokesmen were almost unanimously opposed to the Awakening, grew in numbers by virtue of its appeal to citizens offended by the enthusiasm of the revival.

But such a chronicle of sectarian division and proliferation obscures the fact that the "parties" thrown up by the Awakening were hardly so numerous as any listing of denominations might suggest. The fundamental post-Awakening division of the American mind was one that transcended both the inherited denominational structure and that created by the revival. There were in substance only *two* parties on the American religious scene in the period after the Great Awakening. Generally speaking, one consisted of the opponents of the revival, the other of its advocates, each of which over the succeeding years evolved a religious philosophy consistent with its involvement in and attitude toward the Awakening. These parties were of course not organizational entities, though it is true that the tendency of the century was toward more explicit and formal alignments. The parties into which American Protestantism was divided by the Awakening are best understood, and most accurately described, in intellectual terms. Both represented a casting off from the intellectual universe of Protestant scholasticism, and each marked the independent fulfillment of one of the strains that in Puritanism had been held in precarious balance: "piety" and "reason."

Such a division within Protestantism has long been acknowledged to be the intellectual characteristic of the eighteenth century. Indeed from one perspective what happened in America seems "merely one variant of a universal occurrence in Western culture." In England and on the Continent, as well as in the colonies, the "educated classes" turned to the "generalities of eighteenth-century rationalism," and the "spiritual hungers of the lower classes" found expression in revivals, in Pietism or what is called Evangelicalism.[5] Such a division has been characterized by a recent chronicler of the Great Awakening in New England as the divergence and confrontation of the eighteenth-century forces of "Pietism" and the "Enlightenment."[6] However, the evangelical religion of the colonies differed markedly from the pietism of Europe, and the "rational religion" that arose to thwart the revival impulse was hardly identical to the faith of the Encyclopedists. The Great Awakening in America was a unique and profound crisis in the history of the "indigenous culture."

First of all, it perhaps needs to be stressed that the revival in America, unlike that promoted by the Wesleys in England, built and throve on the preaching of Calvinist doctrine. The "work of God is carried on here," George Whitefield wrote to John Wesley in early 1740, "(and that in a most glorious manner) by doctrines quite opposite to those you hold."[7] The doctrines to which Whitefield referred were those of Wesley's sermon, *Free Grace,* in which the English evangelist had propounded what, in the parlance of the day, was deemed an

"Arminian" theory of salvation. "Arminianism," a name derived from that of the Dutch theologian, Jacobus Arminius (1560–1609), had originally referred to the belief that grace is not irresistible, as Calvin had argued, but conditional. By the eighteenth century, however, the term was used less rigorously, often in conjunction with the names of such Trinitarian heresies as Pelagianism and Socinianism, to refer to any of a number of vague ideas expressive of impatience with the "rigid" and "harsh" doctrines of Calvinism. It was against such an "Arminianism," more appropriately called "rationalism," that the proponents of the American revival thought they were contending.

The Arminianism of the colonies had few affinities with the warmer faith of the Wesleys. Here it was the official theology only of the Church of England, which ascribed to man the power to work out his own salvation largely through the use of his rational powers. In the first quarter of the eighteenth century, moreover, not a few Congregational and Presbyterian preachers were also suggesting that man was not so depraved, nor God quite so sovereign, as orthodox doctrine had argued. Such an undermining of Calvinism was in fact part of the inevitable working out of Puritanism's own modifications of strict Calvinist doctrine. The "covenant theology" itself had made God something less than an arbitrary and inscrutable being, and the doctrine of "preparation" had come to imply, over the course of the century, that man was capable of "willing" his own salvation.

The opening charge of the American revival was thus the sermon of 1735 in which Edwards strove to restore the reformation doctrine of "justification by faith alone" as the "principal hinge" of American Protestantism. In so challenging Arminianism, however, Edwards revealed that the two "schemes" which he contrasted—the "evangelical" and the "legal"—were hardly those traditionally identified with the terms Calvinist and Arminian. For Edwards, in presenting evidence of "God's approbation of the doctrine of justification by faith alone," pointed, not to the Pauline epistle, but to the numerous and "remarkable conversions" experienced in Northampton in 1735.[8] The focus of debate was turning from the theoretic manner of God's operations to what He was actually accomplishing, and over the next decade it moved even further away from the traditional issues of the seventeenth century. During the Great Awakening the contest of ideas was often phrased in the older terms. In 1740, for instance, the young Presbyterian revivalist, Gilbert Tennent, declared that "we may as easily reconcile Light and Darkness, Fire and Water, Life and Death, as Justification partly by Works, and partly by Grace."[9] But even for Tennent, who yielded to no man in the rigor of his Calvinism, the "principal hinge" of the "evangelical scheme" was no longer a point of doctrine. Though the issue was at first whether the Awakening was a genuine "Work of God," the challenge of criticism and the response of evangelical spokesmen were such that the focus of analysis quickly shifted from the will of God to the nature of man. In this context, the crux of Calvinism became the existential reality of the emotional conversion experience.

Similarly, the party that Edwards and Tennent opposed was not perfectly characterized as an Arminian one. The advocates of what Edwards styled the "legal scheme" eventually took to themselves, by virtue presumably of their opposition to the "oppressive" doctrines of Calvinism, the name of "Liberals." But their most distinguishing intellectual mark was the notion that man is—or should be—a rational being, one who derives his standards of virtuous behavior from an observation of the external world. A rationalist strain had of course been present in American Puritanism from the beginning. One of the classic assumptions of the Puritan mind was that the will of God was to be discerned in nature as well as in revelation. But in the late seventeenth century, and with greater boldness by the 1720's, voices had been heard in the colonies proclaiming that a knowledge of God's will was best derived, not from His word, but from His works. The articulation of such a "religion of nature," attended as it was by the reversion of several of Connecticut's more prominent young ministers to Episcopalianism, was one of the developments that prompted the attack in the 1730's on Arminianism. But with the Awakening the avowal of a rational or "reasonable" theology was no longer limited to colonial Anglicans. The notion that Christianity is pre-eminently a rational religion permeated the thinking of Old Side Presbyterianism, the Old Lights of Connecticut, and the Liberal clergy of the neighborhood of Boston.

It was in Massachusetts that the creed of reason was most conspicuously developed into a partisan ideology. There it emerged, in the decades after the Awakening, as "the instrument of a group, or of an interest"[10]—the group opposed to the "enthusiasm" of the revival and the seeming unreason of evangelical religion. The premises of rational religion were first unfolded in the criticisms of the Awakening published by the leading Boston Liberal, Charles Chauncy. But the manifesto of Congregational Liberalism was probably Ebenezer Gay's 1759 Harvard Dudleian Lecture, *Natural Religion.* Here Gay summarized the Liberal thesis that God had formed men as rational beings so they "might learn from his Works, what is good, and what is required of them." The lessons of Scripture could only confirm what man was able to discover from the "Constitution of Things, in their respective Natures and Relations."[11] That Massachusetts Liberals were not alone in evolving such a theology is indicated by the fact that the magnum opus of colonial rationalism was the *Elementa Philosophica* of the Anglican spokesman, Samuel Johnson of Connecticut. And this volume, in turn, was recommended by Benjamin Franklin to all who would properly understand the true nature and bases of morality.

In sharp contrast to this studiously rationalistic religion of nature stood the "Calvinism" evolved in the decades after the Awakening. Actually the Calvinists of eighteenth-century America were hardly subscribers to the theology of the *Institutes.* All were familiar with, and frequently quoted, Edwards' classic disclaimer of "dependence on Calvin."[12] If—as Samuel Hopkins explained of Edwards—their "Principles were *Calvinistic,*" they "called no man, Father."[13] They assumed the designation of Calvinist only, as one New Jersey Presbyterian announced, because such terms were "exceeding useful" when one wished "to express Complex Ideas." Yet the idea that essentially defined American Calvinism was acknowledged to be a rather simple one—a belief in the "inward operation of the holy spirit in regeneration."[14] Herein they followed Jonathan Edwards in emphasizing the role of the "affections" in religion and in making virtue dependent on the reception of a "vital indwelling principle" from the Holy Spirit.

In truth, the partisans of evangelical and emotional religion were all in some degree under the intellectual dominion of Jonathan Edwards. Samuel Hopkins would undoubtedly have liked to consider himself Edwards' only begotten intellectual offspring. But he, like the Edwards of whom he wrote, "thought and judged for himself, and was truly very much of an Original."[15] Just as close to Edwards in idea and spirit (and perhaps closer) were the multitude of New Light and New Side preachers, Separatists and Baptists, who, despite their minor differences with Edwards, acknowledged him to be "the greatest pillar in this part of zion's building." Joseph Bellamy, Edwards' student and friend, invariably cited his writings as the best books "on experimental religion and vital piety since the days of inspiration." The Baptist Isaac Backus, though at one time in disagreement with Edwards over the qualifications of the ministry, was always ready to acknowledge him a writer of "pure truth" and, in later years, spoke of him as "our Edwards."[16] Ebenezer Frothingham, who was distraught when Edwards refused to accept the leadership of the Separates, continued to praise him as a defender of the revival and as a theologian and, after Edwards' death, saluted him as one who had "doubtless gone to heaven."[17] Indeed a variety of ministers and men cherished the memory of the "late divine, whose praise is in all the churches," and for all of them Edwards' legacy consisted in the "many valuable volumes" which, as Gilbert Tennent consoled himself, this "ascending elijah" had left as his mantle to American Calvinism.[18] So well did they wear it, indeed, that the Calvinist ministry, averse as they were to invoking "great names" in support of ideas, were nevertheless more accurately "Edwardeans."*[19] Perhaps not until Calhoun similarly convinced two generations of Southerners that, like Edwards, he spoke with "almost superhuman wisdom,"[20] were the axioms and postulates of so broad a movement ever thus provided by one individual nor its inspiration and significance so readily discernible in his writings.

For three and more decades the Calvinists (or Edwardeans) of America debated with the Liberals the questions of the nature of man and the character of God. In this confrontation the party lines of the revival were preserved essentially intact—and even reinforced. To be sure, not all the critics of the Awakening were full-blown rationalists. But as one defender of the revival observed, "the principal and most *inveterate Opposers*" were men of "Arminian and *Pelagian* Principles." The others, those whom he styled "only Deputy or second Hand Opposers," could not, however, long deny their fundamental differences with the Liberal opponents of the Awakening.[21] Moreover, on the issues of the freedom of the human will, man's original sin, and, perhaps most importantly, the place of the emotions in religious experience, they came to acknowledge their affinities with the evangelical religion of the Awakening and of Edwards.

Of course there remained a number of American clergymen for whom the federal (or covenant) theology and its metaphysic continued to have some meaning. Generally of an older generation than either the partisans of the revival or its more vehement critics, they persisted in defining the minister's role as that of "pointing out those middle and peaceable Ways, wherein the Truth generally lies, and guarding against Extreams on the right Hand and on the Left."[22] But their formulas proved untenable in the post-Awakening era, as did for the most part those of the new generation of moderates who, in an effort to straddle or avoid

---

* Though some Calvinist ministers from William Tennent to David Austin considered themselves the successors of John Baptist (and dressed accordingly) and though others conceived their function as that of the apostles Paul and James, Edwards was alone in contending consistently that the Christian minister was a "type of the Messiah." The notion of a peculiar analogue between pre-Christian society and pre-Awakening America, which filled all of Edwards' speculations on the millennium, frequently led him (particularly in the heady ecstasies of the Awakening) to conclusions as to his personal role in the redemption of mankind which other Calvinists implicitly accepted. At one point Edwards privately remarked that "if it was plain to all the world of Christians that I was under the infallible guidance of Christ, and I was sent forth to teach the world the will of Christ, then I should have power in all the world." Edwards never attained to this eminence, but neither his thinking nor that of his colleagues is fully understandable without an appreciation of their lurking suspicion that he probably deserved it.

the central issues of the period, evolved a creed comparable to that of second-generation Puritanism.

While there were more than two theologies at work in post-Awakening America, the intellectual life of American Protestantism was clearly dominated and substantially defined by the spokesmen of rationalism and of evangelical religion. Part I of this study is devoted to an exploration and interpretation of the nature and significance of this contest of ideas. The assumption on which the analysis proceeds is that of the essential similarity of all Liberals, regardless of denominational commitment, and of the evangelicals of whatever sectarian persuasion.

To be sure, one of the bitterest debates of the period was that which came to rage between the more Liberal Presbyterians and Congregationalists and the representatives of an equally rational Episcopalianism. Likewise the Baptists of the Middle Colonies argued with New Side Presbyterians, and the New England Separates with the New Lights who remained within the Congregational Church. By the beginning of the Seven Years War, indeed, such "disputings" had, according to Isaac Backus, the leader of New England's Baptists, brought the Church "in all parts" of the colonies "into terrible circumstances." And by 1760 Gilbert Tennent was complaining that the Christian Church of America had become, "by her numerous and scandalous Divisions," a "Torment to herself, a Grief to her Friends, and the Scorn of her Enemies."[23] Backus and Tennent, as well as such Liberals as Charles Chauncy, had programs for healing these divisions. These led in some instances to a realignment of parties, but in others served only to perpetuate and further encourage division. Any analysis of the intellectual history of eighteenth-century America must necessarily concern itself with such developments, but like denominational multiplicity itself, they should not obscure—they did not at the time—the fundamental cleavage between rationalists and evangelicals.

Indeed the lack of any sharp intellectual differences among the participants in these intestine debates was testimony to the American religious mind's acceptance of the fact that in the years after the Awakening it had only two viable intellectual options. The only vehement debates within rationalism and evangelicalism were ecclesiastical, and the matter of church structure was, in the context of post-Awakening America, something of a "thing indifferent." Such contests represented efforts merely to refine, or to define somewhat more precisely, the character of the two parties between which the fundamental conflict of the era was acknowledged to lie, and to decide the institutional allegiances of Americans presumably already committed to one religious philosophy or the other.

There are many ways of looking at the division brought to America by the Awakening. One historian has concluded that the revival "cut a swath between rich and poor, stimulating the hostility that already divided them," and thus opened the way for "class conflict" in the colonies.[24] Clearly there were divisions and antagonisms among the American people in the period before the Awakening. One New England preacher, surveying the scene just before the impact of the revival had been felt, noted that New Englanders were distinguished by their "want of Brotherly Love (evident by their quarrelsome, litigious Disposition, and Law-Suits without number)."[25] In many communities, disputes had arisen over the use and control of the common lands, and for years nearly every colony was racked by debates over the relative merits of specie and paper currency. The latter issue, revolving about the needs of the merchants for a "medium of trade" and the search by farmers for solutions to the problems of inflation, indebtedness, and the declining productivity of the land, had given rise to fairly hardheaded and prag-matic partisan contests. In each community and province hostility was expressed and exacerbated by such speculative programs as the "land-bank" scheme. All these controversies, in many of which the clergy participated, reflected the diffi-culty Americans were experiencing in coming to terms with their environment and with the involvement of the British government and economy in their affairs.

Far from stimulating these hostilities, however, the immediate effect of the religious revivals seems to have been a tempering of the fierce social, economic and political antagonisms that had racked the colonies since the beginning of the century. One glory of the Awakening in the eyes of those who approved it was the restoration of social and political concord to the villages and towns of the colonies. In 1741, Jonathan Edwards reported, the politicians and citizens of New England ceased their usual bickerings and contentions, and whole communities enjoyed a union and social harmony greater than that known "at any time during the preceding thirty years."[26] (To many Calvinists it seemed that true concord had departed from the colonies much earlier—in the moment when God's plantations had been converted into trading enterprises and the "God Land" had become, as Roger Williams once apprehended, "as great a God" among the English "as the God Gold was with the Spaniard.")[27] The Calvinist ministry welcomed the Awakening, and long remembered it, as a golden age when men were not divided, personally or as partisans, over acquisition and distribution of the New World's resources.

Even in 1740, however, it escaped no one's notice that those who possessed "a greater measure of this world's goods" were less disposed toward the Awakening, or that evangelical religion held a greater appeal for the "lower classes" of American society.[28] Yet at no time was the division between Calvinist and Liberal one merely of economic or social class—any more than the Great Awakening itself was "a revolt of the backcountry producers from the stringent controls of the mer-cantile aristocracy."[29] Such interpretations of the eighteenth century do as much violence to the American temper as accounts of the Great Migration that portray New England as originally a plantation of trade. The parties and debates of eighteenth-century American religion simply will not yield to the categories of Marx and Beard, for the reason that the fundamental post-Awakening division was an intellectual one—one more aesthetic, in fact, than economic or social. In the more accurate terms of H. Richard Niebuhr, the division was between those who "saw the reality of an order of being other than that walled and hemmed in existence in which a stale institutional religion and bourgeois rationalism were content to dwell," and those who did not.[30] What distinguished Americans, so far as the "great debate" of the eighteenth century was concerned, was differences not of income but, in substance, of taste.

Implicit in the "new light" of the revival was a foreswearing of the pragmatic and rather hardheaded differences in policy that before the Awakening had distin-guished colonial partisanship. But from the moment when the eyes of some citizens of the colonies were taken from their "ordinary secular business" and turned to the "great things of religion," the stage was being prepared for a new kind of party struggle, but one hardly less vehement.[31] In the contest between rational and evangelical religion was embodied, indeed, one of those fundamental value disagreements which, according to many historians, America has from the beginning been free. When Edwards first challenged Arminian rationalism he proclaimed that the differences between his "scheme" and the "legal one" were multiform and irreconcilable. When the "foundation" is so different, he went on to insist, "the whole scheme becomes exceeding diverse and contrary."[32] Over the remainder of the century this contrariety was to be manifested in nearly every area of thought and behavior.

What these many contrasts between Liberalism and Calvinism were, and where they led, is the subject of this volume. The differences were perhaps even more numerous and various than the detailed analyses that follow suggest. But the sharpest differences in the realm of ideas were ones that necessarily ramified throughout American culture. The great debate of the eighteenth century focused on such questions as the nature and needs of the human personality, the pattern and tendency of history (and of American history in particular), the nature of the good society—phrased both as judgment on the social order of colonial America and as conviction as to what the civilization of the New World might and should be—and the role of the intellectual, and of ideas and expression, in translating ideals into practice.

Certain of the differences between evangelical and rational religion emerge from the express utterances of their spokesmen. Others, including some of the more important, must be inferred, or at least confirmed, by way of what amounts to a translation of theological discourse into more instrumental terms. The interpretations that follow often derive from a view of doctrinal positions and developments that does not, confessedly, adhere to the standard rubrics for a history of religious dogma. A fresh look is frequently taken at such formulations as that of the Trinity, or of God's wisdom in the permission of sin. Viewed in conjunction with other ideas, and institutional changes, such doctrines provide insight into the general intellectual pattern and tendencies of the period. Throughout, the goal of analysis has been that of discovering what was ultimately at stake, for the American mind, in a dispute that was not so much a debate between theologians as a vital competition for the intellectual allegiance of the American people.

Obviously such an intellectual history is not a narrative merely but an interpretation as well. My conclusions, however, or perhaps more accurately my hypotheses, are based on an abundance of what is, after all, the only appropriate evidence for the historian of ideas—the recorded thoughts and expression of the men who spoke to and for the people of colonial America. Nearly everything published in the colonies (and not a few items printed elsewhere, or unpublished) has been read—and read always with the hope of determining not merely what was said but what was *meant*. To discover the meaning of any utterance demands what is in substance a continuing act of literary interpretation, for the language with which an idea is presented, and the imaginative universe by which it is surrounded, often tells us more of an author's meaning and intention than his declarative propositions. An understanding of the significance of any idea, or of a constellation of ideas, requires an awareness of the context of institutions and events out of which thought emerged, and with which it strove to come to terms. But full apprehension depends finally on reading, not between the lines but, as it were, through and beyond them.

Almost any reading of the literature of pre-Revolutionary America soon yields the conclusion that many of the ideas apparently held in common by all American Protestants were not in fact shared. By virtue of the disparate intellectual universes out of which the utterances of Calvinism and Liberalism emerged, the same word as employed by each often contained and communicated a quite different meaning. As will be abundantly demonstrated two such words were among the most important in the vocabulary of eighteenth-century Americans: "liberty" and "union." Indeed, in the disparate connotations of these two words was encapsulated nearly the whole of the larger significance of the confrontation of rational and evangelical religion. The conflict between liberalism and Calvinism was not, as is generally assumed, simply a token of the unwillingness of the latter to confess itself an anachronism in an age of reason and science. Rather the intellectual division and debate had implications for both the society of the colonies and its politics, and in such a context rational religion is not so readily identifiable as the more liberal of the two persuasions. Indeed the evidence attests that Liberalism was a profoundly elitist and conservative ideology, while evangelical religion embodied a radical and even democratic challenge to the standing order of colonial America.

From the very outset opponents of the revival sensed in the evangelical impulse a revolutionary potential. The "best of the people of all denominations," reported a Connecticut Anglican in 1742, feared that the "enthusiasts would shortly get the government into their hands and tyrannize over us."[33] Ever afterward critics of evangelical thought were unable to debate with Calvinists (the latter complained) without having "something to say about the mad men of Munster, who they tell us rebelled against their civil rulers."[34] Liberal fears seemed justified when, in the early 1760's, a New Light party took control of the Connecticut legislature. It seemed obvious that the "rigid enthusiasms and conceited notions" of the revival and evangelicalism were the sources of the "republican and mobbish principles and practices" of the insurgent party. The Calvinist ministry, "fond to a madness" of "popular forms of government," were, it was charged, responsible for Connecticut's "revolutionary" change of government.[35] And when, a decade later, America was confronted by genuine revolution, it would often be concluded that what the colonies had awakened to in 1740 was none other than independence and rebellion.

The revival impulse and the divisions it engendered were objectified in the party structure and the political process of the colonies. In 1763 a frightened Connecticut Arminian complained that the New Lights, who within his "short memory were a small Party, merely a religious one," had already "such an Influence as to be nearly the ruling part of the Government." Among his explanations for their rise and success was a "superior Attention to Civil Affairs," but to fix on the civil concerns of Calvinists is to distort both their manner of thinking and the manner in which evangelical religion impinged on colonial politics.[36] For one thing the civil issues that had most concerned the New Lights of Connecticut for two decades were the opposition of the provincial government to the Awakening and its support of the antirevival and seemingly Arminian administration and faculty of Yale College. Even in the 1760's the reigning public issue, so far as Calvinists were concerned, was that which also first introduced a "party spirit" into the politics of Virginia: the rights of evangelical dissenters to religious liberty. It is by no means unimportant that in the Old Dominion Samuel Davies' Presbyterians learned to exact "Bonds from candidates to serve and stand by their Interests" in the House of Burgesses.[37] But such strategies are hardly the whole tale of the involvement of evangelical religion in the political life of the colonies, and it is not the purpose of this study in any case to trace institutional changes and development. The concern here is rather with the history of ideas and their impact on pre-Revolutionary America.

Some Thoughts Concerning the Present Revival of Religion, written and published by Jonathan Edwards in 1742, was in a profound sense the first national party platform in American history. Yet Edwards' thoughts seem totally divorced from all the topics of which partisan issues are presumably made. His thinking reveals the disengagement of the evangelical ministry and populace from the usual institutions and processes of government and politics. Edwards even dismisses as a relatively insignificant matter the outbreak of hostilities between Britain and Spain: "We in New England are now engaged in a more important war"—the battle between the opposition to the revival and those who wanted to encourage and forward it.[38] Three years later the "serious people" of New England refused to enlist for the expedition against Louisburg until the magistrates somehow managed to persuade George Whitefield to bless the venture.[39] Though Edwards eventually hailed the victory at Cape Breton as a Providential dispensation of momentous significance, the Calvinist mind continued to respond in the spirit of the *Thoughts on the Revival* to many of the great events of the next decades. In 1757, at the height of the French and Indian War, Samuel Davies was seeking an *"outpouring of the Spirit"* as the "grand, radical, all-comprehensive blessing" for Virginia.[40] Even on the first day of January, 1775, Calvinist spokesmen were insisting that a revival of religion was the one thing needful, the "Sum of all Blessings," for the American colonies.[41]

Nonetheless, it can be said that Edwards' judgment on the comparative importance of New England's two "wars" proved as prescient as his views on so many other subjects. For Edwards' *Thoughts,* like the Awakening he defended, was in a vital respect an American declaration of independence from Europe, and the revival impulse was one toward intercolonial union. To be sure, the Awakening was in inception a response to the changing conditions of American life as perceived on the level of the local community. But the Calvinist mind was such that Edwards' vision moved quickly outward from Northampton toward making all "New England a kind of heaven upon earth"—and from there to all America.[42] Over the next decades evangelical thought so progressed that Davies sought the blessings of the spirit not for Hanover parish alone, but for his "country," and by 1775 Calvinists were looking for a gracious shower on what by then they saw as their "Nation and Land." The evangelical impulse, promoted almost entirely within the church and through "the ordinary means," was the avatar and instrument of a fervent American nationalism.

The Calvinist commitment to the unity of the American people—part of the fascinating tale of the passage of the American mind out of the theological universe of the eighteenth century into the world of national politics—took thirty-five years to reach overt expression. It is but one instance of what constitutes a major theme of the pages that follow: the manner in which the Awakening, by shattering the communities and the social assumptions inherited from the seventeenth century, allowed the evangelical ministry to offer the American people new commitments, political as well as ethical.

Much of Calvinism's thrust, its radical and emphatic definitions of liberty and equality, emerged more as the premises and assumptions of doctrine than as an articulate program. Still, the Calvinist ministry aspired to understand the times in order that they, like the men of Issachar, might "know what Israel ought to do."[43]

In this respect, something of a watershed for the Calvinist mind was passed in 1755, when Aaron Burr, Edwards' son-in-law, published a sermon on imperial affairs which, omitting the doctrinal section, consisted entirely of commentary and advice on British and colonial government and policy.[44] Over the next decades Calvinist spokesmen grew ever bolder in proposing programs for the accomplishment of what they took to be the general welfare. Many of their policies, indeed most of them, were directed toward the amelioration of domestic conditions—as, for instance, their demand for a "more effectual provision for the Instruction of our Children, in our Common Schools."[45] In the Revolutionary period, domestic and imperial issues merged, and the evangelical scheme was translated into the political imperative that the colonial "poor" not be "squeezed, to support the corruption and luxury of the great."[46]

As the last quotation suggests, the programmatic elements of Calvinism were invariably subordinated to, or conceived within, what the evangelical clergy considered the primary moral dimension of all activity, individual or communal. In the Revolutionary period, and before, the Calvinist mind responded to political challenge in terms of the felt obligation of both ministers and people to "fight sin always."[47] Often the evangelical ministry concluded that "Sin" was the cause of all difficulties, "civil, ecclesiastical, and domestic," and they were ever ready to describe an opposing policy as a "mere ideal project, arising from the DECEITFULNESS of sin." They also ranged rather widely in search of this "dreadful monster" and of means for overcoming and destroying sin.[48] In sum, to the thought of post-Awakening and Revolutionary Calvinism can be traced that enduring quality of the American political mind that Richard Hofstadter has characterized as an impatience with "hard politics." In this sense the American tradition—of Populists and rank-and-file Jacksonians and Jeffersonians—was hardly the child of the Age of Reason. It was born of the "New Light" imparted to the American mind by the Awakening and the evangelical clergy of colonial America.

NOTES

1. "Observations on the Support of the Clergy," *American Museum*, VIII (1790), 254.
2. Jonathan Mayhew, *The Snare Broken . . . May 23d, 1766*, in [Frank Moore, ed.], *The Patriot Preachers of the American Revolution* (New York, 1862), p. 23.
3. Charles Chauncy, *Seasonable Thoughts on the State of Religion in New-England* (Boston, 1743), p. 55.
4. *Some Thoughts Concerning the Present Revival of Religion in New England*, in *The Works of Jonathan Edwards* (10th ed., London, 1865), I, 422.
5. Perry Miller, "Jonathan Edwards and the Great Awakening," *Errand into the Wilderness* (Cambridge, 1956), pp. 156–157.
6. Edwin S. Gaustad, *The Great Awakening in New England* (New York, 1957).
7. Quoted, *George Whitefield's Journals. A New Edition Containing Fuller Material* (London, 1960), p. 19 n.
8. Edwards, *Introduction to Five Discourses*, in *Works*, I, 620.
9. Gilbert Tennent, *A Sermon upon Justification. Preach'd at New-Brunswick . . . in August, Anno 1740* (Philadelphia, 1741), p. 17.
10. Perry Miller, "The Insecurity of Nature. Being the Dudleian Lecture for the Academic Year 1952–1953," *Harvard Divinity School Bulletin: Annual Lectures and Book Reviews*, 1954, p. 31.
11. Ebenezer Gay, *Natural Religion as Distinguish'd from Revealed* (Boston, 1759), pp. 10–11.
12. Edwards, *A Careful and Strict Enquiry into the Modern Prevailing Notions of that Freedom of Will, Which is Supposed to be Essential to Moral Agency*, Paul Ramsey, ed. (New Haven, 1957), p. 131.
13. Samuel Hopkins, *The Life of the Late Reverend, Learned and Pious Mr. Jonathan Edwards* (Boston, 1765), p. 41.

14. Jacob Green, *An Inquiry into the Constitution and Discipline of the Jewish Church* (New York, 1768), p. iii; Nathaniel Whitaker, *A Funeral Sermon, on the Death of the Reverend George Whitefield* (Salem, Mass., 1774), p. 13.

15. Hopkins, *Edwards,* p. 41.

16. David Bostwick, in Francis Alison and David Bostwick, *Peace and Union Recommended; and Self Disclaimed and Christ Exalted,* in *Two Sermons, Preached at Philadelphia, before the Reverend Synod* (Philadelphia, 1758), p. 47; Joseph Bellamy, *A Careful and Strict Examination of the External Covenant,* in *The Works of Joseph Bellamy, D.D.* (Boston, 1850), II, 70; Isaac Backus, *True Faith will Produce Good Work* (Boston, 1767), p. 68; Bellamy, *An Essay on the Nature and Glory of the Gospel,* in *Works,* II, 418.

17. Ebenezer Frothingham, *A Key to Unlock the Door* (n.p., 1767), p. 33.

18. Gilbert Tennent, in David Bostwick, *Self disclaimed, and Christ exalted* (London, 1759), pp. 31 n–32 n.

19. Harvey G. Townsend, ed., *The Philosophy of Jonathan Edwards. From His Private Notebooks* (Eugene, Oregon, 1955), p. 200.

20. Samuel Buell, in William B. Sprague, *Annals of the American Pulpit* (New York, 1859–1865), III, 105.

21. David McGregore, *The Spirits of the Present Day Tried. A Sermon at the Tuesday Evening Lecture in Brattle-Street, Boston, Nov. 3, 1741* (Boston, 1742), p. 19.

22. Nathaniel Appleton, *Faithful Ministers of Christ, the Salt of the Earth, and the Light of the World. Illustrated in a Sermon Preach'd before the Ministers of the Massachusetts-Bay . . . at their Annual Convention . . . May 26. 1743* (Boston, 1743), pp. 20–21.

23. Isaac Backus, *A History of New England* (2 vols., 2nd ed., Newton, Mass., 1871), II, 134; Gilbert Tennent, *A Persuasive to the Right Use of the Passions in Religion* (Philadelphia, 1760), p. 21.

24. John C. Miller, "Religion, Finance and Democracy in Massachusetts," *New England Quarterly,* VI (1933), 29.

25. Edward Holyoke, *The Duty of Ministers of the Gospel to guard against the Pharisaism and Sadducism, of the present Day . . . Preach'd at the Convention of Ministers . . . May 28. 1741* (Boston, 1741), p. 24.

26. Edwards, *Works,* I, ciii.

27. Quoted, Alan Simpson, *Puritanism in Old and New England* (Chicago, 1955), p. 59.

28. Perry Miller, ed., "Jonathan Edwards' Sociology of the Great Awakening," *New England Quarterly,* XXI (1948), 72.

29. Richard Mosier, *The American Temper* (Berkeley, 1952), p. 76.

30. H. Richard Niebuhr, *The Kingdom of God in America* (New York, [1959]), pp. 110–111.

31. Edwards, *A Faithful Narrative of the Surprising Work of God,* in *Works,* I, 348.

32. Edwards, *Five Discourses,* in *Works,* II, 646.

33. Samuel Johnson to the Secretary of the S.P.G., March 25, 1742, in Herbert and Carol Schneider, eds., *Samuel Johnson. His Career and Writings* (New York, 1929), III, 231.

34. Isaac Backus, *An Appeal to the Public for Religious Liberty* (Boston, 1773), p. 50.

35. Quoted, Leonard W. Labaree, *Conservatism in Early American History* (New York, 1948), pp. 66–67.

36. Quoted, Edmund Morgan, *The Stamp Act Crisis. Prologue to Revolution* (Chapel Hill, 1953), p. 228.

37. Quoted, Wesley M. Gewehr, *The Great Awakening in Virginia, 1740–1790* (Durham, N.C., 1930), p. 89.

38. Edwards, *Thoughts on the Revival,* in *Works,* I, 366.

39. John Gillies, *Memoirs of Rev. George Whitefield* (Middletown, Conn., 1838), p. 105.

40. Samuel Davies, "The Happy Effects of the Pouring out of the Spirit," *Sermons on Important Subjects* (4th ed., New York, 1845), I, 345.

41. Samuel Buell, *The Best New-Year's Gift for Young People . . . January 1st, 1775* (New London, n.d.), p. 53.

42. Edwards, *Thoughts on the Revival,* in *Works,* I, 390.

43. Noah Benedict, *Preparation for Death. A Sermon, Delivered at the Funeral of Rev. Joseph Bellamy* (New Haven, 1790), p. 19.

44. Aaron Burr, *A Discourse Delivered at New-Ark in New-Jersey, January 1, 1755. Being a Day set apart for solemn Fasting and Prayer* (New York, 1755), p. [1].

45. Edward Eels, *Christ, the Foundation of the Salvation of Sinners, and of Civil and Ecclesiastical Government: . . . Preached . . . on the Day of the Anniversary Election* (Hartford, [1767]), p. 25.

46. Robert Ross, *A Sermon, in which the Union of the Colonies is Considered and Recommended* (New York, 1776), p. 9.
47. Fellamy, *Election Sermon* (1762), in *Works,* I, 596.
48. Mark Leavenworth, *Charity Illustrated and Recommended . . . a Sermon Delivered . . . on the Day of . . . Election* (New London [1772]), p. 31.

SECTION 7: SUGGESTIONS FOR FURTHER READING

Most of the current literature on the Great Awakening has a regional cast. Important exceptions include a masterful early compilation by Joseph Tracy, *The Great Awakening: A History of the Revival of Religion in the Time of Edwards and Whitefield* (1841), along with Alan Heimert, *Religion and the American Mind: From the Great Awakening to the Revolution* (1966). Both of these works may be supplemented by the shorter accounts of C. B. Cowing, *The Great Awakening and the American Revolution: Colonial Thought in the 18th Century* (1971), and J. M. Bumsted and J. E. Van de Wetering, *What Must I Do To Be Saved? The Great Awakening in Colonial America* (1976). Heimert's methodology and conclusions have been the focus of significant controversy. E. S. Morgan, in the *William and Mary Quarterly,* 3rd ser., 24 (1967), pp. 454–459, and Sidney Mead, "Through and Beyond the Lines," *Journal of Religion,* 48 (1968), pp. 274–288, have been most critical. In turn Heimert receives support from W. G. McLoughlin, "The American Revolution as a Religious Revival: 'The Millenium in One Country'," *New England Quarterly,* 40 (1967), pp. 99–110. For E. S. Morgan's position on possible links between Awakening thought and the Revolution, see "The American Revolution Considered as an Intellectual Movement," *Paths of American Thought,* ed. A. M. Schlesinger, Jr., and Morton White (1963), pp. 11–33, and "The Puritan Ethic and the American Revolution," *William and Mary Quarterly,* 3rd ser., 24 (1967), pp. 3–43.

A number of primary source collections have appeared which offer valuable introductions to the movement. They include Alan Heimert and Perry Miller, eds., *The Great Awakening: Documents Illustrating the Crisis and Its Consequences* (1967), D. S. Lovejoy, ed., *Religious Enthusiasm and the Great Awakening* (1969), R. L. Bushman, ed., *The Great Awakening: Documents on the Revival of Religion, 1740–1745* (1970), J. M. Bumsted, ed., *The Great Awakening: The Beginnings of Evangelical Pietism in America* (1970), D. B. Rutman, ed., *The Great Awakening: Event and Exegesis* (1970), and P. N. Carroll, ed., *Religion and the Coming of the American Revolution* (1970). None of these works reprint selections from the Bible, the source book of theological differences in the Awakening. Relative to the new Birth message, a reading of the books of Acts, Romans, Ephesians, and Thessalonians I and II is mandatory for the scriptural context.

The New England phase of the Awakening has been analysed in a number of excellent studies. The best include E. S. Gaustad, *The Great Awakening in New England* (1957), C. C. Goen, *Revivalism and Separatism in New England, 1740–1800: Strict Congregationalists and Separate Baptists in the Great Awakening* (1962), Joseph Haroutunian, *Piety Versus Moralism: The Passing of New England Theology* (1932). Also of interpretive value are Emil Oberholzer, *Delinquent Saints: Disciplinary Action in the Early Congregational Churches of Massachusetts* (1956), G. J. Goodwin, "The Myth of 'Arminian-Calvinism' in Eighteenth-Century New England," *New England Quarterly,* 41 (1968), pp. 213–237, and J. E. Van de Wetering, "God, Science, and the Puritan Dilemma," *New England Quarterly,* 38 (1965), pp. 494–507.

An old and descriptive account of the upsurge in the middle colonies is C. H. Maxson's *The Great Awakening in the Middle Colonies* (1920), which must be supplemented by L. J. Trinterud, *The Forming of an American Tradition: A Re-examination of Colonial Presbyterianism* (1949), Dietmar Rothermund, *The Laymen's Progress: Religious and Political Experience in Colonial Pennsylvania, 1740–1770* (1962), and J. B. Frantz, "The Awakening of Religion among the German Settlers in the Middle Colonies, *William and Mary Quarterly,* 3rd ser., 33 (1976), pp. 266–288, along with Lodge's valuable article. The standard general study of the southern experience in the Awakening is W. M. Gewehr, *The Great Awakening in Virginia, 1740–1790* (1930), which now may be supplemented by the more interpretive investigations of Rhys Isaac in two articles, "Religion and Authority: Problems of the Anglican Establishment in the Era of the Great Awakening and the Parsons' Cause," and "Evangelical Revolt: The Nature of the Baptists' Challenge to the Traditional Order in Virginia, 1765 to 1775," both in the *William and Mary Quarterly,* 3rd ser., 30 (1973), pp. 3–36, and 31 (1974), pp. 345–368, along with D. T. Morgan's "The Great Awakening in North Carolina, 1740–1755: The Baptist Phase," *North Carolina Historical Review,* 45 (1968), pp. 264–283.

Many biographies have been written about the Awakening's leaders and opponents. Significant studies of Jonathan Edwards include O. E. Winslow, *Jonathan Edwards, 1703–1758: A Biography* (1940), Perry Miller, *Jonathan Edwards* (1949), E. H. Davidson, *Jonathan Edwards: The Narrative of a Puritan Mind* (1968), and R. L. Bushman, "Jonathan Edwards as Great Man: Identity, Conversion, and Leadership in the Great Awakening," *Soundings*, 52 (1969), pp. 15–46. The latter is a psychohistorical analysis. S. C. Henry's *George Whitefield: Wayfaring Witness* (1957), should be compared with W. H. Kenney, 3d, "George Whitefield, Dissenter Priest of the Great Awakening," *William and Mary Quarterly*, 3rd ser., 26 (1969), pp. 75–93. Other valuable biographies include James Tanis, *Dutch Calvinistic Pietism in the Middle Colonies: A Study in the Life and Theology of Theodorus Jacobus Frelinghuysen* (1968), W. G. McLoughlin, *Isaac Backus and the American Pietistic Tradition* (1967), G. W. Pilcher, *Samuel Davies: Apostle of Dissent in Colonial Virginia* (1971), L. L. Tucker, *Puritan Protagonist: President Thomas Clap of Yale College* (1962), E. S. Morgan, *The Gentle Puritan: A Life of Ezra Stiles, 1727–1795* (1962), C. W. Akers, *Called Unto Liberty: A Life of Jonathan Mayhew* (1964), and H. E. Bernhard, *Charles Chauncy: Colonial Liberal, 1705–1787* (1948).

Social historians have also been investigating the causes and consequences of the Great Awakening. R. L. Bushman maintains in *From Puritan to Yankee: Character and Social Order in Connecticut, 1690–1765* (1967), that tensions caused by the increasing commercialization of New England society were released through revivalism. Bushman's interpretation should be analyzed in the context of the J. M. Bumsted essay presented in this section, and with C. B. Cowing, "Sex and Preaching in the Great Awakening," *American Quarterly*, 20 (1968), pp. 622–644, J. M. Bumsted, "Revivalism and Separatism in New England: The First Society of Norwich, Connecticut, as a Case Study," *William and Mary Quarterly*, 3rd ser., 24 (1967), pp. 588–612, James Walsh, "The Great Awakening in the First Congregational Church of Woodbury, Connecticut," *William and Mary Quarterly*, 3rd ser., 28 (1971), pp. 543–562, P. J. Greven, Jr., "Youth, Maturity, and Religious Conversion: A Note on the Ages of Converts in Andover, Massachusetts, 1711–1749," *Essex Institute Historical Collections*, 108 (1972), pp. 119–134, G. F. Moran, "Conditions of Religious Conversion in the First Society of Norwich, Connecticut, 1718–1744, *Journal of Social History*, 5 (1972), pp. 331–343, H. S. Stout, "The Great Awakening in New England Reconsidered: The New England Clergy as a Case Study," *Journal of Social History*, 8 (1974), pp. 21–47, and T. L. Smith, "Congregation, State, and Denomination: The Forming of the American Religious Structure," *William and Mary Quarterly*, 3rd ser., 25 (1968), pp. 155–176. An older article which argues that the Awakening in Massachusetts had lower-class, class conflict, overtones is J. C. Miller, "Religion, Finance, and Democracy in Massachusetts," *New England Quarterly*, 6 (1933), pp. 29–58, which also represents a departure point for the J. M. Bumsted essay appearing in these pages.

A "New" American Culture and Identity

SECTION 8

In spite of the spectacular religious enthusiasm of the Great Awakening, the dominant trend in eighteenth-century thought was away from theology and toward Enlightenment rationality. During the "Age of Reason" in Europe more and more people came to believe that the mind of man had the inherent power to conquer all problems and to produce higher levels of harmony and progress, indeed a utopia in human relationships. In the provinces, the changing intellectual milieu may be epitomized in the pattern of declension affecting the Winthrop family of Massachusetts. The first John Winthrop gave himself wholeheartedly to the founding of an orderly corporate biblical community. Yet his grandsons, Fitz and Wait, were much less spiritually oriented than their grandfather. Two generations later John Winthrop IV (1714–1779) cast almost all Calvinist doctrine aside. He immersed himself in scientific inquiry and the inductive method of reasoning. He studied the mysteries of astronomy, calculus, and the human sciences even before assuming the Hollis Professorship of Mathematics and Natural Philosophy at Harvard College. One of his most carefully drawn arguments was that earthquakes occurred from natural causes—they should no longer be considered as afflictions thrust upon society by a dissatisfied Old Testament God, as John Winthrop would have argued a hundred years before. The scientific orientation of John IV as compared to the religious concerns of John I provide a mirror to changing intellectual currents in the provinces as a reflection of the European Enlightenment.

John Winthrop IV preferred the tools of systematic observation and inductive logic. He was one among several provincial students of science who insisted that immutable natural laws controlled the universe. Such men no longer felt that the universe was subject to God's whims, although most believed that God had set the laws in motion, and then stepped aside so that man could achieve his destiny. Laws were laws, and they were discoverable, as the profoundly influential English mathematician Sir Isaac Newton had demonstrated in his investigations of gravity. The best way to guarantee human progress was to explore for universal laws, to prove their existence, and to spread that knowledge to other individuals of rationalist temperament, all with the prospect of uplifting the human condition.

Benjamin Franklin, with his electrical experiments, was without a doubt the most widely regarded of the early American men of science. Other notable researchers were the botanists John Bartram of Philadelphia and Dr. Alexander Garden of Charleston, the men of multiple scientific interests like Lieutenant

Governor Cadwallader Colden of New York and Dr. William Douglass of Boston. They and others formed the first American scientific community—Brooke Hindle in the first selection ahead refers to them as part of the provincial "natural history circle." They dedicated themselves to the systematic classification of human knowledge about all subjects, but they preferred to provide solutions to problems in physics and plant and animal existence. Even though these provincial scientists constituted a minor note in the larger community of Enlightenment learning during the dawning "Age of Reason," they were the harbingers of rationalism in American thought and, perhaps, of a new maturity in American culture and identity.

The spreading fascination with scientific inquiry, even though largely European in origin, may indicate that the provinces had passed through the most rudimentary stages of settlement and internal cultural development. Individuals who must carve new communities out of the wilderness and devote all their energy to producing enough food in order to avoid starvation in the face of hostile elements rarely have time to read widely, let alone to contemplate and write about philosophical and scientific questions. But it can be argued that once hostile colonial elements, whether disease, climatic factors, or in the colonial experience the Eastern Woodland Indian nations, have been overcome, once the basic conditions for assured survival and sustenance have been met, once the economy shows signs of growth, development, and prosperity, and once urban centers emerge to function as points of informational and cultural exchange, at least some citizens may devote themselves with greater ease to the realm of unexplored human knowledge. The heightened activity in secular learning among the colonists suggests that American society may have been more firmly established as a viable, separate entity by the mid-eighteenth century.

Indeed, "maturity" may be an important way of conceptualizing colonial Americans about to be swirled into the vortex of revolution. Some historians, as did many Anglo-Americans of the time, have written in terms of the appearance of an "adult" phase of culture and identity by midcentury. With a dawning sense of adulthood, a feeling which many English leaders consciously chose to ignore, other elements may have come together that resulted in a successful rebellion against a "parent" state insensitive to growth and maturity.

Certainly well before the Revolution many provincials had begun to take pride in their un-English ways and habits. Some felt that a unique civilization was blossoming in the western part of the British empire, even if Great Britain refused to recognize that assumption. We have already seen that the provinces, relative to the English and European models, represented societies more susceptible to economic opportunity, less rigid in the traditional definition of class lines, and more equalitarian in their social and political relationships, even if wealth, social standing, and political power were becoming unbalanced through time. The very fact that some Americans wanted to more closely Anglicize or Europeanize provincial society meant that a pattern of divergence from old World habits, attitudes, and life-styles had occurred. Yet what caused the divergence? What were the distinctive qualities that set apart a possible new American identity and culture from its English antecedents?

Late in the nineteenth century a young historian, Frederick Jackson Turner, who had a major influence upon what twentieth-century Americans have thought about their past, expounded his famous frontier thesis: that the distinctiveness of the American people and their culture could be traced to the interaction of their

European cultural heritage with the vast open space (the free land frontier) of the American environment. Somehow the frontier worked to destroy Old World institutional values and norms. European blueprints did not adapt that readily to the New World environment. Thus to Turner it was the frontier experience that resulted in a novel way of life as well as an unique American identity. Americans became more individualistic in temperament, dissatisfied with fixed social conventions, and determined to live by the code of democratic equalitarianism. To Turner the frontier was the source of American democracy.

The writings of Turner still influence our assumptions about the putative distinctiveness of American character and culture. But the Turner thesis, even if possessing the remotest form of explanatory validity, certainly does not encompass all the factors that should be taken into consideration. It may also be that the free land frontier was much more a source of myths which Americans have believed about themselves and their past than an actual determinant of democracy, as maintained by Richard Slotkin ahead. Then again the frontier may have been relatively unimportant in creating a separate American culture and identity. It may have been developing urban centers like Philadelphia which focused values, as suggested by Frederick B. Tolles, or it may have been conditions associated with warfare and economic development, as postulated by Max Savelle in the two other selections which complete this volume. Clearly, something more deeply imbedded than political differences seemed to be setting Americans apart from their English superiors after midcentury. Was it the interaction of Old World cultures with the American environment and Indian nations? Or were other elements more significant?

The essays that follow consider a maturing American culture and sense of identity within the context of European influences. We must determine whether Americans on the eve of revolution thought of themselves as unique or, perhaps, even more important, as having a new mission to fulfill because of the feeling of being "called out" as a destined people. Not only must we ask how such thinking developed, but we must also ask why, and we must consider the long-term impact that the sense of being both American and unique had on United States history from the Revolution to the present.

29. Shattered Dreams and Unexpected Accomplishment

Brooke Hindle

More than once Americans have been accused of being overly concerned with the practical applications of knowledge. Information must have some use for them, or it is considered to be of no value. If the utility of knowledge is deeply imbedded in the way Americans approach learning today, then the same characteristics tended to determine the interests of early American men of science, according to Brooke Hindle (b. 1918), who is the director of the National Museum of History and Technology of the Smithsonian Institution in Washington, D.C. The first colonial scientists, Hindle reminds us, were usually amateurs, individuals with leisure time available for experimentation. Although they regularly shared correspondence with major European scientists and were heavily dependent on them, the provincial amateurs preferred to investigate problems with utilitarian features.

In the passages from Professor Hindle's book *The Pursuit of Science in Revolutionary America* ahead, the author describes the original attempt to found an intercolonial scientific organization, the American Philosophical Society, to facilitate the exchange of information. These primitive organizational efforts did not fare well. It was left for individuals like Benjamin Franklin to demonstrate the utility of scientific experimentation through his electrical investigations as a spur to organized inquiry. No one could have shown more dramatically than Franklin how useful knowledge can come from the inductive scientific method. Why was it that early Americans placed so much value upon the practical results of science? Could it be that utilitarianism already had become a vital part of the provincial American identity and values? If so, why?

Every one of the active American naturalists complained of the thinness of the intellectual environment he met in America. Each of them missed the libraries, the publications, and, most of all, "the conversation of the learned" that would have been open to him in Europe. The gradual process of maturing might have been expected to bring all of those things in its train but it was not necessary to wait passively for this enrichment. Colden, Bartram, Mitchell, Garden, and Clayton all took part in efforts to create a community that would encourage scientific activity.

Cadwallader Colden was the first to suggest the formation of an intercolonial

Source: From Brooke Hindle, *The Pursuit of Science in Revolutionary America, 1735–1789* (Chapel Hill: University of North Carolina Press, 1956), pp. 59–79. Footnotes omitted. Reprinted by permission of the University of North Carolina Press and the Institute of Early American History and Culture.

scientific community in the form of a society or academy. This was the most logical starting point in the eighteenth century when the academy was the primary focus of scientific activity. Despite the much heralded decline of the Royal Society of London, it remained the point at which most British science was centered; while for the French world, the same function was performed by the Académie des Sciences. Despite its faults, the Royal Society's *Philosophical Transactions* was the medium of regular, scientific intelligence in all the areas where English was spoken and in many where it was not. Throughout Europe, the formation of academies was still in full flood in the first half of the eighteenth century with the establishment of such societies at Madrid, Vienna, Upsala, Bordeaux, Marseilles, St. Petersburg, and Edinburgh—all of them patterned after the Royal Society or the Académie des Sciences. Colden was making the proper approach when he wrote his friend William Douglass in 1728 suggesting the formation of "a Voluntary Society for the advancing of Knowledge."

The society would include members in each province but, he suggested, "because the greatest number of proper persons are like to be found in your Colony . . . the Members residing in or near Boston [ought to] have the chief Direction." In 1728, it was reasonable to look to Boston for leadership in a project of this sort. Boston then was and for many years had been the principal cultural center in the British colonies. Its attainments in science were particularly notable if fellowship in the Royal Society could be used as an index, for of the eight residents of the continental colonies elected to the Royal Society before 1728, seven were Bostonians. Moreover, real contributions to the advance of science had been made by Paul Dudley, Thomas Robie, and Zabdiel Boylston as well as by William Douglass, all of them still living in the area when Colden made his suggestion. Colden may also have known of Increase Mather's attempt in Boston to establish a philosophical society as early as 1683.

Boston could be proud of its citizens who had contributed to science and of its many cultural accomplishments but it is clear that it had not developed a scientific community. Colden, of course, had sought to create one through the formation of his proposed organization; yet organizations are seldom the starting point in the formation of any kind of community. More often they are based upon previously existing, though informal, relationships. Such had been the experience of the two greatest academies in the West: the Royal Society of London had grown out of both the "invisible college" and the Oxford Philosophical Society; the Académie des Sciences had developed when Colbert provided official recognition of the long continued but irregular meetings held by a group of French scientists. Lacking such a background, Douglass was well-advised in not doing anything to implement Colden's suggestion.

Eight years later, Douglass wrote to Colden to announce the formation of a medical society in Boston, recalling as he did so the New Yorker's earlier suggestion of "a sort of Virt[u]oso Society or rather correspondence." On the face of it, Douglass' medical society had little relationship to Colden's project. His was not a scientific but a medical society which planned to publish short pieces on medical subjects from time to time. Even as he wrote, Douglass announced that the first number of these "Medical Memoirs" was ready for the press. Somehow it failed to be published and the four medical essays it was to contain have been lost. The society itself continued for some years; indeed, Dr. Alexander Hamilton found it still functioning under the leadership of Douglass in 1744.

This relationship of a medical society in being to a philosophical society that remained an aspiration was closer than it might seem. Even as late as 1736, there was no scientific community anywhere in America except for the medical fraternity which flourished in each of the larger colonial towns. These medical communities had intercolonial and international relationships. They were the most coherent groups of men who had had some kind of scientific training to be found in the colonies. In addition, the physicians had a more immediate motive of expediency which encouraged association and joint effort. Their early organizations were always in some measure dedicated toward improving the conditions of their own profession, toward providing such things as the licensing of practitioners and the regulation of rates. The physicians were associated by material interests as well as by intellectual curiosity.

Douglass's society was only the first such organization of which traces remain. In 1749, a society was meeting weekly in New York and in 1755, the "faculty of physic" in Charleston organized under the presidency of Dr. John Moultrie. The Charleston organization was primarily concerned with the "better Support of the Dignity, the Privileges, and Emoluments of their Humane Art," but its agreement that physicians should collect fees at each visit aroused a furore in the press. The twofold aim of these societies was best demonstrated by the Boston organization which in addition to its interest in publishing memoirs and observing surgical operations, sought to obtain a system of licensing practitioners in Massachusetts.

All of these societies were in a sense surface manifestations of an American medical community which was already a part of the much larger European medical community. The Americans were related to the Europeans not only through medical studies undertaken by some in Europe and through continuing personal correspondence, but also most effectively through publications. The Royal Society itself had always devoted attention to medical subjects and some Americans had access to its *Philosophical Transactions* both as readers and as contributors. The Americans were also served by two more specialized periodicals published by medical societies: from Edinburgh, the *Medical Essays and Observations,* often called simply the *Edinburgh Essays* which began to appear in 1733, and from London, the *Medical Observations and Inquiries* of Dr. John Fothergill's society beginning in 1757. The *Medical Observations and Inquiries* particularly welcomed American papers from its foundation, recognizing that there were "physicians of great experience and abilities" in the colonies. The general magazines in England and Scotland published medical papers too, the *Gentleman's Magazine* being particularly notable for the number of American essays it saw fit to print. In lieu of medical periodicals in America, the newspapers and the short-lived magazines frequently published medical essays of a type that belonged in a journal. When to all of these facilities was added the publication of medical pamphlets and books on both sides of the Atlantic it is clear that physicians in America were furnished with intellectual outlets as well as means of professional enlightenment.

A large proportion of their writing was intended to influence the lay public rather than to advance knowledge. The great debate over inoculation brought a flood of articles designed to win support for or condemnation of the practice. Inoculation was fought out before the public and before the colonial legislatures in terms of absolute prohibition, regulation, establishment of inoculation hospitals, and specific technique to be used. Every epidemic of smallpox as well as other diseases brought newspaper articles on treatment. Questions of autopsy, quarantine, and care of the poor were similarly of public interest. The publication, however, most certain to sell was the home medical guide for which there was a constant demand.

Americans also made studies of specific diseases often resulting in scholarly medical papers which conformed to the standards of the British periodicals and books they read. Most frequently, they wrote such case reports as John Bard's account of an extra-uterine foetus or Thomas Bond's account of a worm that had been lodged in a patient's liver. Some studies were made in the colonies to provide specific information that seemed important in the light of prevailing medical theory. Such were the numerous efforts to correlate the incidence of sickness with weather conditions; the meteorological studies of Lionel Chalmers, a Scottish physician of Charleston, even approached a climatological determinism as far as disease was concerned. Other papers attempted to support the virtues of some new specific which had been discovered in America. Occasionally these studies brought fame and fortune to individuals although not one of the drugs so rewarded lived up to the claims of its advocate. One of the most dramatic examples of the promotion of a new medicine was the case of John Tennent of Virginia, who wrote much in support of the virtues of Seneca snake root, even journeying to England in support of his claims. Although it had been originally presented as a rattlesnake cure, Tennent claimed its utility in a wide variety of disorders. Before the defects of his own character disgraced him, he won election to the Royal Society and a £100 grant from the Virginia Assembly. The legislature of South Carolina showed still more gullibility when it granted upwards of £500 to a man who claimed to have discovered a sovereign cure for syphilis.

With all the vitality the medical community could boast, it was not a substitute for a scientific community and it did not satisfy the needs that had led Colden to suggest an intercolonial scientific society. These needs came to seem still more imperative to John Bartram as he extended his study of natural history, leading him to address his own suggestion of a scientific academy to Peter Collinson in 1739. While Collinson was right in asserting that an academy with paid professors was beyond the capacity of Pennsylvania, Philadelphia was in the midst of an impressive development. The Library Company of Philadelphia, into which Collinson succeeded in introducing Bartram, was in 1739 only the most striking evidence of a rapidly developing capacity to sustain cultural activity of a varied character.

Collinson made a penetrating observation when he told Bartram, "Your Library Company I take to be an essay towards . . . a society [such as you suggested]." The Library Company was a remarkable institution. Because it was operated on the subscription principle, regular planned book purchases became possible with the result that its collections grew rapidly and rationally. Because its purchases were directed by men seeking general enlightenment, it differed considerably from the large libraries collected by colleges for the use of graduate students in theology. It soon held the finest collection of scientific books in the country. It became a good nucleus for the formation of a scientific community because it served not only the members of the Library Company, but also the general public, particularly the city artisans who made much use of the reading privileges freely extended to all.

In addition to serving as the most effective library in the colonies, the Library Company presented the appearance of a museum or a scientific society because of the natural history specimens and scientific apparatus which were acquired. In several cases, shares in the company were given in return for curiosities: for some stuffed snakes, for a dead pelican, for the robes of Indian chiefs, for an old sword, for a set of fossils. In 1738, John Penn, one of the proprietors of Pennsylvania, recognized the general importance of the organization when he presented a "costly Air-Pump" rejoicing that the Library Company was "the first [institution] that encouraged Knowledge and Learning in the Province of Pennsylvania." The directors of the Library did not at all consider such a gift a strange thing with which to burden a library. Indeed, they asserted it to be directly in support of their objective which was "the Improvement of Knowledge." Members of the proprietary family continued to donate scientific apparatus, contributing a pair of sixteen-inch globes, a telescope, and an electric machine before 1749.

This breadth of function demonstrated by the Library Company occurred at many other places in the colonies. In Massachusetts, the dominant intellectual institution was Harvard College, so it was about Harvard that scientific apparatus and a heterogeneous collection of curiosities as well as a library clustered. At Newport, a learned society dating from 1730, "The Society for the Promotion of Knowledge and Virtue by a Free Conversation," had a library engrafted upon it when Abraham Redwood, inspired by a trip to Philadelphia, donated £500 for the purpose of buying books. The Redwood Library followed. At Charleston, the example of the Philadelphians was followed in 1748 with the formation of the Charleston Library Society which came to embrace apparatus and a museum as well as a collection of books. Few intellectual agencies of this period were very specialized.

Philadelphia's much copied subscription library was only one evidence of its continually expanding intellectual vitality. Behind this increasing ability to sustain cultural activities lay a profitable trade and a population that was beginning to grow so fast that it would soon exceed Boston's. Its people came of many nations and many faiths and they retained varied contacts with the Old World. As wealth, learning, and leisure became more common, the city began to provide more encouragement for writers, teachers, musicians, painters, and those who were interested in science. Throughout the eighteenth century, it pioneered in more and more ways. For science, one of the most important foundations of these years was the college which opened its doors in 1751, the first colonial college not under the control of any one religious sect. The following year, the Pennsylvania Hospital began to receive patients as the first general hospital in the colonies. Both of these institutions acquired libraries, museums, and collections of apparatus of their own.

John Bartram's suggestion of a scientific academy came just as Philadelphia was entering this period of flowering. Very significantly, the natural history circle in America was just beginning at this time too. Because of both of these developments, Bartram was not defeated by Collinson's lack of encouragement. He found a receptive audience in America.

Benjamin Franklin was approaching a turning point in his career when John Bartram began to interest him in his ideas. Bartram said that Franklin was the only printer in the city who had ever made a success of that trade, but however that may be, Franklin's success was unquestionable. In 1743, he began to plan for ultimate retirement by inviting David Hall to come over from Edinburgh with the idea of making him a partner if the arrangement worked out. He did not make his famous withdrawal from the business until 1748 but that was no sudden decision. By that time, his energies were turning in many directions at once: to the organization of fire companies, to interest in the Masons, to education, and more significantly to science. Franklin's interest in learning was an essential part of him; he once said that he could not remember a time when he was unable to read. His Junto of 1727 had been only a mutual improvement club but one of the questions asked of new members had been, "Do you love truth for truth's sake?" The Library Company had been even more clearly an effort to further learning. Franklin's promotion of the subscription scheme of 1742 in favor of Bartram's explorations had shown the scientific direction in which his thoughts were steadily turning.

Franklin always displayed the warmest affection toward John Bartram but in 1742 the relationship between the two men was almost the reverse of what it became after the Philadelphia printer had attained world renown. In 1742, John Bartram was a recognized member of the natural history circle who corresponded not only with Peter Collinson but also with Gronovius, Dillenius, Catesby, and Sir Hans Sloane, president of the Royal Society, as well as with several American naturalists. Franklin knew at firsthand the value Collinson placed upon Bartram's work. To Franklin, Bartram represented attainment in an area which was increasingly claiming his own attention. When his friend talked of his European correspondence and of such Americans as Colden, Clayton, and Mitchell, whose work was applauded by the Europeans and who already constituted the beginning of an American scientific community, Franklin listened carefully. Together the two men tried to plan a society which could be built upon the American natural history circle.

Franklin knew little of this group except through Bartram, but he did know Philadelphia and it was clear that any scientific society must have a nucleus at some one point where the efforts of the corresponding naturalists throughout the colonies could be centered. There were several men in the city who were ready to support such an effort, the most important being Thomas Bond, who was personally acquainted with some of the leading European naturalists as a result of his medical studies abroad. The others were men with whom Franklin had been associated in the Junto and in the management of the Library Company. There were Thomas Godfrey, who had won recognition from the Royal Society for his quadrant; Phineas Bond, who had studied in Europe like his brother; Thomas Hopkinson, an Oxford man; Samuel Rhoads, a successful builder; William Parsons, a surveyor; and William Coleman, a merchant.

Another Philadelphian belonged in this group, too. Franklin and Bartram were ready to place the name of James Logan at the head of their list for Logan was undoubtedly the most distinguished scientist in the area. Yet, despite his own scientific accomplishments, despite his wide European acquaintance, and despite his means and past examples of patronage, he refused to countenance the new learned society. A Quaker aristocrat of a touchy temperament, James Logan had already discouraged Bartram and Colden from depending upon him. His defection was a serious loss but in Bartram's stalwart words, the projectors "resolved that his not favoring the design would not hinder our attempt and if he would not go along with us we would Jog along without him."

In 1743 Franklin devoted much thought to the promotion of knowledge. it was in that year that he drew up a proposal, which he did not publish, for the formation of an academy in Philadelphia. He did publish, however, his *Proposal for Promoting Useful Knowledge among the British Plantations in America* urging the establishment of an American learned society. Although it was issued from Franklin's press and printed in broadside form over Franklin's signature, Bartram called it "our Proposals." There are many indications that it was in fact a joint product. It was clearly written with the natural history circle in mind. It appeared to be a full implementation of the suggestion Colden had made to Douglass some fifteen years earlier. The announced purpose was identical: "That one Society be formed of *virtuosi* or ingenious men residing in the several Colonies, to be called *The American Philosophical Society* who are to maintain a constant correspondence."

The enumeration of subjects to which the society would devote its attention revealed the basis of the whole plan. First mention was made of botany and medicine: "All new discovered plants, herbs, trees, roots, &c, their virtues, uses, &c.; methods of propagating them, and making such as are useful, but particular to some plantations, more general, improvements of vegetable juices, as cyders, wines, &c.; new methods of curing or preventing diseases." These were exactly the things that interested the natural history circle in general and John Bartram in particular. The proposal also mentioned geology, geography, agriculture, mathematics, chemistry, and the crafts but omitted entirely any mention of physics or astronomy and showed little understanding in the suggestions relating to the physical sciences. It was intended to cover all knowledge, "all philosophical experiments that let light into the nature of things, tend to increase the power of man over matter, and multiply the conveniences or pleasures of life," but it was formulated from the viewpoint of a naturalist.

The Philadelphians who associated themselves with the enterprise were expected to serve the essential role of receiving scientific papers from distant members, considering them, and redirecting them to other members. Each resident member was given a particular post, Bartram being the botanist and Thomas Bond the physician while Franklin was simply the secretary. These three were the effective leaders of the group. They counted upon support from the "many in every province in circumstances that set them at ease, and afford[ed them] leisure to cultivate the finer arts and improve the common stock of knowledge." Members were to bear their own expenses without any plan to seek public or private aid except that Franklin agreed to frank all of their correspondence. Each member would pay for a quarterly abstract of society papers. The basis of support would be individual means and leisure just as it was in the natural history circle.

At first, the society grew very well. During the summer of 1743, Franklin, meeting Cadwallader Colden for the first time, won his support. Both Colden and John Mitchell visited Philadelphia in 1744, after their election to membership. John Clayton was at least informed of the society. In New York and New Jersey, a surprising number of men proved eager to accept membership. James Alexander and Chief Justice Robert Hunter Morris, who a little later was elected to fellowship in the Royal Society, were among this group, although most of the men were political figures of wealth and position without notable scientific interests. Franklin reported that there were "à Nummber of others in Virginia, Maryland, Carolina, and the New England Colonies, who we expect to join us, as soon as they are acquainted that the Society has begun to form itself" Despite this promise, Bartram refused to mention it to any of his European correspondents "for fear it should turn out poorly."

When the Europeans did find out about it from Colden and from Clayton, they all became anxious to know how it was progressing. Colden was noncommittal in his report, declaring, "I cannot tell what expectations to give you of that undertaking," but Collinson immediately became enthusiastic. His tepid view of Bartram's first suggestion was forgotten when it appeared that a society had actually been formed. "I can't enough commend the Authors and promoters of a Society for Improvement of Natural knowledge," he wrote, "Because it will be a Means of uniteing Ingenious Men of all Societies together and a Mutual Harmony be got . . . I expect Something New from your New World, our Old World as it were Exhausted." To Peter Collinson, the advantages to be anticipated from such a society lay within the realm of natural history. He repeated what he had often said before, "I certainly think [they] cannot Labour Long when Such wonders are all around them Ready brought forth to their hands and to Which Wee are great strangers Butt because you See them Every Day they are thought Common and not worth Notice."

Unexpected support was given the struggling group by one of those travelling lecturers who were so much a part of the colonial scene, a Dr. Adam Spencer of Edinburgh. Spencer was not a quack, like many of the itinerants; he came with recommendations from Dr. Richard Mead and other prominent London physicians as "a most judicious and experienced Physician and man midwife." He was working his way down the coast from Boston to the West Indies when he reached Philadelphia. There, Franklin became so interested in his demonstrations that he agreed to act as his agent. To Dr. Thomas Cadwalader he lent important assistance in the preparation of his *Essay on the West-India Dry-Gripes,* a pamphlet which inaugurated medical publication in Philadelphia with a commendable treatment of several cases of lead poisoning caused by distilling rum through lead pipes. Spencer's lectures on physiology and the diseases of the eye proved popular but he found that the greatest response followed his lectures on electricity. After attending one of the meetings of the Philosophical Society he extended his encouragement to the Philadelphia group. He even offered to promote the society as well as he could by taking copies of Franklin's *Proposal* with him to the West indies. Nearly a year later he was still thinking about the society when he talked with Dr. John Mitchell on his way through Virginia.

Encouragement was offered from many quarters, but it was not sufficient to sustain the society. After his visit to Philadelphia in the fall of 1744, Colden wrote Franklin in concern lest the whole project be abandoned. The following summer, Franklin was still not ready to admit that it had collapsed though he did declare, "The members of our Society here are very idle Gentlemen; they will take no Pains." Thomas Bond, however, said that Franklin was at fault. Out of this bickering came a resolution by Bartram, Bond, and Franklin to revive the society and make it effective. John Bartram felt this might easily be done, "if we could but exchange the time that is spent in the Club, Chess and Coffee House for the Curious amusements of natural observations." The real trouble was that there had never been an integrated scientific community in Philadelphia and the society failed to create one. It was because of inadequate local support that the noble aspirations for an intercolonial learned society were dissipated.

Benjamin Franklin was the only one who did not give up. Upon Cadwallader Colden's suggestion, he decided to publish an American Philosophical Miscellany. This would be a scientific journal issued monthly or quarterly and it was hoped that it might "in time produce a Society as proposed by giving men of Learning or Genius some knowledge of one another." By taking upon himself the whole job of compiling and by permitting anonymous papers to appear in it, Franklin would not jeopardize the reputation of anyone. After the Pennsylvania Assembly adjourned in 1746, he was able to get together enough papers to make up five or six numbers of the miscellany. Many of them had been submitted to the society while it was attempting to carry out its announced aims; others Franklin obtained independently. Most of them have since been lost although copies of some and hints about others remain—enough to reveal the general character of the collection.

The most important known papers came from or through members of the natural history circle. John Mitchell submitted to the society an essay on yellow fever which was later given to Benjamin Rush by Franklin and became the basis of his famous "cure" in the yellow fever epidemic of 1793. When Franklin asked Mitchell for permission to publish this account in his miscellany, Mitchell refused because he said it was not complete enough. He may have been more ready to see his essay on the pines of Virginia published, however, and another which he had ready for the society in September 1745. Cadwallader Colden wrote one medical paper himself which he sent to Franklin and he forwarded another written by Dr. Evan Jones on the effects and treatment of rattlesnake bites. Joseph Breintnall also wrote a letter on a rattlesnake bite which he may have offered to Franklin before he sent it to the Royal Society for publication in the *Philosophical Transactions* of 1746. Dr. Isaac DuBois wrote a paper on an epidemic fever about this time which found its way to Colden's hands. it may well have been intended for the society or for the miscellany. A description of a newly invented wooden cannon was sent to Franklin from an undisclosed source. Franklin himself worked out a theory to account for the shorter time consumed in crossing the Atlantic from America to Europe than from Europe to America, a theory which Colden offered to support if he wanted to publish it in his miscellany. Fortunately this was not published, for his solution, involving the rotation of the earth, was incorrect. He kept working on the problem until he did find the correct explanation—the gulf stream.

The proposed American Philosophical Miscellany never appeared. The enthusiasm that had led to the organization of the Philosophical Society had expended itself, leaving insufficient energy to establish this sort of journal. The dream of an American learned society could not be fulfilled until other factors had been added to the environment. When Peter Kalm visited Philadelphia in 1748, he was told that the impact of the War of Austrian Succession on the colonies had killed the American Philosophical Society. That judgment was not fair. It is true that the declaration of war was published in Pennsylvania in July 1744 but the province raised no troops until 1746, and Franklin did not become involved in the preparations until the middle of 1747. By that time both the society and the miscellany were quite dead.

The American Philosophical Society had failed even though it had been based in part upon an already existing intercolonial scientific group—the natural history circle. It had failed because its local base had been too feeble and limited. It had not made use of the nonscientific but "curious" elements of the city's population. Merchants and gentlemen, in particular, had not been brought into the society as they were brought into another project of scientific interest which was launched in 1753 and 1754. In those years, two expeditions were sent from Philadelphia by the North West Company in search of the northwest passage. Franklin reported that the subscription for the first voyage in the sixty-ton schooner *Argo* amounted to £1300. Not only were Philadelphia merchants involved, but some even from

Maryland, New York, and Boston. They were ready to contribute generously because of the great possibilities of profit that lay in finding the passage, but at the same time they realized the scientific importance of the exploration. Although both expeditions failed in their objective, they did bring many leading Philadelphians into direct contact with an effort to advance knowledge. Some of the Eskimo utensils brought back by Captain Charles Swaine were presented by the North West Company to the Library Company of Philadelphia to add to its collection of curiosities. The American Philosophical Society had not succeeded similarly in enlisting the support of the mercantile community—a group which in England formed one of the most important sources of support of the Royal Society.

As a matter of fact, before Franklin became interested in the northwest passage and even before the war claimed his attention he had already turned away from the abortive society to a new enthusiasm. His developing interest in science was first attracted and then absorbed in the study of electricity which was then becoming something of a popular fad in Europe. Peter Collinson recognized it as another wave of interest in a scientific wonder, reporting, the "Phenomena of the Polypus Entertained the Curious for a year or two past but Now the Ventuosi of Europe are taken up In Electrical Experiments." The people of Europe and America began to read articles on the subject in their magazines and to see advertisements of lecturers who drew sparks from subjects' eyes and gave electrical shocks to their patrons. Half parlor magic and half academic study, it offered a rare opportunity for scientific achievement to those who held truth as their goal, even though they might not have had the formal mathematical training required for astronomical studies or the years of botanical observation needed to permit the recognition of new genera.

It was probably the itinerant lecturer, Adam Spencer, who gave Franklin his first knowledge of electricity when the Philadelphian visited Boston in the summer of 1743. The following spring, Spencer provided more information while he was lecturing in Philadelphia. In 1746, Franklin saw William Claggett in Newport and talked to that colonial lecturer about electricity. If he read the *American Magazine* in 1745 or 1746, he ran across accounts of French and German electrical experiments, and he could have found electrical papers in the *Philosophical Transactions* even earlier. Electricity was in the air and no alert man could have avoided knowing about it. Adam Spencer was, at best, only one source of information.

Peter Collinson was much more. Sometime before 1747, he sent to the Library Company of Philadelphia a glass tube for conducting electrical experiments and an account of German experiments in electricity with directions for repeating them. These things arrived at an opportune moment—just after Franklin had seen the philosophical society collapse and the philosophical miscellany prove unrealistic. His one scientific publication of these years, *An Account of the New-Invented Pennsylvanian Fireplace,* described an important invention and was well received, but it was not enough to satisfy his growing appetite for scientific work. Confronted with Collinson's donations, Franklin threw himself into the study of electricity to a point where it "totally engrossed" his attention as it had never been engaged before. The "Philadelphia Experiments" followed.

Several Philadelphians shared Franklin's enthusiasm and explored with him the possibilities of electricity. His three most important associates were Thomas

Hopkinson, who had been designated president of the American Philosophical Society; Philip Syng, a silversmith and Junto crony; and Ebenezer Kinnersley. Kinnersley, an unemployed Baptist clergyman, became the most original and important of the men behind Franklin. He worked out significant experiments himself describing them in letters which were included in later editions of Franklin's *Experiments and Observations* and in the *Philosophical Transactions*. He lectured successfully on electricity in several American towns. Franklin, in his own letters, made careful reference to the aid he received from these associates, but as one reviewer aptly put it, "These acknowledgements . . . are neither numerous or important enough to produce any considerable diminution of the Author's fame as a philosopher."

Franklin's work also demonstrated his continuing relationship with the natural history circle. One of his published letters was addressed to John Mitchell, now in England, another to Cadwallader Colden, and a third to John Lining. Mitchell did only a little work on electricity, but Lining came to devote to this study all the time he could spare from his indigo planting. Colden showed interest for a time, and his son, David, did some worthwhile experimental work. Some years later, Alexander Garden experimented with the electrical eel in a study which nicely combined electricity and natural history. John Bartram, however, would not be deflected from his botany. It was not that he was unresponsive but he told Colden, "I take this to be the most Surpriseing Phenomena that we have met with and is wholy incomprehensible to thy friend John Bartram."

First and last, it was Peter Collinson, at the heart of the natural history circle, who was Franklin's most important support. He was even more essential in communicating Franklin's experiments to the world than he had been in initiating them. Collinson did not read Franklin's first letter containing experiments to the Royal Society, but to a small circle of friends including William Watson, one of the leading experimenters in England. Watson quoted extensively from it in a letter of his own which he did read to the Royal Society with the result that portions of Franklin's very first letter found their way into the *Philosophical Transactions*. Collinson directed later letters to Edward Cave who put two of them in his *Gentleman's Magazine* and then, in 1751, published a collection of Franklin's letters with a preface by John Fothergill under the title, *Experiments and Observations on Electricity*. It was Collinson who introduced Franklin to the world.

Franklin's book was the most important scientific contribution made by an American in the colonial period. In it, his ability to construct hypotheses that were often brilliant and to check them with adequate experiments was made clear for the first time. His most important accomplishments were in the realm of pure theory where he was able to show how his single-fluid concept fitted the observed conditions more satisfactorily than the two-fluid theory then widely accepted under the stimulus of Charles Dufay's writings. Franklin also suggested the terminology that became so widely useful, calling one charge negative and the other positive—the presumption being that a deficiency of electric fluid caused the negative state. According to Franklin, the flow of current was from positive to negative and although modern knowledge has revealed that the electrons flow in the opposite direction, the Franklinian terminology and direction of flow are still used by electricians. At many points, notably when confronted with an example of induction, Franklin showed the ability to grasp the essential nature of the phenomenon and to fit it into his conceptual scheme.

Obscuring his more basic conclusions were the dramatic suggestions Franklin made concerning lightning. First, he suggested that lightning was an electrical phenomenon—not a new idea but now based upon a careful comparison of their properties. Then he devised two experiments to test this hypothesis. The guard house experiment, in which a man stood inside an insulated house on top of a steeple surmounted by a lightning rod from which he could draw off electricity, was performed first in France, but Franklin performed his more famous kite experiment before anyone else. The hypothesis was proven and the way cleared for the great utilitarian accomplishment of his study—the lightning rod. Franklin was led to the suggestion of the lightning rod by his study of the electrical effect of points. It is not clear whether he actually used one before he made the suggestion in his almanac, but at any rate, the idea was quickly taken up. Lightning rods soon sprouted in London and Paris as well as in Philadelphia until they became Franklin's greatest advertisement.

The response that met Franklin's work was overwhelming. His book passed through five English and three French editions, and was translated into German and Italian as well. In England, the Royal Society awarded him its Copley Medal and admitted him to fellowship without requiring him to request the election, sign the register, or pay the usual fees—a rare honor. In France, the King directed his own "Thanks and Compliments in an express Manner to *Mr. Franklin of Pennsylvania*" while the Académie des Sciences elected him one of its eight associés éstrangers. In America, Harvard, Yale, and William and Mary granted him honorary degrees. Franklin became a world celebrity.

His work in electricity was significant but it was not enough to account for the reputation he won—a reputation which seemed to transcend that of any of his contemporaries, European or American, literary or political. His experiments were only the foundation of the great esteem he met. He had made his discoveries when electricity was a world-wide fad and while general interest was at a peak. His invention of the lightning rod was a spectacular justification of the faith of the eighteenth century that all knowledge was useful. The very fact that he was an American added to the charm of his achievement in an age which celebrated the virtues of the simple society and distrusted scholastic learning. His work in electricity, however, gave the world only its first view of the capacities of a genius. Franklin was then able to pass from the little world of Philadelphia to the great world of London and Paris, there to demonstrate the same breadth of interest, keenness of perception, and warmth of humanity that had distinguished his earlier performances. Indeed, Franklin improved with age until he became the very epitome of the learned philosopher.

Franklin's achievements were accepted as the achievements of an American and in him, for the first time, an American was admitted as a peer of the leading scientists of the western world. This was recognition of an altogether different character from that which had been accorded the natural history workers in America. They, too, had been honored, encouraged, and regarded with continuing esteem. Yet, much of their accomplishment had resulted from their great advantage of position. They had been field workers doing work that no one in Europe could do. Franklin had enjoyed no similar advantage from being in America. Presumably, he should have been able to carry through his experiments and make his speculations even more successfully in Europe where he would have had the advantages of the great libraries and the conversation of the leading thinkers. Instead, he had flowered in America—not as a species of wild life, but as a product of the cultural milieu of Philadelphia and an associate of the natural history circle. Franklin's work was not simply field work which could be fitted into some European's scheme of organization. He developed the theory himself from facts he had found himself and in concert with other Americans. This was a prodigy; an American scientist of the first magnitude! It is likely that some part of the great recognition Franklin received was a result of the understanding of that important fact.

30. The Culture of Early Pennsylvania

Frederick B. Tolles

Professor Frederick B. Tolles (b. 1915) of Swarthmore College, who has written extensively on Quakers and the emergence of American culture, has speculated that urban centers like Philadelphia, rather than frontier areas, were the real seedbeds of a distinctive American culture. Looking at various cultural groups in Pennsylvania during the eighteenth century, Tolles in the following essay points out that ethnic groups which moved out onto the frontier did not readily mingle and fuse their cultural traits. By settling in distinct enclaves they avoided sustained interaction. German pietist sects and the Welsh were particularly exclusionist and conscious of their cultural heritage, and they worked to preserve Old World habits and traditions. In the dynamically expanding commercial center of Philadelphia, by comparison, the pattern was quite different. Individuals could not so easily come into contact with different cultural traditions. It was in the City of Brotherly Love, as a case study, that "cultural pluralism" gave rise to American "cultural growth." The city was the arena in which new American traditions formed out of a fusion of Old World habits and life-styles.

Assuming the reasonableness of Professor Tolles's observations, how much weight can we attach to a "melting pot" conception of cultural growth? Is it not also possible, given the dominance of Quaker influences in Philadelphia, that non-Quakers subordinated their own habits and absorbed the more firmly planted Quaker cultural traits? Does cultural pluralism, as personified in prerevolutionary Pennsylvania, necessarily result in cultural interaction and fusion?

Benjamin West has a lot to answer for. Everyone knows his painting of William Penn's treaty with the Indians; it is one of our national icons, "as indelibly impressed on the American mind," it has been said, "as . . . Washington's crossing of the Delaware." The lush greens of its foliage, the tawny flesh tones of its noble savages, the sober drab of its Quaker plain dress have fixed forever in our consciousness a stereotype of early Pennsylvania. There he stands under the great elm at Shackamaxon, portly and benignant, the Founder of the Quaker commonwealth, eternally dispensing peace and yard goods to the Indians. If it is mostly legend—for there is no documentary record of a treaty at Shackamaxon—it is at least an inspiring one, quite as much so as that of Pocahontas laying her lovely head on Captain John Smith's breast or Squanto instructing the Pilgrim Fathers

Source: Frederick B. Tolles, "The Culture of Early Pennsylvania," *Pennsylvania Magazine of History and Biography,* 81 (1957), pp. 119–137. Footnotes omitted. Reprinted by permission of Frederick B. Tolles and the *Pennsylvania Magazine of History and Biography.*

in the mysteries of maize culture. And whatever its faults as a document or as a painting, it has the merit of a certain truth to history, for, unlike the founders of Jamestown and Plymouth, the Quaker founders of Pennsylvania did contrive by fair dealing and generosity to stay at peace with the local Indians for three quarters of a century. As a matter of fact, it is worth pausing a moment to note that the autumn of 1956 marked the two-hundredth anniversary of the ending of that remarkable experiment in peaceful race relations.

What is wrong, then, with West's vast, idyllic canvas as a symbol of early Pennsylvania? It is not the anachronisms that bother me. True, the architectural background is composed of brick buildings that could not have been standing in 1682; true, West portrays Penn as stout and middle-aged when in fact he was still young and athletic, and dressed him in the Quaker Oats costume of shadbelly coat and cocked hat that Friends did not wear for half a century to come. No, the mischief lies in the aura, the atmosphere, of the painting—the air of smug and stupid piety combined with the stolid respectability of the successful bourgeois. No one will deny that the early Quakers were a "God-fearing, money-making people"—least of all I, who have written a book on the proposition that they had one foot in the meetinghouse and the other in the countinghouse. It is probably unfair to demand of a painter that he project the life of the mind of his canvas; perhaps it takes a modern abstractionist to portray a pure idea. Yet I cannot help regretting that the most widely current stereotype of early Pennsylvania should suggest a cultural and intellectual desert.

Besides, early Pennsylvania was not, of course, just Quaker. Everyone who has seen *Plain and Fancy* knows about the Amish, who have been here for a long time, and everyone who has a taste for the quaint and the indigestible knows about "hex signs" on barns (which have nothing to do, of course, with witches) and shoofly pie. If we don't know about the Scotch-Irish, it is not for want of zeal on the part of their descendants, who would have us believe that they fought the Indians and won the American Revolution all by themselves. And if we happen to be Bryn Mawr graduates we are vaguely conscious that the college campus and its surroundings were once peopled by Welshmen, who left the landscape strewn with odd-sounding place names like Llanerch, Bala-Cynwyd, and Tredyffrin (many of which, incidentally, were chosen from a gazetteer by a nineteenth-century president of the Pennsylvania Railroad looking for distinctive names for his suburban stations).

What I want to suggest is that early Pennsylvania had a genuine and important culture or complex of cultures, that there was something more to it than simple Quaker piety and commercialism on the one hand and ethnic quaintness on the other. I am going to side-step one basic problem by refusing to define exactly what I mean by "culture." The anthropologically minded will be annoyed by my irresponsible tendency to use the term now as Ruth Benedict would use it and again perhaps as Matthew Arnold would use it. In justification of this slipshod procedure I can only plead that I am merely an unscientific historian, not a "social scientist."

"Early Pennsylvania" I will define more strictly. By this term I shall mean Pennsylvania east of the Susquehanna and south of the Blue Mountains in the period down to about 1740. But I must immediately point out that this area was never a self-contained or self-conscious regional unit. It was part of a larger geographical whole. The men in the gray flannel suits have been trying hard in recent years to impress upon us the concept "Delaware Valley, U.S.A." The colonial Pennsylvanian knew without being told that he lived in the valley of the Delaware. He first saw his new home from the deck of a ship sailing up the great river. His prosperity and his comfort depended in large measure on the commerce that carried his farm products down the river to the West Indies and southern Europe, that brought back up the river the textiles and hardware he needed and could not manufacture for himself. The Delaware united West Jersey, Pennsylvania, and the Lower Counties (which eventually became the state of Delaware) into a single economic province, and linked it with the rest of the Atlantic community. It also unified the valley into a single "culture area." The Quakers' Yearly Meeting embraced Friends on both sides of the river, and met alternately at Philadelphia on the west bank and Burlington on the east. The Anglicans also thought of the valley as a unit, a single missionary field to be saved from "Quakerism or heathenism." I shall restrict myself, however, to that portion of it which originally formed the province of Pennsylvania proper—the counties of Bucks, Philadelphia, and Chester.

The Founder of Pennsylvania, we must be clear, was neither a narrow-minded religious zealot on the one hand nor a mean-spirited Philistine on the other. William Penn was a man of broad intellectual culture in Matthew Arnold's sense, educated at Oxford, on the Continent, and at Lincoln's Inn; he was a Fellow of the Royal Society and the associate not only of kings and courtiers, but of the reigning intellectuals of the day—men like Samuel Pepys, the diarist, John Locke, the philosopher, Sir William Petty, the political economist. He was a man of wide reading. The list of books he bought to bring to America on his second visit suggests his range; it included the poems of Milton, a copy of *Don Quixote*, the works of John Locke, the latest travel books by William Dampier and Father Hennepin, the Roman histories of Livy and Suetonius. Penn was a good Quaker and a shrewd real-estate promoter, but he was also—though one would scarcely guess it from Benjamin West's canvas—a Restoration egg-head, as much at home with the philosophers of the Royal Society as with the Indians of the Pennsylvania forest. The example of such a man was enough to insure that Pennsylvania would not be a cultural desert. And Penn's commitment to a sophisticated ideal of religious freedom meant that the intellectual life of his colony would never stagnate for want of controversy and the creative clash of opinions.

It is true that, by and large, the English Quakers who sailed with Penn on the *Welcome* or followed him on other ships did not come, as he did, from the leisure class. Quakerism in the seventeenth century took root in the lower orders of society, among yeoman farmers, husbandmen, artisans, shopkeepers, hired servants, men and women who worked with their hands. The farmers among them, poverty-stricken dalesmen from the moors of northern England, headed straight for the rich uplands of Bucks and Chester counties. (As late as the middle of the eighteenth century, the people of Chester still spoke in a broad Yorkshire dialect.) Within a few years they were producing flour and meat for export. With the proceeds they built those neat stone farmhouses with their projecting pent roofs and door hoods that are so charming when one comes upon them in the midst of the split-levels and ranch houses of Philadelphia's exurbia.

They had little beyond the rudiments of reading and writing, these rural Friends, and few books beyond the Bible and Barclay's *Apology*. They had little time for reading, and besides, their Quakerism enjoined upon them a sober, plain way of life. But if their lives seem drab, remember the clean lines, the satisfying proportions, the functional perfection of the stone meetinghouse where they gathered on First Day to worship God in the living silence. In that simple structure form followed function with a faithfulness that Frank Lloyd Wright might envy, and every superfluity was stripped away to leave its purpose revealed in utter purity. The Pennsylvania Friends even anticipated a favorite device of the modern architect; they installed sliding panels with which they could break up the "flow of space" and convert their oblong meetinghouses into two rooms for the men's and women's meetings for business.

Howard Brinton calls the period from 1700 to 1740 the Golden Age of Quakerism in America. He is thinking primarily of the rural Quakers of Bucks and Chester counties when he describes, with a touch of nostalgia, the "unique Quaker culture" of the period.

> In the Quaker communities the meeting was the center, spiritually, intellectually, and economically. It included a library and a school. Disputes of whatever nature were settled in the business sessions of the meeting. The poor were looked after, moral delinquents dealt with, marriages approved and performed. . . . Each group, centered in the meeting, was a well-ordered, highly integrated community of interdependent members. . . . This flowering of Quakerism was not characterized by any outburst of literary or artistic production. Its whole emphasis was on life itself in home, meeting and community. This life was an artistic creation as beautiful in its simplicity and proportion as was the architecture of its meeting houses. The "Flowering of New England" has been described in terms of literature, but the flowering of Quakerism in the middle colonies can be described only in terms of life itself.

Quaker life in Philadelphia soon fell into a different pattern. Eventually the cleavage between rural and urban Quaker culture would split the society of Friends into two factions, Hicksite and Orthodox (and one might even suggest that the recent healing of the schism was made easier by the blurring of that sharp line of cleavage in our twentieth-century suburban culture). The material basis for the rise of urban Quaker culture was Philadelphia's amazing growth and prosperity. Last of the major colonial cites to be founded, William Penn's "green country town" quickly outstripped New York, Newport, and Charleston, and by 1740 was pressing the much older town of Boston hard for primacy in wealth and population.

By 1740 the Quakers were already a minority group in the Quaker City, but they had been the prime movers in the town's economic expansion and they still controlled a large share of its trade and its visible assets. Most of the early immigrants had been craftsmen and shopkeepers. They practiced the economic ethic of Poor Richard long before Benjamin Franklin, that Johnny-come-lately, arrived in Philadelphia. Working diligently in their callings, they quickly transformed a primitive frontier into a complex provincial market town and business center. The tons of wheat and flour, the barrels of beef and pork, the lumber, the bales of furs that poured into Philadelphia from the farms in the hinterland provided, of course, the substance of Philadelphia's flourishing export trade. But it was the diligence and business acumen of the Quaker merchants that translated those raw goods into prosperity for the whole region.

But prosperity, it must be admitted, had its effects on Philadelphia Quakerism. As wealth increased, plainness—what Friends called "the simplicity of Truth"—declined. As early as 1695 Philadelphia Yearly Meeting was warning its male members against wearing "long lapp'd Sleeves or Coates gathered at the Sides, or Superfluous Buttons, or Broad Ribbons about their Hatts, or long curled

Perriwiggs," and cautioning women Friends against "Dressing their Heads Immodestly, or Wearing their Garments undecently . . . or Wearing . . . Striped or Flower'd Stuffs, or other useless and Superfluous Things." Obviously, the Yearly Meeting wouldn't have bothered to discourage its members from wearing these abominations unless some Friends were actually doing so. But the clever Quaker could find ways to outwit the meeting, could practice conspicuous consumption without violating the letter of the discipline. In 1724 Christopher Saur, the German printer, noted that "plainness is vanishing pretty much" among the Philadelphia Friends. It was still noticeable in their clothes, "except," he added, "that the material is very costly, or is even velvet." In other words, the Philadelphia Friends were becoming worldly, and there were Jeremiahs— especially among the country Friends—who insisted that vital Quakerism varied inversely with the prosperity of its adherents.

I am not concerned at the moment with moral judgments. I am concerned with "culture," loosely defined, and I must therefore point out that the Quaker aristocrats of Philadelphia were receptive not only to the fashions of the "world's people," but to their architecture, their books, their ideas as well, though there was always something sober and substantial about Quaker houses, libraries, and intellectual pursuits, as there was about Quaker clothes. If rural Pennsylvania Quakerism flowered in ordered and beautiful lives, the Quakerism of Philadelphia flowered in many realms of the mind and spirit, particularly in the fields of organized humanitarianism, science, and medicine. Since they had no use for a learned clergy, the Quakers were slow to establish colleges: Haverford, which began as a secondary school in 1833, did not become a college until 1856; Swarthmore was not founded till 1864, and Bryn Mawr came still later, in 1885. But the humane and learned institutions which gave Philadelphia its cultural preeminence in the pre-Revolutionary years—the American Philosophical Society, the Library Company, the Pennsylvania Hospital, even the College of Philadelphia, which became the University of Pennsylvania—all owed more than a little to the solid and generous culture of the Quaker merchants.

If I limit myself to mentioning the cultural interests and achievements of just one Philadelphia Quaker—James Logan—it is because he is the one I know best. I will not contend that Logan was either a typical Philadelphian or a representative Friend. The breadth and reach of his mind would have made him an exceptional man in any time or place; and as for his Quakerism, he sat so loose to it that Philadelphia Monthly Meeting had to deal with him repeatedly for breaches of the discipline. But a résumé of James Logan's contributions in the realm of "high culture" should lay to rest any lingering suspicions that early Philadelphia was a Sahara of the intellect.

Logan came to Philadelphia in 1699 as William Penn's secretary. At one time or another over the next half century, he occupied nearly every responsible public office in the province, including those of chief justice and acting governor. He was Pennsylvania's leading fur merchant, her ablest and most respected Indian diplomat. He was the builder of Philadelphia's most distinguished early Georgian mansion—the house called Stenton, which still stands in its elegant Quaker simplicity amid the ugliness of industrial North Philadelphia. He assembled a library of three thousand volumes which I do not hesitate to call the best-chosen collection of books in all colonial America. Unlike most other colonial libraries, it is still intact at the Library Company of Philadelphia. And unlike many other colonial libraries, it was a scholar's working library. Logan's marginal annotations make it clear how closely he studied his learned books in many tongues. He carried on a correspondence in Latin—the universal language of scholarship—with Dr. Johann Albertus Farbricius of Hamburg, the most erudite classicist of his age, and his commentaries on Euclid and Ptolemy were published in Hamburg and Amsterdam. He made a translation of Cicero's essay on old age which Benjamin Franklin, its publisher, hailed as "a happy omen that Philadelphia shall become the seat of American Muses." He designed and carried out some experiments on the generation of Indian corn that botanists all over Europe cited for a century or more as proof that sex reared its head in the plant kingdom. He was certainly one of the first Americans to understand and use Sir Isaac Newton's method of fluxions, or calculus. He made contributions to the science of optics, which were published in Holland, and several of his scientific papers were read before the Royal Society of London and printed in its *Philosophical Transactions*. He crowned his intellectual life by writing a treatise on moral philosophy which, unfortunately, was never finished and never published. That treatise, which exists only in fragments, may have been suggested by an offhand remark of the great John Locke that it should be possible to construct a rational science of morals: Logan called it in typical eighteenth-century fashion, "The Duties of Man Deduced from Nature."

James Logan, I repeat, was not a typical Philadelphia Quaker, but the example of such a man—and remember he was the leading public figure of his day—could not fail to stimulate others to the intellectual life. Indeed, the three men who are usually called Philadelphia's first scientists—Benjamin Franklin, John Bartram, the botanist, and Thomas Godfrey, the inventor of the mariner's quadrant—all owed a great deal to Logan's encouragment and patronage.

Here then, were two conflicting, or at least divergent, Quaker cultures in early Pennsylvania. A third—perhaps we should call it a subculture—flourished transiently in the frontier region west of the Schuylkill, known as the "Welsh Tract." It is difficult to form an accurate picture of the early Welsh community. There are massive works on the subject, but they are all heavily genealogical in emphasis, and read more like stud books than works of history. They seem more concerned with providing a suitable ancestry for later generations of Philadelphians than with disclosing the actual outlines of life in the Welsh Tract.

Were the settlers of Merion, Haverford, and Radnor rich or poor? We get no clear answer because the truth is obscured by a conflict of myths. On the one hand, to fit the legend of America as a land of opportunity, a haven for the oppressed, they must be poor men, fleeing from persecution. On the other hand, to satisfy our itch for highborn ancestors, they must be aristocrats, country squires, gentlemen to the manner born. The size of some of the early landholdings and the inventories of some personal estates suggest that a few wealthy Welshmen did take up their residence on the Main Line in the 1680's and 1690's. But alongside the purchasers of two and three thousand acres who signed themselves "gentleman" were scores of yeomen, grocers, tailors, and the like, who settled on one hundred or one hundred fifty acres. The bulk of the Welsh immigrants were probably of "the middling sort" of people who gave the North American colonies and eventually the United States their overwhelmingly middle-class character.

Neither poverty nor persecution really explains that emigration from Wales which started as soon as William Penn opened the doors of Pennsylvania and lasted till some Quaker communities in Wales were all but depopulated. Professor

A. H. Dodd, a learned student of Welsh history, has pointed out that if poverty had been at the root of this folk movement, it would have stemmed from the economically backward region of Anglesey and Caernarvon rather than from fertile and prosperous Merionethshire, Radnorshire, and Montgomeryshire. And had persecution been the main impetus, the stream of emigration would have slacked off with the coming of toleration in 1689, instead of continuing as it did into the next century.

If we would identify the fundamental "cause" of the Welsh migration, we must recognize that it was not the "pushing" factors of poverty or persecution at home, but the strong "pulling" force of a dream—the powerful but delusive dream of a new Wales in the western wilderness, in which, as the Welsh immigrants put it themselves, "we might live together as a civil society to endeavor to decide all controversies and debates amongst ourselves in a Gospel order, and not to entangle ourselves with laws in an unknown tongue." So the first Welsh settlers extracted from William Penn a verbal promise that they should have a 40,000-acre enclave west of the Schuylkill where they could speak their own language, practice their own customs, and hold their own courts in splendid isolation.

Their attempt to transplant their ancient culture and preserve it intact did not prosper. Within a few decades they had lost their identity and merged with the fast-growing American society around them. They blamed William Penn for the failure of their dream. It was true that his governor, confronted with a solid Welsh voting bloc, followed the time-honored principle of divide and rule: he split the Welsh Tract in two by running a county line through the middle of it, throwing Haverford and Radnor into Chester County, leaving only Merion in Philadelphia County. But the experiment, one suspects, was doomed from the start. The Welsh, after all, were a bilingual people, as fluent in English as their own tongue; they kept their records in English, and there is little evidence that distinctive Welsh laws or customs were observed in the Tract. It was not long before David ap Rees became David Price, Ellis ap Hugh became Ellis Pugh, and Edward ap John became plain Edward Jones.

It is not clear how long even such national traits as the love of music persisted. Thomas Allen Glenn found it pleasant "to think that often through the wild woodland of Colonial Merion there has echoed the burthen of some ancient British war song, chanted ages ago in battle against the legions of Imperial Rome." But Charles H. Browning, who compiled the fullest account of Welsh life in Pennsylvania, could not find "even a tradition that the Welsh Friends over the Schuylkill were inclined to music, singing and dancing." There is a revealing story about Edward Foulke, one of the pioneer settlers of Gwynedd. While he was still in Wales and not yet joined with the Quakers, people used to collect on Sundays at his house on at Coed-y-foel in Merionshire to join him in song, for Edward was a fine singer. But he and his wife presently became uneasy in their mind about this idle way of spending the Lord's Day. Thereafter, when his musical friends gathered and he was tempted to "undue levity," he would get out the Bible and read it aloud. It was surprising, says an old account, how quickly "the light and unprofitable portion of his visitors" melted away. When Edward Foulke came to the Quaker settlement of Gwynedd in 1698, it is safe to assume that he left his harp behind. The war songs of the ancient Britons may have rung out in the Merion Woods, but the echo that Thomas Allen Glenn thought he caught over the centuries was more likely the sound of the psalms of David sung in the Baptist chapels of the Welsh Tract. In any case there is little reason to think that the Welsh Friends after a few decades in America differed much from their English coreligionists.

The original settlers of Germantown seem to have suffered a like fate. The late Professor William I. Hull was convinced that they were predominantly Dutch, not German in culture, and Quaker, not Mennonite, in religion. But whatever their origins, they quickly became Philadelphia Friends, like the Welsh. Their very names were Anglicized from Luykens to Lukens, from Kunders to Conard, from Schumacher to Shoemaker. Those Dutchmen who were not assimilated to Anglo-Saxon Quakerism were presently swallowed up by the great tide of Swiss and Germans who came to Pennsylvania after 1709—the people who, to add to the general confusion, are known as "Pennsylvania Dutch."

I cannot here attempt a definition or characterization of Pennsylvania Dutch culture. All I can do is make a few observations about it and suggest two excellent books on the subject—Fredric Klees's *The Pennsylvania Dutch* and the symposium called *The Pennsylvania Germans*, edited by Ralph Wood. In the first place, Pennsylvania Dutch culture was never a single entity, a uniform way of life. Though we tend to think of it as a unity, it was and is a congeries of cultures with roots in many different geographical areas and religious traditions. Among the immigrants from continental Europe who came to Pennsylvania in a trickle during the first twenty-five years and in a flood thereafter were Alsatians and Württembergers and Swiss, a scattering of French Huguenots who had lived temporarily in the Rhine Valley, and, ultimately, some Bohemians, Silesians, and Moravians, who came to America by way of Saxony. In religious terms they fell into three broad categories: the sects or plain people, the church people, and the Moravians. All of them were pushed out of central Europe by religious persecution and economic hardship; all were pulled toward Penn's colony by the promise of religious freedom and economic opportunity. It is the sects—the Mennonites, the Amish, the Dunkers, the Schwenkfelders, the Protestant monks and nuns of Ephrata, the mystical Society of the Woman in the Wilderness—who have attracted most attention because of their peculiarities. But it was the church people—the Lutherans and the Reformed—who predominated, and it was they who established the characteristic Pennsylvania Dutch way of life. When Count Zinzendorf, the leader of the Moravians, came to Pennsylvania with a noble ecumenical dream of uniting all the German religious groups, he soon discovered how stubborn these theological and cultural differences were.

What these people had in common was chiefly that they spoke a different, a "foreign," tongue. They were, said a supercilious Philadelphian, "so profoundly ignorant as to be unable to speak the English language." Hence arose the familiar stereotype, the notion that they were boors, stupid, stolid clods—in a word, "the dumb Dutch." Yet they were beyond all comparison the best farmers in colonial America. From the beginning their great barns, their neat farmyards, their care in fencing their livestock, their systematic rotation of crops, their infallible instinct for fertile limestone soil, their industry and good management drew favorable comment in a land notorious for wasteful and slovenly farming. "It is pretty to behold our back settlements," wrote Lewis Evans in 1753, "where the barns are large as palaces, while the owners live in log huts; a sign, though, of thriving farmers." Evans' reference to the log cabin is a reminder that we owe that symbol of the American frontier to the Germans and to the Swedes, who had settled earlier along the Delaware River. It was no invention of the American pioneer, but a cultural importation from the forest lands of central and northern Europe. As a matter of fact, we are indebted to the Pennsylvania Dutch for the two other major symbols of the frontier—the Conestoga wagon, and the so-called Kentucky rifle. And consider their rich and various folk art. Beside the gay and colorful designs of tulips and hearts, distelfinks and peacocks with which they covered their dower chests and pottery and baptismal certificates, most of what passes for early American folk art seems pale and anemic. Finally, be it remembered that the plain people of the Pennsylvania Dutch country have maintained a vital and satisfying religious life longer than almost any other group in America. Even today the simple piety of a Mennonite farmer is a real and impressive thing in the midst of much false and superficial religiosity.

Theirs was a peasant culture, and it has kept its peasant character for two centuries in a country where peasantry has always been alien. Professor Robert Redfield's general description of peasant values describes their outlook pretty accurately: "an intense attachment to native soil; a reverent disposition toward habitat and ancestral ways; a restraint on individual self-seeking in favor of family and community; a certain suspiciousness, mixed with appreciation, of town life; a sober and earthy ethic." Unquestionably, early Pennsylvania Dutch life was limited, lacking in intellectual quality, wanting in many of the higher values of civilized life. And yet, having said that, one immediately asks: where in early America except in the Moravian towns of Bethlehem and Nazareth and Lititz could one hear Bach and Handel, Haydn and Mozart, performed by full orchestra and chorus?

The tide of German immigration set toward the full around 1710 and reached the flood at mid-century. Hardly had the old settlers begun to adjust to these newcomers with their strange tongue and stranger ways before they became aware of a new inundation of land-hungry immigrants—the people who have always been known in America as the Scotch-Irish—Scottish and Presbyterian in culture, Irish only in that they had been living for a longer or shorter period in Ulster. They came in waves, the first after 1717, the second about ten years later, the third around the year 1740. Their coming in such crowds and their free-and-easy attitude toward details like land titles took even James Logan aback, although he was a Scotch-Irishman himself. They simply squatted, he complained, wherever they found "a spot of vacant ground." When challenged to show title, he added, a little sadly, their standard response was that it was "against the laws of God and nature that so much land should lie idle while so many Christians wanted it to labor on and raise their bread."

It was actually James Logan who assigned them their historic role in America. It happened that the Indians across the Susquehanna were growing restive just as the first wave of Scotch-Irish settlers were reaching Philadelphia. Though Logan was a Quaker, he did not share William Penn's faith in pacifism. Recalling from his own childhood how gallantly the Protestants of Ulster had defended Londonderry and Inniskillen against the Roman Catholic forces of James II, he "thought it might be prudent" to plant a settlement of these tough, bellicose Ulstermen on the Susquehanna "as a *frontier* in case of any disturbance." Logan used the term "frontier" with a specific, limited meaning; he meant a border garrison, a strong point on the edge of hostile territory. But the word was destined to vibrate with special overtones for Americans as the outer edge of settlement crept across the continent. And on nearly every American frontier, the Scotch-Irish—those doughty, Bible-quoting, whiskey-drinking, gun-toting, Indian-fighting Presbyterians whom James Logan planted in his garrison town of Donegal on the Susquehanna—would be the defenders of the marches, the tamers of the wilderness, the advance agents of the white man's civilization.

They were not crude, uncultivated roughnecks, these Scotch-Irish frontiersmen. They were pious Presbyterians, and they insisted on a learned ministry and a literate congregation. "The schoolhouse and the kirk went together," says Carl Wittke, "wherever the Scotch-Irish frontier moved." "These fortresses against ignorance and the devil," adds Louis B. Wright, "paralleled a chain of blockhouses and forts against the French and Indian. The Scots were as eager to fight one as the other." New Englanders have a habit of attributing the spread of popular education over the country to the heirs of the Yankee Puritan. But some of the credit rightfully belongs to the Scotch-Irish Presbyterian, who kept the lamp of learning lighted on many an American frontier. As early as 1726 the Reverend William Tennent established a "Log College" on Neshaminy Creek in Bucks County, and the "Log College" was the seed out of which Princeton University grew.

A cultural map of the settled portion of Pennsylvania in 1740 would show a band of Quaker country roughly parallel with the Delaware River and extending back twenty-five or thirty miles, its western outposts near Coatesville, Pottstown, and Quakertown. Behind it would be a broad belt of Pennsylvania Dutch country, anchored at Bethlehem to the northeast and at Lancaster to the southwest. Still farther west in the Susquehanna Valley would be a sparse strip of Scotch-Irish settlement, overlapping on its eastern side with the Pennsylvania Dutch country and swinging eastward in upper Bucks County, near where Neshaminy Creek joins the Delaware. There were a hundred thousand people in all, perhaps more. Scattered over these broad culture areas would be small pockets of people with different backgrounds—English and Welsh Baptists in the Quaker country, a handful of Roman Catholic and Jewish families in Philadelphia, four or five thousand Negroes, slaves and freedmen, and, here and there, some remnants of the ancient inhabitants of Pennsylvania—the Lenni Lenape or Delaware Indians.

Two of these "pocket groups" demand special mention. Along the Delaware south of Philadelphia lived several hundred descendants of the "old colonists"—the Swedes, Finns, and Dutch who had brought the white man's culture to the Delaware Valley long before William Penn. By the end of a century, however, they had lost most of their distinguishing characteristics and had merged with the English culture around them. In Philadelphia there was a strong and growing Anglican community, which worshiped in style in the Palladian elegance of Christ Church. Already some of the leading Quaker families had moved so far from their plainer country brethren that they began to drift over to the more fashionable Church of England. The cultural traditions of early Pennsylvania, it is clear, were in constant flux, forever forming new combinations, new patterns, in the prevailing atmosphere of social freedom and economic plenty. The variety and interrelations of these traditions give early Pennsylvania culture its peculiar significance in the development of American life.

It was this region primarily that Hector St. John de Crèvecoeur had in mind when he asked his famous question, "What then is the American, this new man?" and sketched out the answer which has done duty for most of us ever since. The

American, said Crèvecoeur, is the product of a "promiscuous breed" of "English, Scotch, Irish, French, Dutch, Germans, and Swedes." Settling in the New World, he leaves behind him "all his ancient prejudices and manners [and] receives new ones from the new mode of life he has embraced, the new government he obeys, and the new rank he holds." Here, says Crèvecoeur, "individuals of all nations are melted into a new race of men, whose labors and posterity will one day cause great changes in the world." The prophecy in Crèvecoeur's last words has unquestionably come true, but his account of the process by which his American, "this new man," was created is too simple.

The familiar image of the melting pot seems to imply "a giant caldron in which foreigners are boiled down into a colorless mass—as insipid as any stew." Clearly that is not an accurate image of early Pennsylvania. To be sure, some groups melted. The Welsh apparently did. So did the Dutch in Germantown and the Swedes along the Delaware. But the Germans, by and large, did not. Indeed they seem to have become self-consciously German for the first time in Pennsylvania: "the impact of American life," says Caroline Ware, "tends to accentuate rather than to obliterate group consciousness" among immigrants. Some Philadelphia Quakers became Episcopalians, but the great majority did not; and there was never any *rapprochement* between the Quakers of the east and the Scotch-Irish Presbyterians of the west. Indeed, the political history of colonial Pennsylvania is a story of continuous struggle, not primarily between social classes or economic groups, but among cultural and religious blocs. Not assimilation but what might be called "selective interaction" was the rule. It seems likely, for example, that the plain dress and the plain architecture of the Amish—or at least some elements thereof—were not brought to America by the immigrants, but were borrowed, once they had arrived, from the broadbrim hat, the plain bonnet, and plain meetinghouse of the Quakers. By way of return, the Pennsylvania Dutchman put scrapple and sticky cinnamon buns on Quaker City breakfast tables. It has even been suggested that we owe apple pie to the Pennsylvania Dutch, though as a New Englander, I shall require further evidence before I can accept *that* revolutionary thesis. In any case, this process of selective borrowing seems to be how American civilization was created, and there is no better laboratory in which to observe it at work than early Pennsylvania.

My final observation takes me from the popular culture of bonnets and scrapple back to the level of "high culture." It is fairly well known that from about 1740 to the end of the eighteenth century Philadelphia was the intellectual and cultural capital of North America. In science, in medicine, in humanitarianism, in music and drama and *belles lettres* its pre-eminence was unquestioned. How shall we explain this remarkable quick maturing in the youngest of the colonial towns? Not simply, I submit, on the ground that it was the largest and most prosperous city in the American colonies. I for one have never been convinced that high culture is a function of a high rate of income. Nor can we attribute it *all* to that displaced Bostonian, Benjamin Franklin. No, I think we shall find the source of colonial Philadelphia's flowering in the richness, the variety, and above all, in the creative interaction of the elements in its cultural hinterland.

There is nothing in Benjamin West's idyllic painting of Penn and the Indians that foreshadows the Philadelphia of Franklin and Rittenhouse, of Benjamin Rush and Charles Brockden Brown, of the American Philosophical Society and the

Pennsylvania Hospital and the College of Philadelphia. But William Penn, it should be clear by now, was more than a benign dispenser of peace and yard goods to the Indians. By opening the doors of Pennsylvania to people of every nation and every religion, he established a situation of cultural pluralism and thereby created the conditions for cultural growth. And the atmosphere was freedom.

31. Regeneration Through Violence

Richard Slotkin

Unlike Professor Tolles, Richard Slotkin (b. 1942), who teaches in the English department at Wesleyan University, falls within the traditional mold of Frederick Jackson Turner in that he sees in the frontier an explanation of an emerging American identity. But Professor Slotkin's observations are very different from those of Turner's. Turner, as the premier historian of the American West, wrote often about the free land frontier separating "savagery" from "civilization." Turner's backcountry was the actual source of rugged individualism and democratic institutions in the evolving American experience. But to Slotkin, the Indians in the wilderness were essential to the formation of the myth of an American as opposed to a European type, a myth which even to this day is a central part of the lore of historical reality. Among the first generation of settlers, establishing their "Englishness" was all important, as personified in the captivity narratives. In time that literary convention gave way to a new myth-hero, that of the hardy hunter and farmer (the Daniel Boone type) who lived in close harmony with nature and the land, but who was always ready to defend his freedom against hostile and sinister (Indian-like) influences.

Slotkin suggests that a sense of national character or culture is nothing more than myth presented as reality. His concern is with the origin and use of myth in describing the process by which Englishmen in America established a sense of unique identity. All important to this process was the Indian as a negative reference type. By the Revolution the image among the white settlers had become that of the hunter and farmer living in republican simplicity and virtue, suspended between the "brute savagery" of the Indian and the vice and corruption of the European.

If Slotkin is correct, then how might the drift in literary conventions help to explain the timing of the American Revolution? Was a sense of unique identity essential to the separation from Great Britain? How can we be sure that anyone believed the myth outside of literary circles?

The mythology of a nation is the intelligible mask of that enigma called the "national character." Through myths the psychology and world view of our cultural ancestors are transmitted to modern descendants, in such a way and with

Source: From Richard Slotkin, *Regeneration Through Violence: The Mythology of the American Frontier, 1600–1860* (Middletown, Conn.: Wesleyan University Press, 1973), pp. 3–5, 6–9, 14–23. Footnotes omitted. Copyright © 1973 by Richard Slotkin. Reprinted by permission of Wesleyan University Press.

such power that our perception of contemporary reality and our ability to function in the world are directly, often tragically affected.

American attitudes toward the idea of a national mythology have been peculiarly ambivalent. There is a strong antimythological stream in our culture, deriving from the utopian ideals of certain of the original colonists and of the revolutionary generation, which asserts that this New World is to be liberated from the dead hand of the past and become the scene of a new departure in human affairs. Nonetheless, we have continually felt the need for the sense of coherence and direction in history that myths give to those who believe in them. The poets of the early years of the republic—taught, as part of their classical education, that national mythologies are embodied in literature and begin with national epics in the manner of Homer—attempted to fabricate an "American epic" that would mark the beginning of a national mythology, providing a context for all works to come after. Their concept of myth was essentially artificial and typically American: they believed, in effect, that a mythology could be put together on the ground, like the governments of frontier communities or the national Constitution, either by specialists or by the spontaneous awakening of the popular genius. Like the Constitution, such myth-epics would reflect the most progressive ideas of American man, emphasizing the rule of reason in nature and in human affairs, casting aside all inherited traditions, superstitions, and spurious values of the past. The freedom and power of man were to be asserted against the ideas of necessity, of historical determinism, of the inheritance of guilt and original sin. From Barlow's *Columbiad* and Dwight's *Greenfield Hill* in the late eighteenth century, through Whitman's "Song of Myself" and Melville's *Moby-Dick* in the nineteenth, to Hart Crane's *The Bridge* and Williams's *Paterson* or the "great American novel" in the twentieth, American writers have attempted the Homeric task of providing, through epic poetry or epic fiction, a starting point for a new, uniquely American mythology. Even scholarly critics who address themselves to the problem of the "myth of America" have a marked tendency to engage in the manufacture of the myth they pretend to analyze in an attempt to reshape the character of their people or to justify some preconceived or inherited notion of American uniqueness. Such critics are themselves a part of this national phenomenon of myth-consciousness, this continual preoccupation with the necessity of defining or creating a national identity, a character for us to live in the world.

Works like the *Columbiad* and *The Bridge,* whatever their artistic merit, failed (at least in their authors' lifetimes) to achieve that quasi-religious power throughout the whole of a culture that is the characteristic attribute of true myth. The premises of such works do not take into account the facts that myth-making is a primary attribute of the human mind and that the process of mythogenesis in a culture is one of continuous activity rather than dramatic stops and starts. True myths are generated on a subliterary level by the historical experience of a people and thus constitute part of that inner reality which the work of the artist draws on, illuminates, and explains. In American mythogenesis the founding fathers were not those eighteenth-century gentlemen who composed a nation at Philadelphia. Rather, they were those who (to paraphrase Faulkner's *Absalom, Absalom!*) tore violently a nation from the implacable and opulent wilderness— the rogues, adventurers, and land-boomers; the Indian fighters, traders, missionaries, explorers, and hunters who killed and were killed until they had mastered the wilderness; the settlers who came after, suffering hardship and

Indian warfare for the sake of a sacred mission or a simple desire for land; and the Indians themselves, both as they were and as they appeared to the settlers, for whom they were the special demonic personification of the American wilderness. Their concerns, their hopes, their terrors, their violence, and their justifications of themselves, as expressed in literature, are the foundation stones of the mythology that informs our history.

The failure of writers and critics to recognize and deal with the real mythological heritage of their time and people has consequences that go beyond the success or failure of their literary works. A people unaware of its myths is likely to continue living by them, though the world around that people may change and demand changes in their psychology, their world view, their ethics, and their institutions. The antimythologists of the American Age of Reason believed in the imminence of a rational republic of yeomen farmers and enlightened leaders, living amicably in the light of natural law and the Constitution. They were thereby left unprepared when the Jeffersonian republic was overcome by the Jacksonian Democracy of the western man-on-the-make, the speculator, and the wildcat banker; when racist irrationalism and a falsely conceived economics prolonged and intensified slavery in the teeth of American democratic idealism; and when men like Davy Crockett became national heroes by defining national aspiration in terms of so many bears destroyed, so much land preempted, so many trees hacked down, so many Indians and Mexicans dead in the dust.

The voluminous reports of presidential commissions on violence, racism, and civil disorder have recently begun to say to us what artists like Melville and Faulkner had earlier prophesied: that myths reach out of the past to cripple, incapacitate, or strike down the living. It is by now a commonplace that our adherence to the "myth of the frontier"—the conception of America as a wide-open land of unlimited opportunity for the strong, ambitious, self-reliant individual to thrust his way to the top—has blinded us to the consequences of the industrial and urban revolutions and to the need for social reform and a new concept of individual and communal welfare. Nor is it by a far-fetched association that the murderous violence that has characterized recent political life has been linked by poets and news commentators alike to the "frontier psychology" of our recent past and our long heritage. The first colonists saw in America an opportunity to regenerate their fortunes, their spirits, and the power of their church and nation; but the means to that regeneration ultimately became the means of violence, and the myth of regeneration through violence became the structuring metaphor of the American experience. . . .

MYTHOGENESIS

A mythology is a complex of narratives that dramatizes the world vision and historical sense of a people or culture, reducing centuries of experience into a constellation of compelling metaphors. The narrative action of the myth-tale recapitulates that people's experience in their land, rehearses their visions of that experience in its relation to their gods and the cosmos, and reduces both experience and vision to a paradigm. Reference to that myth or to things associated with it—as in religious ritual—evokes in the people the sense of life inherent in the myth and all but compels belief in the vision of reality and divinity implicit in it. The believer's response to his myth is essentially nonrational and religious: he recognizes in the myth his own features and experience, the life and appearance of his ancestors, and the faces of the gods who rule his universe, and he feels that the myth has put him in intimate contact with the ultimate powers which shape all of life. Thus myth can be seen as an intellectual or artistic construct that bridges the gap between the world of the mind and the world of affairs, between dream and reality, between impulse or desire and action. It draws on the content of individual and collective memory, structures it, and develops from it imperatives for belief and action.

The ultimate source of myth is the human mind itself, for man is essentially a myth-making animal. He naturally seeks to understand his world in order to control it, and his first act in compassing this end is an act of the mind or imagination. On the basis of limited, finite experience, he creates a hypothetical vision of a universal, infinite order and imposes that hypothesis on his perception of the phenomena of nature and his own behavior. He tests his vision by acting in accordance with the principles of behavior that seem to be demanded by reality as he envisions it. Insofar as that behavior is consistent with the universal order, it will seem to prosper him and acquire the name of virtue. Aside from its function as a guide to behavior, his vision is regarded as a source of power, since it tells him how to propitiate and control the forces that order the world. Thus myth-visions, which are generated by the mind, ultimately affect both man's perception or reality and his actions. Myth describes a process, credible to its audience, by which knowledge is transformed into power; it provides a scenario or prescription for action, defining and limiting the possibility for human response to the universe.

In order to understand the process of myth-making in America and to establish criteria by which we can discover and define both the nature of the "American myth" and the manner and time of its emergence, we must begin by examining the state of mind that transforms experience, perception, and narration into the materials of a myth. Philip Wheelwright calls this state of mind the "mythopoeic mode of consciousness" and finds it present in the psychology of both the myth-making artist and the artist's people—his audience. The mythopoeic mode of consciousness comprehends the world through a process of thought- and perception-association, a process of reasoning-by-metaphor in which direct statement and logical analysis are replaced by figurative or poetic statement: the sudden, nonlogical perception and expression of "an objective relation between parts of reality, or between objective and subjective realities." The nature of the mythopoeic perception, in both maker and audience, is mystical and religious, drawing heavily on the unconscious and the deepest levels of the psyche, defining relationships between human and divine things, between temporalities and ultimates.

> There is a strong tendency of the different experiential elements to blend and fuse in a non-logical way. And not only that, but the self-hood of the observer tends to blend with them; that is to say he becomes a full participant and not a mere observer. Finally, there is a blending, or partial blending, of worshipper and sacred objects and ceremonial acts with certain transcendent Presences.

Myth-making, by this definition, is simultaneously a psychological and a social activity. The myth is articulated by individual artists and has its effect on the mind of each individual participant, but its function is to reconcile and unite these individualities to a collective identity. A myth that ceases to evoke this religious response, this sense of total identification and collective participation, ceases to *function* as a myth; a tale that, through the course of several generations—or even several retellings within one generation—acquires this kind of evocative power has evolved into myth.

The mythopoeic mode of consciousness is dependent on—but distinct from—the myth-artifact, which is the actual tale or some sacred image or object connected with the myth-narrative. The artifact symbolically embodies the mythopoeic perception and makes it concrete and communicable. The legends and stories we commonly call myths are simply the artifacts of the myth, and they retain their mythic powers only so long as they can continue to evoke in the minds of succeeding generations a vision analogous in its compelling power to that of the original mythopoeic perception. The myth-artist, priest, or fabulist uses the artifacts of myth to evoke the "sense" of the myth and its complex of affirmations in the audience. He may use these artifacts in two ways—either deliberately, in an effort to make propaganda for his cause, or unconsciously, under the compelling association of perceived event and inherited mythology.

As artifacts, myths appear to be built of three basic structural elements: a protagonist or hero, with whom the human audience is presumed to identify in some way; a universe in which the hero may act, which is presumably a reflection of the audience's conception of the world and the gods; and a narrative, in which the interaction of hero and universe is described. Hero and universe may be readily abstracted as "images," which may in turn be evocative enough to become equated in our minds with the whole of the myth itself. The narrative as a whole is more difficult to abstract, since its action defines (explicitly and implicitly) the relationship of hero to universe and of man to God—and so establishes the laws of cause and effect, of natural process, and of morality. It is the narrative which gives the images life by giving them a mode of interaction.

Images of the hero and the universe are devices that enable us to identify with (and thus enter) the world of the myth, and these may change fairly rapidly to accommodate new perceptions or requirements of the myth-makers and their audience. This is certainly the case with American mythology, in which (as Henry Nash Smith shows in *Virgin Land*) the image of the wilderness east of the Mississippi changes from "desert" to "Garden" in a century and a half, while that of the Great Plains exhibits a similar change in less than half that time—from its purchase in 1803 to the realization of its economic potential before the Civil War. However, while the images may readily exhibit changes in response to the play of social and psychological forces, the narrative or narratives which relate them to each other have or acquire a certain fixity of form. Their structure and character may be more clearly articulated through the passage of time and the operation of historical forces on the mind of the audience, but their essential nature remains substantially the same. Only truly radical alterations of the images of hero and universe effect significant changes at the narrative structural level of the myth, for such changes (by definition) reflect a fundamental alteration of the culture's conception of the relationship of man to the universe, a revolution in world view, cosmology, historical and moral theory, and self-concept. Hence such changes may be seen as marking the point at which a new epoch of cultural history or perhaps even a new culture can be said to begin. . . .

NATIONAL MYTHOLOGY: A SUMMARY VIEW

The universal archetype is essential to myth, since all myth, to be credible, must relate the problems and aspirations of particular cultures to the fundamental conditions of human existence and human psychology. But the viability of myth also depends upon the applicability of its particular terms and metaphors to the peculiar conditions of history and environment that dominate the life of a particular people. This principle of distinction is implied in Joseph Campbell's definition of myth as "traditional metaphor addressed to ultimate questions." The ultimate, archetypal questions of human existence are spoken to by the myth; but the success of the myth in answering these questions for a people depends upon the creation of a distinct cultural tradition in the selection and use of metaphor. It is in their development of traditional metaphors (and the narratives that express them) that the mythologies of particular cultures move from archetypal paradigms to the creation of acculturated, even idiosyncratic myth-metaphors.

In this process of traditionalization it is the artifact of myth—the narrative—that exhibits change and development. Thus it is in this stage that the nature of the artifact, the medium through which the mythic perception is transmitted, becomes of crucial importance. In addition, it is at this stage that the role of the artist, the intelligent manipulator of media and artifacts, becomes important as a means of controlling and directing the development of myth, limiting or augmenting its power to induce the mythopoeic affirmation in its audience. It is at this stage that various cultures move away from the universal vision of the archetype toward some particular interpretation of the archetypal narrative that will reflect their characteristic approach to life. It is at this point that the Christian variant of the myth-narrative of the dead-and-resurrected god diverges from the Norse or the Dionysian, and it is here that the farming culture's version of the sacred marriage varies from that of the hunting or the industrial culture. Hence it is at this point that myth provides a useful tool for the analysis of the particularity of a human culture.

The Europeans who settled the New World possessed at the time of their arrival a mythology derived from the cultural history of their home countries and responsive to the psychological and social needs of their old culture. Their new circumstances forced new perspectives, new self-concepts, and new world concepts on the colonists and made them see their cultural heritage from angles of vision that noncolonists would find peculiar. The internal tension between the Moira and Themis elements in their European mythologies (and the psychological tension that is the source of this myth-duality) found an objective correlative in the racial, religious, and cultural opposition of the American Indians and colonial Christians. This racial-cultural conflict pointed up and intensified the emotional difficulties attendant on the colonists' attempt to adjust to life in the wilderness. The picture was further complicated for them by the political and religious demands made on them by those who remained in Europe, as well as by the colonists' own need to affirm—for themselves and for the home folks—that they had not deserted European civilization for American savagery.

Added together, these conditions ensured that the colonists would be preoccupied with defining, for themselves and for others, the precise nature of their constantly changing relationship to the wilderness. This made for a highly self-conscious literature with a tendency toward polemic and apology, in which the colonist simultaneously argued the firmness and stability of his European character and (paradoxically) the superiority of his new American land and mode of life to all things European. The fact that the colonial experience began in the age of the printing press gave this kind of literature wide currency. The very nature of print made it the perfect medium for this sort of literature, allowing the writer to draw on a vast vocabulary of literary conventions in making his case for America.

This set of circumstances created a pattern of evolution for the American myth that is somewhat different from the pattern suggested by Wheelwright for primitive cultures. The colonists whose writings form the body of the mythology were working in a literary tradition and a medium of communication that had been highly structured and conventionalized through centuries of European practice. The primary sources from the New World, written by early explorer-conquerors, are couched in the imagery of this romantic European mythology and seem at this distance highly artificial and literary. References to images of the Golden Age, as depicted by Greek and Latin poets, abound both in the writings of court and church historians and in the accounts by the explorers themselves. Howard Mumford Jones notes that Columbus's first description of the New World is colored by the traditional imagery of the earthly paradise:

This island and all others are very fertile to a limitless degree. . . . In it there are many harbours on the coast of the sea, beyond comparison with others which I know in Christendom, and many rivers, good and large, which is marvellous. Its lands are high, and there are in it very many sierras and very lofty mountains, beyond comparison with the island of Teneriffe. All are most beautiful, of a thousand shapes, and all are accessible and filled with trees of a thousand kinds and tall, and they seem to touch the sky. And I am told that they never lose their foliage, as I can understand, for I saw them as green and lovely as they are in Spain in May, and some of them were flowering, some bearing fruit, and some in another stage, according to their nature. And the nightingale was singing, and other birds of a thousand kinds. . . . In it are marvellous pine groves, and there are very large tracts of cultivable lands, and there is honey, and there are birds of many kinds, and fruits in great diversity. In the interior are mines of metal. The people of this island . . . go naked. . . . They never refuse anything which they possess, if it be asked of them; on the contrary they invite anyone to share it, and display so much love as if they would give their hearts. . . . And they do not know any creed, and are not idolators; only they believe that power and good are in the heavens. . . .

As Jones notes, the description is generalized, abstracted, and vague to a fault; and the nightingales are either pure fiction or the error of a perception dominated by conventional imagery, since no such birds exist in the New World. The accounts of the conquest of Mexico written by Cortés, Gómara, and Díaz del Castillo reflect the strong influence of secular chivalric romances. Díaz's Indians, viewing the ruins of Mexico City, speak "in much the same way that we would say: 'Here stood Troy.'"

The later myth-literature of the Colonial and early national periods was intended as a kind of consummatory myth-making: an attempt by artful moderns to recapture the unsophisticated, passionate, believing spirit of the primitive "natural" man. In so doing, these later writers (Cooper, Longfellow, Melville, and others) reached back to the only sources of truly primary American myth— the myths of the Indian aborigines and the personal narratives of the unsophisticated, almost primitive colonials (and their slicker, sensationalistic successors of the popular press) who fabricated a mythology out of their real and imagined experiences with the Indians. The story of the evolution of an American mythology is, in large measure, the story of our too-slow awakening to the significance of the American Indian in the universal scheme of things generally and in our (or his) American world in particular. As Kenneth Rexroth says:

> Our memory of the Indians connects us with the soil and the waters and the nonhuman life about us. They take for us the place of nymphs and satyrs and dryads—the spirits of the places. They are our ecological link with our biota—the organic environment which we strive to repudiate and destroy. . . . the flooding tide, full of turmoil and whirlpools, of the unconscious, or the id, or the "dark forces of the blood"—the actual, savage environment that reason and order and humane relationships can penetrate but cannot control.

Thus the evolution of the American myth was a synthetic process of reconciling the romantic-conventional myths of Europe to American experience—a process which, by an almost revolutionary turn, became an analytical attempt to destroy or cut through the conventionalized mythology to get back to the primary source of blood-knowledge of the wilderness, the "Indian" mind, the basic, Moiratic, myth-generating psychology of man. Yet our only sources of primary knowledge about the Indian mind (aside from a few incompetent studies of Indian ritual and legendry by missionaries) were works by those who regularly battled the Indians or by those who stayed with them as war captives or adopted tribesmen. These were the people who lived near or among the Indians, learning their modes of thought and behavior so well that they could successfully fight them or even integrate themselves into Indian society. Even at the source of the American myth there lies the fatal opposition, the hostility between two worlds, two races, two realms of thought and feeling.

"The land was ours before we were the land's," said Robert Frost. The process by which we came to feel an emotional title to the land was charged with a passionate and aspiring violence, and "the deed of gift was many deeds of war." Because of the nature of myth and the myth-making process, it is a significant comment on our characteristic attitudes toward ourselves, our culture, our racial subgroupings, and our land that tales of strife between native Americans and interlopers, between dark races and light, became the basis of our mythology and that the Indian fighter and hunter emerged as the first of our national heroes. In order to understand the complex and many-leveled influence of our history on our mythology, and of mythology on our culture, we must understand the nature of the peculiar forces that shaped mythology in America.

Generally speaking, the basic factors in the physical and psychological situation of the colonists were the wildness of the land, its blending of unmitigated harshness and tremendous potential fertility; the absence of strong European cultures on the borders; and the eternal presence of the native people of the woods, dark of skin and seemingly dark of mind, mysterious, bloody, cruel, "devil-worshipping." To these must be added the sense of exile—the psychological anxieties attendant on the tearing up of home roots for wide wandering outward in space and, apparently, backward in time. The sense of loss was heightened by the inevitable lapsing of communication with the homeland, the divergence of colonial from homeland historical experience, and the rise of new generations more acculturated or acclimated to the wilderness, less like the remembered grandparents in the fixed image of Europe. Exploration of new lands was one necessity imposed on them; fighting Indians, enduring captivity among them, and attempting to convert or enslave them were others. All emigrants shared the anxious sense that they had been, willingly or unwillingly, exiled from their true homes in the motherlands of Europe; all faced the problem of justifying their emigration to more stable folk at home, of trying to sell them either actual land or the idea of a colony. All felt impelled to maintain traditions of religious order and social custom in the face of the psychological terrors of the wilderness. Later, the sons of these emigrants strove to justify their title to the land they took for their own.

Around each of these problems a body of literature with distinct formal conventions gathered: narratives of discovery, narratives of Indian war and captivity, sermons, and colonization and anticolonization tracts. These accounts purport to be first- or second-hand reports of day-to-day events and topography in the new world. The authors usually had ulterior motives in publishing them—a desire to explain or justify, through imaginative reconstruction of events, a course of action they had taken or their right to possess the land; or simply an attempt to persuade potential European settlers of the beauties and wealth of the strange new world. In any case, their appeal to the reader was carried by the metaphors that, implicitly or explicitly, informed their accounts. At the outset these metaphors were drawn from a purely European context, either the literature of the classical age and medieval and Renaissance romances, or the religious and political thought of the Reformation. Gradually these metaphors, constantly adjusted to suit American conditions, began to metamorphose, to take on some of the shape and coloration of the colonists' experience of America and her landscape.

As American society evolved through years of historical experience, the differentiated literary forms were gradually drawn together by writers who more or less deliberately sought to create a unified and compelling vision of the total American experience—an American myth. This process of reintegration was logically inevitable. The more a writer or preacher understood of the American environment, the less he could simplify or compartmentalize his approach to analyzing it. One could not discuss exploration, for example, without mentioning the chance of Indian attack and captivity. One could not maintain religious discipline by purely theological argument or pure civic force, if parishioners were willing and capable of seeking their fortune by itinerating on the edges of the wilderness; so sermons merged with accounts of frontier hardship. Any work capable of attaining that unified and compelling vision of the whole American experience would have to contain in its terms—narrative, character, imagery, values—the sum total of all these experiences reduced to as basic and universal archetype of all the colonists' experiences, the one presenting the most vital psychological difficulties, and present its vision in terms appropriate to the historical experience of a wilderness people.

Printed literature has been from the first the most important vehicle of myth in America, which sets it apart from the mythologies of the past. The colonies were founded in an age of printing, in large part by Puritans, who were much inclined toward the writing and printing of books and pamphlets and the creating of elaborate metaphors proving the righteousness of their proceedings. Since Americans turned readily to the printed word for the expression and the resolution of doubts, of problems of faith, of anxiety and aspiration, literature became the primary vehicle for the communication of mythic material, with the briefest of gaps between the inception of an oral legend and its being fixed in the public print. How this occurred is one of the chief issues to be dealt with in this study. For the student of the historical development of America as a culture, the visibility of the several stages in the evolution of "traditional metaphors addressed to ultimate questions" is an invaluable aid. It also presents several difficulties. In order for us to examine myth, we must rely on artifacts which are translations of the mythopoeic perception of reality. A tale handed down in the oral tradition from generation to generation presents, if examined at a late period, a distorted and adulterated image of the original. As a vehicle of myth, literature enjoys the advantage of formal permanence. The process of writing, however, necessitates a certain distortive distancing between the author and his experience—a distortion compounded where the author has the experience only at second hand or where he attempts to recall it after the passage of many years. Furthermore, myth as literature is subject to the movements of the literary marketplace. Authors and publishers interested in book sales might deliberately shape their narratives to suit current fashion; moreover, writers desiring a wide reputation shaped their narratives to English audiences as much as, or more than, to American audiences, introducing extraneous characterizations of their material which have little to do with the American colonists' attempts to understand their situation in their own terms.

On the whole, the development of narrative literature in the first two hundred and fifty years of American history is one of the best guides to the process by which the problems and preoccupations of the colonists became transformed into "visions which compel belief" in a civilization called America. Repetition is the essence of this process. Certain instances of experience consistently recurred in each colony over many generations; translated into literature, these experiences became stories which recurred in the press with rhythmic persistence. At first such repetition was the result of real recurrence of the experiences. The Indian war and captivity narratives, for example, grew out of the fact that many pious and literate New Englanders were continually falling into the hands of the Indians or attempted to explain their actions in battle. Once in literary form, the experience became available as a vehicle for justifying philosophical and moral values which may have been extrinsic to the initial experience but which preoccupied the minds of the reading public. Thus Cotton Mather and others wrote "improvements" of the captivity narratives and used them in jeremiads and revival sermons. Through repeated appearances and recastings in the literary marketplace, a narrative which proved viable as a bestseller or a vehicle for religious or commercial persuasions would be imitated by more or less professional writers (where such existed) or those emulous of literary or ecclesiastical reputation. Thus the experience would be reduced to an imitable formula, a literary convention, a romantic version of the myth. When enough literature had been written employing the convention, it might become a sort of given between writer and audience, a set of tacit assumptions on the nature of human experience, on human and divine motivations, on moral values, and on the nature of reality. At this point the convention has some of the force of myth: the experience it portrays has become an image which automatically compels belief by a culture-wide audience in the view of reality it presents. Thus in tracing the development of the conventions of narrative literature, we are tracing the development—by accretion of symbols characteristic of cultural values—of a distinct world vision and an accompanying mythology emerging from the early experiences of Europeans in the wilderness.

The cultural anxieties and aspirations of the colonists found their most dramatic and symbolic portrayal in the accounts of the Indian wars. The Indian war was a uniquely American experience. Moreover, it pitted the English Puritan colonists against a culture that was antithetical to their own in most significant aspects. They could emphasize their Englishness by setting their civilization against Indian barbarism; they could suggest their own superiority to the home English by exalting their heroism in battle, the peculiar danger of their circumstances, and the holy zeal for English Christian expansion with which they preached to or shot at the savages. It was within the genre of colonial Puritan writing that the first American mythology took shape—a mythology in which the hero was the captive or victim of devilish American savages and in which his (or her) heroic quest was for religious conversion and salvation. As their experience in and love for America grew, however—and as non-Puritans entered the American book-printing trade—the early passion for remaining "non-American" (or non-Indian) became confused with the love the settlers bore the land and their desire to gain intimate knowledge of and emotional title to it. If the first American mythology portrayed the colonist as a captive or a destroyer of Indians, the subsequent acculturated versions of the myth showed him growing closer to the Indian and the wild land. New versions of the hero emerged, characters whose role was that of mediating between civilization and savagery, white and red. The yeoman farmer was one of these types, as were the explorer or surveyor and, later, the naturalist.

But it was the figure of Daniel Boone, the solitary, Indian-like hunter of the deep woods, that became the most significant, most emotionally compelling myth-hero of the early republic. The other myth-figures are reflections or variations of this basic type. In numerous popular narratives devoted to Boone's career, the experience of America that first appears in the captivity and Indian war narratives is reduced to a paradigm. The values, beliefs, and experience of life for which the captives and Indian-killers or -converters had spoken were concentrated in this new figure and in the narratives that define his ways of relating to the cosmos. Moreover, these older values were compounded with the newer, more acclimated view of America symbolized by the farmer and the naturalist or surveyor. The figure and the myth-narrative that emerged from the early Boone literature became archetypal for the American literature which followed: an American hero is the lover of the spirit of the wilderness, and his acts of love and sacred affirmation are acts of violence against that spirit and her avatars.

In its structure this myth-narrative follows a variation of the initiation into a new life or a higher state of being or manhood that is a myth-theme as old as mankind. The boy's coming of age, the fall, the Christian conversion, and the success myth (the American dream of perpetual self-improvement and -transcendence) are variations of the basic theme. Usually the experience of initiation is portrayed as an individual accomplishment, an experience of life which each man must come to in his turn. In America, however, the experience of initiation into a new life was shared by all members of colonial society simultaneously during a certain, relatively brief period of time. The pivotal position of the Indian war narratives and John Filson's legend of Boone's "baptism by combat" in the development of American mythology and literature is explained by their applicability to the universal problem of the colonial period: the problem of acculturation, of adjusting the mores and world view of one's native culture to the requirements of life in an alien environment. The English colonists had to remake their values, their concepts of law and religion, and their images of their role and place in the universe in order to survive in the wilderness. This necessity was difficult to acknowledge, since the colonists felt it their duty to remain loyal to their English heritage. It was far easier to define their cultural identity by negative means, through attacking or condemning alien elements in their society, by casting our heretics like Roger Williams and John Underhill, whose ideas were strange or whose behavior smacked of an Indian-like lack of orthodox discipline. The Indian wars, in which culture was pitted against culture, afforded a perfect opportunity for this sort of definition by repudiation. In opposing the Indian culture, the Puritan symbolically affirmed his Englishness. Even as social and religious issues grew complex and clouded, as men who had been orthodox in England grew heretical in America, as men grew unsure about whether the true church was presbyterian or congregational, antinomian or orthodox, English or universal or American, there remained a fundamental simplicity in the opposition between Indian and settler.

Writers of the Indian war narratives, a circle which included both actual participants and clerical outsiders like the Mathers, generally composed their accounts as if their audience's belief in certain concepts of morality and theology and the frontier could be taken for granted. Their works were unconscious experiments, designed to test the power of certain ideas of human experience (and in particular the American experience) to produce conviction in an audience. Revival preachers employed Indian war tales as a tool for arousing pious anxiety in their congregations; land speculators used them as advertising ploys; representatives of social, religious, and political factions used them to justify their particular conceptions of the truth. Frontiersmen used them to mock the ways of town-bred tenderfeet; town-bred preachers used them in chastising the restless indiscipline of frontier life.

Any experiment was successful to the extent that its assumptions about life, America, Indian, God, and the wilderness coincided with those of its particular audience. But during the first centuries of its existence, colonial society was fragmented into hostile cultural enclaves and rival governments, each speaking for separated and isolated fragments of that society. Even after the Revolution, sectional and local differences persisted and to some degree intensified. This heterogeneity, coupled with the constant pressure of European immigration and expansive emigration to the frontier made for a constant agitation of issues, values, and ideas. In this fluid culture, the success of any given attempt at myth-making was usually brief, until Filson's first study of Daniel Boone appeared in 1784. This figure caught and held the national attention for half a century, despite varying sectional evaluations of the moral and social character of the frontier hero.

32. The Genesis of an "American" Nationalism

Max Savelle

Max Savelle (b. 1896), emeritus professor of history at the University of
Washington, has concluded that a sense of national identity existed in America
by the 1750s, but the sources were different from those suggested by Professor
Slotkin. The new nationalism emanated from various factors, including improved
intercolonial communications and the existence of a hated enemy to the north—
French Canada. Anti-Catholicism and the fear of popery helped to unite the
colonists in their hatred of the French; the same feelings also helped to foster
provincial support for the home government's struggle to wrest Canada from
French control during the American phase (the French and Indian War) of the
international Seven Years' War (1755–1763). What the provincials learned,
according to Professor Savelle, from this international war for empire was that
they could unite, fight together, and defeat a common European enemy.
American settlers fought with ability, moreover, even though British regular
officers often showed contempt for American military prowess.

Obviously, a developing sense of national pride had serious implications for
British-American imperial relationships, once the French were no longer the
common enemy. Yet how do we reconcile the diverse findings of Tolles, Slotkin,
and Savelle? How do we explain the seeming Europeanization of late provincial
society in the context of an emerging American identity? Finding an answer to
that question may be a key to understanding the national experience of
postrevolutionary America and the insecurity citizens of the republic felt in
creating a new nation.

A common loyalty to a common American purpose and ideal was beginning to
emerge among the Americans even before 1750. And it was this new American
self-consciousness in all things, this new loyalty to America, that was to give the
Americans an intellectual and emotional sense of unity of purpose and ideal. It
was the conflict with the mother country over the question of taxation, to be sure,
that galvanized this American self-consciousness into dramatic literary expression
and political action; but its beginnings lie farther back than that: its roots are
deeply embedded in the earliest American experience.

The people of the British colonies in America did not yet, in the year 1750,
constitute a homogeneous social entity. For the British Empire in this hemisphere

Source: From Max Savelle, *Seeds of Liberty: The Genesis of the American Mind* (Seattle:
University of Washington Press, 1948), pp. 564–581. Footnotes omitted. Reprinted by permission of
Max Savelle and the University of Washington Press.

484 / A "NEW" AMERICAN CULTURE AND IDENTITY

was composed of a congeries of disparate settlements and societies from the primitive trading posts on the shores of Hudson Bay and British Guiana to the highly sophisticated societies of New York, Virginia, or Jamaica. Yet thirteen of the twenty-odd colonies were passing, more or less consciously, through a process that was at once drawing them together toward homogeneity and distinguishing them, as a single unit, from all the others. For these thirteen, located along the eastern seaboard of the continent, were being subtly fused by a number of forces that were daily becoming more powerful.

Among these forces were the influences exerted by increased commercial, social, and intellectual intercourse between colonies. As roads from one colony to another appeared, finally binding them together on one long string from Portsmouth to Savannah, the spreading consciousness of a common cultural tradition could not fail to grow. This development seems to have been an almost inevitable consequence of the expansion of populations that brought the people of one colony to rubbing elbows with the people of the next. As the means of communication were expanded and improved, travel increased; and the traveler from Boston in Charleston, for example, found that the citizens of the two places had much in common. Travel and writing led to intercolonial marriages; and as the number of colleges increased and their fame spread, more and more young men crossed intercolonial boundaries in quest of education. These intellectual and social and economic forces making for closer association were well under way by the middle of the century.

One of the most obvious of these forces was the binding effect of intercolonial trade. And the continued growth of intercolonial economic relations gave impetus to the already well-developed consciousness of the differentness of American economic interests from those of the mother country. The appearance of an American self-consciousness in the realm of economic affairs, in fact, had had its beginning very early in the history of the colonies, and had sprung originally from the realization that their economic interests diverged, at many important points, from those of the mother country. The Navigation Acts and the Acts of Trade had been efforts to force American economic life into the imperial pattern, but they had been only partially successful; and many Americans such as Franklin had begun to question, as early as about 1750, the validity of the entire system. But the formulation of a positive feeling of economic nationalism did not really appear until the conflict with the mother country over the program, initiated about 1764, to make the old imperial system really effective. The colonies, thrown on the defensive, were forced to elaborate reasons for their opposition to the mother country, and some Americans went on beyond their economic philosophy in defense of their liberties to emotional glorifications of the economic grandeur and destiny of America as a whole or of one's own province as a separate unit. Such, for example, was the sentiment of Daniel Dulany, writing in Virginia in 1765:

> Let the manufacture of *America* be the symbol of dignity, the badge of virtue, and it will soon break the fetters of distress. A garment of linsey-woolsey, when made the distinction of real patriotism, is more honourable and attractive of respect and veneration, than all the pageantry, and the robes, and the plumes, and the diadem of an emperor without it. Let the emulation be not in the richness and variety of foreign productions, but in the improvement and perfection of our own. . . . I have in my younger days seen fine sights, and been captivated by their dazzling pomp and glittering splendor; but the sight of our representatives, all adorned in compleat dresses of their own leather, and

flax, and wool, manufactured by the art and industry of the inhabitants of *Virginia,* would excite, not the gaze of admiration, the flutter of an agitated imagination, or the momentary amusement of a transient scene, but a calm, solid, heart-felt delight. Such a sight would give me more pleasure than the most splendid and magnificent spectacle the most exquisite taste ever painted, the richest fancy ever imagined, realized to the view . . . as much more pleasure as a good mind would receive from the contemplation of virtue, than of elegance; of the spirit of patriotism, than the ostentation of opulence.

The solid intellectual bases for an American national feeling were being laid in the 1740's and 1750's. One of the greatest of the agencies for such a development was the post-office, of which, significantly enough, Benjamin Franklin became the head in 1753. Franklin had actively sought the office of Deputy Postmaster-General for America, partly because he thought it might be remunerative, but also, as he said in his letter to Peter Collinson, because he felt sure the post-office could be made an effective agency for the development of an active intercolonial intellectual exchange. He believed the work of the Philosophical Society would be extended by it, and that Philadelphia might well become the cultural capital of America.

There were probably not many men in America who saw the intellectual maturity of America as Franklin saw it in 1743, or believed that the colonies were culturally so mature. Yet the organization and the success and permanence of the American Philosophical Society may be taken, perhaps, as evidence that in 1743 and the years following there was enough and sufficiently widespread intercolonial interest in intellectual matters to permit of this year being used as the marker of the birth of an American cultural self-consciousness. For the exchange of ideas and associations that resulted must have given considerable impetus to the growth of a sense of a common American intellectual life.

Even if Franklin had been alone in his effort to draw the colonies together culturally, as he was not, his own sponsoring of an intercolonial cultural development was a significant manifestation of his early "Americanism"; and if in 1743 he was giving form to an American cultural life, twenty years later he was beginning to see in America the very heart and center of the culture of western civilization.

Meanwhile, a cultural self-consciousness was also appearing in other lines of literary production, one of the most notable of which was history. It is probably not without significance, and highly symptomatic of the dawning self-consciousness of the Americans, that Dr. William Douglass's *Summary, Historical and Political, of the British Settlements in North-America,* which was intended to cover the entire Anglo-American colonial area on the continent of North America, appeared between the years 1747 and 1752. The fact that it was not completed does not diminish the significance of the author's conception; for he gave the first important literary and documentary expression to an American continental self-consciousness.

One of the most important manifestations of the awakening cultural self-consciousness of the Americans was the deliberate effort of William Smith and his circle of young littérateurs and artists in Philadelphia to make for America a place in the cultural sun. All of the magazines that were launched between 1740 and 1760 show this cultural objective, in one way or another; and the *American Magazine,* published by Smith and his circle, is full of literary and historical expressions of it.

The Americans, indeed, were slowly but surely awakening to a realization of their own traditions and a sense of their own glorious future as a distinct people, in all the realms of their thinking. Already, for example, American patriots were beginning to extol the humanitarianism of America as a refuge for the poor and the oppressed, and the virtues of "The American, this new man," as the product of the melting-pot. Poor Richard expressed this popular sentiment in 1752 when he sang the praises of this country as a place

> Where the sick Stranger joys to find a Home,
> Where casual Ill, maim'd Labour, freely come;
> Those worn with Age, Infirmity or Care,
> Find Rest, Relief, and Health returning fair.
> There too the Walls of rising Schools ascend,
> For Publick Spirit still is Learning's Friend,
> Where Science, Virtue, sown with liberal Hand,
> In future Patriots shall inspire the Land.

But the love of one's country inspired by its humanitarian welcome to the poor and suffering of the world was looked upon with a jaundiced eye by those hundred-per-cent patriots who feared the possible un-American activities and influence of the foreigners on our soil. This was the sort of fear which, mixed with religious distrust, led to the passage of the Connecticut "Act Providing Relief against the evil and dangerous Designs of Foreigners and Suspected Persons"; this was the fear, also, that led William Smith to write his diatribes against the Pennsylvania Germans, and William Douglass to pour out the vials of his wrath against the Quakers in his bitter exclamation that "the pusilanimous Doctrine of not defending themselves by force against an invading Enemy is very absurd: PRO PATRIA *is not only a Law of Nations, but of Nature.*"

Even Franklin, in almost the same moment when with the popular voice of Poor Richard he was extolling the national melting-pot, could privately express his fear that the Germans might prove to be too un-American in their influence to be absorbed:

> This will in a few Years become a *German* Colony: Instead of their Learning our Lanugage, we must learn their's, or live as in a foreign country. Already the *English* begin to quit particular Neighbourhoods surrounded by *Dutch* [Germans], being made uneasy by the Disagreeableness of disonant Manners; and in Time, Numbers will probably quit the Province for the same Reason. Besides, the *Dutch* under-live, and are thereby enabled to under-work and under-sell the *English*; who are thereby extreamly incommoded, and consequently disgusted, so that there can be no cordial Affection or Unity between the two Nations.

The split in nationalistic pride between those who glorify the melting-pot and those who fear the un-American activities of foreigners whose ideals do not exactly coincide with their own is no new thing; it has apparently been one of the dialectical strains within American nationalistic feeling almost from the beginning.

The same sort of dialectical strain has also been present in the religious aspects of American patriotism. For, despite the established principle of religious toleration, the nationalistic self-consciousness of the Americans of the eighteenth century expressed itself strongly and repeatedly as committed to the dissenting Protestant way. This was especially visible in the diatribes against Roman Catholic France, but it was also visible even in the resistance of many Americans against the possibility of an expansion of Anglicanism and, most particularly, to the movement for the establishment of an Anglican bisphopric here. Jonathan Mayhew had voiced this fear in the preface to his famous sermon on unlimited submission in 1750. Twelve years later his convictions had taken on a distinctly nationalistic tinge:

> We [Britishers] are still farther distinguished and favoured of God, by having been born and bred in a *protestant* country, and a *reformed* part of the christian church; instead of a roman-catholic country, & in the errors, superstitions and idolatries of the church of Rome. For had the latter been our lot, we should probably, the most of us, have been enslaved to those delusions, and the papal tyranny to this day. And those of us, whom God should have given light and courage to cast them off, might have suffered a cruel persecution; and "for conscience towards God endured grief"; as protestants now do, even in France itself, from a pretended most polite, humane and refined, but really *barbarous* people in some respects. . . .

But Americans were favored, even above other Britons, not only on the count of religion, but also because of America's happy isolation from Europe's turmoil and her precious civil liberties:

> If we come to our own country in particular; we have here enjoyed, of late, almost all the blessings of peace, in a time of war and tumult among the nations of Europe. We have also been favoured with general health. Our invaluable civil rights and privileges are preserved to us. I do not say, that they have even been struck at, in any instance or degree—But if they have, they are not wrested from us: And may righteous heaven blast the designs, tho' not the soul or the body of that man, whoever he be amongst us, that shall have the hardiness and presumption to attack them!

The growth of something approximating a nationalistic religious outlook was accompanied by a corresponding development in concepts of education. For now, to the concept of education as a promoter of social aims, molder of preachers, disseminator of the arts and sciences, and trainer of young people in the skills required for making a living, was added an increasing weight of suggestion that education had a civic duty to perform in the training of citizens; and since the Americans were coming to have a poignant sense of their own traditions, history was thought of as being the subject most likely to inculcate the civic virtues. Thus in 1749 Cadwallader Colden wrote to Franklin:

> While you keep the great end of education in view, that is, to enable men and incline them to be more useful to mankind in general, and to their own country in particular, and at the same time to render their own life more happy, you cannot be in danger of taking wrong steps, while all of them tend to that end. . . . It is a common opinion, that the power and strength of a nation consist in its riches and money. No doubt money can do great things; but I think the power of a nation consists in the knowledge and virtue of its inhabitants, and, in proof of this, history shows us that the richest nations, abounding most in silver and gold, have been generally conquered by poor, but, in some sense, virtuous nations. If riches be not accompanied with virtue, they on that very account expose a nation to ruin, by their being a temptation for others to invade them, while luxury, the usual consequence of riches, makes them an easy prey.

Colden was using the language of nationalism and national civic virtue in education. But it must be remembered that his was a "Tory" nationalism; also that he was an aristocrat in education; and that as he grew older and more bitter over the political radicalism of the assembly party in New York, he thought of education as an instrumentality for training aristocratic leaders who would know to whom their supreme loyalty should attach. The important thing to notice here, of course, is that Colden, like so many of his American contemporaries, was feeling his way toward a clear concept of the nation, and was thinking of education as a mechanism for promoting the national civic virtues and national happiness.

Franklin believed strongly in the educational value of history, not merely for the promotion of the social ideal and the virtues of citizenship, but also for inculcation in the student of the peculiar virtues and advantages of his own people: "If the new *Universal History* were also read, it would give a connected idea of human affairs, so far as it goes, which should be followed by the best Modern histories, particularly of our mother country; then of these colonies; which should be accompanied with observations on their rise, increase, use to Great Britain, encouragements and discouragements, the means to make them flourishing, and secure their liberties."

This was written in 1749. Yet there is unquestionably present in this recommendation a consciousness of the peculiar differentness of the colonies, of their common problems, and the preciousness of their liberties. It is this idealization of the abstract qualities of one's own people that is the essence of nationalism. If this was not nationalism itself, then it was surely the psychological germ from which an American nationalism was to grow.

But it was in the face of a common enemy that the nationalistic feelings of the Americans found the freest and most intense expression in the 1750's. For at this point "Tory" feelings and "American" feelings could merge; an the approach of the Seven Years' War was unquestionably the great catalyst that precipitated the most eloquent expressions of America's nascent nationalism. This strong anti-Gallican animosity had been vocal, in fact, since the War of the Austrian Succession (King George's War) and the thrill of general exultation that ran through all the colonies over the capture of Louisbourg in 1745 by a little band of New Englanders. Poems and essays in celebration of that event were published in the newspapers of the south as well as the north; the following lines taken from a poem in the *Maryland Gazette* are typical of a number of poems like it:

And what avail'd their Demilunes,
Their Parapets, and brazen Guns,
    They were but Frenchmen still;
Their feeble Genius soon gave Place
To bold New-England's hardy Race,
    Led on by Pepp'ral's skill.

As for New England, it was beside itself; and a man so chaste in his language as Charles Chauncy was impelled to exult: "I scarce know of a Conquest, since the Days of *Joshua* and the *Judges,* wherein the Finger of God is more visible. . . . And now as the Conclusion of all, May it please the good and gracious God to over-rule this glorious Conquest to an happy Issue, the Good of our *Nation* and *Land.* . . . And may the happy Period come on, when Nation shall no more lift up Sword against Nation, nor the Alarm of War be heard on Earth."

And Nathaniel Ames poured his patriotic feelings into his almanac in the form of a prayer to the Goddess of Victory for yet greater favors:

Hail, Victory! Thy Aid we still implore,
Thy *Britain* conquers; send her Thunder o'er:
We only for her moving Castles wait;
But they, alas! have been detain'd by Fate.
Great-Britain's Forests float upon the Floods,
And dreadful Lions dwell within those Woods;
Awake their sleeping Fury, make 'em roar,
And all the Beasts on Canadensis Shore
Shall fear, and all their Native Rage forsake,
And Trembling seize those Coasts, ev'n to Quebeck. . . .
  Proud of thy special Favours heretofore,
Like Beggars once indulg'd we ask for more;
Thou know'st which Way the ridged Fates incline,
If on our Side, give one propitious Sign,
And lo Ten Thousand bold *Americans* will join,
With chearful Hearts to extirpate a Race
Of Superstitious Papists false and base.

This deep and intense fear and hatred of a common enemy, the sentiment that might be called a sense of the "Gallic peril," was expressed in many places and in many ways. It appears again and again in the newspapers and in the pamphlets, especially in the mid-century armed truce between 1748 and 1754. The French were the great enemy of all the colonies except the small, coast-bound provinces like Rhode Isand, Connecticut, New Jersey, and Delaware; and as population had expanded even farther and farther westward, the inevitability of eventual conflict had become increasingly apparent to everybody, including the French themselves. The governors of New France repeatedly warned their mother country, especially the Marquis de la Galissonnière, of the irrepressible expansiveness of the British Americans. But the French forts built along the frontier from Crown Point in the north to Fort Toulouse in the south appeared to the British colonists only the visible evidence of an aggressive French determination at least to hem them in along the seaboard. The alarmists, however, saw a greater threat than that and warned their readers that the French would reach out to the coast itself ard, it might be, one day drive the British from the Atlantic coastal plain altogether, or, worse still, reduce all the Americans to slavery. One of the easiest ways, obviously, for the French to do this, would be by alienating the "foreigners" along the frontier. The French had lately been active along the Ohio, building forts and establishing control over the Indians; since the Quakers of Pennsylvania were pacifists, it seemed to William Smith that it would be extremely easy, even what the French actually designed, to make, by way of Pennsylvania, a breach in the solid front of the English colonies.

Many Americans were in a state of deathly fear of the French and their iniquitous designs, and the sermons of the period sought to whip their audiences into a fervor of patriotic defense of American soil and liberties. Here is an example from Jonathan Mayhew:

And what horrid scene is this, which restless, roving fancy, or something of an higher nature, presents to me, and so chills my blood! Do I behold these territories of freedom, become the prey of arbitrary power? . . . Do I see the slaves of Lewis with their Indian allies, dispossessing the free-born [American] subjects of King George, of the inheritance received from their forefathers, and purchased by them at the expense of their ease, their treasure, their blood! . . . Do I see a protestant, there, stealing a look at his bible, and being tak[en] in the fact, punished like a felon! . . . Do I see all liberty, property, religion, happiness, changed, or rather transubstantiated, into slavery, poverty, superstition, wretchedness!

Freedom of property, freedom to work, freedom to worship, the free pursuit of happiness; these American freedoms were threatened by Louis XV of France, monstrous symbol of dictatorial government menacing the liberty of the world, and especially American freedom! This was an ideological war; and the forces of nationalistic emotion were called upon to defend the American-English ideal of liberty against the rapacious Juggernaut of popish authoritarianism. If there ever was a war of Anglo-American aggressive expansionism, the Seven Years' War in America was that war. Yet that did not prevent the intellectual leaders from preaching, in all sincerity of conviction, and the people from believing, that it was a holy war in the name of an ideal, the ideal of "British" (American) liberty and self-government. Samuel Davies, in Virginia, could pull out all the stops on the organ of his eloquence to stir the Virginians to patriotic self-sacrifice:

and shall these Ravages go on uncheck'd? Shall *Virginia* incur the Guilt, and the ever-lasting Shame of tamely exchanging her Liberty, her Religion, and her All, for arbitrary *Gallic* Power, and for Popish Slavery, Tyranny, and Massacre? Alas! are there none of her Children, that enjoyed all the Blessings of her Peace, that will espouse her Cause, and befriend her now in the Time of her Danger? Are *Britons* utterly degenerated by so short a Remove from their Mother-Country? Is the Spirit of Patri-otism entirely extinguished among us? And must I give thee up for lost, O my Country! and all that is included in that important Word?

And James Sterling, of Annapolis, "pathetically" urged the Maryland Assembly to patriotic action:

Let me tell you, my worthy countrymen, the eyes of your constituents are now upon you. . . . The eyes of your sister-colonies are upon you, who will be agitated by shame or rivalship to take their measures from your pattern. Assume then the glory of making your pattern the master-spring of their motion!—The eyes of your venerable mother-nation will be upon you, who requires and expects, that . . . you wou'd imitate her parliaments in a suitable conduct, when French invasions are threaten'd; and no longer be amus'd, like our commissaries in Paris, by the futile and timespinning wrangles, or by all the stale chicanery of a treaty-making and treaty-breaking race; but crush at a blow the crocodile in the eggshell.—Nay, gentlemen, the Argus' eyes of the very French are upon you, who, by their various and conceal'd emissaries, undisguis'd jesuits, pardoned rebels, and traiterous malcontents, will have dispatched to them at Quebec, or even Paris, the accounts of your proceedings. . . . O then . . . O permit not the zeal of a true public spirit to cool in your breasts; but . . . improve it in yourselves; kindle, increase it in others; and transmit the hallowed principle to your children's children, to latest posterity; till only the day of Judgment and the kingdom of Christ put a period to the British dominion in our *new world*; or till time shall be lost in eternity!

Many of the Americans, if not all, were being drawn swiftly and deeply into the continental mood of nationalistic self-defense. The Albany Congress, with its plan for intercolonial union, was more a practical effort at defense than a sounding-board of psychological nationalism; yet its members were moved by the same patriotic sentiments that were moving the souls of so many other Americans; and William Livingston reported that "The speakers [at the conference] . . . were not many; but of those who spoke, some delivered themselves with singular energy and eloquence. All were inflamed with a patriotic spirit, and the debates were nervous and pathetic [fervent]. This assembly . . . might very properly be compared to one of the ancient Greek conventions, for supporting their expiring liberty against the power of the Persian empire, or that Lewis of Greece, Philip of Macedon."

Samuel Davies probably expressed the common mood of most Americans when he said, in 1756: "Now what can be more important, what more interesting, than our country! Our country is a word of the highest and most endearing import: it includes our friends and relatives, our liberty, our property, our religion: in short, it includes our earthly all. And when the fate of our country and all that it includes, is dreadfully doubtfull . . . every mind that has the least thought, must be agitated with many eager, dubious expectations. This is the present situation of our country. . . ." And Nathaniel Ames, intellectual mentor for thousands of New England almanac-readers, could in 1758, with uncanny prescience, cry down the years to the Americans of the future:

The Curious have observ'd, that the Progress of Humane Literature (like the Sun) is from the East to the West; thus has it travelled thro' Asia and Europe, and now is arrived at the Eastern Shore of *America.* As the Coelestial Light of the Gospel was directed here by the Finger of GOD, it will doubtless, finally drive the long! long! Night of Heathenish Darkness from *America:*—So Arts and Sciences will change the Face of Nature in their Tour from Hence over the Appalachian Mountains to the Western Ocean; and as they march thro' the vast Desert, the Residence of wild Beasts will be broken up, and their obscene Howl cease for ever;—Instead of which, the Stones and Trees will dance together at the Music of *Orpheus,*—The Rocks will disclose their hidden Gems,—and the inestimable Treasures of Gold & Silver be broken up. Huge Mountains of Iron Ore are already discovered; and vast Stores are reserved for future Generations: This Metal more useful than Gold and Silver, will employ millions of Hands, not only to form the martial Sword, and peaceful Share, alternately; but an Infinity of Utensils improved in the Exercise of Art, and Handicraft amongst Men. Nature thro' all her Works has stamp'd Authority on this Law, namely, "That all fit Matter shall be improved to its best Purposes."—Shall not then those vast Quarries, that team with mechanic Stone,—those for Structure be piled into great Cities,—and those for Sculpture into Statues to perpetuate the Honor of renowned Heroes; even those who shall now save their Country,—*O! Ye unborn Inhabitants of America! Should this Page escape its destin'd Conflagration at the Year's End, and these Alphabetical Letters remain legible,—when your Eyes behold the Sun after he has rolled the Seasons round for two or three Centuries more, you will know that* in Anno Domini 1758, *we dream'd of your Times.*

The final climax of American nationalistic conviction eventually came in the realm of political thought, which epitomized the whole struggle of the Americans and their culture-complex for self-expression. And this trend toward a political nationalism looked two ways; for while it was expressing itself positively along the lines of the struggle for political self-direction, it was also expressing itself negatively in the increasing resistance to control by the mother country.

Thus in the same years in which the colonists were beginning to sense the reality of their common cause and purpose toward their French and Indian enemies, they were also awakening to a consciousness of the common nature of their problems toward the mother country. Hitherto, of course, and even now, the American's highest loyalty was to England and to his King. But these years marked the moment of his awakening, in the course of his struggle over the prerogative, over the regulation of commerce, and over taxation, to the fact of his differentness from Englishmen: the fact that, somehow, the American and the Englishman, though ruled by the same King, were not the same men, that England and America were not the same society; and that for the American, though he might still be supremely loyal to his King, the society in which he breathed and had his being was American, not English; and his loyalty to his King was really a symbol of his loyalty to his colony, and through it, eventually, to "America." Jonathan Mayhew's sermon on unlimited submission was a clear warning to the English crown to govern the colonies according to the social compact between them, delivered without for a moment contemplating a reduction of American loyalty. With the same candor within the bounds of "British" loyalty Franklin was criticizing the mother country for her shortsightedness in insisting upon the Navigation Acts. A wise mother, he said, would not do it; and he was speaking for all the colonies, not just one or several.

That some such feeling of differentness was taking shape in Franklin's mind between 1750 and 1755, despite his enthusiastic expansionist imperialism, is clear from his writing during this period touching upon the relations of the colonies to the mother country, economic as well as political. For he not only criticized the unwisdom of Parliamentary restraints upon colonial trade, but, more positively, suggested a greater imperial union, with the colonies enjoying a much more important place in imperial deliberations, representation in an imperial parliament, and greater recognition of the uniqueness of the way of life of the colonies as a distinct unit in the Empire. In his eighteenth-century quest for a natural order in human affairs corollary to the order in the physical universe, he was discovering, or thought he was, the natural processes by which societies are formed. The American society had been formed by the natural process; it was different from the society from which it sprang; and it must be respected as being so. There began to be implicit in Franklin's criticisms of England a principle, the nationalistic counterpart of his sociological and economic thinking, of the naturalistic origins and peculiarities of nations. This principle, gradually becoming clearer in his own mind as it found expression in his political thoughts on the nature of the British Empire between 1765 and 1775, did not, as yet, conflict with the principle of loyalty to the King. Franklin was an ardent and patriotic Briton; but he was also a patriotic American, fired with a sense of the future greatness of his native land.

The growing feeling of criticism of England and the nebular beginning of an intercolonial solidarity were not confined to the struggle of the assemblies against the prerogative, nor even to politics. The manifold activities of the colonial agents in England also reflect the increasing complexity of the problem of forestalling interference in colonial affairs; and the agents were now finding it increasingly to their advantage to present a common front. A very significant case of this sort of co-operative action took place between 1750 and 1753, when the northern colonial agents in London found themselves lined up in a solid front against the sugar-planters of the British West Indies and their agents for the preservation of the trade of the northern colonies with the French West Indies. The proposed restrictions upon that trade, said the northern agents, would paralyze the northern colonies economically; moreover, the restrictions would constitute a violation of the American's rights as Englishmen. Significantly, their protest was based upon the economic differentness of the colonies from England.

This united effort of the agents was successful. The passage of the Sugar Act in 1764 brought the agents together again, and from then on they were regularly instructed to co-operate on questions of common interest; after the Stamp Act of 1765 they met together regularly to formulate joint policies. The significant development here was, of course, the emergence of a united, cooperative front toward the mother country among the colonies through their agents in England. The common front represented in the colonial mind the idea of common interests and a common cause.

During the Seven Years' War in America the feeling of difference between "Americans" and "Englishmen" was heightened by their relationships in military operations. The British soldiers and officers looked down upon their cruder American cousins and infuriated them by their own discrimination and patronizing attitude. This is well illustrated at the time of Braddock's defeat, when, though everybody deplored the disaster itself, there was more than a little grim satisfaction in American commentaries which pointed to it as a lesson to teach the supercilious British that the Americans knew more about warfare in America and claimed that British honor was saved, after all, by the Americans, without whom the disaster would have been far greater than it was.

This mood of American importance in imperial affairs was no passing fancy, either. For there were numerous Americans who felt that it was to the colonials that victory was due, and that the mother country actually owed them a debt of gratitude for making possible so great an expansion of the Empire. This is the theme, for example, in Daniel Dulany's *Considerations on the Propriety of Imposing Taxes on the Colonies,* published in 1765, where he said:

> It is presumed that it was a notable service done by *New England,* when the militia of that colony reduced *Cape-Breton,* since it enabled the *British Ministers* to make a peace less disadvantageous and inglorious than they otherwise must have been constrained to submit to, in the humble state to which they were then reduced. . . . It is evident that the general exertion of the colonies in North America, during the last war [1754–63], not only facilitated, but was indispensably requisite to the success of those operations by which so many glorious conquests were achieved, and that those conquests have put it in the power of the present illustrious Ministers to make a peace upon terms of so much glory and advantage, as to afford an unexhaustible subject during their administration, and the triumph of toryism, at least, for their ingenious panegyrists to celebrate.

Dulany demolishes the idea that England protected the colonies out of generosity. Great Britain was fighting for its life, and the colonies were an important factor in saving it. Far from taxing or exploiting the "Americans" (note the use of the term), England should feel only gratitude and respect for them:

> An *American,* without justly incurring the imputation of ingratitude, may doubt, whether some other motive, besides pure generosity, did not prompt the *British Nation* to engage in the defence of the colonies. He may be induced to think that the measures

taken for the protection of the plantations, were not only connected with the interests, but even necessary to the defence of *Great Britain* herself, because he may have reason to imagine that *Great Britain,* could not long subsist as an independent kingdom after the loss of her colonies.

Dulany was an American fully aware of the principle, then current in European diplomacy, that the balance of power among the great commercial states of Europe depended, in large measure if not entirely, upon the possession of profitable colonies in the new world. What he did was to turn that principle to the profit of the Americans by claiming that it was they who had preserved and increased England's weight in the international balance of power by preserving and extending England's colonial holdings for her. She had begged the colonies for their aid, and she had got it, with consequent incalculable success and profit to herself; and she should be grateful. Furthermore, Dulany made so bold as to say that "The frugal *Republicans of North-America* (if the *British* inhabitants there are to be distinguished by a *nickname,* because it implies that they are enemies to the government of *England,* and ought therefore to be regarded with a jealous eye)" should be acknowledged to know more about their own affairs than anybody in England.

The ideas and sentiments in this curious "Who won the war?" argument are clearly the impulses of a young and bumptious nationalism, the more clearly so because they were the feelings of not just one American, but probably most of them. The Americans were thinking of themselves now as different from their English cousins and as entitled to the respect due to a people that has arrived at political and cultural maturity. As Franklin put it in a letter to Lord Kames in 1767:

> Every man in England seems to consider himself a piece of a sovereign over America; seems to jostle himself into the throne with the King, and talks of *our subjects in the colonies.* . . . But America, an immense Territory, favored by nature with all the advantages of climate, soils, great navigable rivers, lakes, &c., must become a great country, populous and mighty; and will, in a less time than is generally conceived, be able to shake off any shackles that may be imposed upon her, and perhaps place them on the imposers. . . . And yet there remains among that people so much respect, veneration, and affection for Britain, that, if cultivated prudently, with a kind usage and tenderness for their privileges, they might be easily governed still for ages, without force or any considerable expense. But I do not see here a sufficient quantity of the wisdom, that is necessary to produce such a conduct, and I lament the want of it.

Franklin was warning England of the psychological facts. But a subtle and significant change had now taken place in his mind. He no longer spoke of Americans as identical with Britons, or of the colonies as part of England. They were separate; they had only respect and reverence for the great traditions and ideals of the British way of life and all that that could mean; but they were now a separate people, among the other British peoples.

The loyalties of the Americans were becoming more and more sharply divided. The American mentality was growing conscious of this divergence, thinking of itself as a distinct, "American" entity within the Empire, and of England and its people as alien to itself. This was a psychological phenomenon, a factor of profound importance for the future of the Empire and for America. From Franklin's position of 1767 it was but a short step to Jefferson's position of 1774, which spoke of Englishmen as foreigners to America, and to the eloquent Patrick Henry's "I am an American." Or to that of John Randolph, who warned the mother country, on the eve of the Revolution:

> The Histories of dependent States put it beyond a Doubt that America, when she is able to protect herself, will acknowledge no Superiority in another. That she will be capable, some Time or other, to establish an Independence, must appear evident to every One, who is acquained with her present Situation and growing Strength. But although it must be apparent to everyone that *America* will, in short Period, attain to a State of Maturity, yet, if *Great Britain* could be prevailed on to govern her Colonies to their Satisfaction, from the force of Habit, and the good Impressions which a pleasing Intercourse must occasion, I am persuaded that she would procrastinate our Separation from her, and carry on an exclusive Trade with us, so long as she is able to maintain her Weight in the political scale of *Europe*; but, on the contrary, if she persevere in her Rigour, and the Colonies will not relax on their Part, the Parent will probably soon be without a Child, and the Offspring become unable to support itself.

What the Americans were driving for was a recognition, by the mother country, of the now self-confident American national personality. The child had grown up and become a man. Psychologically, the American Revolution was a war to force the mother country to admit this basic fact. The Americans were perfectly willing, even anxious, given the mother country's admission of their national maturity, to remain members of the imperial family. But that was just the tragic point at which British nationalism found itself in conflict with British-American nationalism, and since neither one could accept the ideal and the point of view of the other, the British-American mind became the American mind, simply.

SECTION 8: SUGGESTIONS FOR FURTHER READING

The most succinct general survey of all aspects of provincial culture, including art, architecture, literature, music, theater, and science, remains L. B. Wright, *The Cultural Life of the American Colonies, 1607–1763* (1957). For the rich variety of general commentary about early American culture Wright's findings may be supplemented by Michael Kraus, *The Atlantic Civilization: Eighteenth-Century Origins* (1949), C. L. Rossiter, *Seedtime of the Republic* (1953), Max Savelle, *Seeds of Liberty: The Genesis of the American Mind* (1948), A. M. Schlesinger, Sr., *The Birth of a Nation: A Portrait of the American People on the Eve of Independence* (1968), and T. J. Wertenbaker, *The Golden Age of Colonial Culture* (2nd ed., 1949). More specialized studies of significance include Carl Bridenbaugh, *Myths and Realities: Societies of the Colonial South* (1952), John Clive.and Bernard Bailyn, "England's Cultural Provinces: Scotland and America," *William and Mary Quarterly,* 3rd ser., 11 (1954), pp. 200–213, F. B. Tolles, *Quakers and the Atlantic Culture* (1960), T. J. Wertenbaker, *The Founding of American Civilization: The Middle Colonies* (1938), and L. B. Wright, *The First Gentlemen of Virginia: Intellectual Qualities of the Early Colonial Ruling Class* (1940).

No one has explained the nature of the new intellectualism in America more gracefully than H. F. May, *The Enlightenment in America* (1976). This outstanding study may be supplemented with R. N. Gummere, *The American Colonial Mind and the Classical Tradition: Essays in Comparative Culture* (1963), and with the primary documents contained in Adrienne Koch, ed., *The American Enlightenment* (1965). May does not ignore the Enlightenment's bearing upon trends in religious thought, especially in terms of Calvinist theology. For greater detail students should consult Perry Miller, "From the Covenant to the Revival," *The Shaping of American Religion,* vol. I, ed. J. W. Smith and A. L. Jamison (1961), pp. 322–368, N. S. Fiering, "Will and Intellect in the New England Mind," *William and Mary Quarterly,* 3rd ser., 29 (1972), pp. 515–558, Bernard Bailyn, "Religion and Revolution: Three Biographical Studies," *Perspectives in American History,* 4 (1970), pp. 87–124, H. M. Morais, *Deism in Eighteenth-Century America* (1934), Conrad Wright, *The Beginnings of Unitarianism in America* (1955), and B. E. Steiner, "New England Anglicanism: A Genteel Faith?," *William and Mary Quarterly,* 3rd ser., 27 (1970), pp. 122–135.

The impact of the Englightenment upon scientific inquiry and the appearance of an American science community is treated in Brooke Hindle, *The Pursuit of Science in Revolutionary America, 1735-1789* (1956), the source of the first reading. Also of value are R. P. Stearns, *Science in the British Colonies of America* (1970). S. A. Bedini, *Thinkers and Tinkers: Early American Men of Science* (1976), and J. H. Wilson, "Dancing Dogs of the Colonial Period: Women Scientists," *Early American Literature,* 7 (1973), pp. 225-235. R. H. Shryock, *Medicine and Society in America, 1660-1860* (1960), sketches the role of physicians while John Duffy, *Epidemics in Colonial America* (1953), looks at medical techniques in the context of diseases. Definitive introductions to a major provincial leader of rationalist temperament are Carl Van Doren, *Benjamin Franklin* (1938), and D. F. Hawke, *Frankin* (1976). D. J. Boorstin, *The Lost World of Thomas Jefferson* (1948), examines the small but brilliant circle of Enlightenment figures in contact with Thomas Jefferson.

For years the history of early American education was explained within the context of the growth of particular educational institutions. Bernard Bailyn's *Education in the Forming of American Society: Needs and Opportunities for Study* (1960), changed that when the author stressed that education must be understood in the context of social units like the family and of cultural transmission through the generations. The new approach may be seen in K. A. Lockridge, *Literacy in Colonial New England: An Inquiry into the Social Context of Literacy in the Early Modern West* (1974), L. A. Cremin, *American Education: The Colonial Experience, 1607-1763* (1970), and James Axtell, *The School upon a Hill: Education and Society in Colonial New England* (1974). Institutional history of the finest quality, however, is available in S. E. Morison, *Three Centuries of Harvard, 1636-1936* (1936), and D. C. Humphrey, *From King's College to Columbia, 1746-1800* (1976), which go far beyond the parochial interests of most filiopietistic school historians.

An important body of literature has touched upon the question of a dawning sense of American nationalism, and the conclusions generally have been similar to those of Max Savelle, *Seeds of Liberty,* from which the last selection is taken. For a unique, quantitative approach see R. L. Merritt, *Symbols of American Community, 1735-1775* (1966), which may be read in conjunction with R. N. Miller, "American Nationalism as a Theory of Nature," *William and Mary Quarterly,* 3rd ser., 12 (1955), pp. 74-95, and Paul Varg, "The Advent of Nationalism, 1758-1776," *American Quarterly,* 16 (1964), pp. 160-181.

Indulging in such sweeping concepts as American culture and identity has many pitfalls, and the pitfalls are carefully outlined in D. M. Potter, *People of Plenty: Economic Abundance and the American Character* (1958). To Potter the concept and reality of plentitude has had a striking impact upon the behavior of all Americans. The formative role of abundance in the minds of early settlers is covered in L. B. Wright, *The Dream of Prosperity in Colonial America* (1965). Potter also comments on Frederick Jackson Turner's frontier thesis and finds it deficient. Several of Turner's classic essays have been collected in *The Frontier in American History* (1920), a good place to begin when asking whether there was a developing American identity before the Revolution. The role of the wilderness and Indians in shaping a sense of Americanism has been brilliantly discussed in Richard Slotkin, *Regeneration Through Violence: The Mythology of the American Frontier* (1973), the source of the third selection. Also helpful are Alan Heimert, "Puritanism, the Wilderness, and the Frontier," *New England Quarterly,* 26 (1953), pp. 361-382, P. N. Carroll, *Puritanism and the Wilderness: The Intellectual Significance of the New England Frontier, 1629-1700* (1969), and James Axtell, "The Scholastic Philosophy of the Wilderness," *William and Mary Quarterly,* 3rd ser., 29 (1972), pp. 335-366.

By comparison Michael Kammen, *People of Paradox: An Inquiry Concerning the Origins of American Civilization* (1973), stresses the importance of logically opposite ideas in forming an American society, culture, and identity. Two important primary source statements should be helpful in sorting out the possibilities. They include Benjamin Franklin's *Autobiography,* and J. Hector St. John de Crèvecoeur's *Letters from an American Farmer,* both of which have been reprinted in multiple editions. It was Crèvecoeur who asked during the Revolution: "What, then, is the American, this new man?" Finding the answer has not been easy.

77 78 79 80 9 8 7 6 5 4 3 2 1